Squiggles by Sharon
Volume 2

Sharon McEnearney

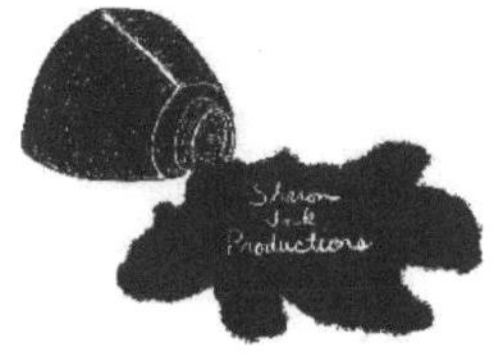

Sharon Ink Productions, LLC

To request permissions, contact Sharon McEnearney at
sharonmcenearney@squigglesbysharon.com

Paperback ISBN: 978-1-7368318-4-7
Ebook ISBN: 978-1-7368318-5-4

Sharon Ink Productions, LLC
www.squigglesbysharon.com

Printed by IngramSpark in the USA

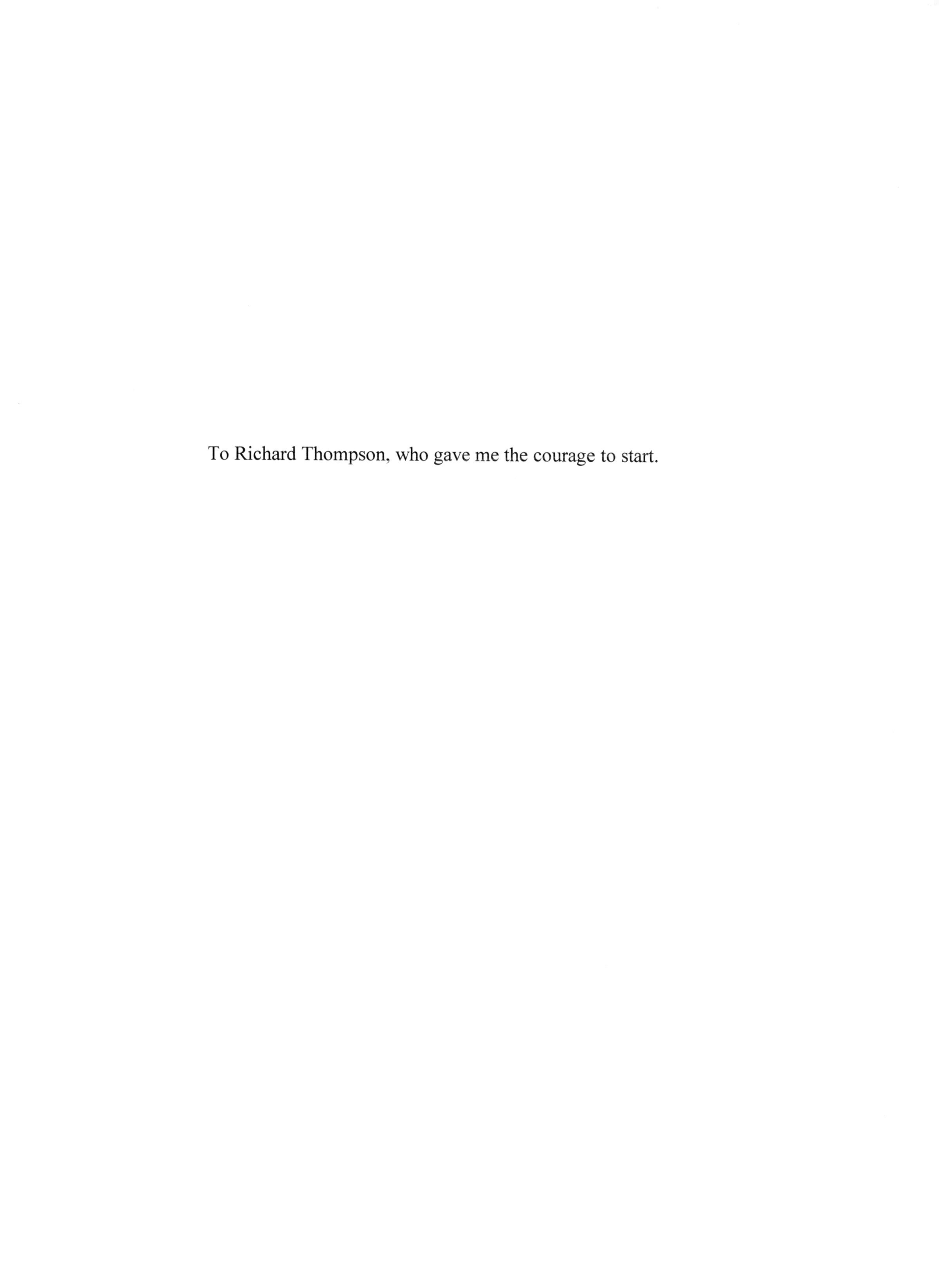

To Richard Thompson, who gave me the courage to start.

A Note From Sharon

My name is Sharon McEnearney (pronounced *Mack-N'-Ernie*) and I whole-heartedly welcome you to the second anthology of my daily comic strip, *Squiggles by Sharon*. Thank you for reading, for following on Instagram/Facebook and commenting, and most importantly for buying this book. It seems like every book introduction includes a thank-you to the author's family, audience, therapist, whomever it was that helped get the book from brain to bookstore, but those thank you's are not without warrant. Publishing a book truly takes a village, so thank you. Quite frankly I can't believe I'm even talking about *Volume 2*. **TWO!** College Sharon would have laughed if you told her this is where things would be by the year 2022, yet here we are. Year 2 is compiled, and Year 3 is well underway. Cartooning isn't exactly the typical career choice with a Chemical Engineering degree. Making blueprints for the future is truly a fool's errand after all!

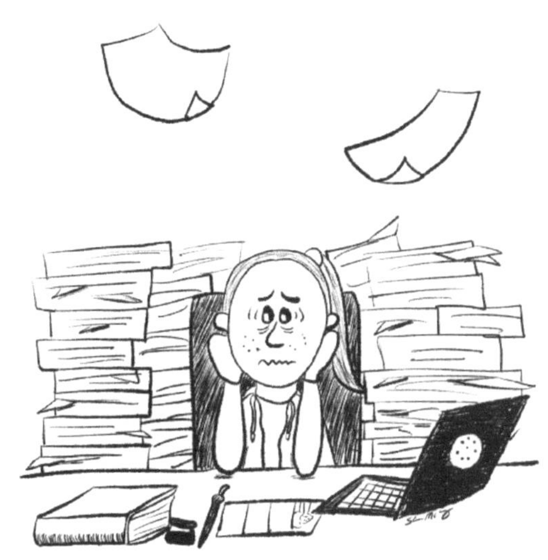

Sharon in the year 2021

The second year of *Squiggles* has – mostly – been a joy to write. Any artist who tells you it's easy or fun all the time is just a naturally enthusiastic person, because there were certainly times when I wanted to throw in the towel. Juggling *Squiggles* with my full-time job (doing lab research on malaria treatment drugs) is not always easy. Then add the stress of everyday life, and it seems only natural that the thought crossed my mind on numerous occasions that I simply did not have the time to dedicate to a daily comic strip. I felt like I would just drown in a sea of paper. See the self-portrait on the left for an accurate emotional depiction.

So, I had a choice. Should I give up on *Squiggle*s? After all, my 9 to 5 job at least pays me money – and I hear that makes the world go 'round! On the other hand, doing this comic strip makes *my personal world* go 'round. The more I thought about it, the more it dawned on me that I couldn't envision a world where I wasn't doing this four-panel comic strip. I need *Squiggles*. It makes me happy and that's worth fighting for. The times when I'm at my lowest, I hear Rocky Balboa's voice in *Rocky IV* when he says, "going in one more round when you don't think you can, that's what makes all the difference in your life." I've always admired that kind of perseverance when facing down a seemingly impossible challenge, and it keeps me going when I don't think I can. I'm happy to report, perseverance really does make all the difference. In a world that encourages us not to care about the things that make us happy, I promise life is better when you dare to make your own meaning. Squiggles is an important part of my meaning, and I hope it can be just a little part of yours too.

Sharon McEnearney
Arlington, VA
April 17, 2022

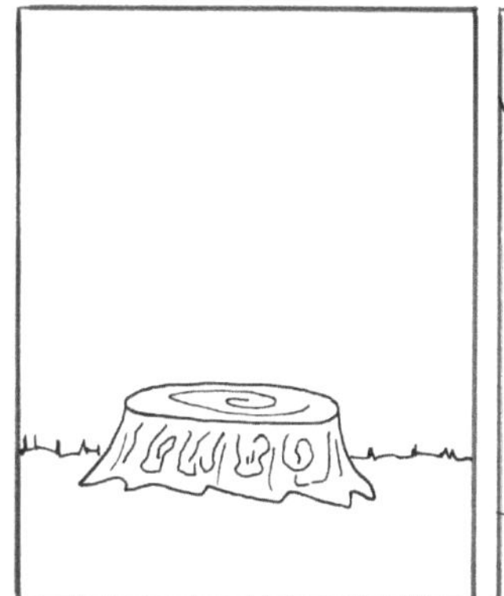

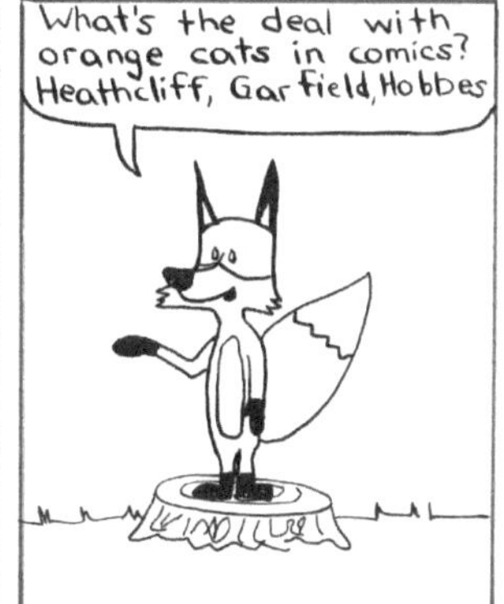
What's the deal with orange cats in comics? Heathcliff, Garfield, Hobbes

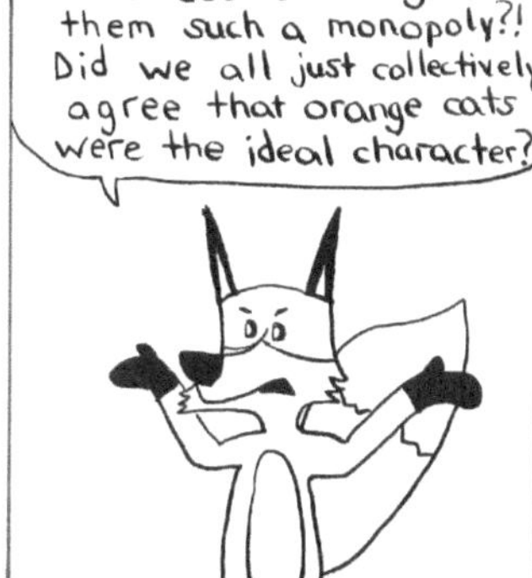
Who decided to give them such a monopoly?! Did we all just collectively agree that orange cats were the ideal character?

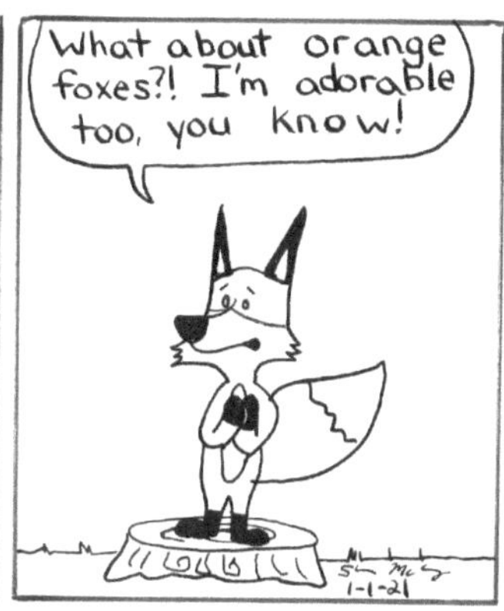
What about orange foxes?! I'm adorable too, you know!
1-1-21

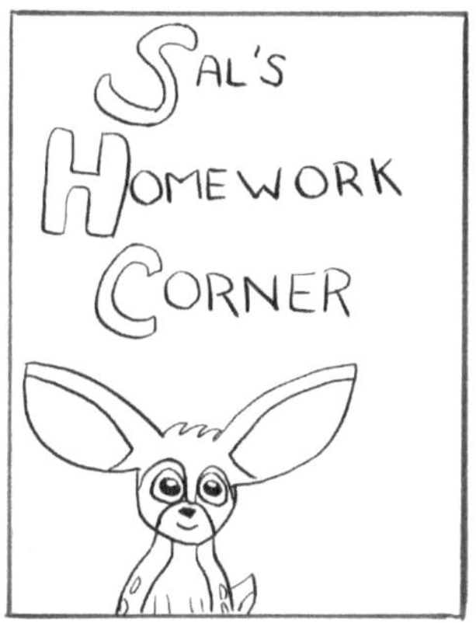
SAL'S HOMEWORK CORNER

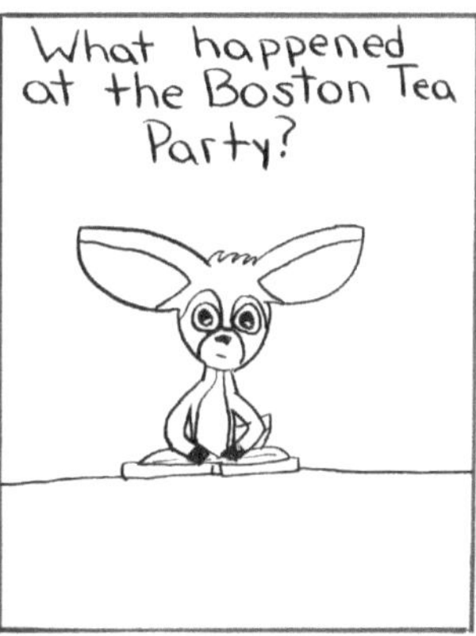
What happened at the Boston Tea Party?

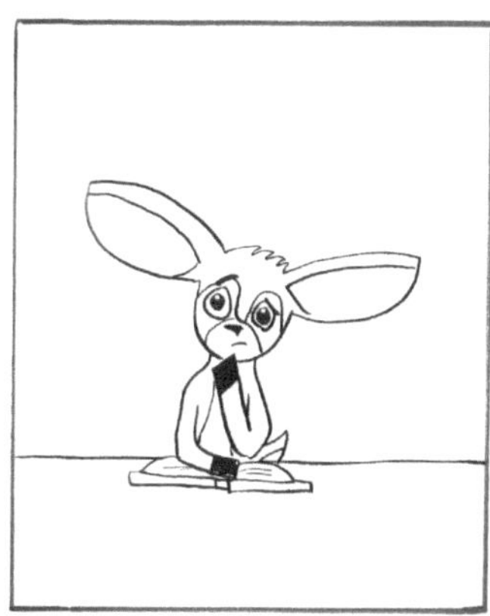

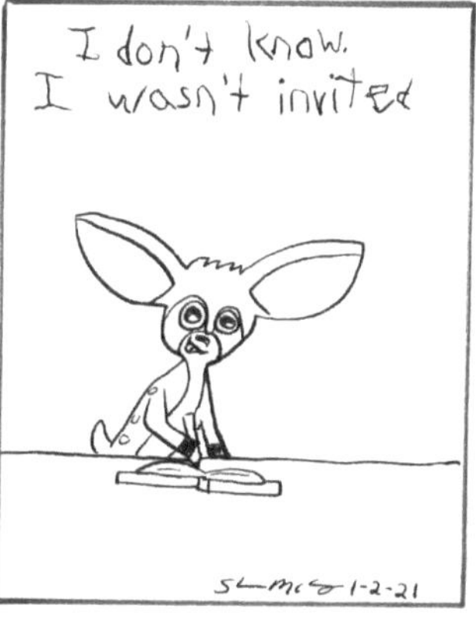
I don't know. I wasn't invited
1-2-21

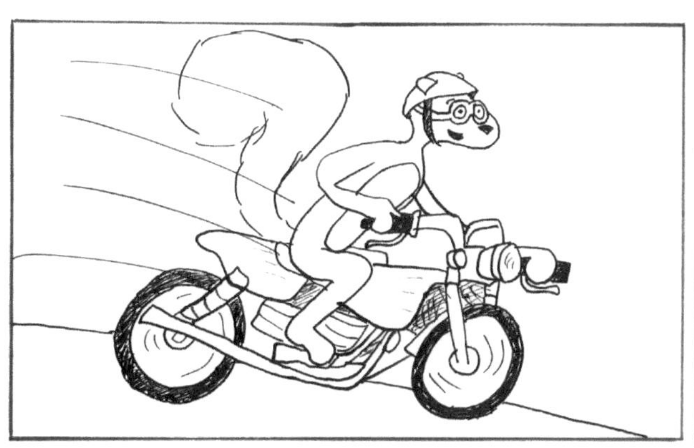

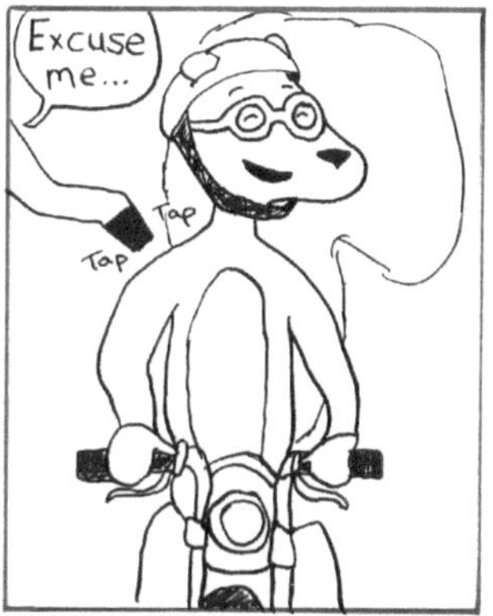
Excuse me...
Tap
Tap

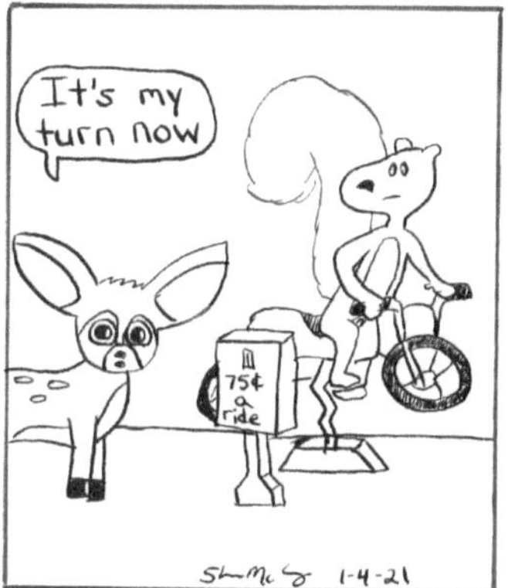
It's my turn now
75¢ a ride
1-4-21

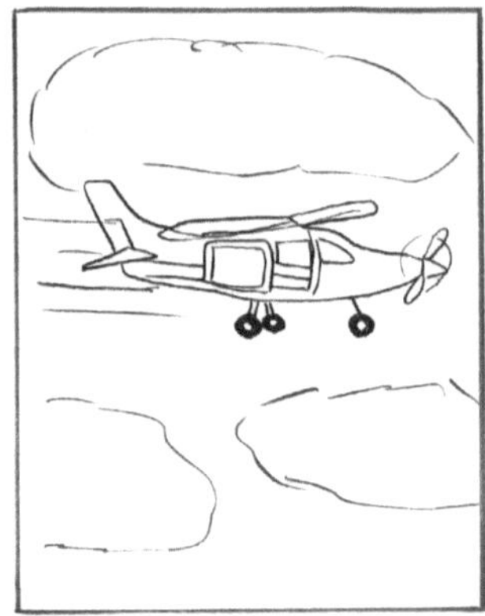

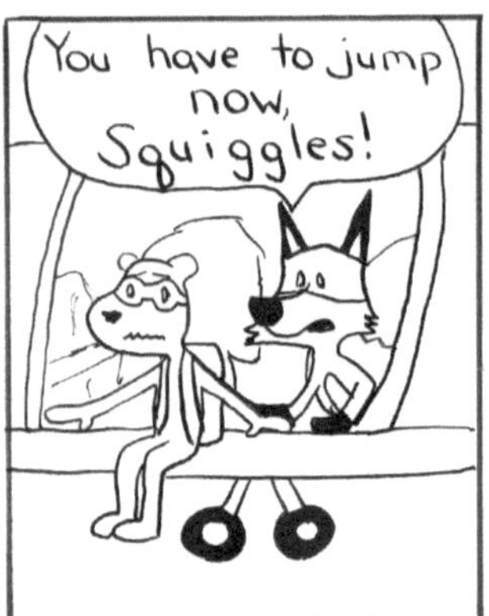
You have to jump now, Squiggles!

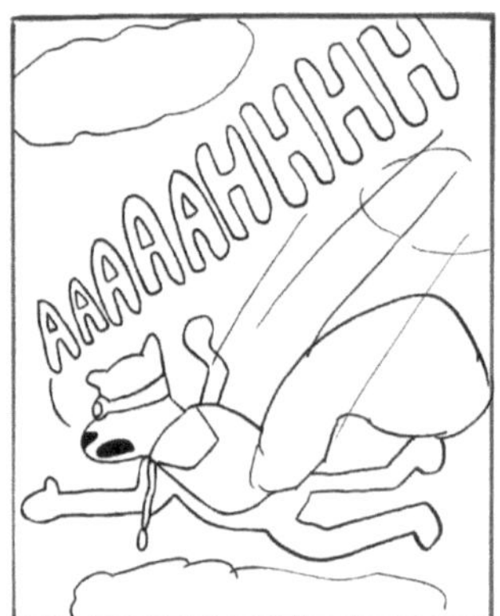
AAAAAHHHHH

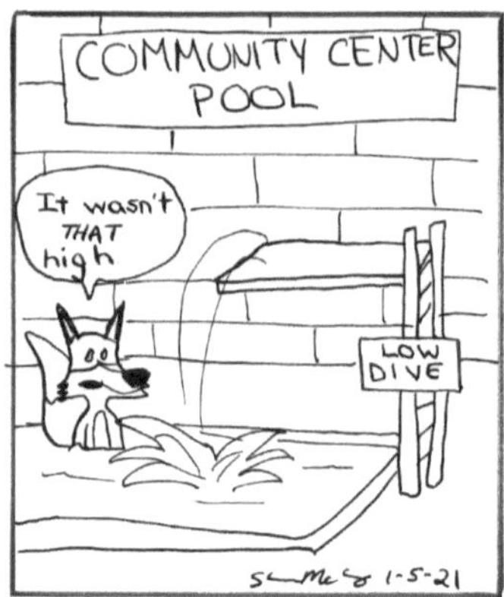
COMMUNITY CENTER POOL
It wasn't THAT high
LOW DIVE
1-5-21

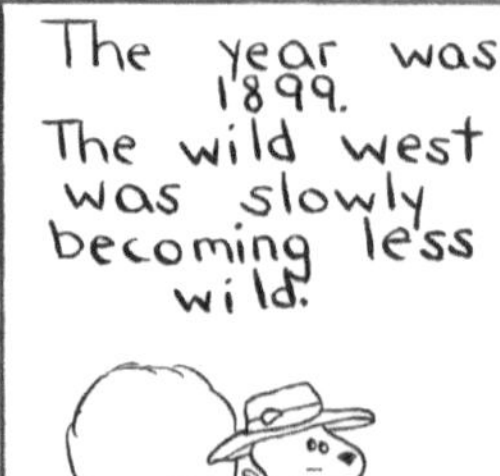
The year was 1899.
The wild west was slowly becoming less wild.

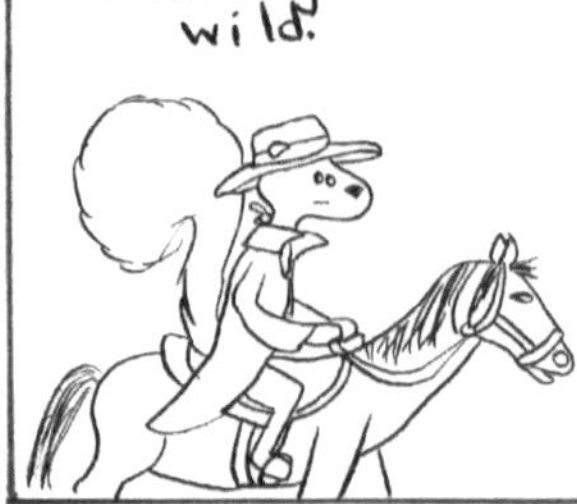

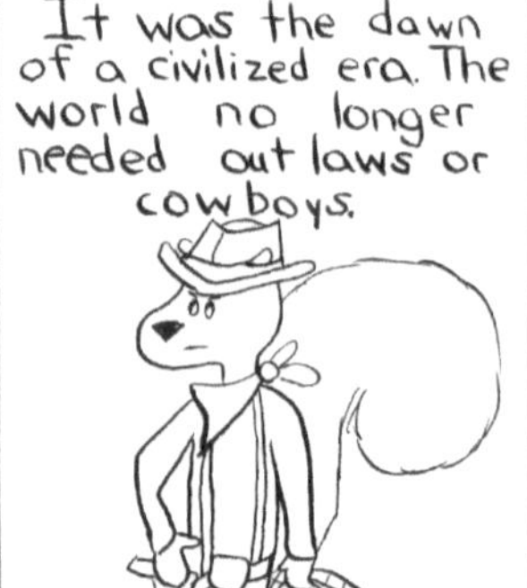
It was the dawn of a civilized era. The world no longer needed outlaws or cowboys.

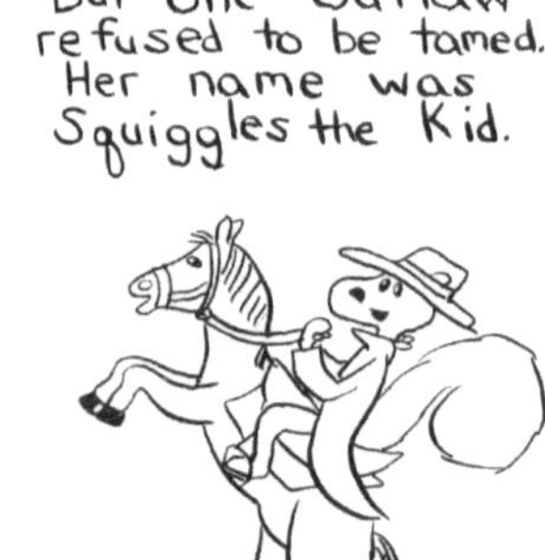
But one outlaw refused to be tamed. Her name was Squiggles the Kid.

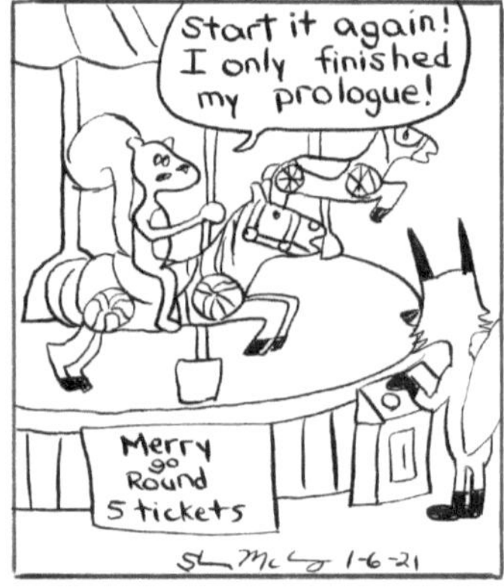
Start it again! I only finished my prologue!
Merry go Round 5 tickets
1-6-21

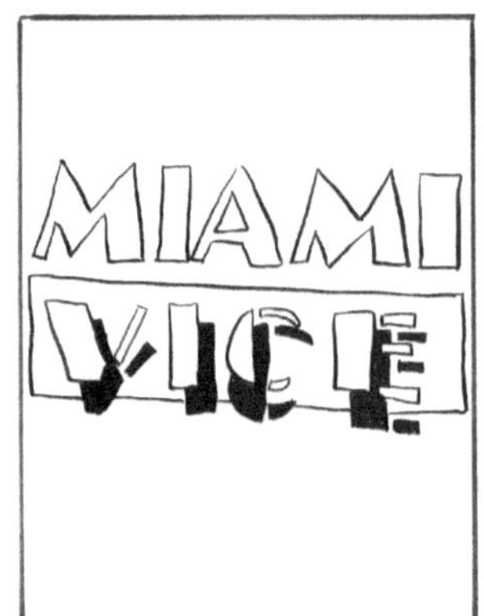
MIAMI
VICE

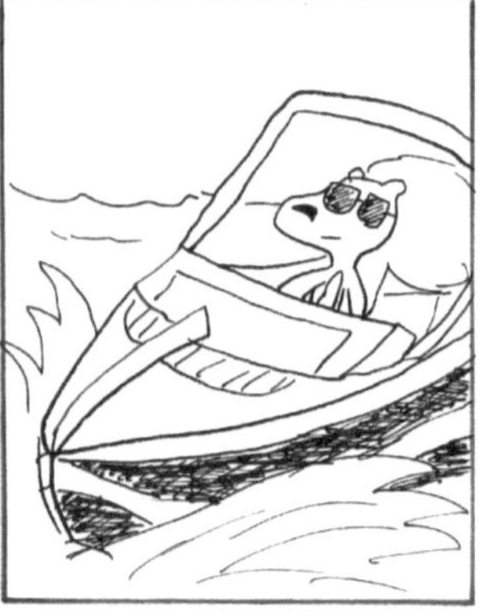

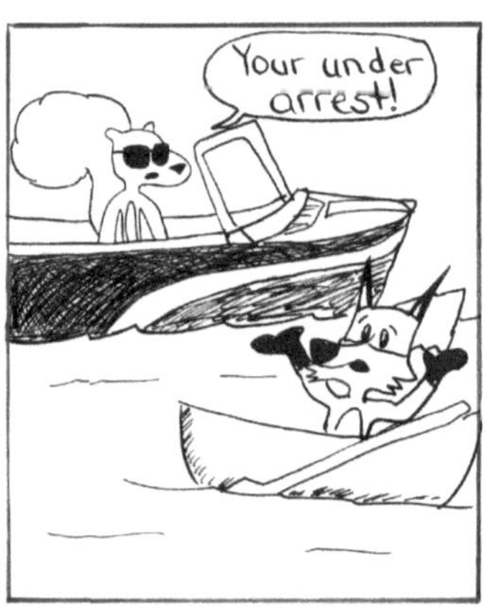
Your under arrest!

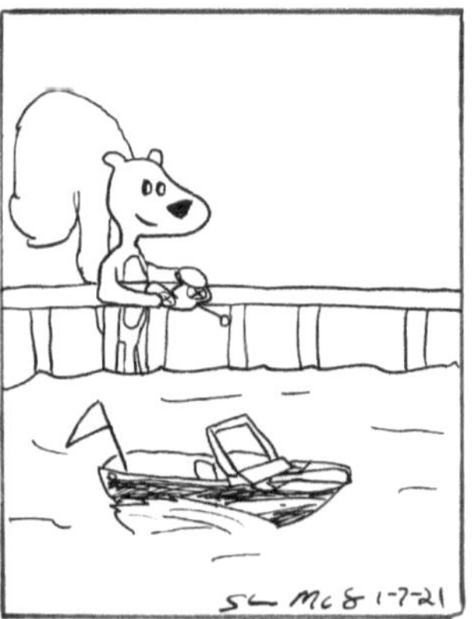
1-7-21

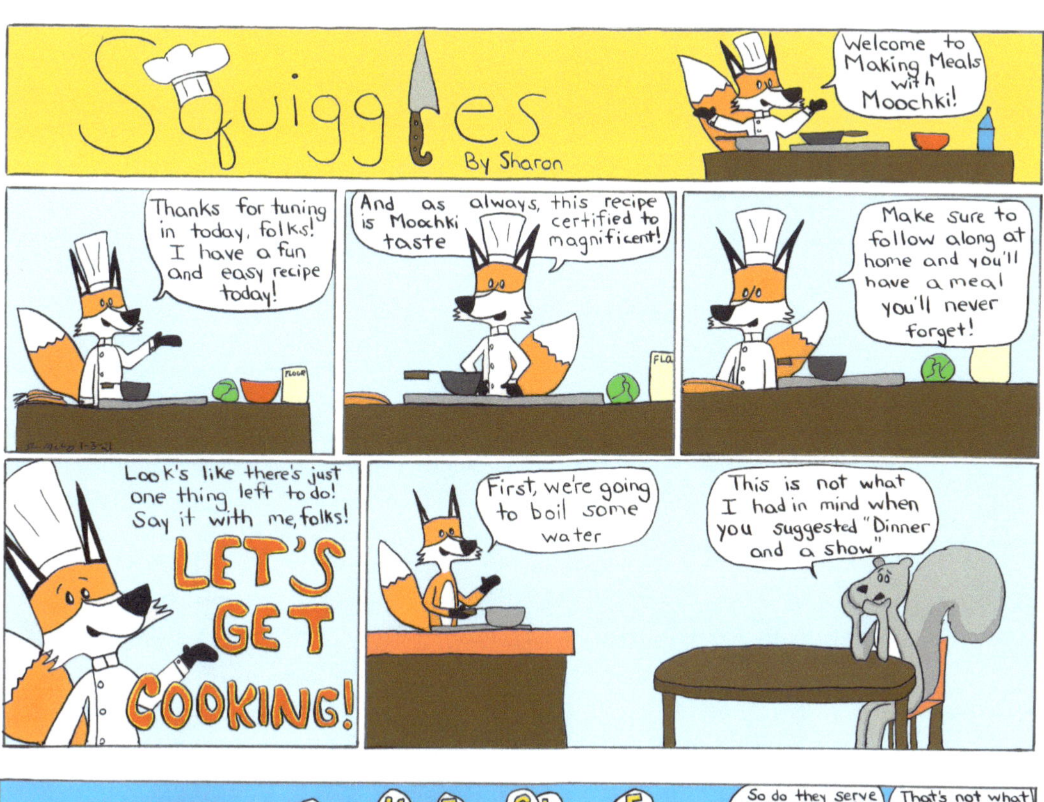

Squiggles
By Sharon
Welcome to Making Meals with Moochki!
Thanks for tuning in today, folks! I have a fun and easy recipe today!
And as always, this recipe is Moochki taste certified to magnificent!
Make sure to follow along at home and you'll have a meal you'll never forget!
Look's like there's just one thing left to do! Say it with me, folks!
LET'S GET COOKING!
First, we're going to boil some water
This is not what I had in mind when you suggested "Dinner and a show"

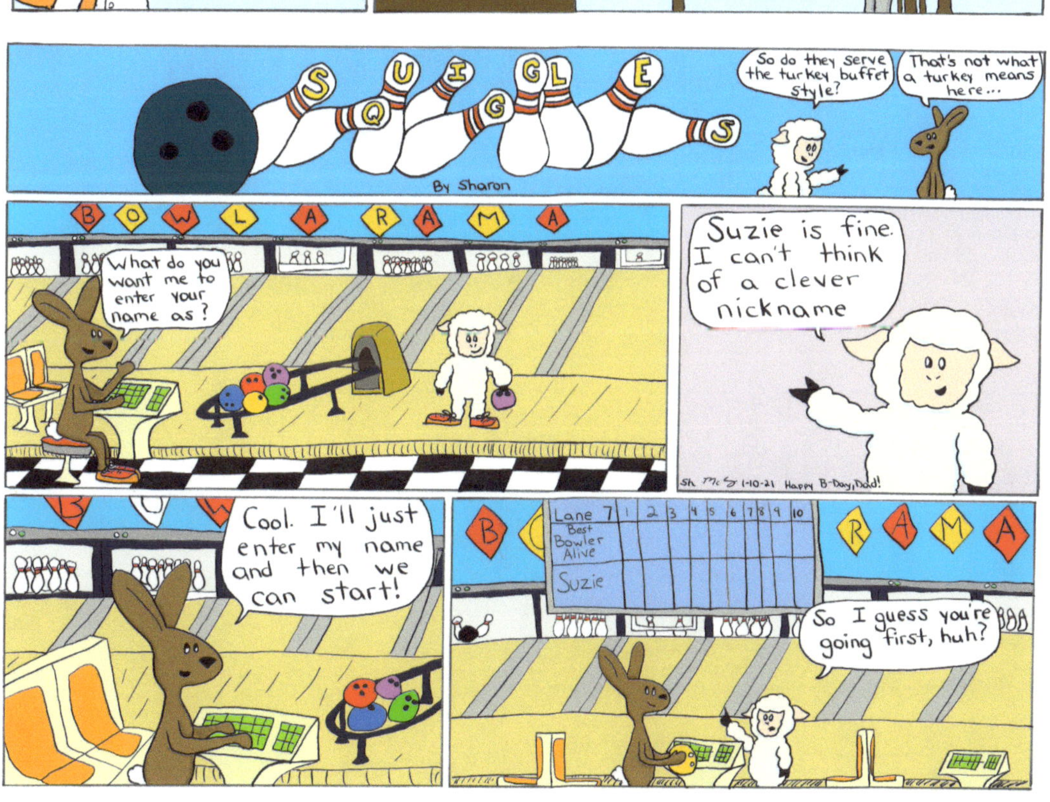

SQUIGGLES
By Sharon
So do they serve the turkey buffet style?
That's not what a turkey means here...
BOWLARAMA
What do you want me to enter your name as?
Suzie is fine. I can't think of a clever nickname
Happy B-Day, Dad!
Cool. I'll just enter my name and then we can start!
Lane 7
Best Bowler Alive
Suzie
So I guess you're going first, huh?

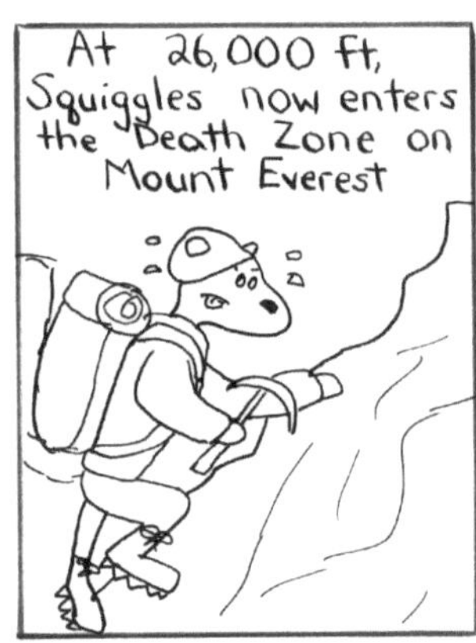

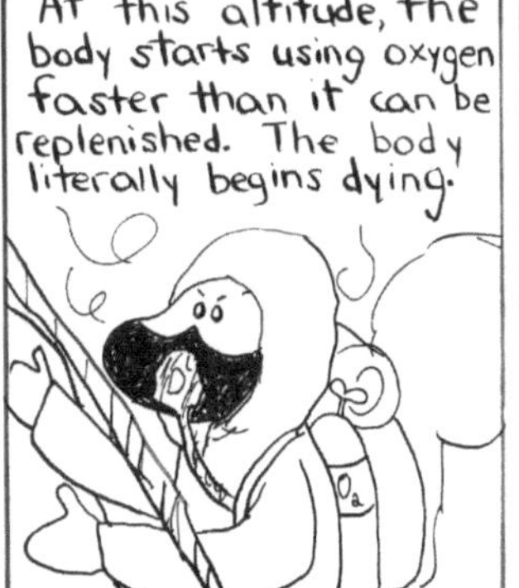

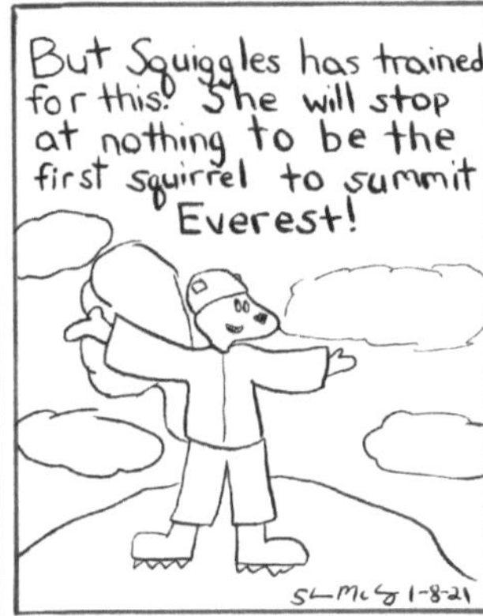

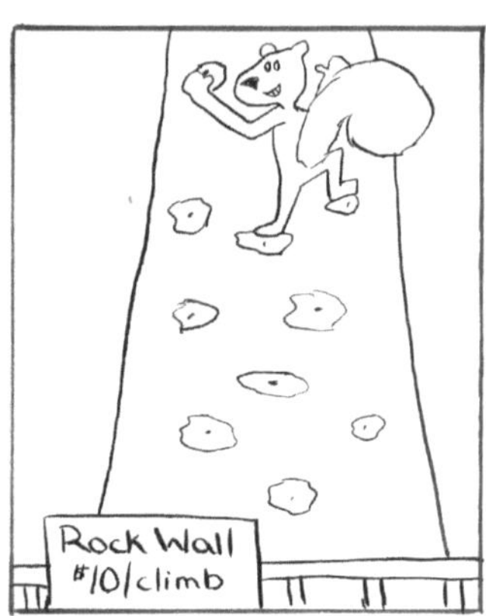

I don't know the future. I didn't come here to tell you how this is going to end. I came here to tell you how its going to begin.

629 000690 55
937 84 301939
496 74 779671

SYSTEM FAILURE

004 679945 17
6 4464040 23
2 7975272 04
3 1444775 32

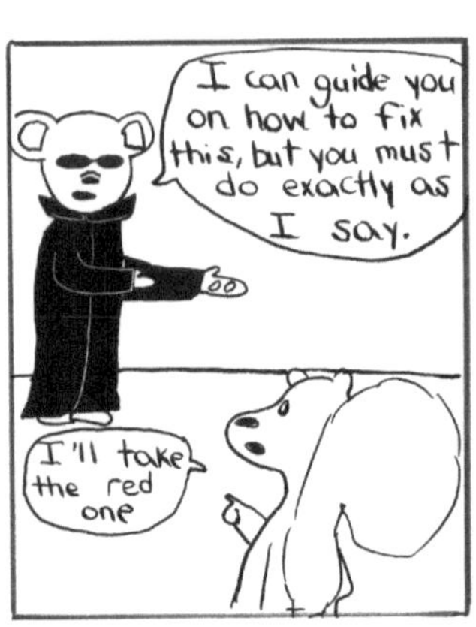

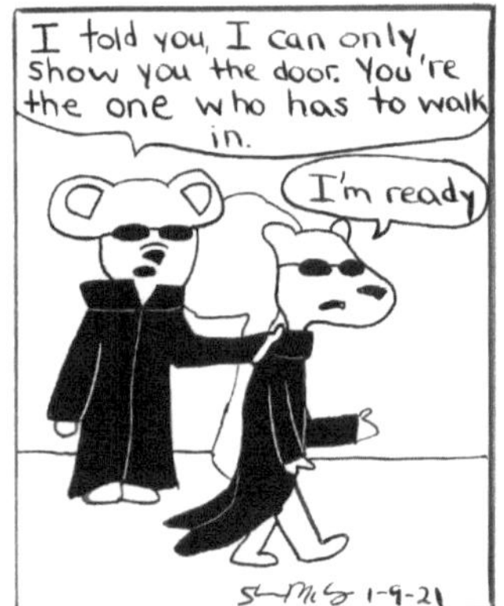

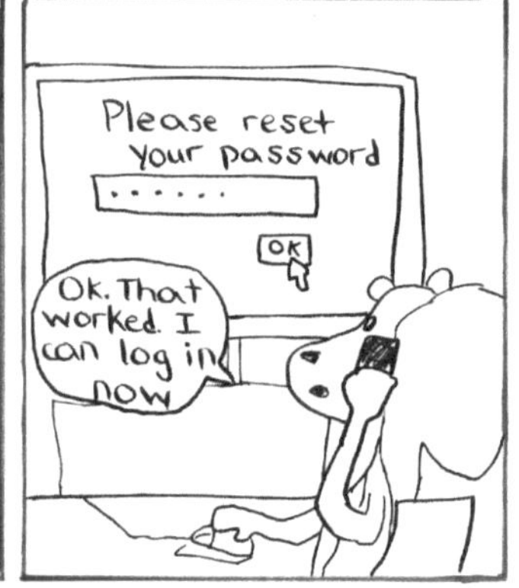

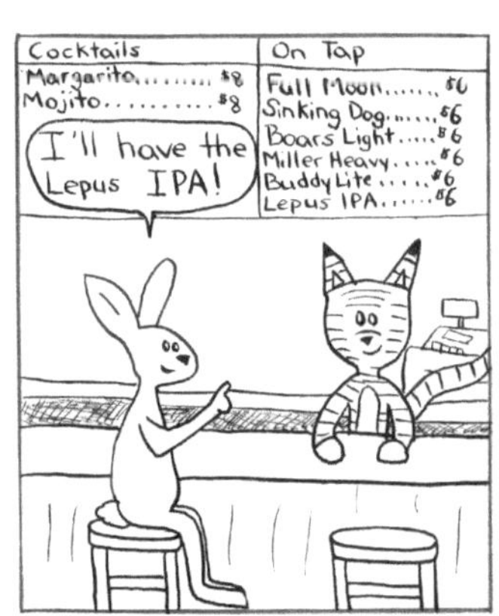

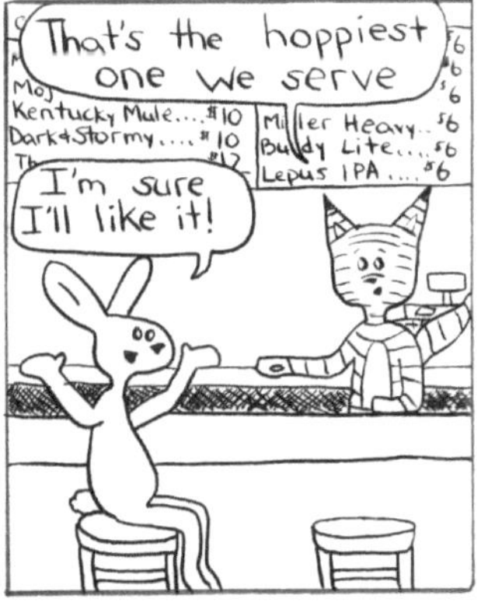

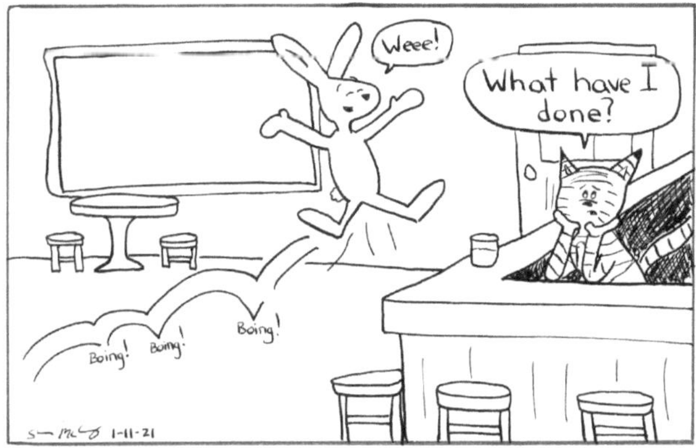

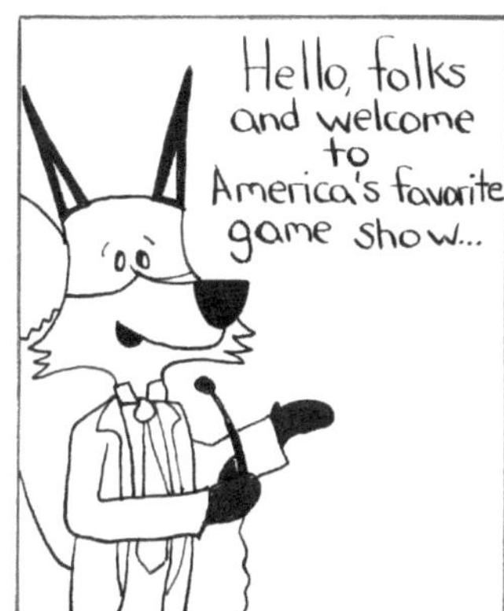
Hello, folks and welcome to America's favorite game show...

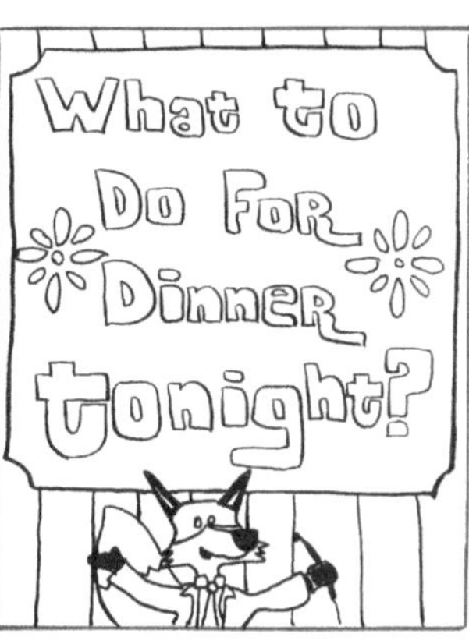
What to Do For Dinner tonight?

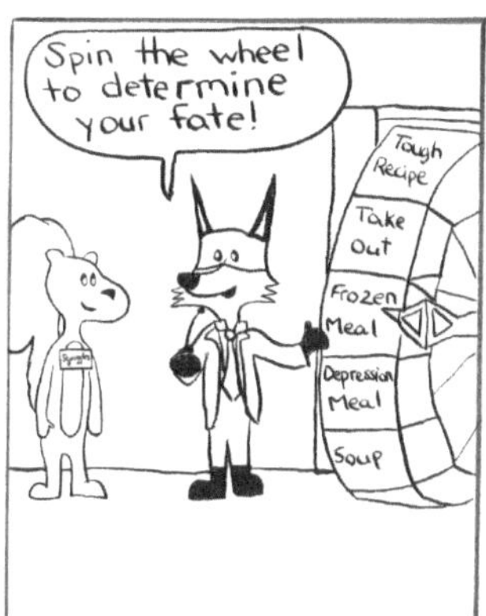
Spin the wheel to determine your fate!
Tough Recipe
Take Out
Frozen Meal
Depression Meal
Soup

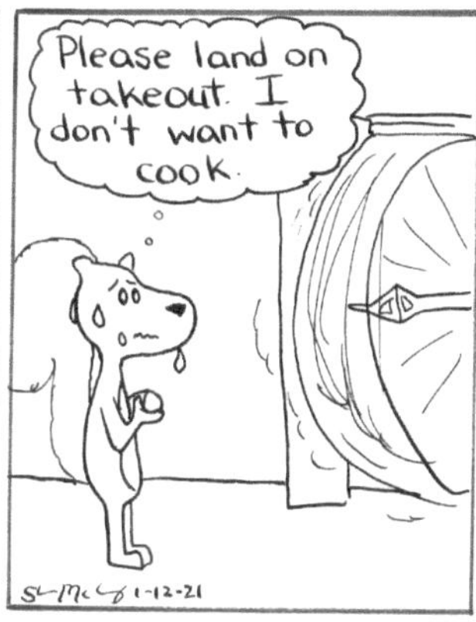
Please land on takeout. I don't want to cook.

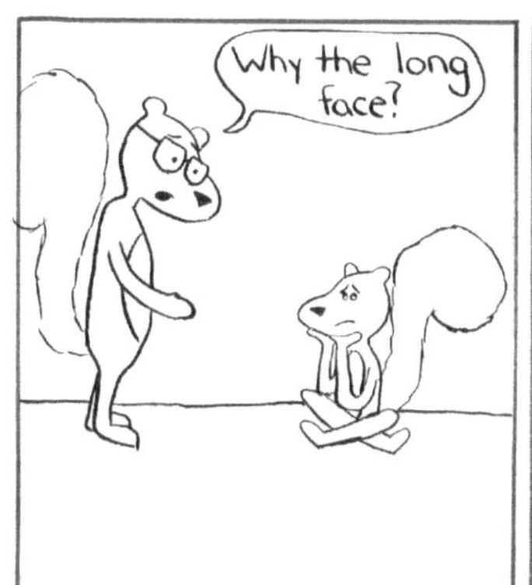
Why the long face?

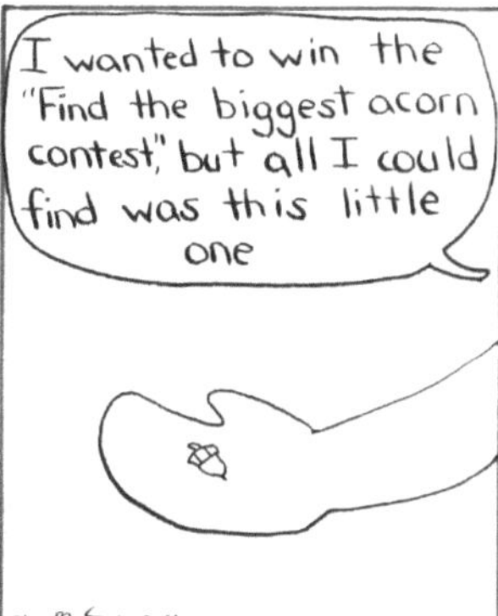
I wanted to win the "Find the biggest acorn contest," but all I could find was this little one

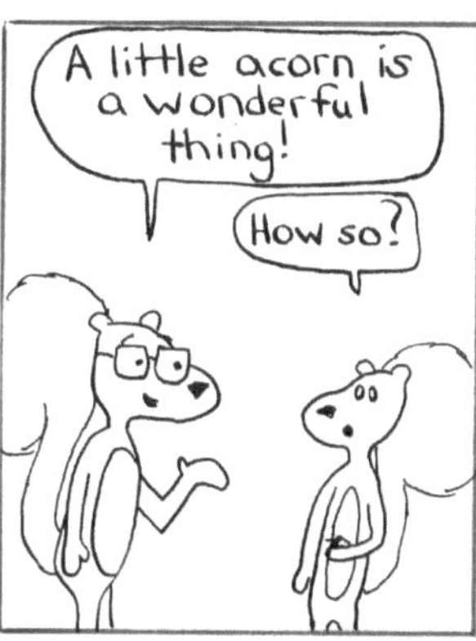
A little acorn is a wonderful thing!
How so?

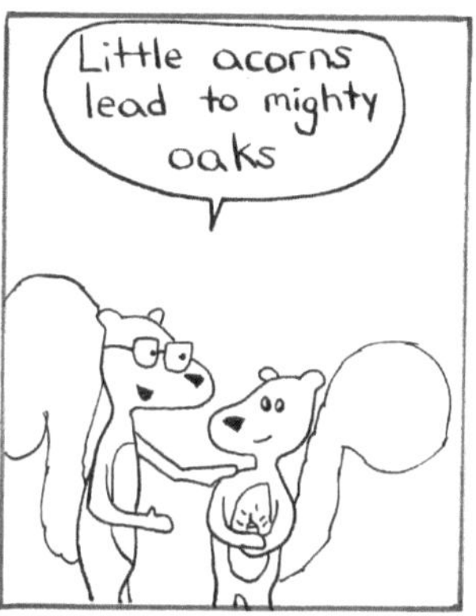
Little acorns lead to mighty oaks

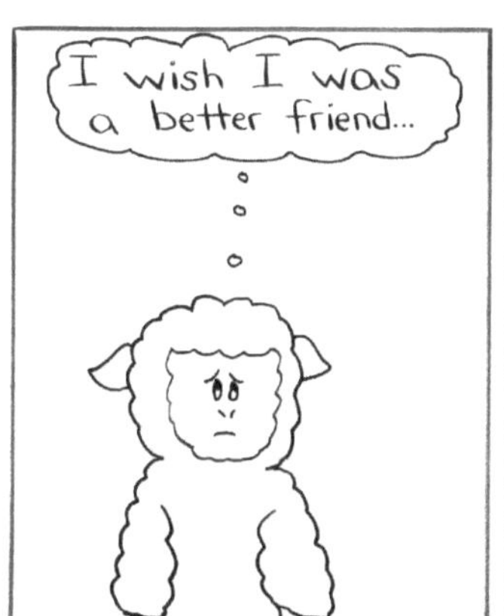
I wish I was a better friend...

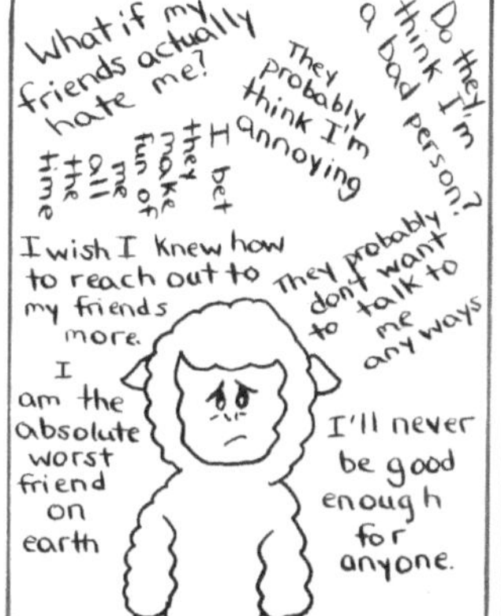
What if my friends actually hate me?
They probably think I'm annoying
Do they think I'm a bad person?
I bet they make fun of me all the time
I wish I knew how to reach out to my friends more.
They probably don't want to talk to me anyways
I am the absolute worst friend on earth
I'll never be good enough for anyone.

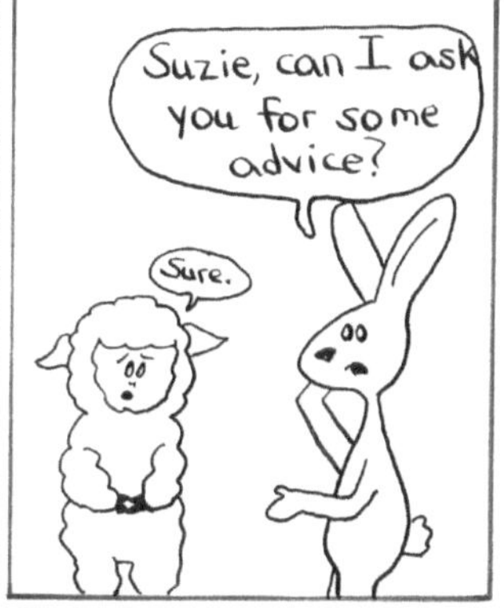
Suzie, can I ask you for some advice?
Sure.

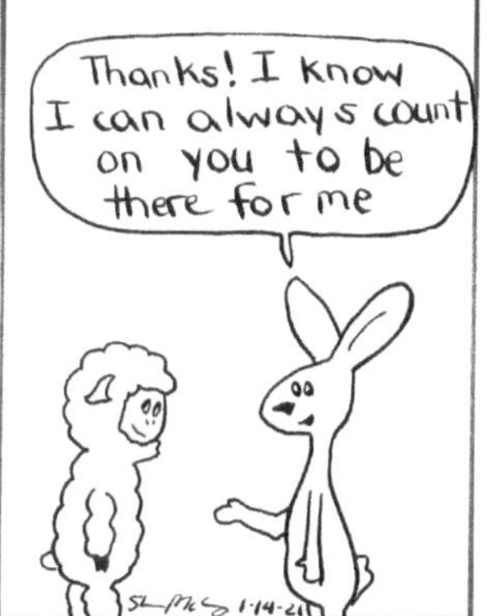
Thanks! I know I can always count on you to be there for me

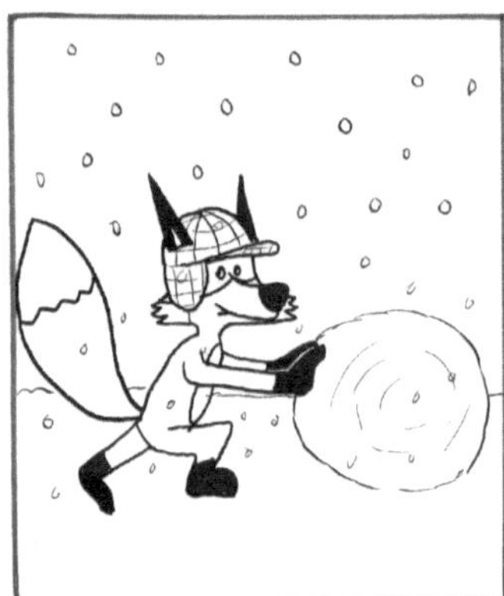

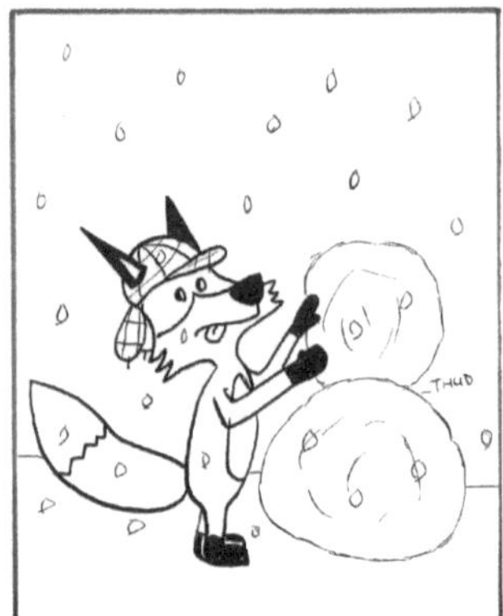

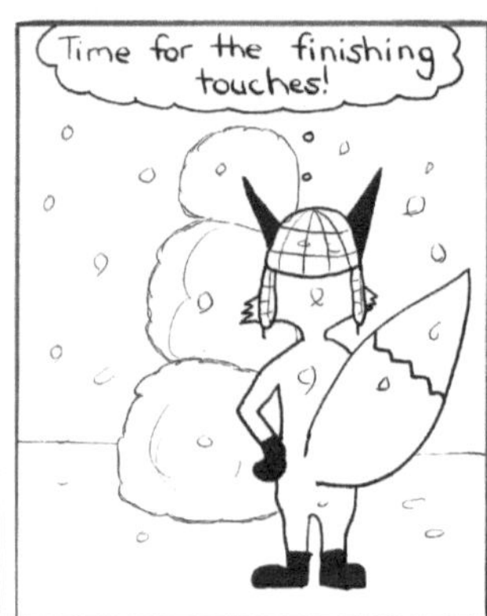

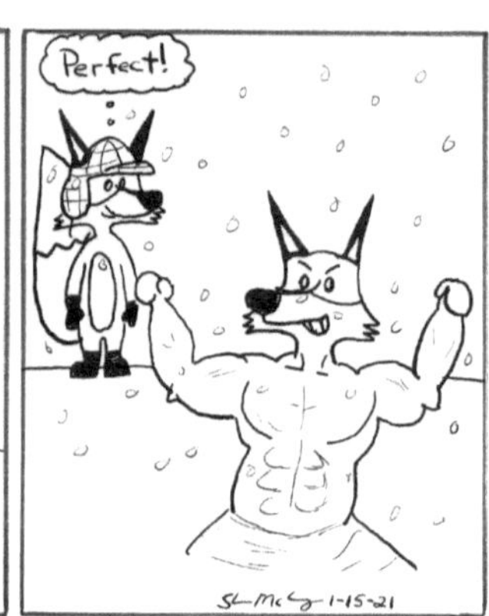

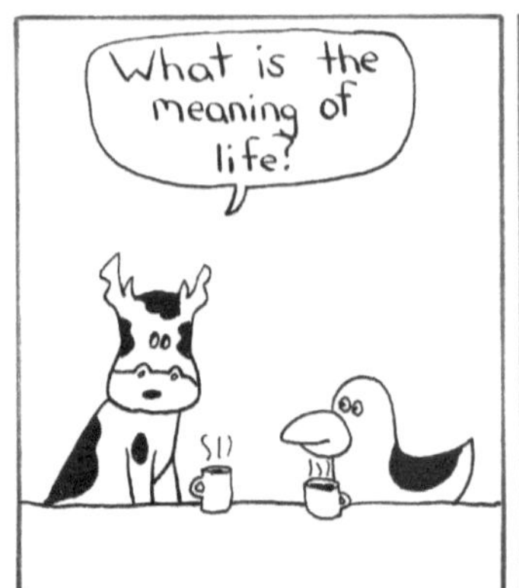

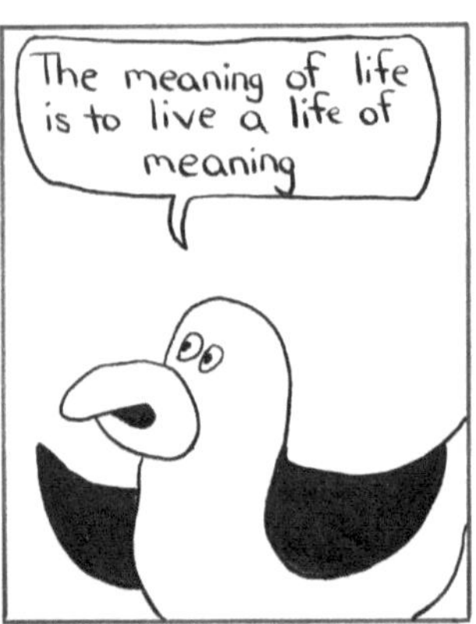

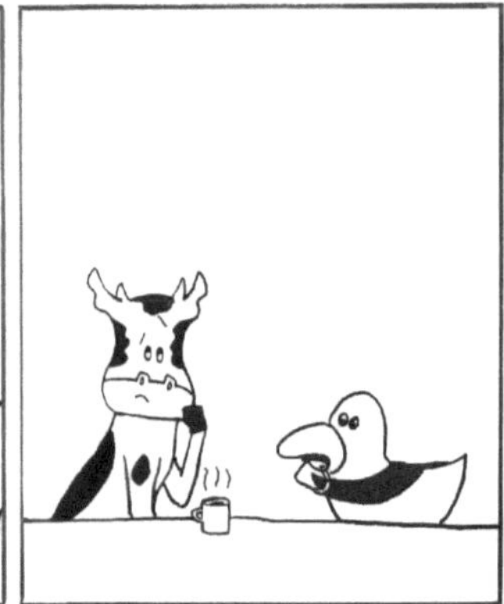

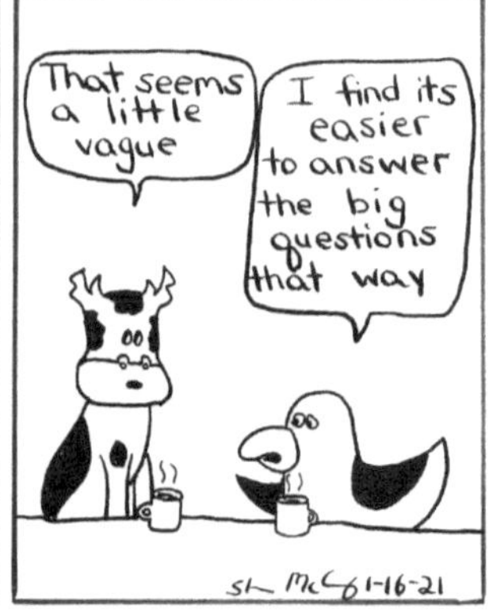

New Years' Resolution Check In:

Squiggles

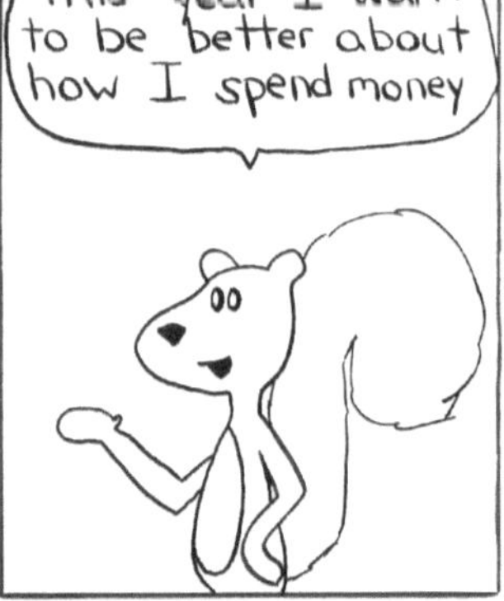

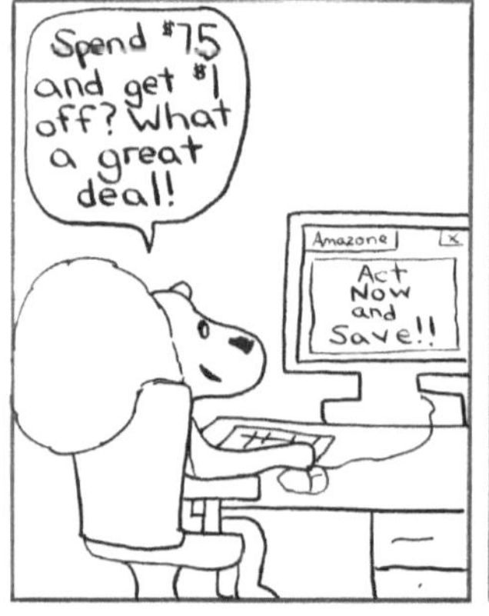

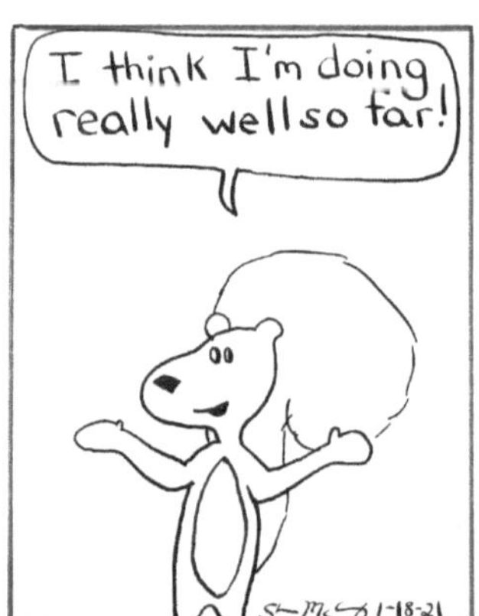

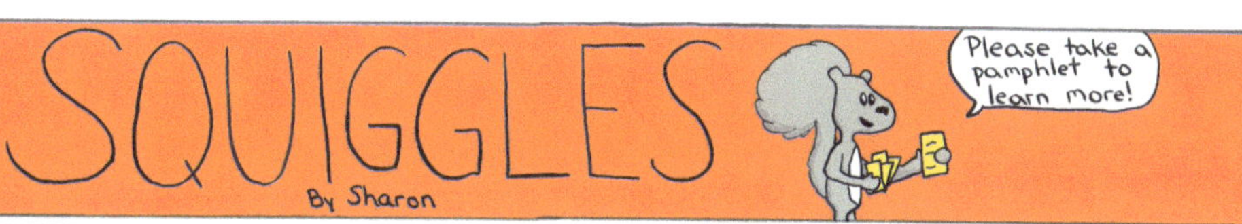
SQUIGGLES
By Sharon
Please take a pamphlet to learn more!

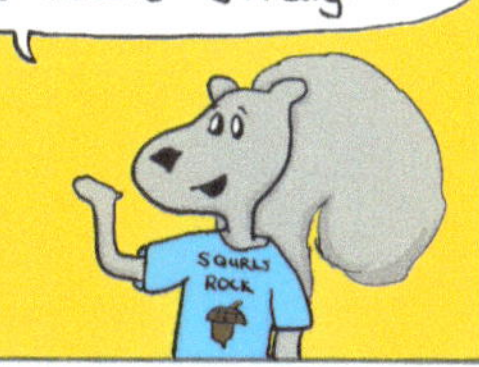
Hi! Squiggles here! Squirrels usually get a bad rep as being pests and kind of stupid, but today I'm going to set the record straight!

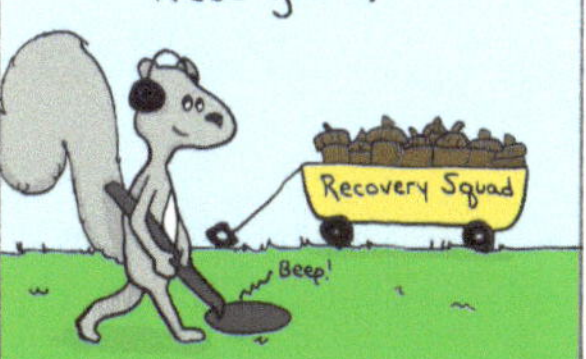
① Squirrels are NOT forgetful. They actually remember the location of nearly 95% of the nuts they bury. Those not recovered help ensure new trees grow!
Recovery Squad
Beep!

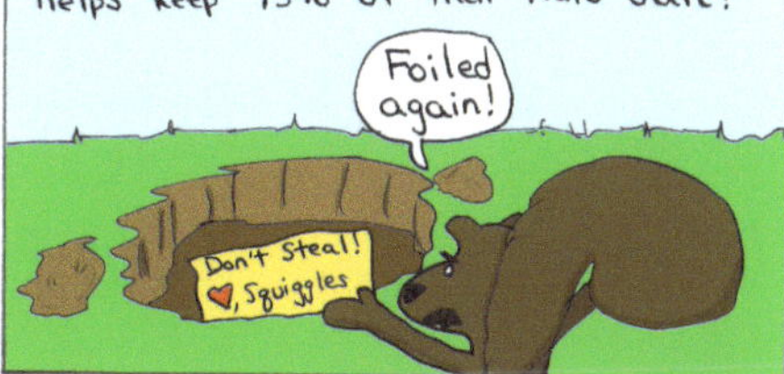
② Speaking of nuts, squirrels know when a potential thief is watching. In fact, if they see a thief, squirrels will pretend to bury a nut to throw the thief off. This helps keep 75% of their nuts safe!
Foiled again!
Don't Steal! ♥, Squiggles

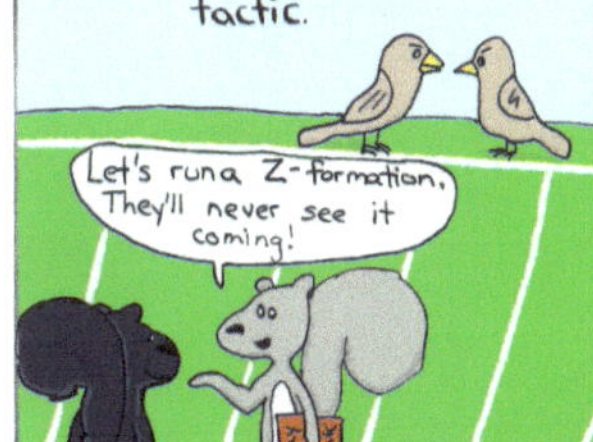
③ Squirrels zig-zag to avoid predators. It has proven to be a beneficial survival tactic.
Let's run a Z-formation. They'll never see it coming!

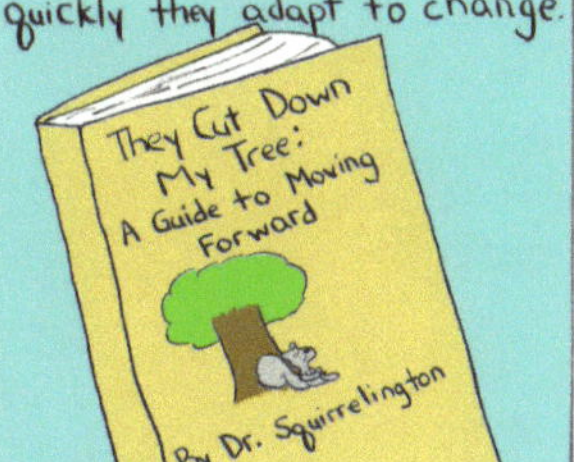
④ Squirrels' intelligence is easy to see if you watch how quickly they adapt to change.
They Cut Down My Tree: A Guide to Moving Forward
By Dr. Squirrelington

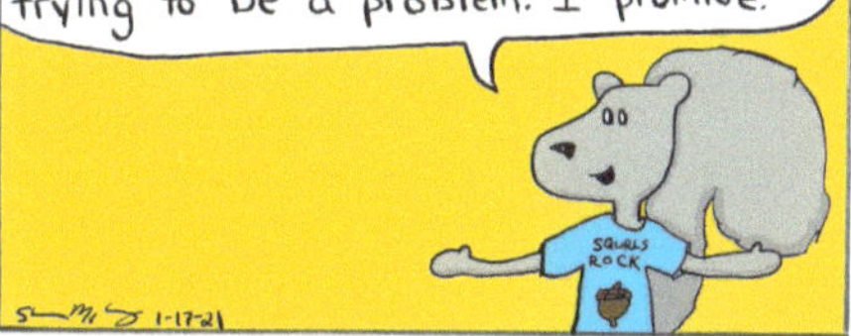
In conclusion, Squirrels are pretty great and do a lot for the tree population. Plus, we're cute! So get to know us better and maybe brake when we try to zig-zag away from your car. We're not trying to be a problem. I promise.
1-17-21

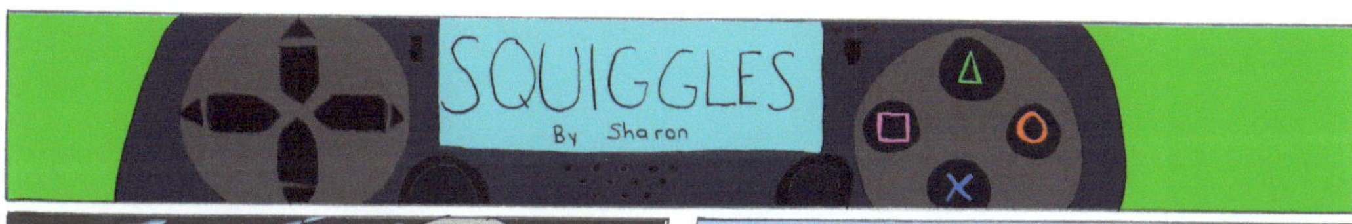
SQUIGGLES
By Sharon

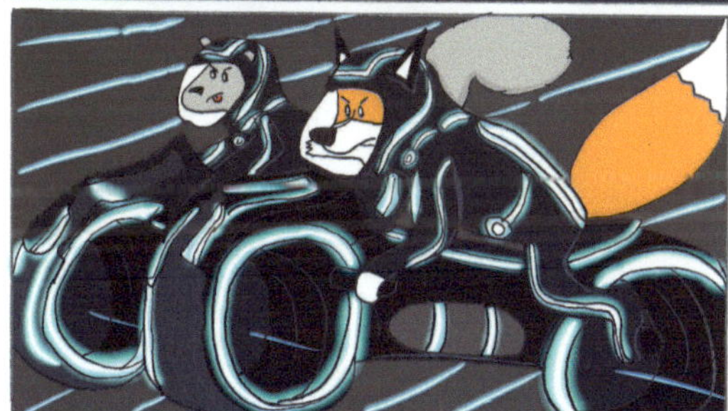

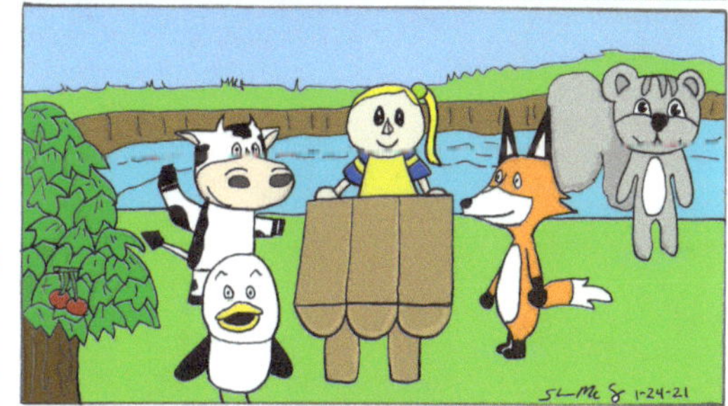
1-24-21

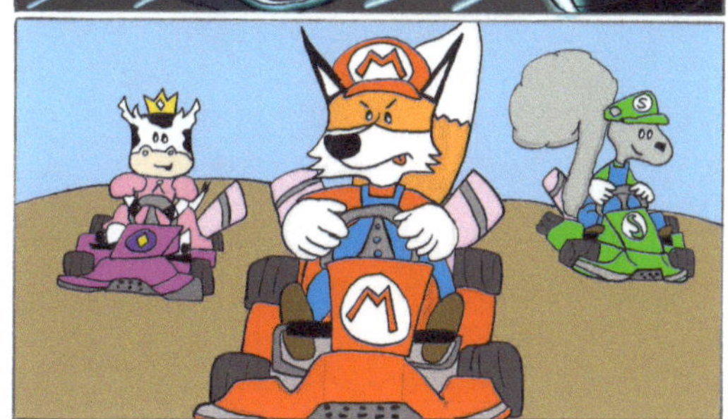

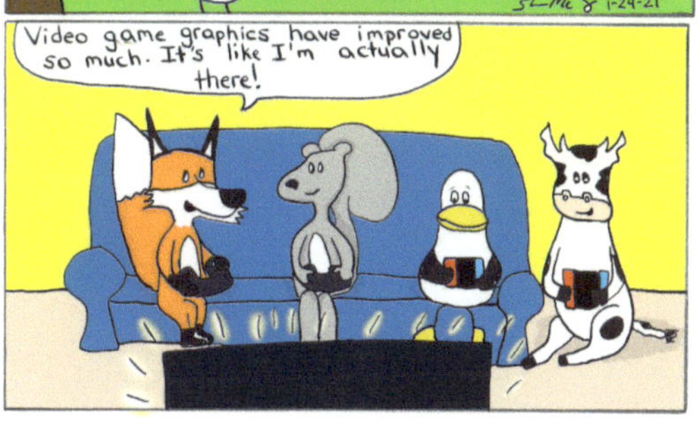
Video game graphics have improved so much. It's like I'm actually there!

New Years' Resolution Check In:

Moochki

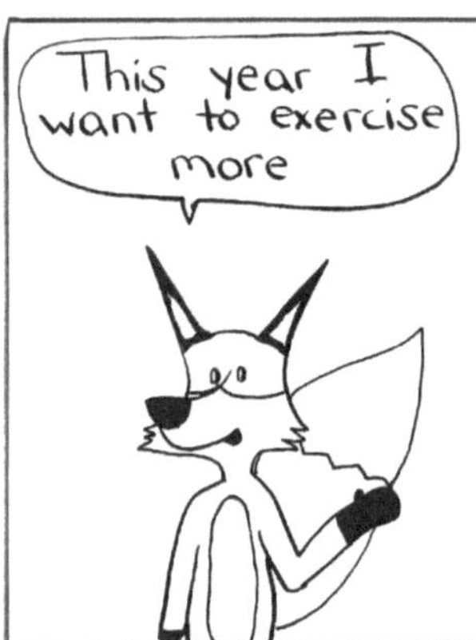

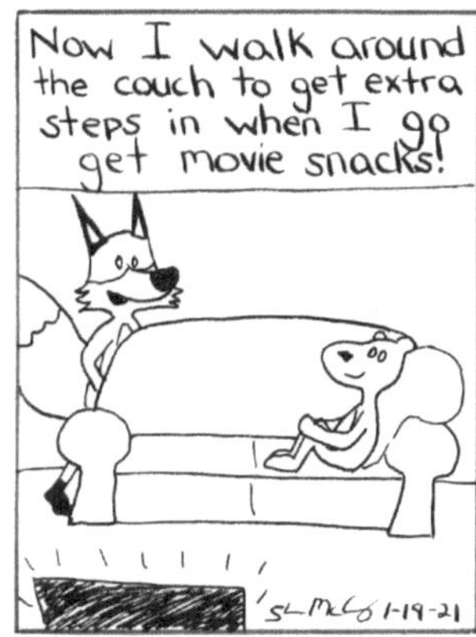

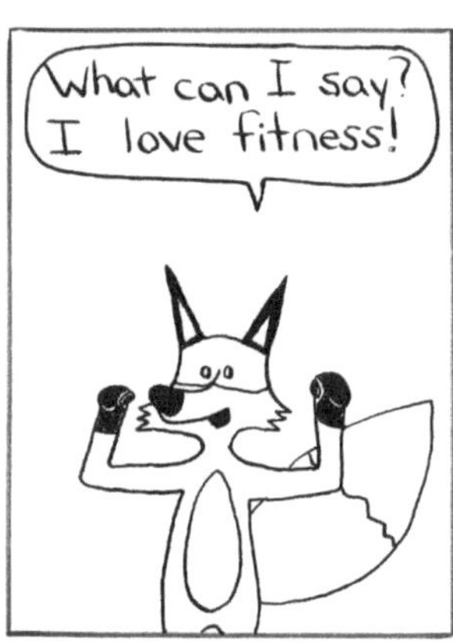

New Years' Resolution Check In:

Suzie

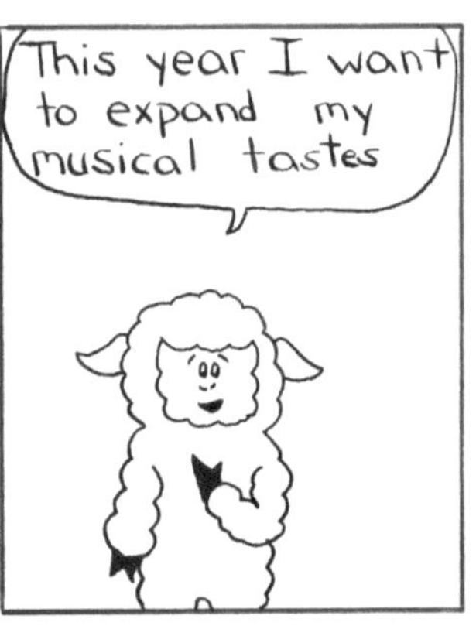

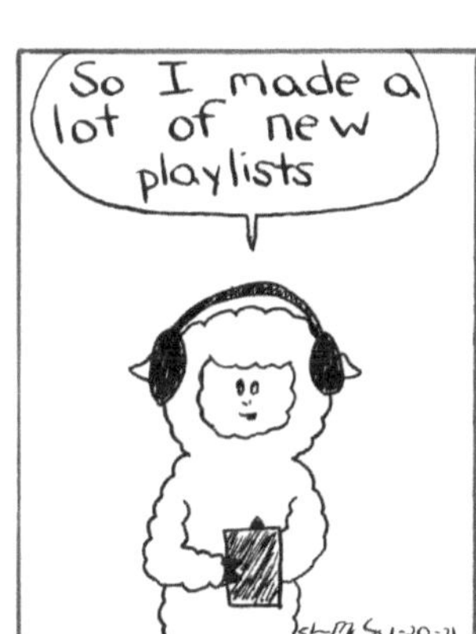

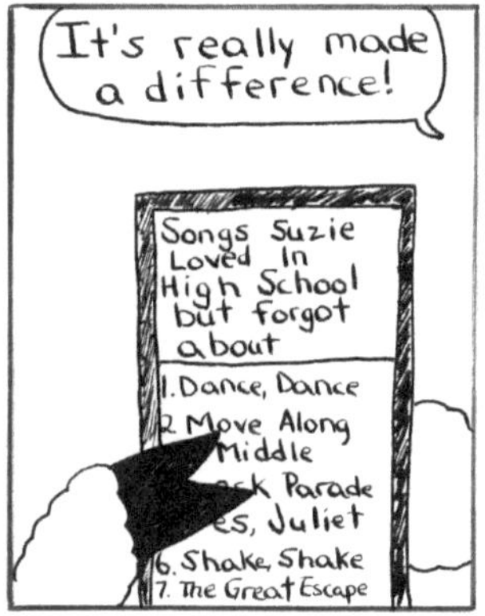

New Years' Resolution Check In:

Bernice

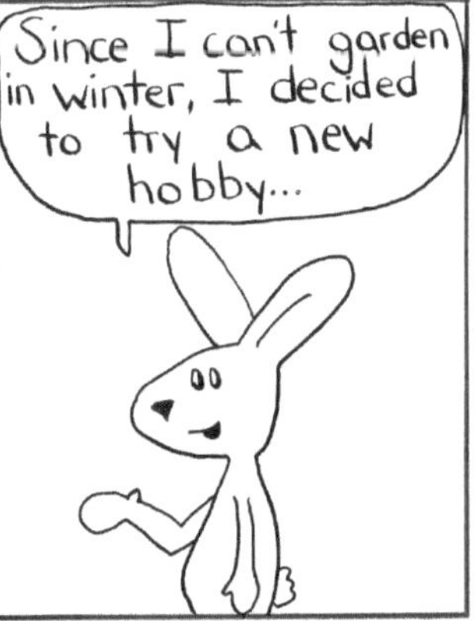

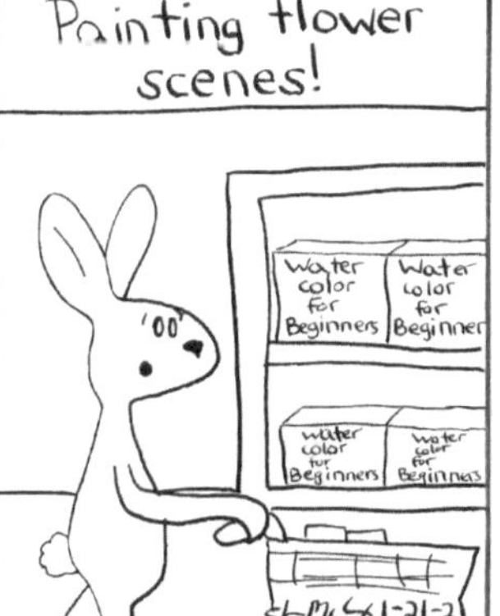

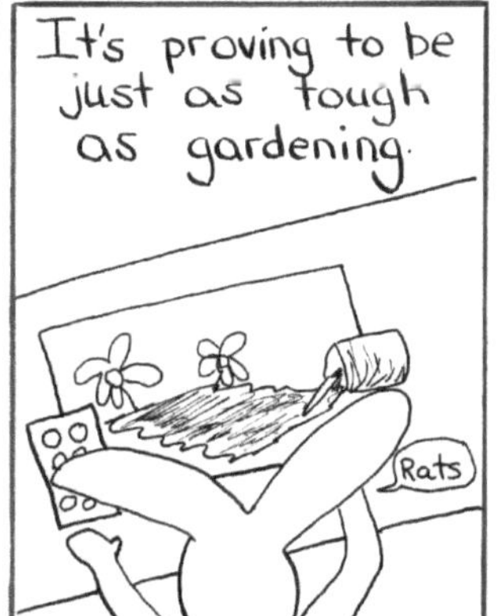

New Years' Resolution Check In:

Harold and Eggplant

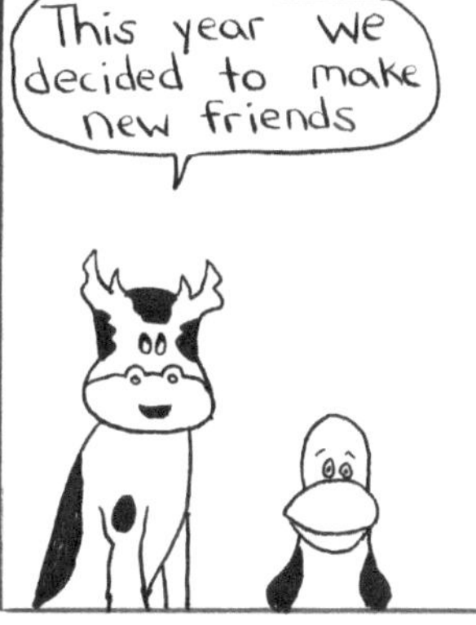

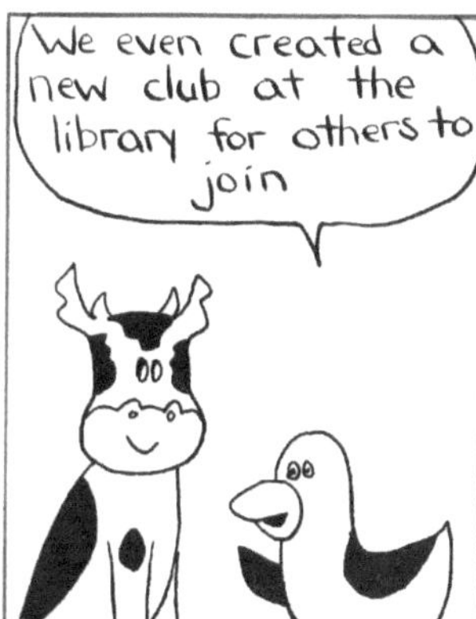

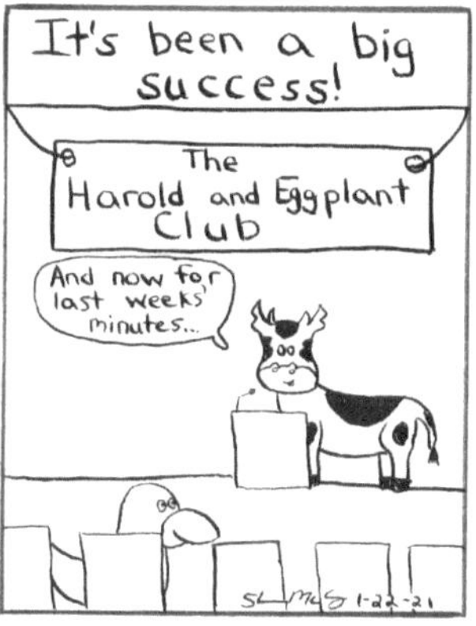

New Years' Resolution Check In:

Paul

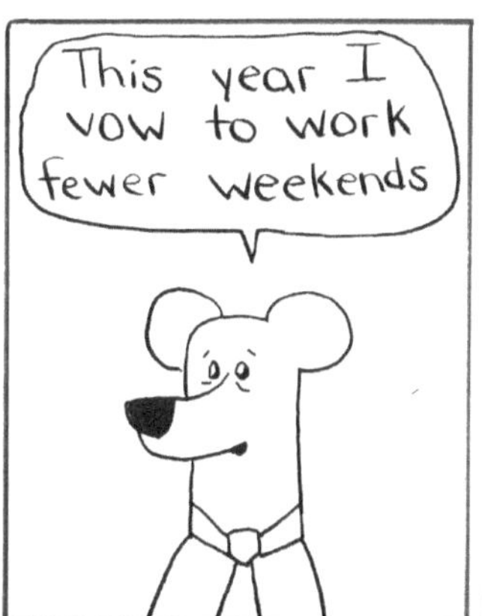

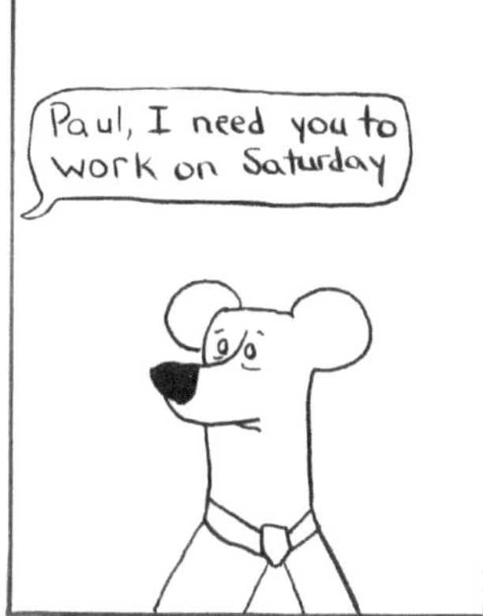

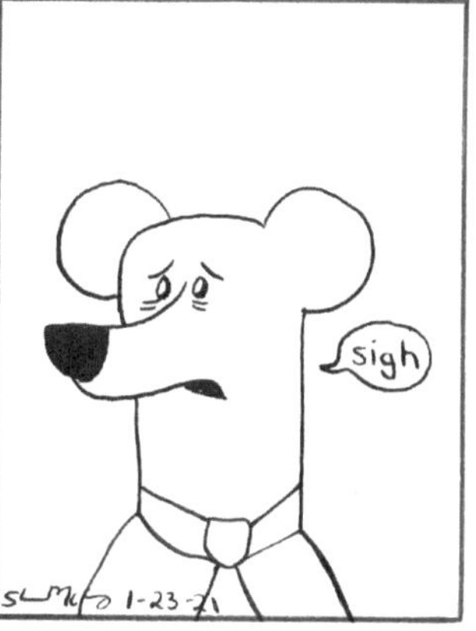

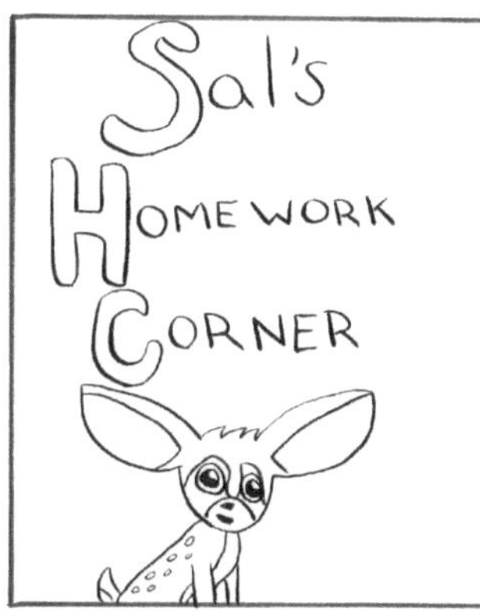

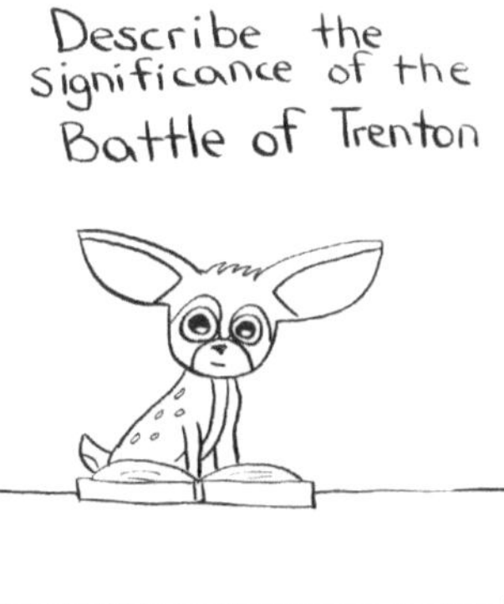

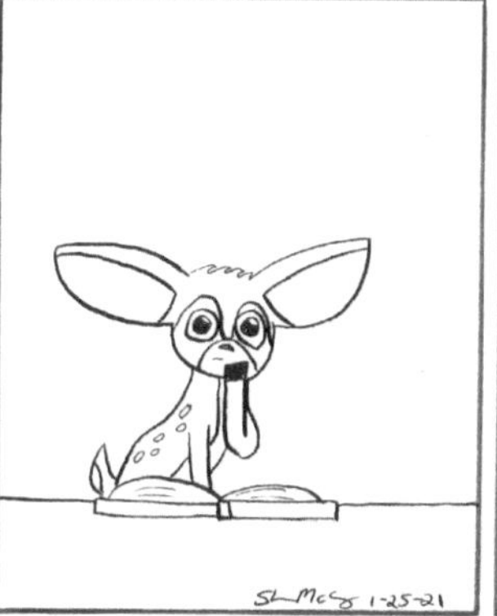

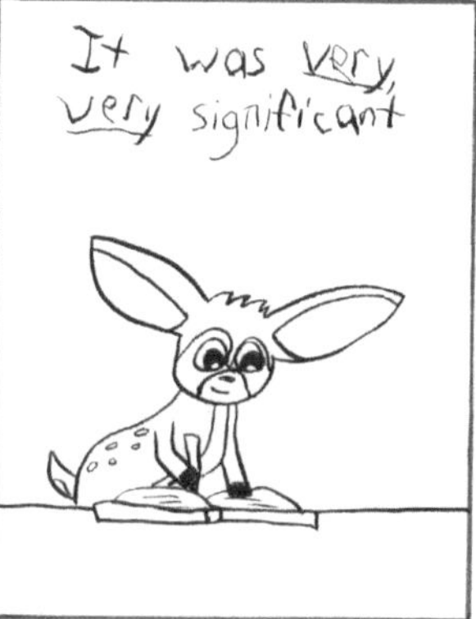

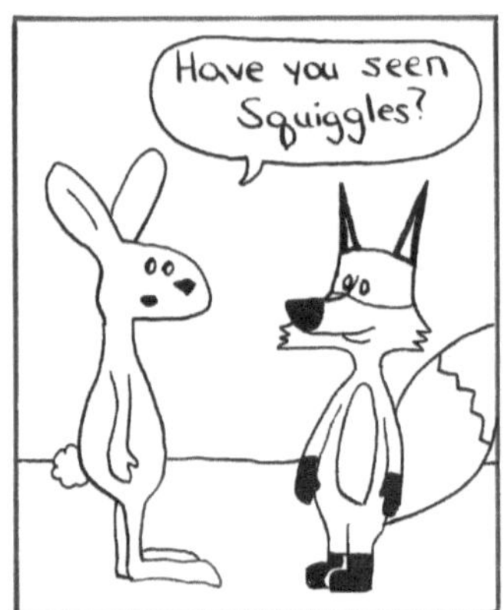
Have you seen Squiggles?

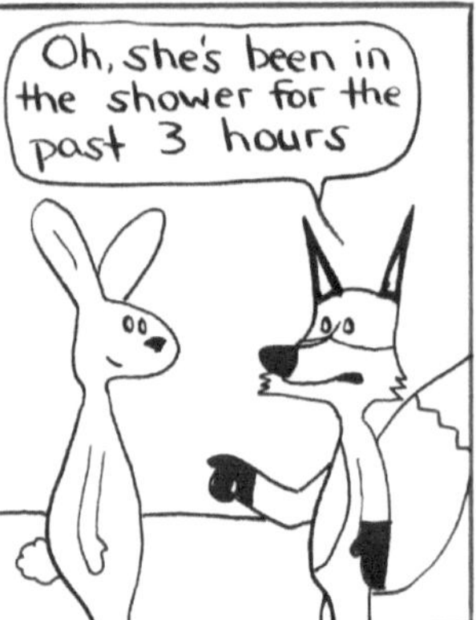
Oh, she's been in the shower for the past 3 hours

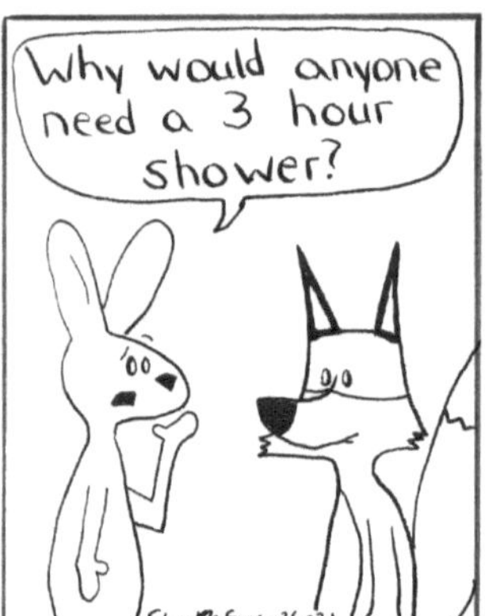
Why would anyone need a 3 hour shower?
1-26-21

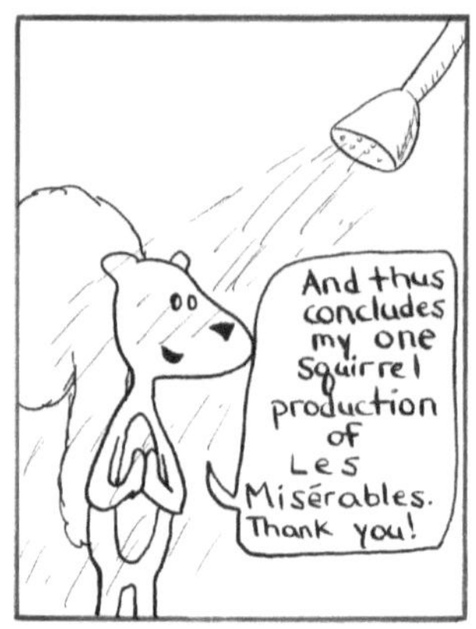
And thus concludes my one Squirrel production of Les Misérables. Thank you!

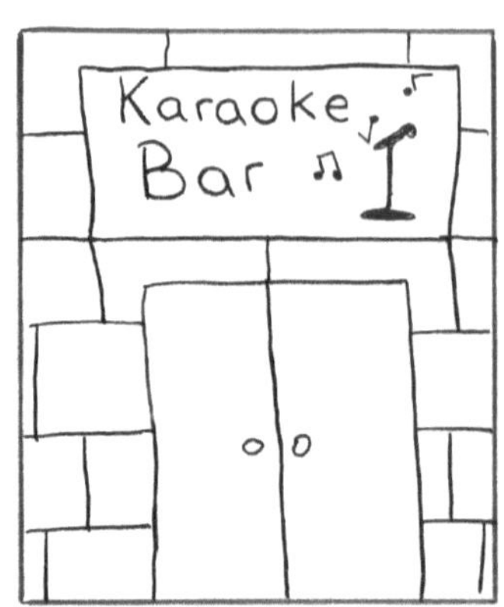
Karaoke Bar

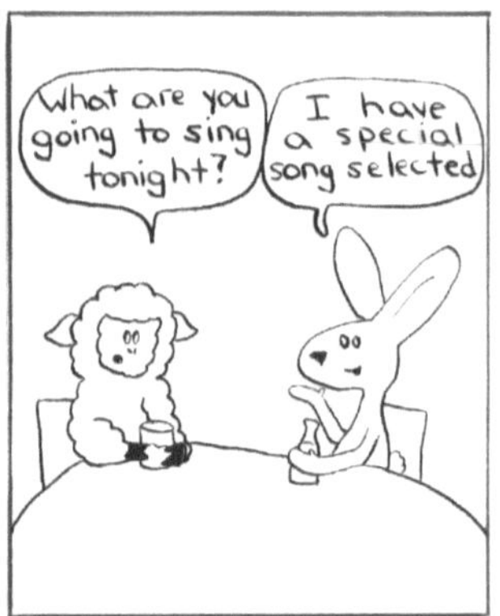
What are you going to sing tonight?
I have a special song selected

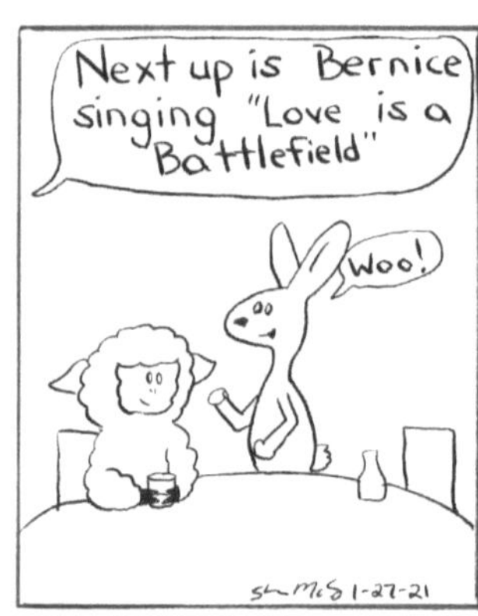
Next up is Bernice singing "Love is a Battlefield"
Woo!
1-27-21

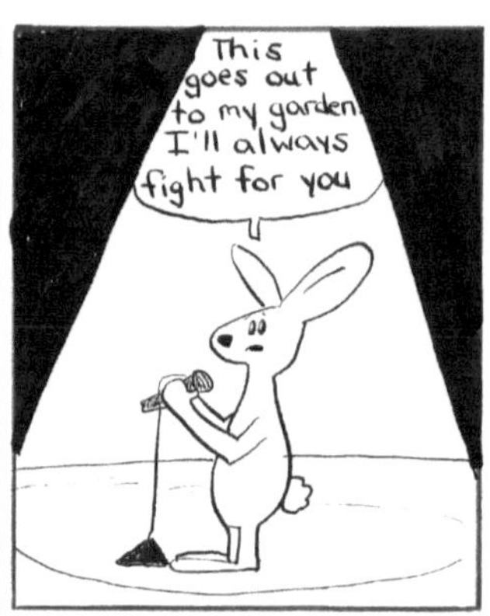
This goes out to my garden I'll always fight for you

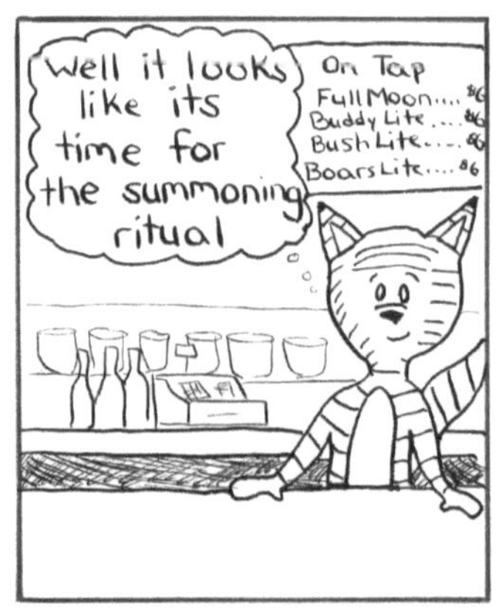
Well it looks like its time for the summoning ritual
On Tap
FullMoon.... $6
Buddy Lite.... $6
Bush Lite.... $6
Boars Lite.... $6

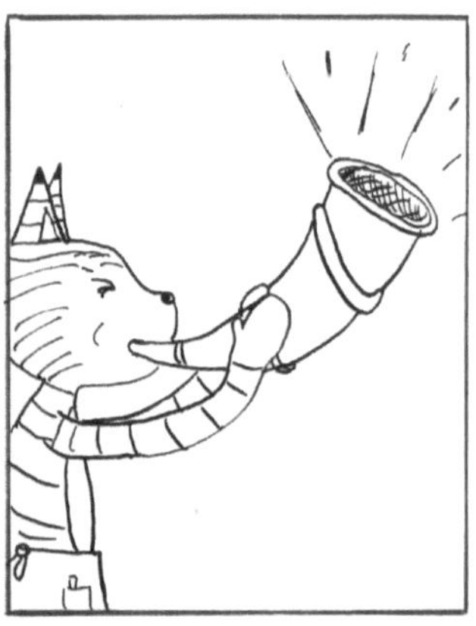

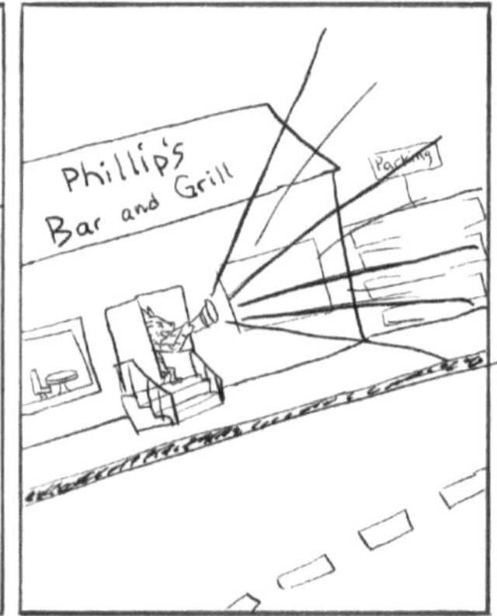
Phillip's Bar and Grill
Parking

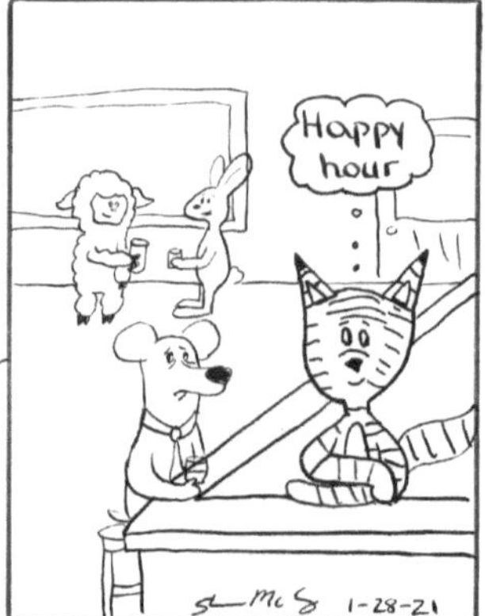
Happy hour
1-28-21

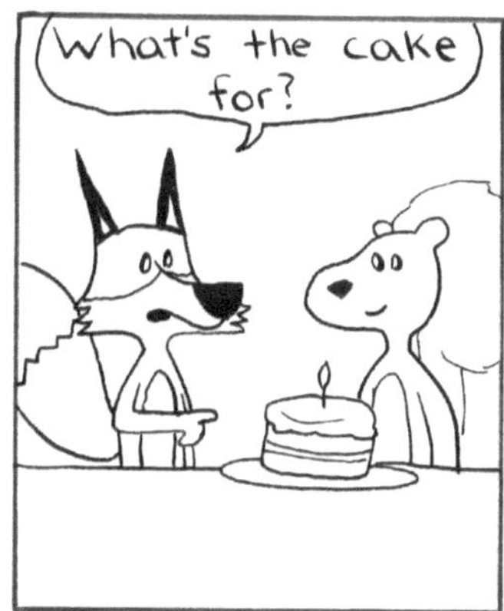
What's the cake for?
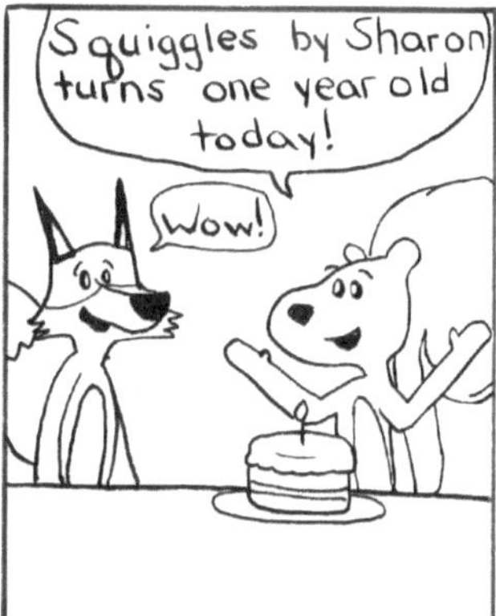
Squiggles by Sharon turns one year old today!
Wow!
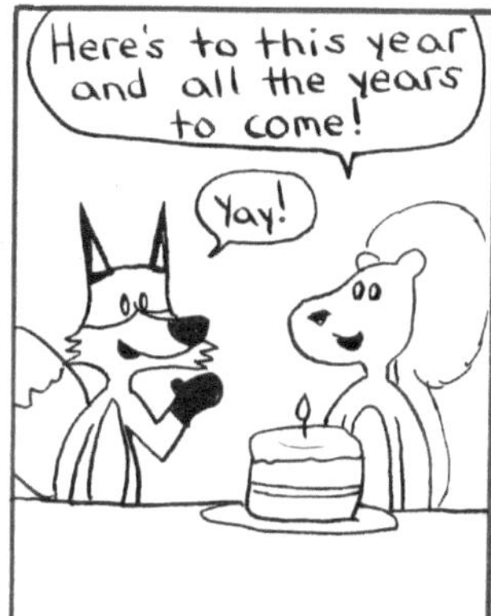
Here's to this year and all the years to come!
Yay!
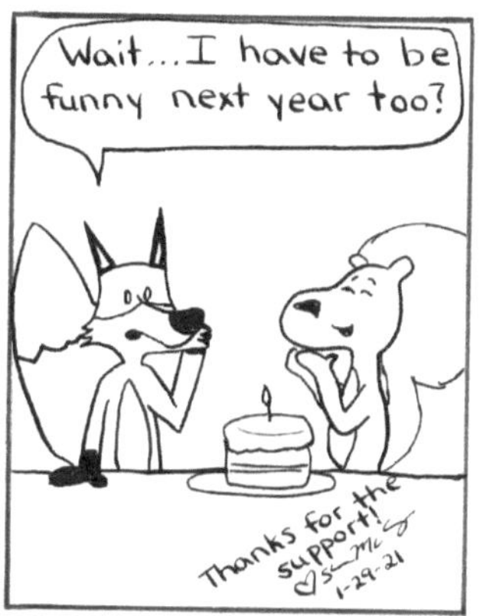
Wait... I have to be funny next year too?
Thanks for the support!
1-29-21
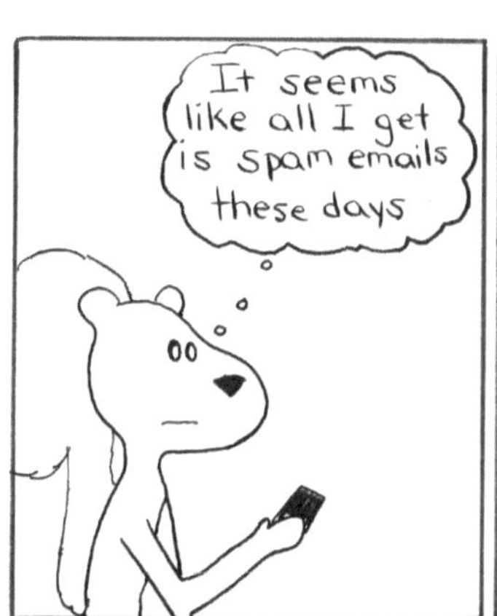
It seems like all I get is spam emails these days
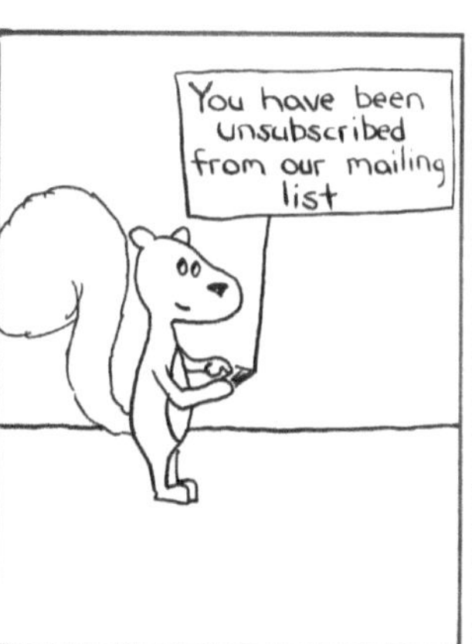
You have been unsubscribed from our mailing list
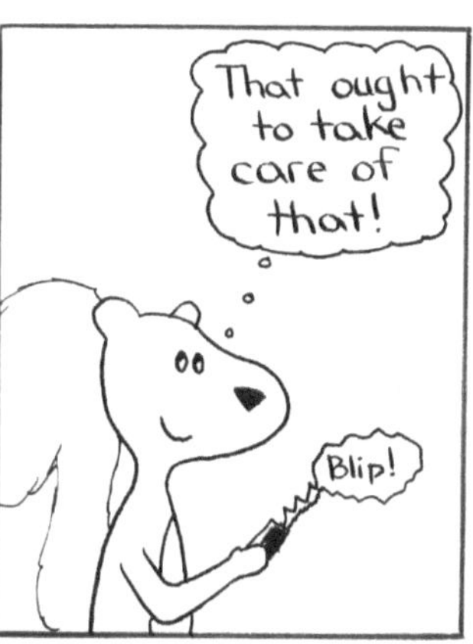
That ought to take care of that!
Blip!
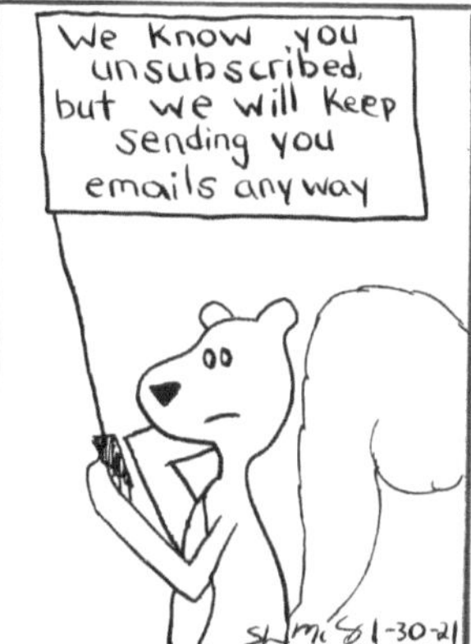
We know you unsubscribed, but we will keep sending you emails anyway
1-30-21

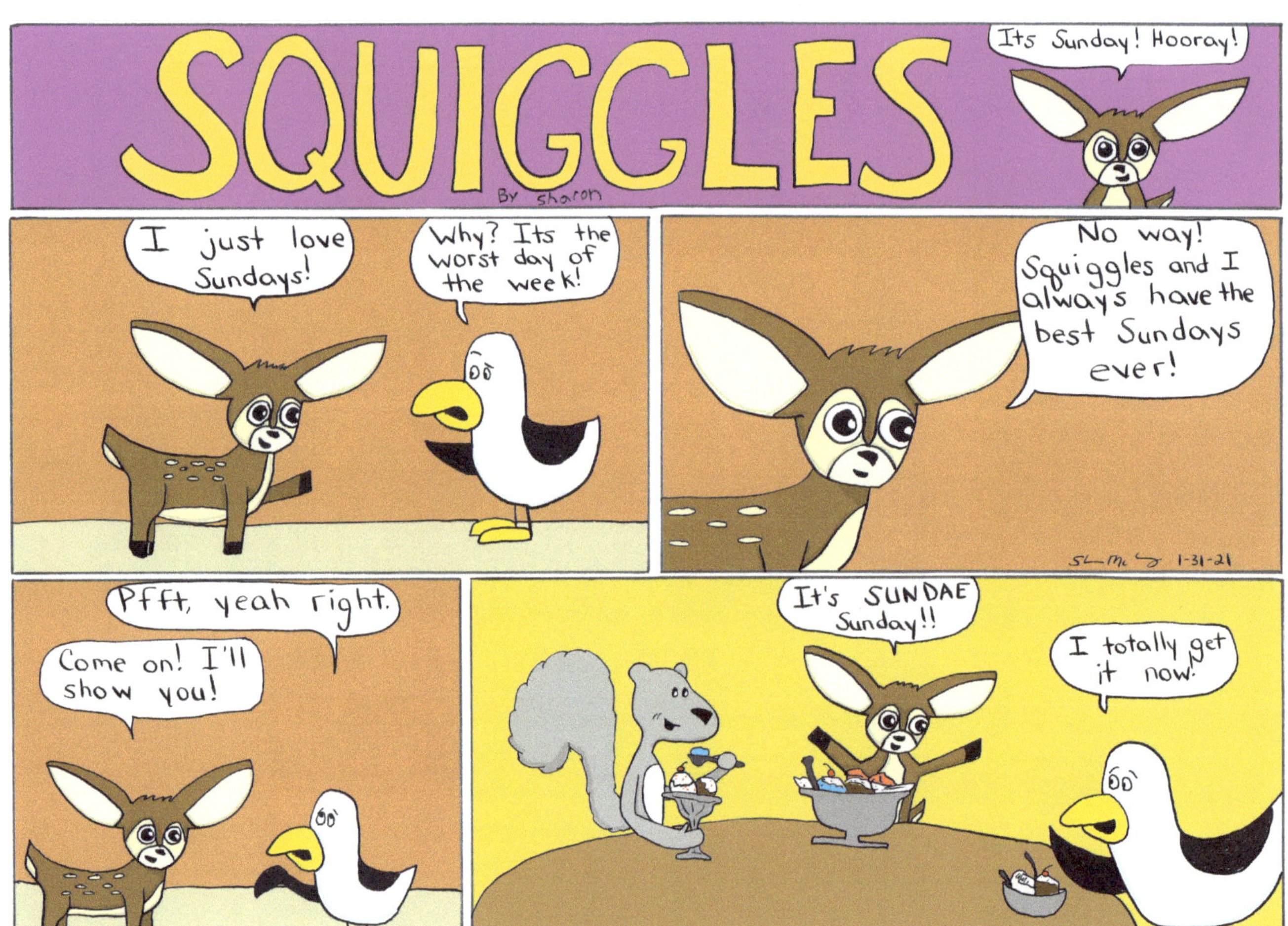
SQUIGGLES
By sharon
Its Sunday! Hooray!
I just love Sundays!
Why? Its the worst day of the week!
No way! Squiggles and I always have the best Sundays ever!
1-31-21
Pfft, yeah right.
Come on! I'll show you!
It's SUNDAE Sunday!!
I totally get it now!

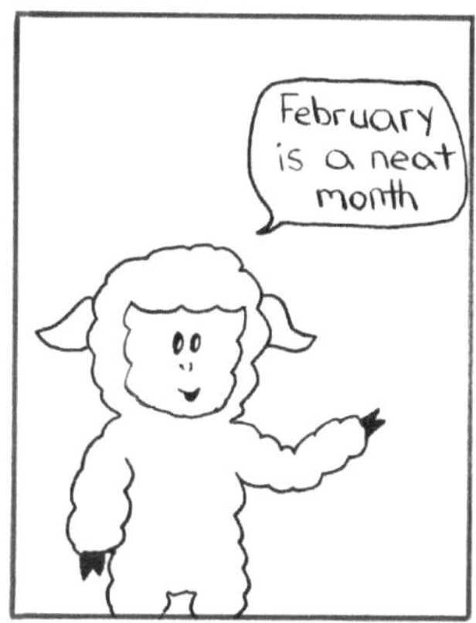
February is a neat month

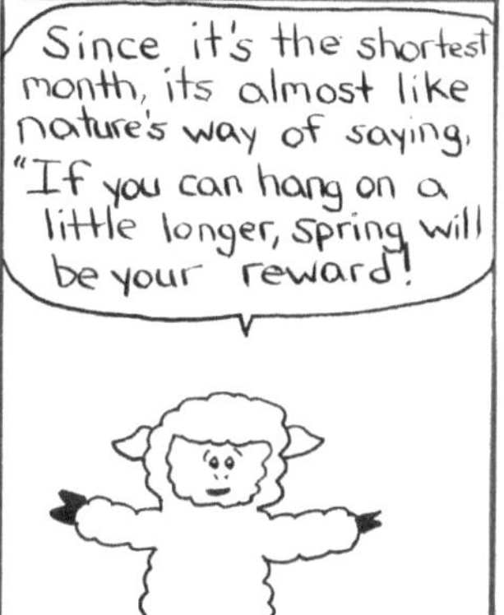
Since it's the shortest month, its almost like nature's way of saying, "If you can hang on a little longer, spring will be your reward!

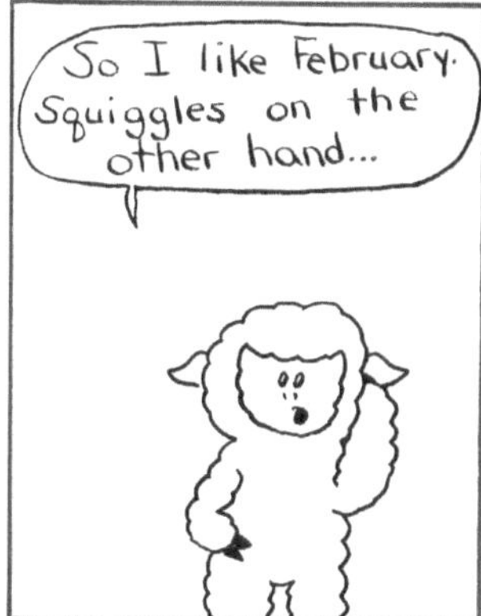
So I like February. Squiggles on the other hand...

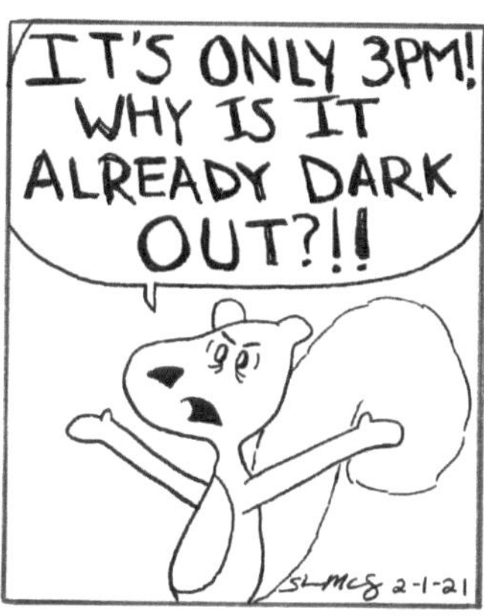
IT'S ONLY 3PM! WHY IS IT ALREADY DARK OUT?!!
SLMcG 2-1-21

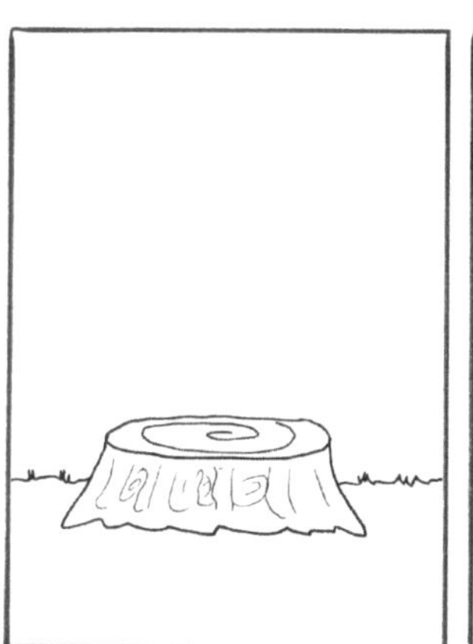

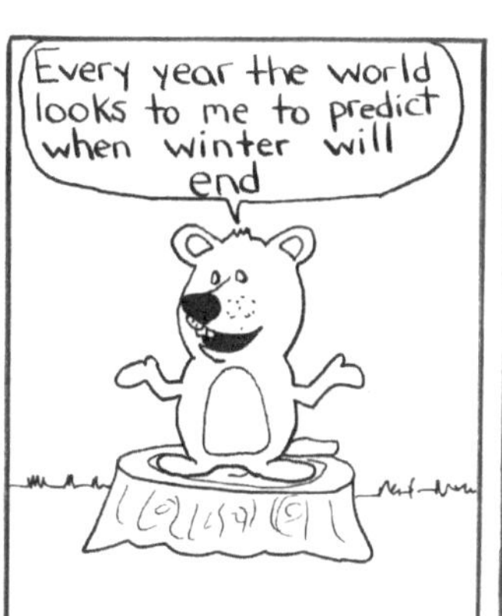
Every year the world looks to me to predict when winter will end

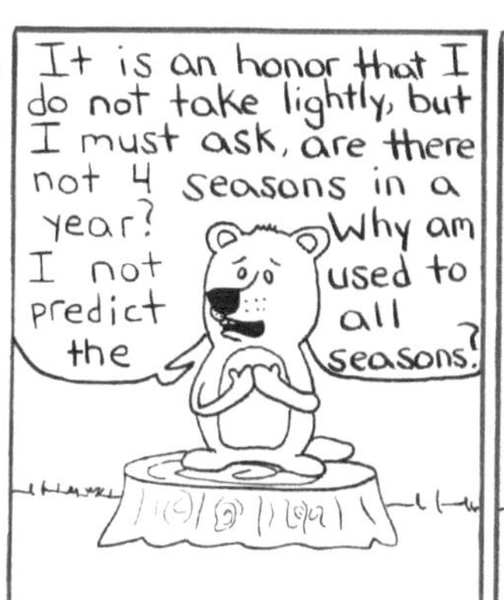
It is an honor that I do not take lightly, but I must ask, are there not 4 seasons in a year? Why am I not used to predict the all seasons?

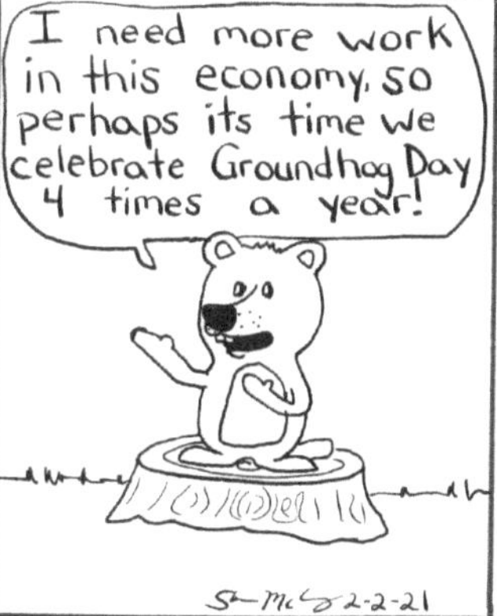
I need more work in this economy, so perhaps its time we celebrate Groundhog Day 4 times a year!
SLMcG 2-2-21

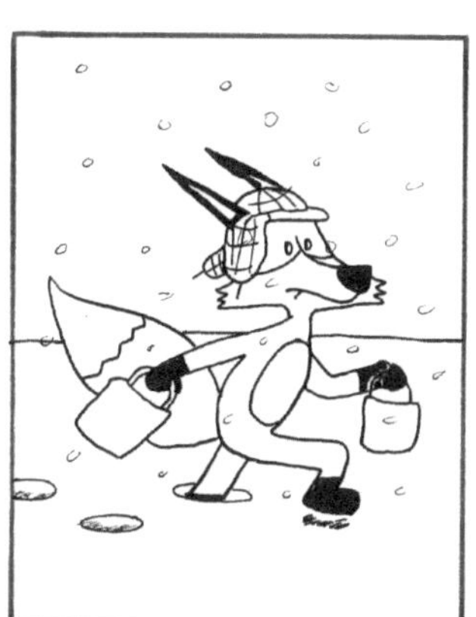

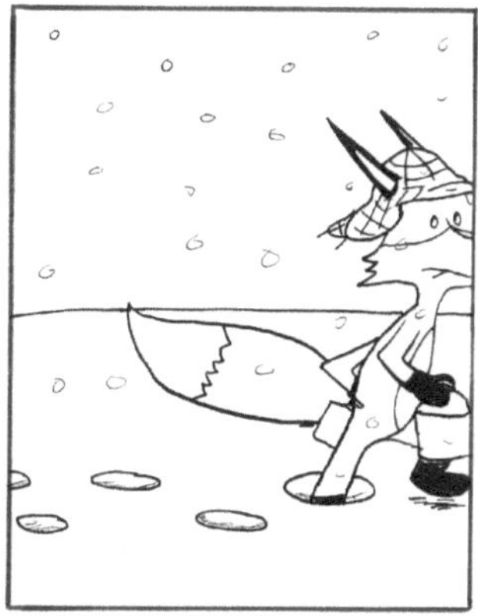

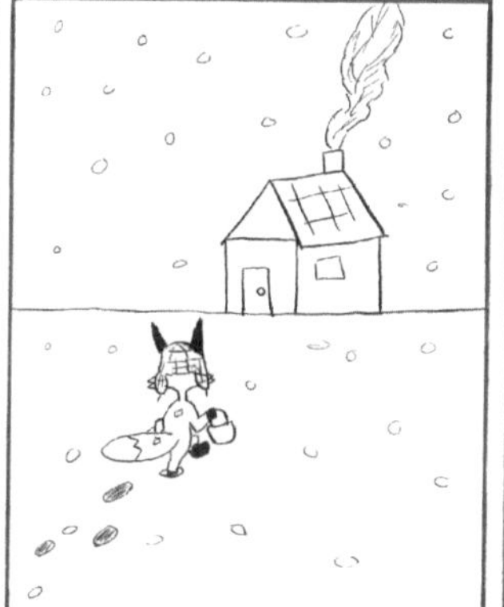

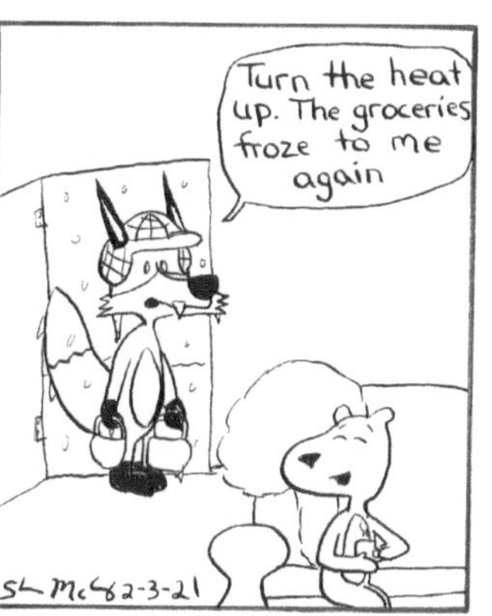
Turn the heat up. The groceries froze to me again
SLMcG 2-3-21

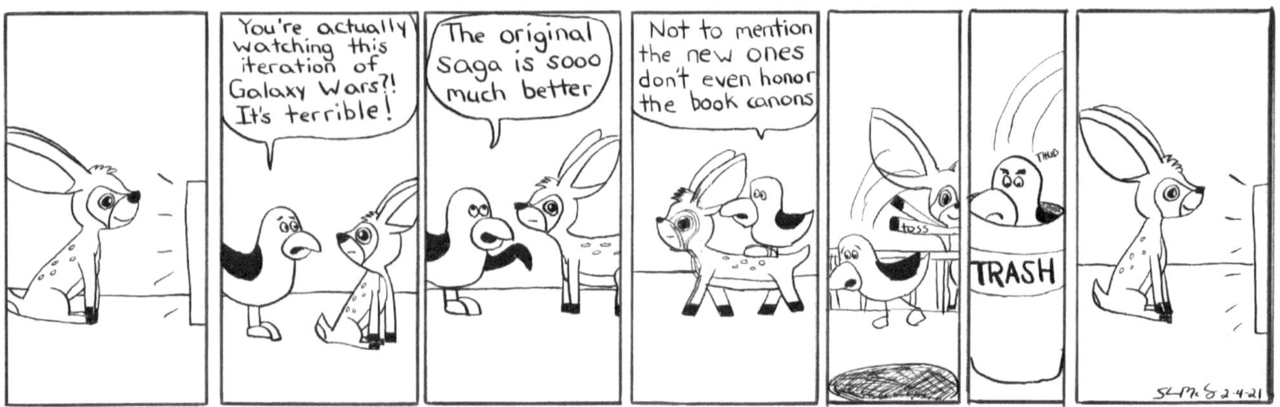
You're actually watching this iteration of Galaxy Wars?! It's terrible!
The original saga is sooo much better
Not to mention the new ones don't even honor the book canons
toss
THUD
TRASH
SLMcG 2-4-21

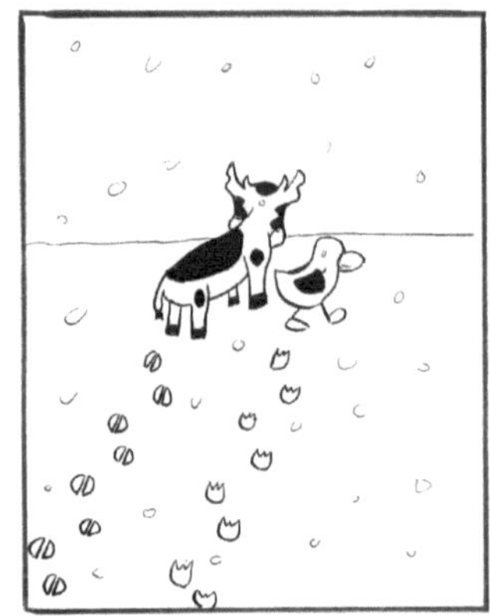

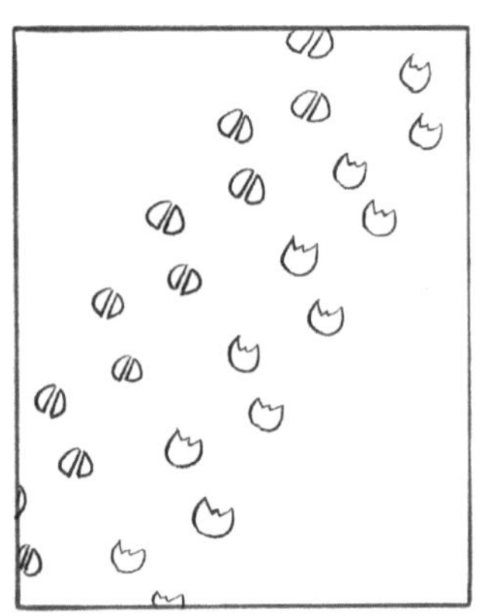

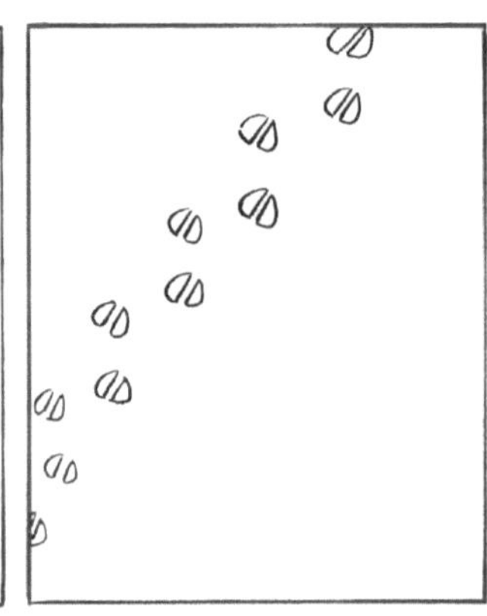

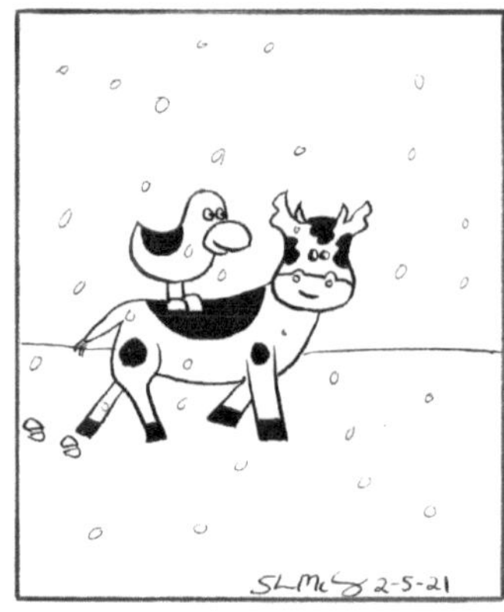
SLMcG 2-5-21

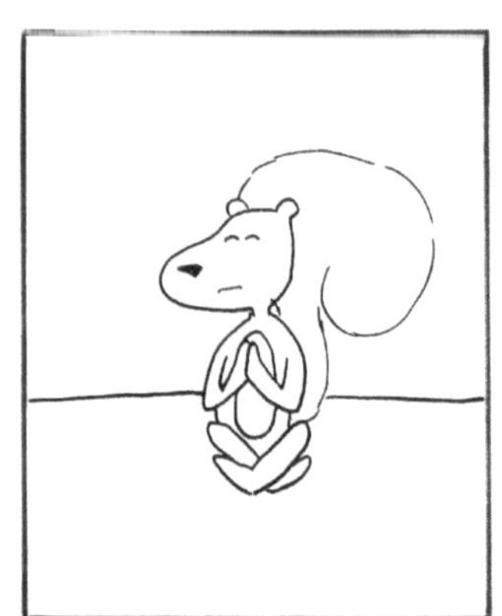

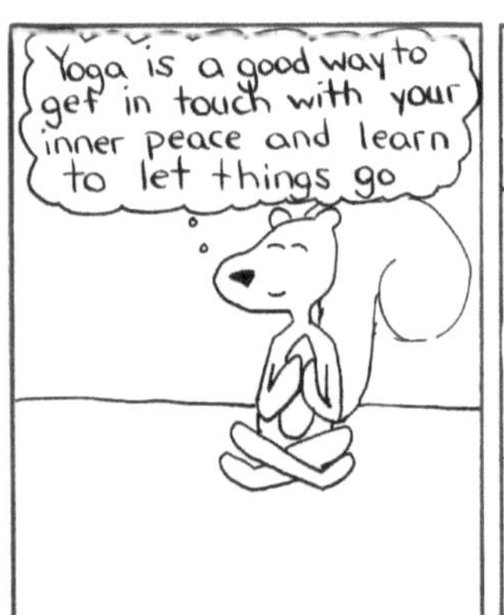
Yoga is a good way to get in touch with your inner peace and learn to let things go

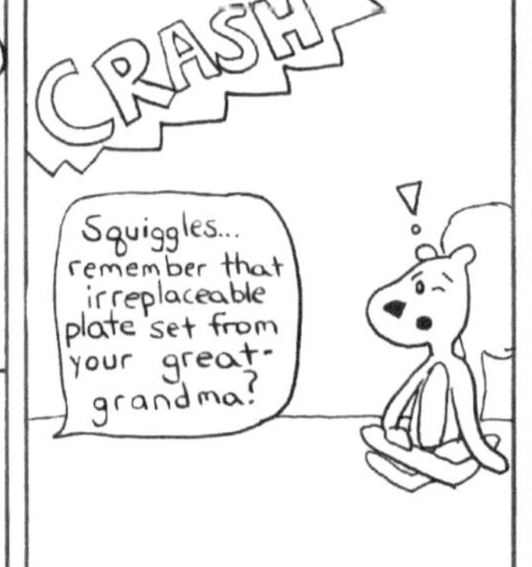
CRASH
Squiggles... remember that irreplaceable plate set from your great-grandma?
!

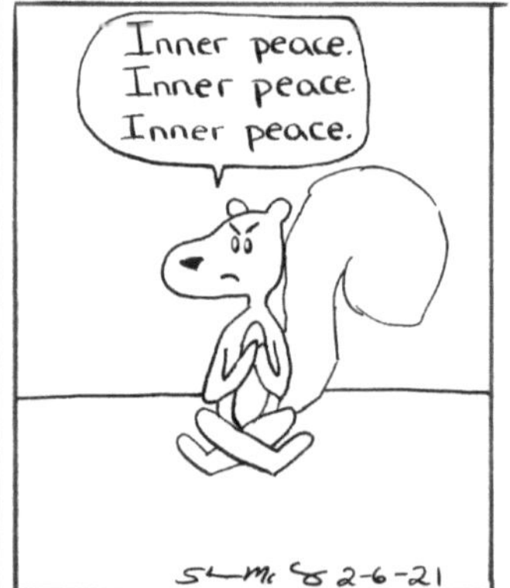
Inner peace. Inner peace. Inner peace.
SLMcG 2-6-21

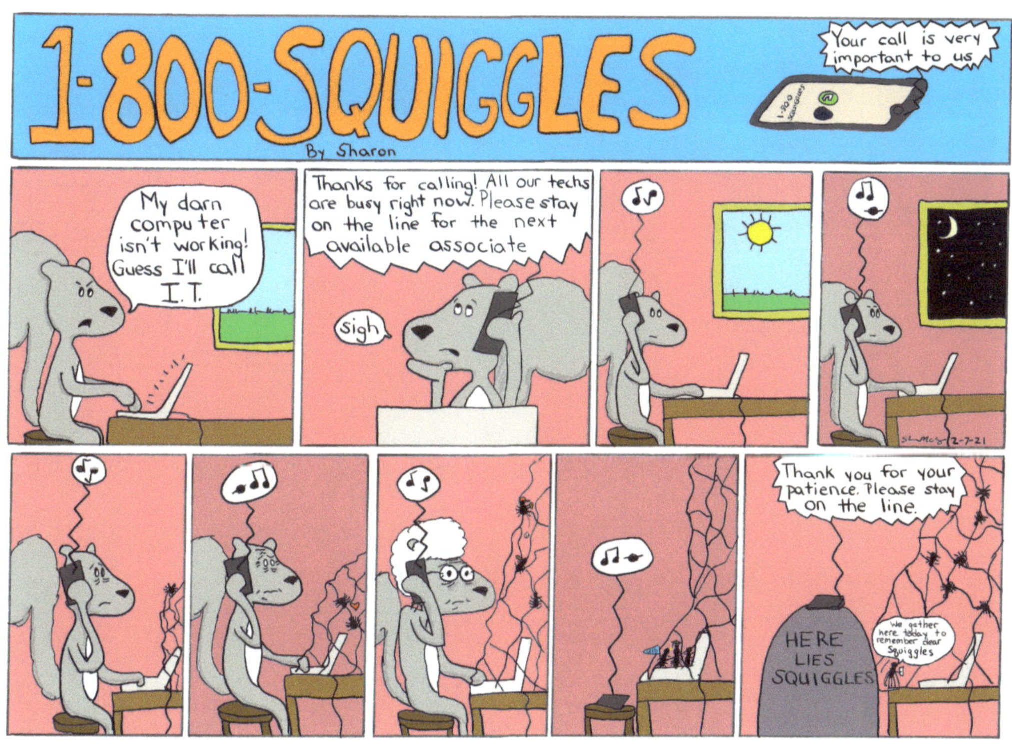
1-800-SQUIGGLES
By Sharon
Your call is very important to us
My darn computer isn't working! Guess I'll call I.T.
Thanks for calling! All our techs are busy right now. Please stay on the line for the next available associate
Sigh
Thank you for your patience. Please stay on the line.
HERE LIES SQUIGGLES
We gather here today to remember dear Squiggles

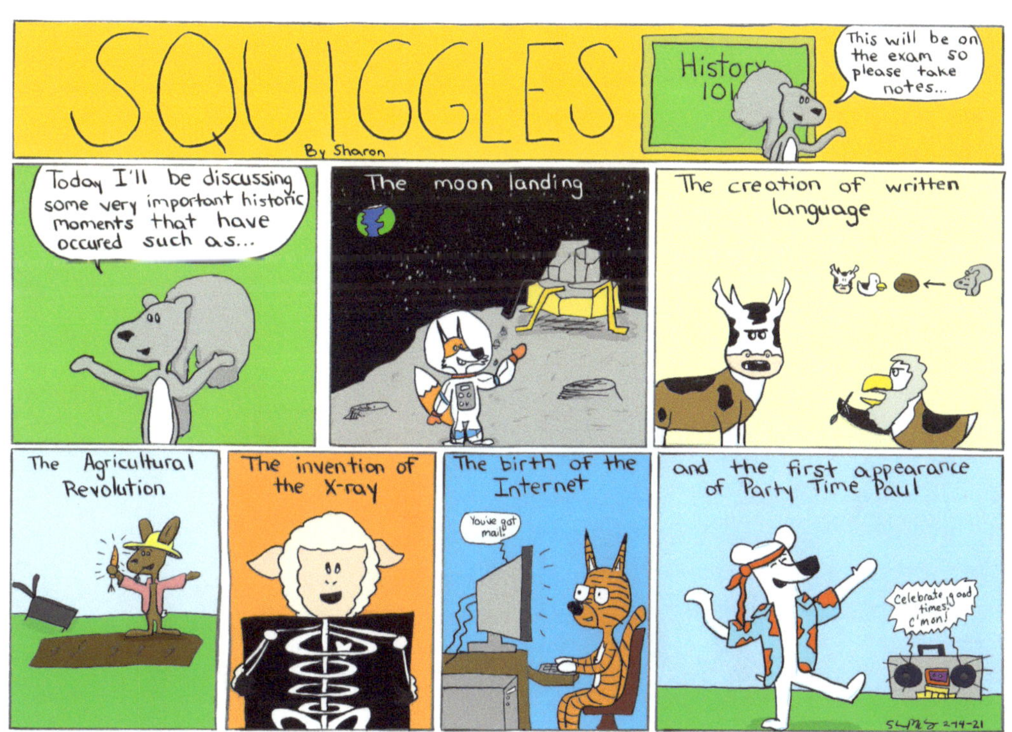
SQUIGGLES
By Sharon
This will be on the exam so please take notes...
Today I'll be discussing some very important historic moments that have occured such as...
The moon landing
The creation of written language
The Agricultural Revolution
The invention of the X-ray
The birth of the Internet
You've got mail!
and the first appearance of Party Time Paul
Celebrate good times, c'mon!

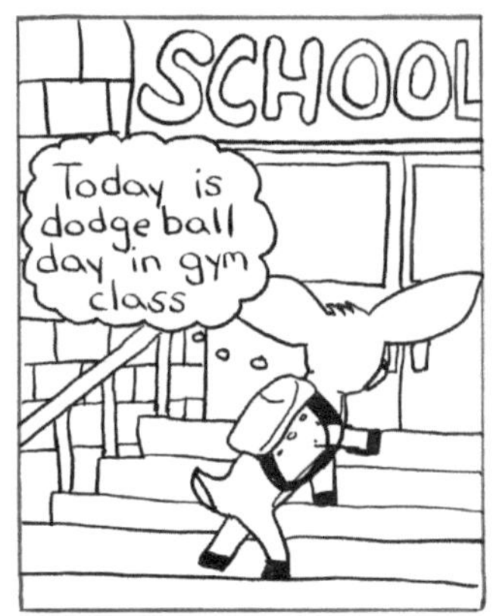
SCHOOL
Today is dodge ball day in gym class
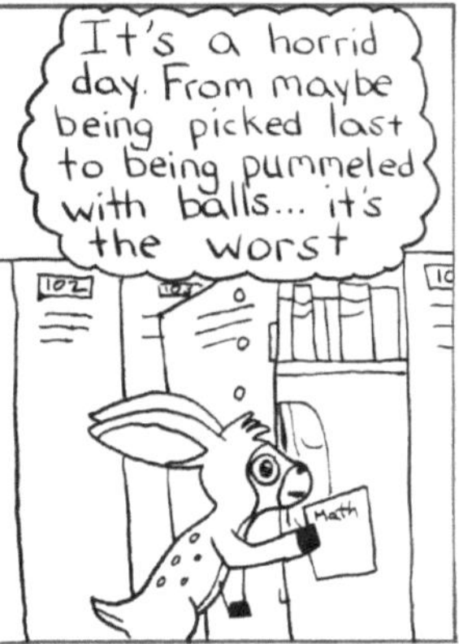
It's a horrid day. From maybe being picked last to being pummeled with balls... it's the worst
102
Math
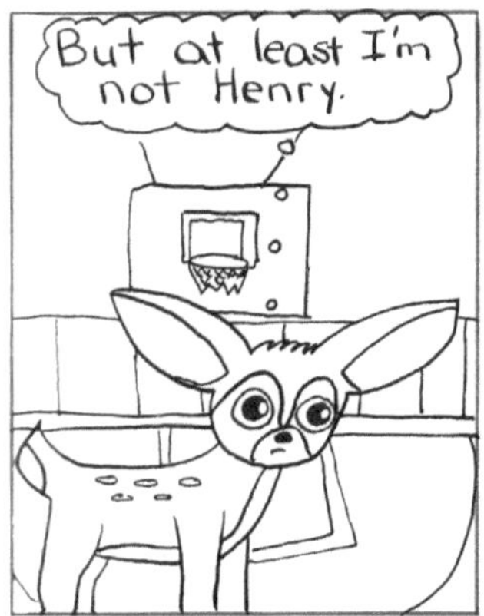
But at least I'm not Henry.
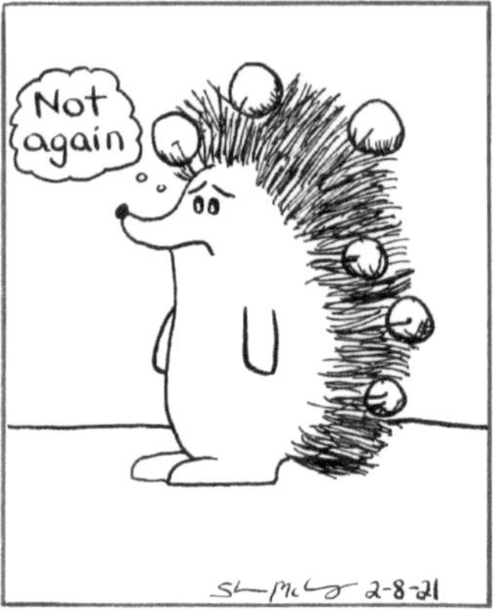
Not again
2-8-21
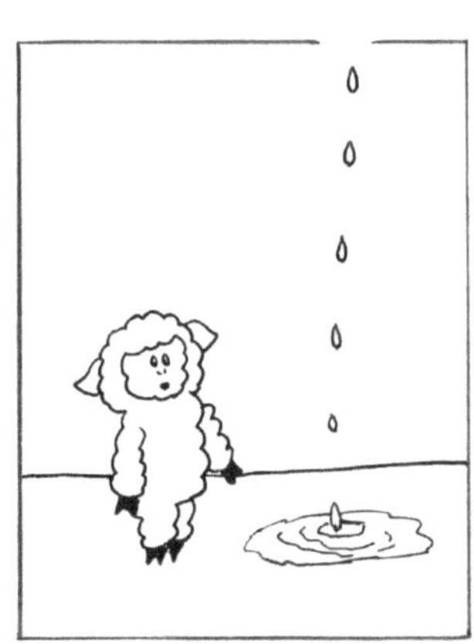
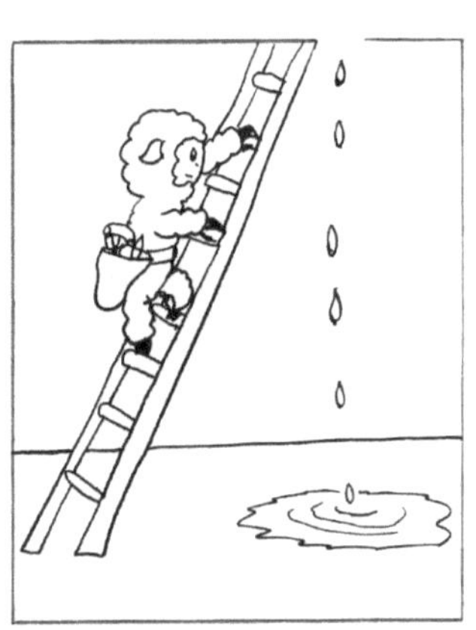
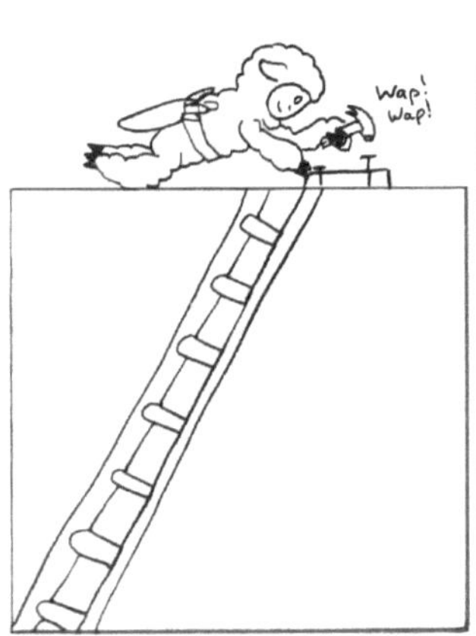
Wap! Wap!
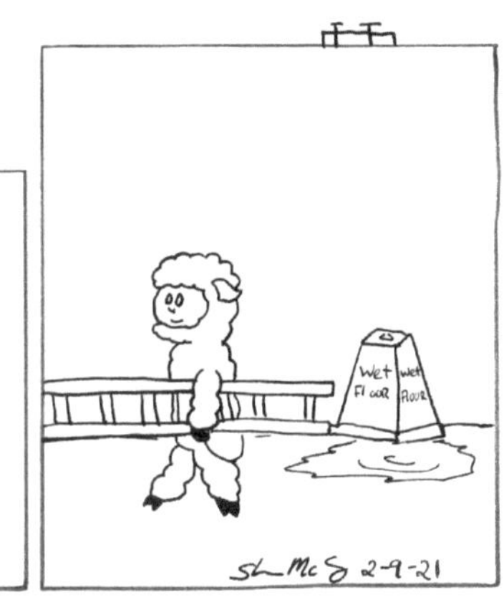
2-9-21
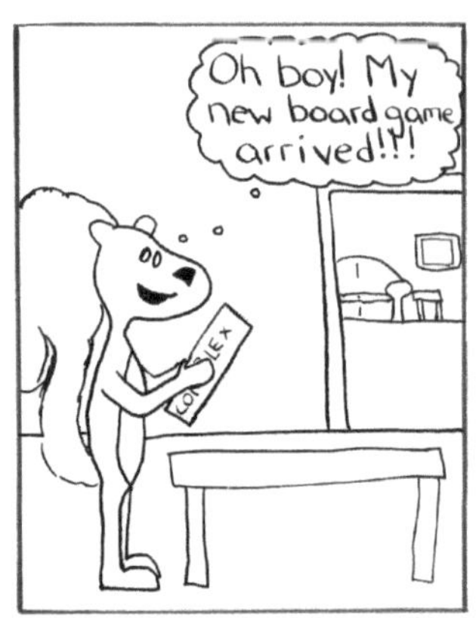
Oh boy! My new board game arrived!!!
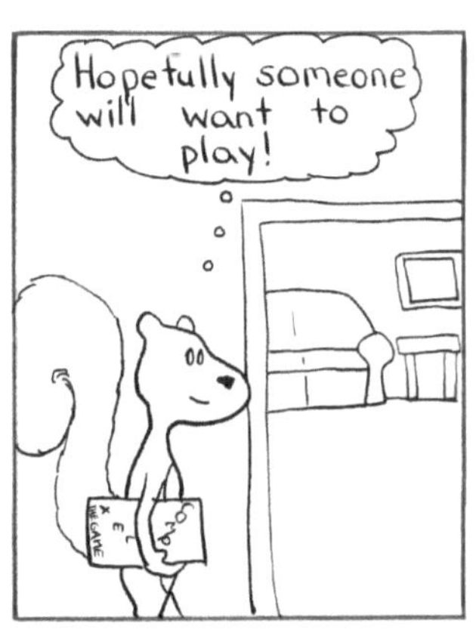
Hopefully someone will want to play!
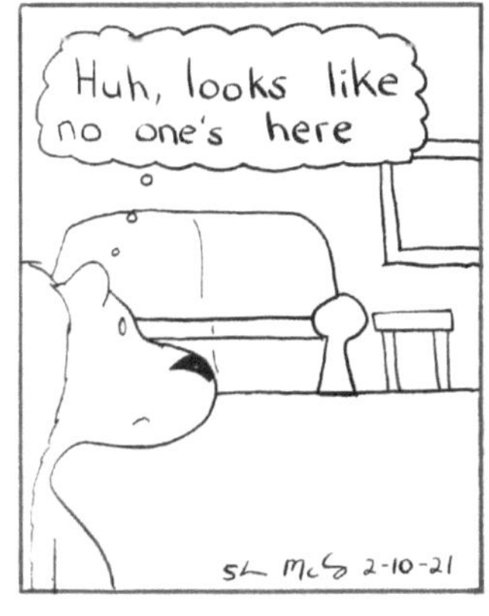
Huh, looks like no one's here
2-10-21
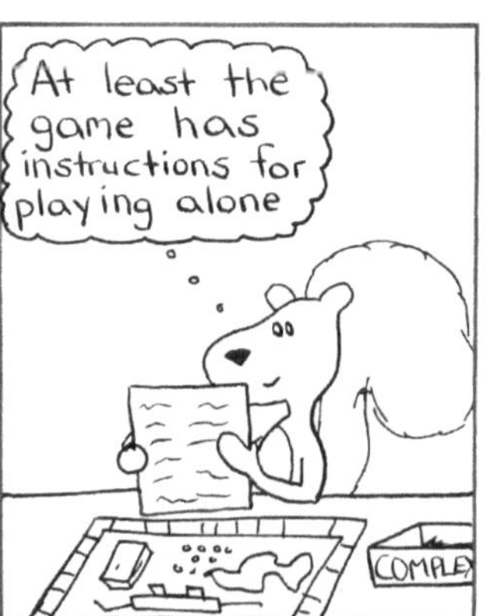
At least the game has instructions for playing alone

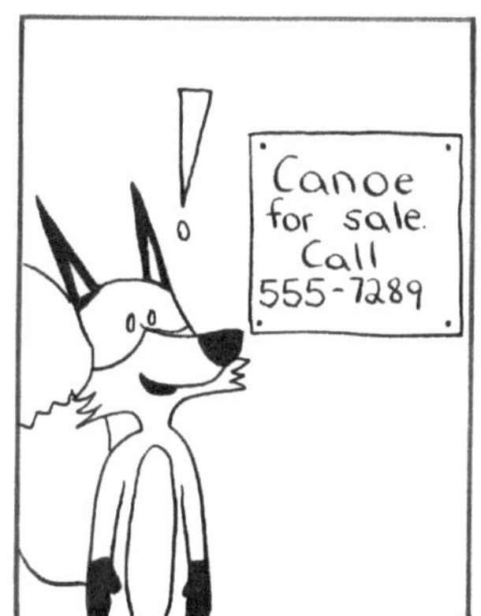
!
Canoe
for sale.
Call
555-7289

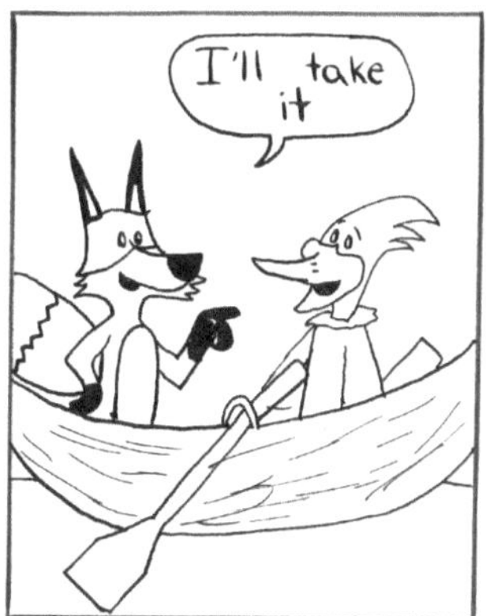
I'll take it

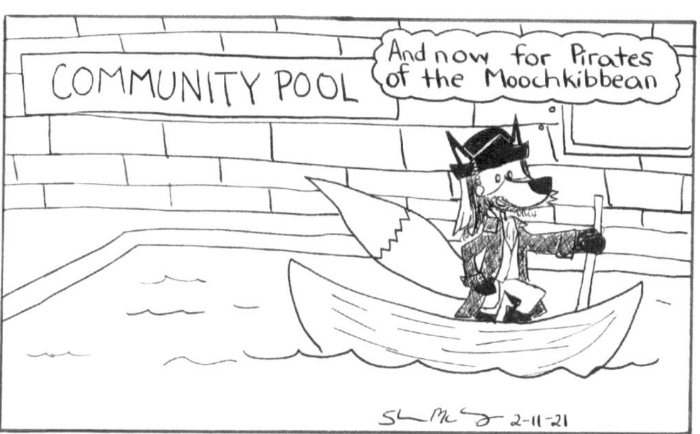
COMMUNITY POOL
And now for Pirates of the Moochkibbean
SL McG 2-11-21

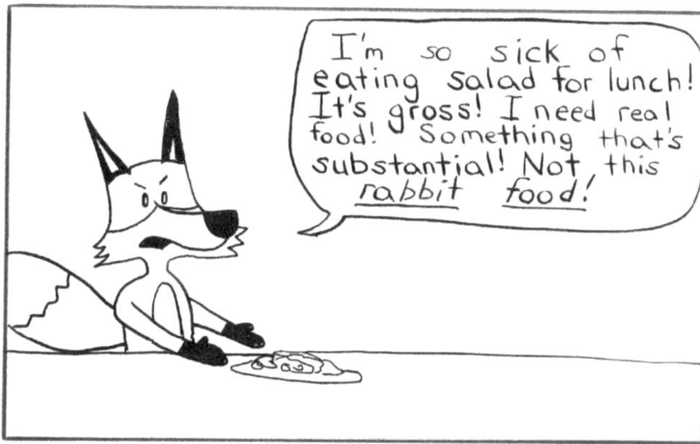
I'm so sick of eating salad for lunch! It's gross! I need real food! Something that's substantial! Not this rabbit food!

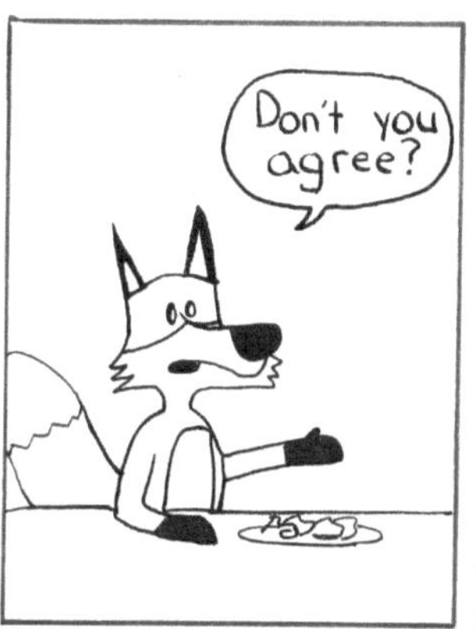
Don't you agree?

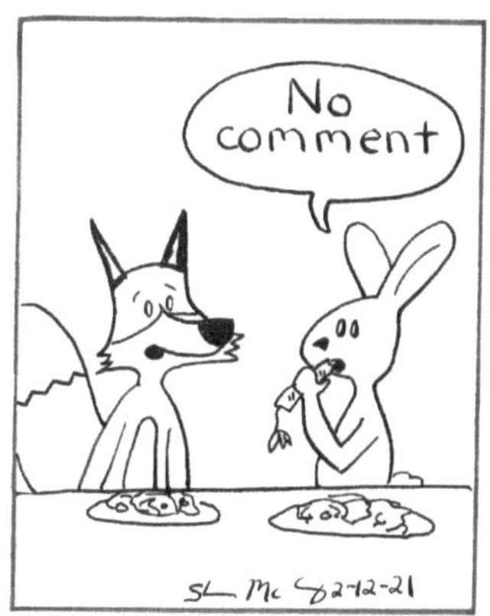
No comment
SL McG 2-12-21

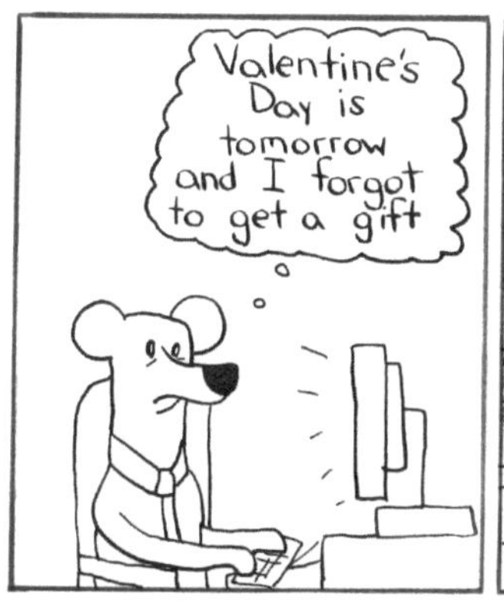
Valentine's Day is tomorrow and I forgot to get a gift

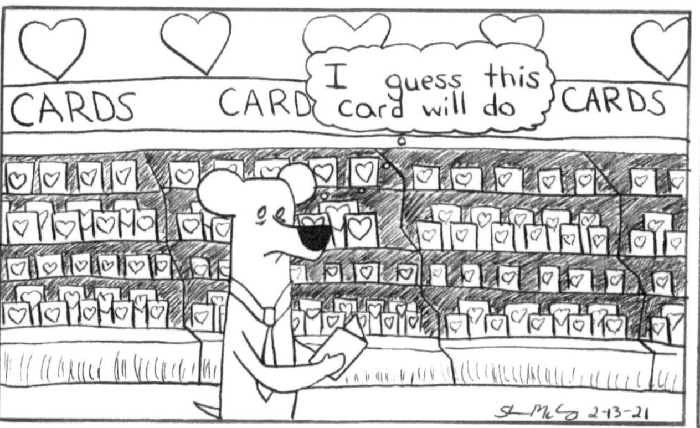
CARDS
CARD
CARDS
I guess this card will do
SL McG 2-13-21

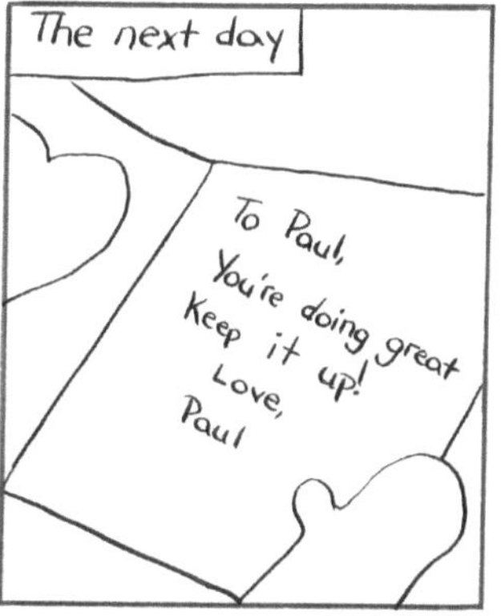
The next day
To Paul,
You're doing great
Keep it up!
Love,
Paul

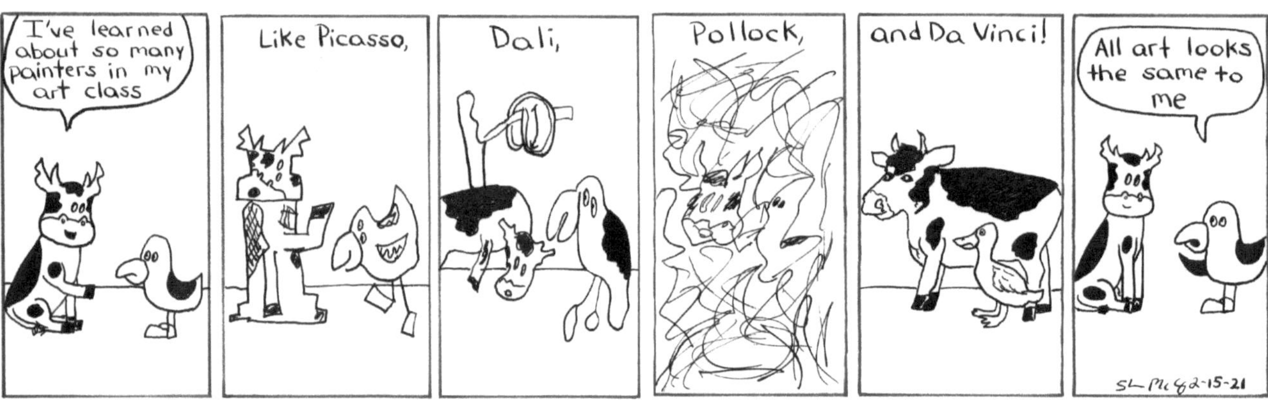
I've learned about so many painters in my art class
Like Picasso,
Dali,
Pollock,
and Da Vinci!
All art looks the same to me
SL McG 2-15-21

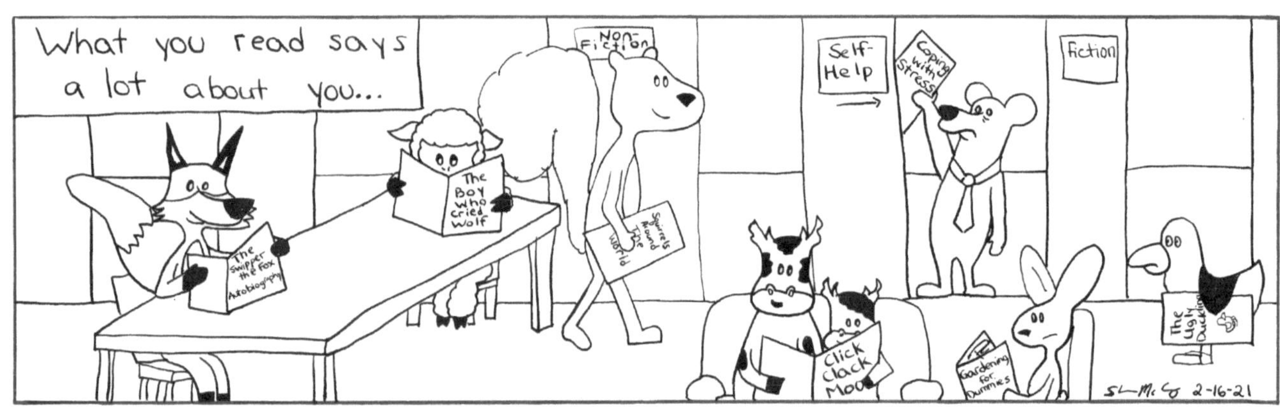
What you read says a lot about you...
Non-Fiction
Self-Help
Coping with Stress
Fiction
The Swipper the Fox Autobiography
The Boy who cried Wolf
Squirrels Around The World
Click Clack Moo
Gardening for Dummies
The Ugly Duckling
SL McG 2-16-21

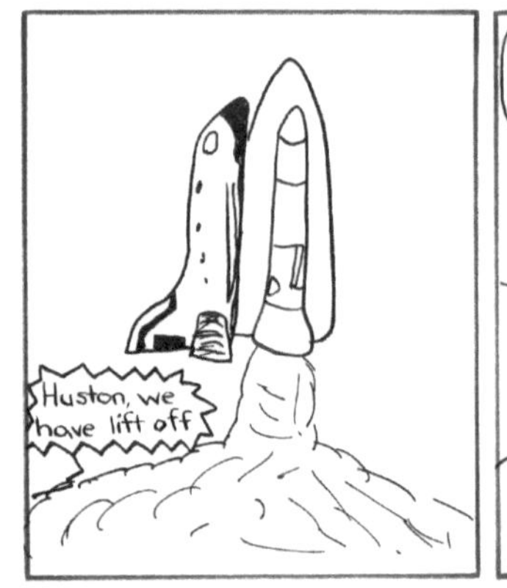
Huston, we have lift off

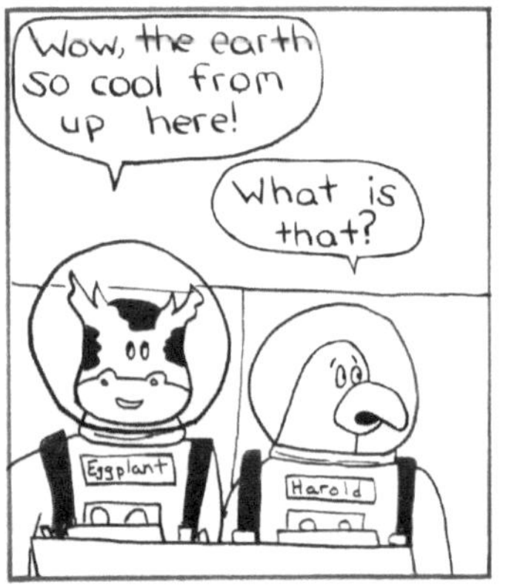
Wow, the earth so cool from up here!
What is that?
Eggplant
Harold

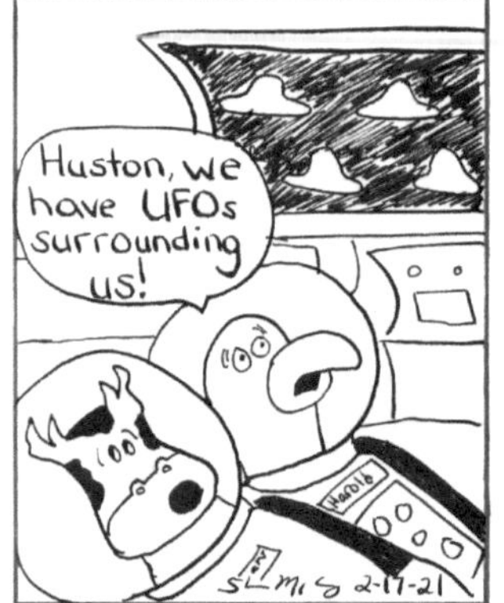
Huston, we have UFOs surrounding us!
Harold
SL McG 2-17-21

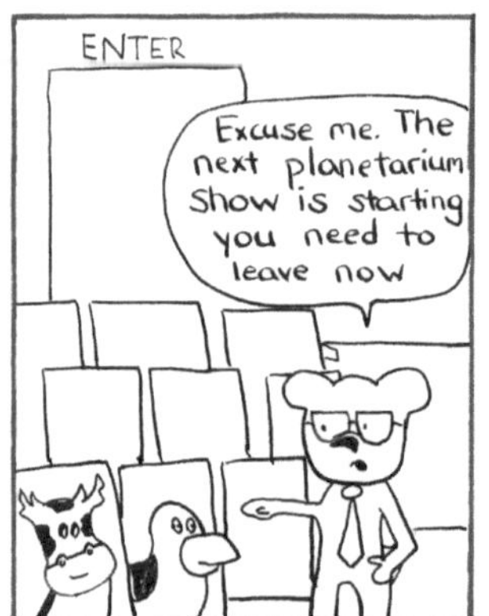
ENTER
Excuse me. The next planetarium show is starting you need to leave now

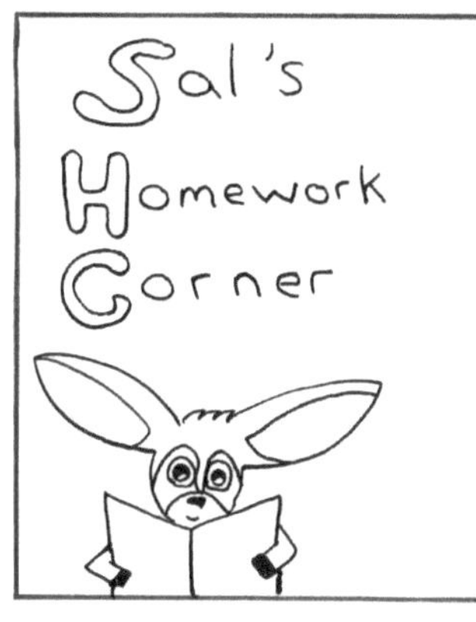
Sal's
Homework
Corner

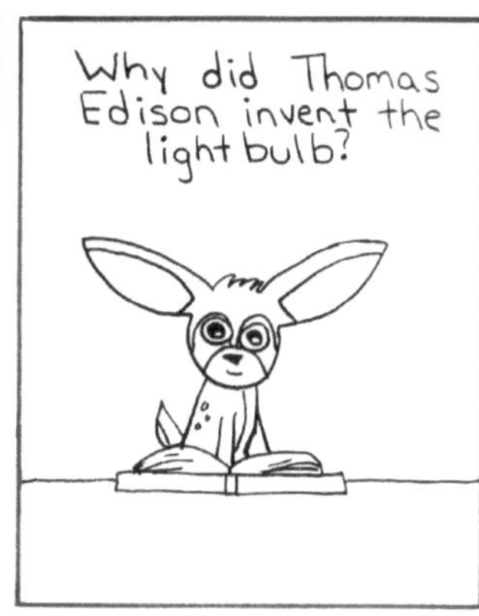
Why did Thomas Edison invent the light bulb?

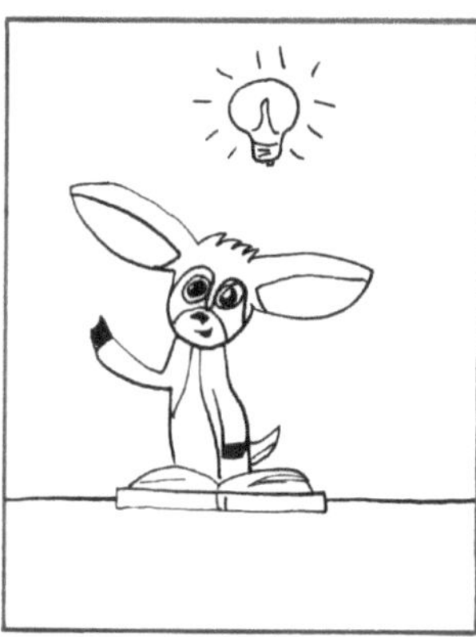

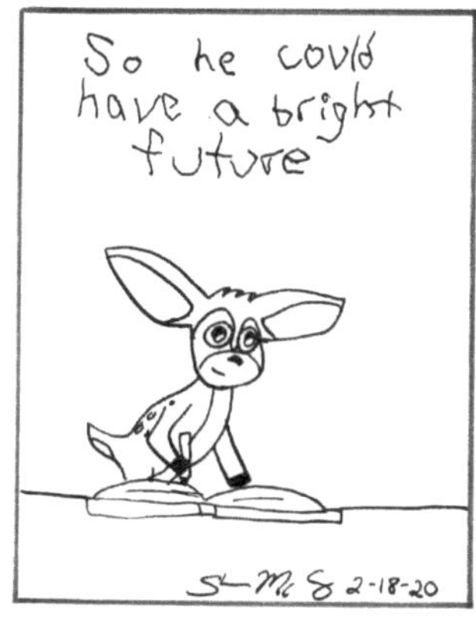
So he could have a bright future
2-18-20

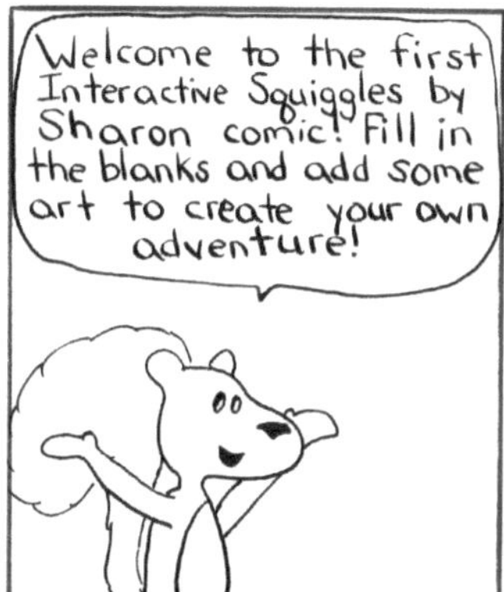
Welcome to the first Interactive Squiggles by Sharon comic! Fill in the blanks and add some art to create your own adventure!

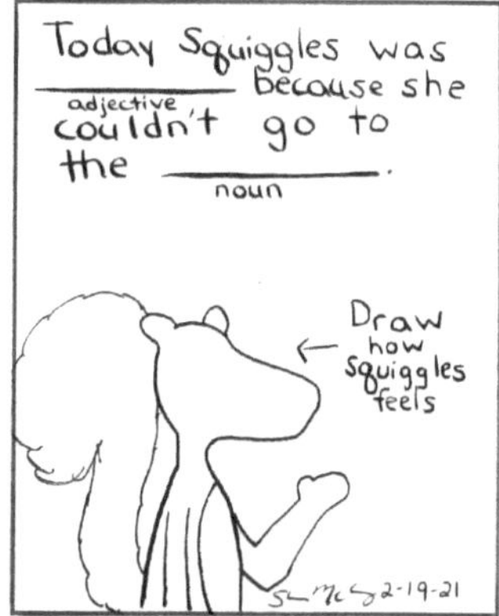
Today Squiggles was ______ because she couldn't go to the ______.
adjective
noun
Draw how Squiggles feels
2-19-21

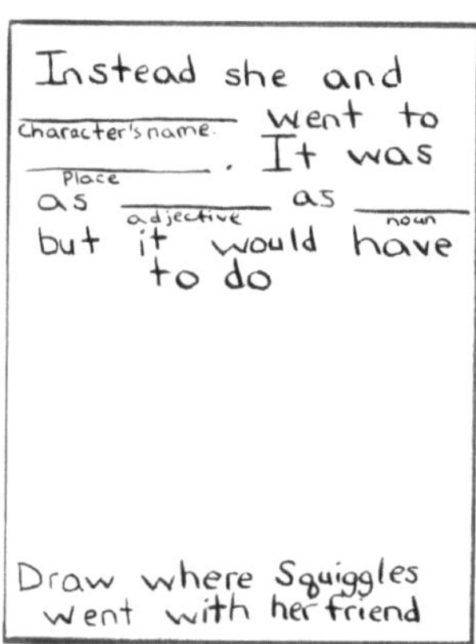
Instead she and ______ went to ______. It was as ______ as ______ but it would have to do
Character's name
Place
adjective
noun
Draw where Squiggles went with her friend

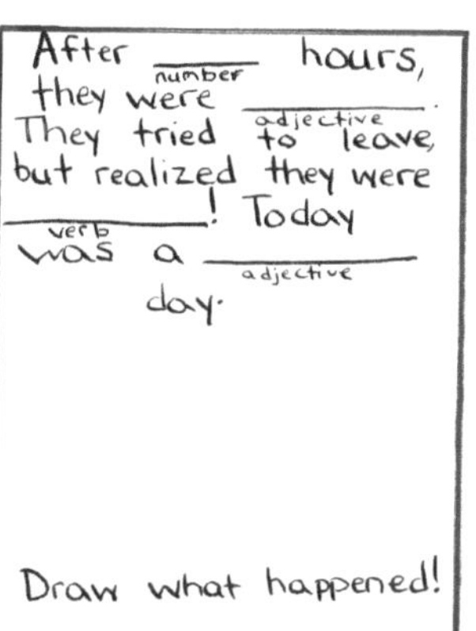
After ______ hours, they were ______. They tried to leave, but realized they were ______! Today was a ______ day.
number
adjective
verb
adjective
Draw what happened!

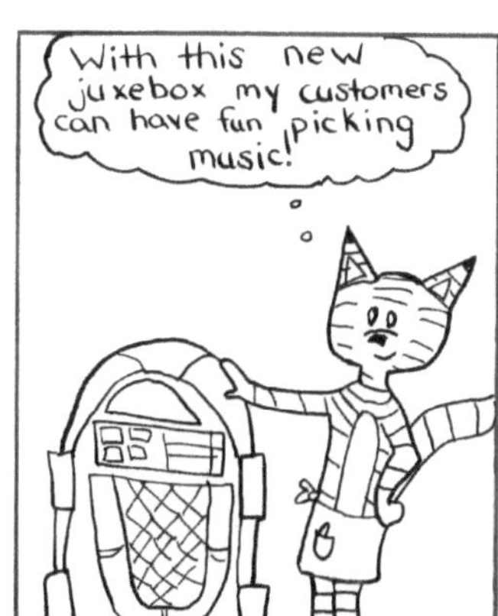
With this new juxebox my customers can have fun picking music!

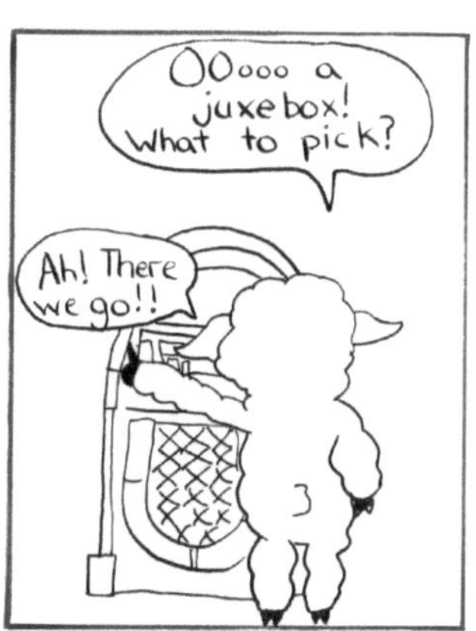
Ooooo a juxebox! What to pick?
Ah! There we go!!

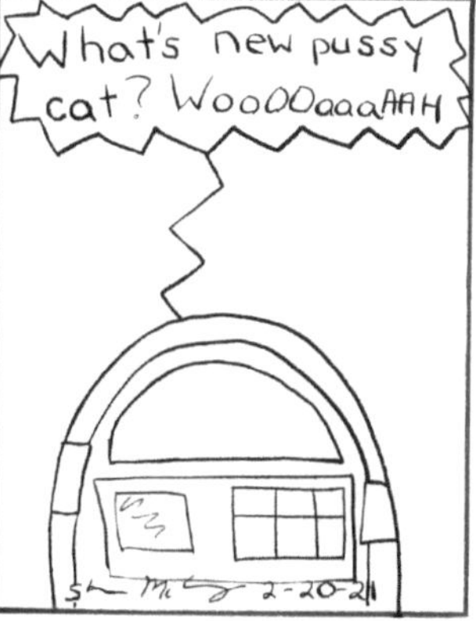
What's new pussy cat? WooOOaaaAAH
2-20-21

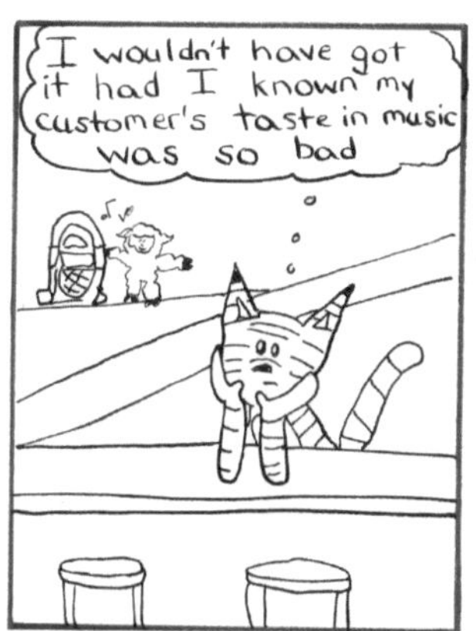
I wouldn't have got it had I known my customer's taste in music was so bad

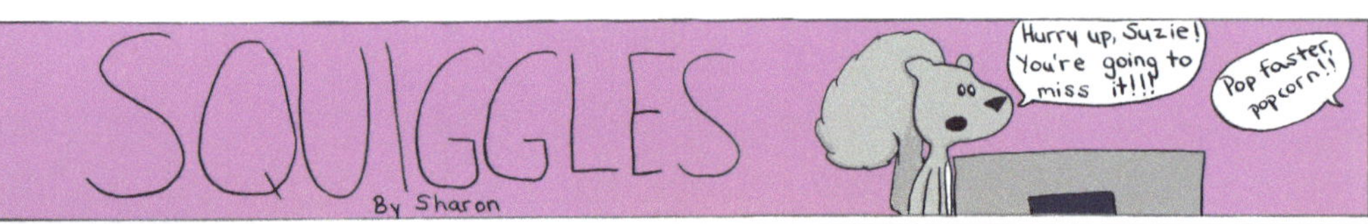
SQUIGGLES
By Sharon
Hurry up, Suzie! You're going to miss it!!!
Pop faster, popcorn!!

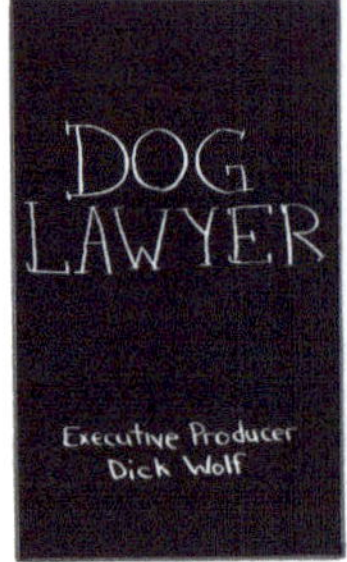
DOG LAWYER
Executive Producer
Dick Wolf

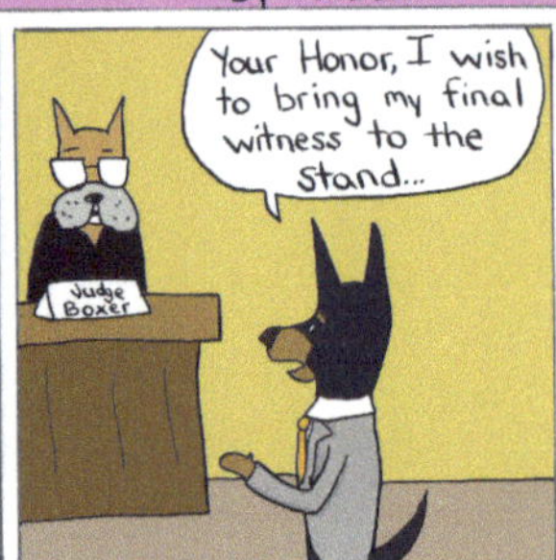
Your Honor, I wish to bring my final witness to the stand...
Judge Boxer

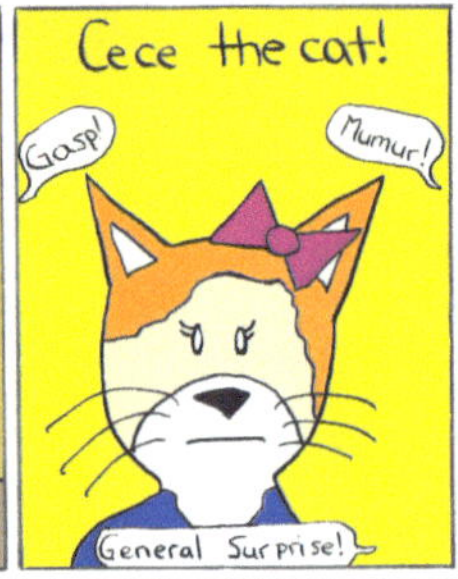
Cece the cat!
Gasp!
Mumur!
General Surprise!

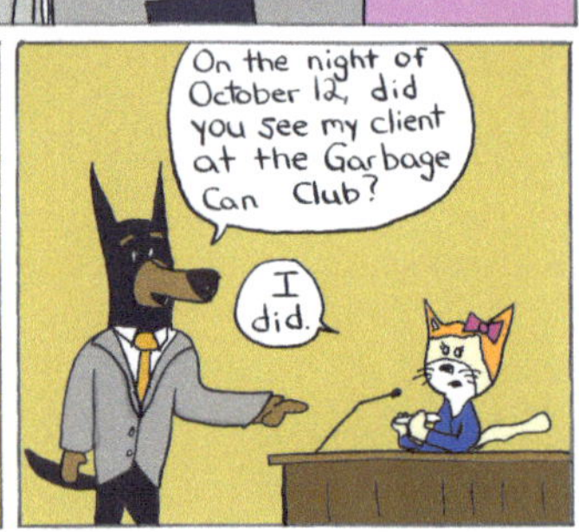
On the night of October 12, did you see my client at the Garbage Can Club?
I did.

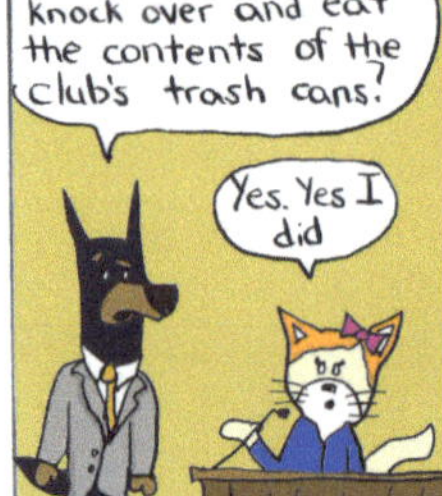
And did you see him knock over and eat the contents of the club's trash cans?
Yes. Yes I did

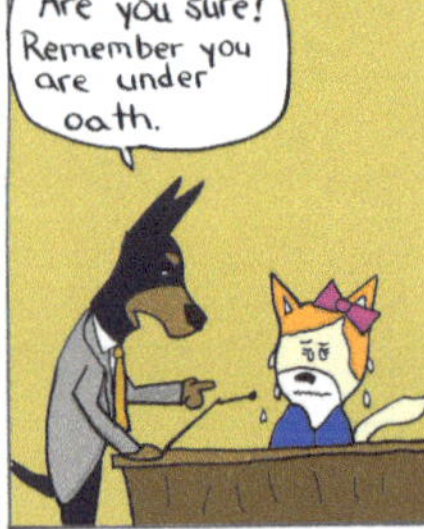
Are you sure? Remember you are under oath.

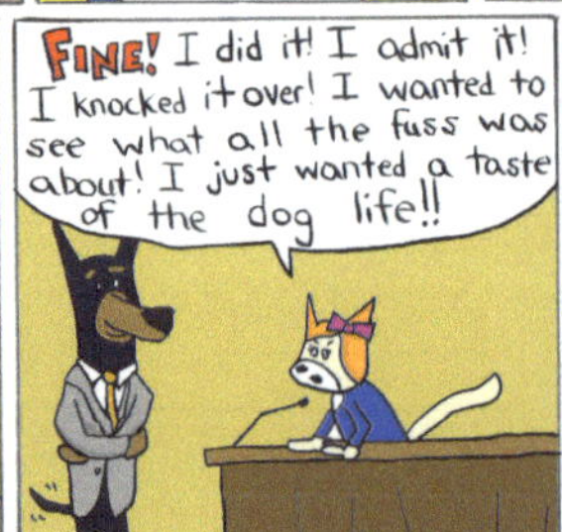
FINE! I did it! I admit it! I knocked it over! I wanted to see what all the fuss was about! I just wanted a taste of the dog life!!

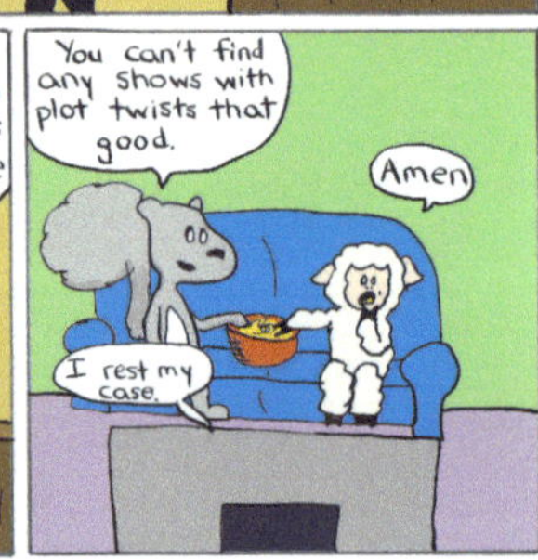
You can't find any shows with plot twists that good.
Amen
I rest my case.

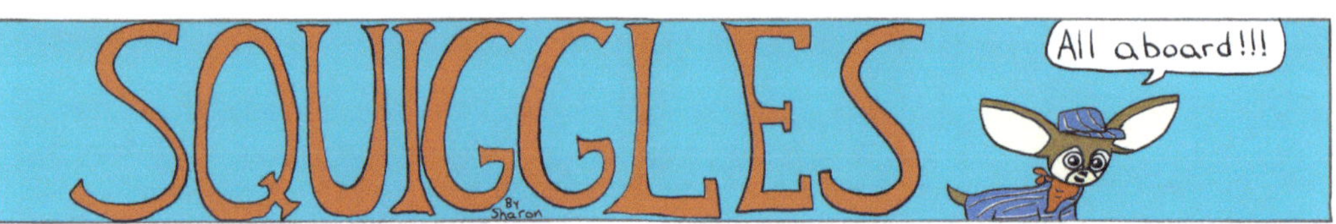
SQUIGGLES
By Sharon
All aboard!!!

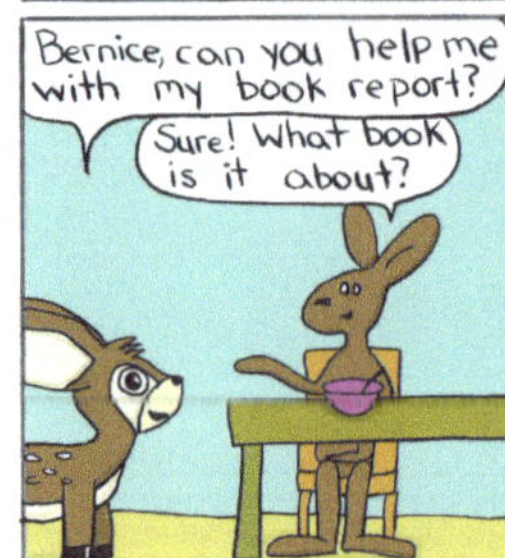
Bernice, can you help me with my book report?
Sure! What book is it about?

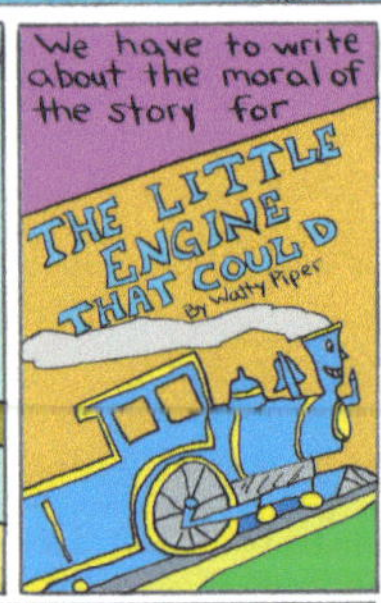
We have to write about the moral of the story for
THE LITTLE ENGINE THAT COULD
by Watty Piper

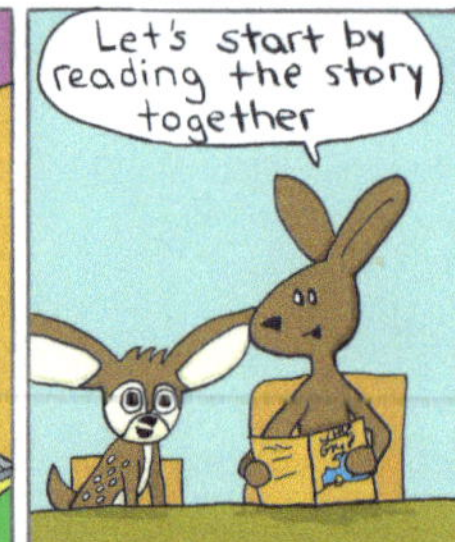
Let's start by reading the story together

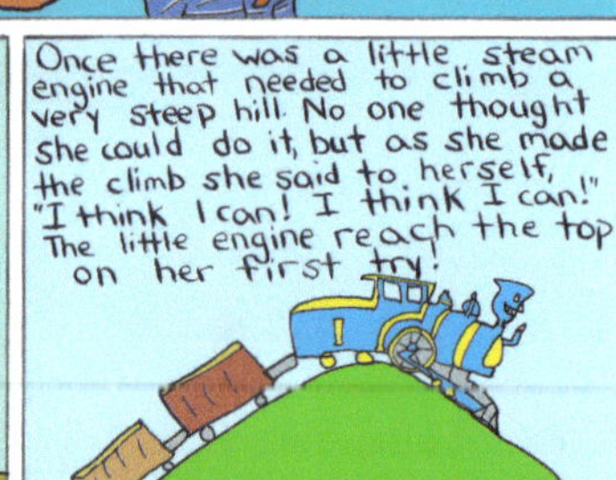
Once there was a little steam engine that needed to climb a very steep hill. No one thought she could do it, but as she made the climb she said to herself, "I think I can! I think I can!" The little engine reach the top on her first try!

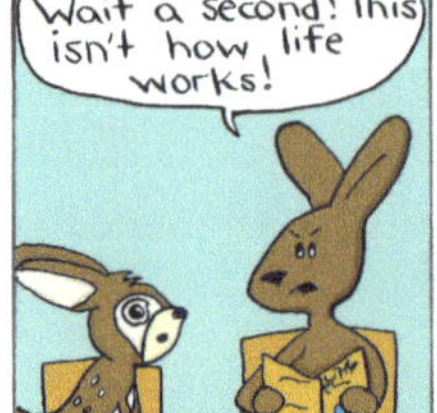
Wait a second! This isn't how life works!

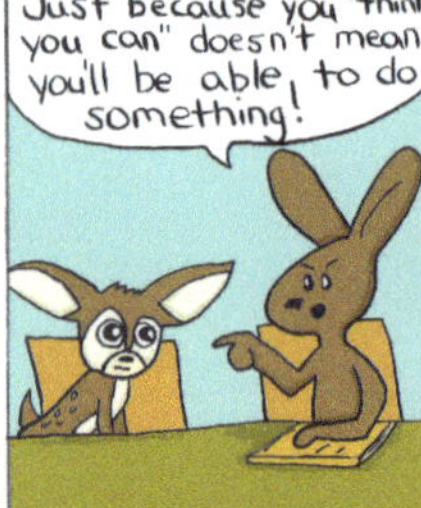
Just because you "think you can" doesn't mean you'll be able to do something!

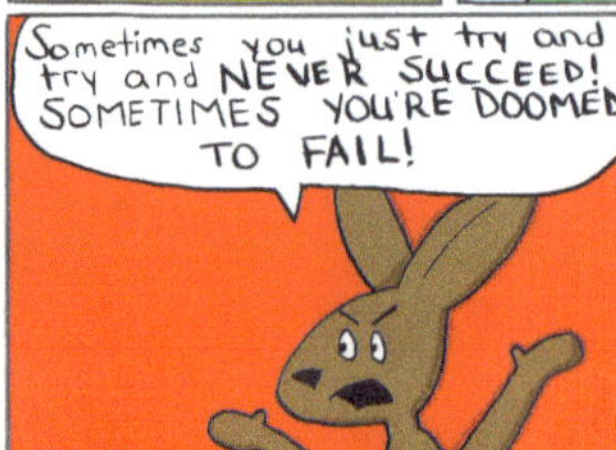
Sometimes you just try and try and NEVER SUCCEED! SOMETIMES YOU'RE DOOMED TO FAIL!

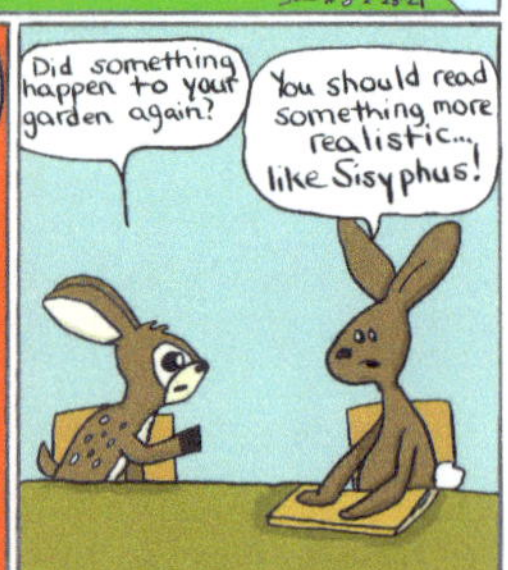
Did something happen to your garden again?
You should read something more realistic... like Sisyphus!

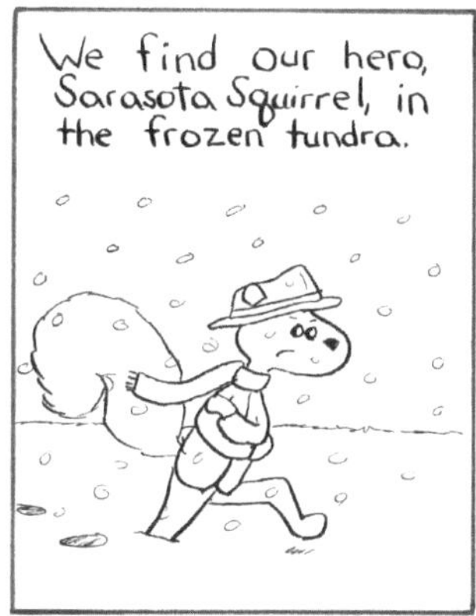
We find our hero, Sarasota Squirrel, in the frozen tundra.

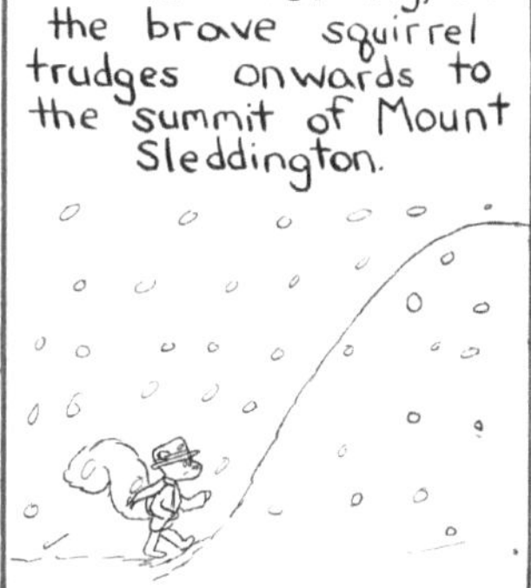
It is freezing, but the brave squirrel trudges onwards to the summit of Mount Sleddington.

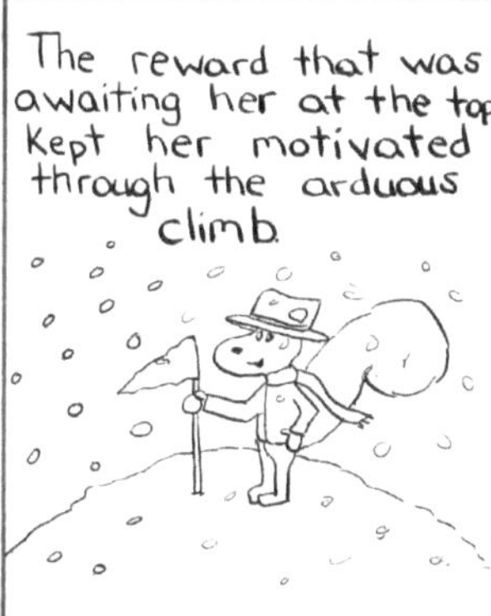
The reward that was awaiting her at the top Kept her motivated through the arduous climb.

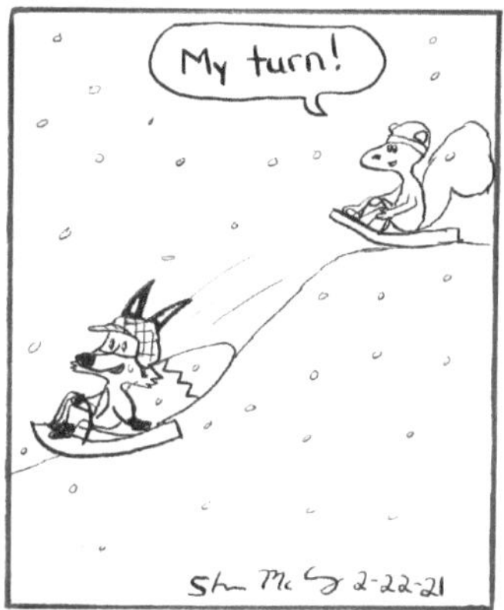
My turn!
2-22-21

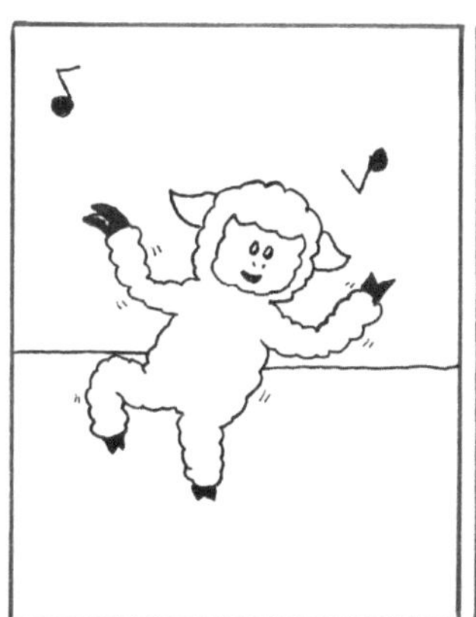

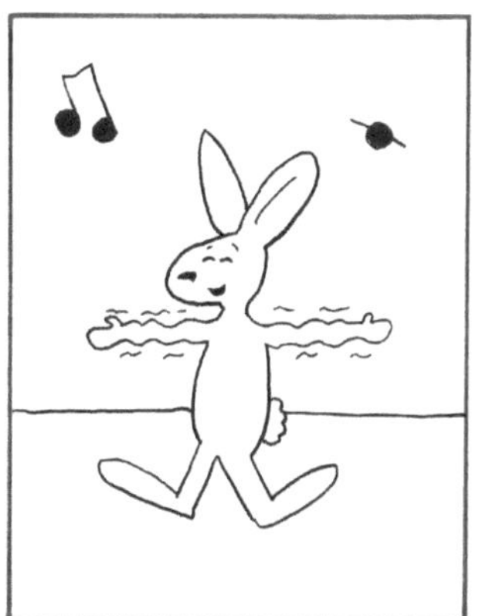

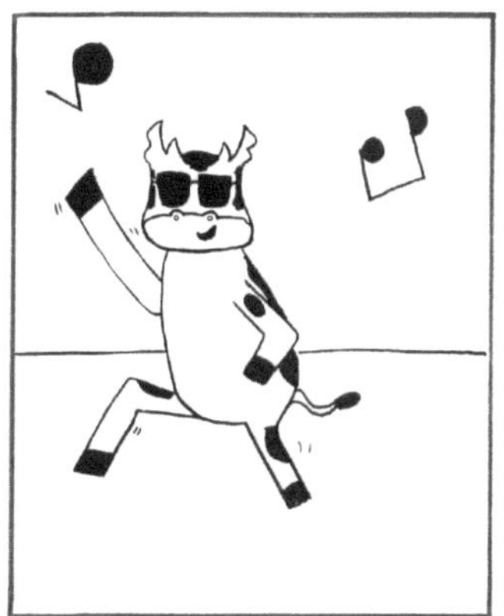

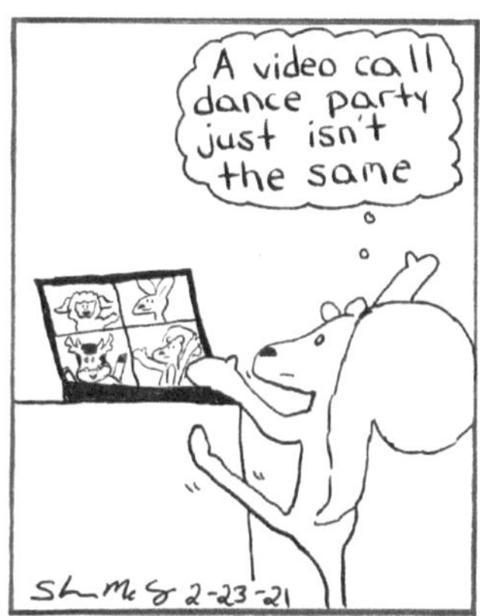
A video call dance party just isn't the same
2-23-21

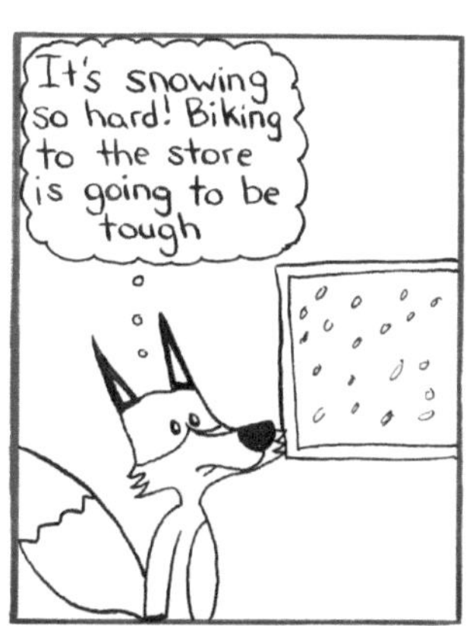
It's snowing so hard! Biking to the store is going to be tough

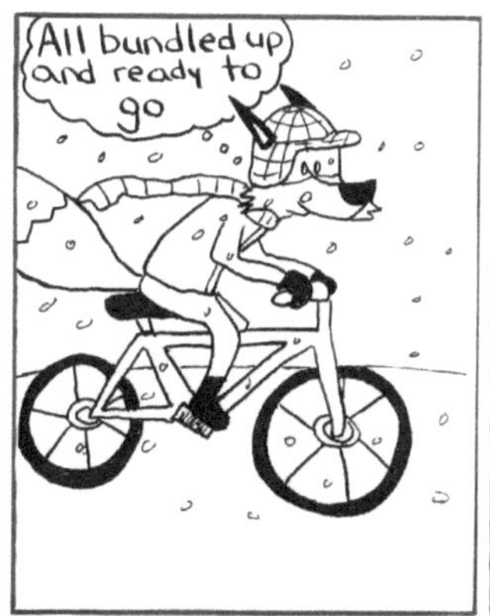
All bundled up and ready to go

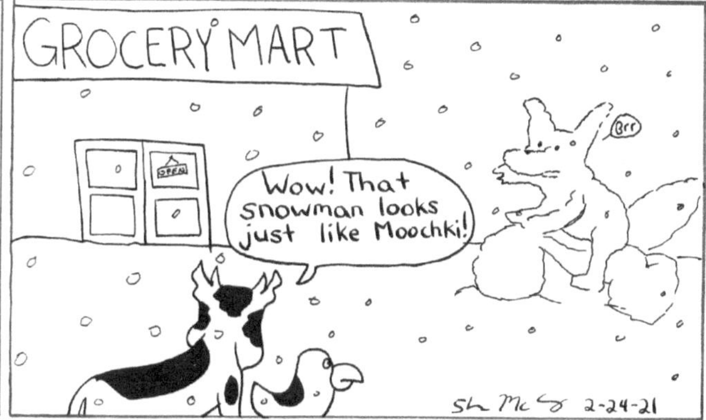
GROCERY MART
OPEN
Brr
Wow! That snowman looks just like Moochki!
2-24-21

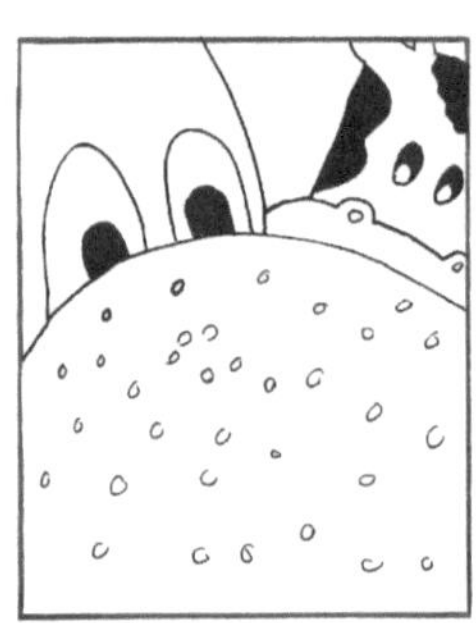

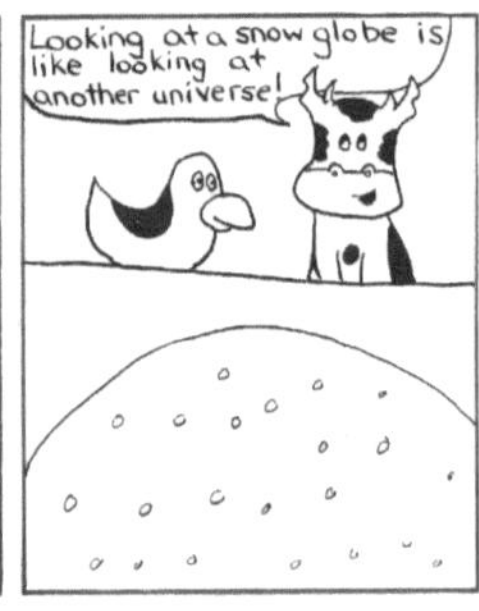

Looking at a snow globe is like looking at another universe!

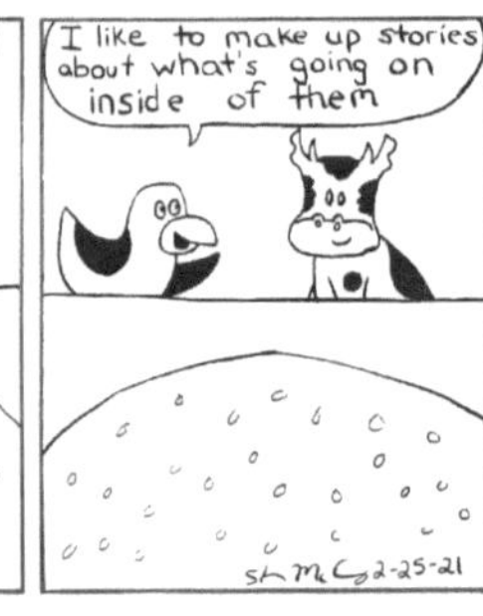

I like to make up stories about what's going on inside of them

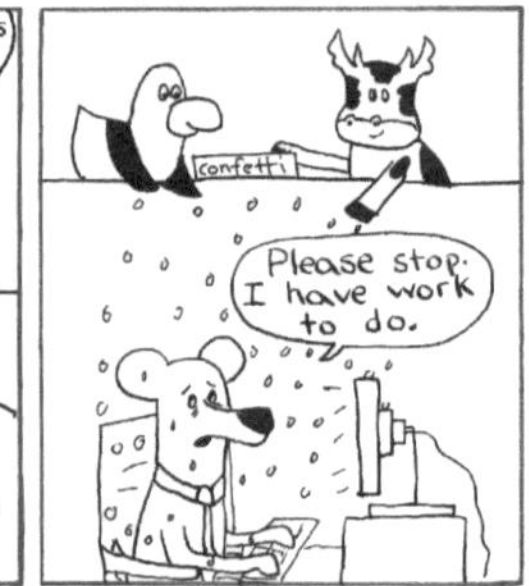

confetti
Please stop. I have work to do.

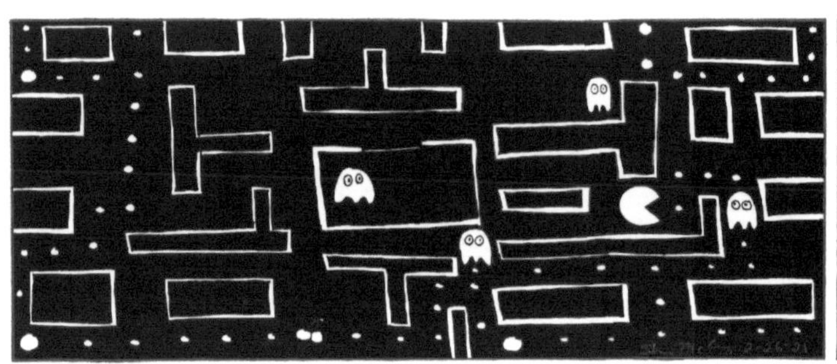

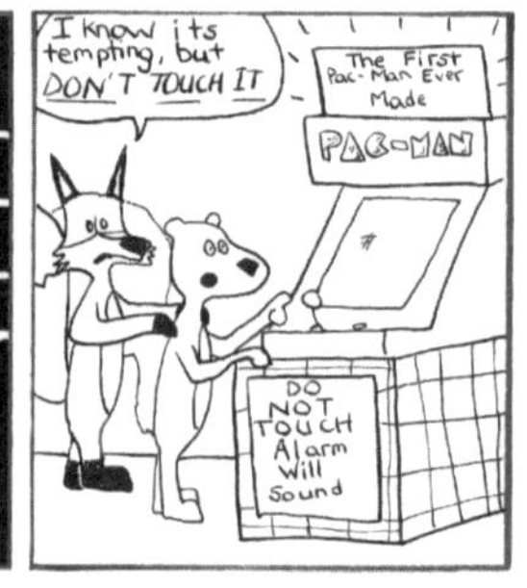

I know its tempting, but DON'T TOUCH IT
The First Pac-Man Ever Made
PAC-MAN
DO NOT TOUCH Alarm will Sound

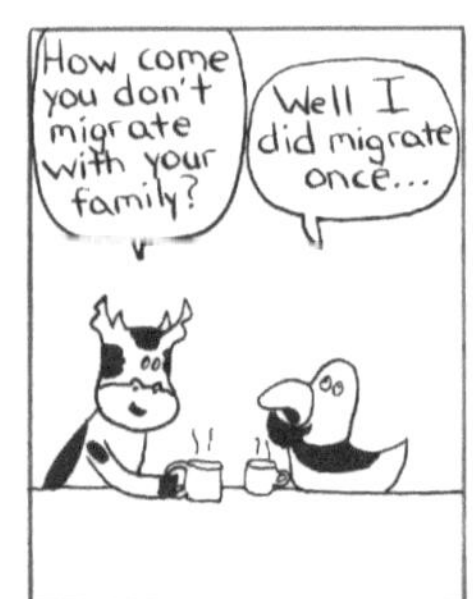

How come you don't migrate with your family?
Well I did migrate once...

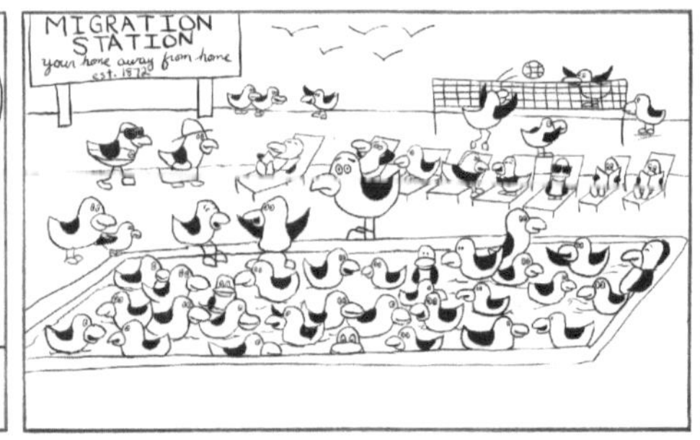

MIGRATION STATION
your home away from home

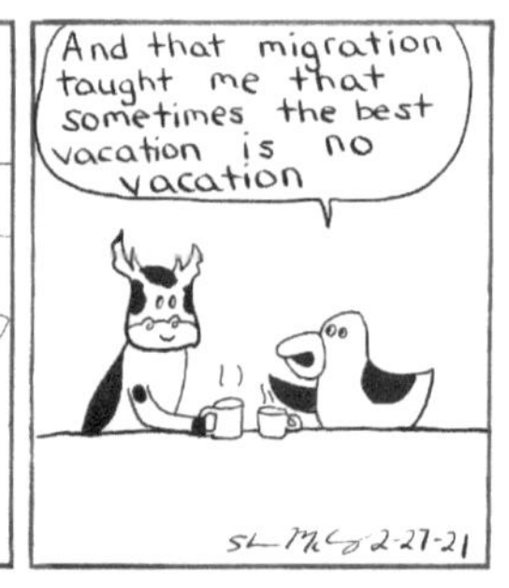

And that migration taught me that sometimes the best vacation is no vacation

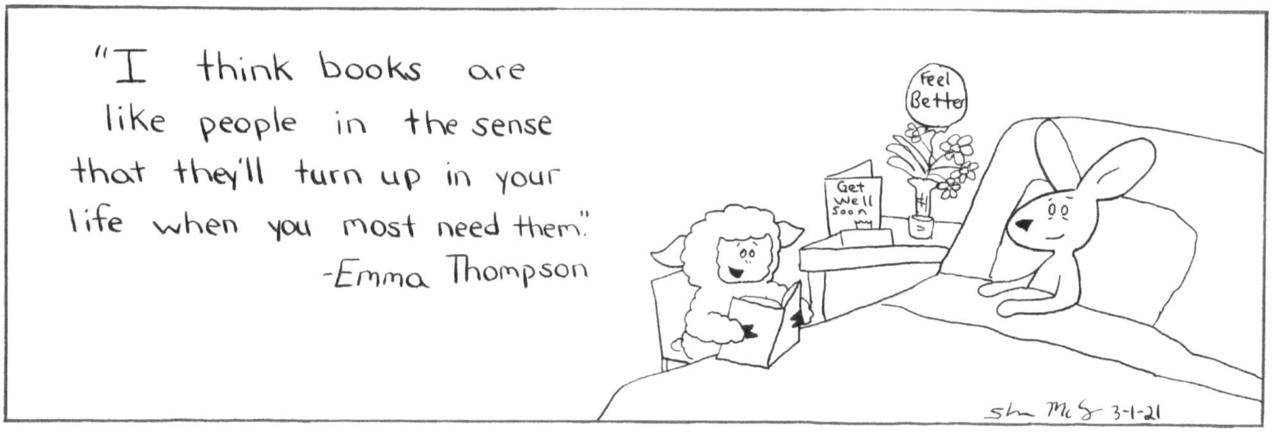

"I think books are like people in the sense that they'll turn up in your life when you most need them."

-Emma Thompson

3-1-21

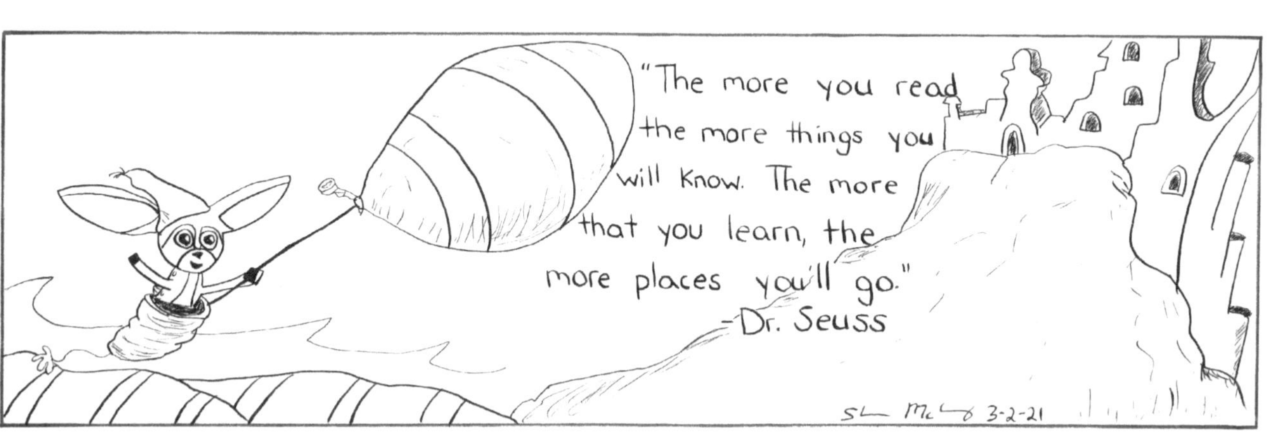

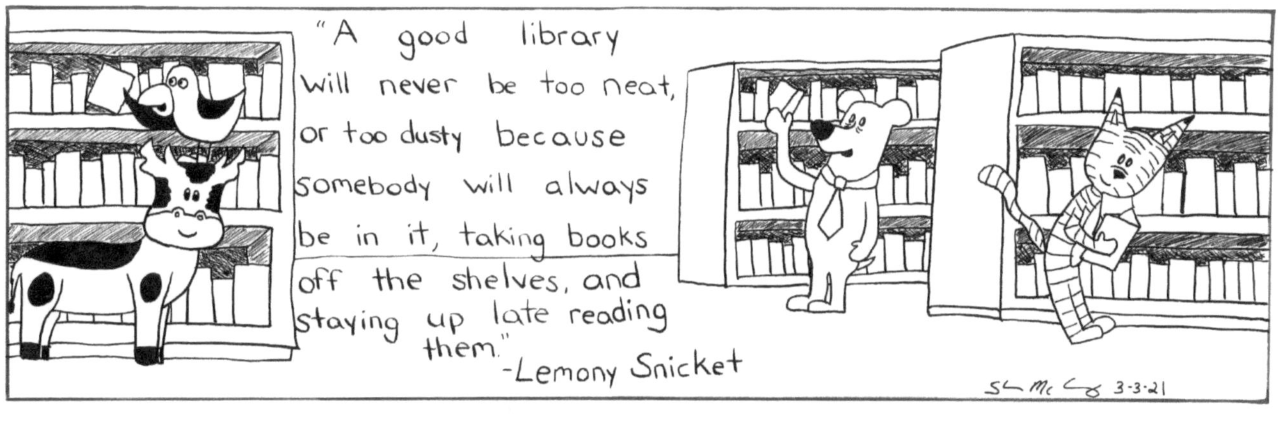

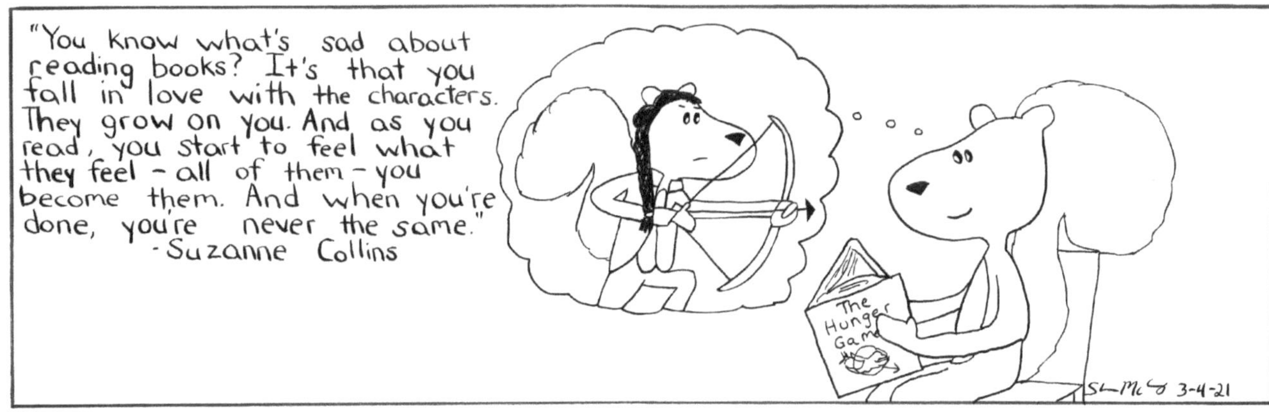
"You know what's sad about reading books? It's that you fall in love with the characters. They grow on you. And as you read, you start to feel what they feel - all of them - you become them. And when you're done, you're never the same."
-Suzanne Collins
The Hunger Games
SL McG 3-4-21

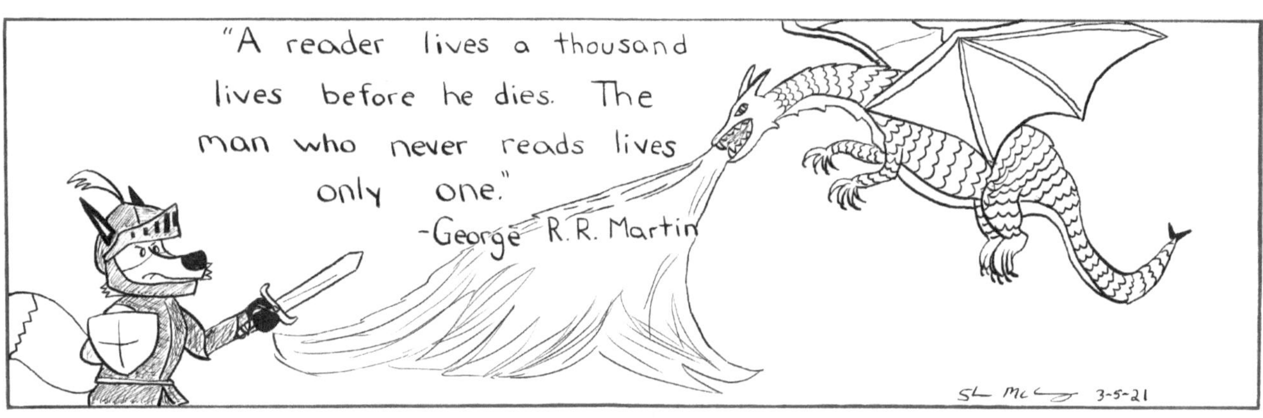
"A reader lives a thousand lives before he dies. The man who never reads lives only one."
-George R.R. Martin
SL McG 3-5-21

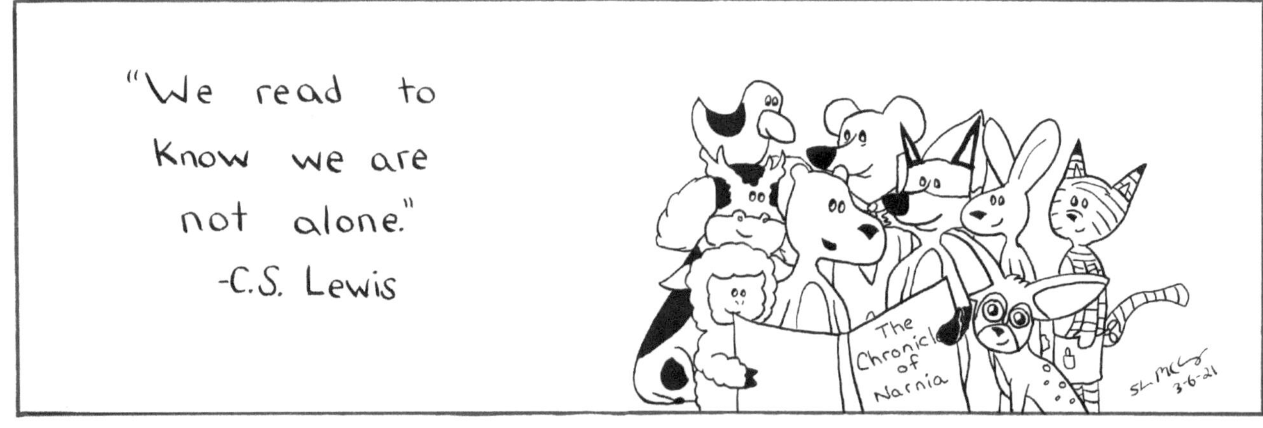
"We read to know we are not alone."
-C.S. Lewis
The Chronicles of Narnia
SL McG 3-6-21

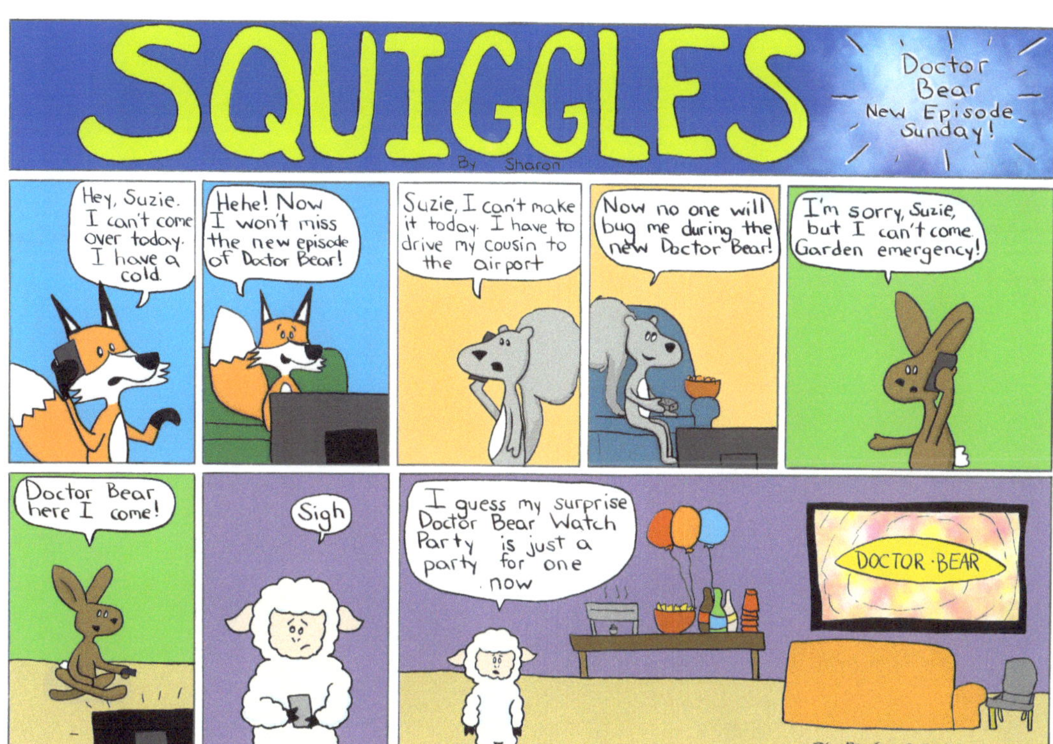
SQUIGGLES
By Sharon
Doctor Bear New Episode Sunday!
Hey, Suzie. I can't come over today. I have a cold.
Hehe! Now I won't miss the new episode of Doctor Bear!
Suzie, I can't make it today. I have to drive my cousin to the airport
Now no one will bug me during the new Doctor Bear!
I'm sorry, Suzie, but I can't come. Garden emergency!
Doctor Bear here I come!
Sigh
I guess my surprise Doctor Bear Watch Party is just a party for one now
DOCTOR · BEAR
3-7-21

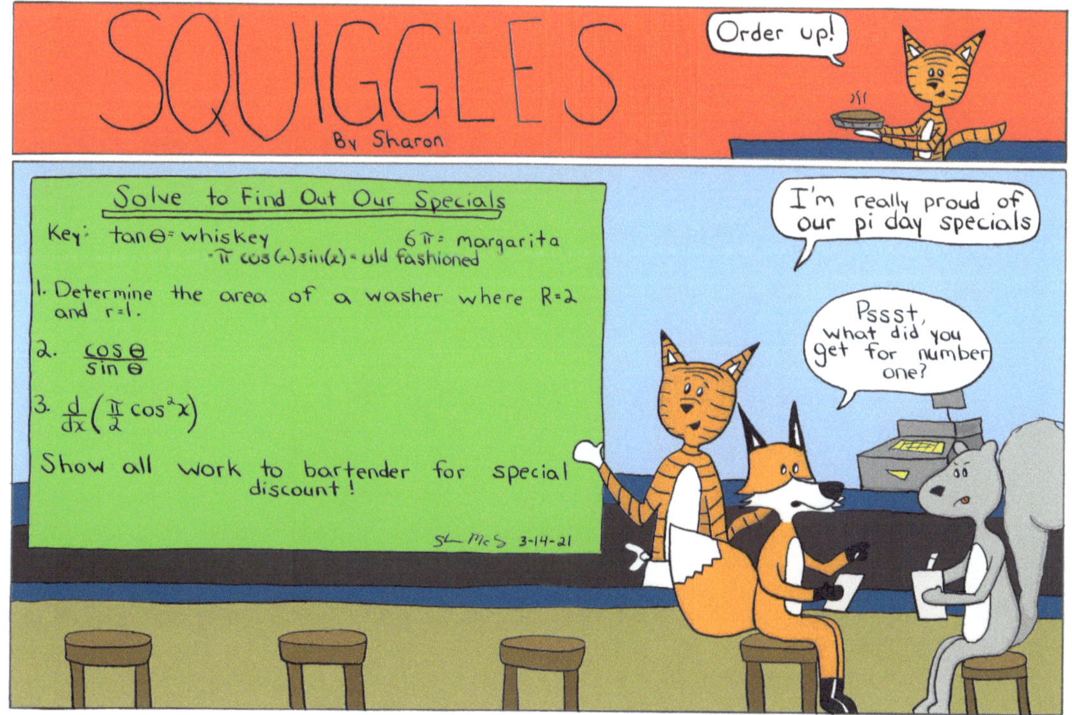
SQUIGGLES
By Sharon
Order up!
Solve to Find Out Our Specials
Key: tanθ = whiskey 6π = margarita
-π cos(x)sin(x) = old fashioned
1. Determine the area of a washer where R=2 and r=1.
2. cosθ / sinθ
3. d/dx (π/2 cos²x)
Show all work to bartender for special discount!
3-14-21
I'm really proud of our pi day specials
Pssst, what did you get for number one?

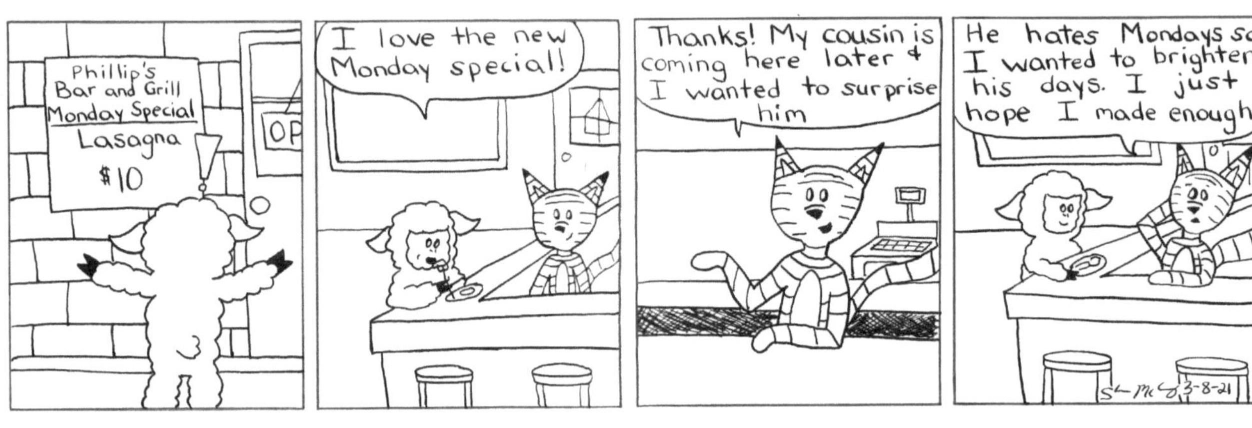
Phillip's
Bar and Grill
Monday Special
Lasagna
$10
OP
I love the new Monday special!
Thanks! My cousin is coming here later & I wanted to surprise him
He hates Mondays so I wanted to brighten his days. I just hope I made enough
3-8-21

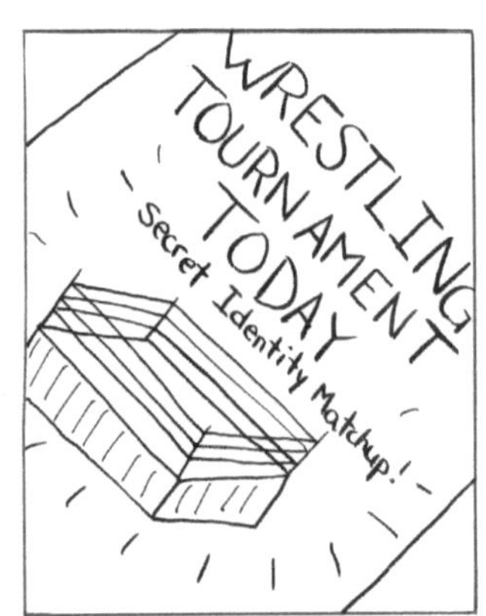
WRESTLING TOURNAMENT TODAY
Secret Identity Matchup!

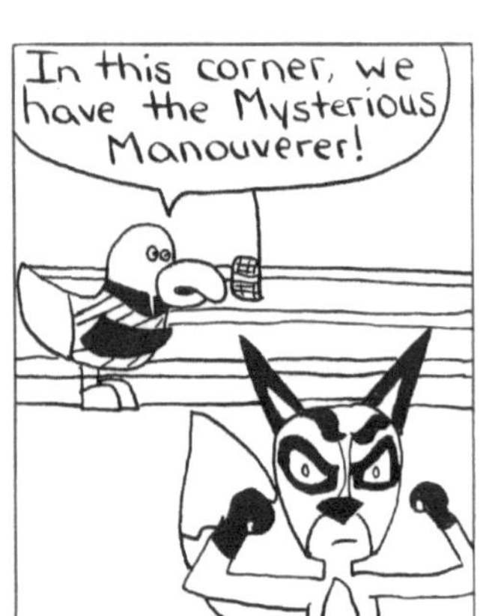
In this corner, we have the Mysterious Manouverer!

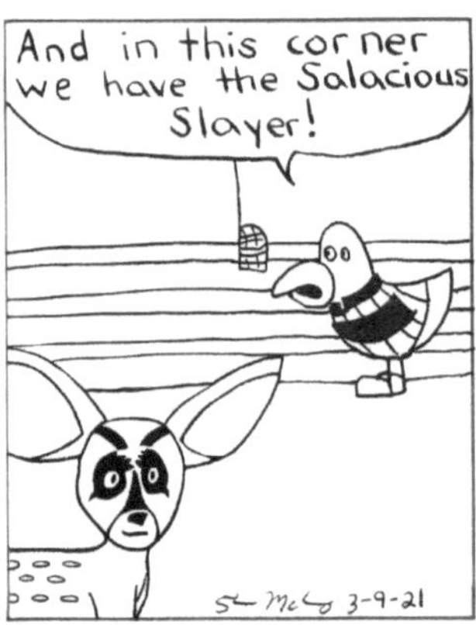
And in this corner we have the Salacious Slayer!
3-9-21

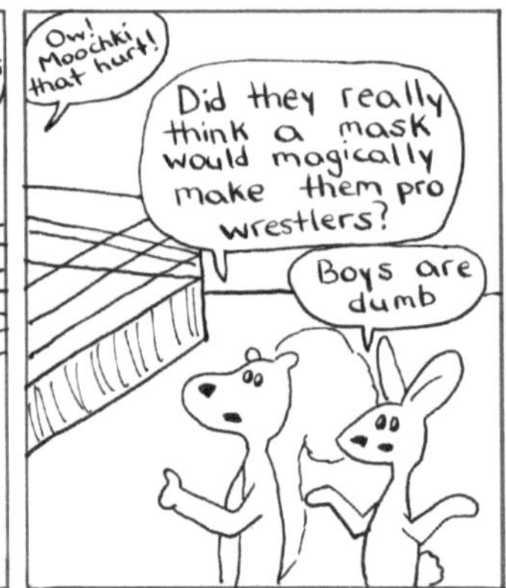
Ow! Moochki that hurt!
Did they really think a mask would magically make them pro wrestlers?
Boys are dumb

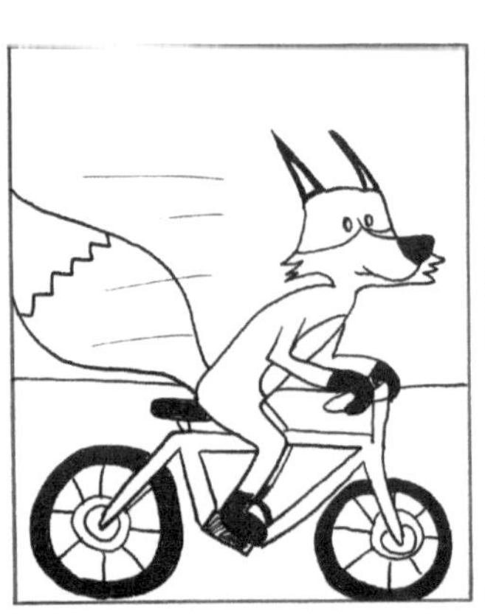

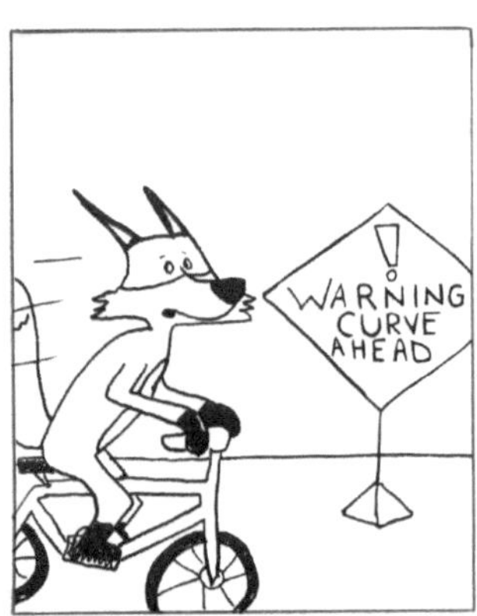
!
WARNING
CURVE
AHEAD

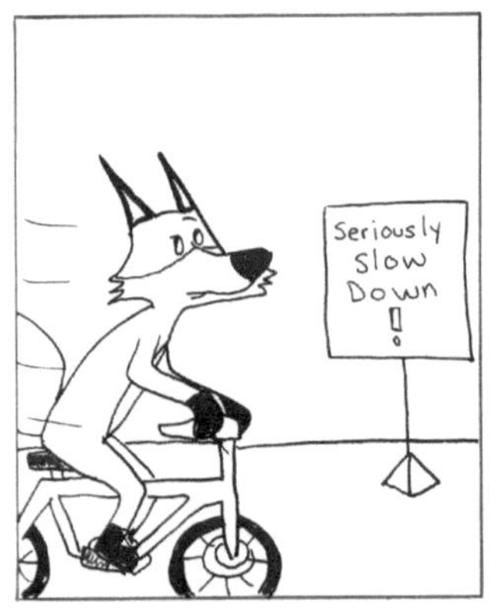
Seriously
Slow
Down
!

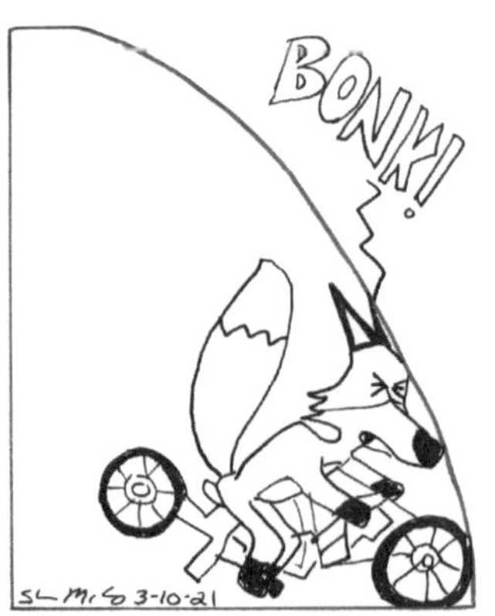
BONK!
3-10-21

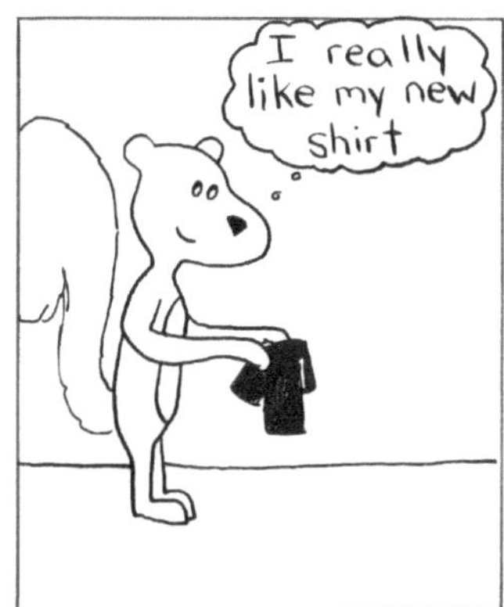
I really like my new shirt
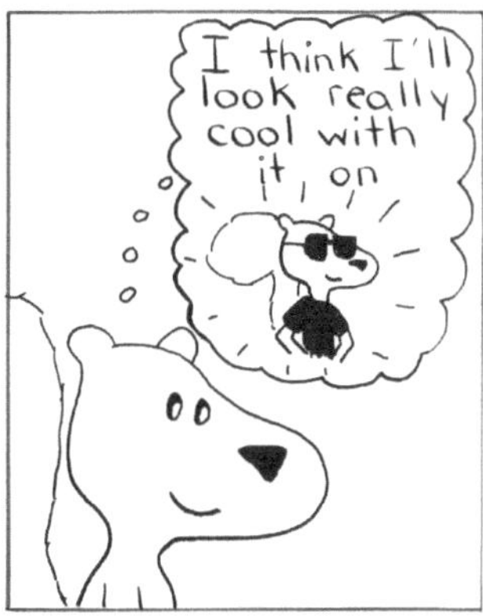
I think I'll look really cool with it on
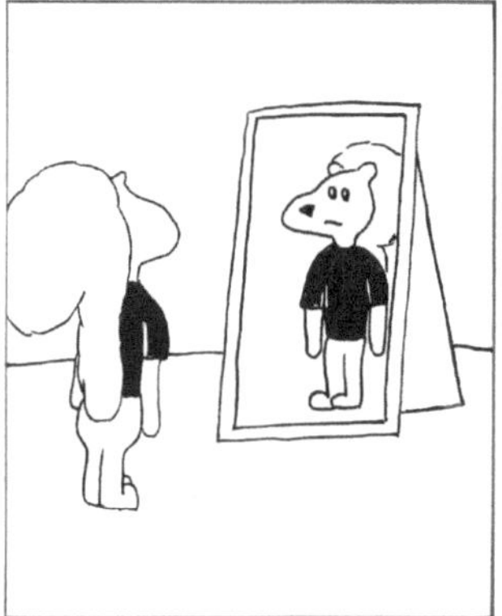
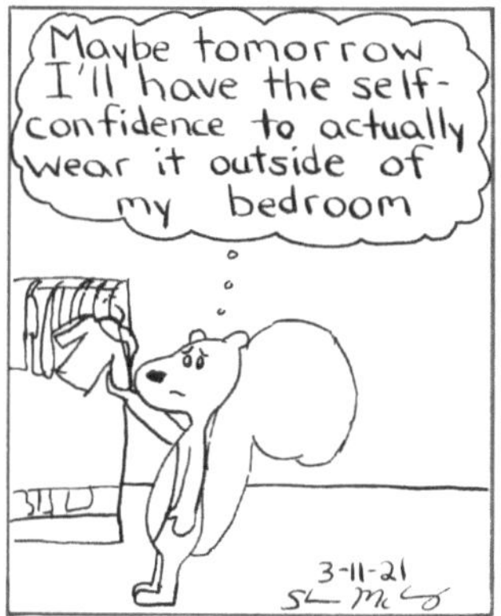
Maybe tomorrow I'll have the self-confidence to actually wear it outside of my bedroom
3-11-21
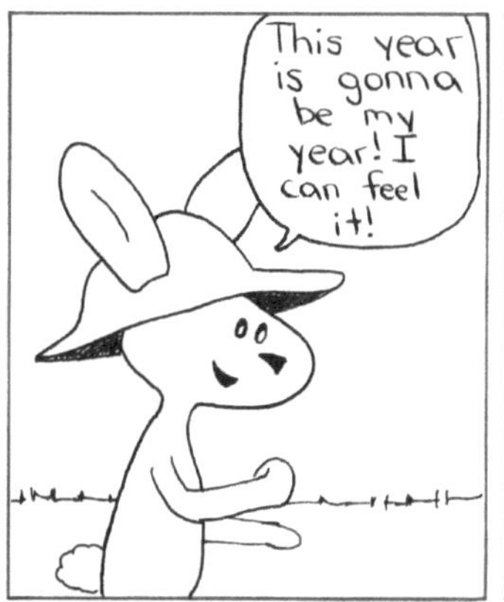
This year is gonna be my year! I can feel it!
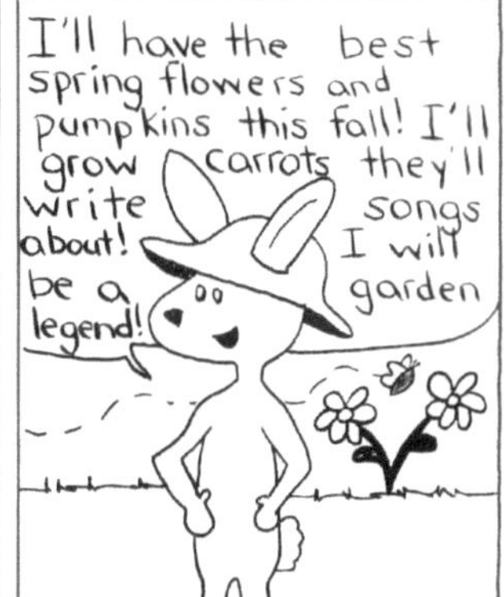
I'll have the best spring flowers and pumpkins this fall! I'll grow carrots they'll write songs about! I will garden be a legend!
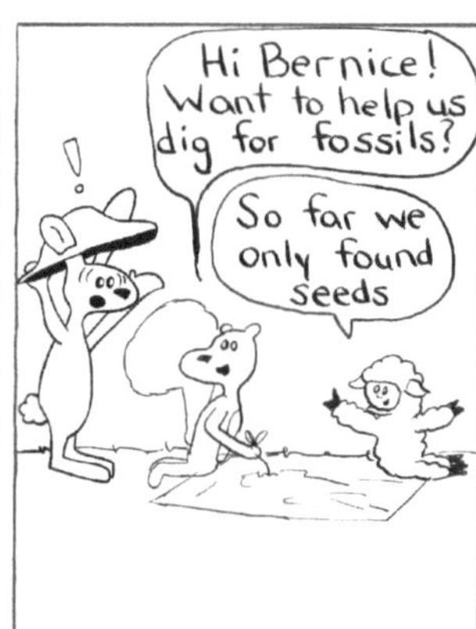
Hi Bernice! Want to help us dig for fossils?
!
So far we only found seeds
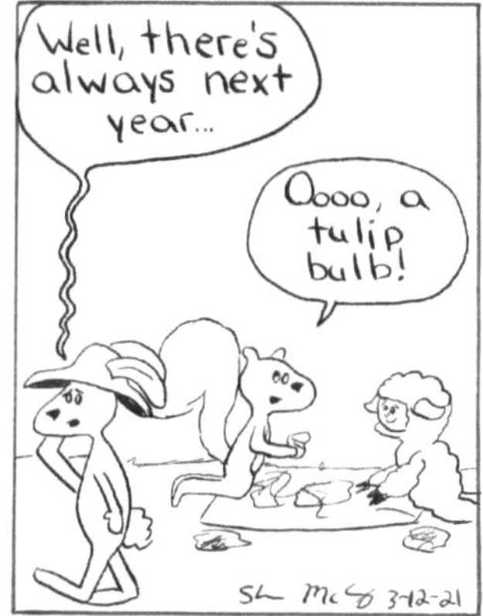
Well, there's always next year...
Oooo, a tulip bulb!
3-12-21
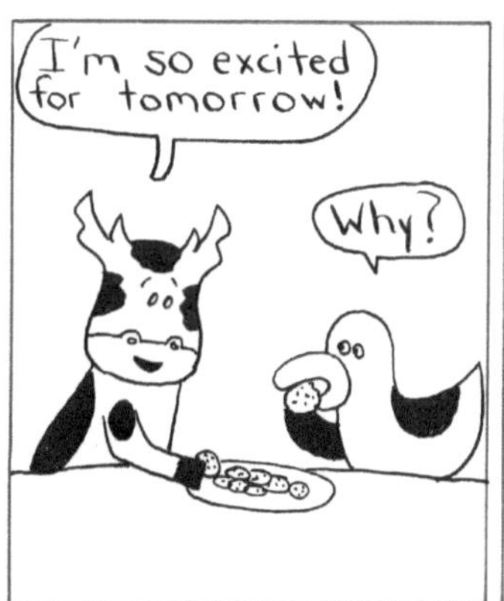
I'm so excited for tomorrow!
Why?
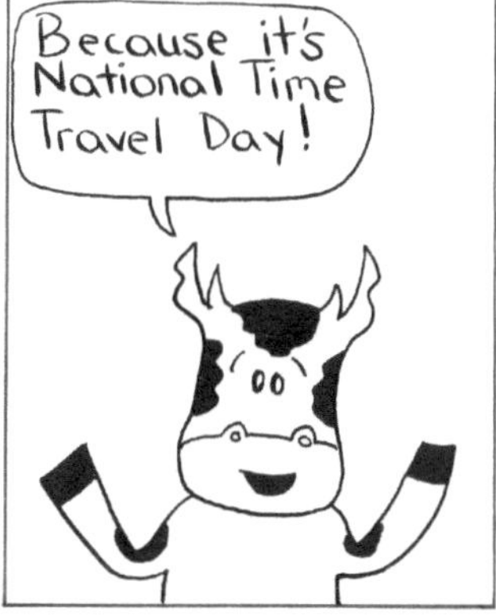
Because it's National Time Travel Day!
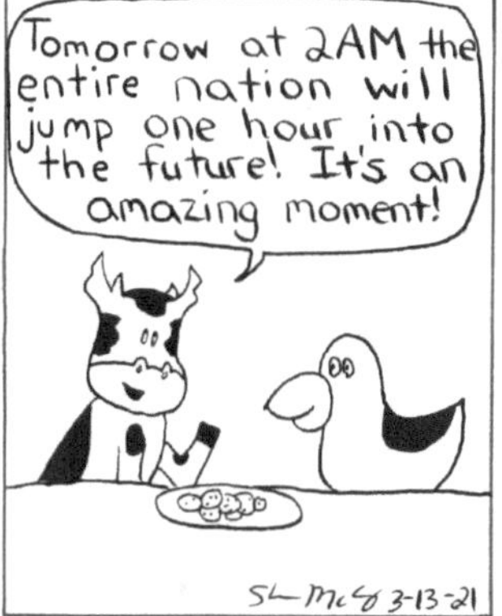
Tomorrow at 2AM the entire nation will jump one hour into the future! It's an amazing moment!
3-13-21
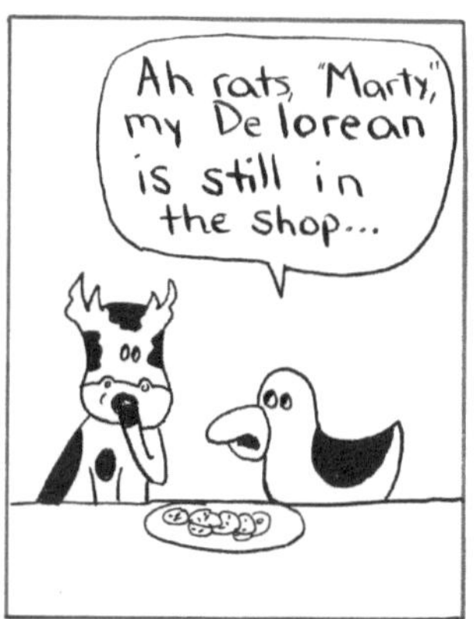
Ah rats, "Marty," my De lorean is still in the shop...

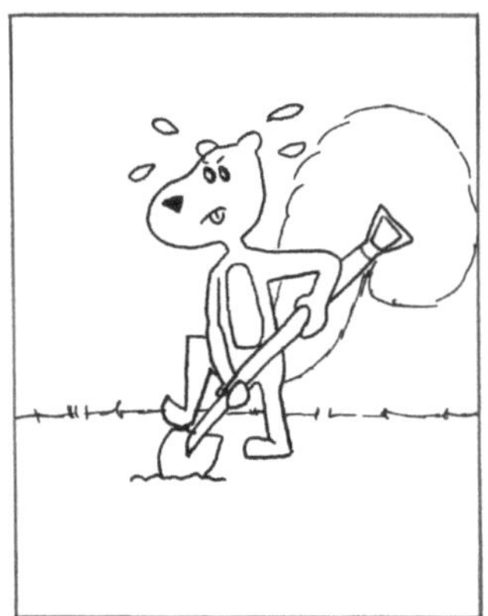

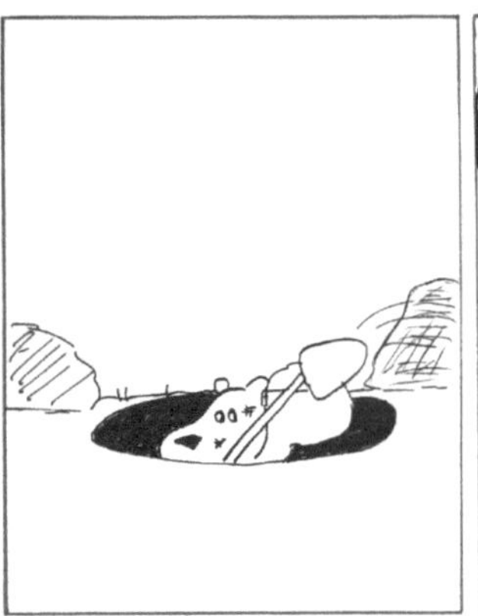

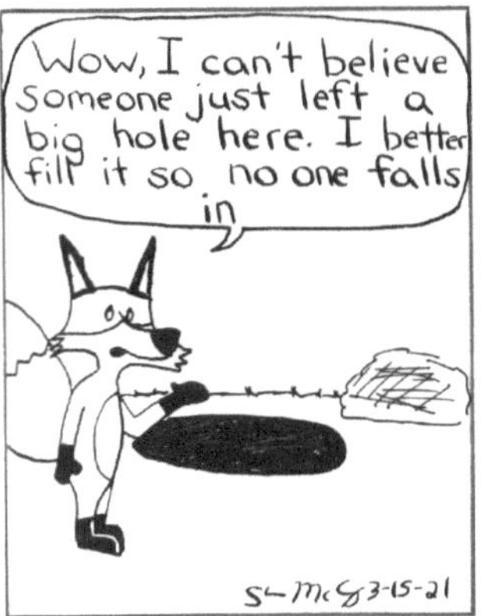

Wow, I can't believe someone just left a big hole here. I better fill it so no one falls in

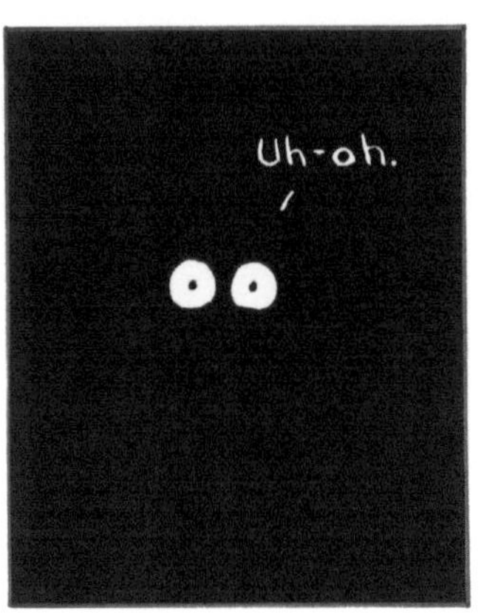

Uh-oh.

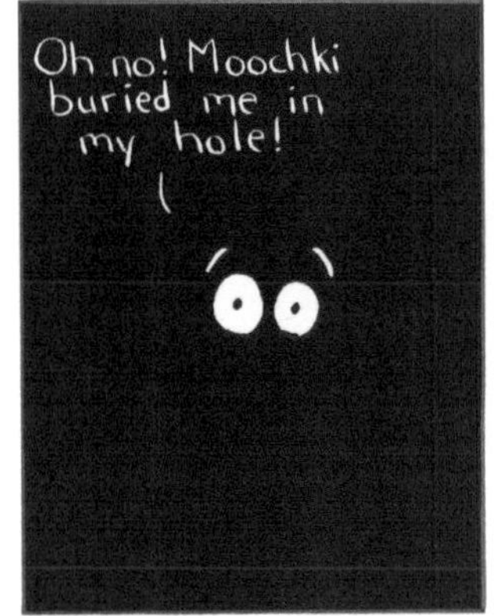

Oh no! Moochki buried me in my hole!

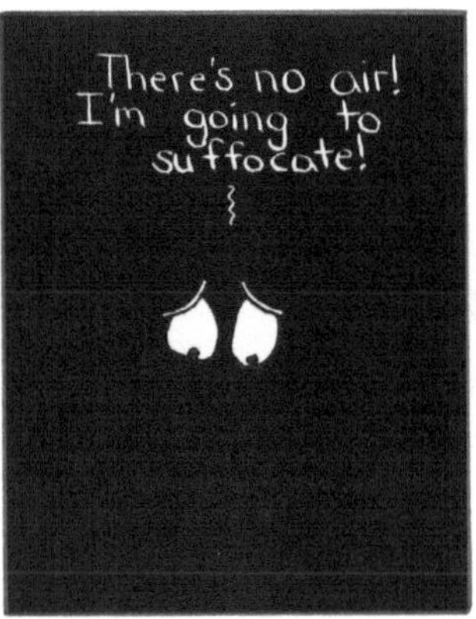

There's no air! I'm going to suffocate!

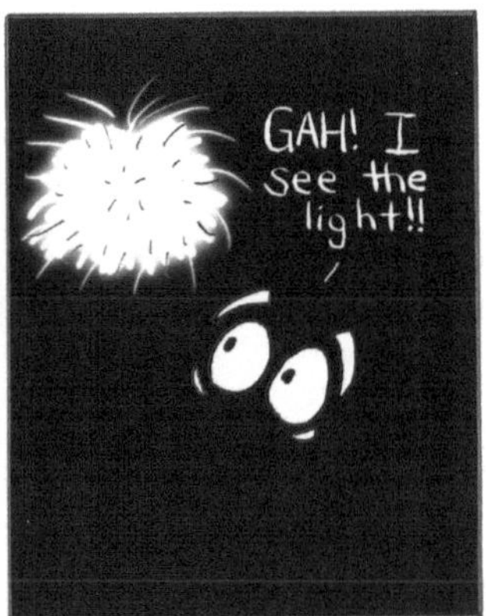

GAH! I see the light!!

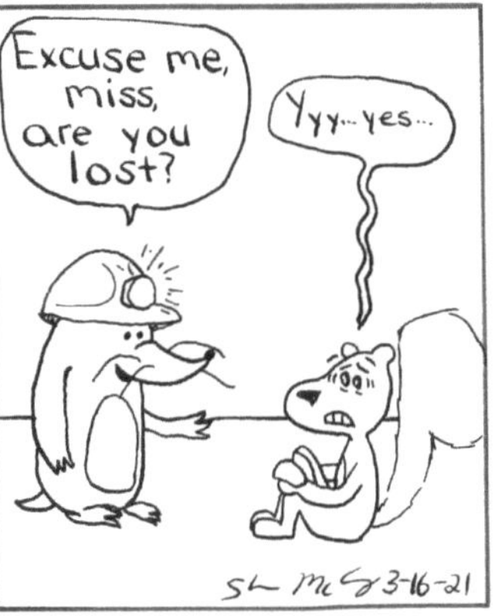

Excuse me, miss, are you lost?
Yyy... yes...

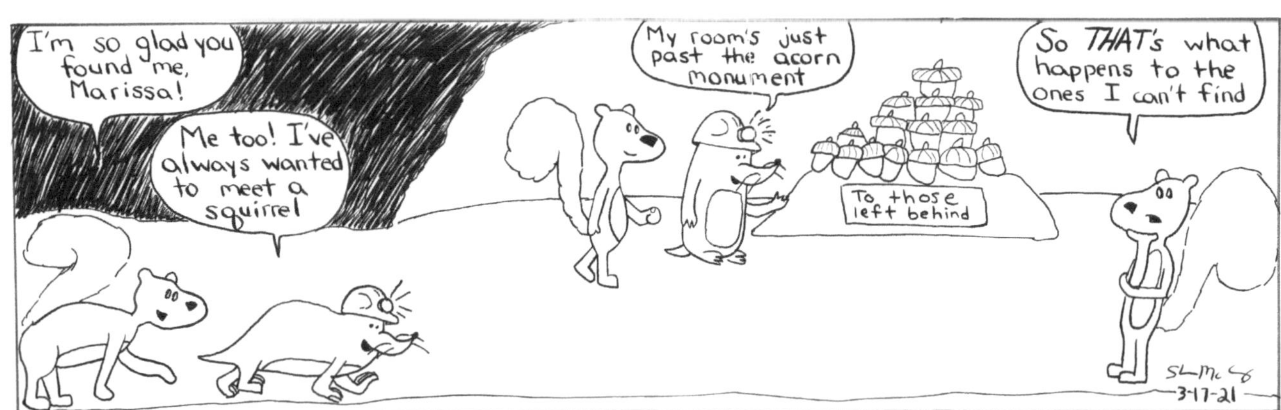

I'm so glad you found me, Marissa!
Me too! I've always wanted to meet a squirrel
My room's just past the acorn monument
To those left behind
So THAT's what happens to the ones I can't find

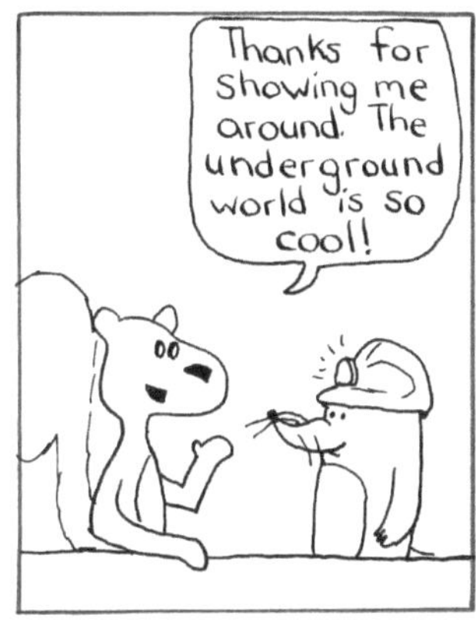
Thanks for showing me around. The underground world is so cool!

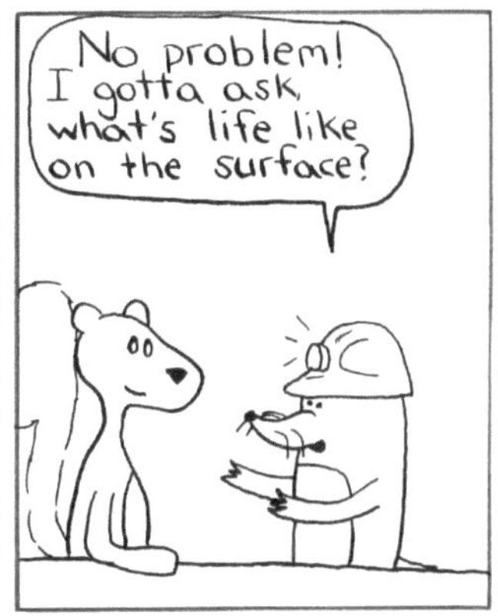
No problem! I gotta ask, what's life like on the surface?

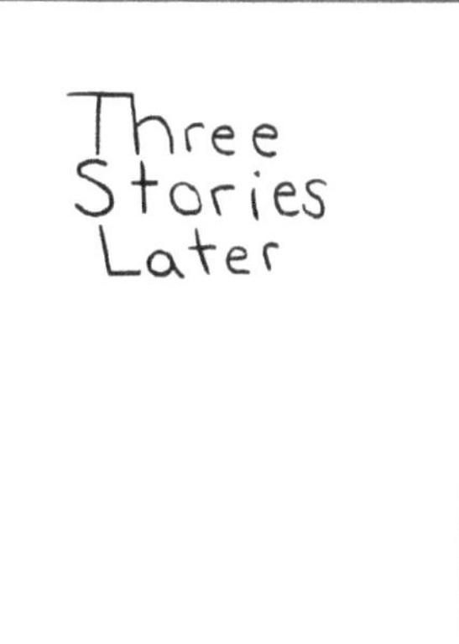
Three Stories Later

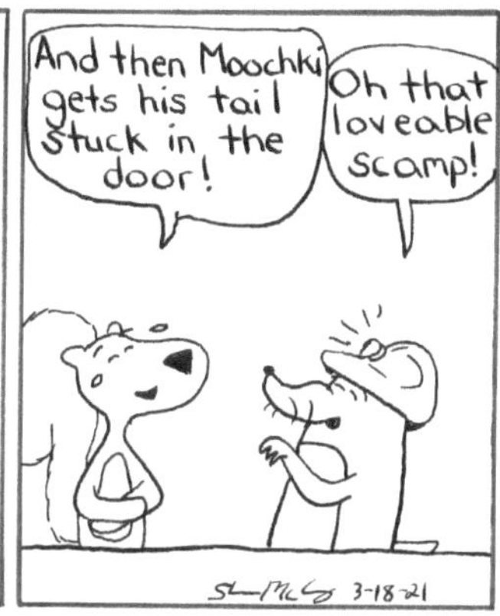
And then Moochki gets his tail stuck in the door!
Oh that loveable scamp!
3-18-21

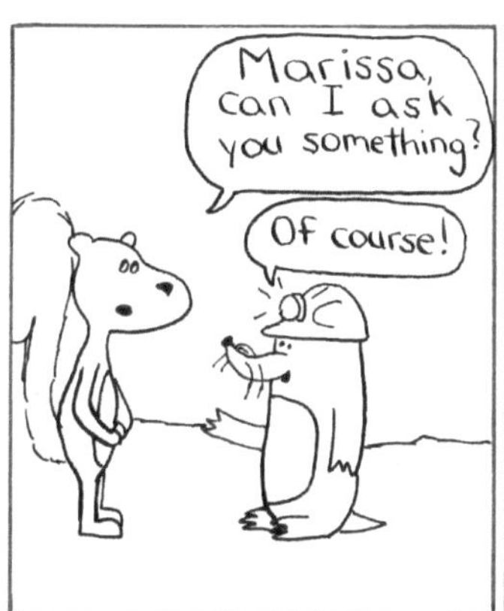
Marissa, can I ask you something?
Of course!

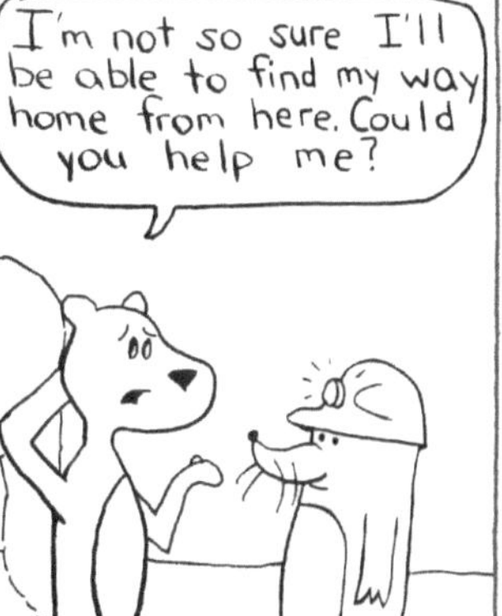
I'm not so sure I'll be able to find my way home from here. Could you help me?

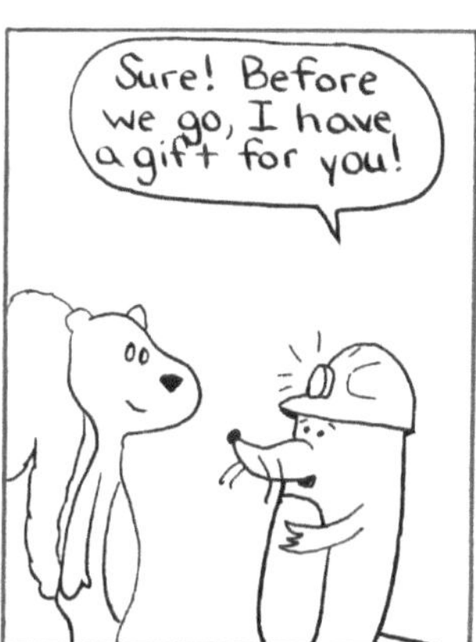
Sure! Before we go, I have a gift for you!

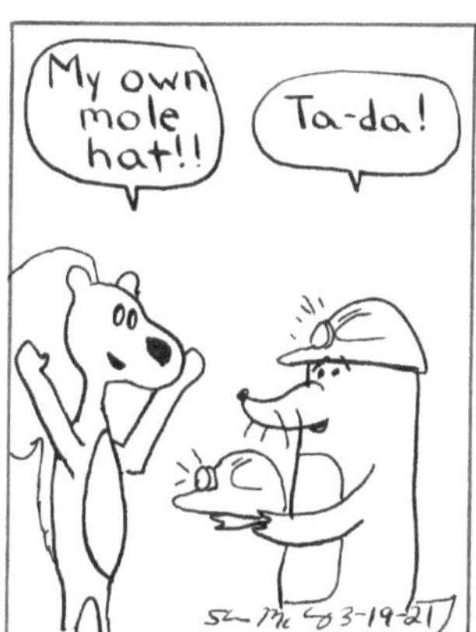
My own mole hat!!
Ta-da!
3-19-21

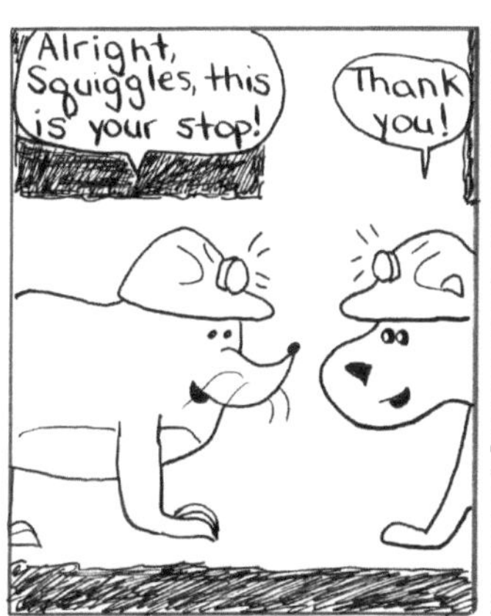
Alright, Squiggles, this is your stop!
Thank you!

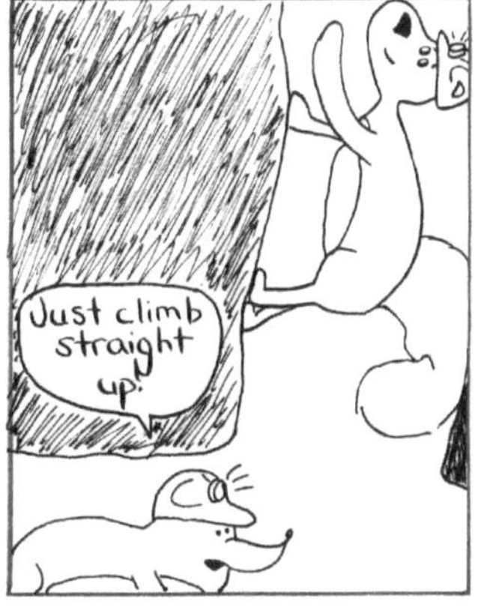
Just climb straight up!

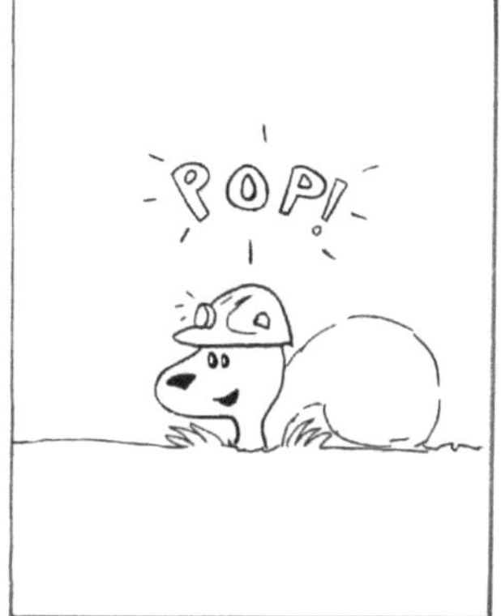
POP!

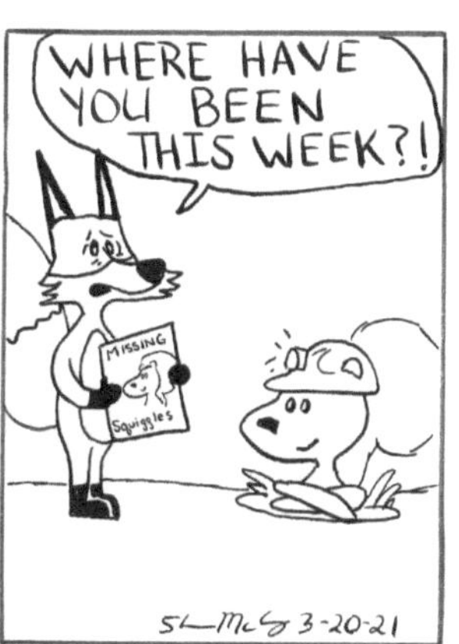
WHERE HAVE YOU BEEN THIS WEEK?!
MISSING
Squiggles
3-20-21

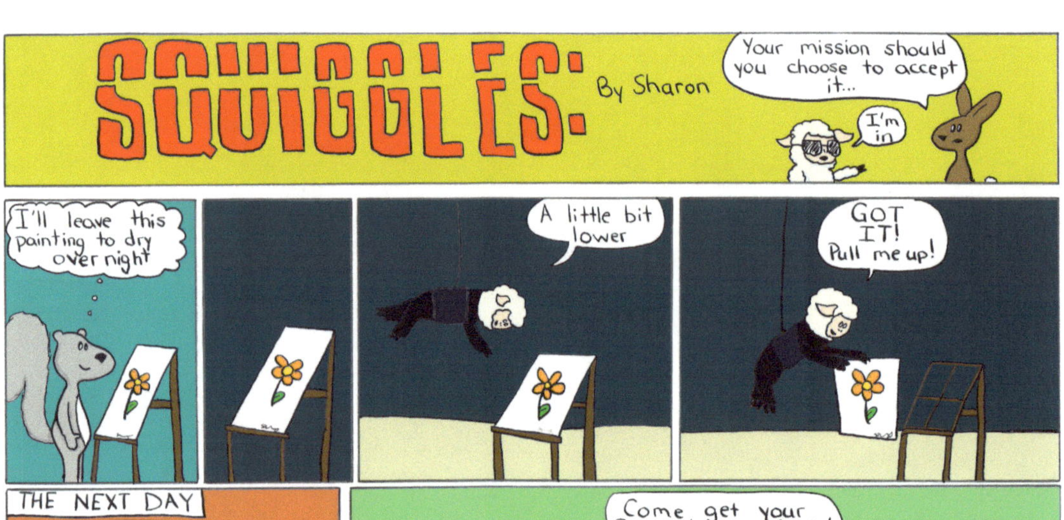
SQUIGGLES:
By Sharon
Your mission should you choose to accept it...
I'm in
I'll leave this painting to dry over night
A little bit lower
GOT IT! Pull me up!
THE NEXT DAY
Where did my painting go? That's the third one to dissappear!
Come get your Squiggles originals!
Only $5!
SL McG 3-21-21

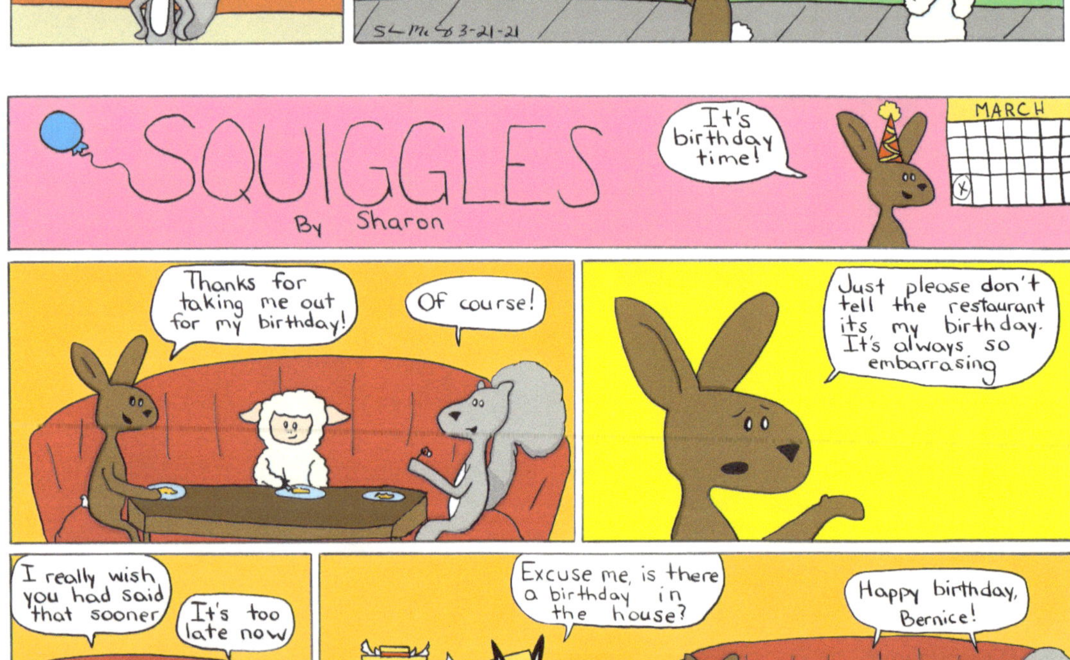
SQUIGGLES
By Sharon
It's birthday time!
MARCH
Thanks for taking me out for my birthday!
Of course!
Just please don't tell the restaurant its my birthday. It's always so embarrasing
I really wish you had said that sooner
It's too late now
Excuse me, is there a birthday in the house?
Happy birthday, Bernice!
SL McG 3-28-21

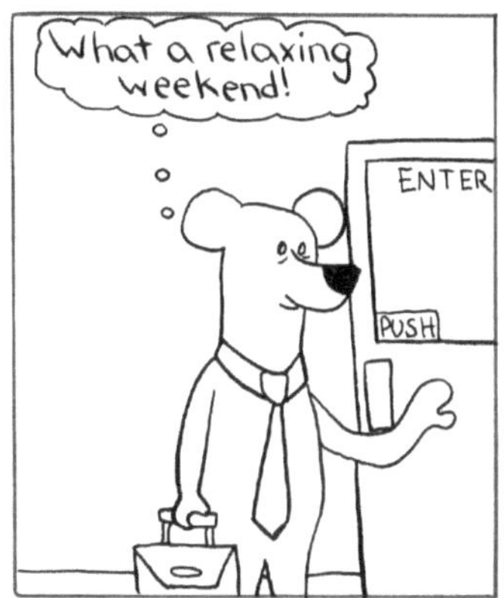
What a relaxing weekend!
ENTER
PUSH

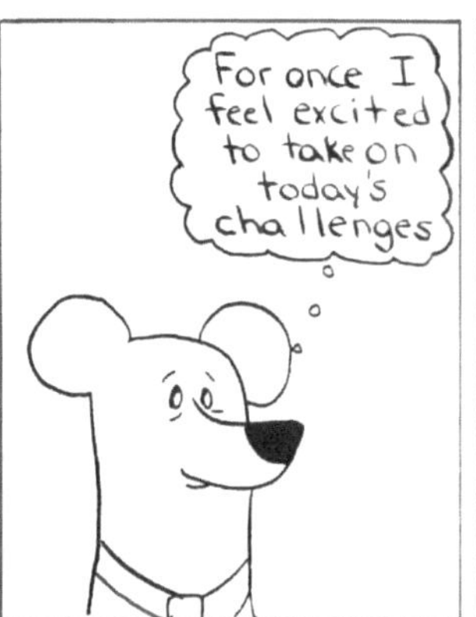
For once I feel excited to take on today's challenges

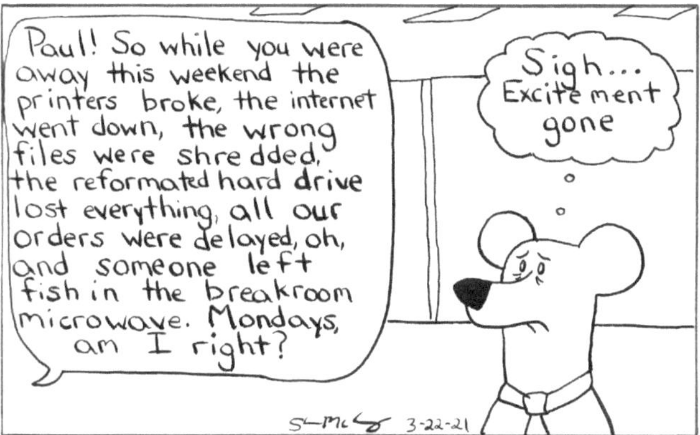
Paul! So while you were away this weekend the printers broke, the internet went down, the wrong files were shredded, the reformated hard drive lost everything, all our orders were delayed, oh, and someone left fish in the breakroom microwave. Mondays, am I right?
Sigh... Excitement gone
SLMcS 3-22-21

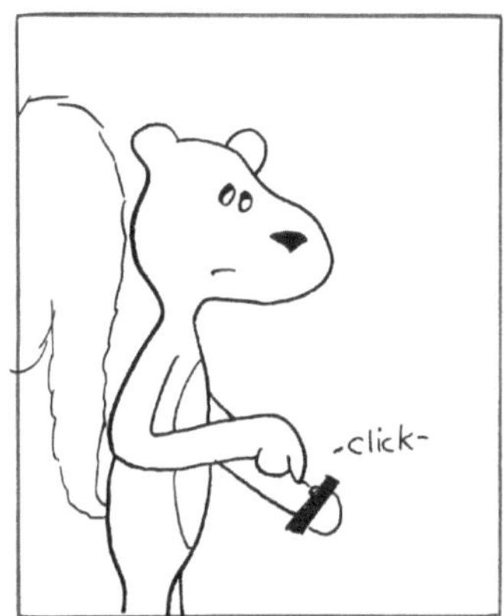
-click-

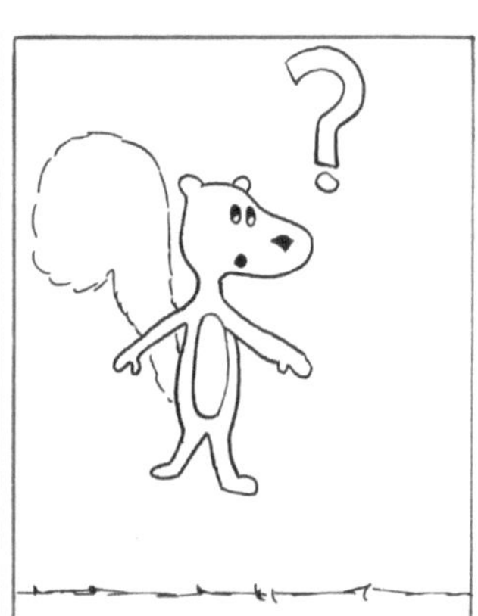
?

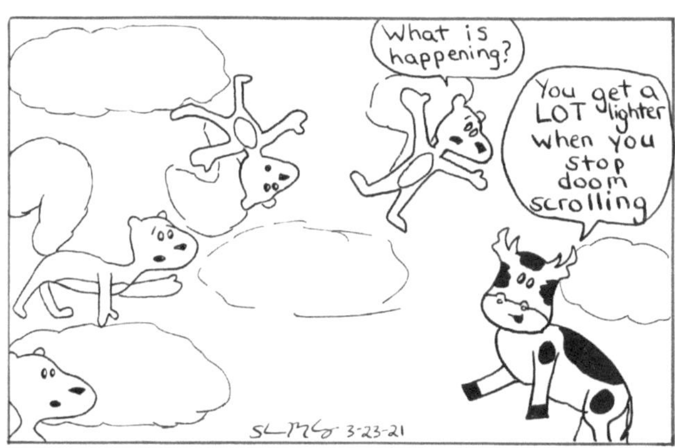
What is happening?
You get a LOT lighter when you stop doom scrolling
SLMcS 3-23-21

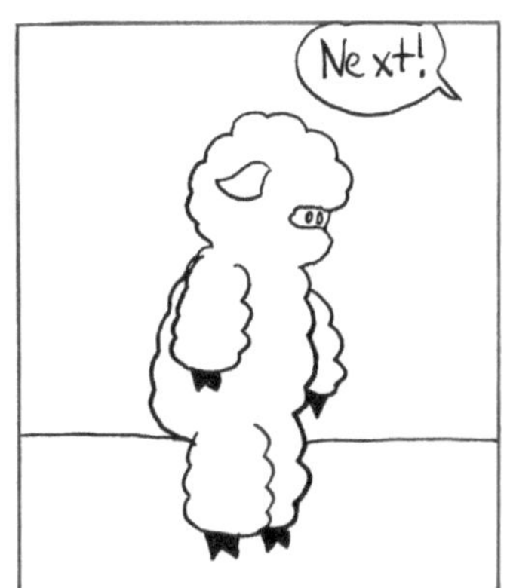
Next!

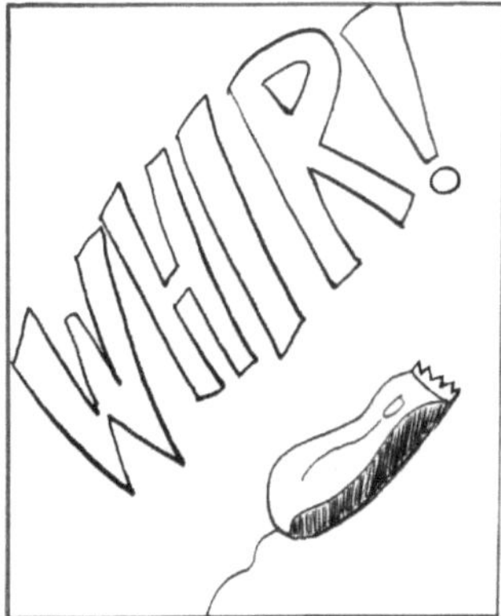
WHIR!

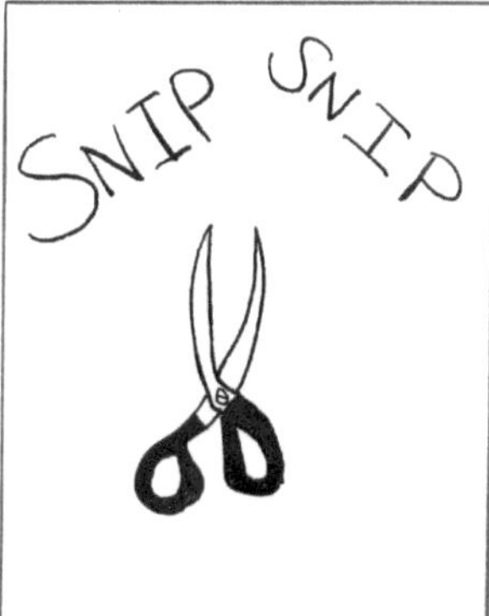
SNIP SNIP

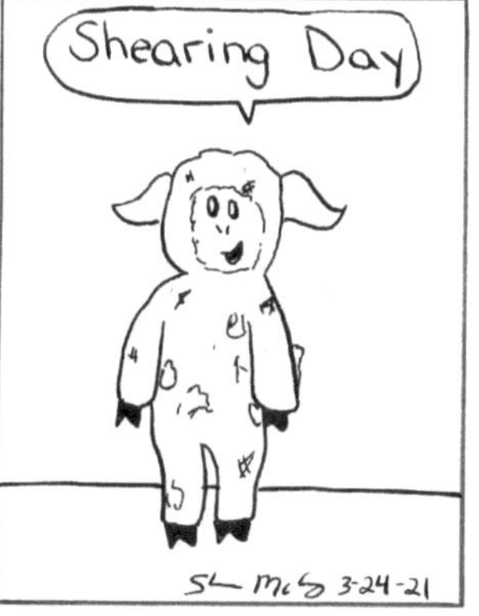
Shearing Day
SLMcS 3-24-21

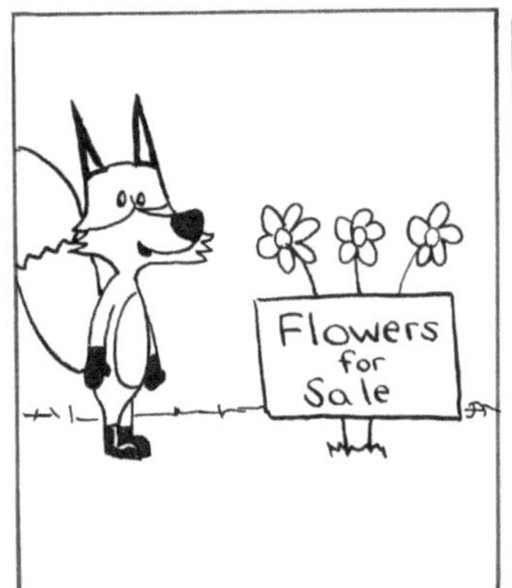
Flowers for Sale
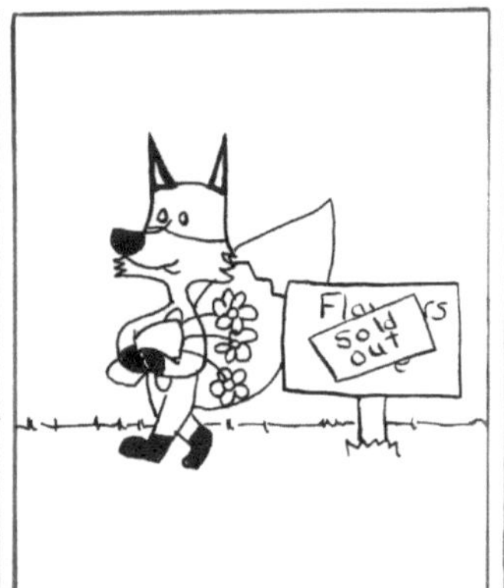
SOLD OUT
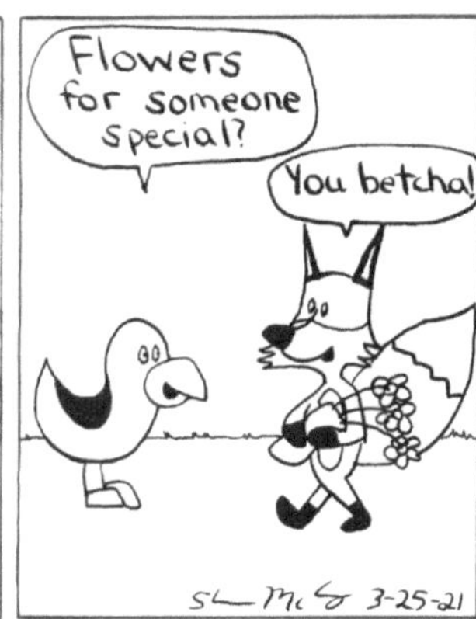
Flowers for someone special?
You betcha!
SL McS 3-25-21
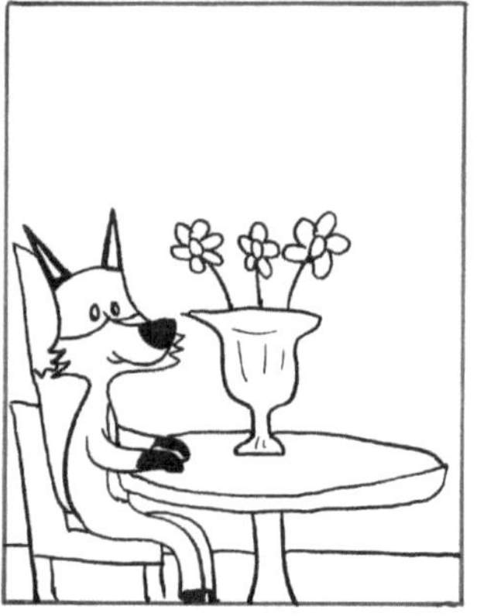
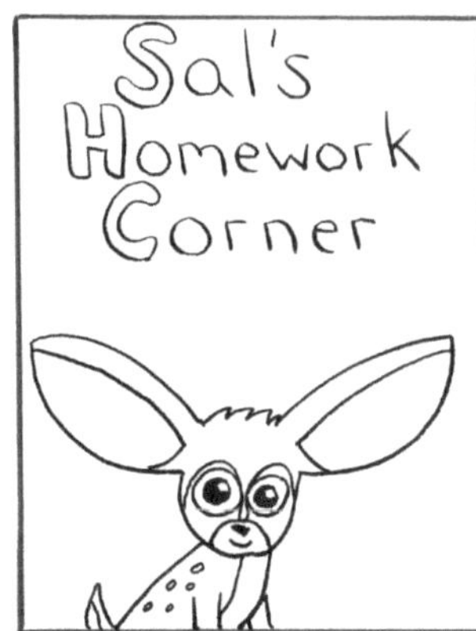
Sal's Homework Corner
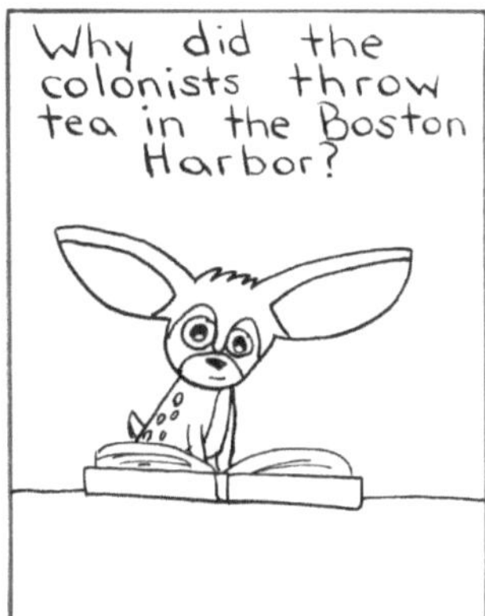
Why did the colonists throw tea in the Boston Harbor?
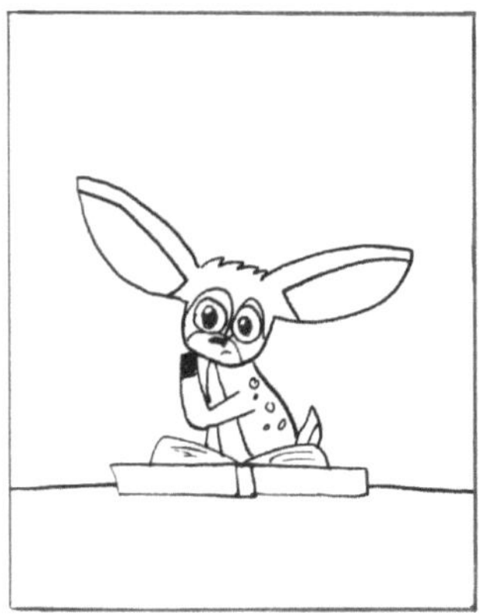
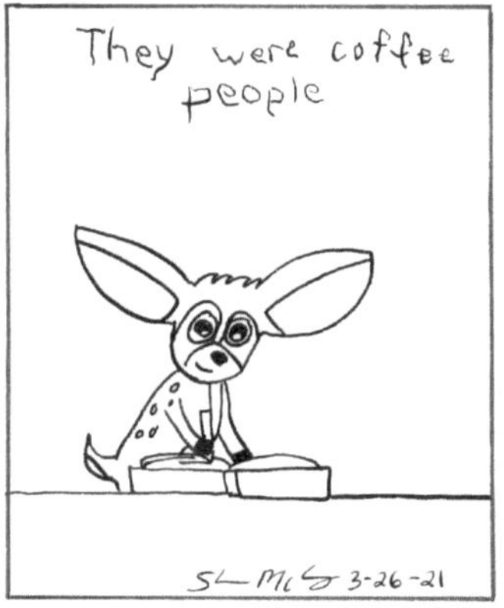
They were coffee people
SL McS 3-26-21
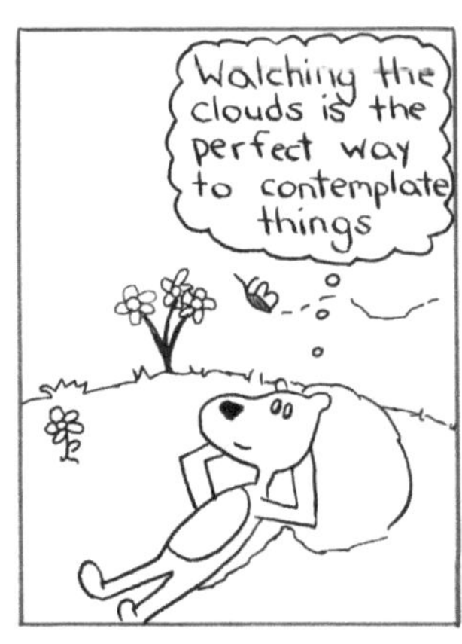
Watching the clouds is the perfect way to contemplate things
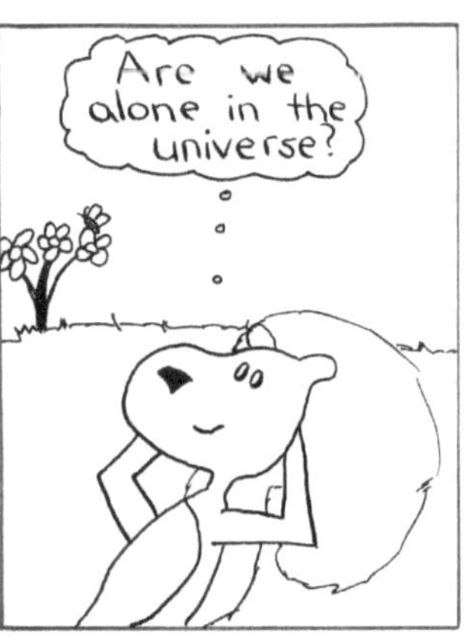
Are we alone in the universe?
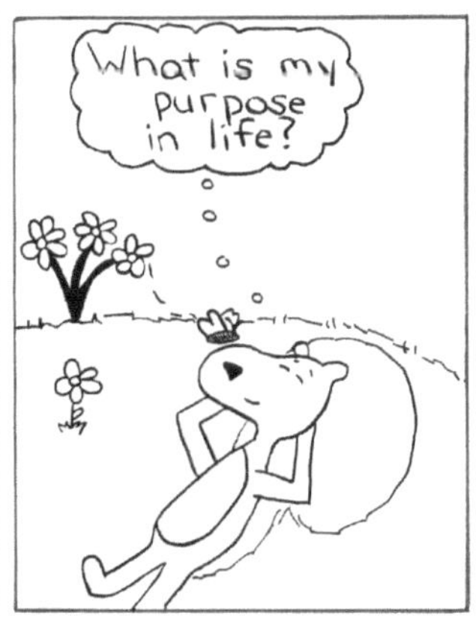
What is my purpose in life?
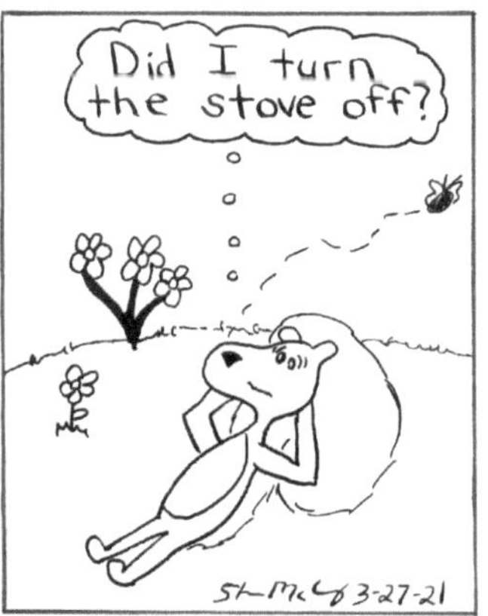
Did I turn the stove off?
SL McS 3-27-21

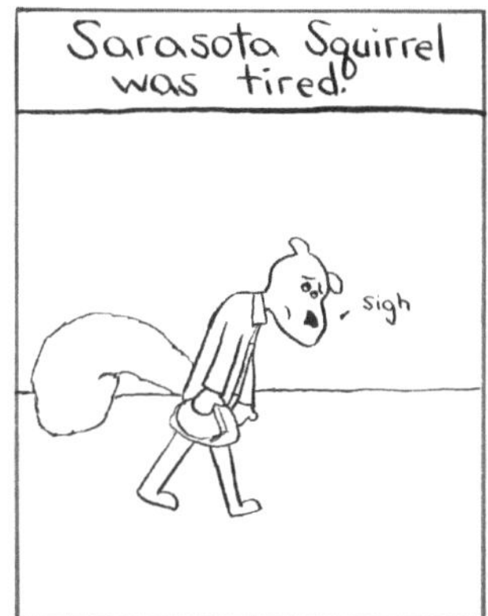
Sarasota Squirrel was tired.
sigh

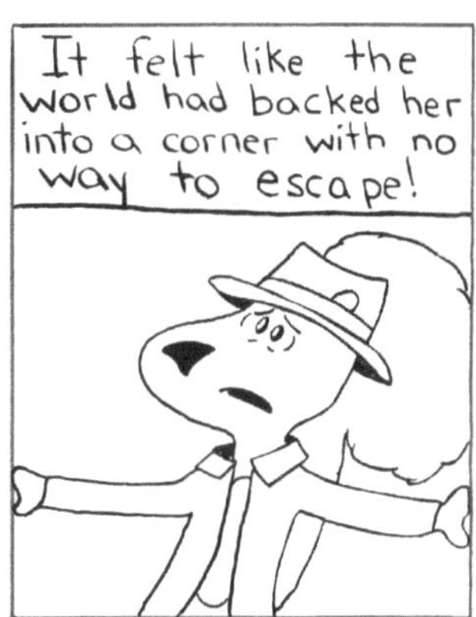
It felt like the world had backed her into a corner with no way to escape!

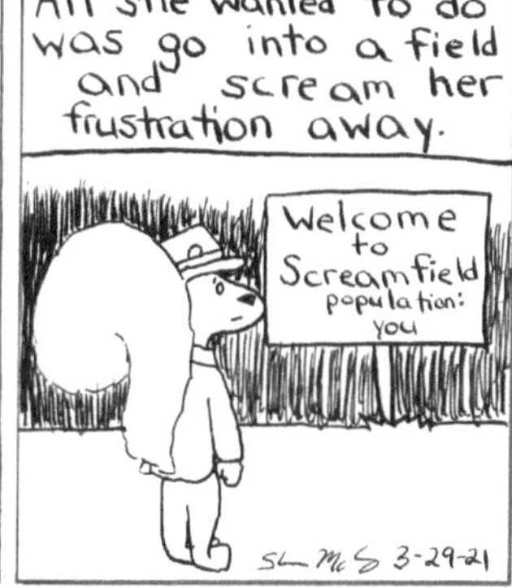
All she wanted to do was go into a field and scream her frustration away.
Welcome to Screamfield
population: you
SL McS 3-29-21

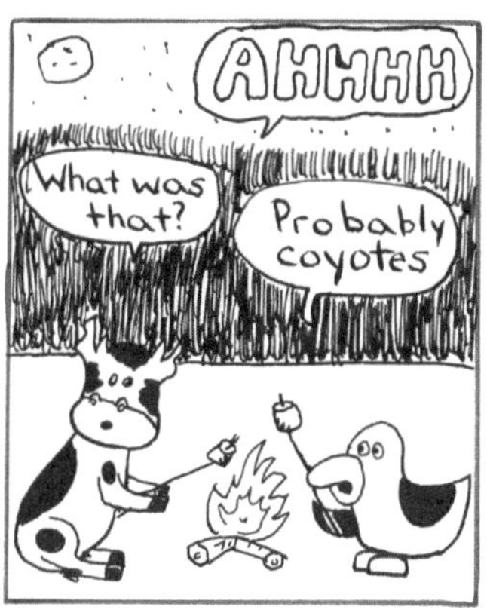
AHHHH
What was that?
Probably coyotes

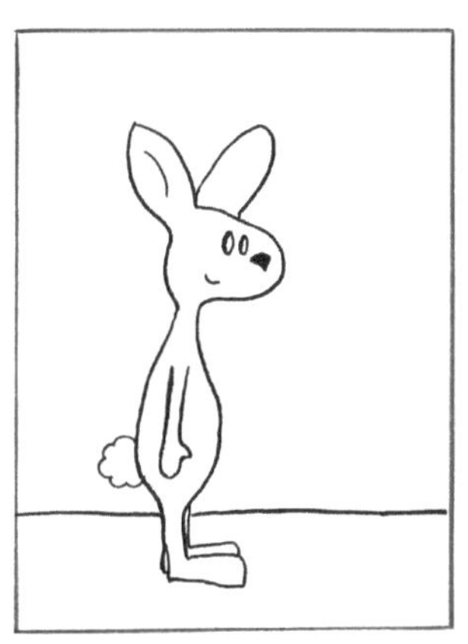

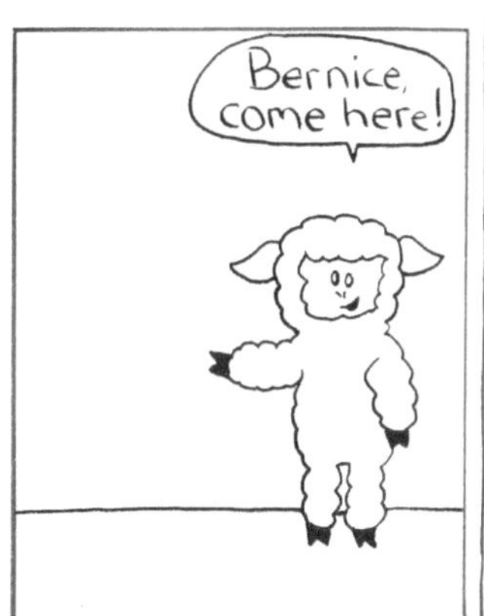
Bernice, come here!

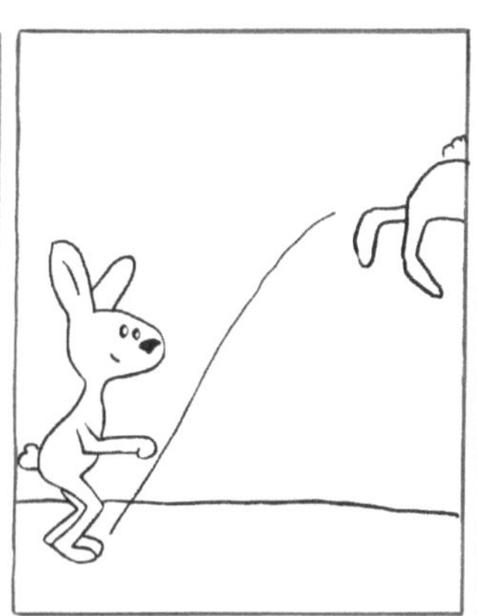

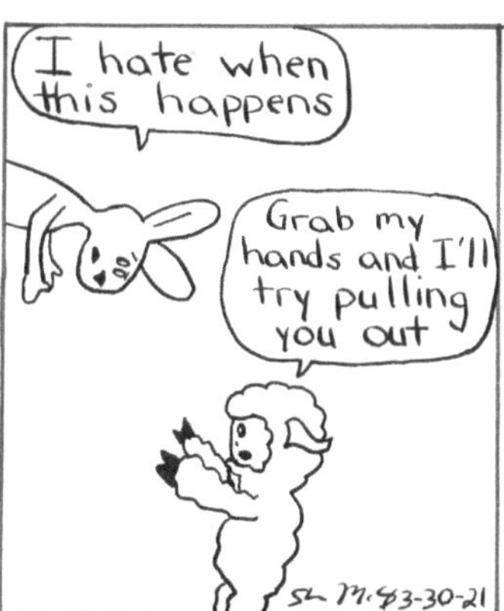
I hate when this happens
Grab my hands and I'll try pulling you out
SL McS 3-30-21

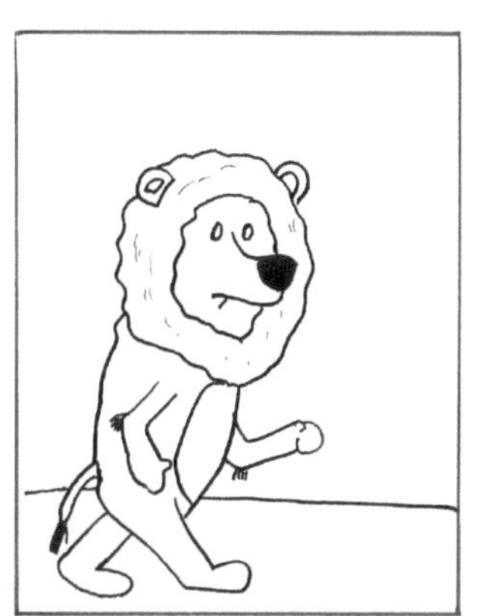

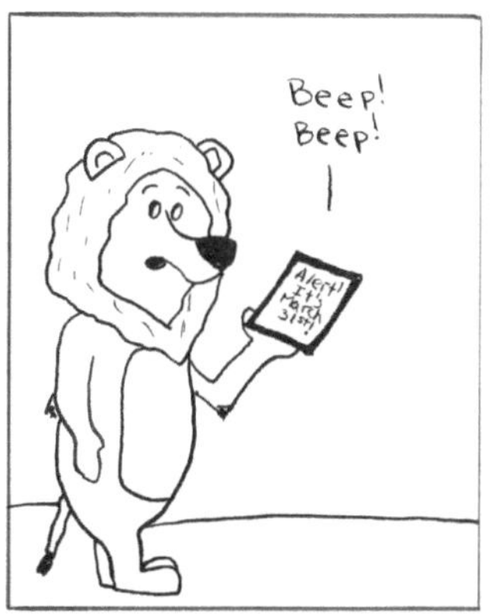
Beep! Beep!
Alert! It's March 31st!

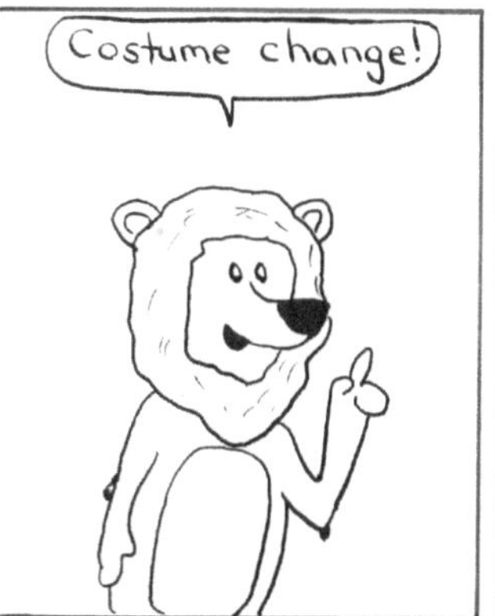
Costume change!

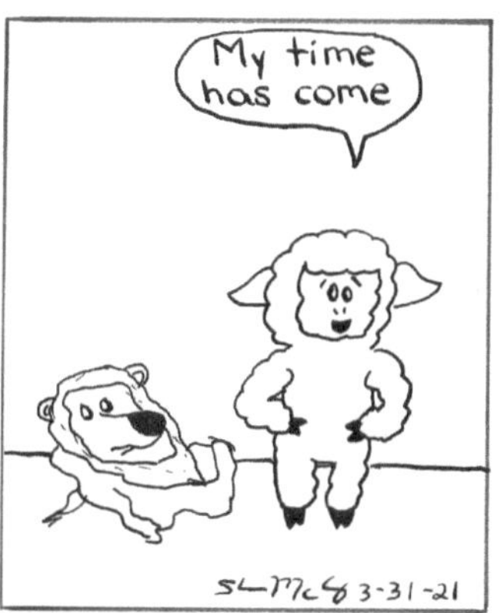
My time has come
SL McS 3-31-21

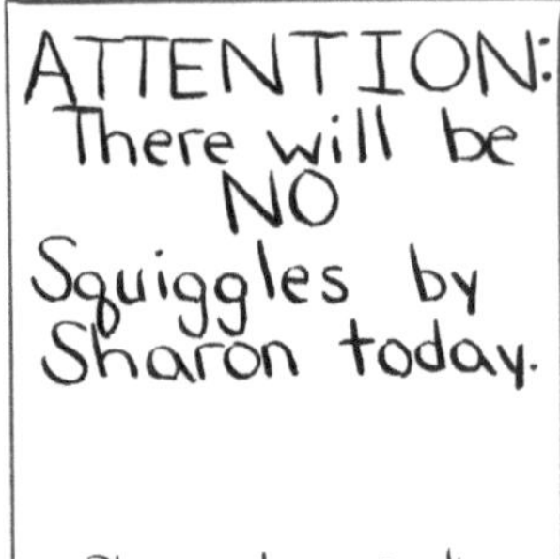
ATTENTION:
There will be NO Squiggles by Sharon today.

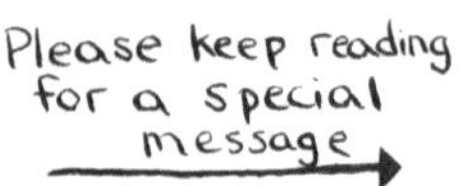
Please keep reading for a special message

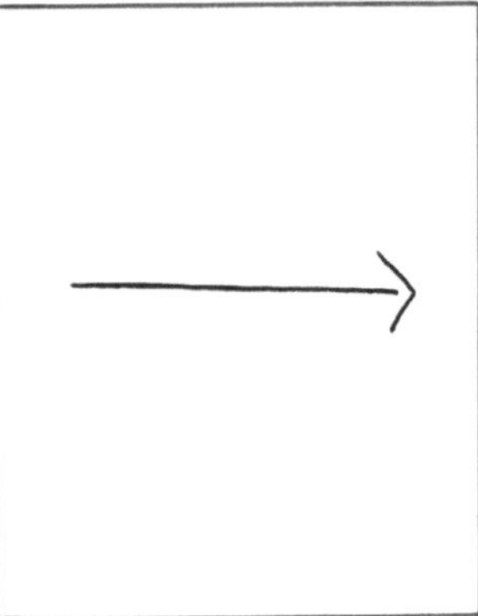

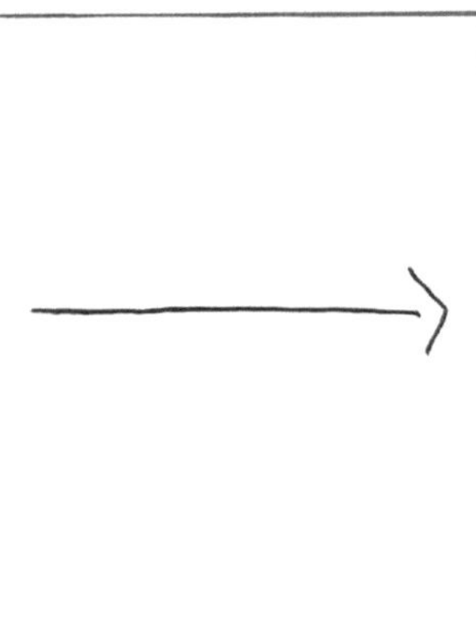

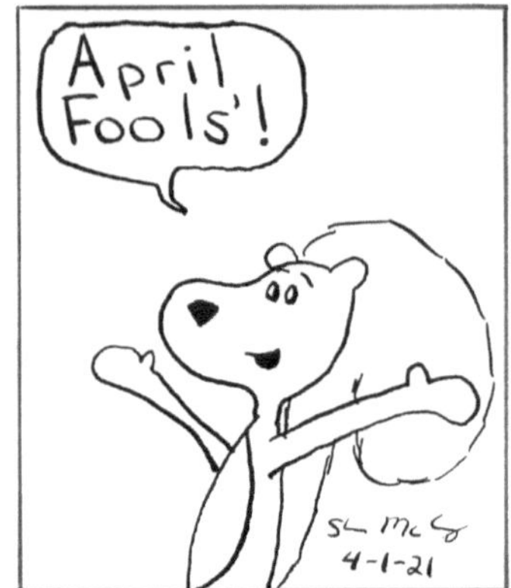
April Fools'!
4-1-21

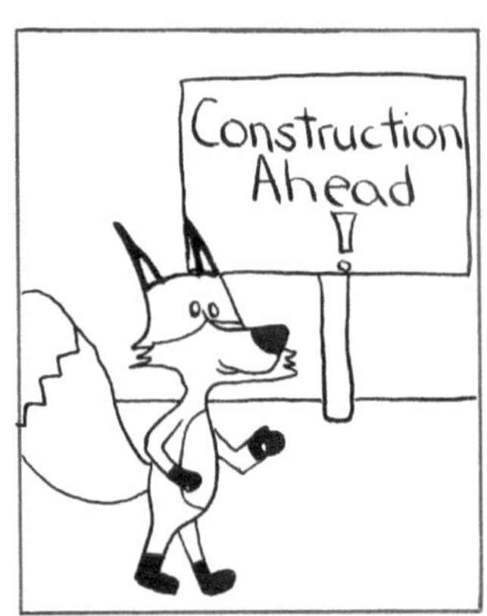
Construction Ahead

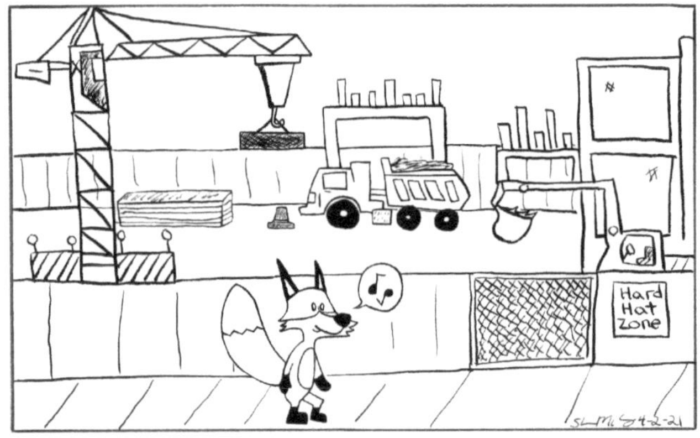
Hard Hat Zone

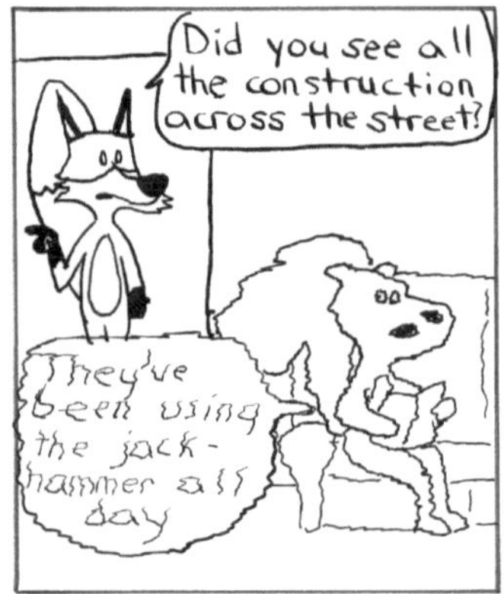
Did you see all the construction across the street?
They've been using the jack-hammer all day

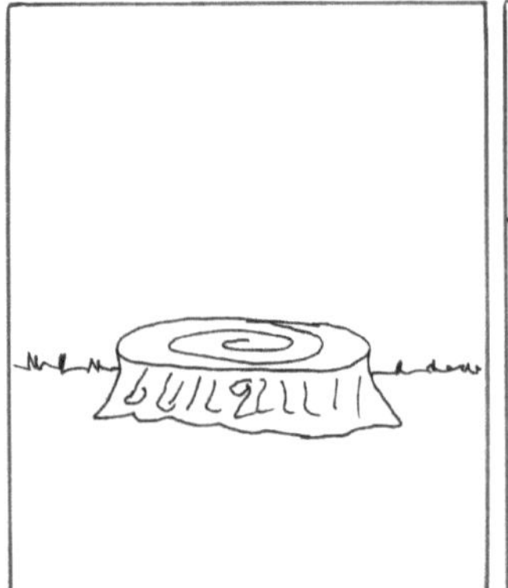

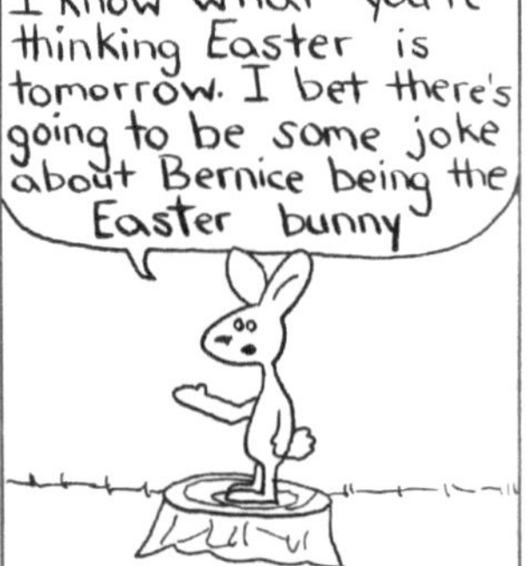
I know what you're thinking Easter is tomorrow. I bet there's going to be some joke about Bernice being the Easter bunny

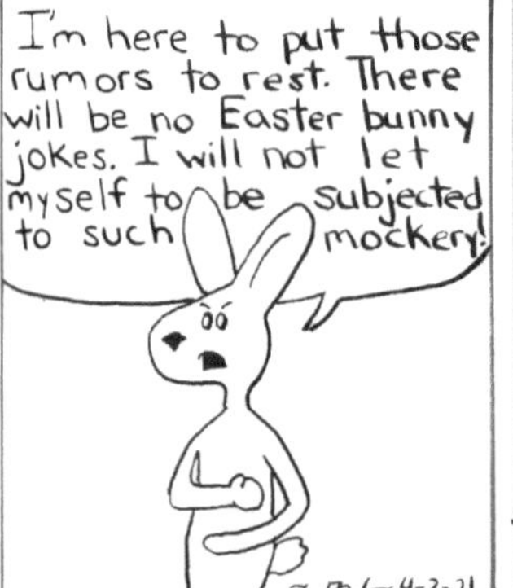
I'm here to put those rumors to rest. There will be no Easter bunny jokes. I will not let myself to be subjected to such mockery!
4-3-21

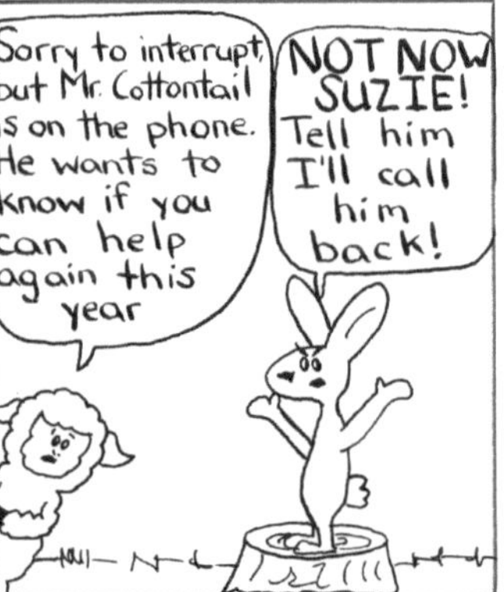
Sorry to interrupt, but Mr. Cottontail is on the phone. He wants to know if you can help again this year
NOT NOW SUZIE! Tell him I'll call him back!

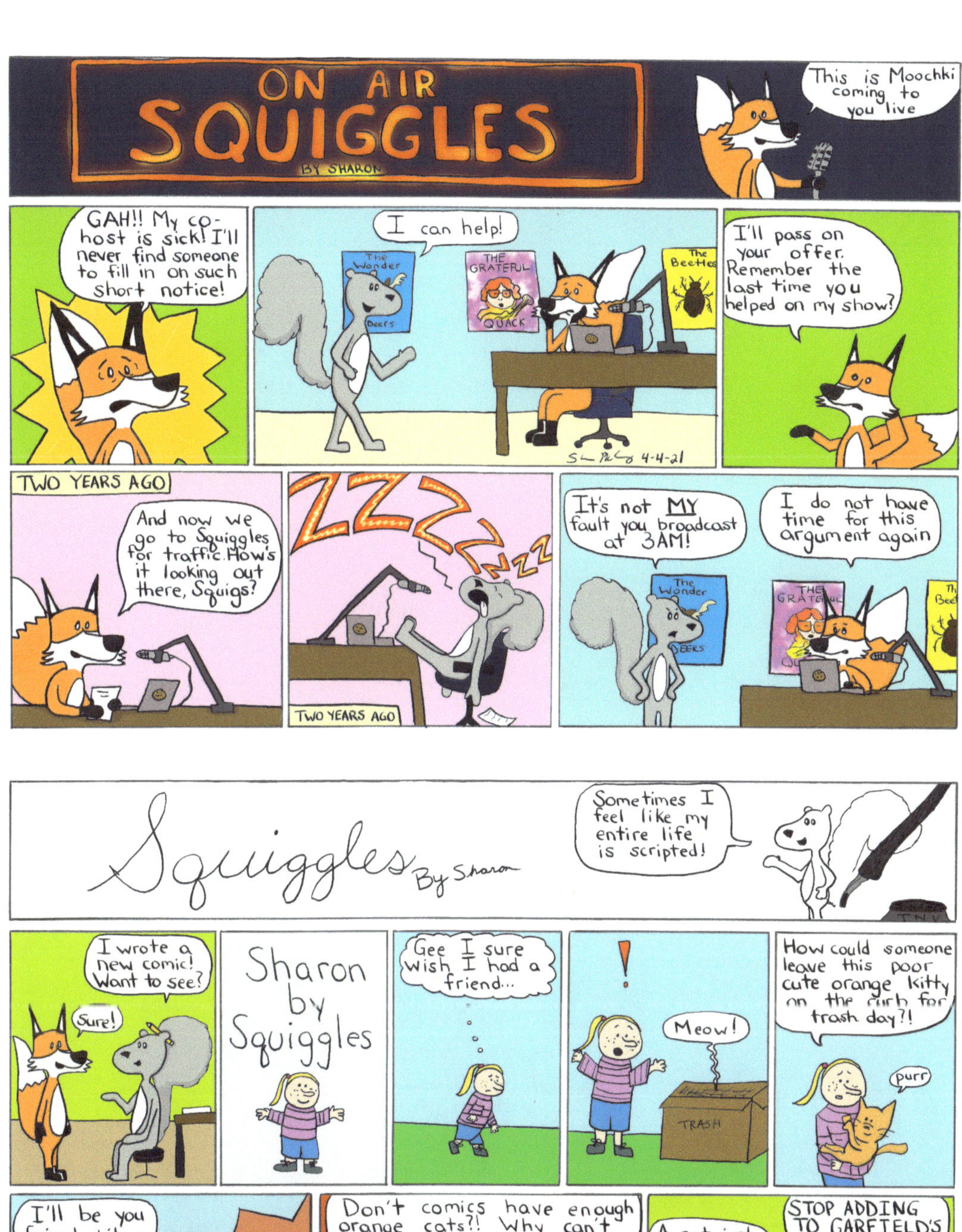
ON AIR
SQUIGGLES
BY SHARON
This is Moochki coming to you live
GAH!! My co-host is sick! I'll never find someone to fill in on such short notice!
I can help!
The Wonder Beers
THE GRATEFUL QUACK
The Beetles
I'll pass on your offer. Remember the last time you helped on my show?
TWO YEARS AGO
And now we go to Squiggles for traffic. How's it looking out there, Squigs?
ZZZZZZ
TWO YEARS AGO
It's not MY fault you broadcast at 3AM!
I do not have time for this argument again
The Wonder Beers
THE GRATEFUL
Squiggles By Sharon
Sometimes I feel like my entire life is scripted!
I wrote a new comic! Want to see?
Sure!
Sharon by Squiggles
Gee I sure wish I had a friend...
!
Meow!
TRASH
How could someone leave this poor cute orange kitty on the curb for trash day?!
purr
I'll be you friend kit—
HOLD IT!
Don't comics have enough orange cats?! Why can't Sharon find a little orange fox?!!
A cat just works better here...
STOP ADDING TO GARFIELD'S MONOPOLY!

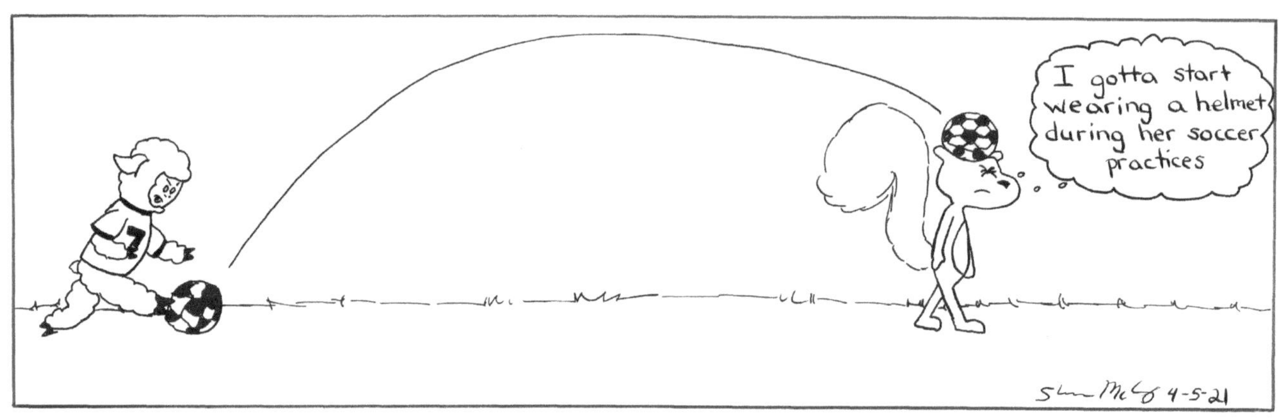
I gotta start wearing a helmet during her soccer practices
Sl McG 4-5-21

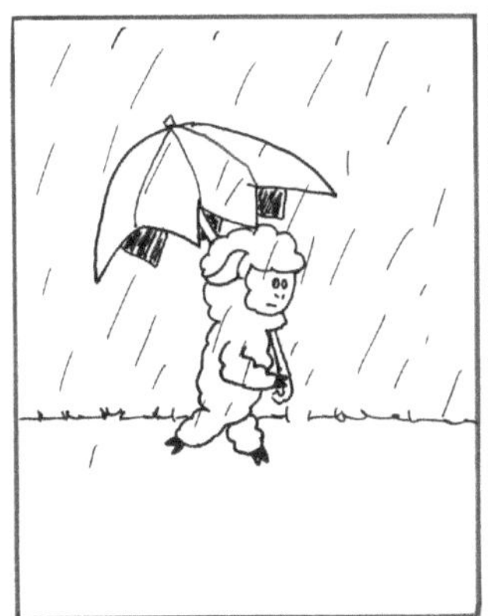

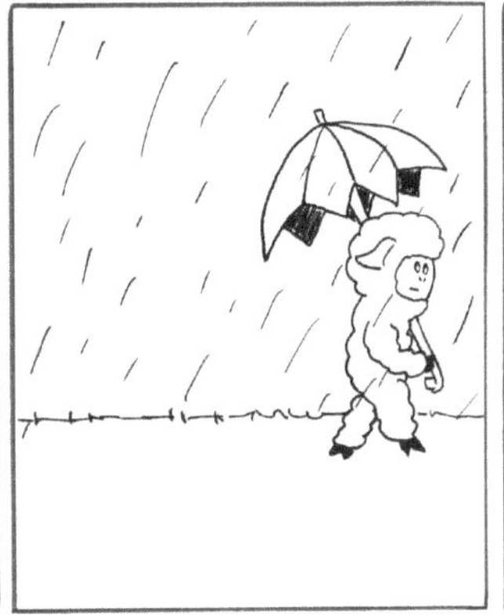

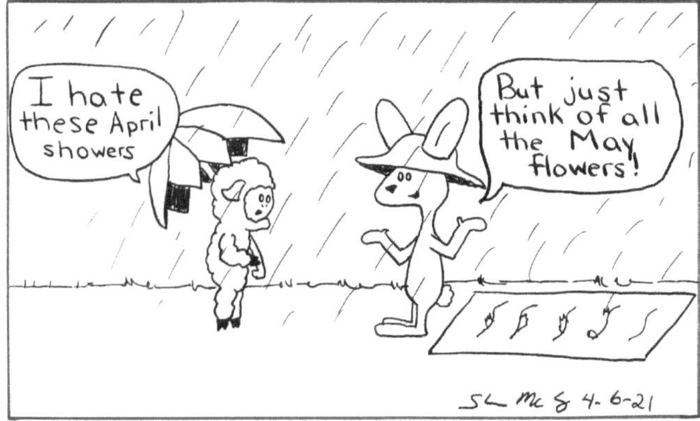
I hate these April showers
But just think of all the May flowers!
SL McG 4-6-21

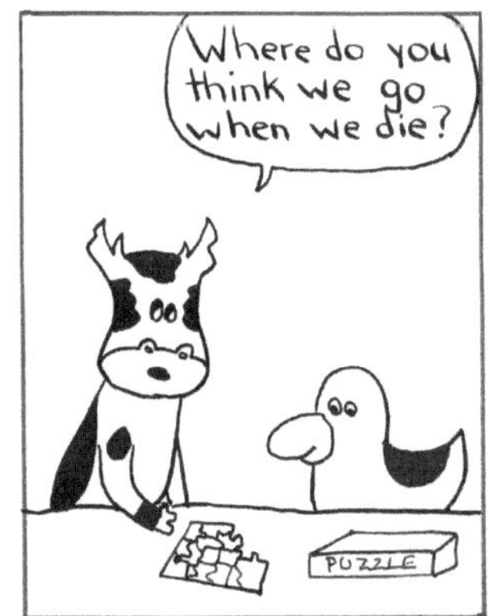
Where do you think we go when we die?
PUZZLE

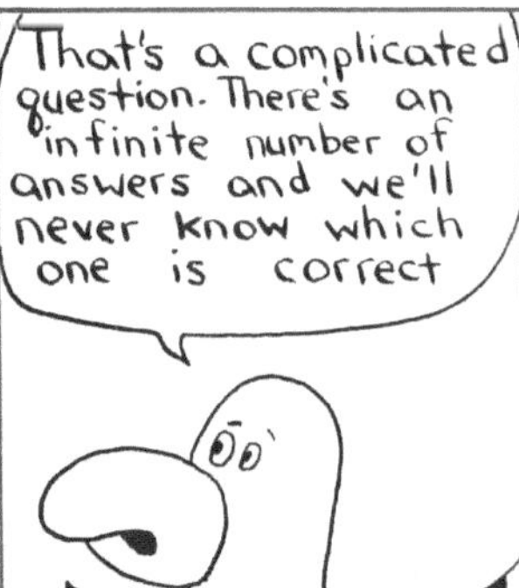
That's a complicated question. There's an infinite number of answers and we'll never know which one is correct

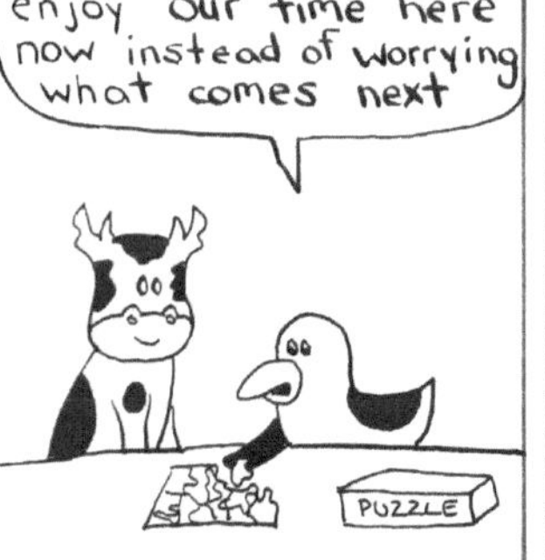
Maybe its best to enjoy our time here now instead of worrying what comes next
PUZZLE

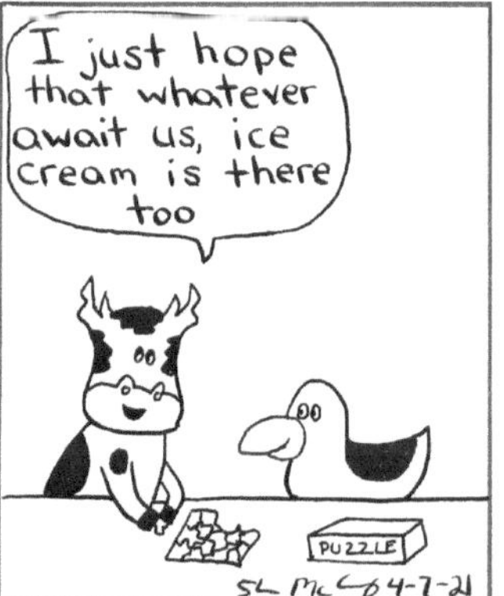
I just hope that whatever await us, ice cream is there too
PUZZLE
SL McG 4-7-21

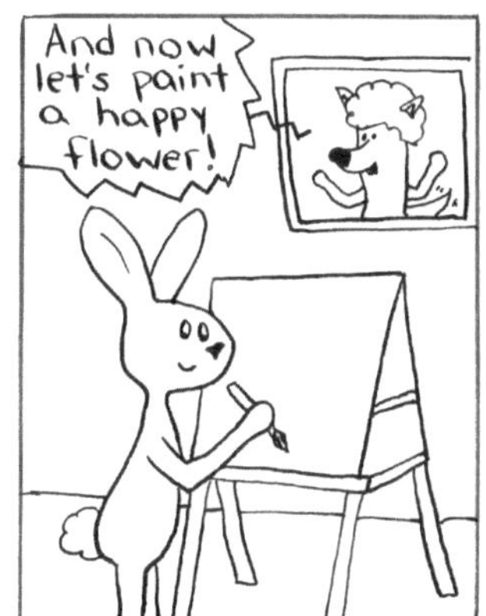
And now let's paint a happy flower!

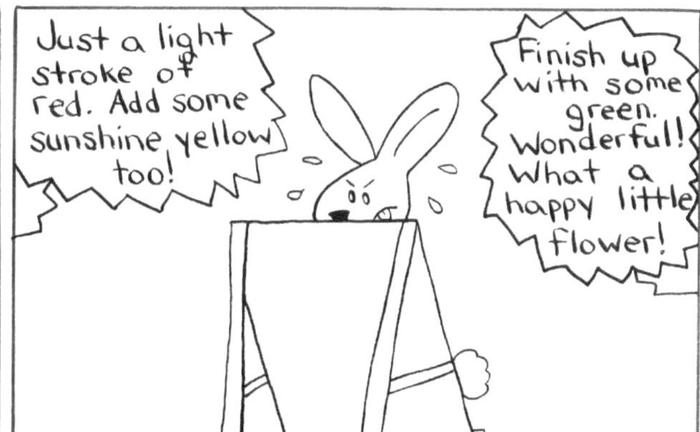
Just a light stroke of red. Add some sunshine yellow too!
Finish up with some green. Wonderful! What a happy little flower!

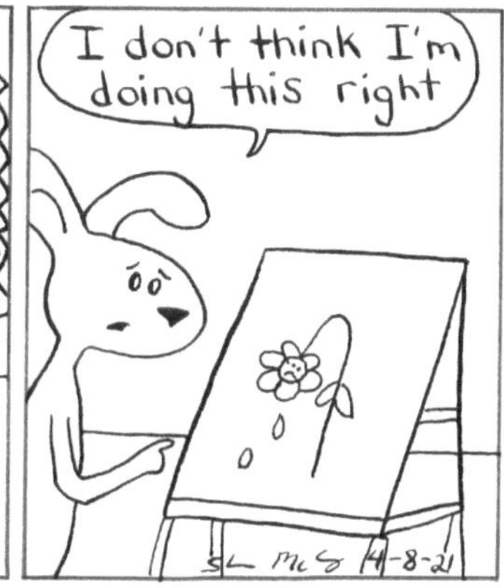
I don't think I'm doing this right
SL McG 4-8-21

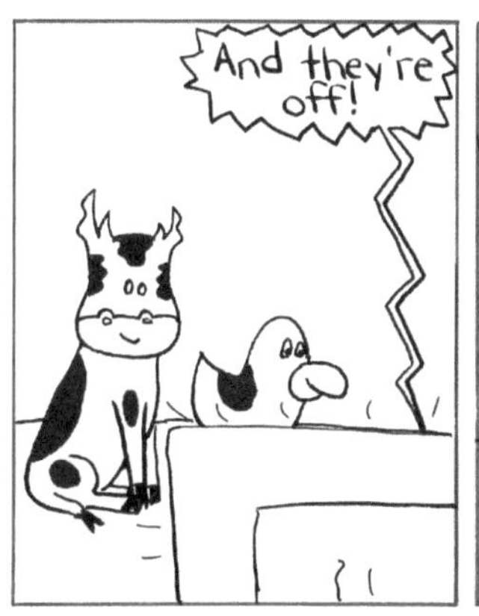
And they're off!

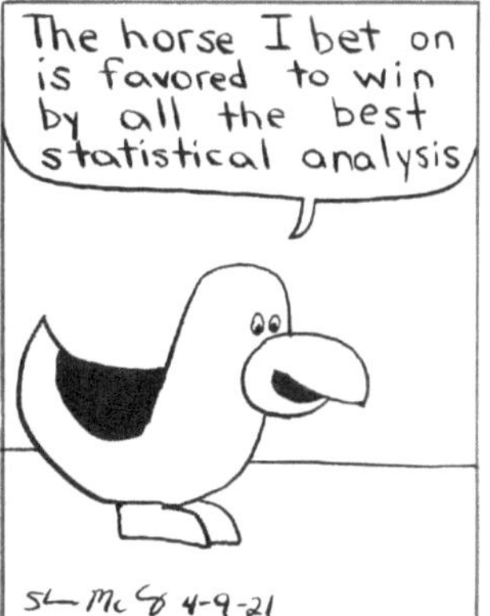
The horse I bet on is favored to win by all the best statistical analysis
SL McG 4-9-21

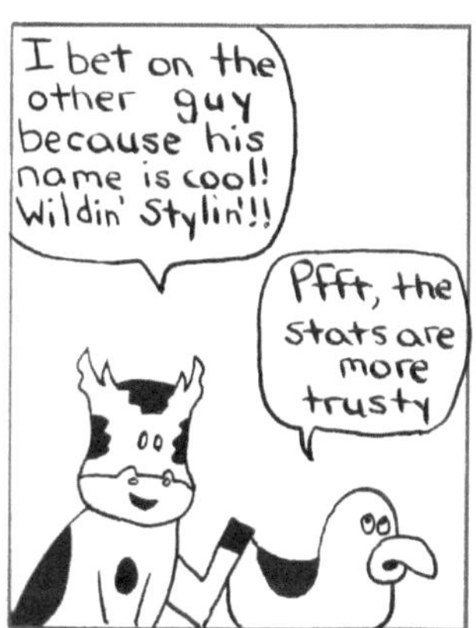
I bet on the other guy because his name is cool! Wildin' Stylin'!!
Pfft, the stats are more trusty

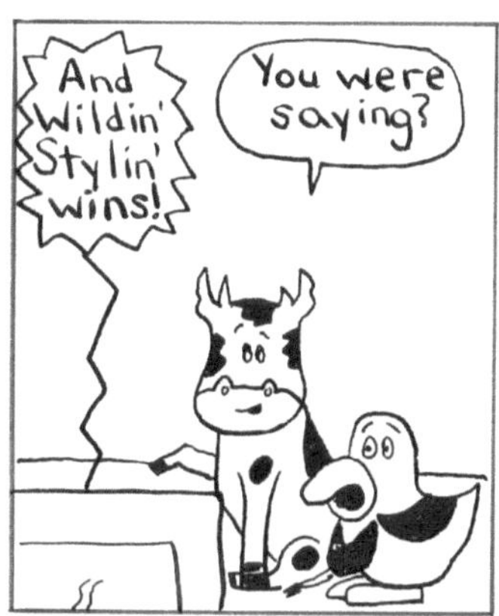
And Wildin' Stylin' wins!
You were saying?

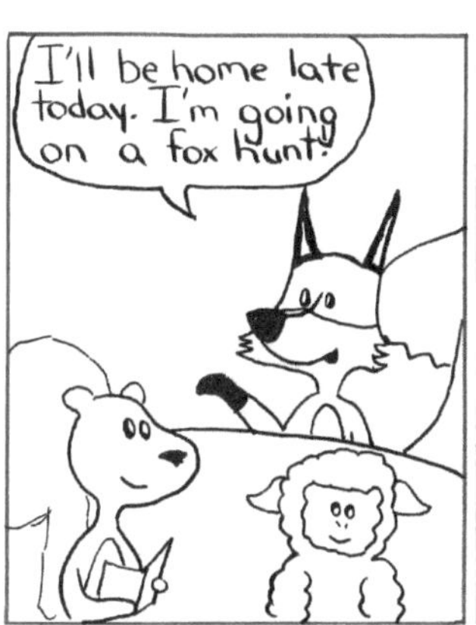
I'll be home late today. I'm going on a fox hunt!

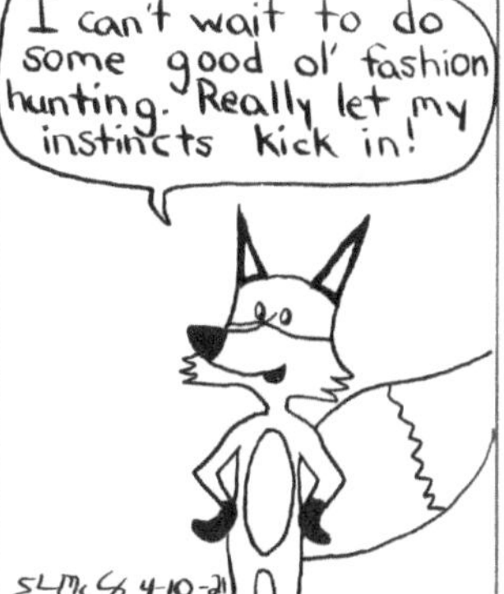
I can't wait to do some good ol' fashion hunting. Really let my instincts kick in!
SLMcG 4-10-21

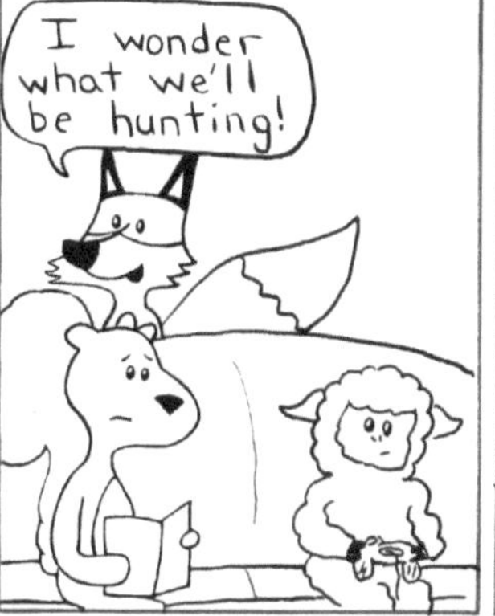
I wonder what we'll be hunting!

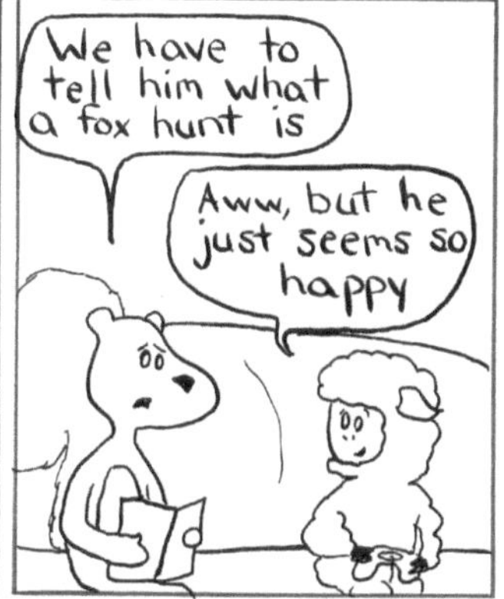
We have to tell him what a fox hunt is
Aww, but he just seems so happy

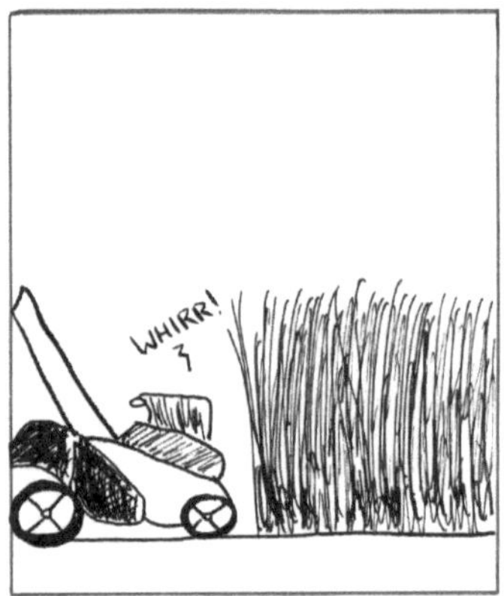
WHIRR!

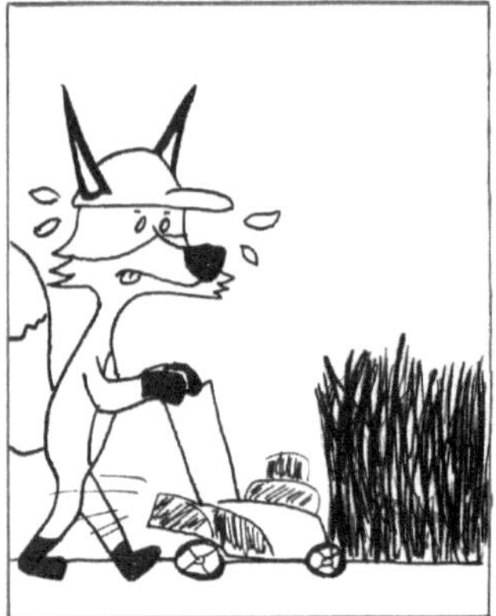

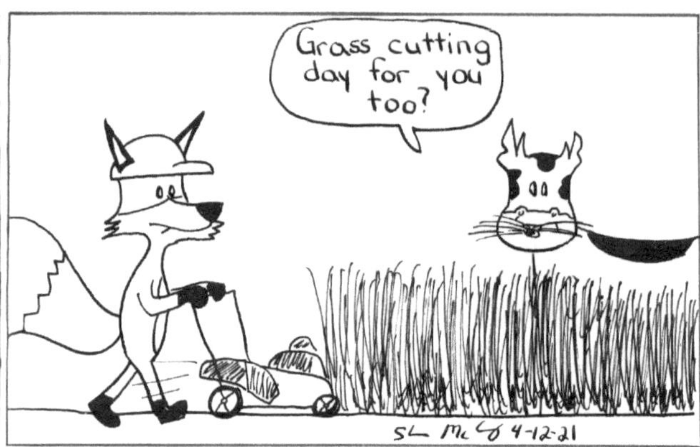
Grass cutting day for you too?
SL Mc 4-12-21

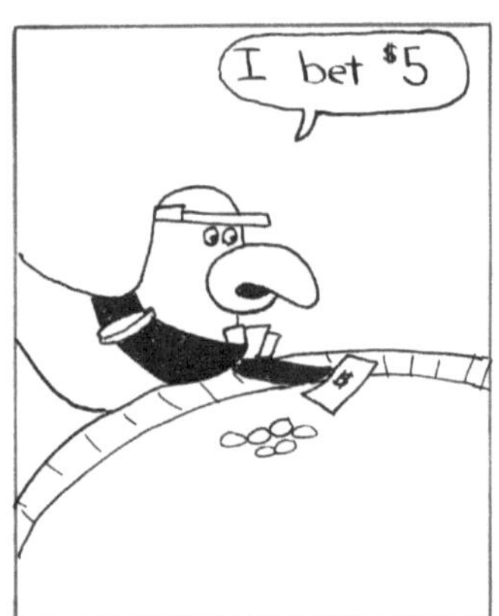
I bet $5

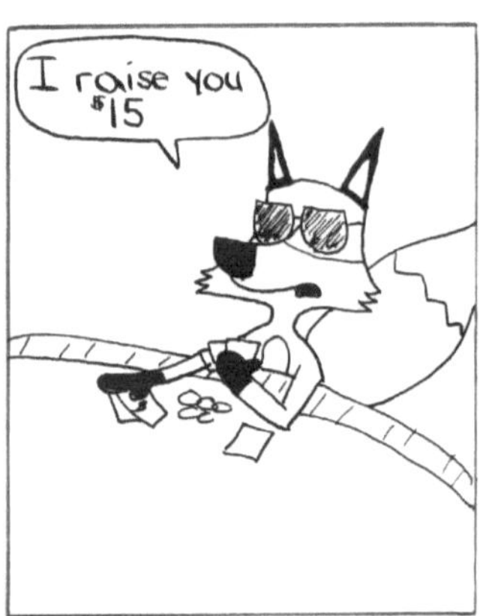
I raise you $15

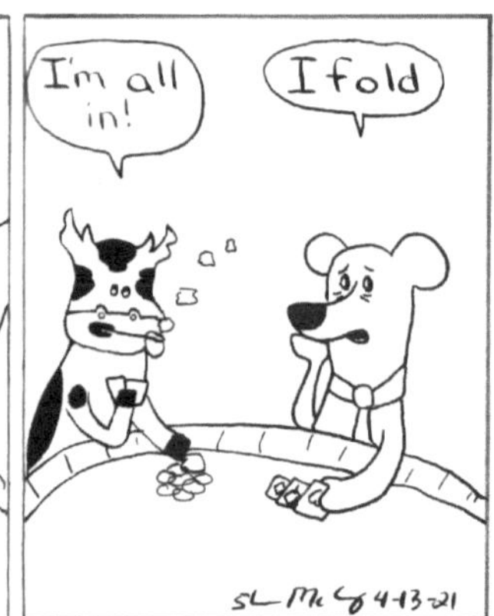
I'm all in!
I fold
SL Mc 4-13-21

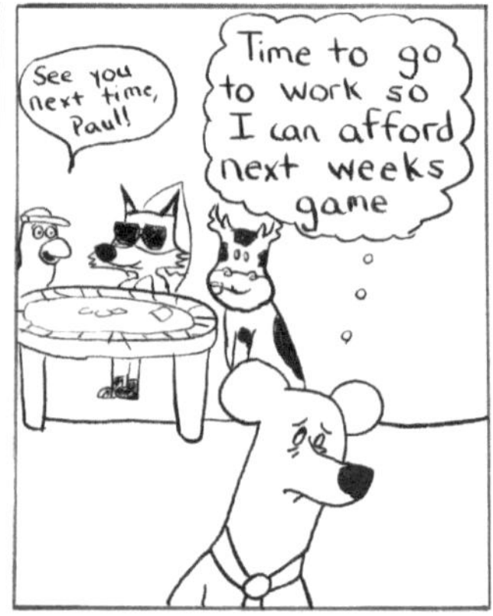
See you next time, Paul!
Time to go to work so I can afford next weeks game

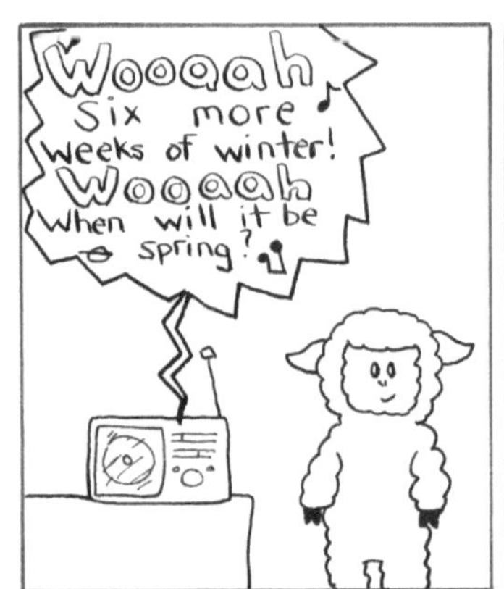
Wooaah Six more weeks of winter! Wooaah When will it be spring?

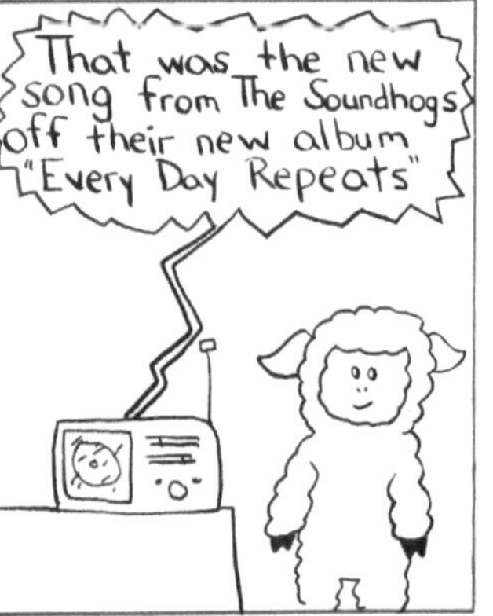
That was the new song from The Soundhogs off their new album "Every Day Repeats"

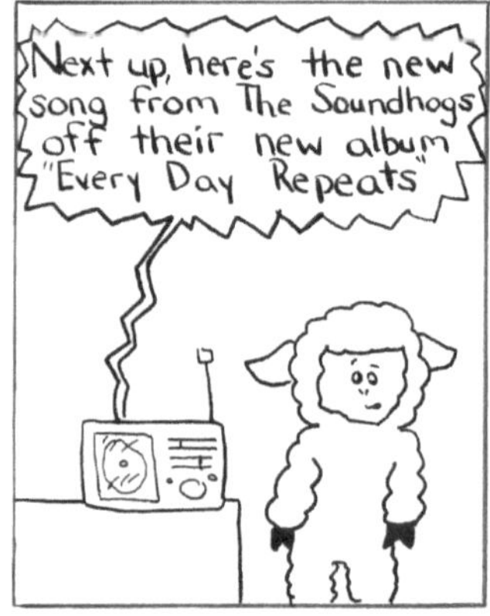
Next up, here's the new song from The Soundhogs off their new album "Every Day Repeats"

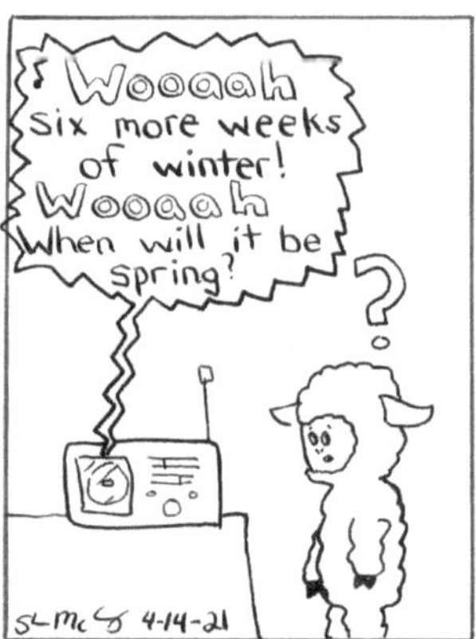
Wooaah Six more weeks of winter! Wooaah When will it be spring?
?
SL Mc 4-14-21

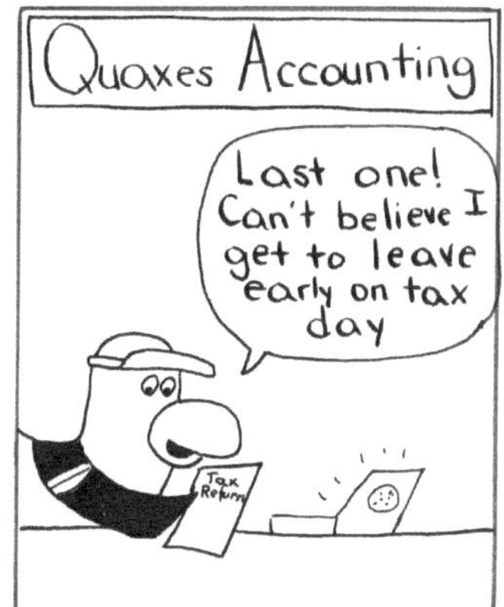
Quaxes Accounting
Last one! Can't believe I get to leave early on tax day
Tax Return

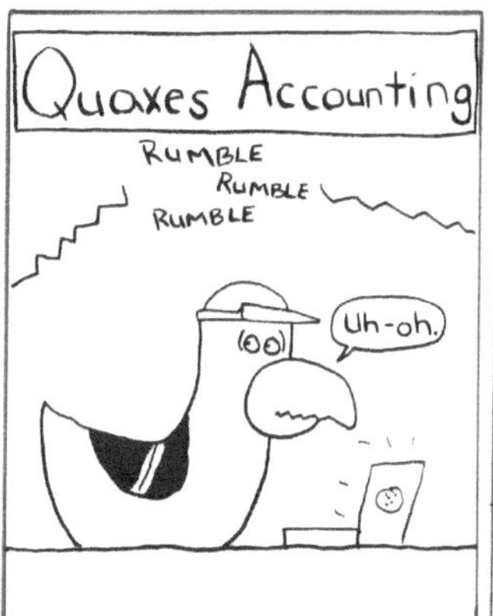
Quaxes Accounting
RUMBLE
RUMBLE
RUMBLE
Uh-oh.

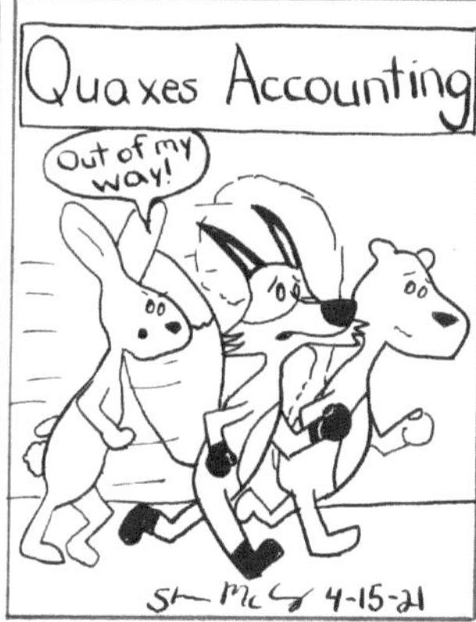
Quaxes Accounting
Out of my way!
SL McG 4-15-21

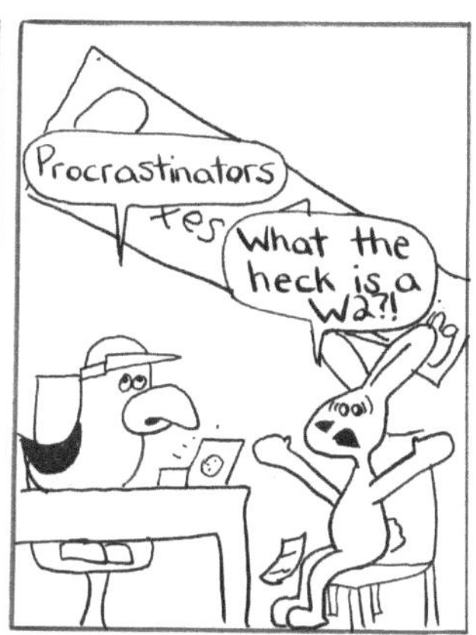
Procrastinators
What the heck is a W2?!

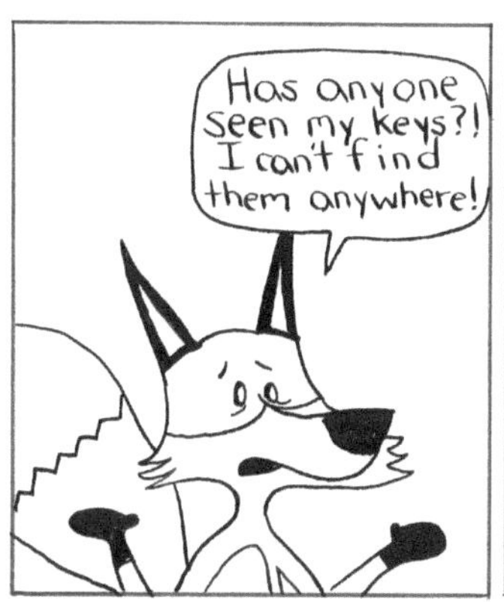
Has anyone seen my keys?! I can't find them anywhere!

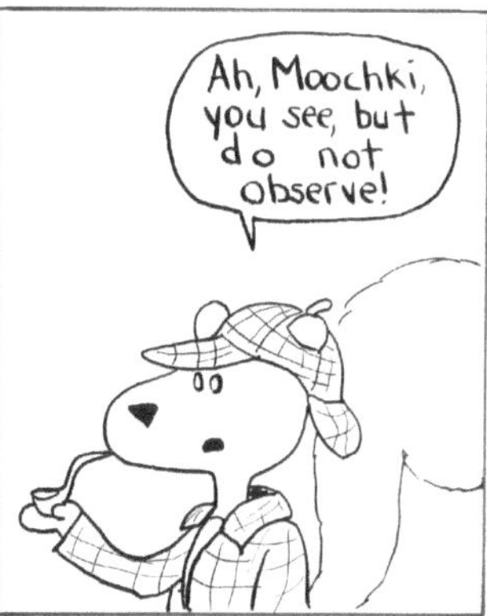
Ah, Moochki, you see, but do not observe!

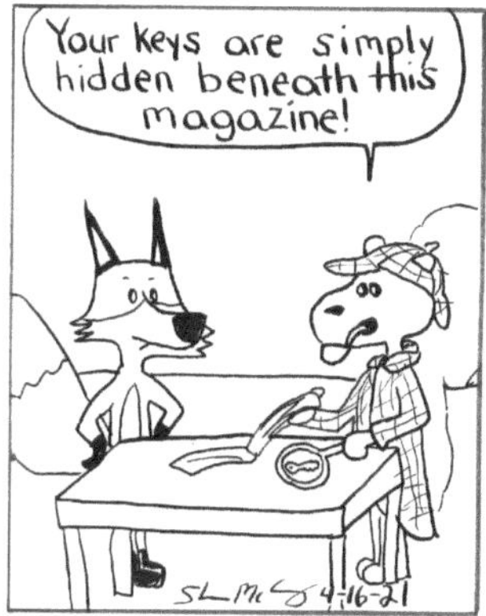
Your keys are simply hidden beneath this magazine!
SL McG 4-16-21

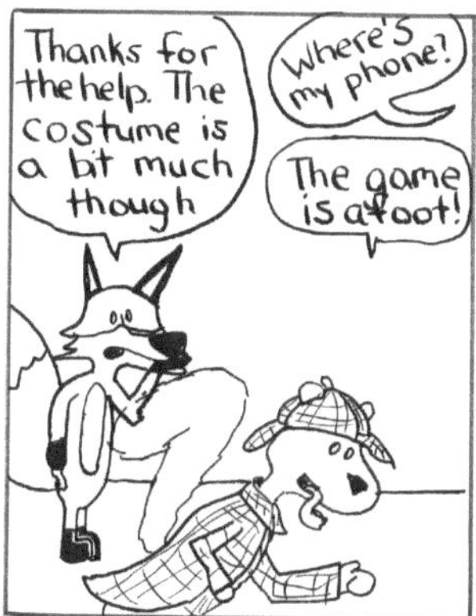
Thanks for the help. The costume is a bit much though
Where's my phone?
The game is afoot!

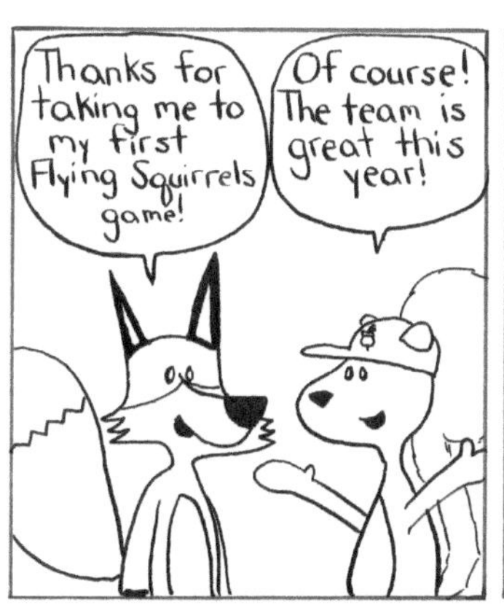
Thanks for taking me to my first Flying Squirrels game!
Of course! The team is great this year!

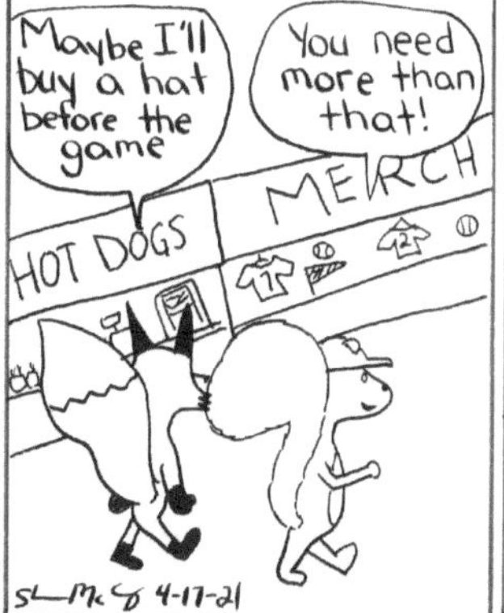
Maybe I'll buy a hat before the game
You need more than that!
HOT DOGS
MERCH
SL McG 4-17-21

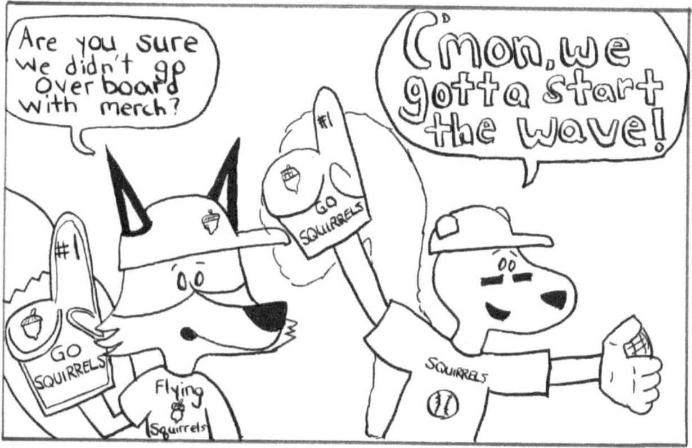
Are you sure we didn't go overboard with merch?
C'mon, we gotta start the wave!
#1
GO SQUIRRELS
#1
GO SQUIRRELS
Flying Squirrels
SQUIRRELS

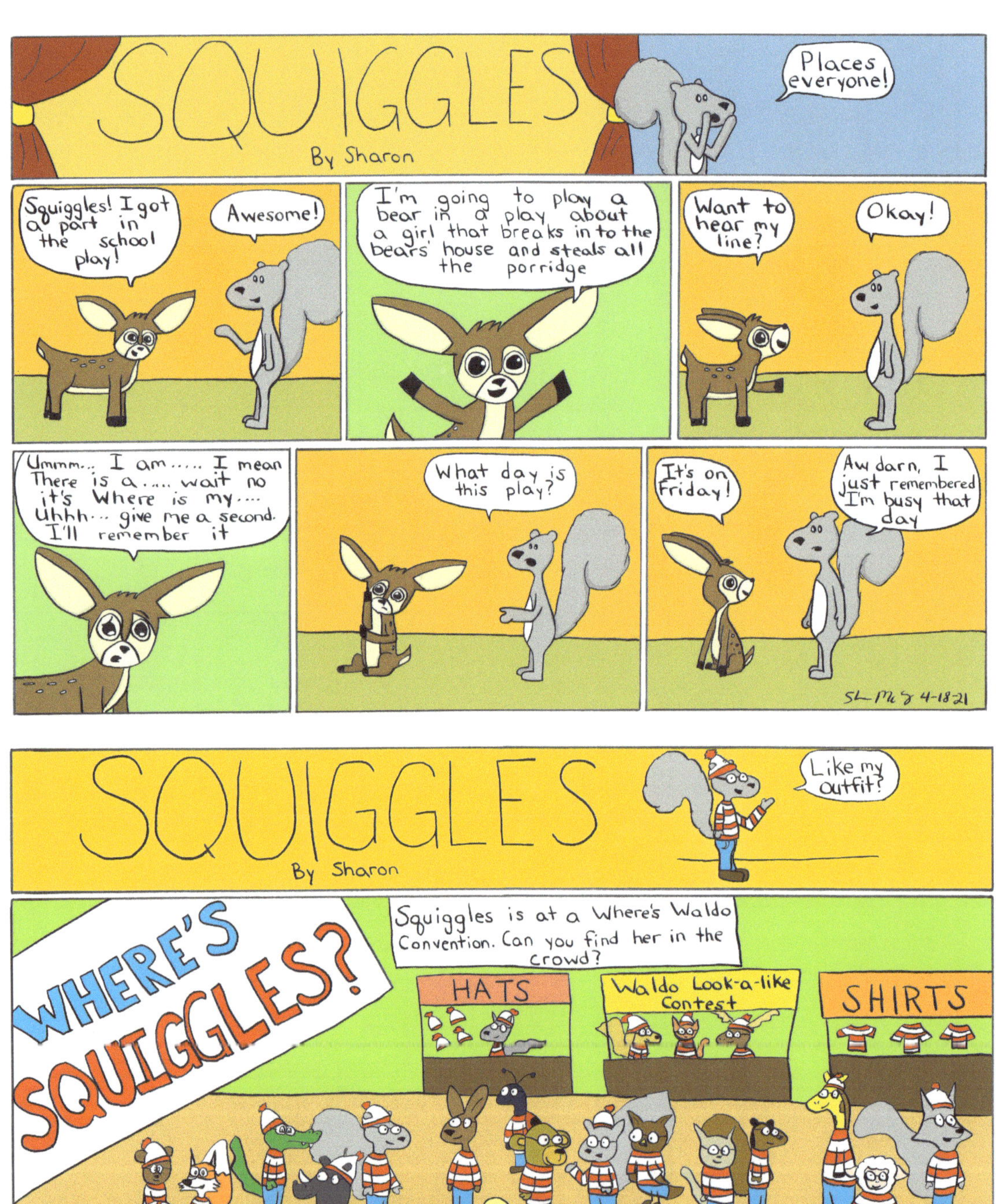
SQUIGGLES
By Sharon
Places everyone!
Squiggles! I got a part in the school play!
Awesome!
I'm going to play a bear in a play about a girl that breaks in to the bears' house and steals all the porridge
Want to hear my line?
Okay!
Ummm... I am..... I mean There is a..... wait no it's Where is my.... Uhhh... give me a second. I'll remember it
What day is this play?
It's on Friday!
Aw darn, I just remembered I'm busy that day
4-18-21
SQUIGGLES
By Sharon
Like my outfit?
WHERE'S SQUIGGLES?
Squiggles is at a Where's Waldo Convention. Can you find her in the crowd?
HATS
Waldo Look-a-like Contest
SHIRTS
4-25-21

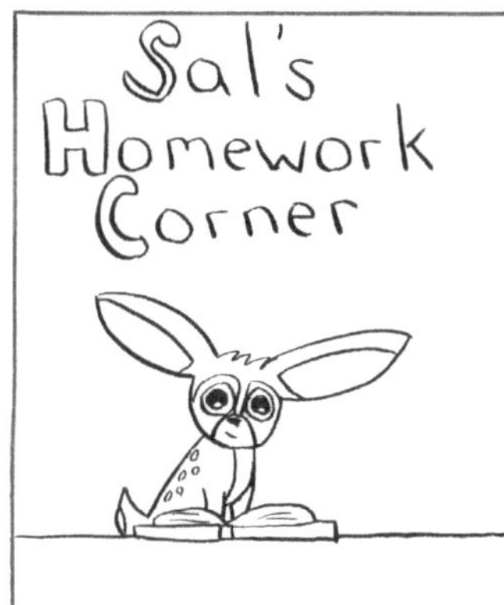
Sal's
Homework
Corner

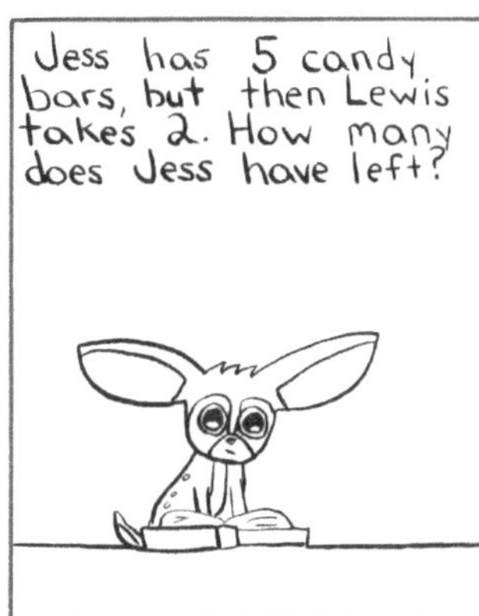
Jess has 5 candy bars, but then Lewis takes 2. How many does Jess have left?

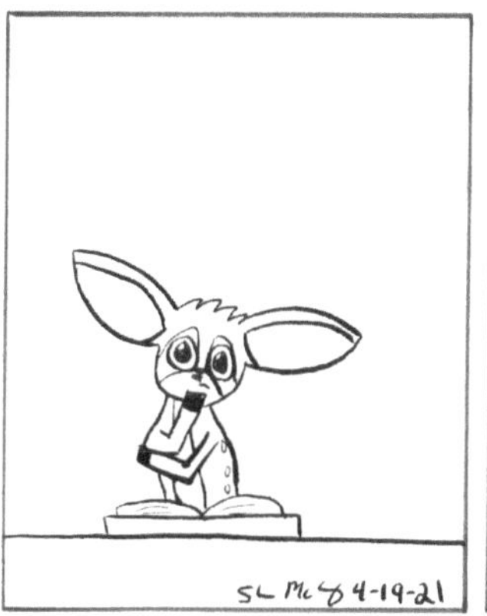
SLMcG 4-19-21

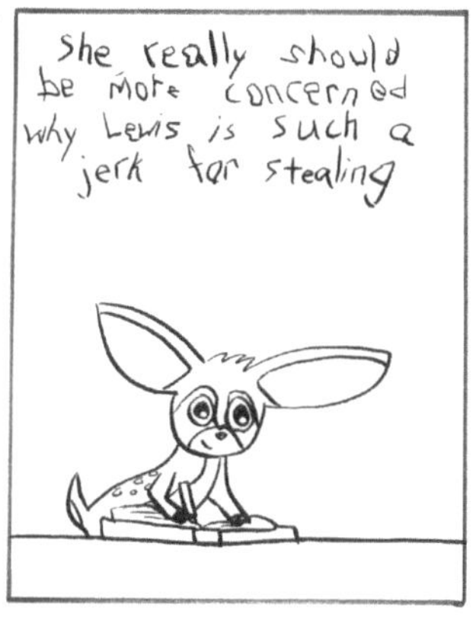
She really should be more concerned why Lewis is such a jerk for stealing

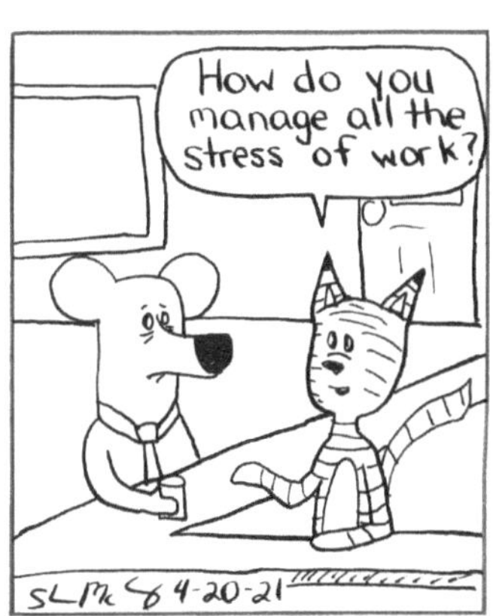
How do you manage all the stress of work?
SLMcG 4-20-21

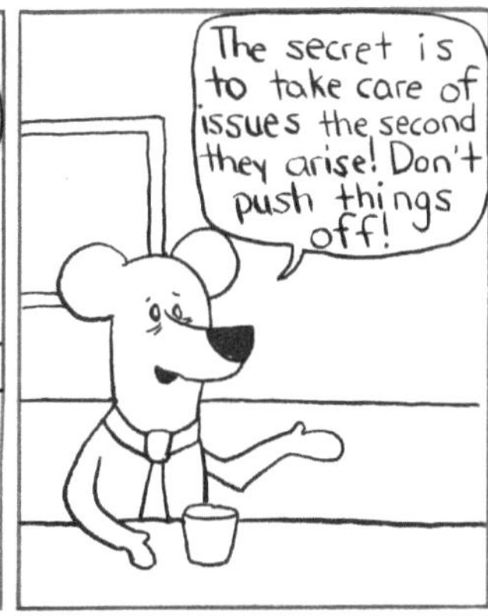
The secret is to take care of issues the second they arise! Don't push things off!

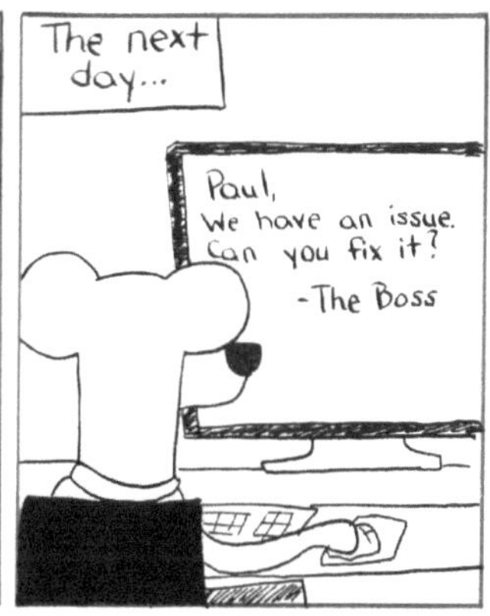
The next day...
Paul,
We have an issue.
Can you fix it?
-The Boss

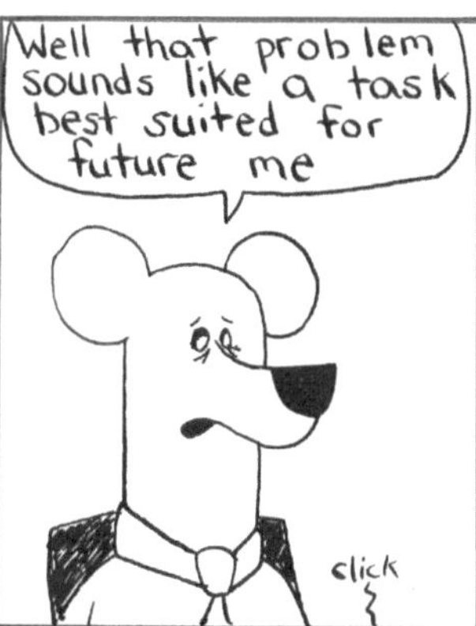
Well that problem sounds like a task best suited for future me
click

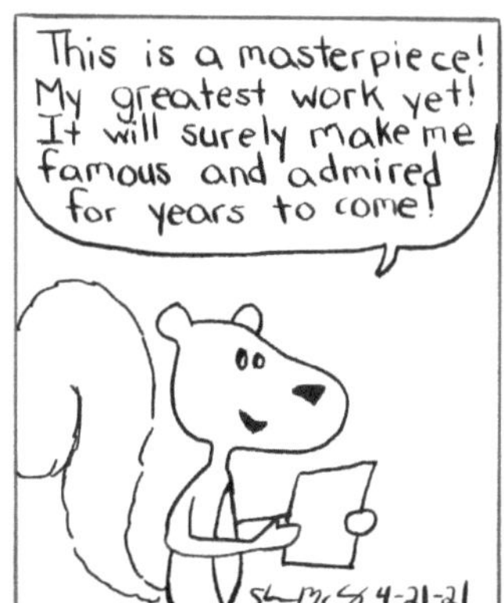
This is a masterpiece! My greatest work yet! It will surely make me famous and admired for years to come!
SLMcG 4-21-21

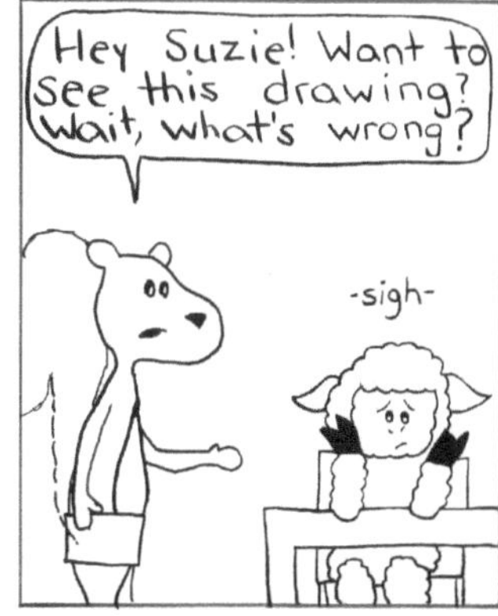
Hey Suzie! Want to see this drawing? Wait, what's wrong?
-sigh-

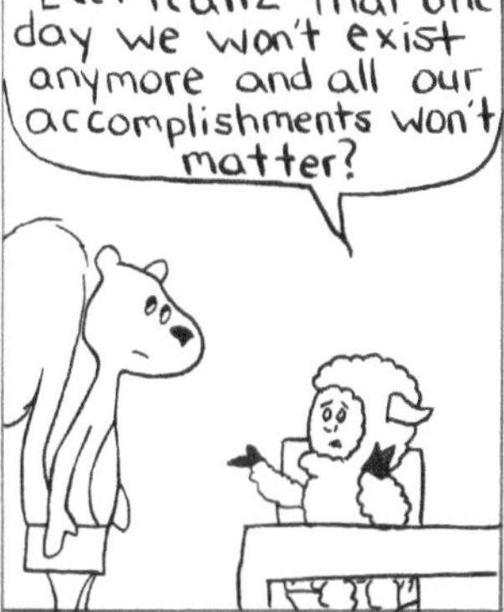
Ever realiz that one day we won't exist anymore and all our accomplishments won't matter?

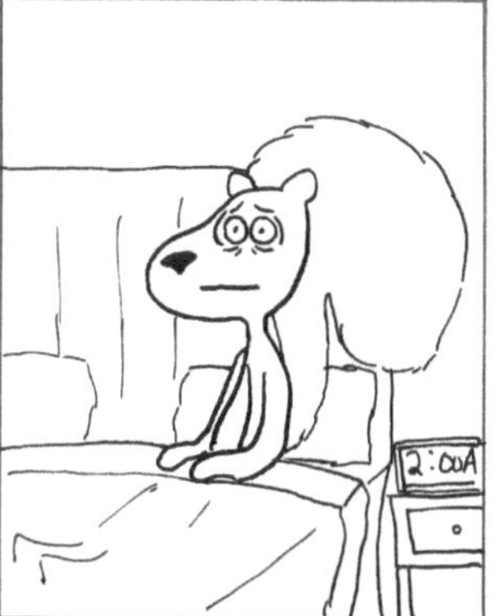
2:00A

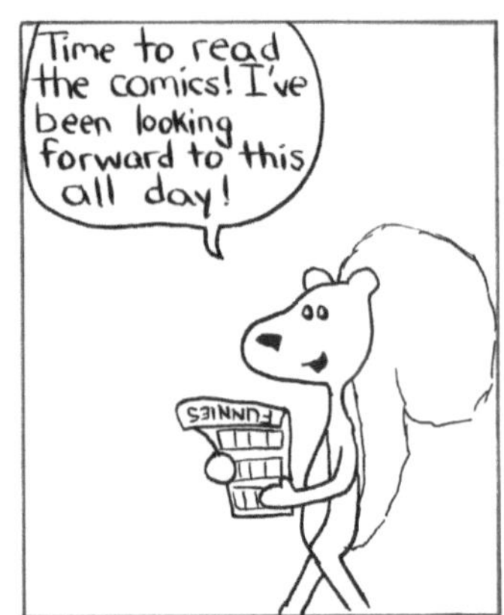
Time to read the comics! I've been looking forward to this all day!

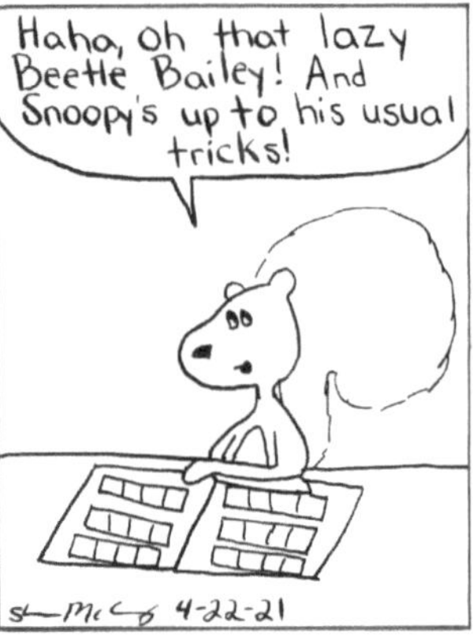
Haha, oh that lazy Beetle Bailey! And Snoopy's up to his usual tricks!
4-22-21

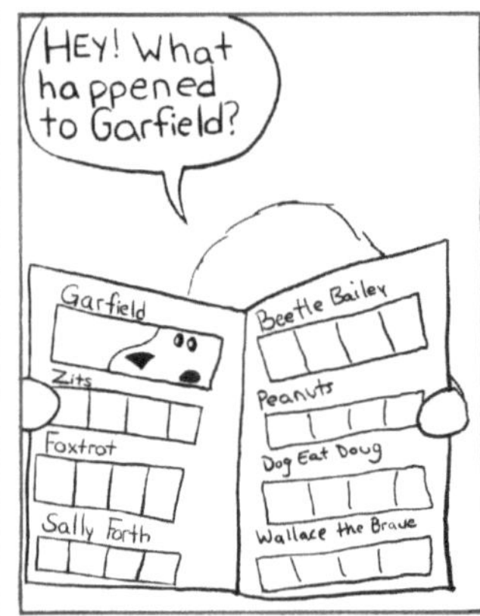
HEY! What happened to Garfield?
Garfield
Zits
Foxtrot
Sally Forth
Beetle Bailey
Peanuts
Dog Eat Doug
Wallace the Brave

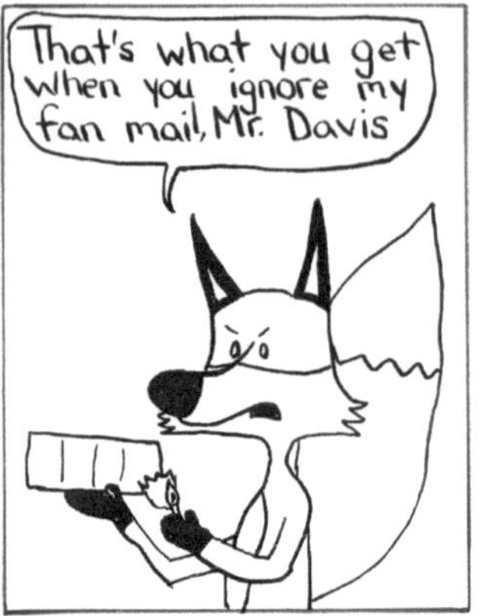
That's what you get when you ignore my fan mail, Mr. Davis

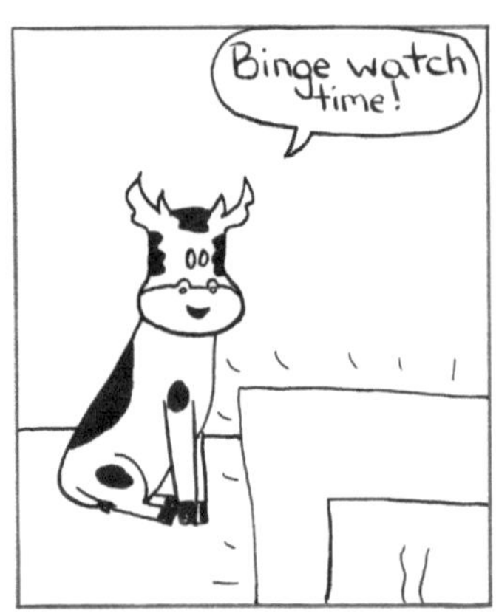
Binge watch time!

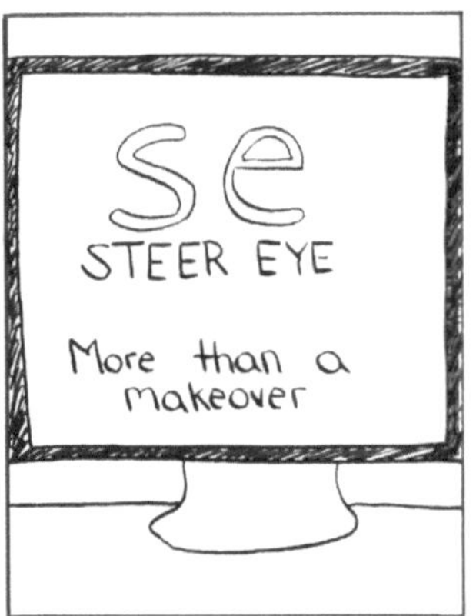
se
STEER EYE
More than a makeover

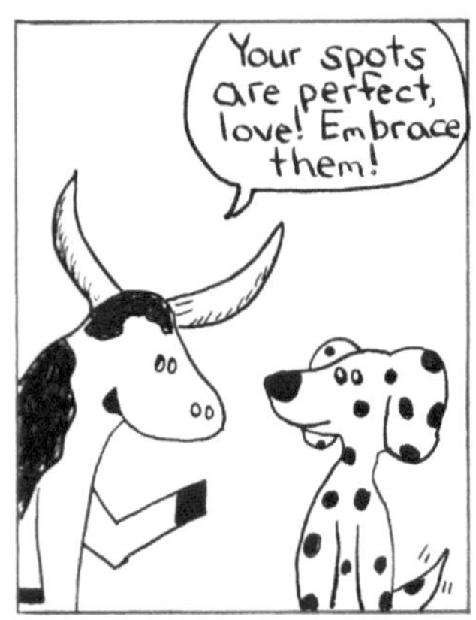
Your spots are perfect, love! Embrace them!

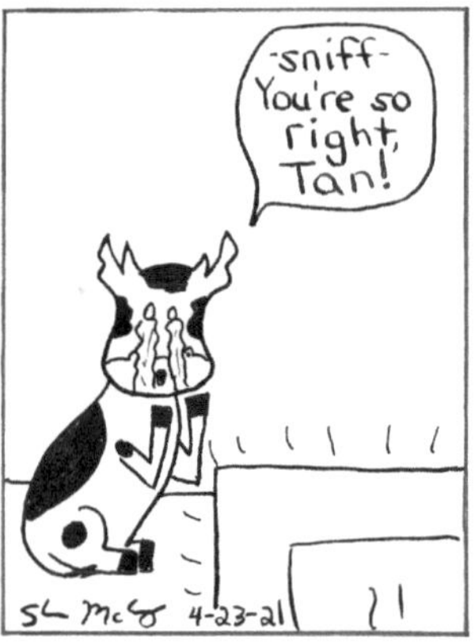
-sniff- You're so right, Tan!
4-23-21

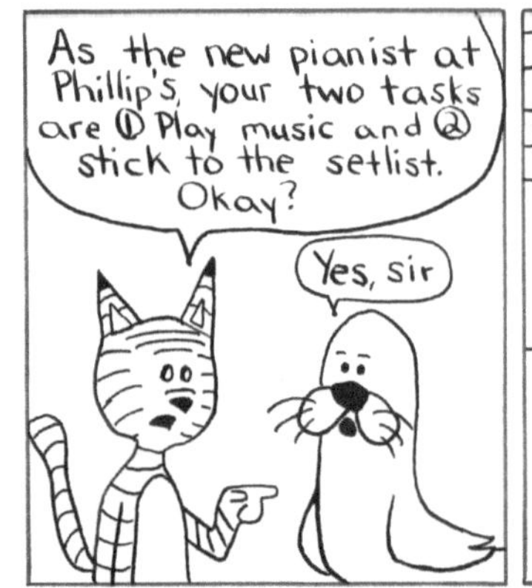
As the new pianist at Phillip's, your two tasks are ① Play music and ② stick to the setlist. Okay?
Yes, sir

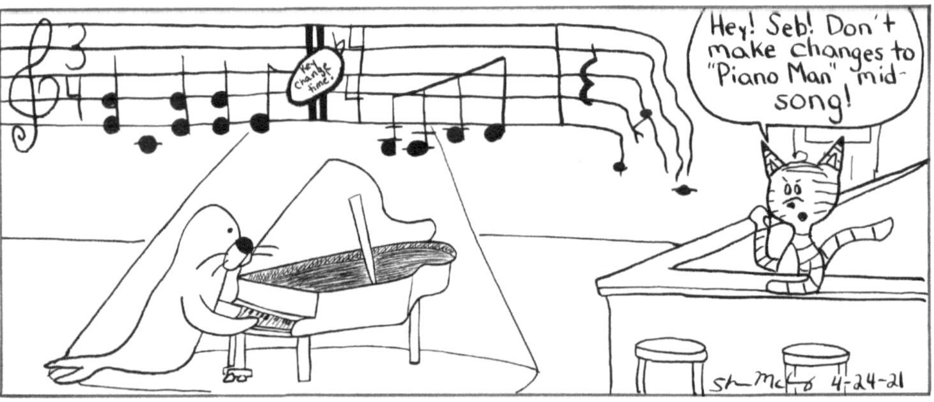
Key change time!
Hey! Seb! Don't make changes to "Piano Man" mid-song!
4-24-21

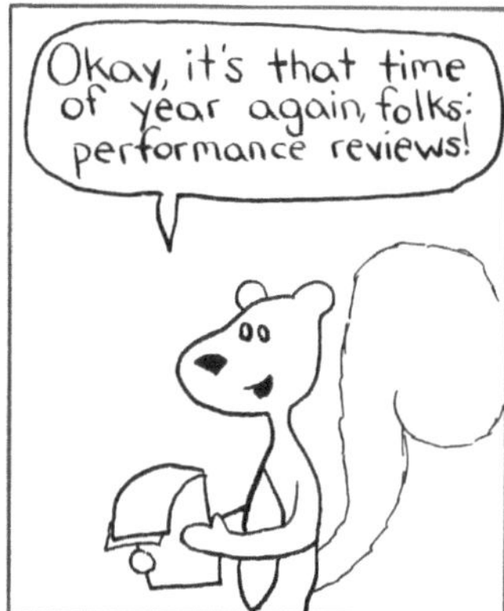
Okay, it's that time of year again, folks: performance reviews!
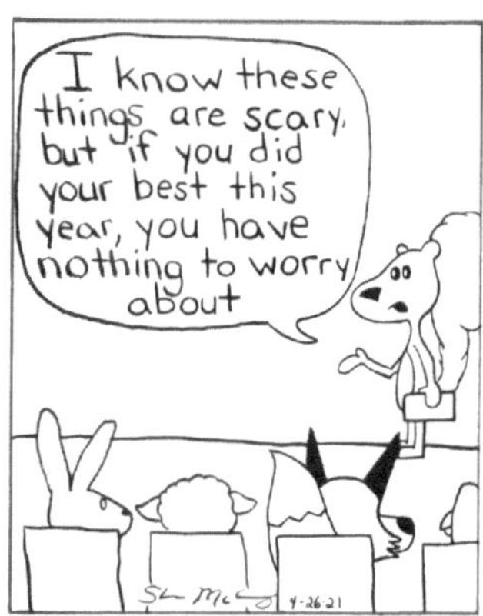
I know these things are scary, but if you did your best this year, you have nothing to worry about
4-26-21
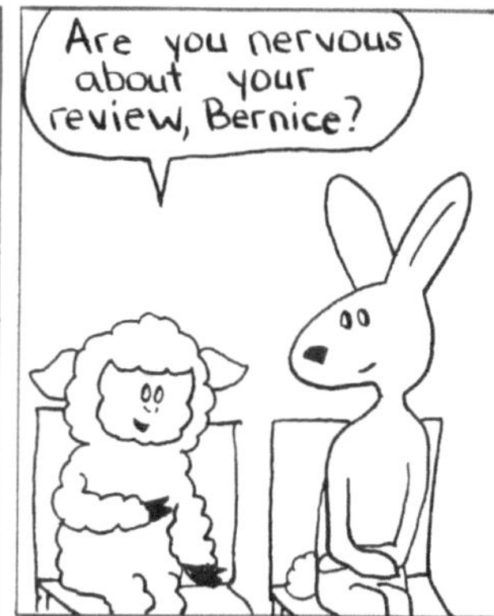
Are you nervous about your review, Bernice?
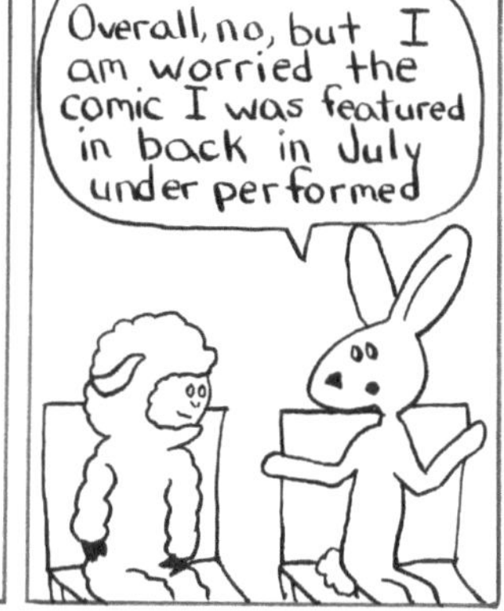
Overall, no, but I am worried the comic I was featured in back in July under performed
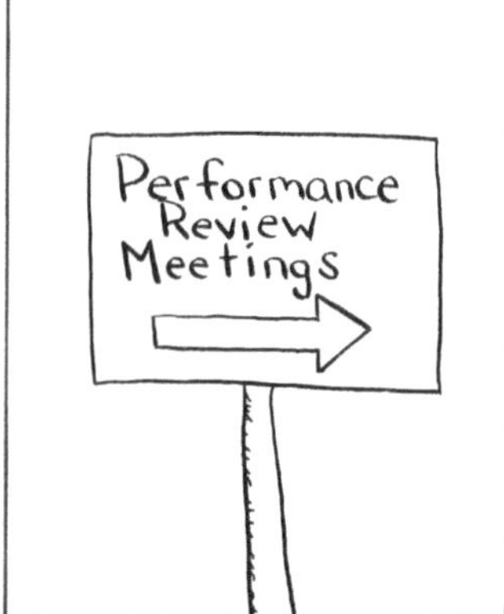
Performance Review Meetings
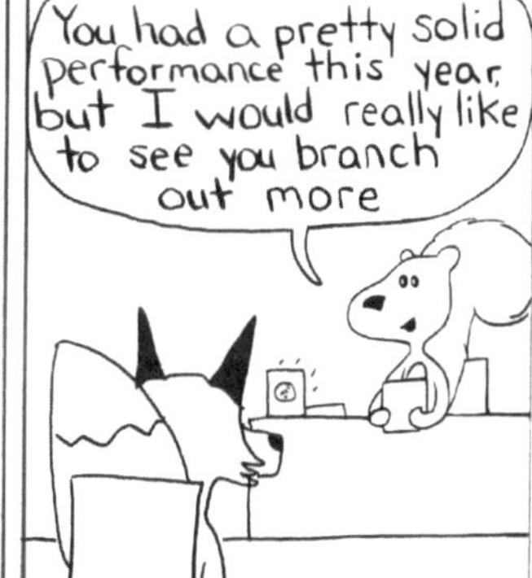
You had a pretty solid performance this year, but I would really like to see you branch out more
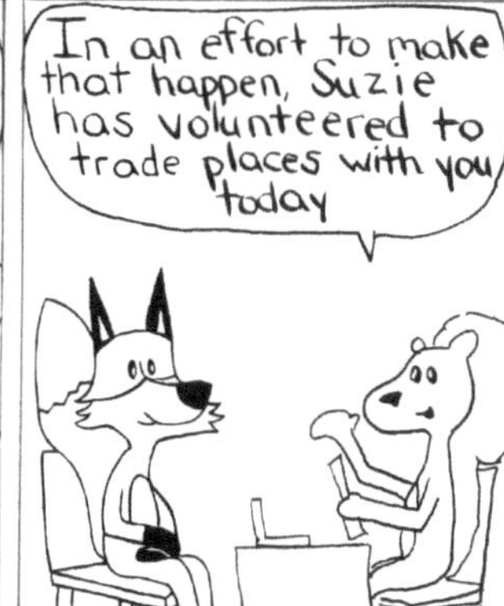
In an effort to make that happen, Suzie has volunteered to trade places with you today
4-27-21
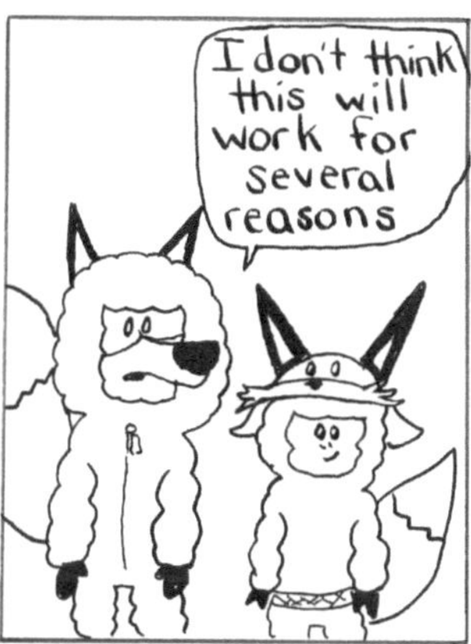
I don't think this will work for several reasons
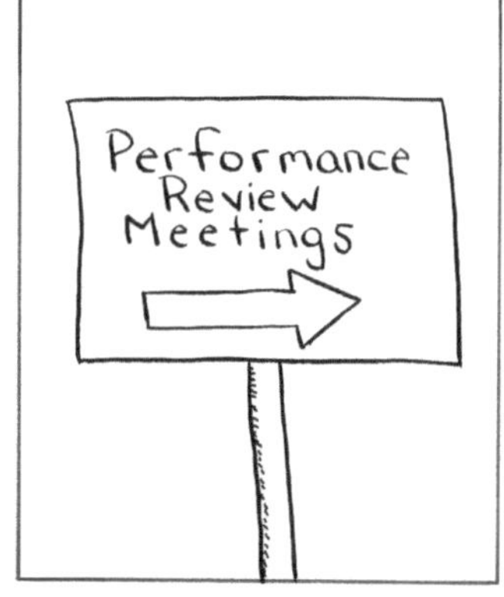
Performance Review Meetings
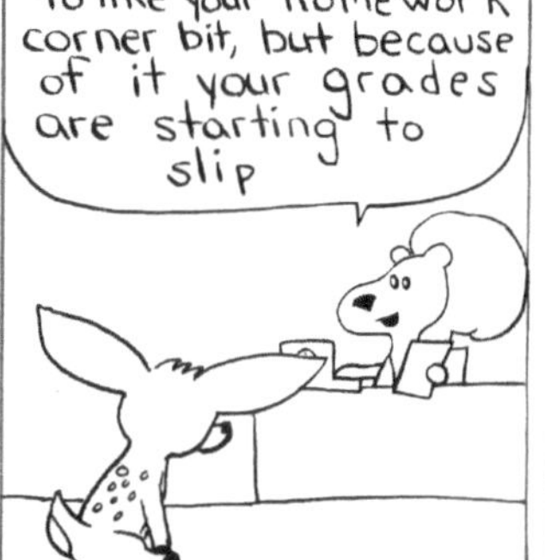
Sal, people really seem to like your homework corner bit, but because of it your grades are starting to slip
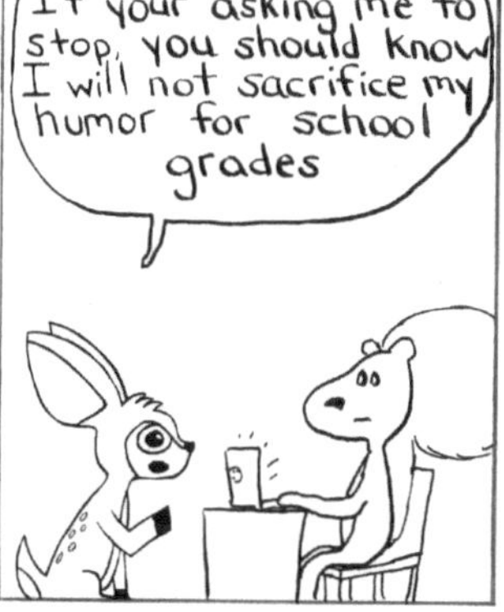
If your asking me to stop, you should know I will not sacrifice my humor for school grades
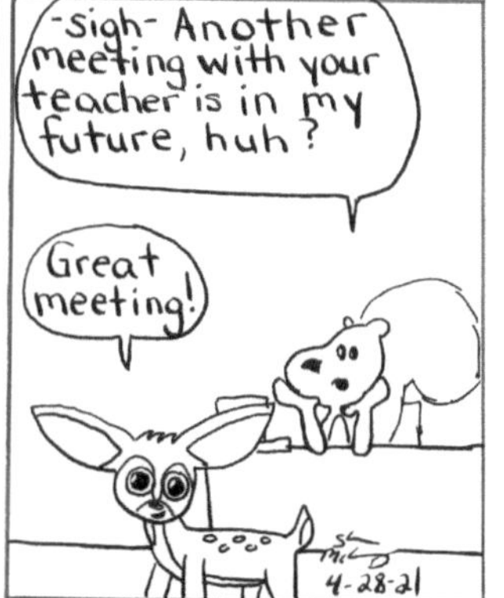
-sigh- Another meeting with your teacher is in my future, huh?
Great meeting!
4-28-21

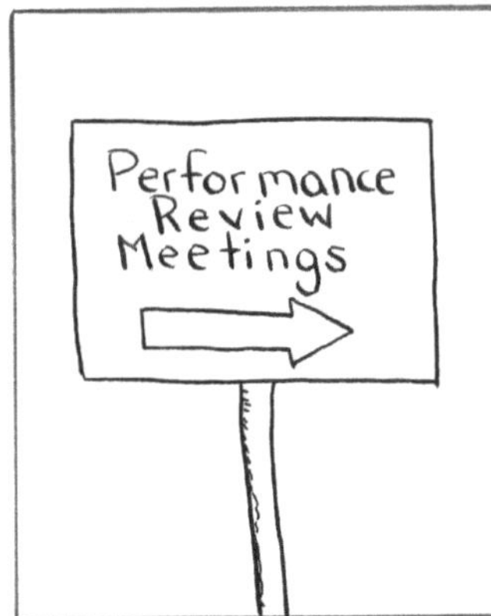

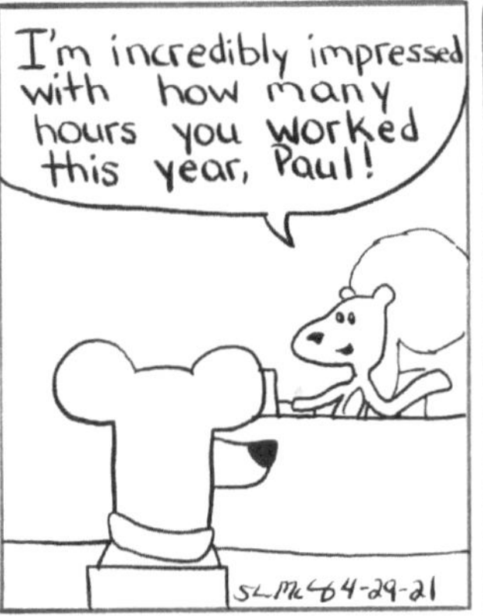

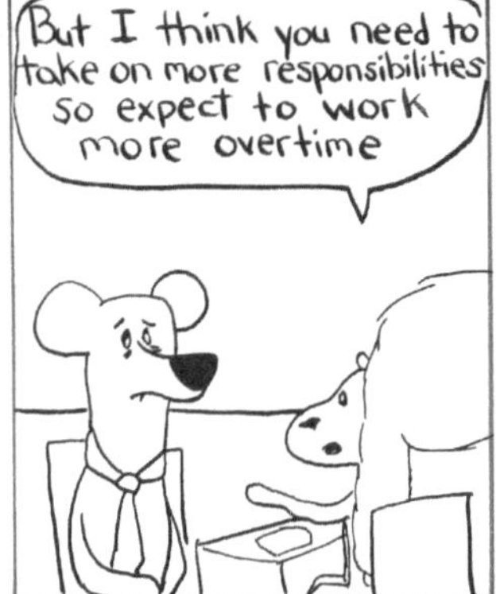

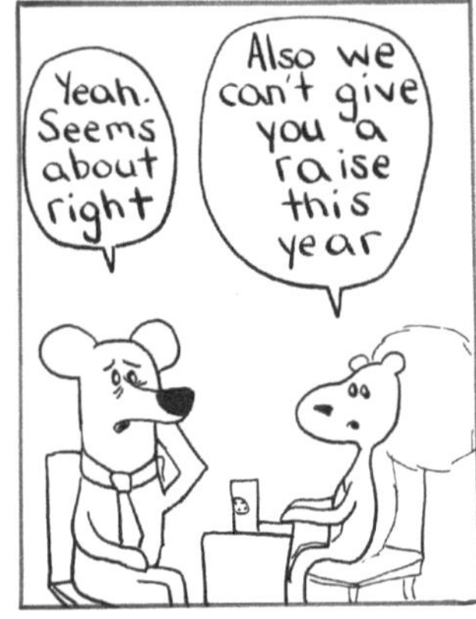

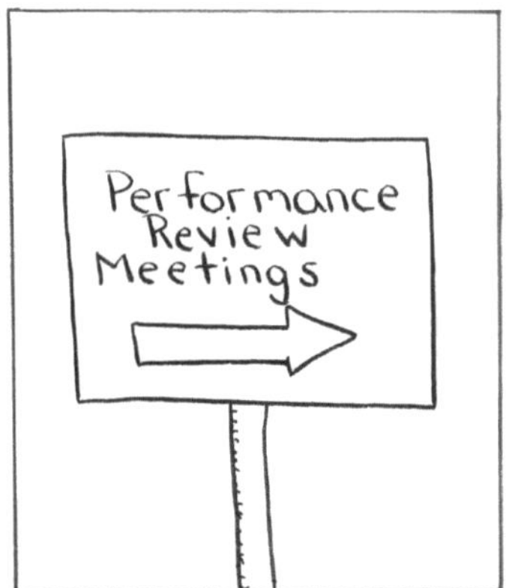

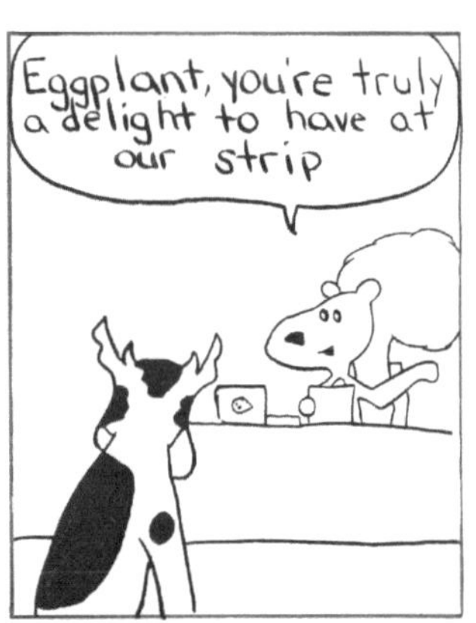

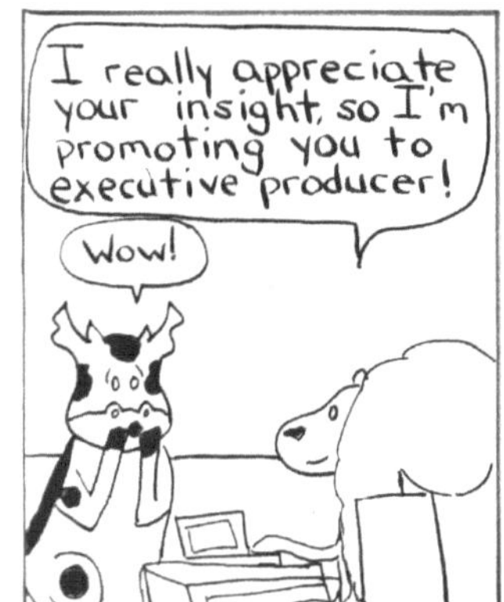

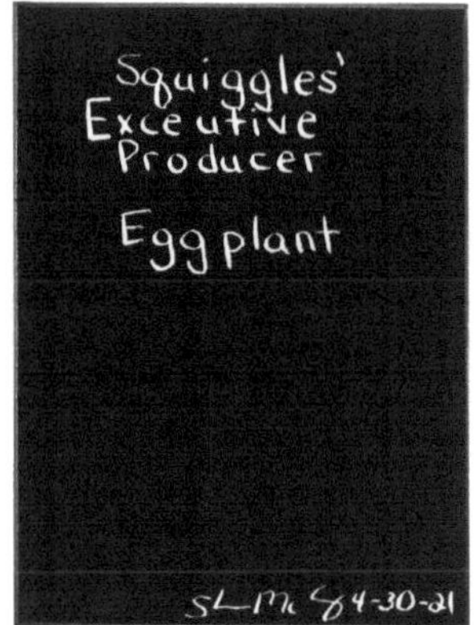

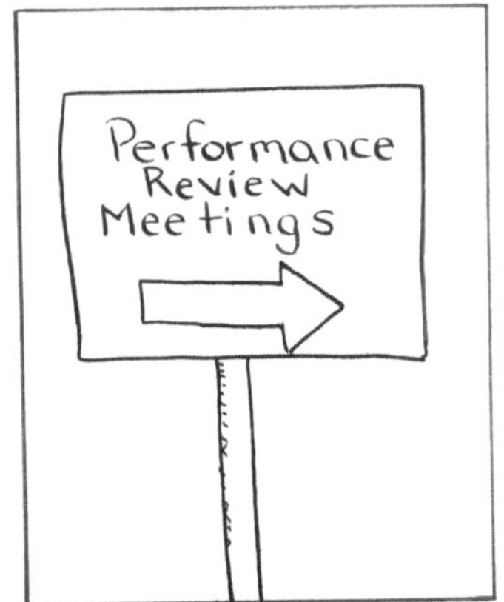

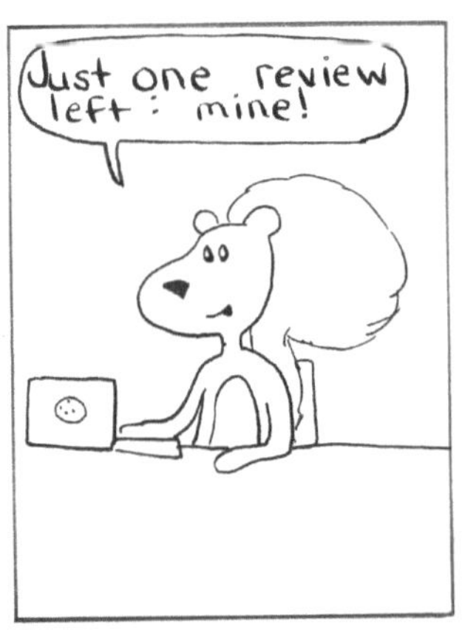

Employee: Squiggles

Review: Squiggles did a phenomenal job this year. The strip would fall apart without her. Keep up the excellent work

Manager Signature: Squiggles

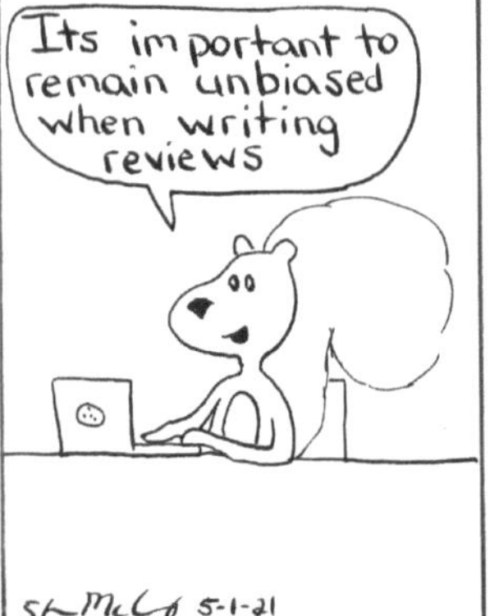

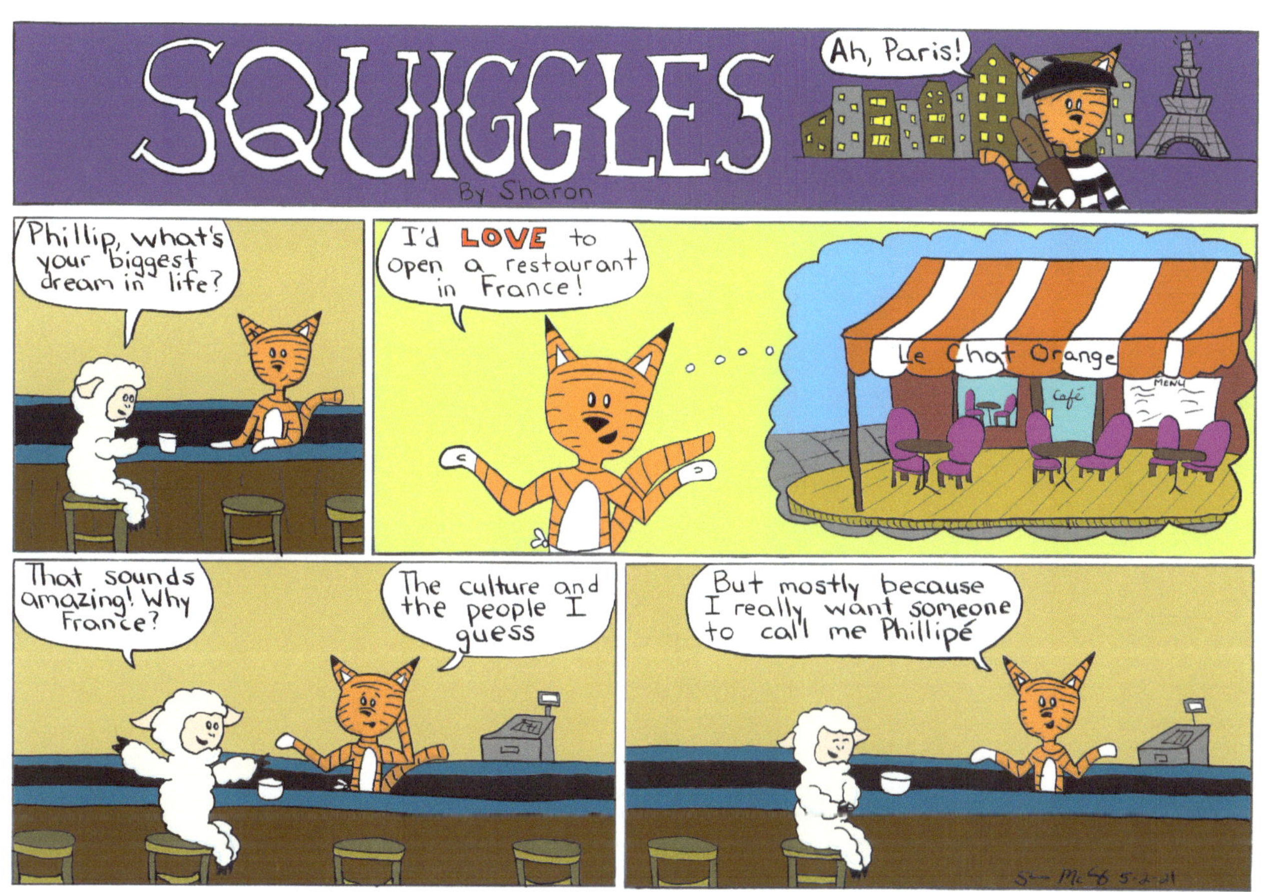
SQUIGGLES
By Sharon
Ah, Paris!
Phillip, what's your biggest dream in life?
I'd LOVE to open a restaurant in France!
Le Chat Orange
Café
MENU
That sounds amazing! Why France?
The culture and the people I guess
But mostly because I really want someone to call me Phillipé

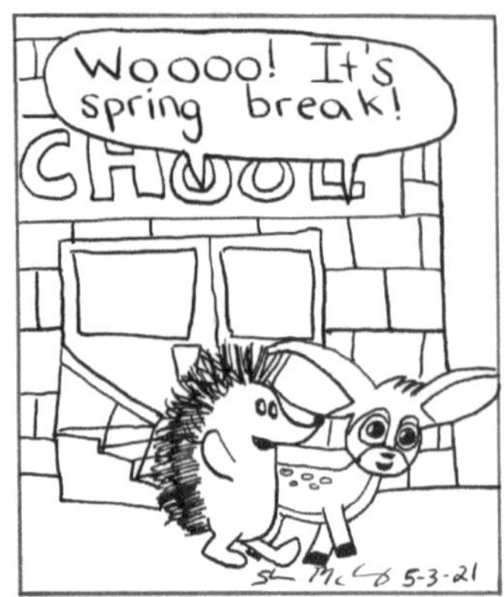
Woooo! It's spring break!
CHOOL
5-3-21

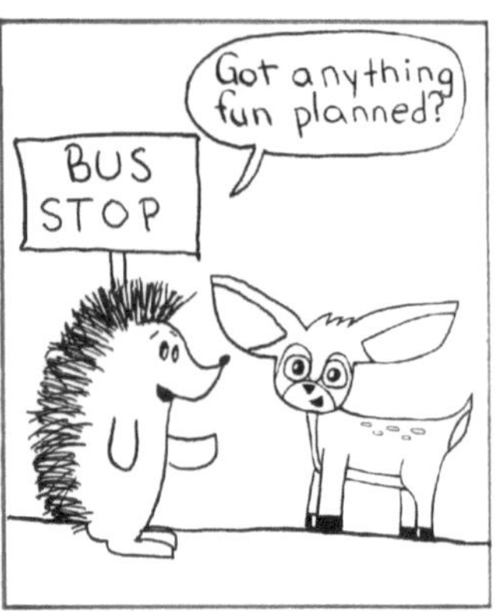
BUS STOP
Got anything fun planned?

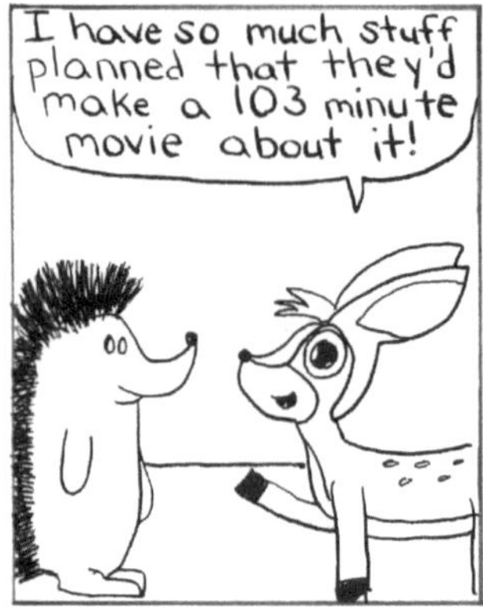
I have so much stuff planned that they'd make a 103 minute movie about it!

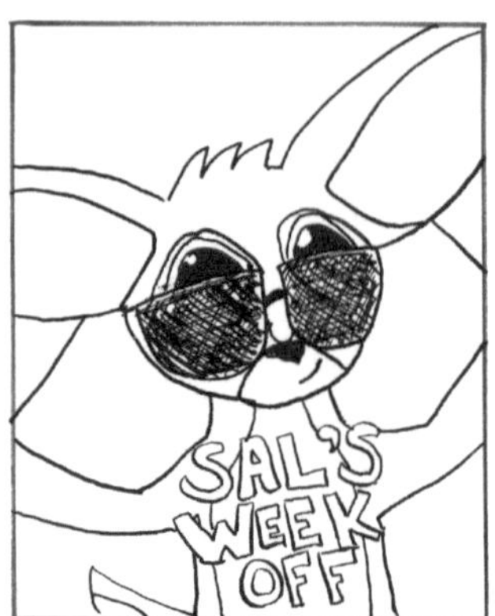
SAL'S WEEK OFF

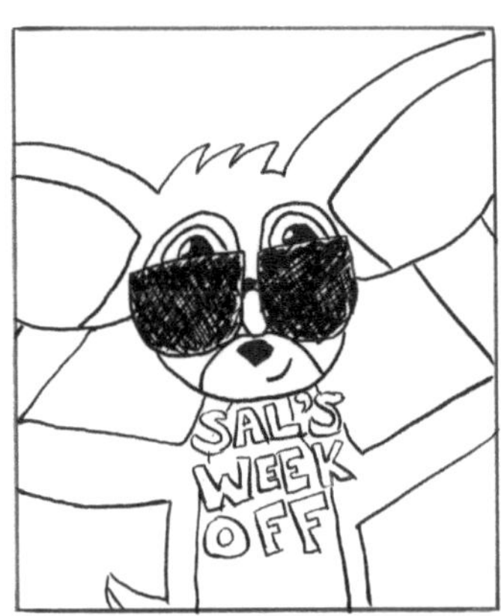
SAL'S WEEK OFF

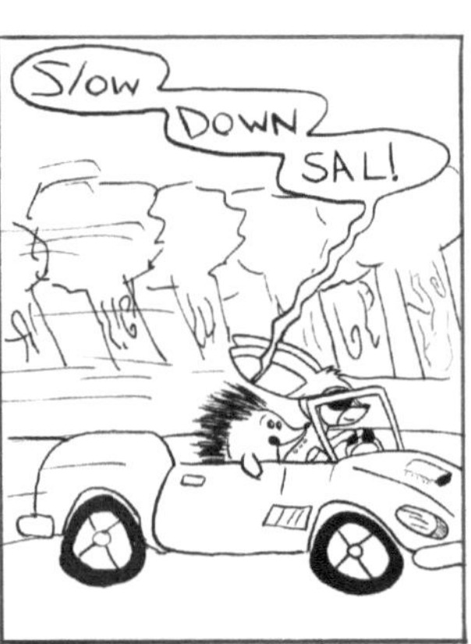
Slow DOWN SAL!

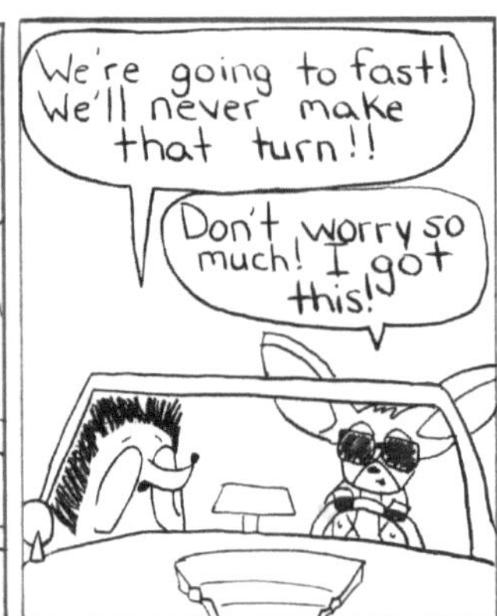
We're going to fast! We'll never make that turn!!
Don't worry so much! I got this!

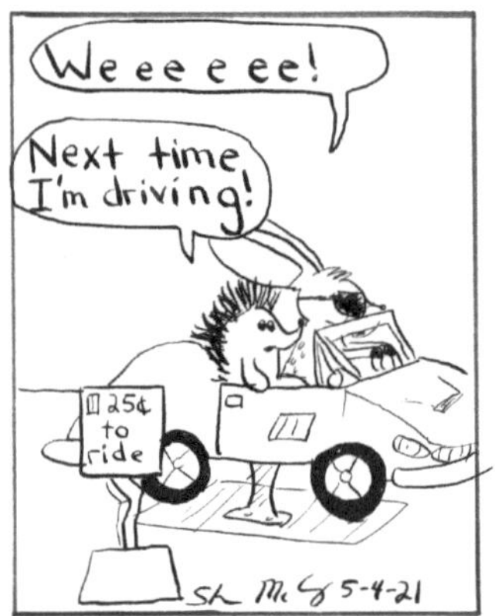
Weeeeee!
Next time, I'm driving!
25¢ to ride
5-4-21

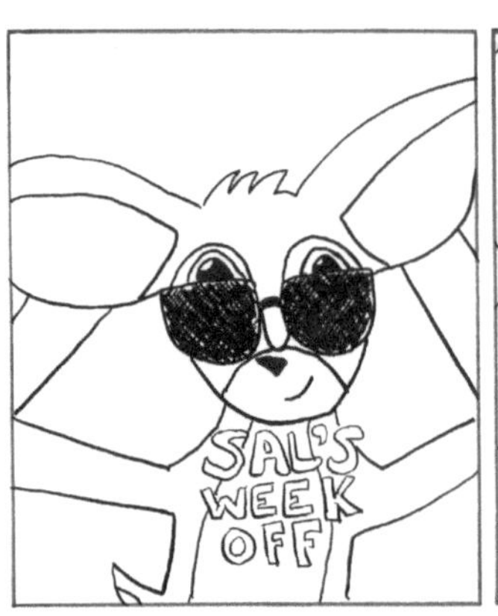
SAL'S WEEK OFF

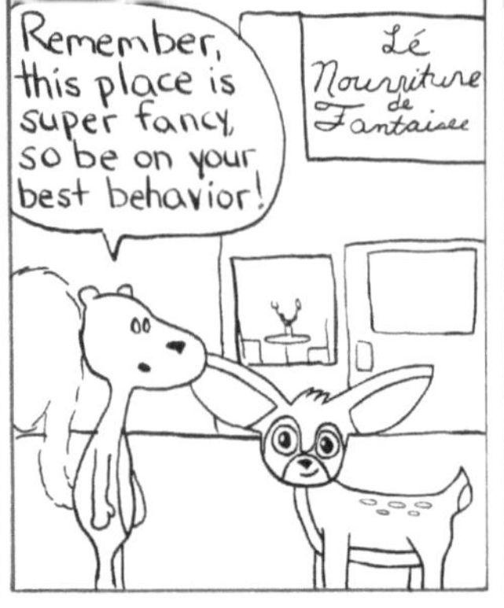
Remember, this place is super fancy, so be on your best behavior!
Lé Nourriture de Fantaisie

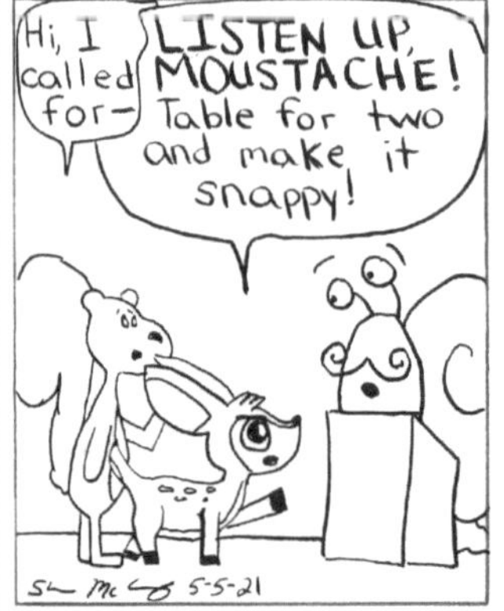
Hi, I called for-
LISTEN UP, MOUSTACHE! Table for two and make it snappy!
5-5-21

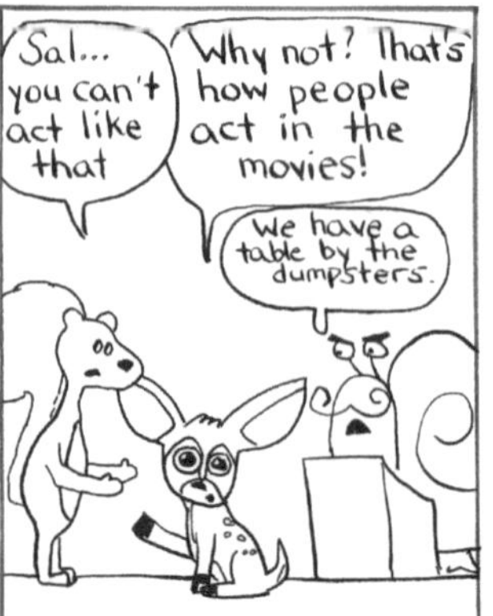
Sal... you can't act like that
Why not? That's how people act in the movies!
We have a table by the dumpsters.

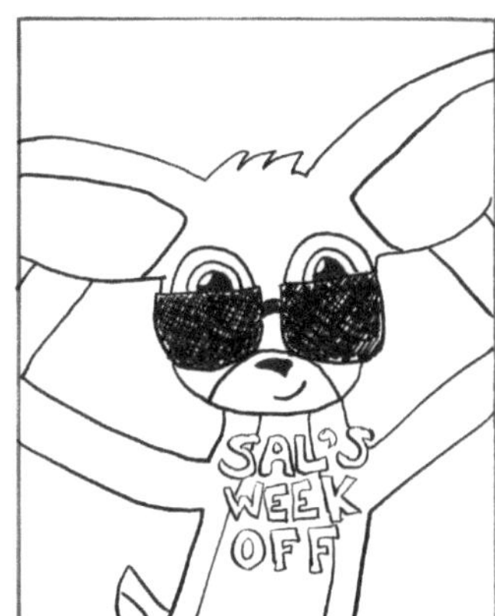
SAL'S
WEEK
OFF
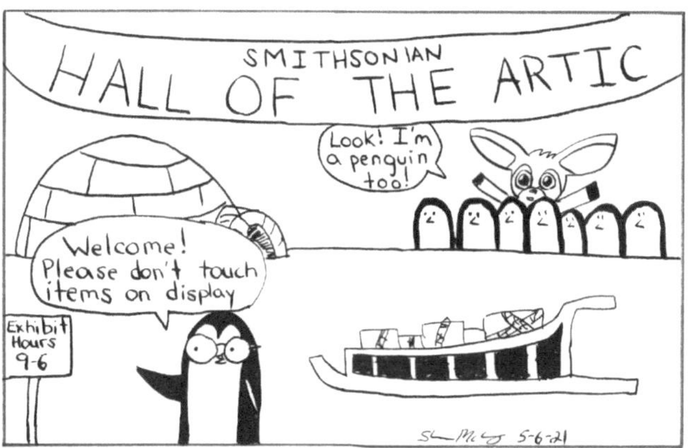
SMITHSONIAN
HALL OF THE ARTIC
Look! I'm a penguin too!
Welcome! Please don't touch items on display
Exhibit Hours 9-6
SL McG 5-6-21
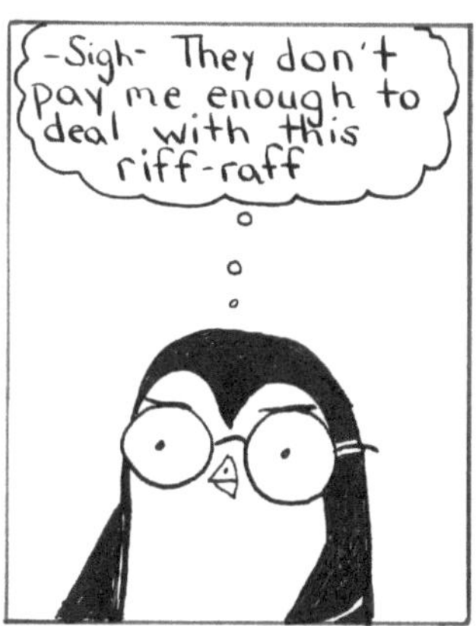
-Sigh- They don't pay me enough to deal with this riff-raff
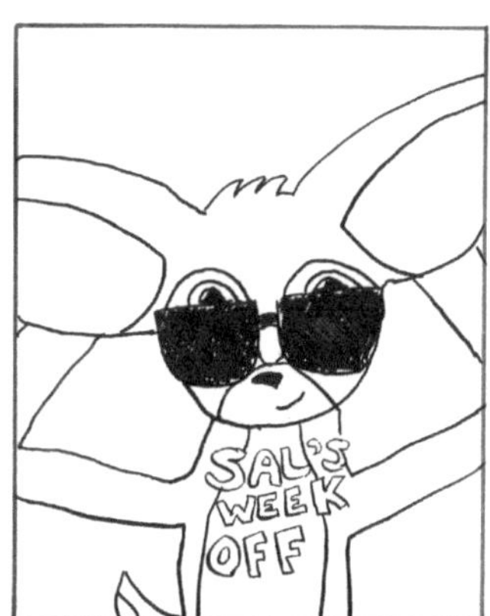
SAL'S
WEEK
OFF
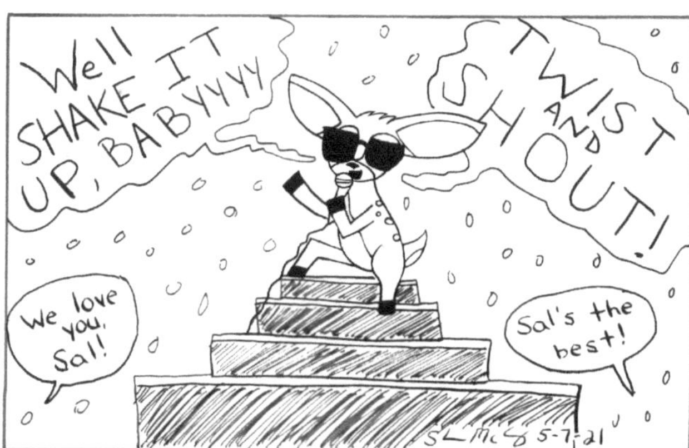
Well SHAKE IT UP, BABYYYY
TWIST AND SHOUT!
We love you, Sal!
Sal's the best!
SL McG 5-7-21
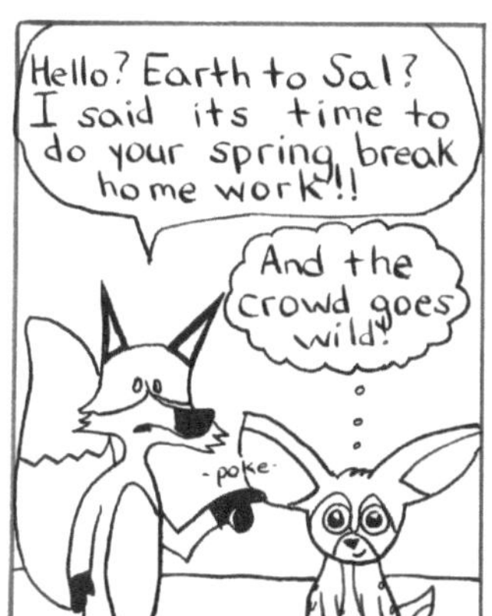
Hello? Earth to Sal? I said its time to do your spring break home work!!
And the crowd goes wild!
-poke-
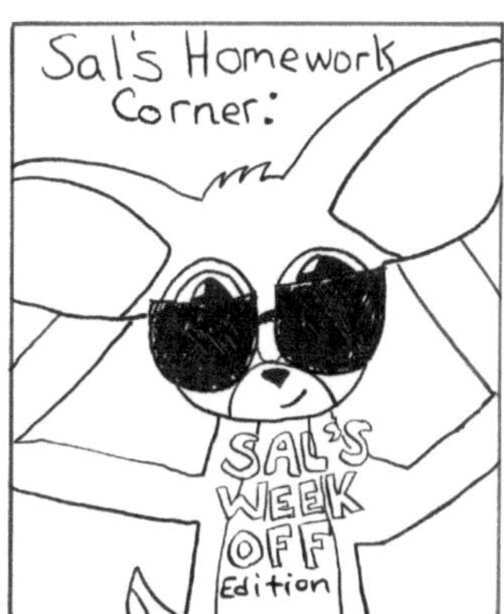
Sal's Homework Corner:
SAL'S
WEEK
OFF
Edition
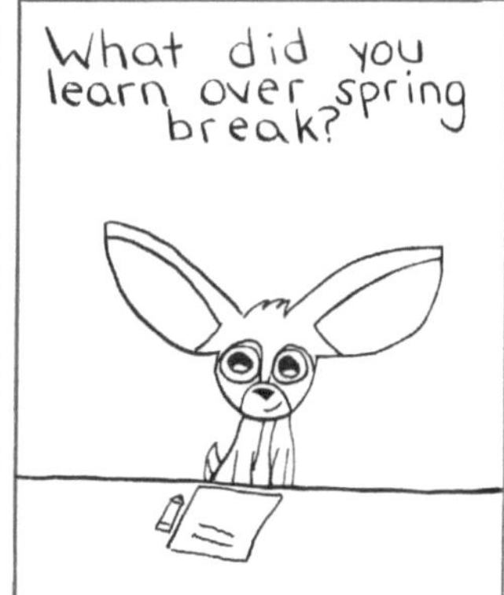
What did you learn over spring break?
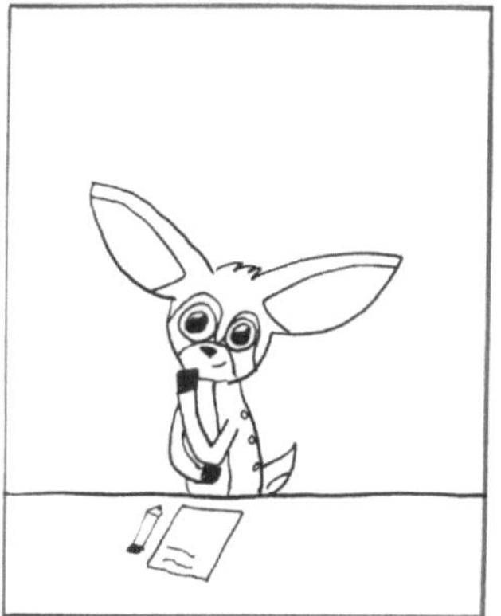
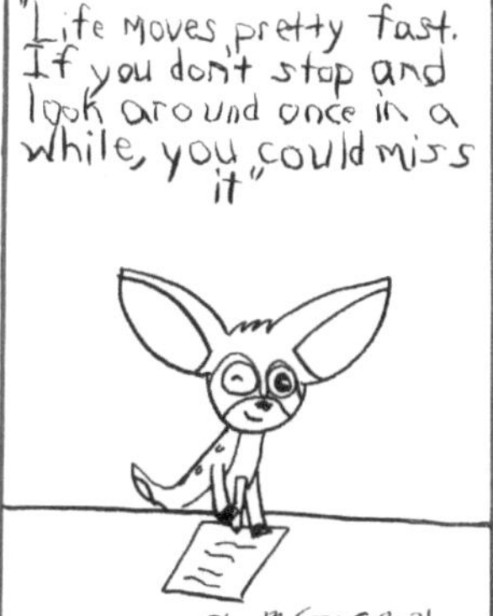
"Life moves pretty fast. If you don't stop and look around once in a while, you could miss it"
SL McG 5-8-21

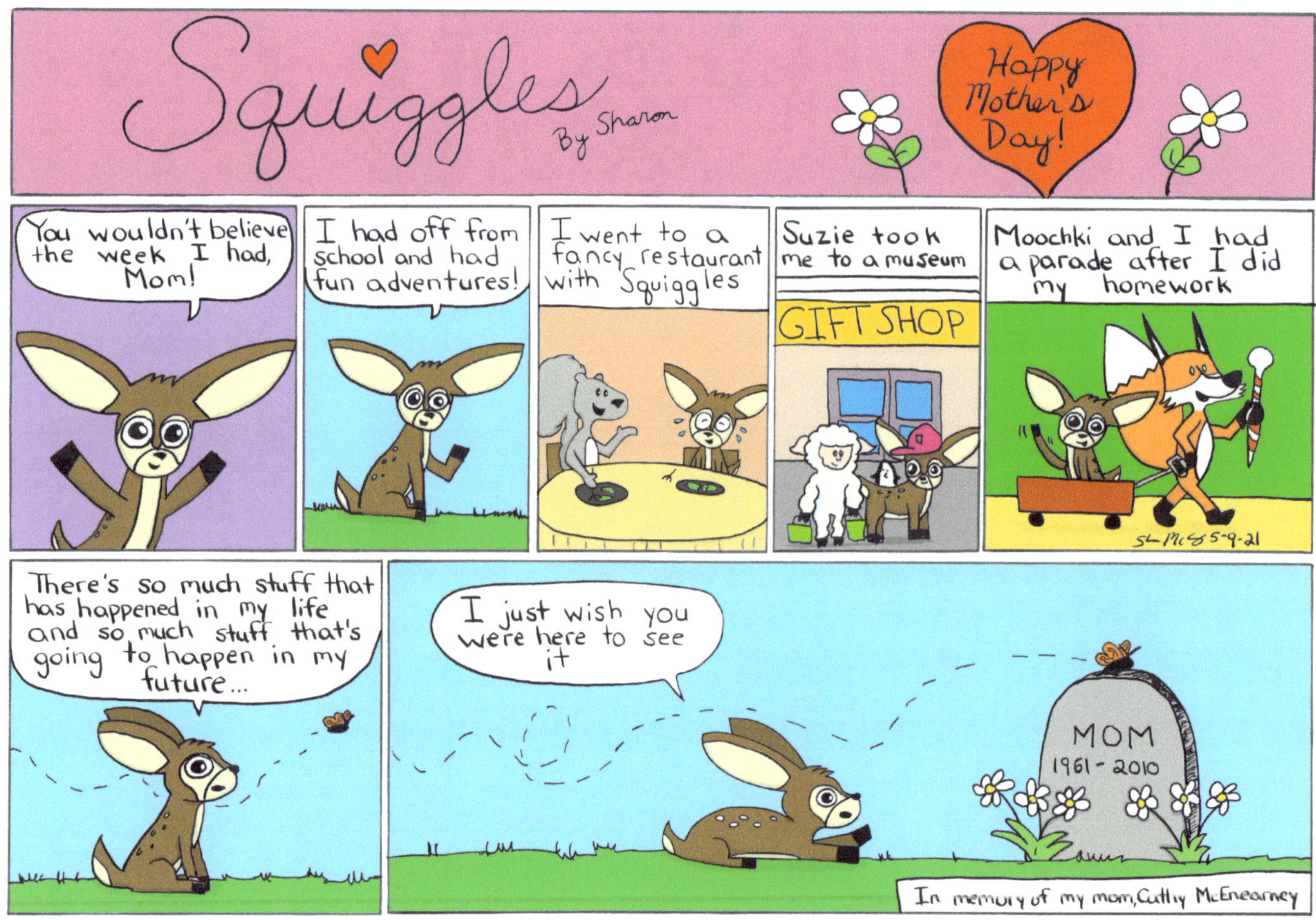
Squiggles
By Sharon
Happy Mother's Day!
You wouldn't believe the week I had, Mom!
I had off from school and had fun adventures!
I went to a fancy restaurant with Squiggles
Suzie took me to a museum
GIFT SHOP
Moochki and I had a parade after I did my homework
SL McS 5-9-21
There's so much stuff that has happened in my life and so much stuff that's going to happen in my future...
I just wish you were here to see it
MOM
1961 - 2010
In memory of my mom, Cathy McEnearney

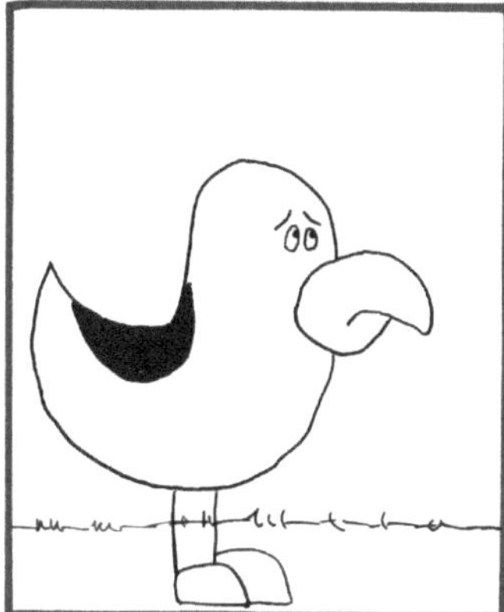
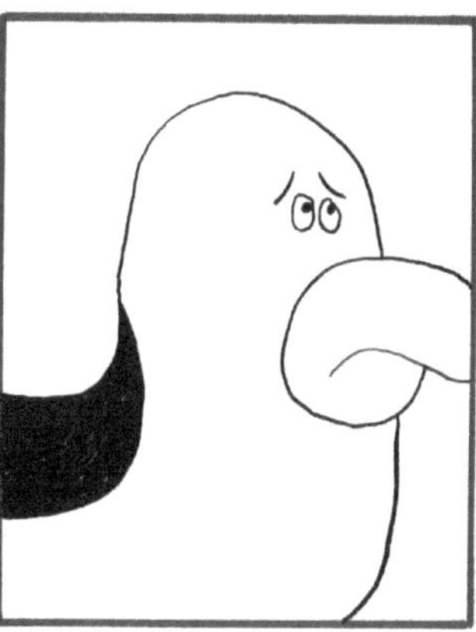
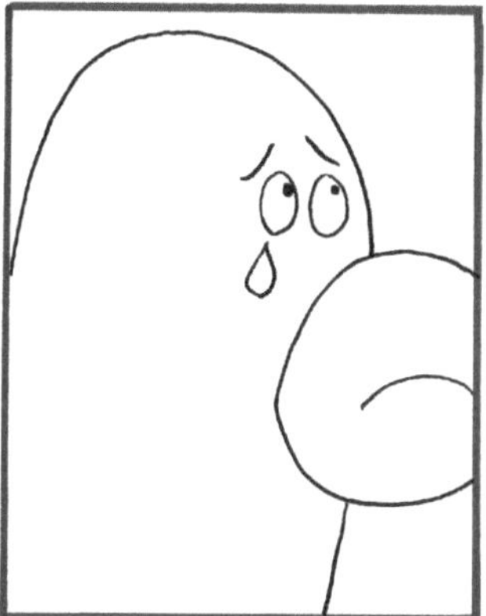
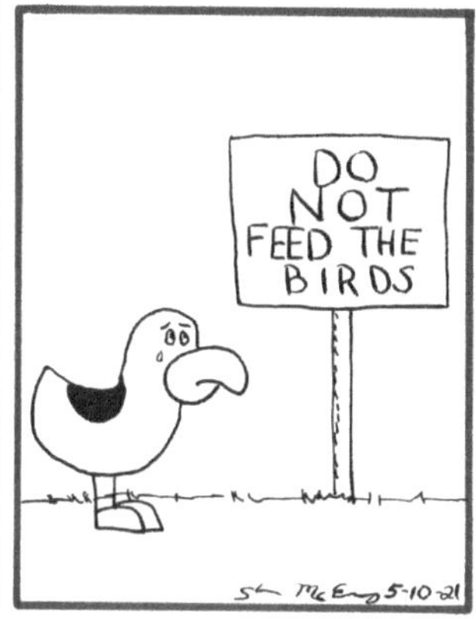
DO
NOT
FEED THE
BIRDS
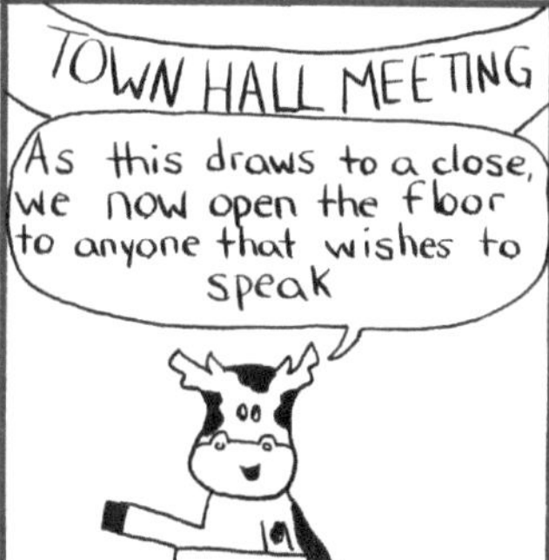
TOWN HALL MEETING
As this draws to a close, we now open the floor to anyone that wishes to speak
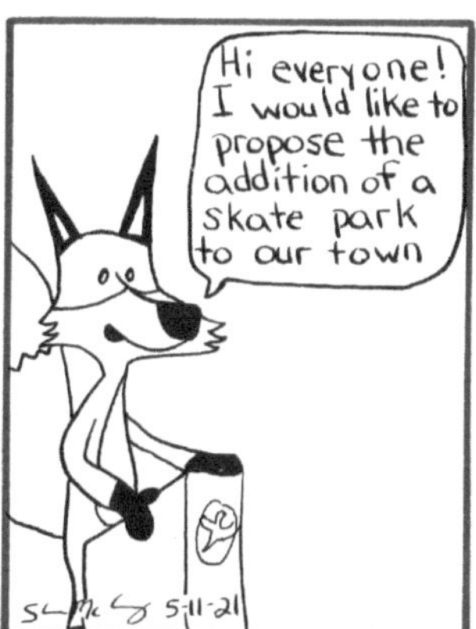
Hi everyone! I would like to propose the addition of a skate park to our town
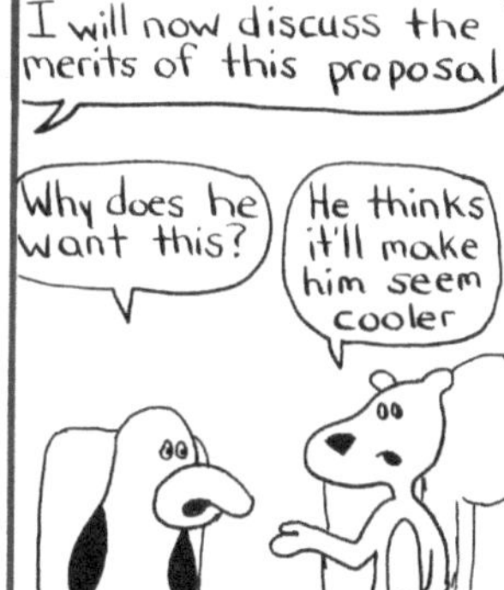
I will now discuss the merits of this proposal
Why does he want this?
He thinks it'll make him seem cooler
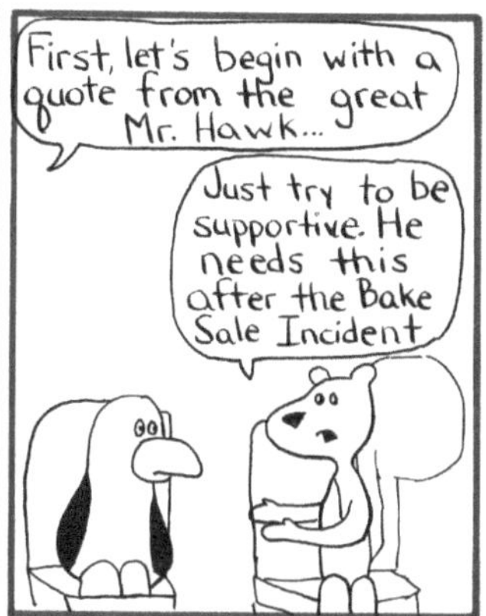
First, let's begin with a quote from the great Mr. Hawk...
Just try to be supportive. He needs this after the Bake Sale Incident
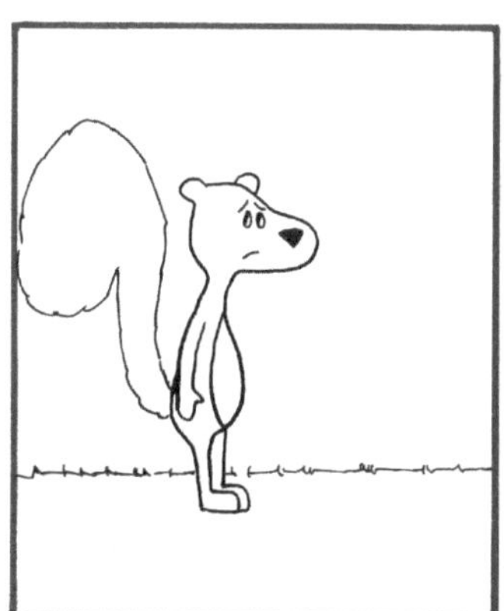
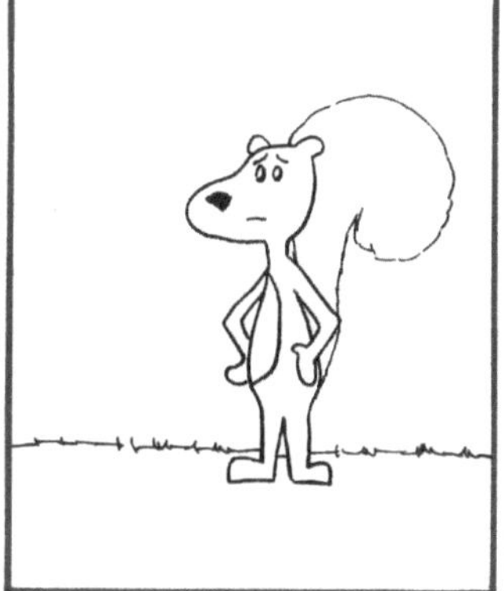
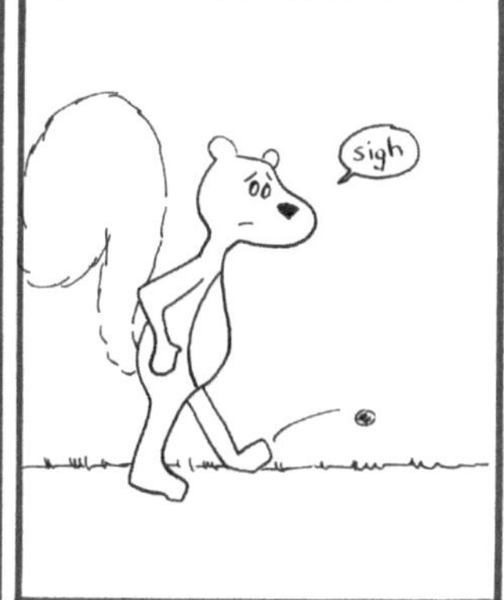
sigh
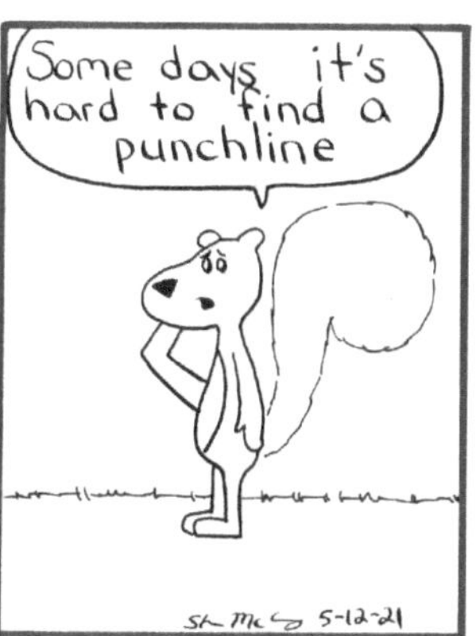
Some days it's hard to find a punchline

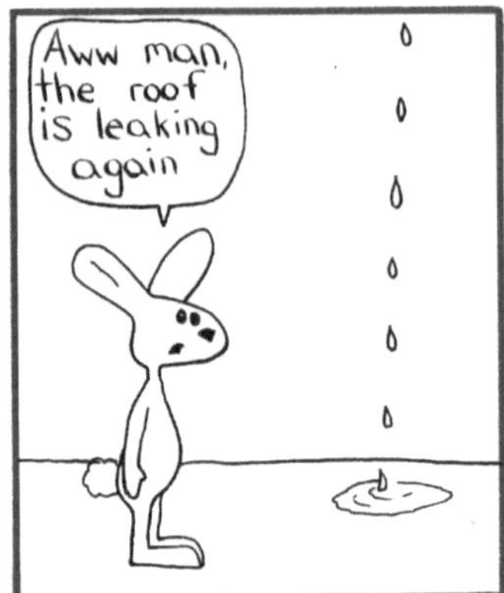
Aww man, the roof is leaking again
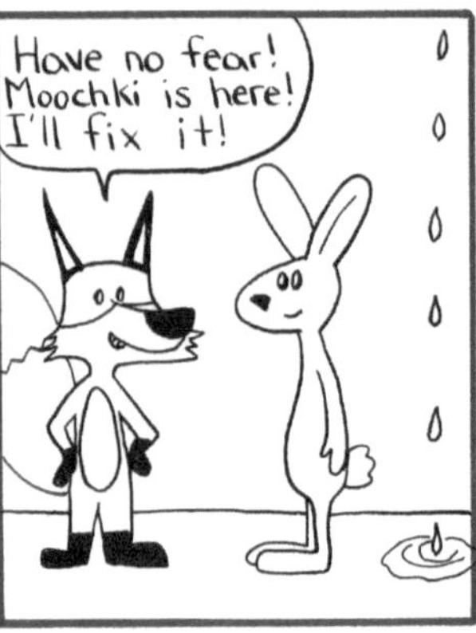
Have no fear! Moochki is here! I'll fix it!
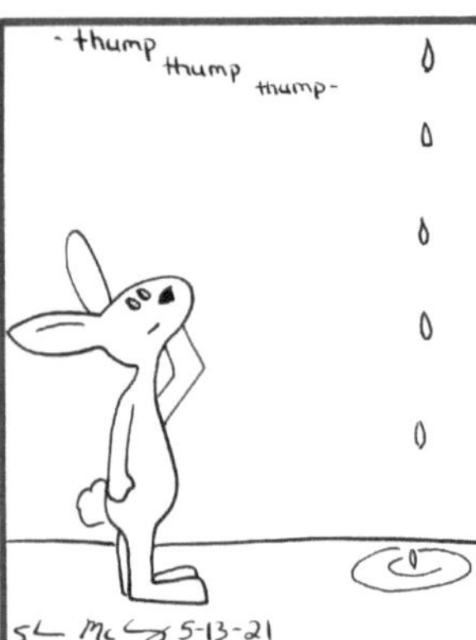
-thump thump thump-
SL McG 5-13-21
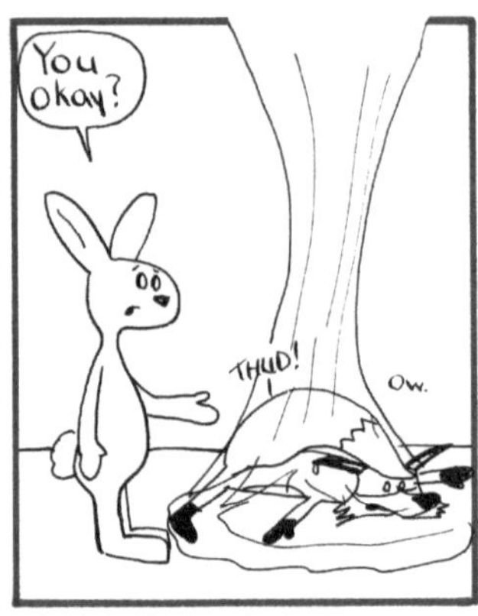
You okay?
THUD!
Ow.
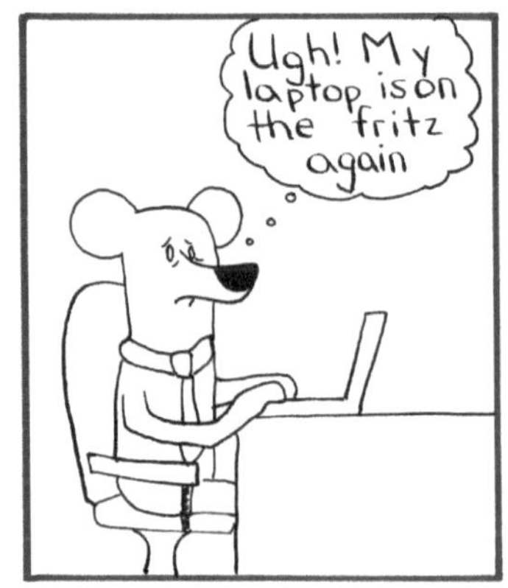
Ugh! My laptop is on the fritz again
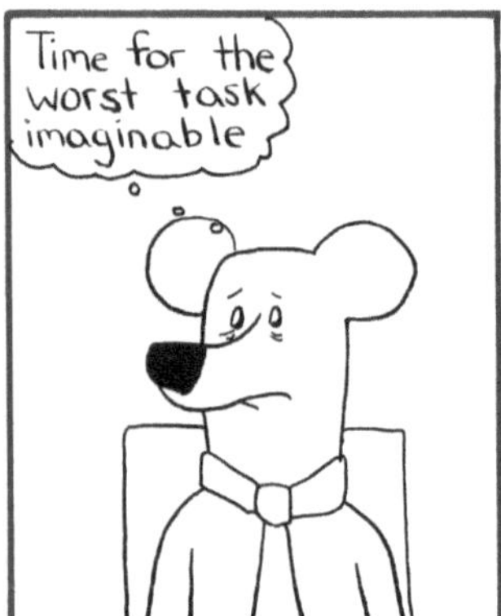
Time for the worst task imaginable
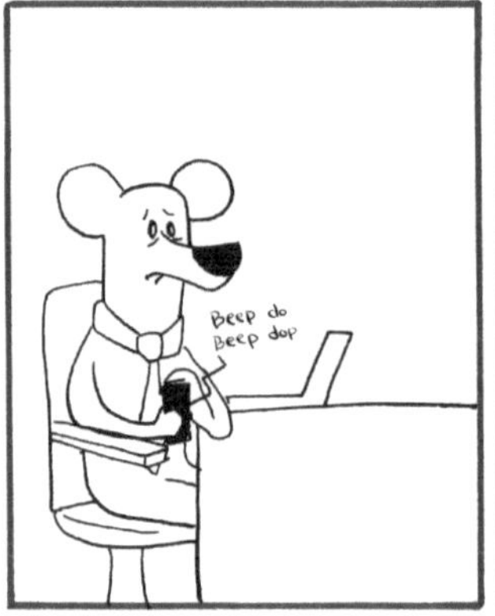
Beep do
Beep dop
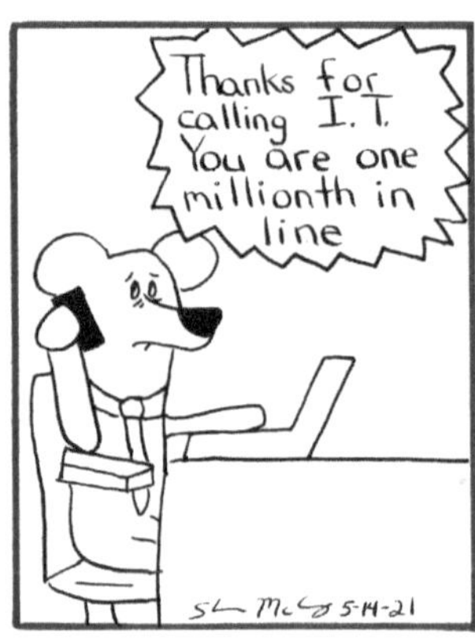
Thanks for calling I.T. You are one millionth in line
SL McG 5-14-21
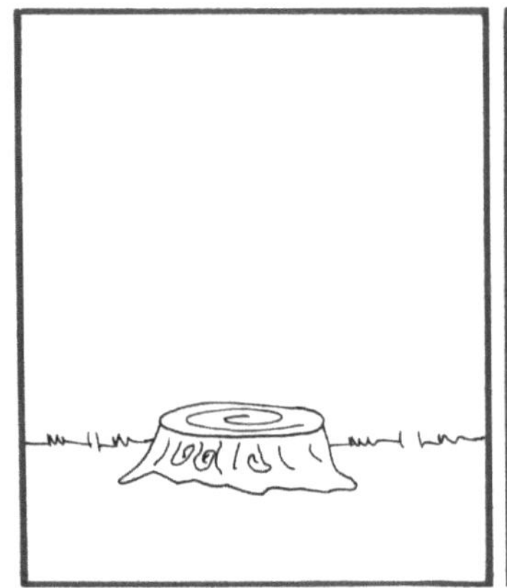
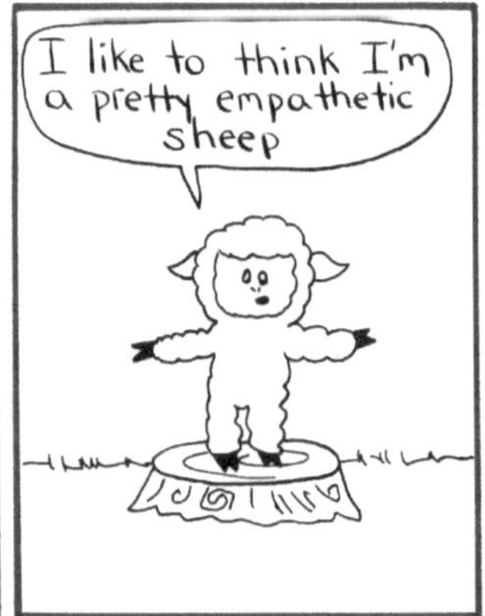
I like to think I'm a pretty empathetic sheep
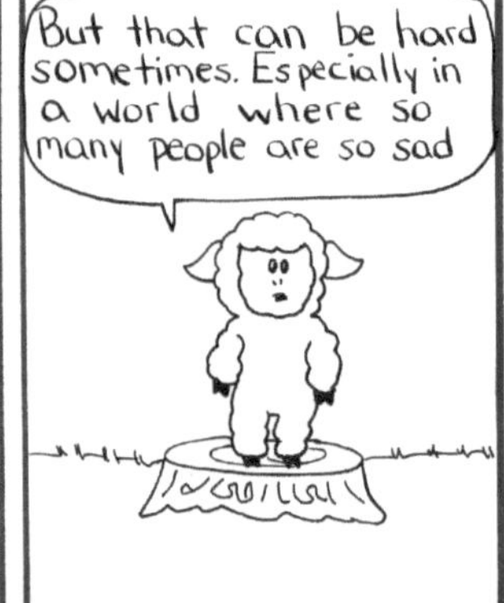
But that can be hard sometimes. Especially in a world where so many people are so sad
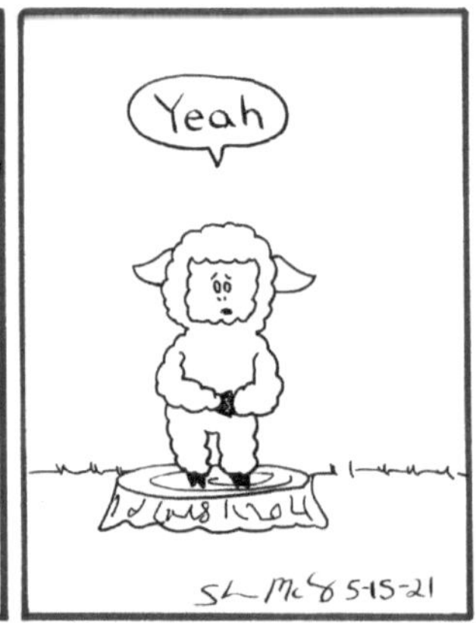
Yeah
SL McG 5-15-21

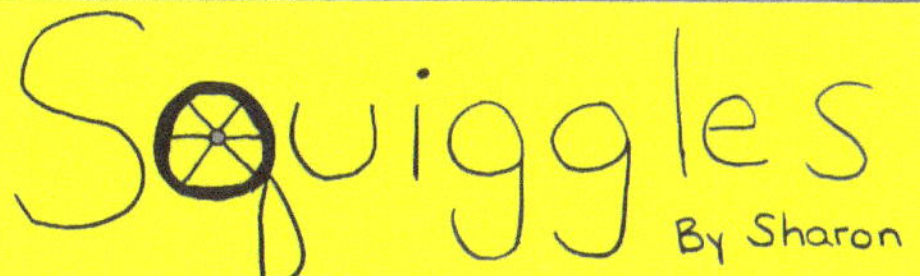
Squiggles
By Sharon

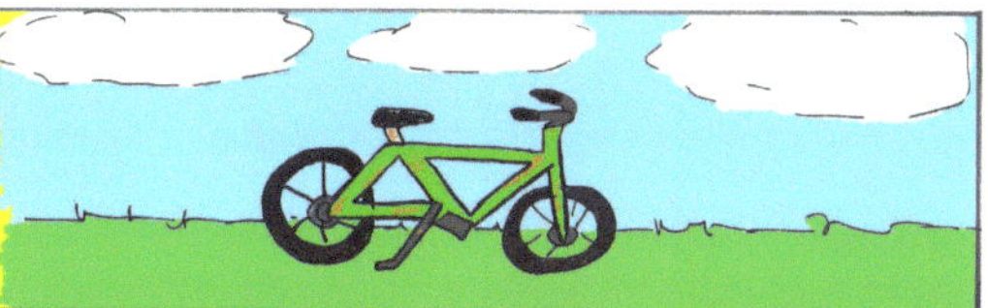

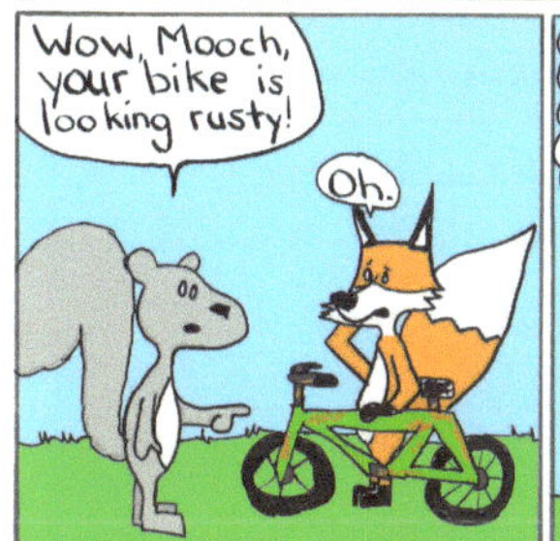
Wow, Mooch, your bike is looking rusty!
Oh.

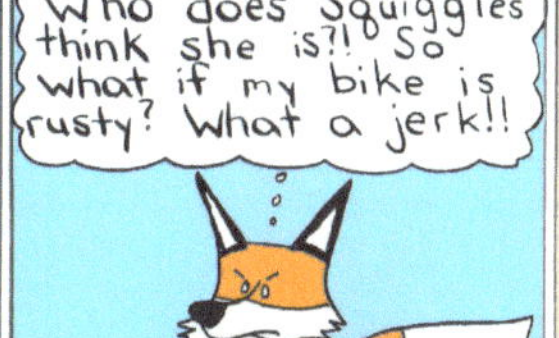
Who does Squiggles think she is?!! So what if my bike is rusty? What a jerk!!

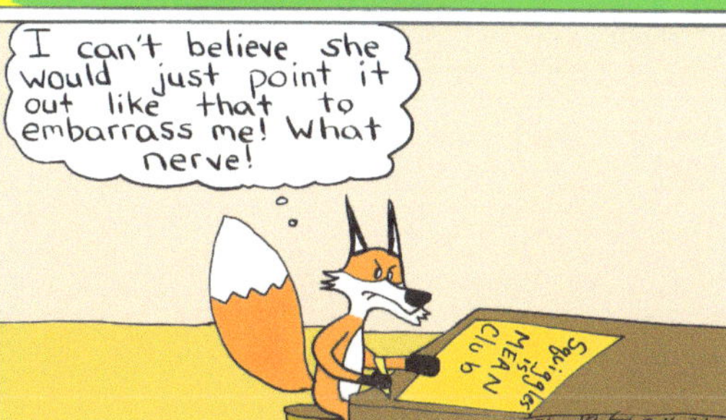
I can't believe she would just point it out like that to embarrass me! What nerve!
Squiggles is MEAN Club

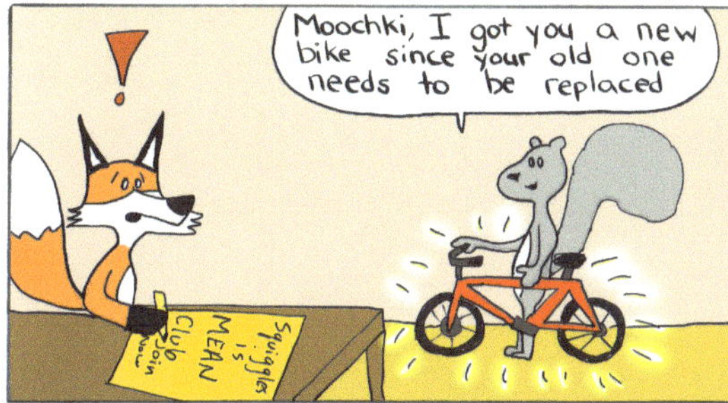
!
Moochki, I got you a new bike since your old one needs to be replaced
Squiggles is MEAN Club

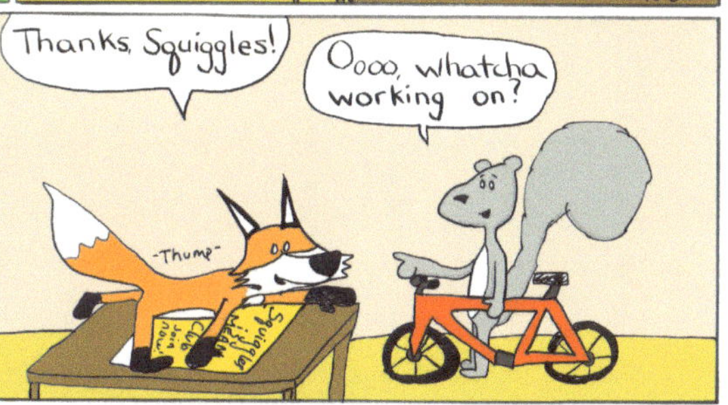
Thanks, Squiggles!
Oooo, whatcha working on?
-Thump-

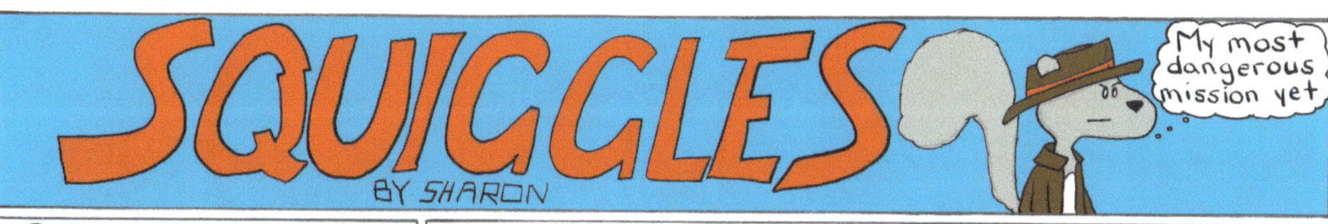
SQUIGGLES
BY SHARON
My most dangerous mission yet

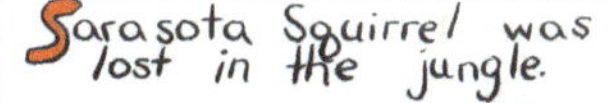
Sarasota Squirrel was lost in the jungle.

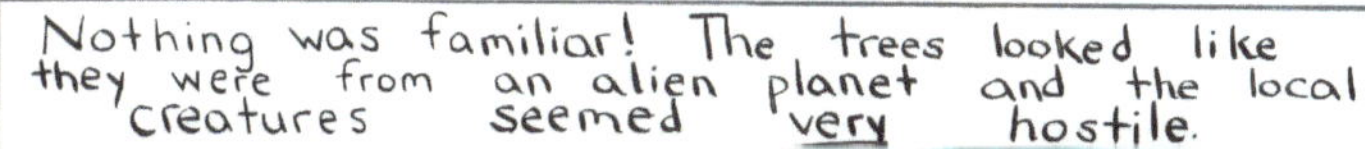
Nothing was familiar! The trees looked like they were from an alien planet and the local creatures seemed very hostile.

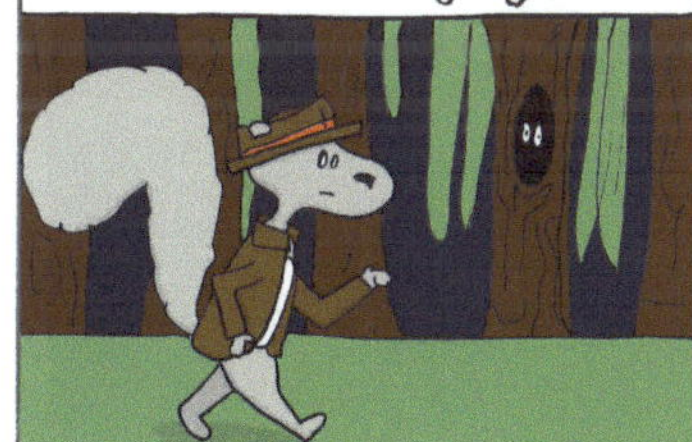

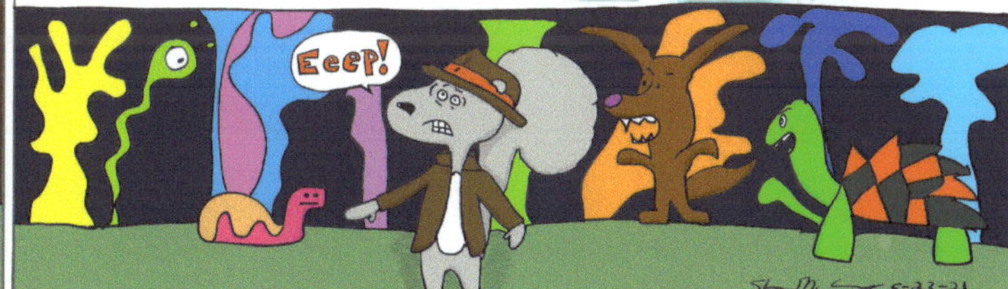
Eeep!

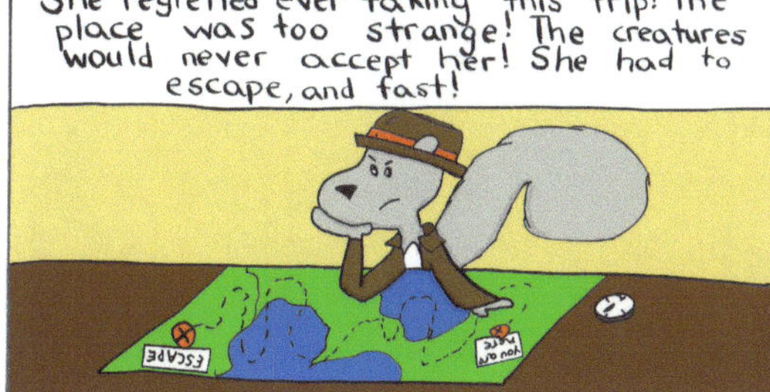
She regretted ever taking this trip! The place was too strange! The creatures would never accept her! She had to escape, and fast!
ESCAPE

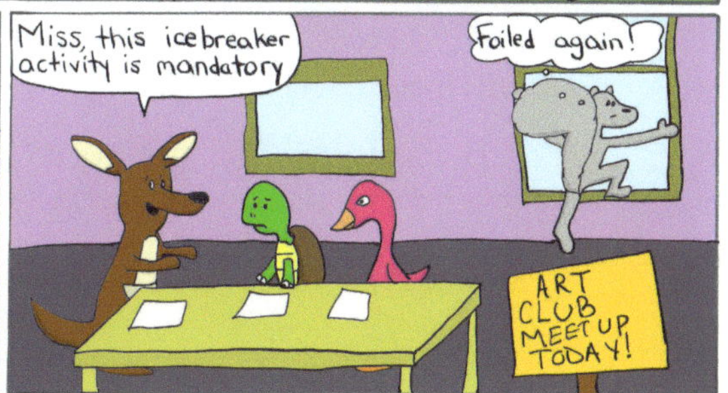
Miss, this icebreaker activity is mandatory
Foiled again!
ART CLUB MEETUP TODAY!

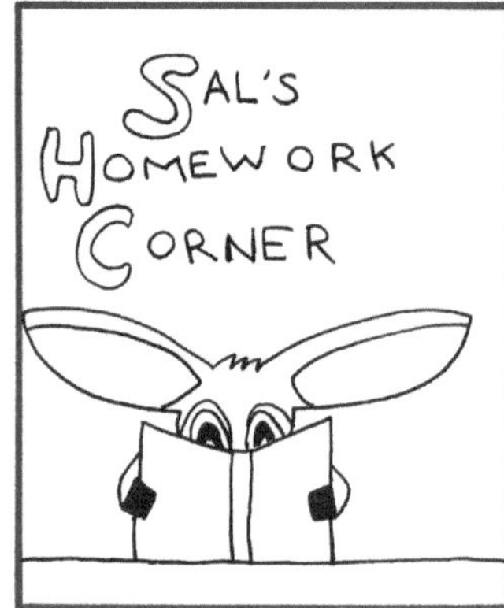
Sal's Homework Corner
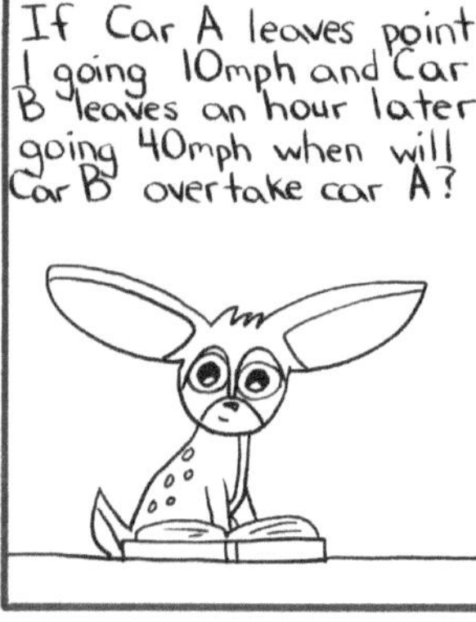
If Car A leaves point 1 going 10mph and Car B leaves an hour later going 40mph when will Car B overtake car A?
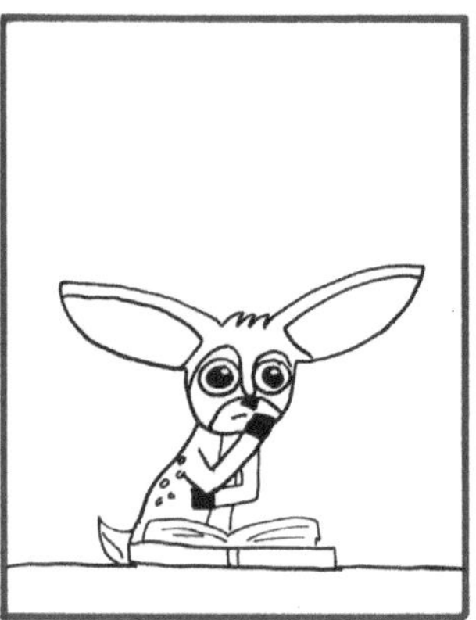
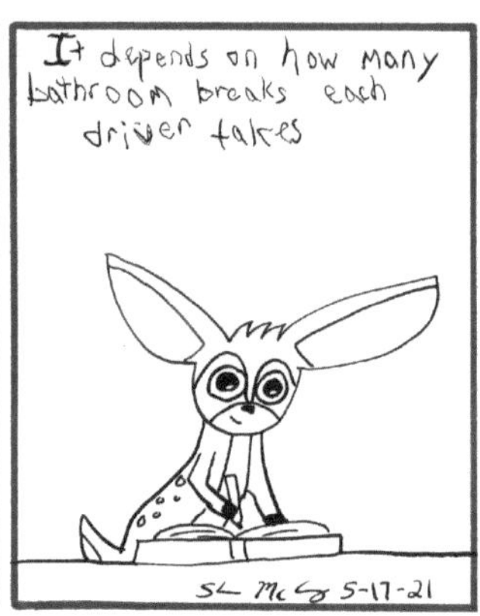
It depends on how many bathroom breaks each driver takes
SL McG 5-17-21
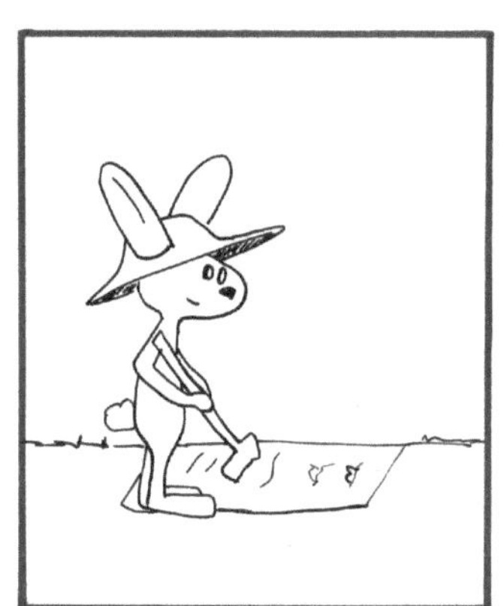
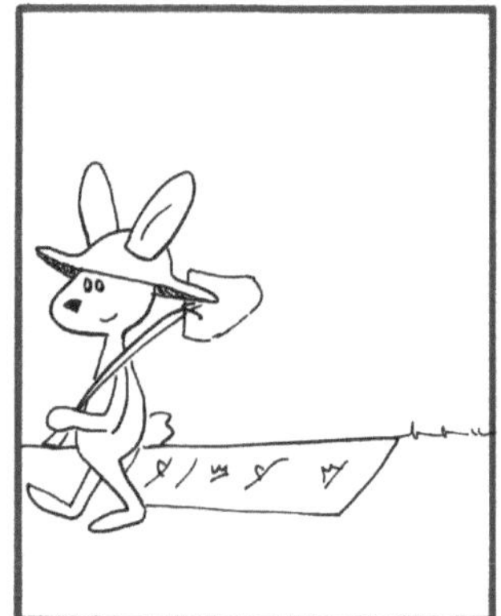
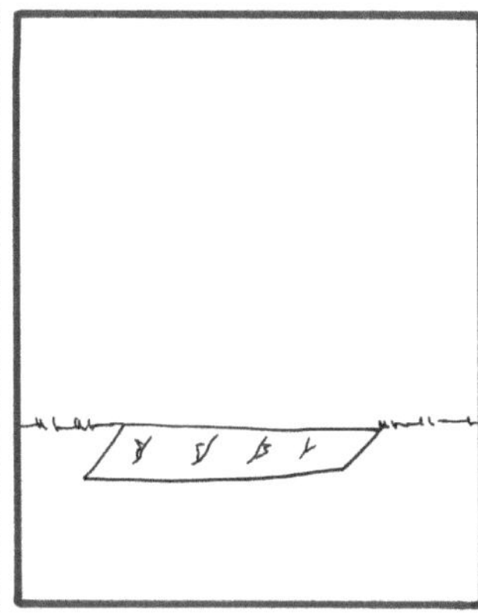
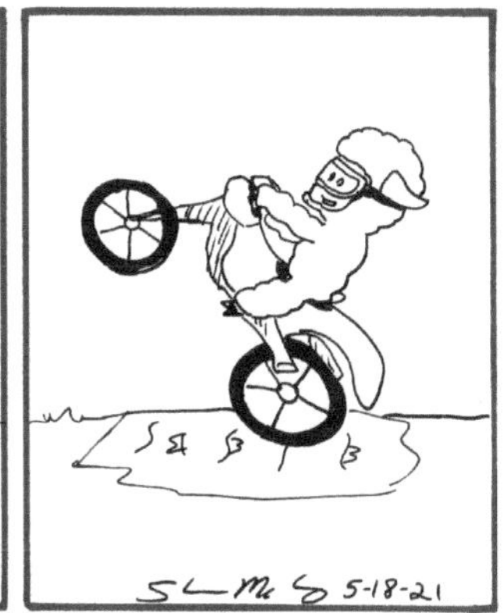
SL McG 5-18-21
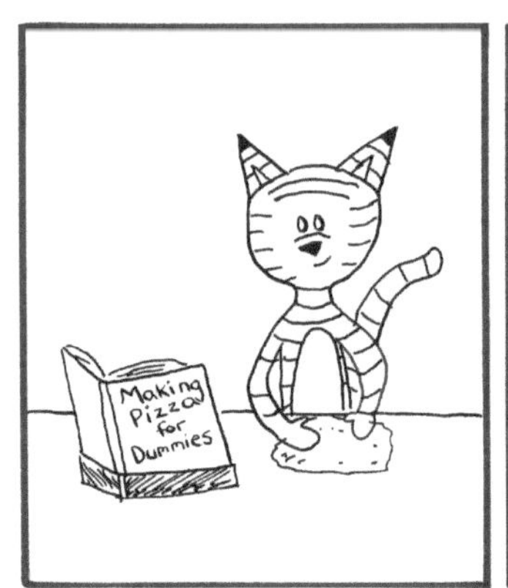
Making Pizza for Dummies
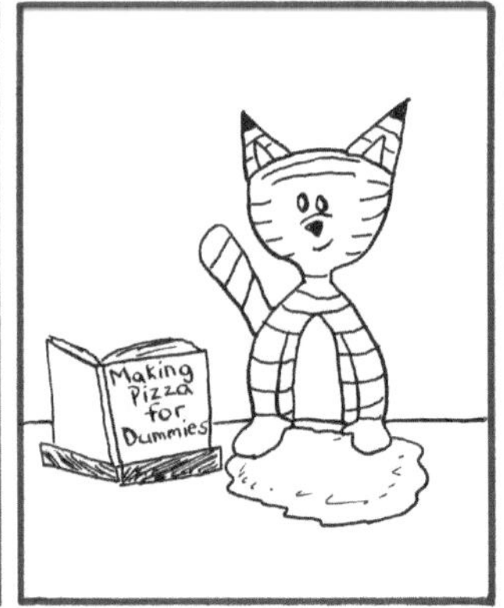
Making Pizza for Dummies
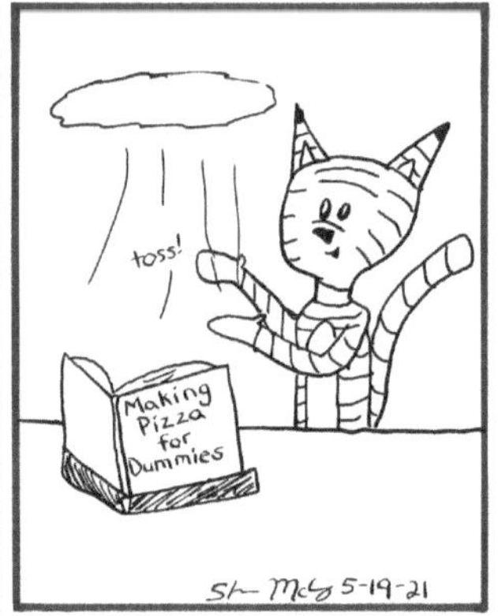
toss!
Making Pizza for Dummies
SL McG 5-19-21
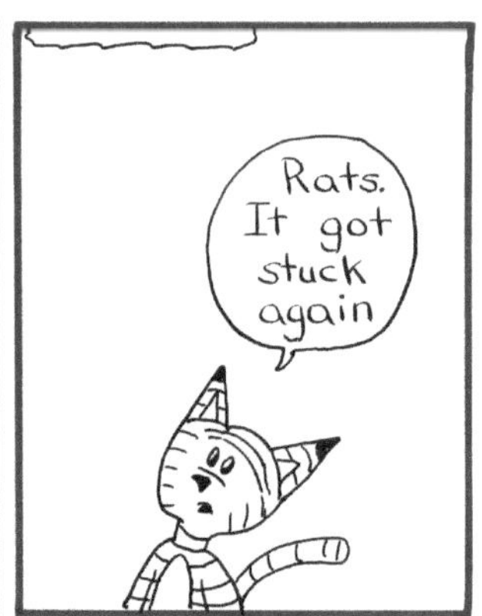
Rats. It got stuck again

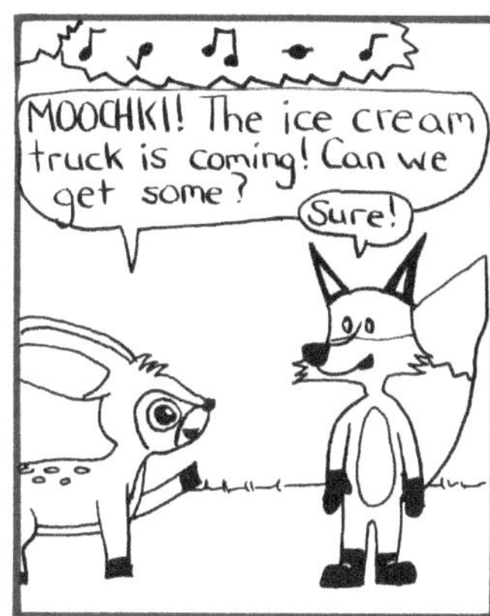
MOOCHKI! The ice cream truck is coming! Can we get some?
Sure!

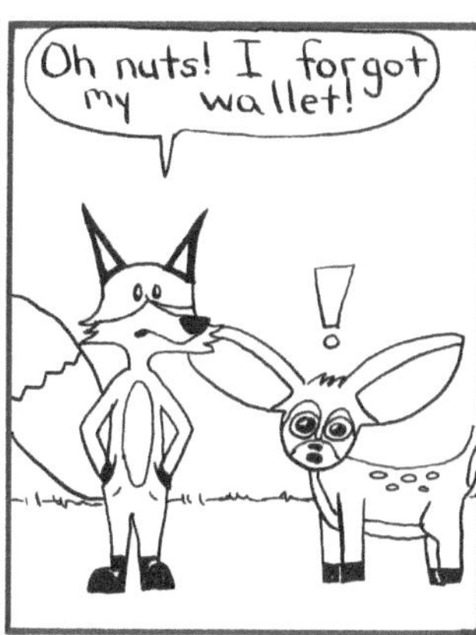
Oh nuts! I forgot my wallet!
!

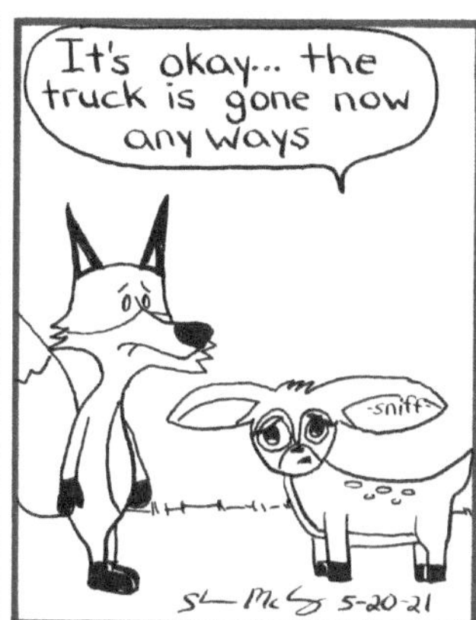
It's okay... the truck is gone now any ways
sniff
SL McG 5-20-21

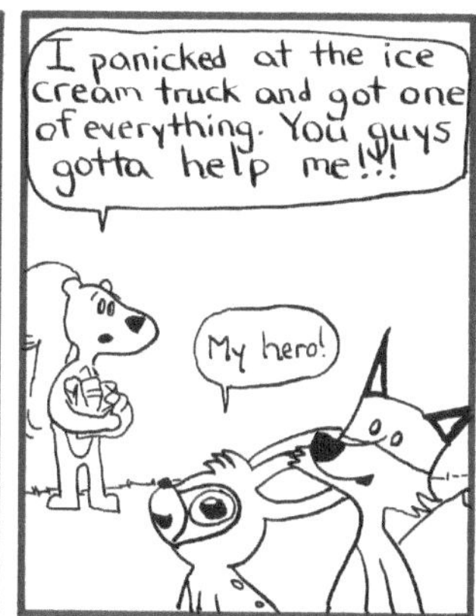
I panicked at the ice cream truck and got one of everything. You guys gotta help me!!!
My hero!

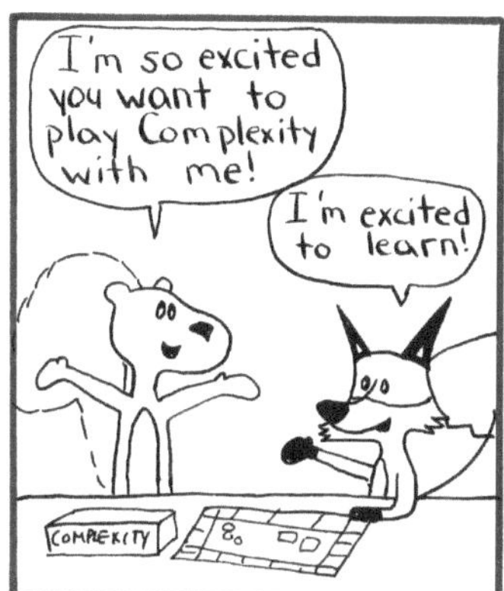
I'm so excited you want to play Complexity with me!
I'm excited to learn!
COMPLEXITY

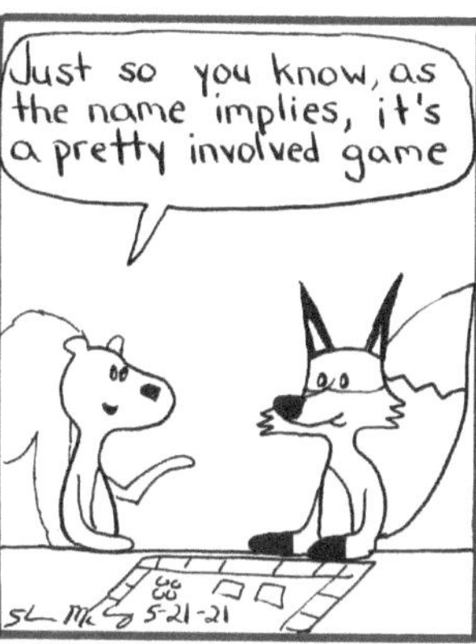
Just so you know, as the name implies, it's a pretty involved game
SL McG 5-21-21

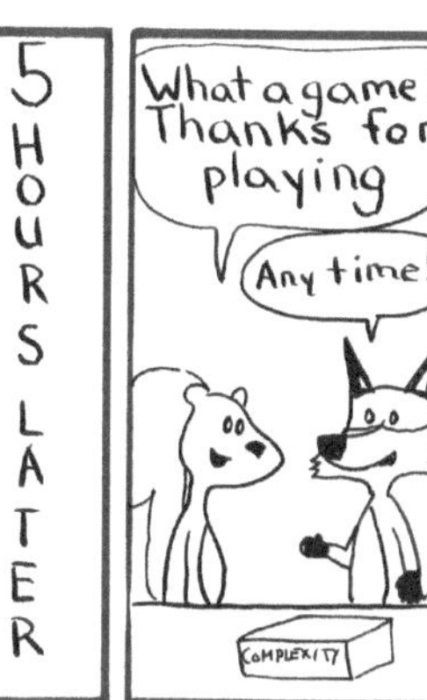
5 HOURS LATER

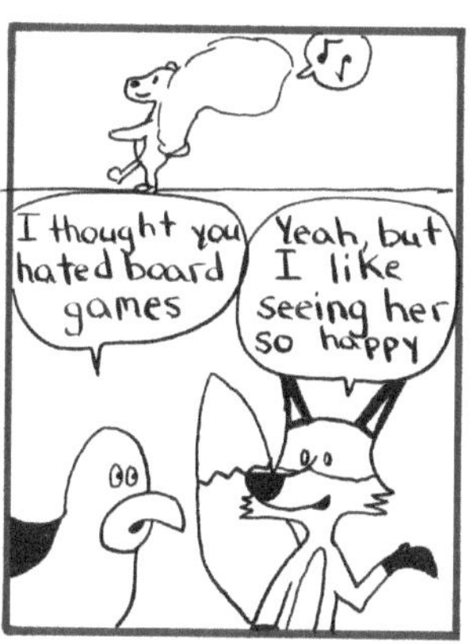
What a game!! Thanks for playing
Any time!
COMPLEXITY

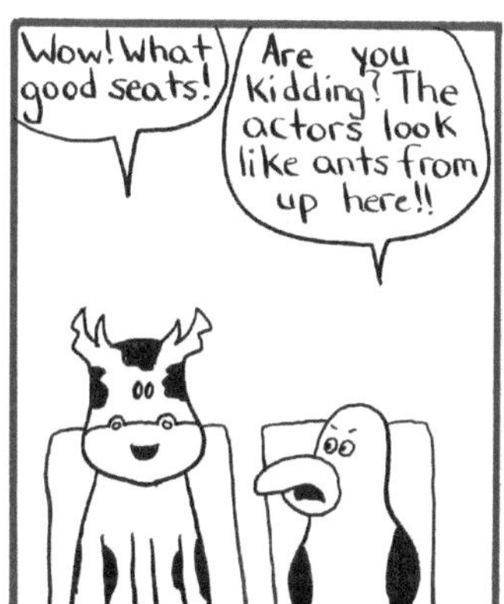
I thought you hated board games
Yeah, but I like seeing her so happy

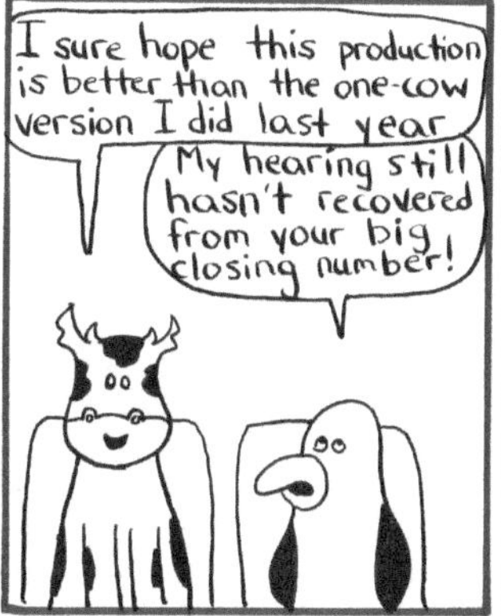
Wow! What good seats!
Are you kidding? The actors look like ants from up here!!

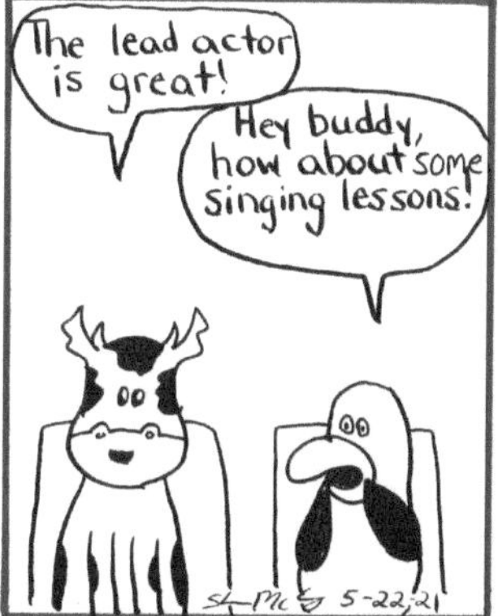
I sure hope this production is better than the one-cow version I did last year
My hearing still hasn't recovered from your big closing number!

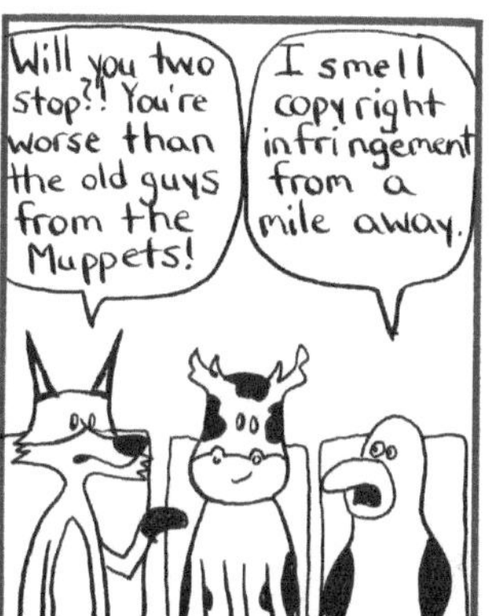
The lead actor is great!
Hey buddy, how about some singing lessons!
SL McG 5-22-21

Will you two stop?! You're worse than the old guys from the Muppets!
I smell copyright infringement from a mile away.

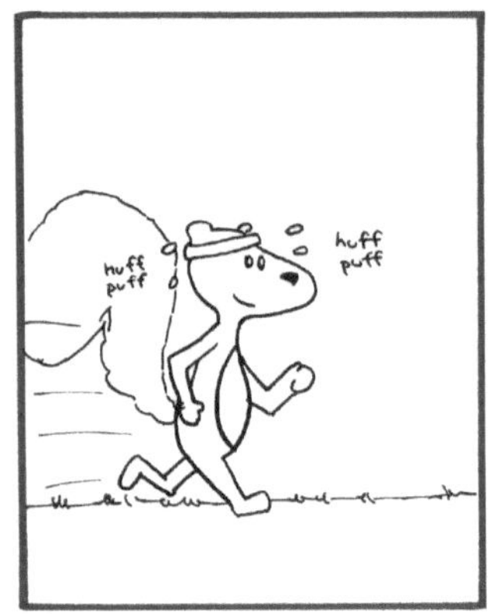
huff
puff
huff
puff

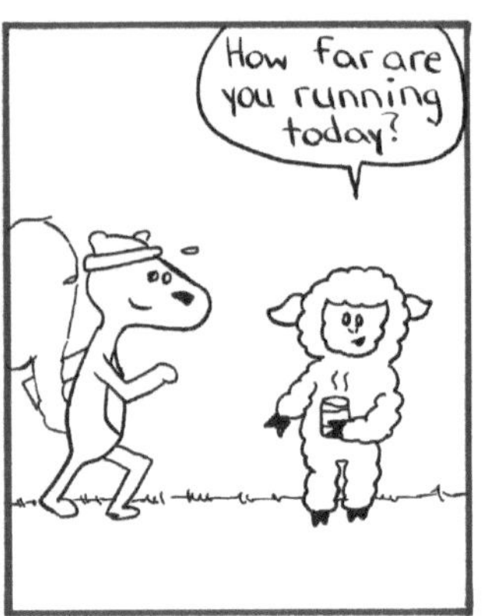
How far are you running today?

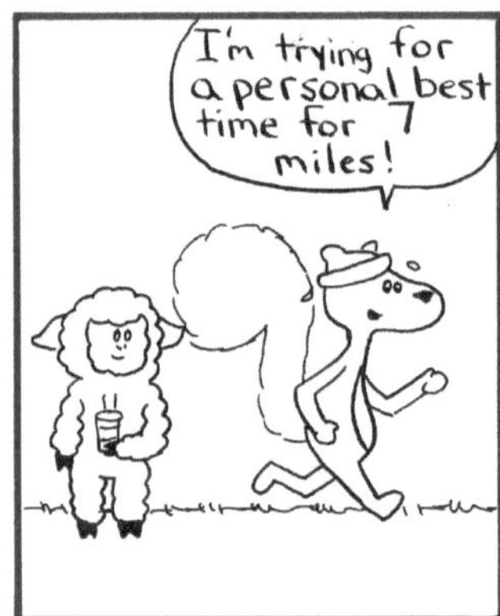
I'm trying for a personal best time for 7 miles!

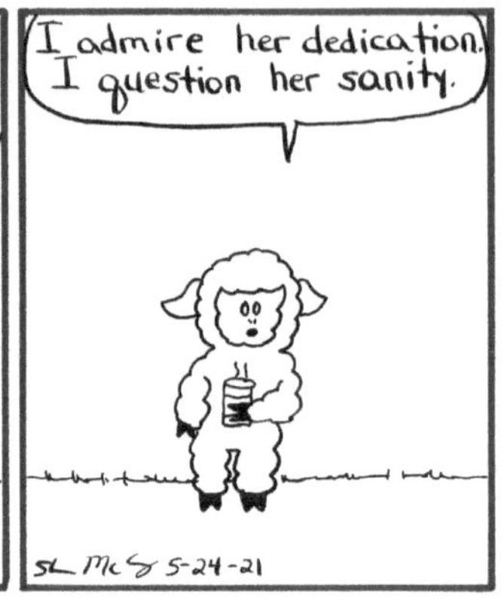
I admire her dedication. I question her sanity.
SL McG 5-24-21

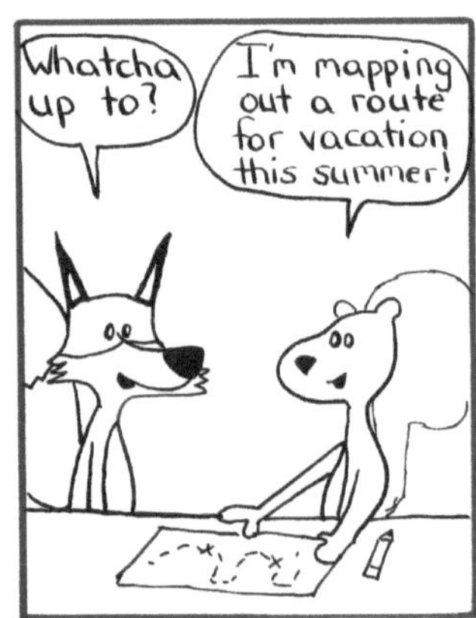
Whatcha up to?
I'm mapping out a route for vacation this summer!

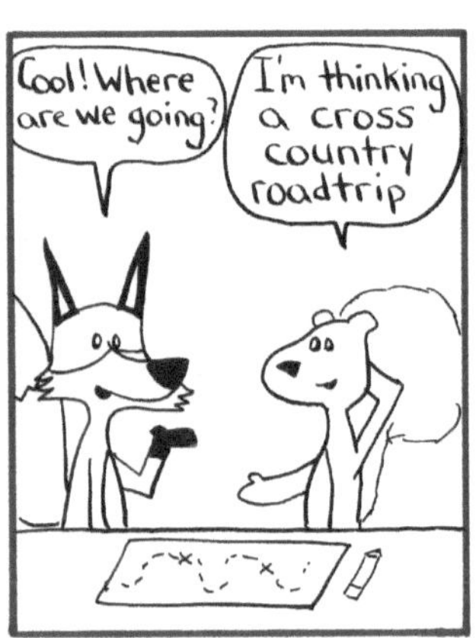
Cool! Where are we going?
I'm thinking a cross country roadtrip

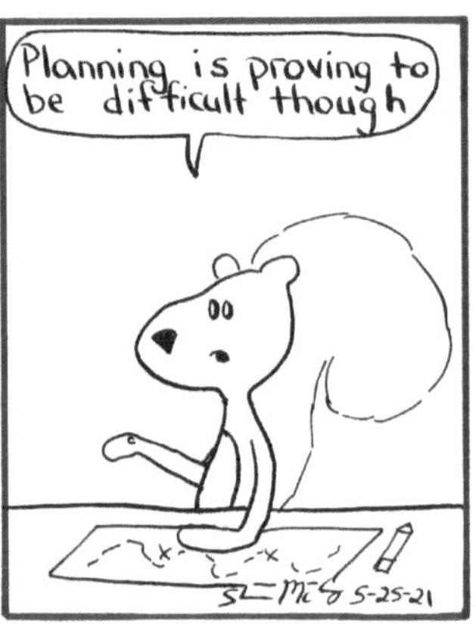
Planning is proving to be difficult though
SL McG 5-25-21

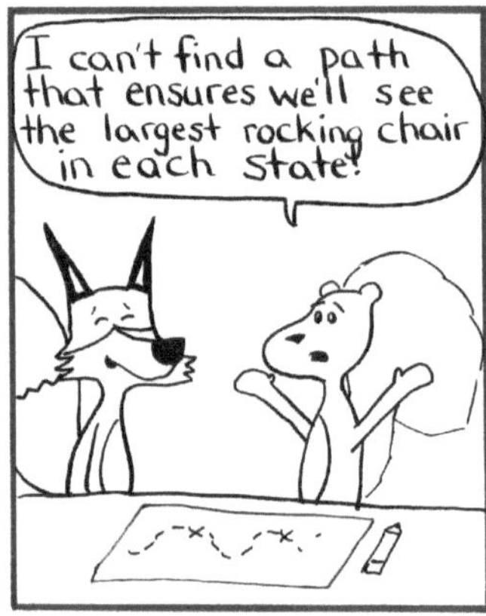
I can't find a path that ensures we'll see the largest rocking chair in each state!

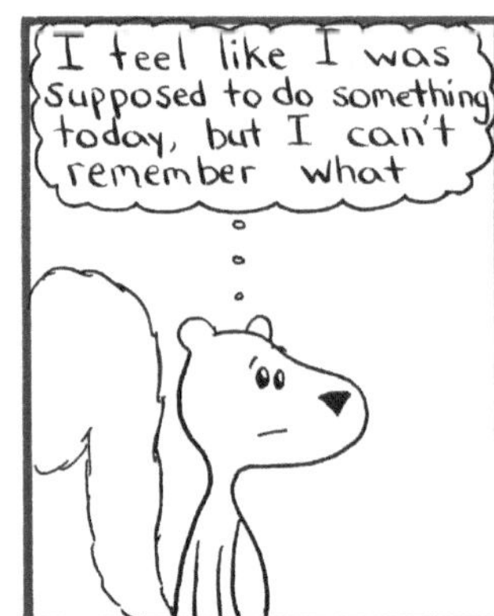
I feel like I was supposed to do something today, but I can't remember what

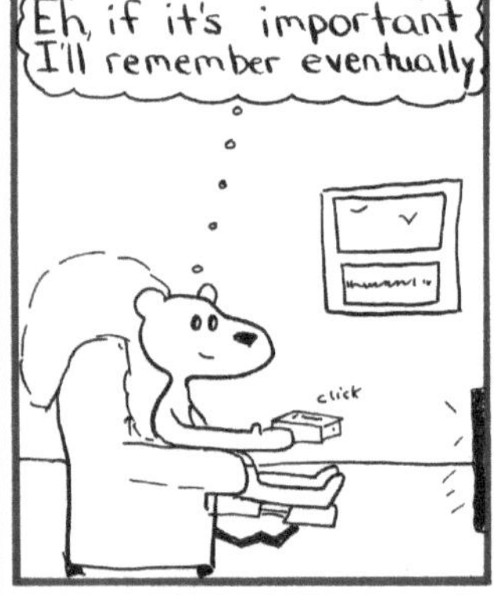
Eh, if it's important I'll remember eventually
click

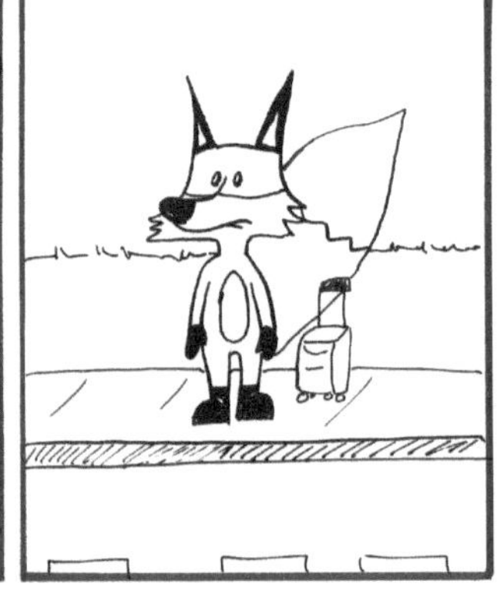

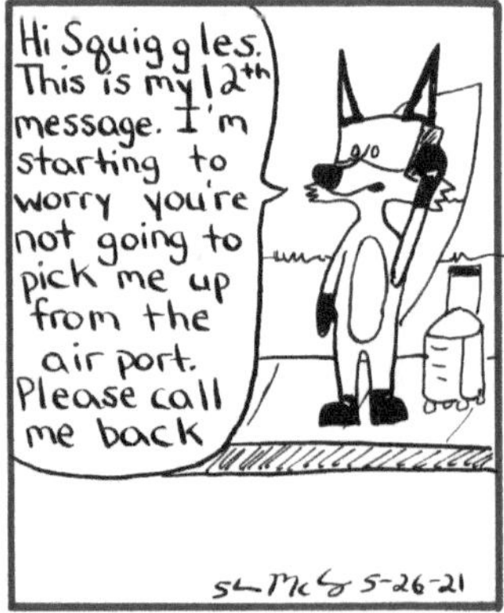
Hi Squiggles. This is my 12th message. I'm starting to worry you're not going to pick me up from the air port. Please call me back
SL McG 5-26-21

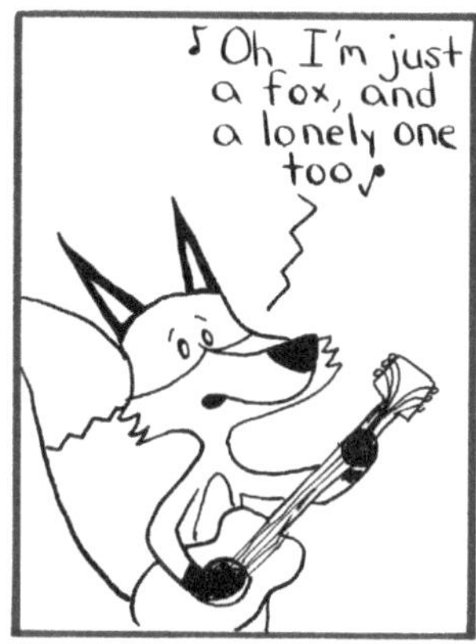
Oh I'm just a fox, and a lonely one too

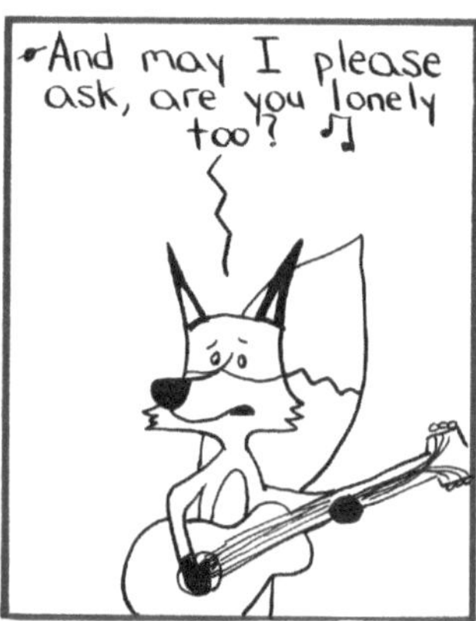
And may I please ask, are you lonely too?

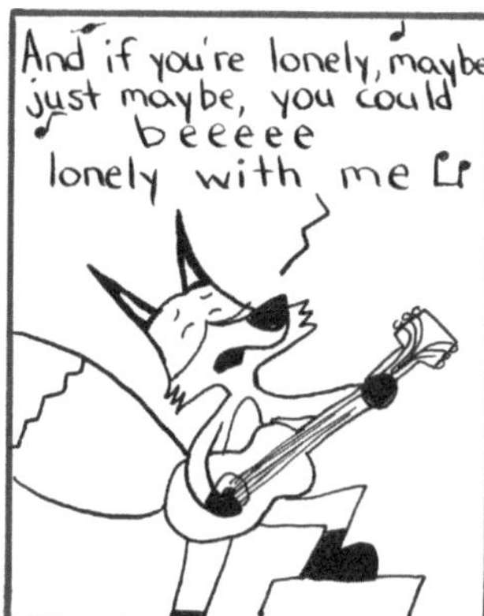
And if you're lonely, maybe just maybe, you could beeeee lonely with me

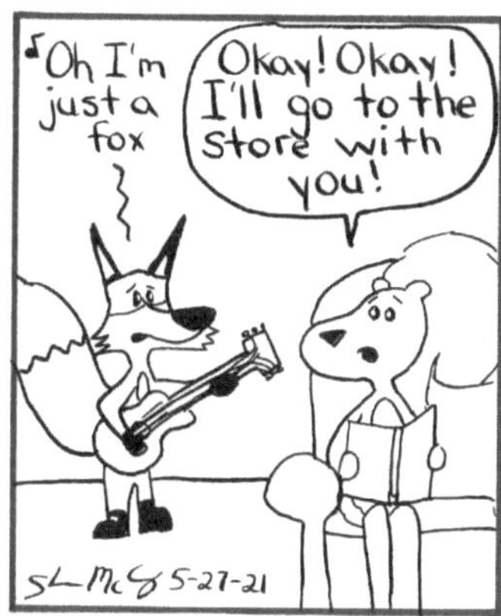
Oh I'm just a fox
Okay! Okay! I'll go to the store with you!
SL McG 5-27-21

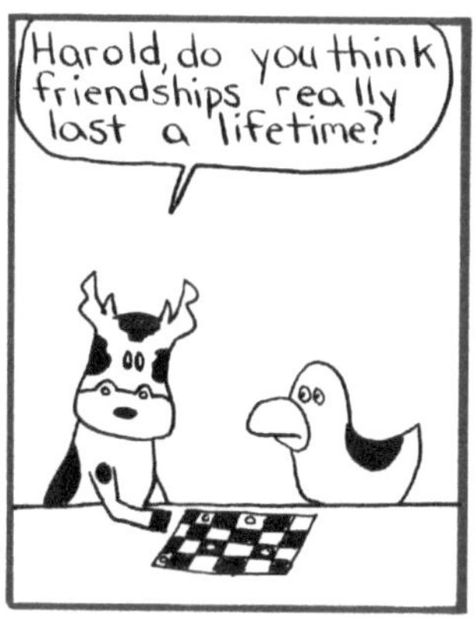
Harold, do you think friendships really last a lifetime?

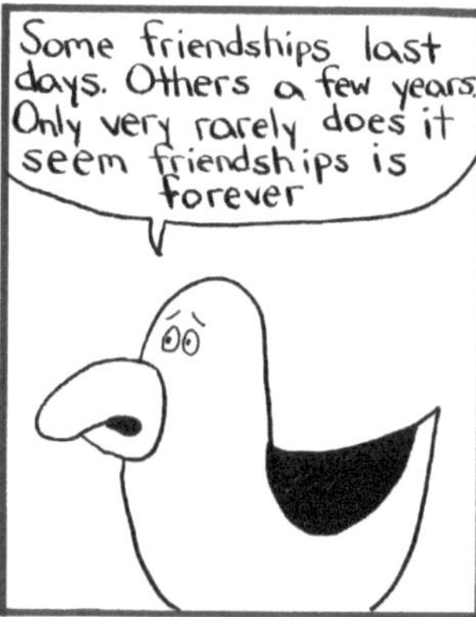
Some friendships last days. Others a few years. Only very rarely does it seem friendships is forever

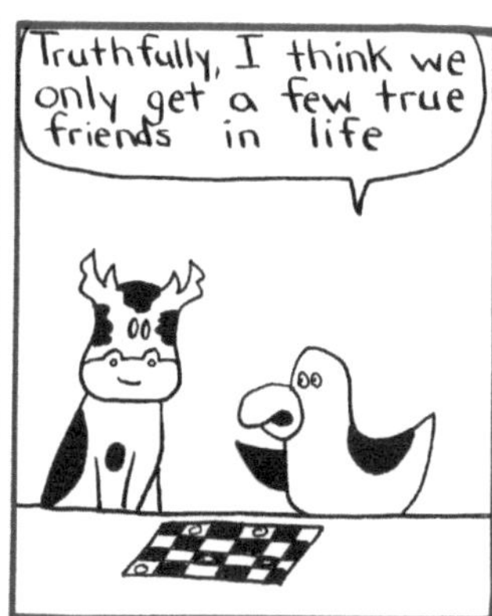
Truthfully, I think we only get a few true friends in life

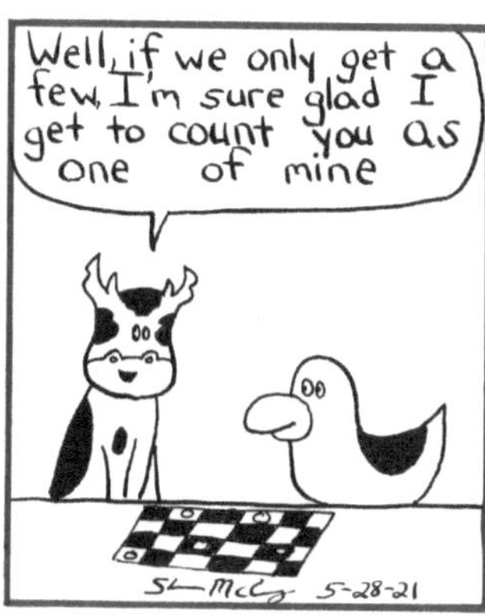
Well, if we only get a few, I'm sure glad I get to count you as one of mine
SL McG 5-28-21

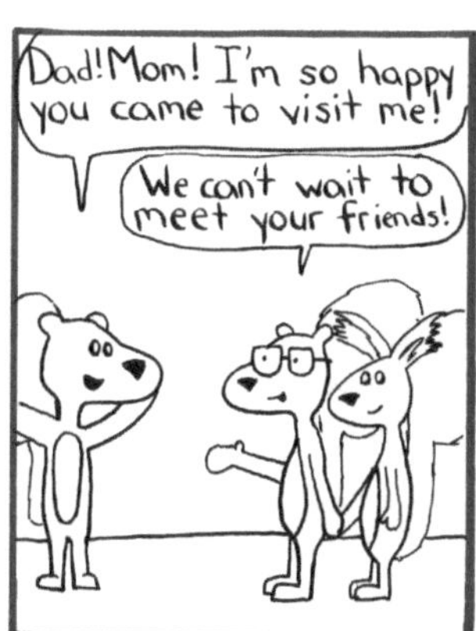
Dad! Mom! I'm so happy you came to visit me!
We can't wait to meet your friends!

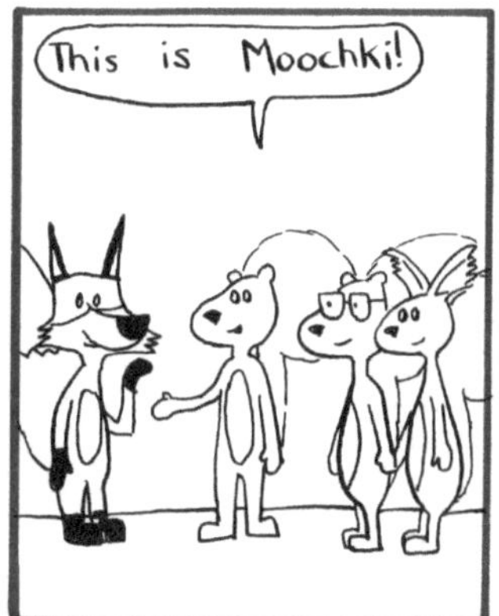
This is Moochki!

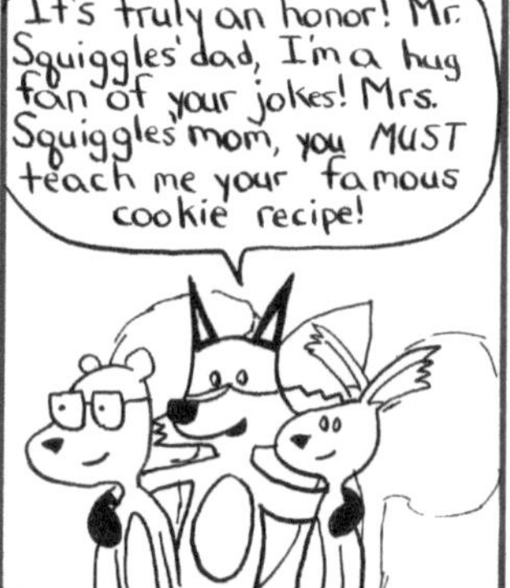
It's truly an honor! Mr. Squiggles' dad, I'm a hug fan of your jokes! Mrs. Squiggles' mom, you MUST teach me your famous cookie recipe!

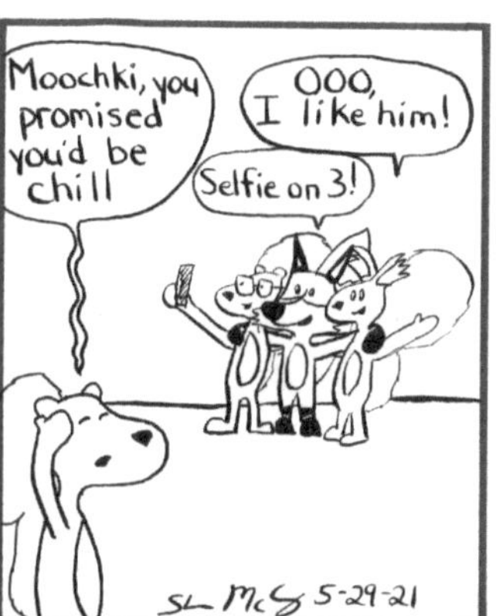
Moochki, you promised you'd be chill
OOO, I like him!
Selfie on 3!
SL McG 5-29-21

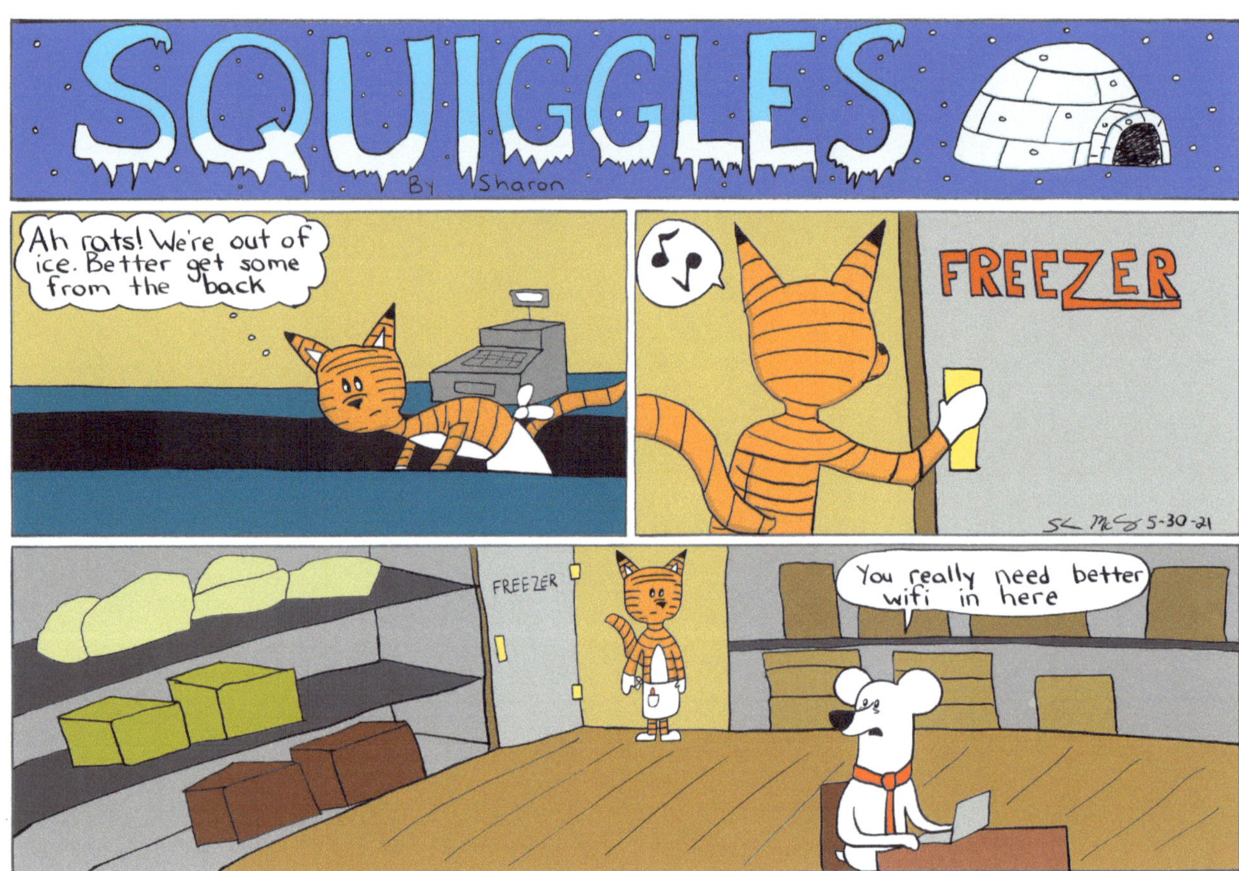
SQUIGGLES
By Sharon
Ah rats! We're out of ice. Better get some from the back
FREEZER
SL McG 5-30-21
FREEZER
You really need better wifi in here

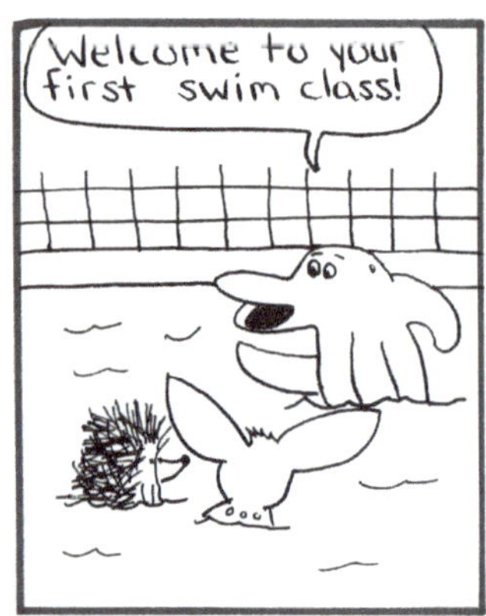
Welcome to your first swim class!

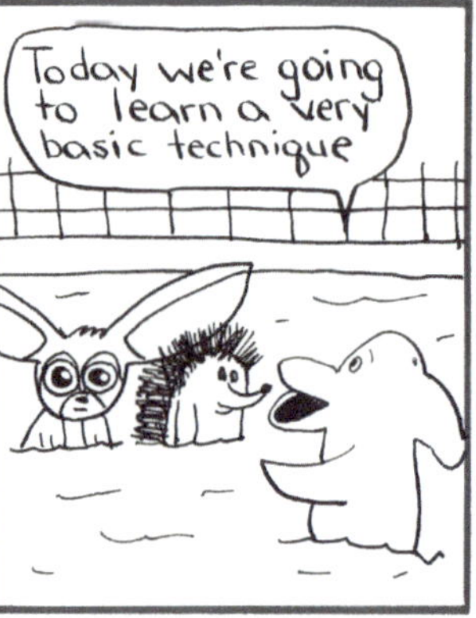
Today we're going to learn a very basic technique

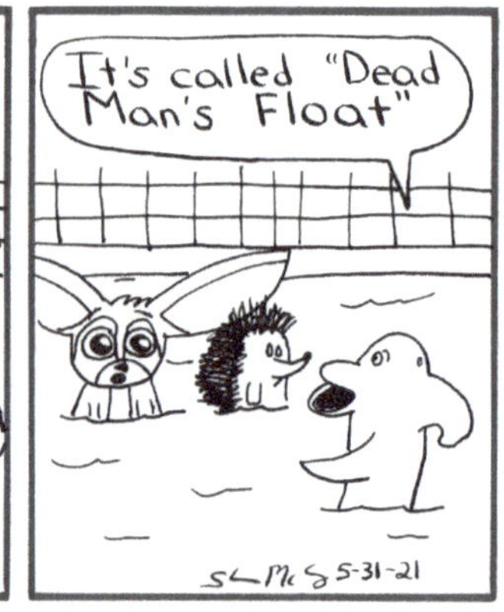
It's called "Dead Man's Float"
SL McG 5-31-21

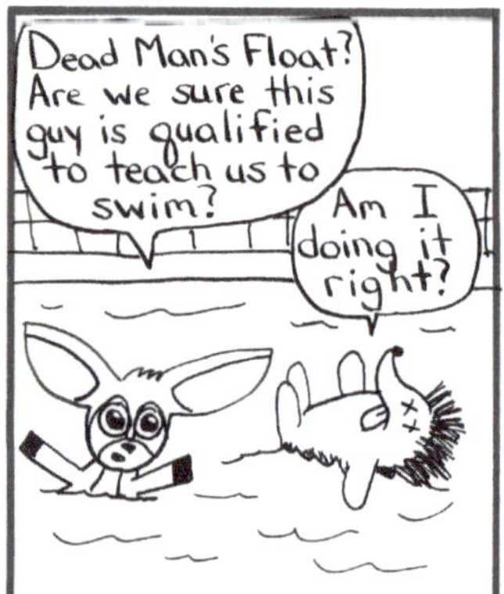
Dead Man's Float? Are we sure this guy is qualified to teach us to swim?
Am I doing it right?

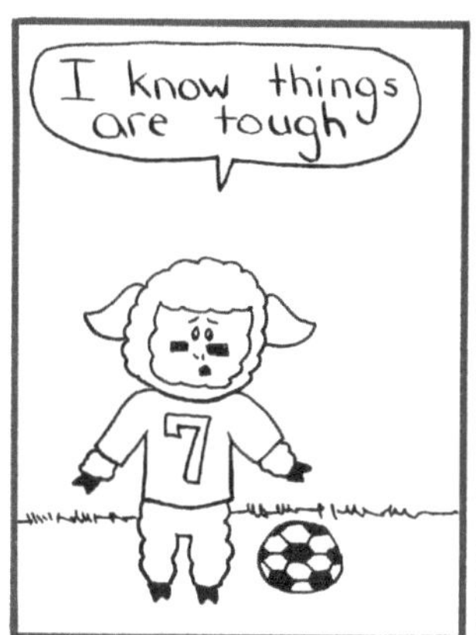
I know things are tough

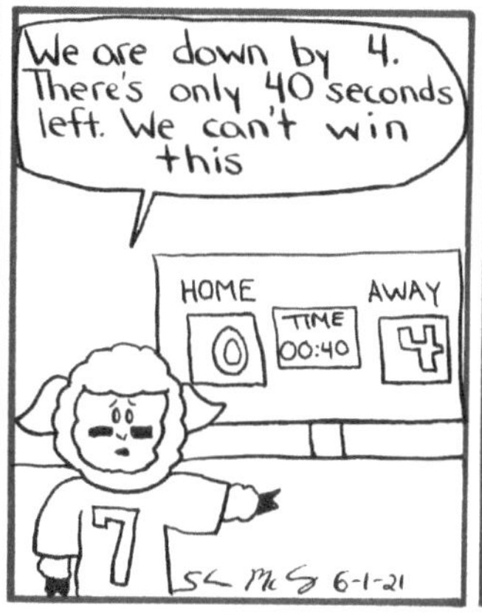
We are down by 4. There's only 40 seconds left. We can't win this
HOME
TIME
00:40
AWAY
0
4
7
SL McG 6-1-21

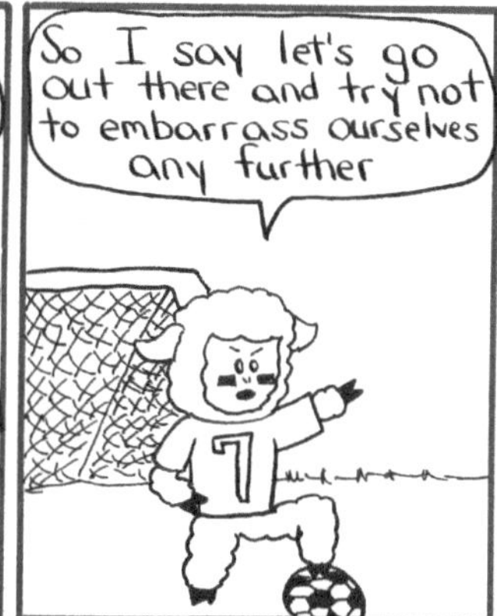
So I say let's go out there and try not to embarrass ourselves any further
7

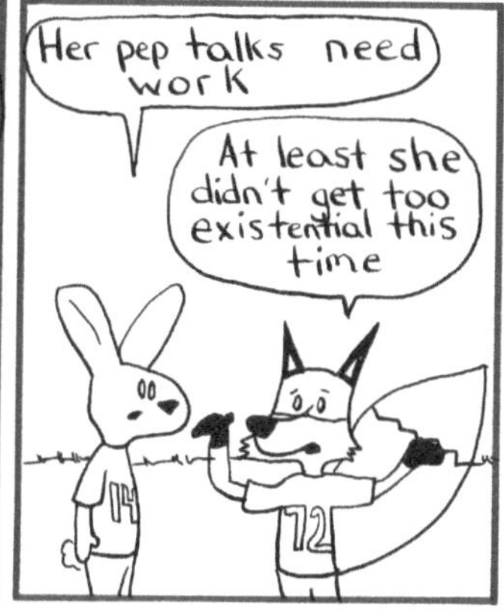
Her pep talks need work
At least she didn't get too existential this time
14
72

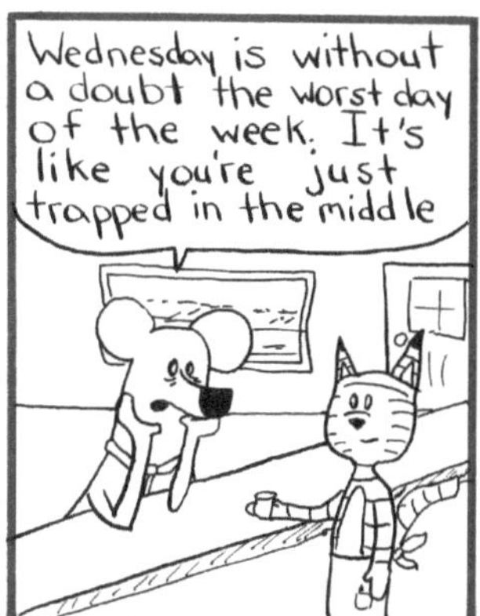
Wednesday is without a doubt the worst day of the week. It's like you're just trapped in the middle

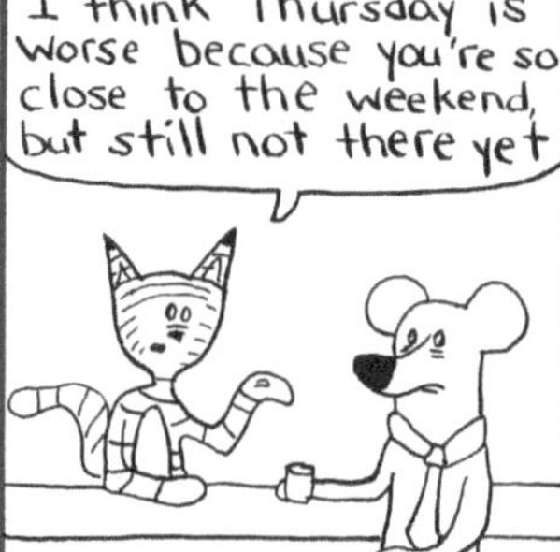
I think Thursday is worse because you're so close to the weekend, but still not there yet

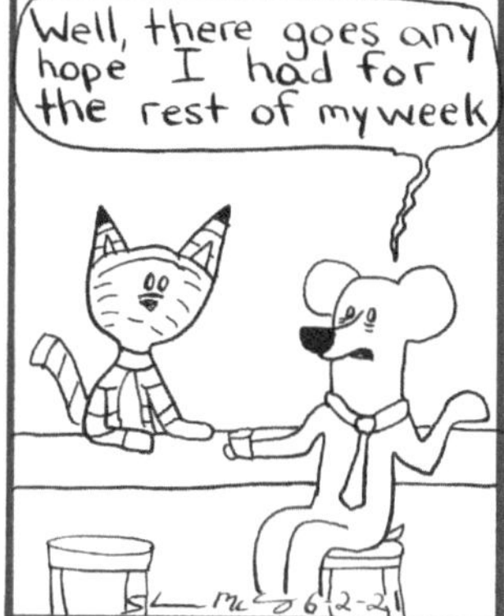
Well, there goes any hope I had for the rest of my week
SL McG 6-2-21

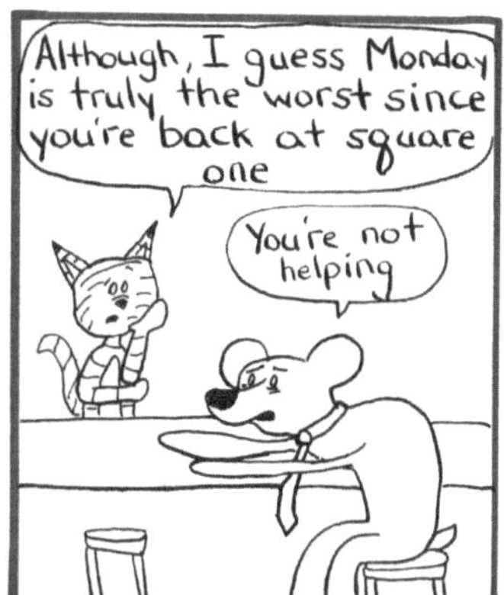
Although, I guess Monday is truly the worst since you're back at square one
You're not helping

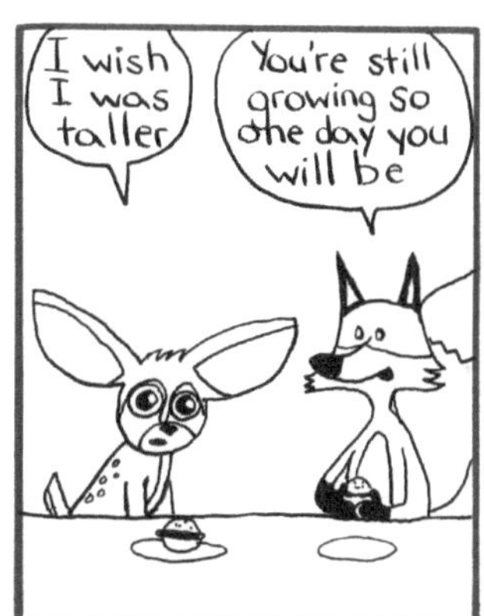
I wish I was taller
You're still growing so one day you will be

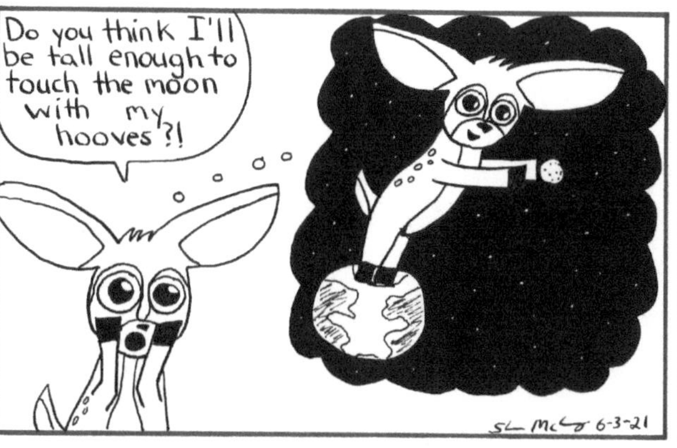
Do you think I'll be tall enough to touch the moon with my hooves?!
SL McG 6-3-21

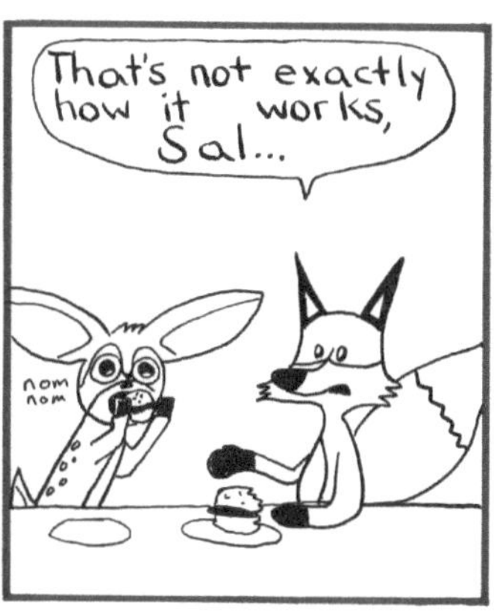
That's not exactly how it works, Sal...
nom nom

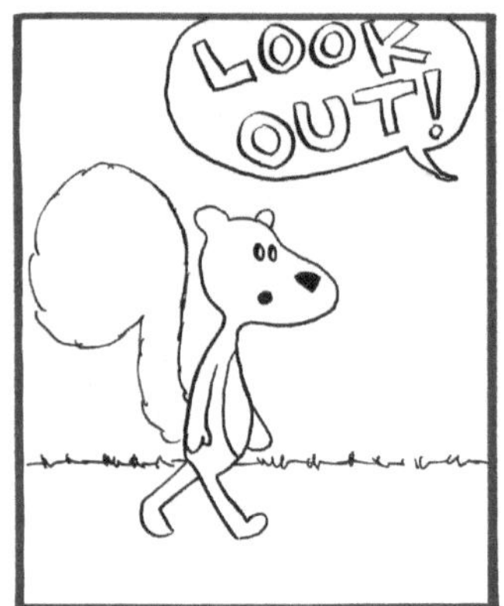
LOOK OUT!
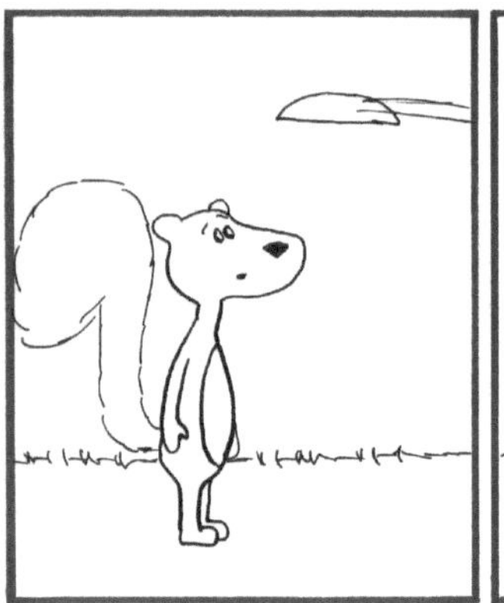
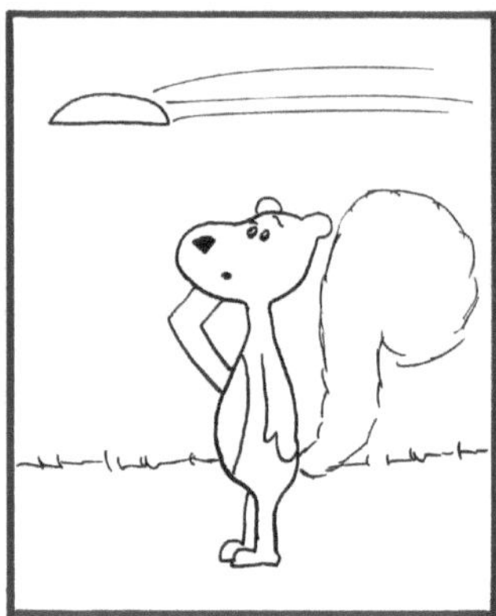
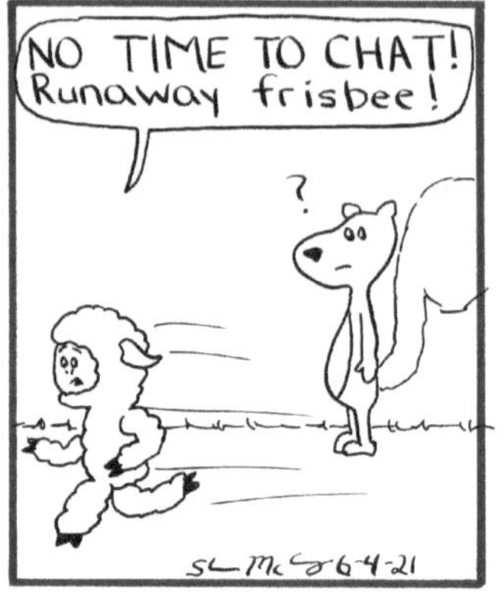
NO TIME TO CHAT! Runaway frisbee!
?
SL McG 6-4-21
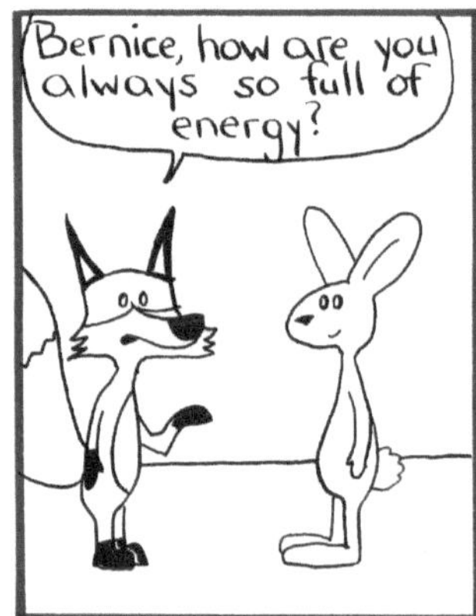
Bernice, how are you always so full of energy?
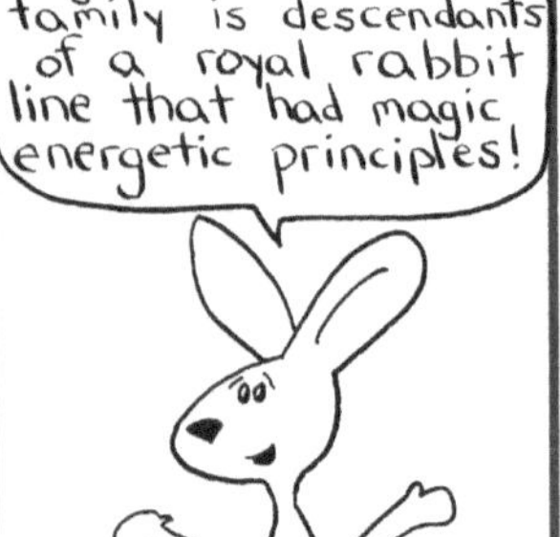
Legend has it my family is descendants of a royal rabbit line that had magic energetic principles!
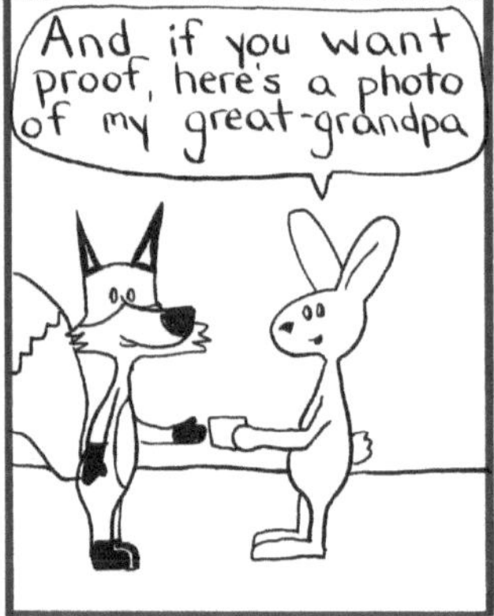
And if you want proof, here's a photo of my great-grandpa
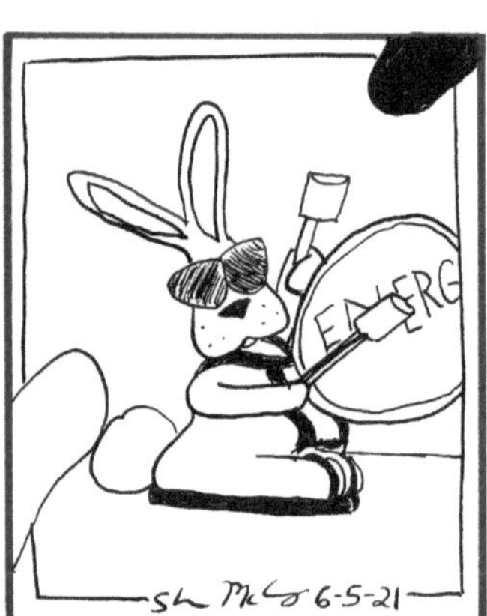
ENERG
SL McG 6-5-21

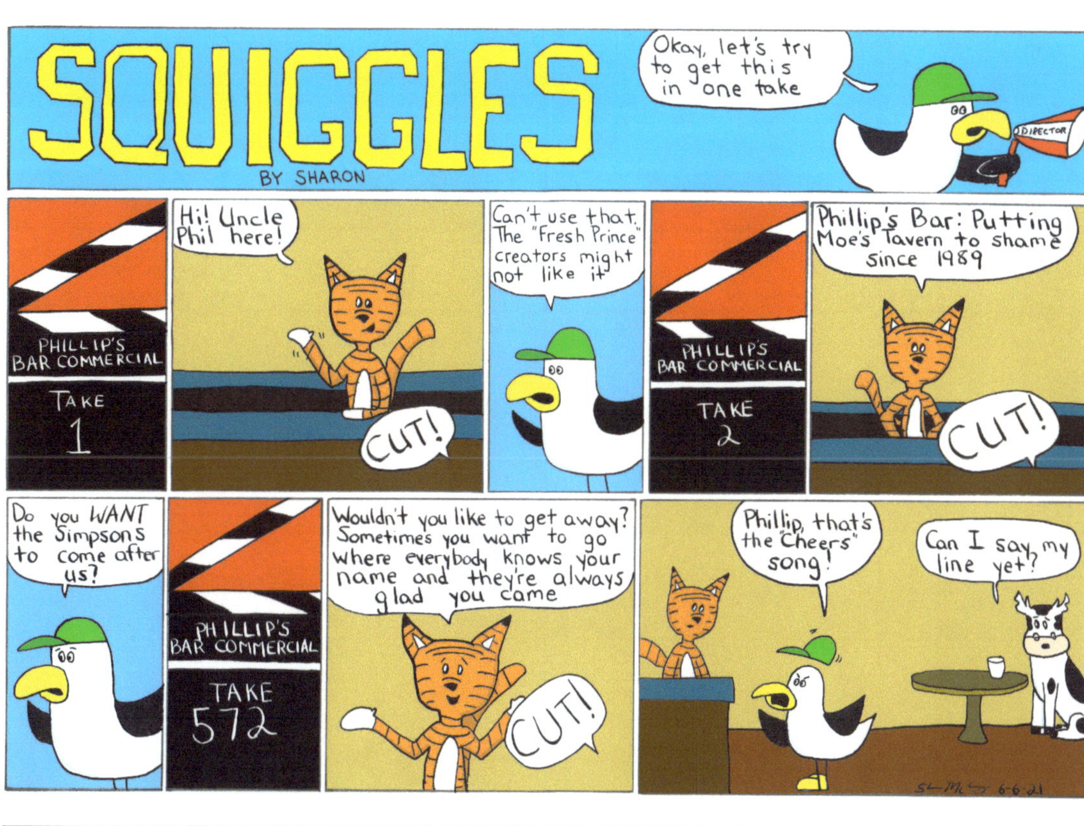
SQUIGGLES
BY SHARON
Okay, let's try to get this in one take
DIRECTOR
PHILLIP'S BAR COMMERCIAL
TAKE 1
Hi! Uncle Phil here!
CUT!
Can't use that. The "Fresh Prince" creators might not like it
PHILLIP'S BAR COMMERCIAL
TAKE 2
Phillip's Bar: Putting Moe's Tavern to shame since 1989
CUT!
Do you WANT the Simpsons to come after us?
PHILLIP'S BAR COMMERCIAL
TAKE 572
Wouldn't you like to get away? Sometimes you want to go where everybody knows your name and they're always glad you came
CUT!
Phillip, that's the "Cheers" song!
Can I say my line yet?
SLM 6-6-21

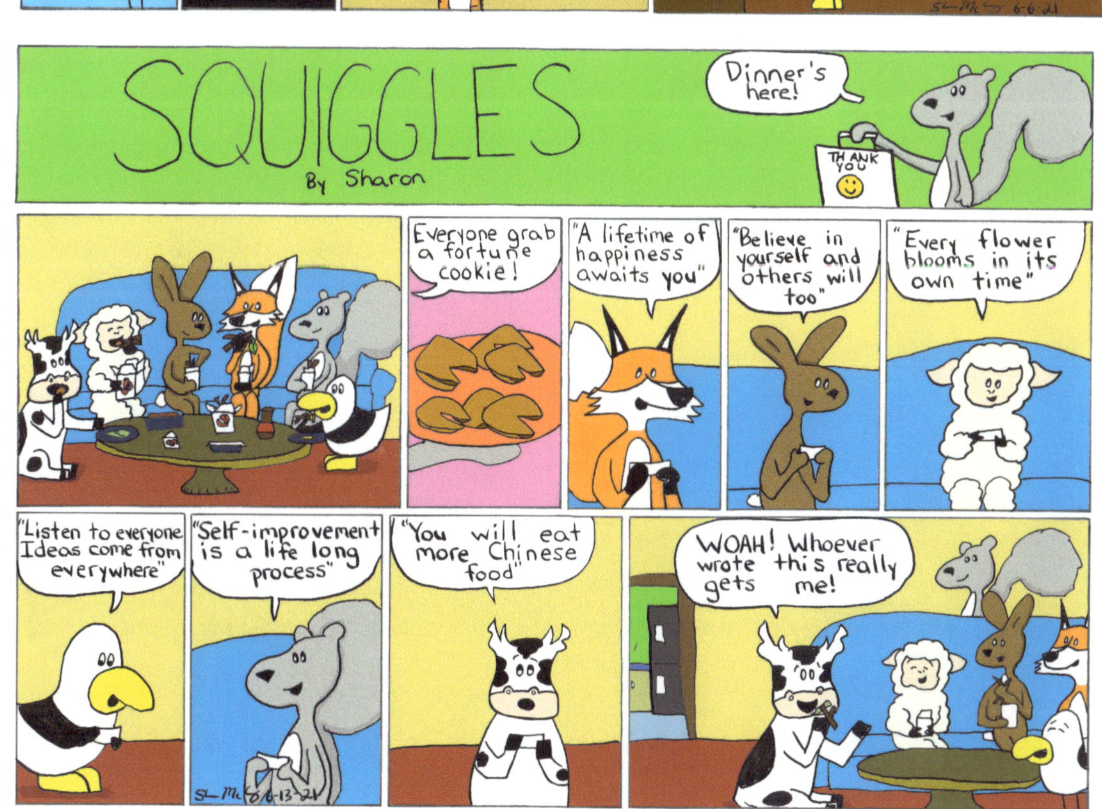
SQUIGGLES
By Sharon
Dinner's here!
THANK YOU
Everyone grab a fortune cookie!
"A lifetime of happiness awaits you"
"Believe in yourself and others will too"
"Every flower blooms in its own time"
"Listen to everyone Ideas come from everywhere"
"Self-improvement is a life long process"
"You will eat more Chinese food"
WOAH! Whoever wrote this really gets me!
SLM 6-13-21

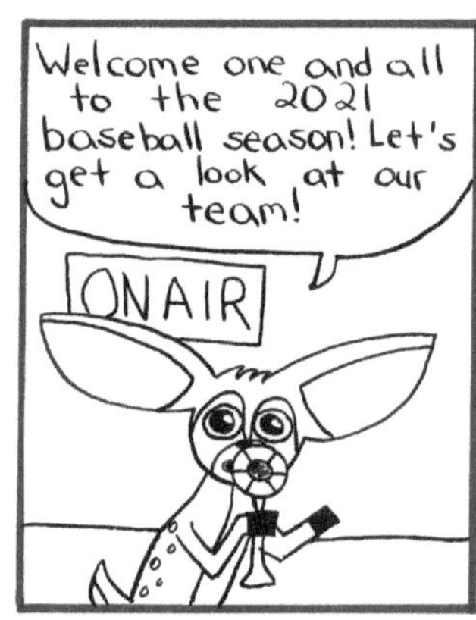
Welcome one and all to the 2021 baseball season! Let's get a look at our team!
ONAIR

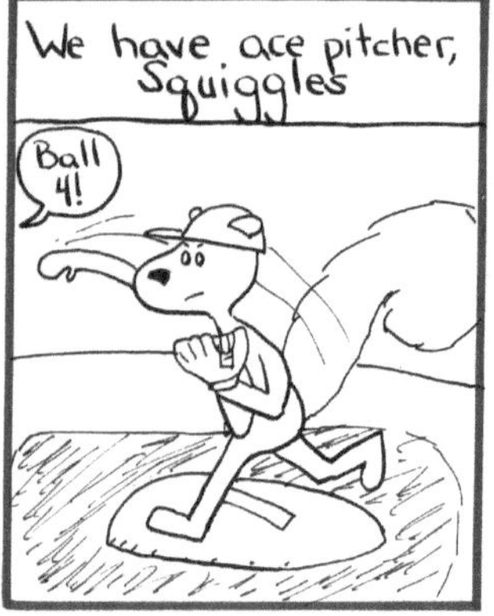
We have ace pitcher, Squiggles
Ball 4!

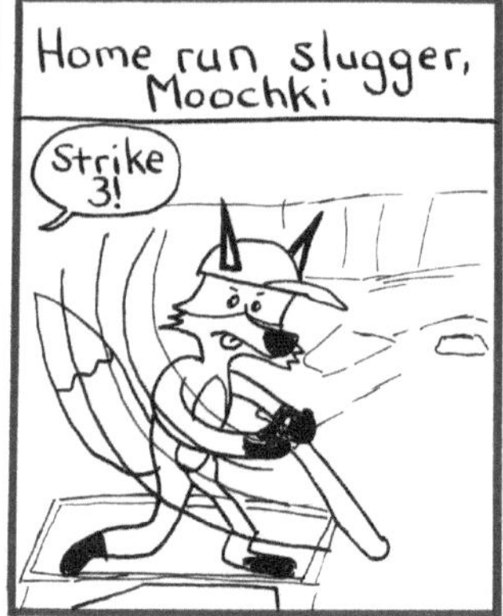
Home run slugger, Moochki
Strike 3!

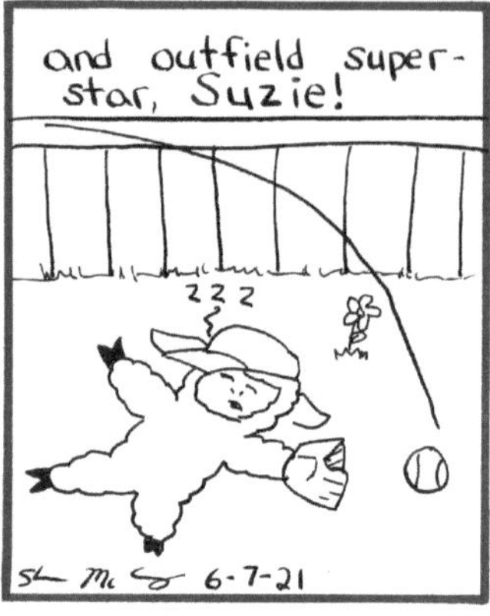
and outfield super-star, Suzie!
zzz
SL Mc 6-7-21

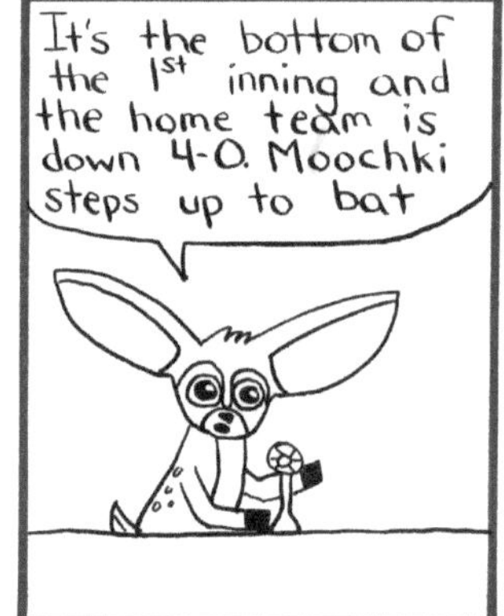
It's the bottom of the 1st inning and the home team is down 4-0. Moochki steps up to bat

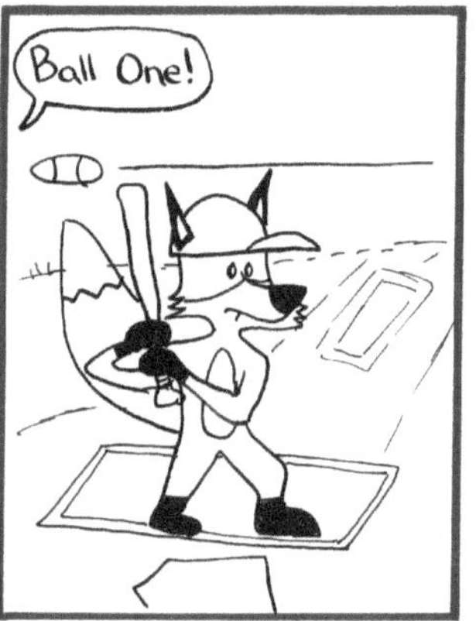
Ball One!

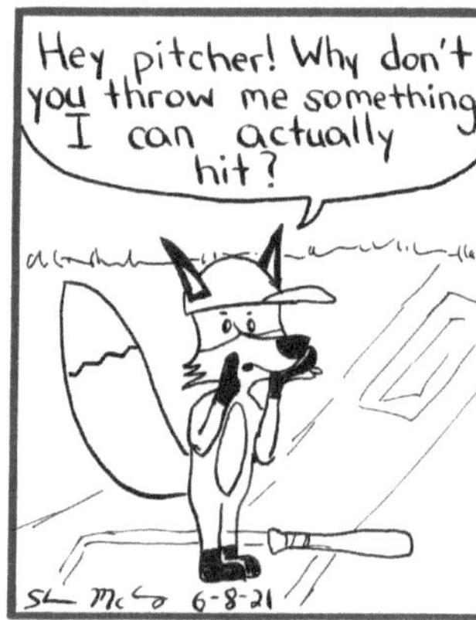
Hey pitcher! Why don't you throw me something I can actually hit?
SL Mc 6-8-21

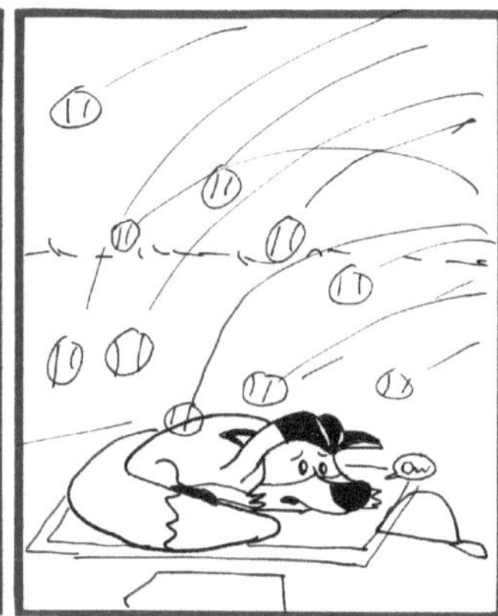

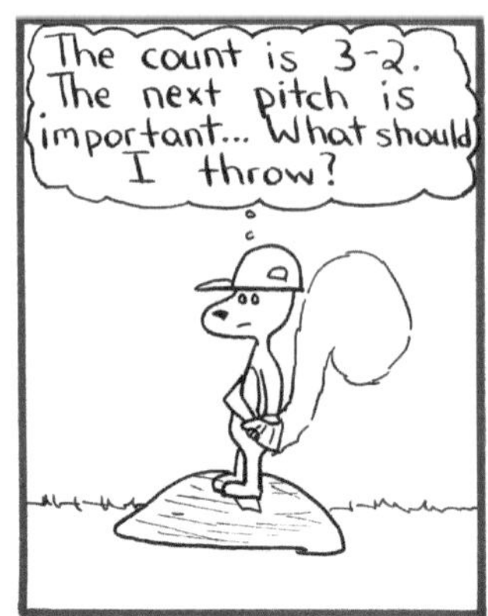
The count is 3-2. The next pitch is important... What should I throw?

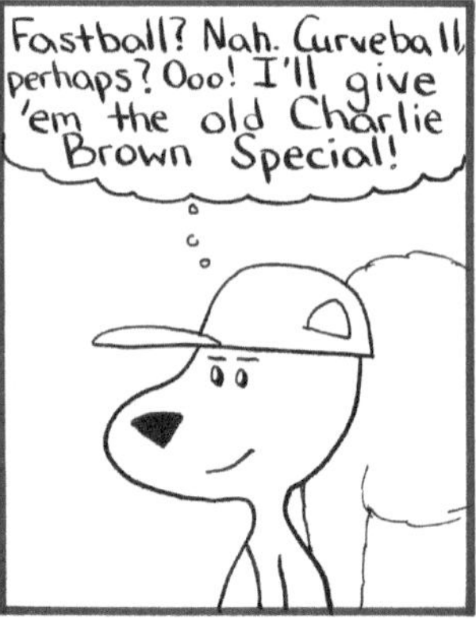
Fastball? Nah. Curveball perhaps? Ooo! I'll give 'em the old Charlie Brown Special!

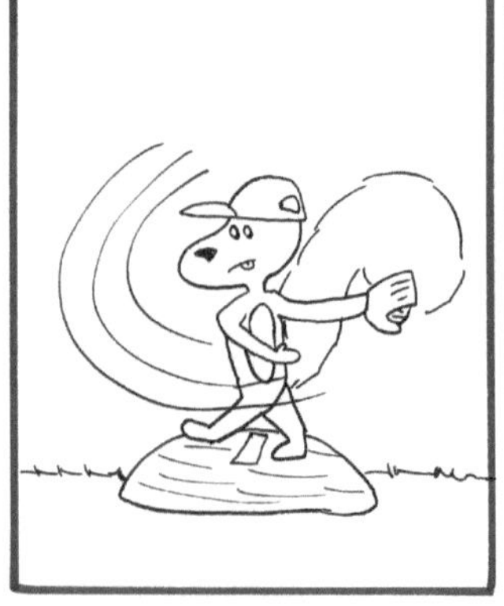

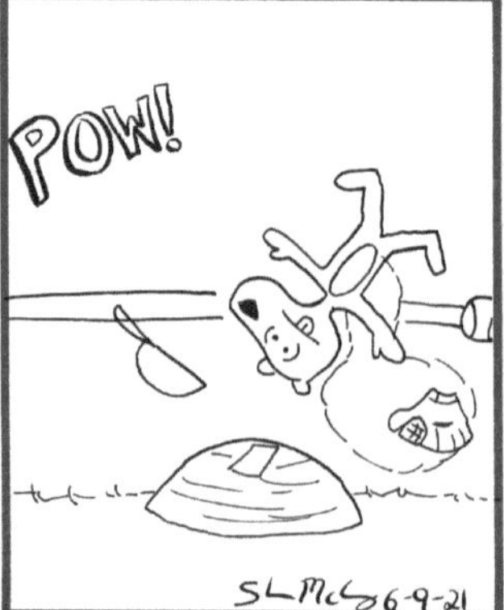
POW!
SLMc 6-9-21

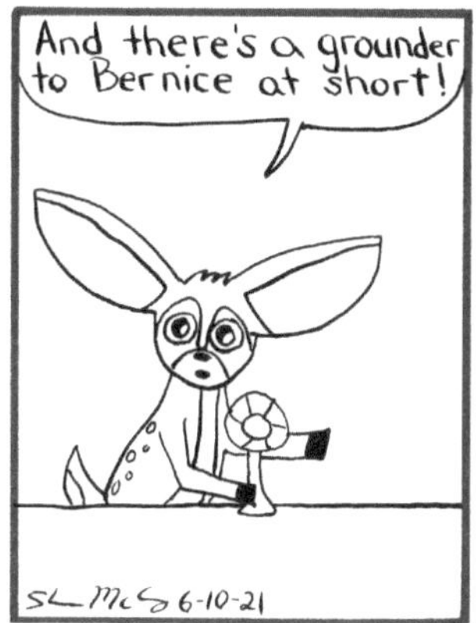
And there's a grounder to Bernice at short!
SL McG 6-10-21
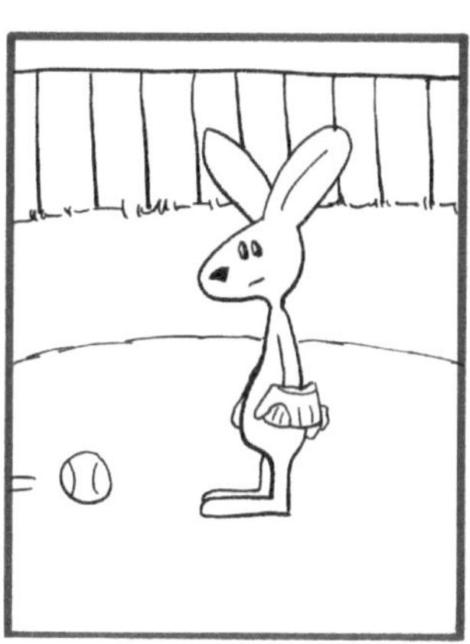
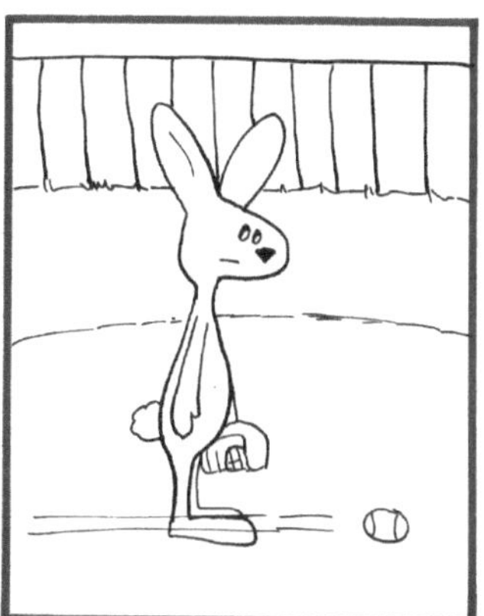
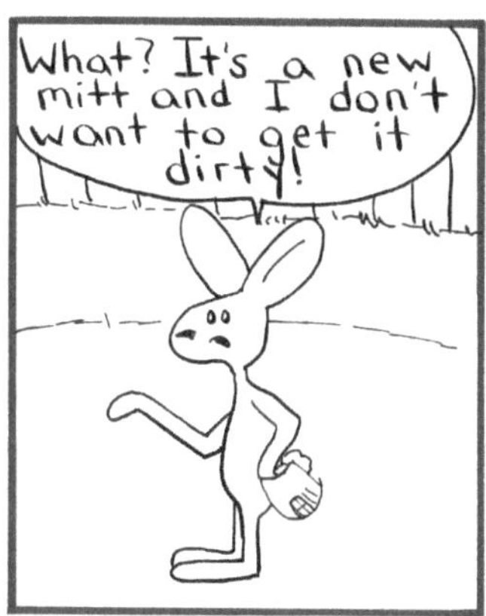
What? It's a new mitt and I don't want to get it dirty!
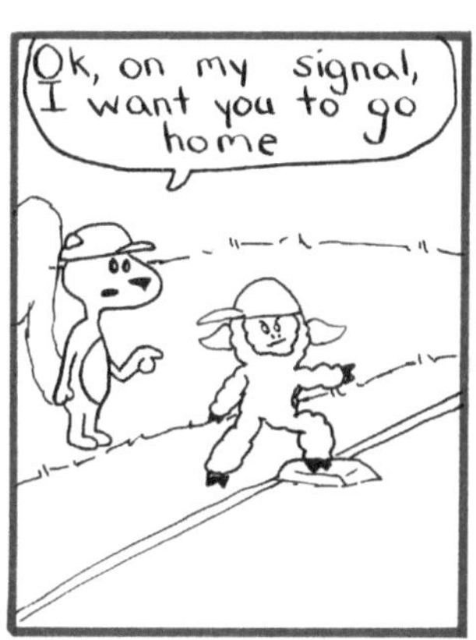
Ok, on my signal, I want you to go home
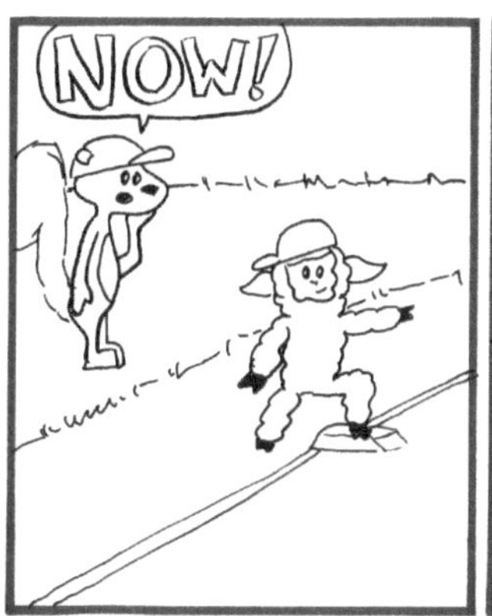
NOW!
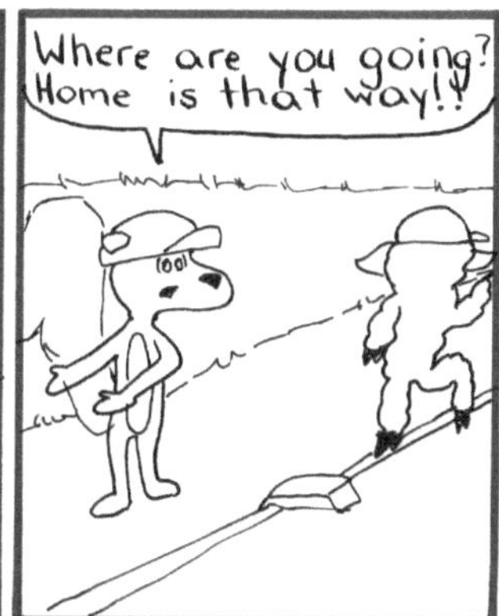
Where are you going? Home is that way!!
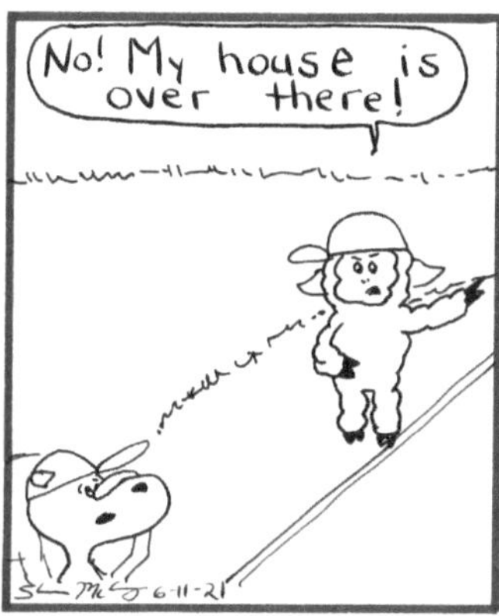
No! My house is over there!
SL McG 6-11-21
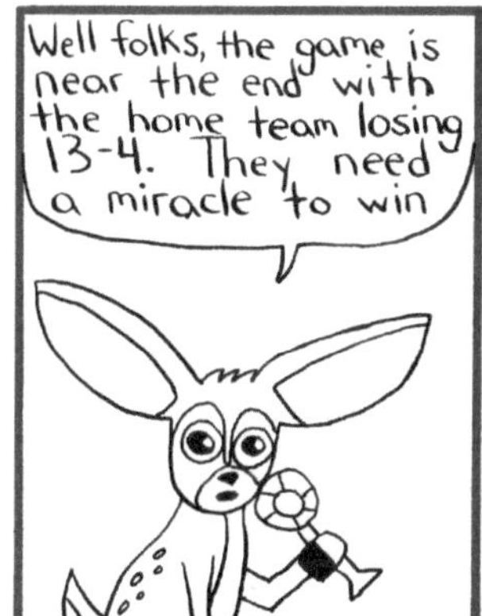
Well folks, the game is near the end with the home team losing 13-4. They need a miracle to win
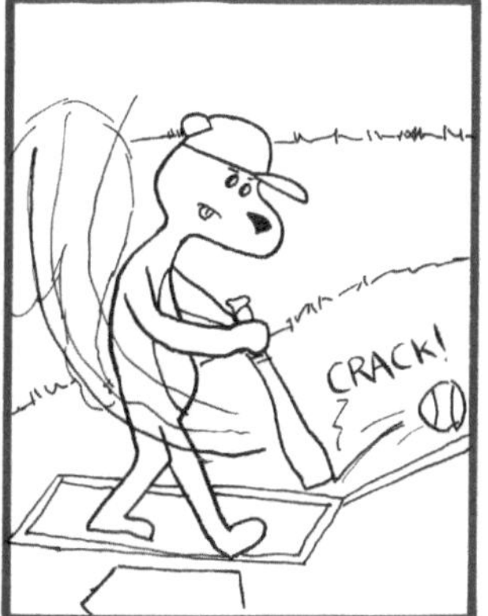
CRACK!
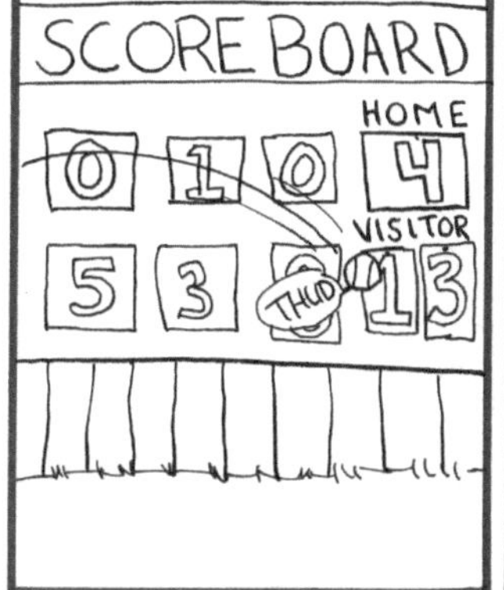
SCORE BOARD
HOME
0 1 0 4
VISITOR
5 3 0 13
THUD
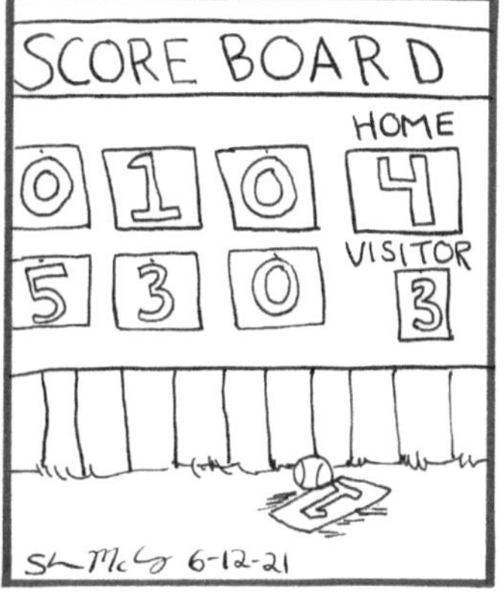
SCORE BOARD
HOME
0 1 0 4
VISITOR
5 3 0 3
SL McG 6-12-21

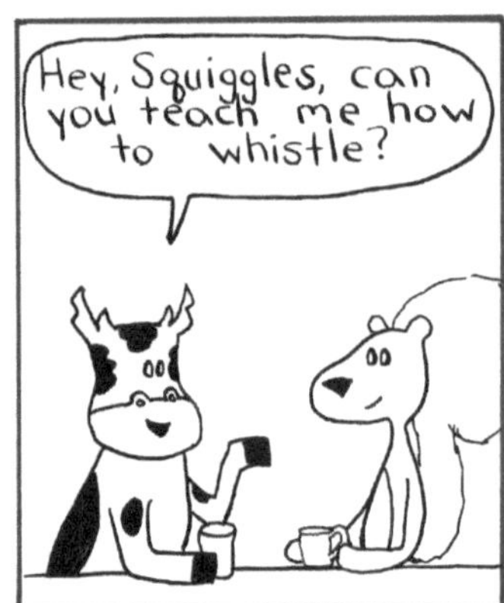
Hey, Squiggles, can you teach me how to whistle?

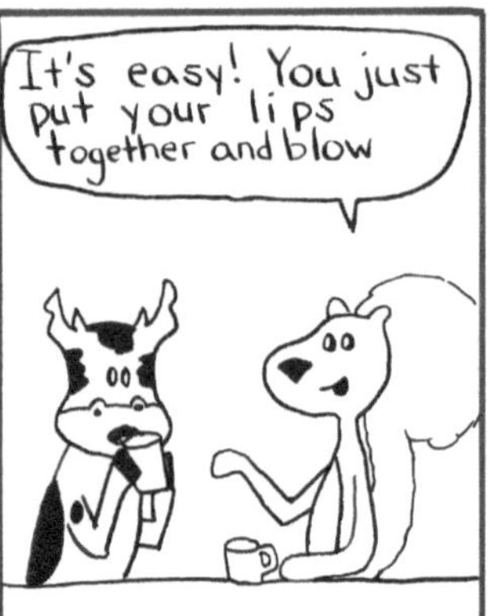
It's easy! You just put your lips together and blow

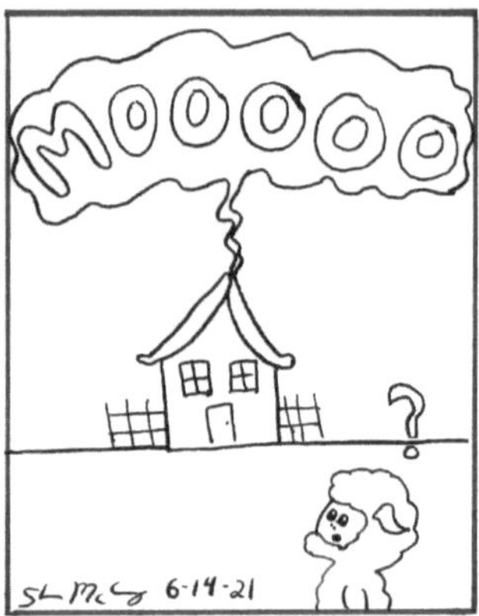
MOOOOO
?
SL McG 6-14-21

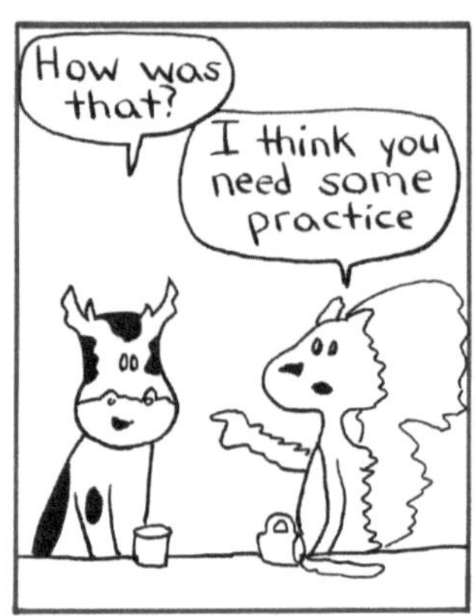
How was that?
I think you need some practice

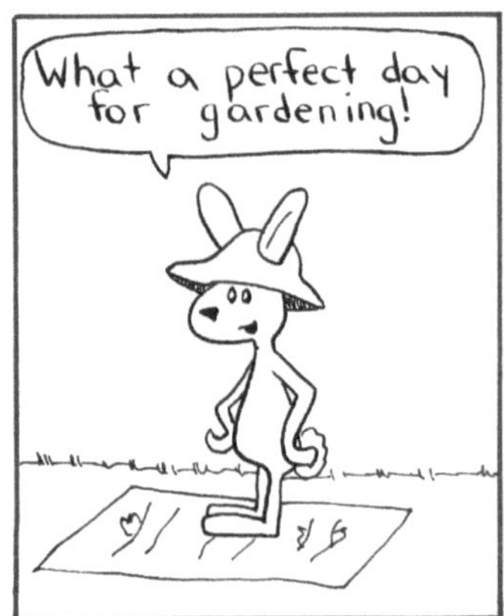
What a perfect day for gardening!

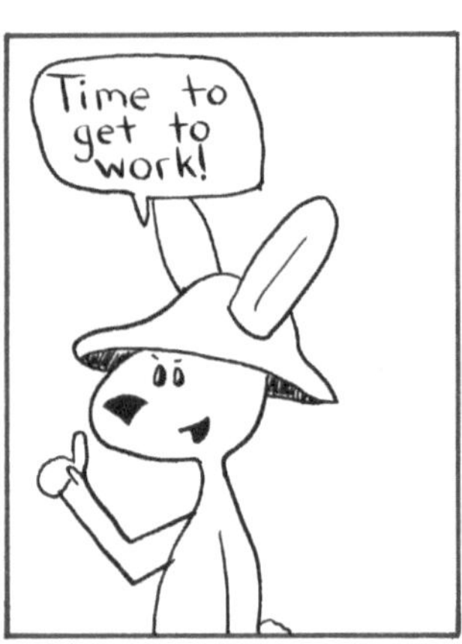
Time to get to work!

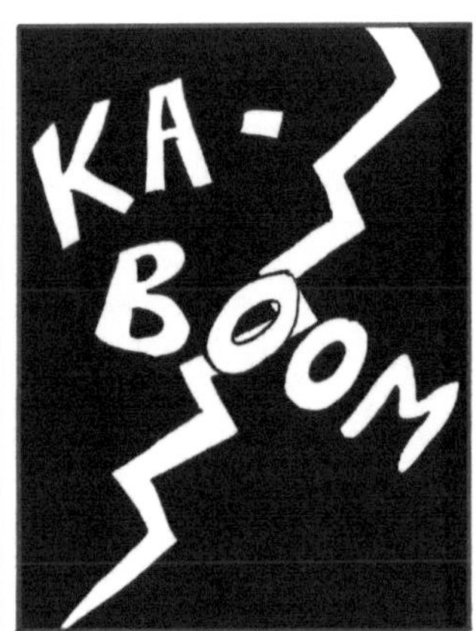
KA-BOOM

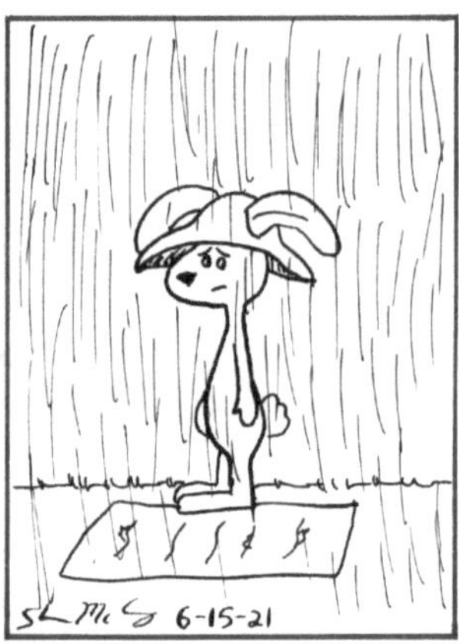
SL McG 6-15-21

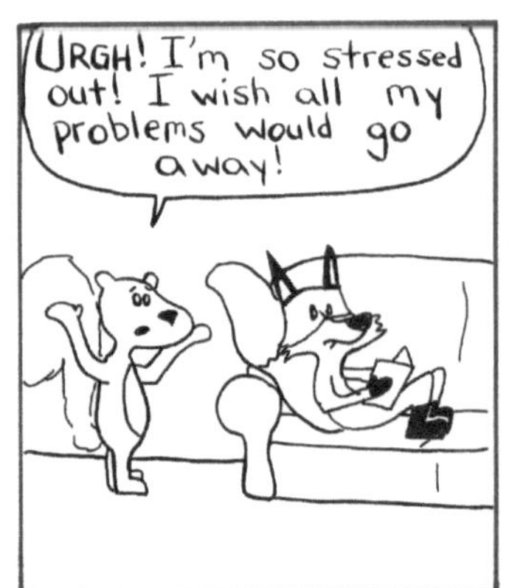
URGH! I'm so stressed out! I wish all my problems would go away!

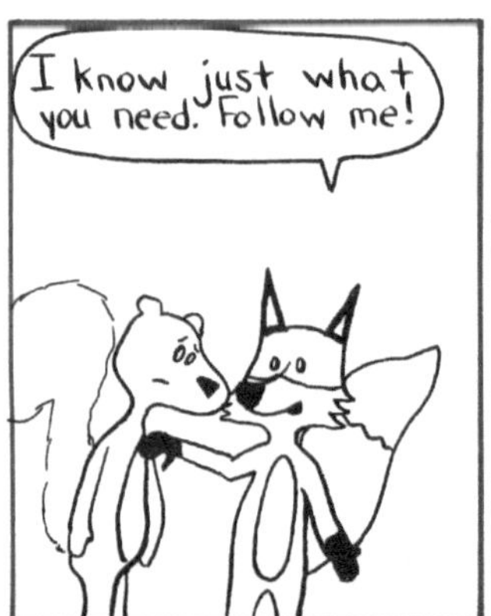
I know just what you need. Follow me!

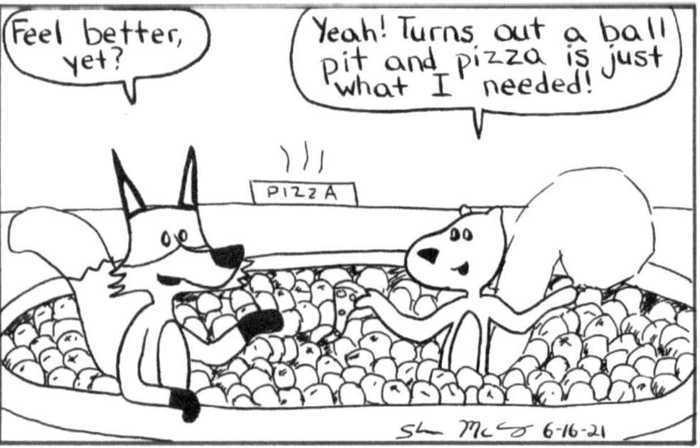
Feel better, yet?
Yeah! Turns out a ball pit and pizza is just what I needed!
PIZZA
SL McG 6-16-21

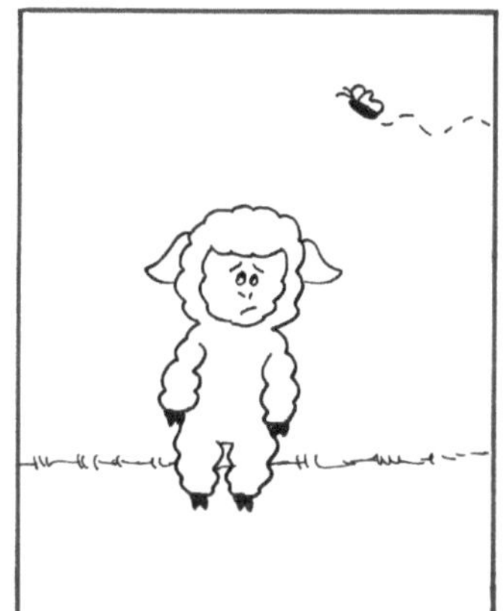

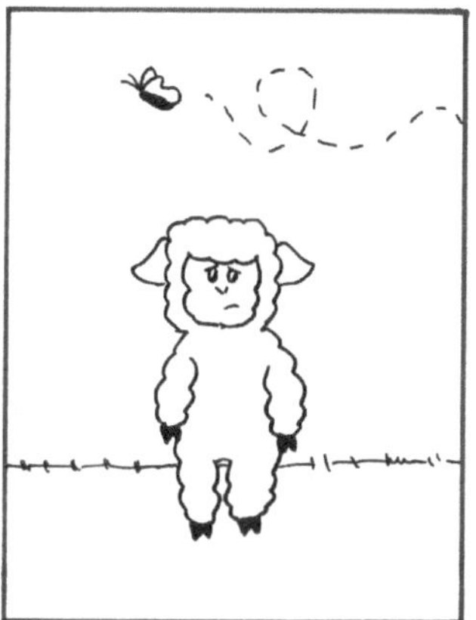

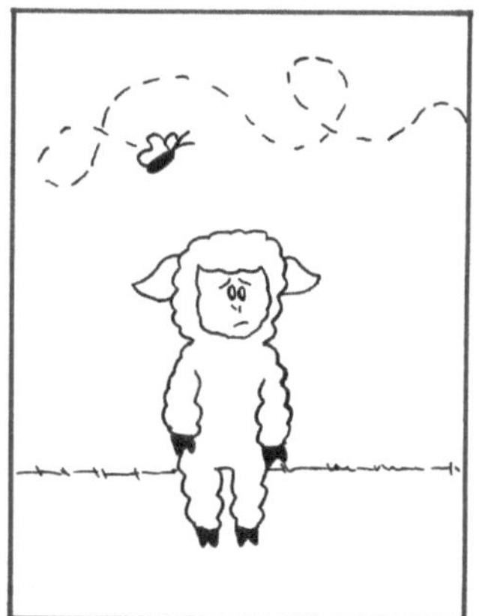

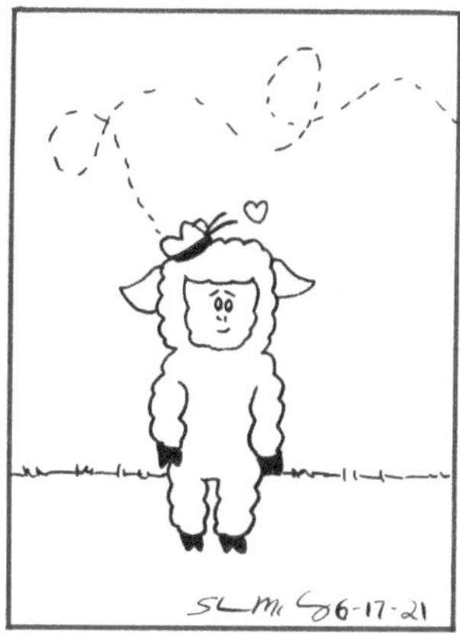
SL McS 6-17-21

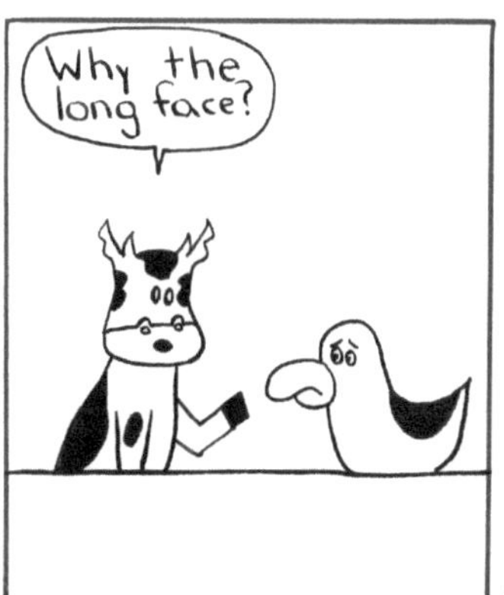
Why the long face?

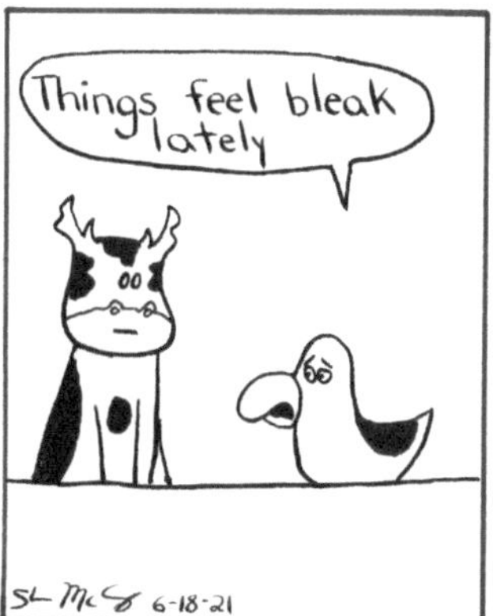
Things feel bleak lately
SL McS 6-18-21

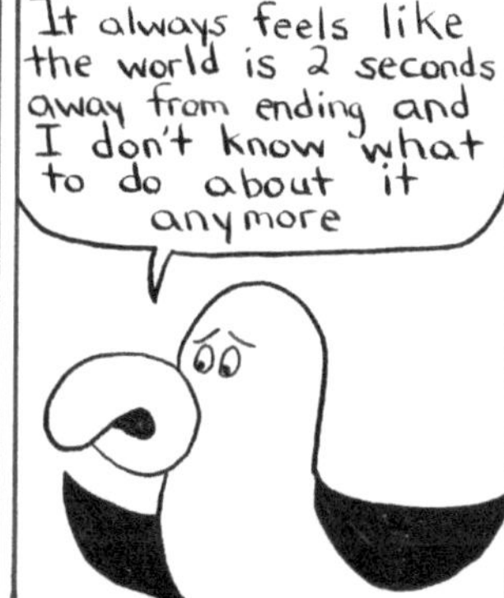
It always feels like the world is 2 seconds away from ending and I don't know what to do about it anymore

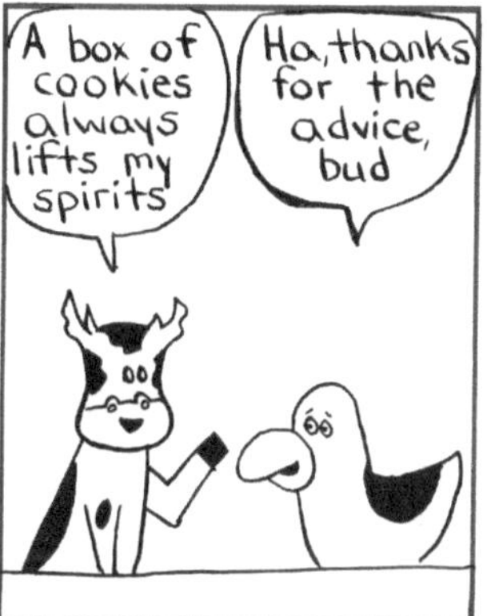
A box of cookies always lifts my spirits
Ha, thanks for the advice, bud

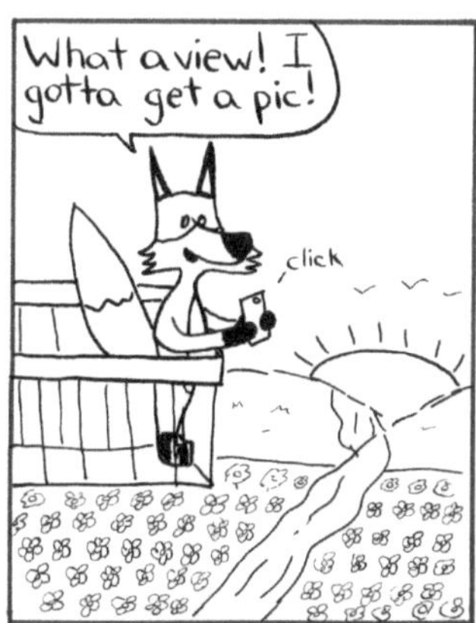
What a view! I gotta get a pic!
click

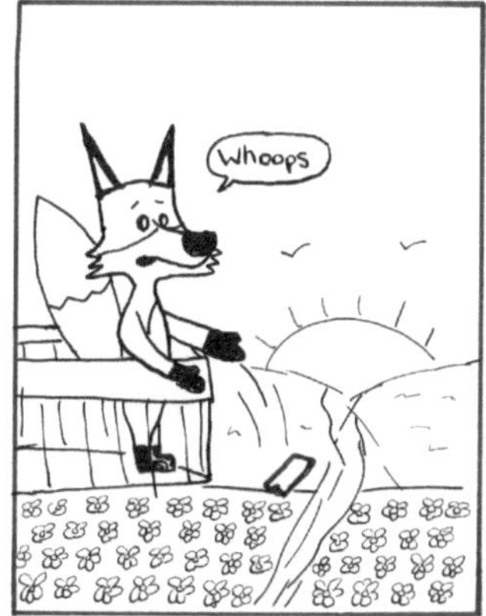
Whoops

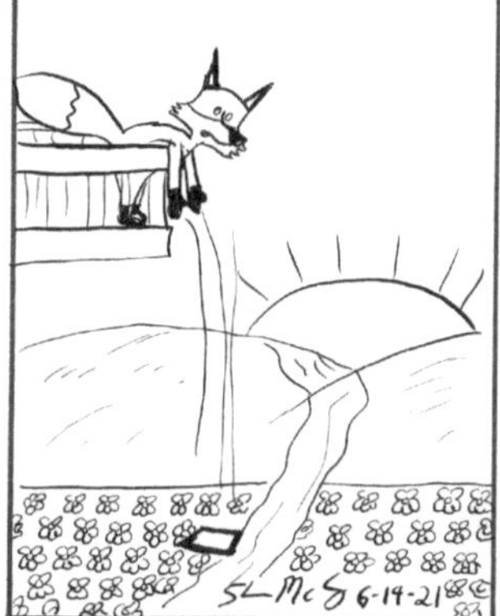
SL McS 6-19-21

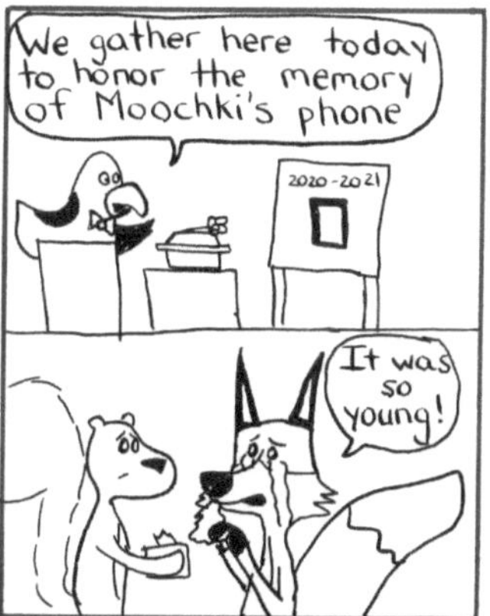
We gather here today to honor the memory of Moochki's phone
2020-2021
It was so young!

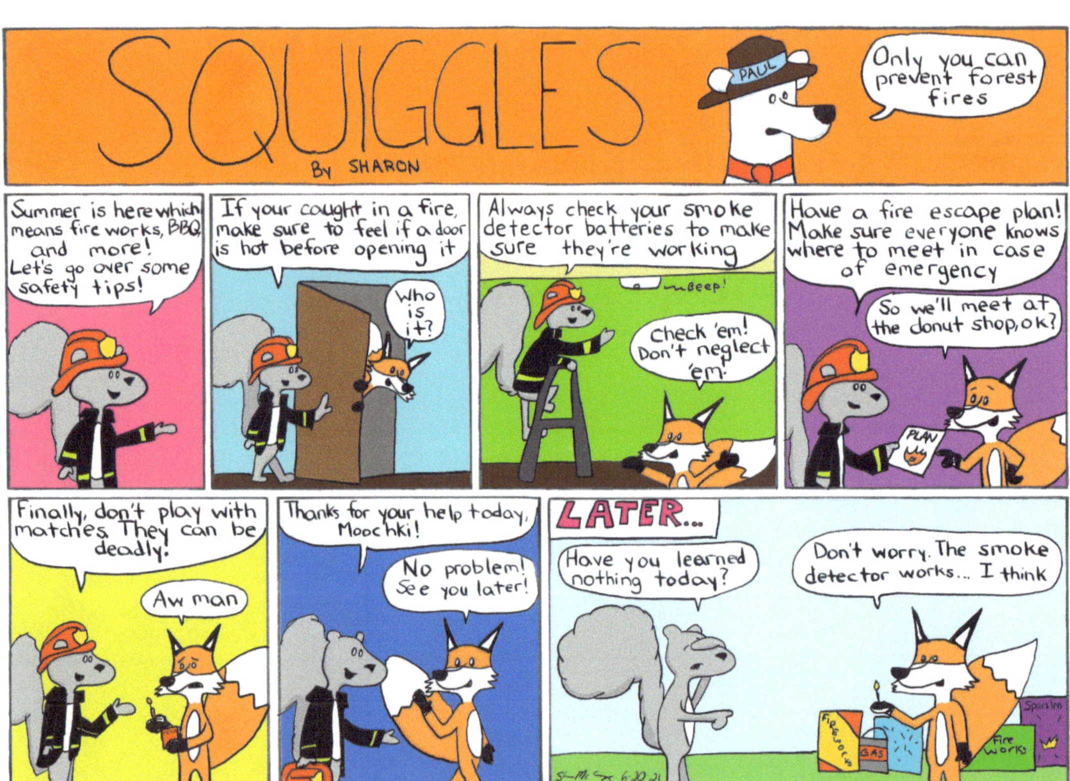
SQUIGGLES
By SHARON
PAUL
Only you can prevent forest fires
Summer is here which means fire works, BBQ, and more! Let's go over some safety tips!
If your cought in a fire, make sure to feel if a door is hot before opening it
Who is it?
Always check your smoke detector batteries to make sure they're working
Beep!
Check 'em! Don't neglect 'em.
Have a fire escape plan! Make sure everyone knows where to meet in case of emergency
So we'll meet at the donut shop, ok?
PLAN
Finally, don't play with matches. They can be deadly!
Aw man
Thanks for your help today, Moochki!
No problem! See you later!
LATER...
Have you learned nothing today?
Don't worry. The smoke detector works... I think
Fireworks
GAS
Sparklers
Fire works
6-20-21

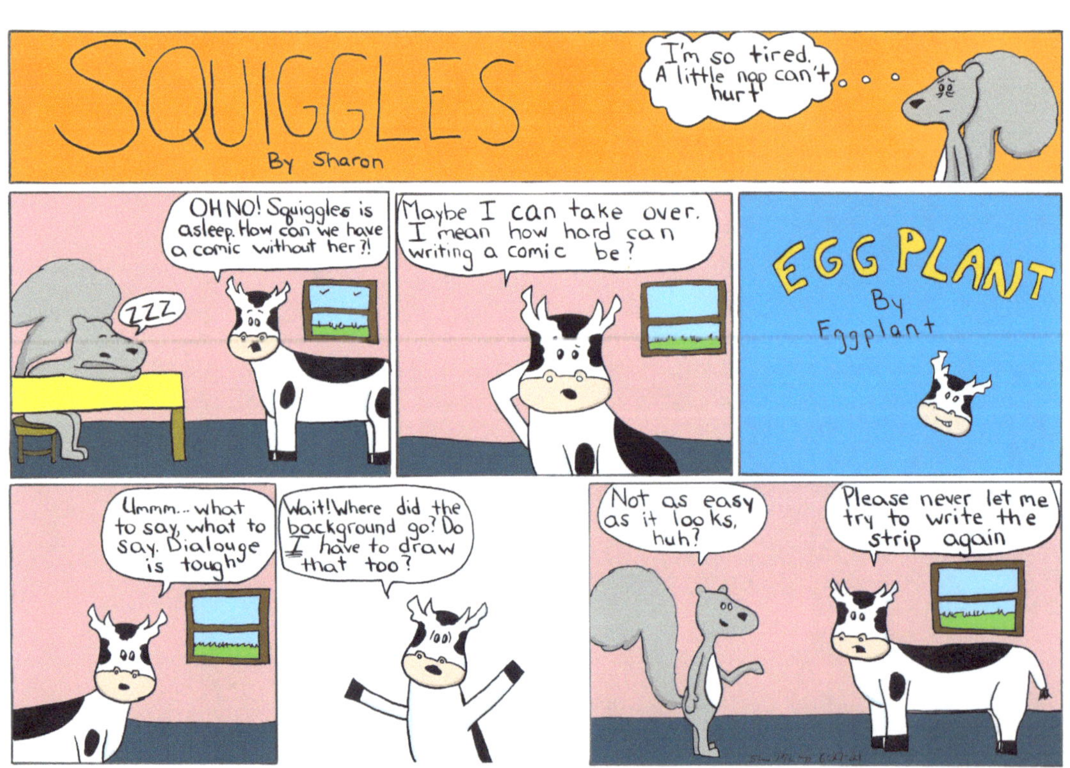
SQUIGGLES
By Sharon
I'm so tired. A little nap can't hurt
OH NO! Squiggles is asleep. How can we have a comic without her?!
ZZZ
Maybe I can take over. I mean how hard can writing a comic be?
EGG PLANT
By
Eggplant
Ummm... what to say, what to say. Dialouge is tough
Wait! Where did the background go? Do I have to draw that too?
Not as easy as it looks, huh?
Please never let me try to write the strip again

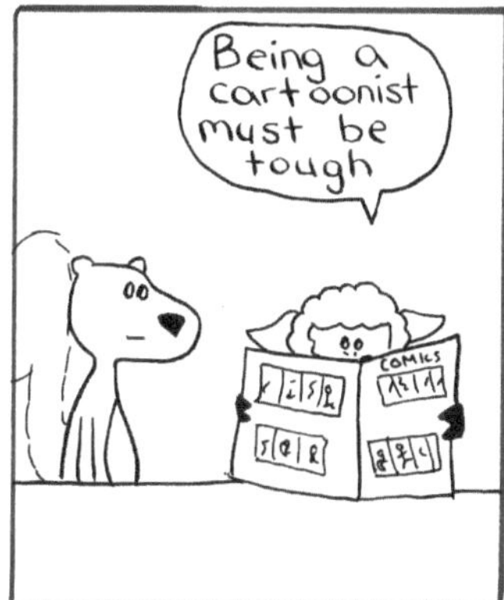
Being a cartoonist must be tough
COMICS
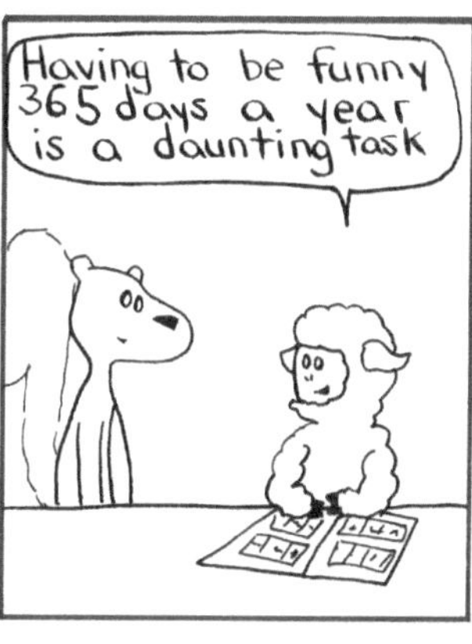
Having to be funny 365 days a year is a daunting task
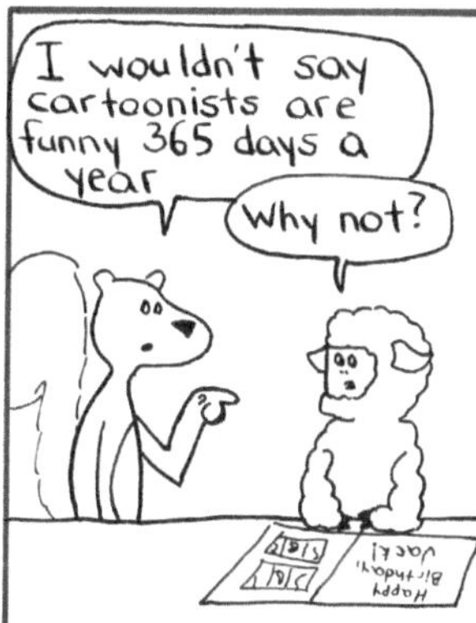
I wouldn't say cartoonists are funny 365 days a year
Why not?
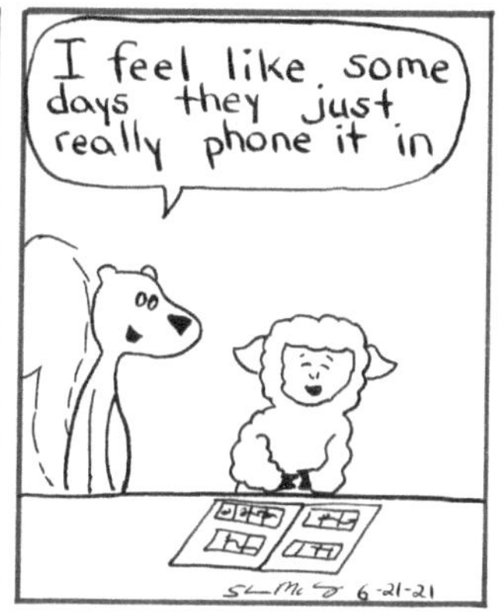
I feel like some days they just really phone it in
6-21-21
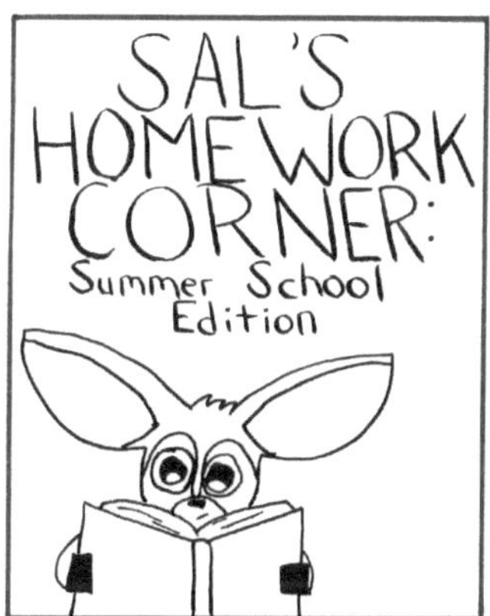
SAL'S HOMEWORK CORNER:
Summer School Edition
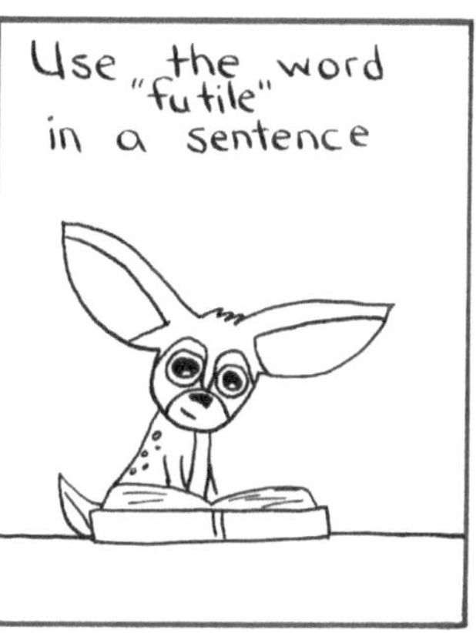
Use the word "futile" in a sentence
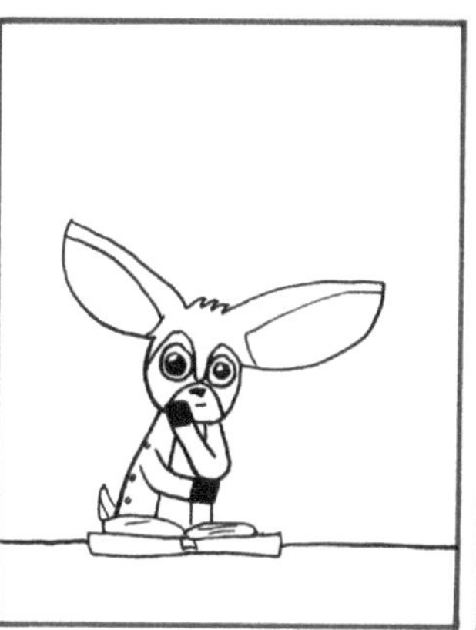
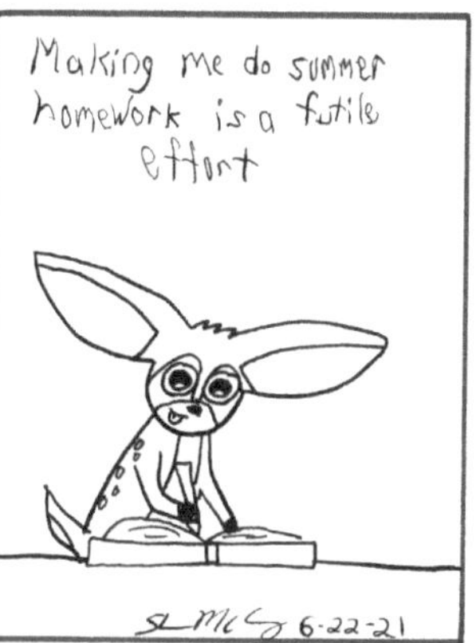
Making me do summer homework is a futile effort
6-22-21
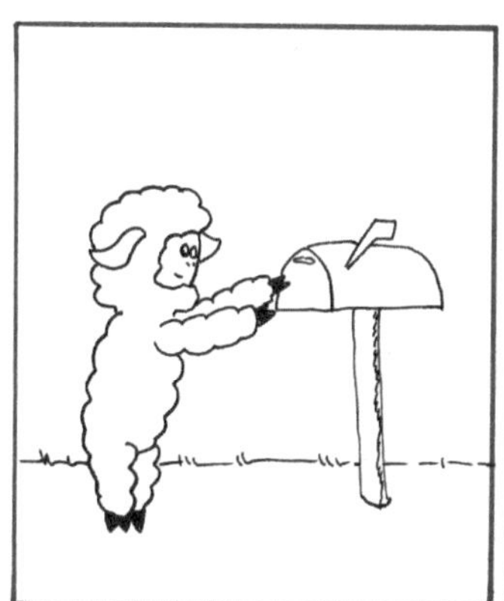
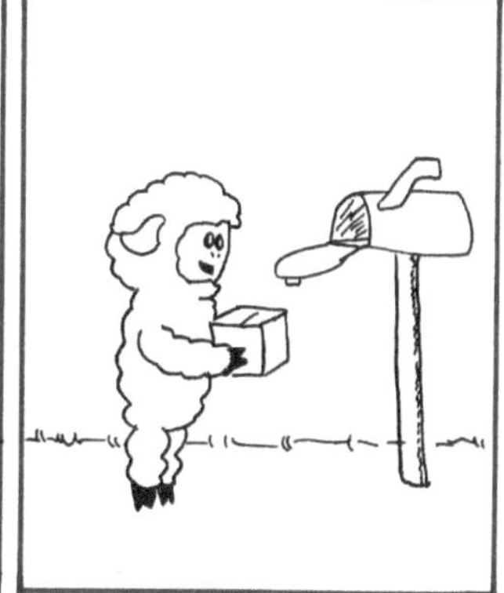
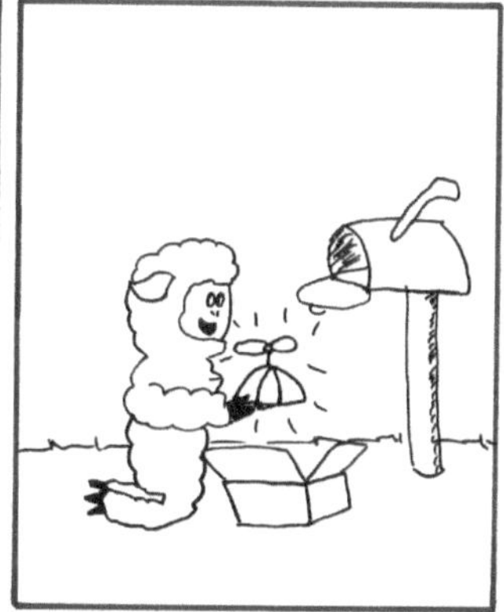
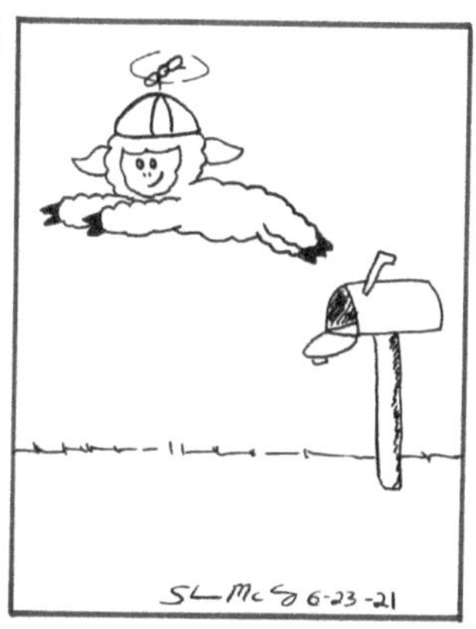
6-23-21

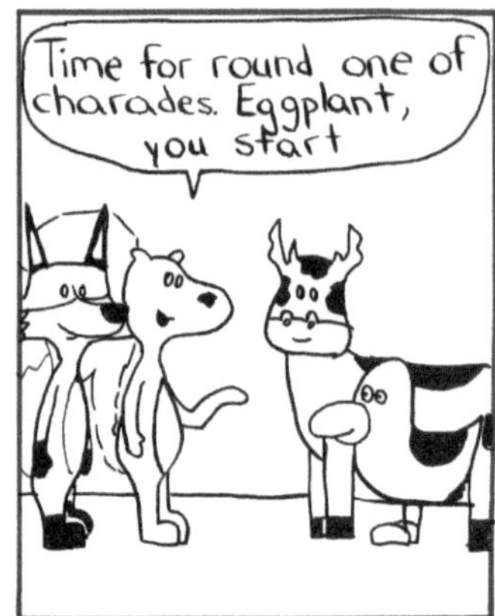
Time for round one of charades. Eggplant, you start

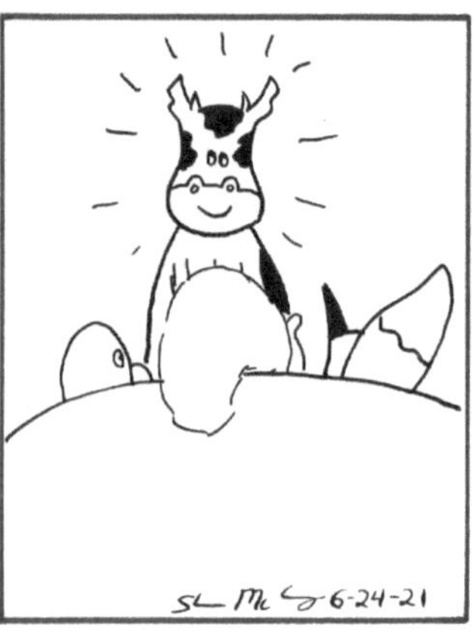
SL McG 6-24-21

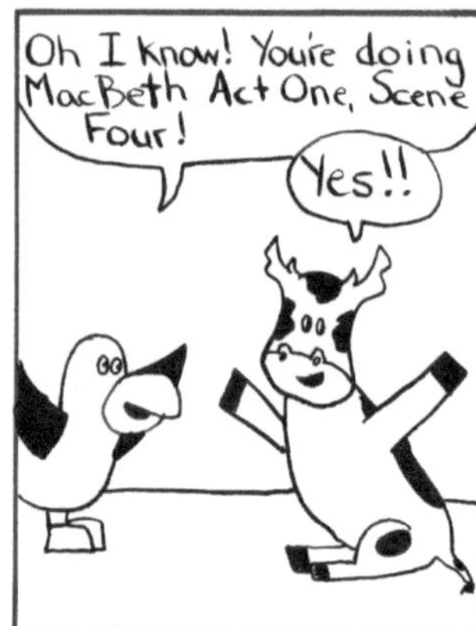
Oh I know! You're doing MacBeth Act One, Scene Four!
Yes!!

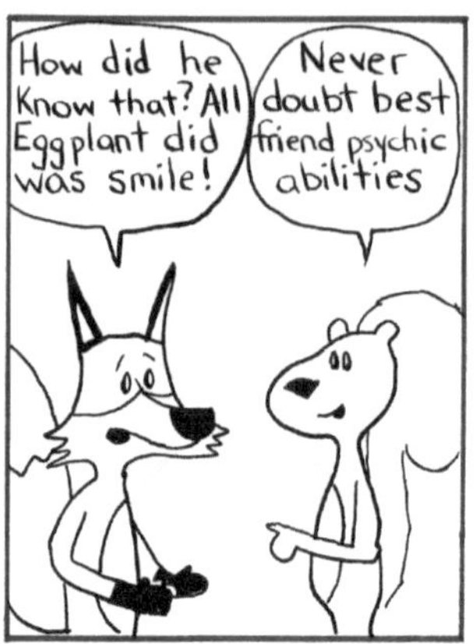
How did he know that? All Eggplant did was smile!
Never doubt best friend psychic abilities

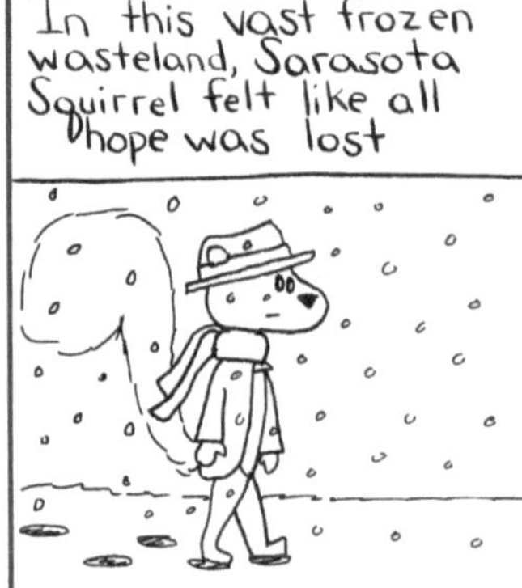
In this vast frozen wasteland, Sarasota Squirrel felt like all hope was lost

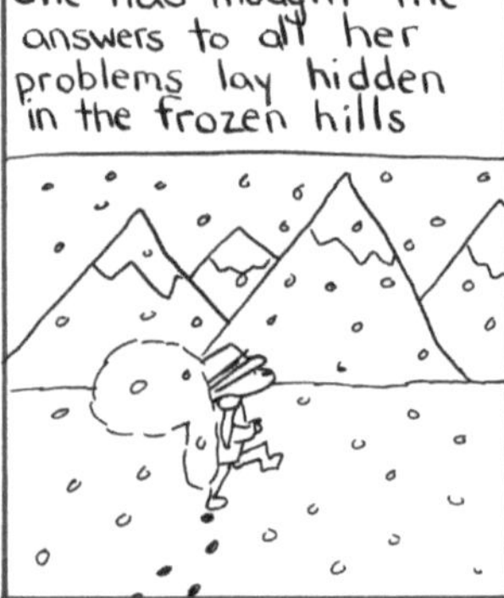
She had thought the answers to all her problems lay hidden in the frozen hills

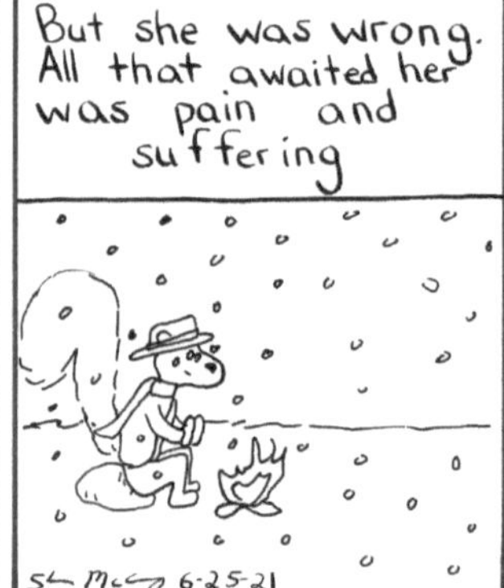
But she was wrong. All that awaited her was pain and suffering
SL McG 6-25-21

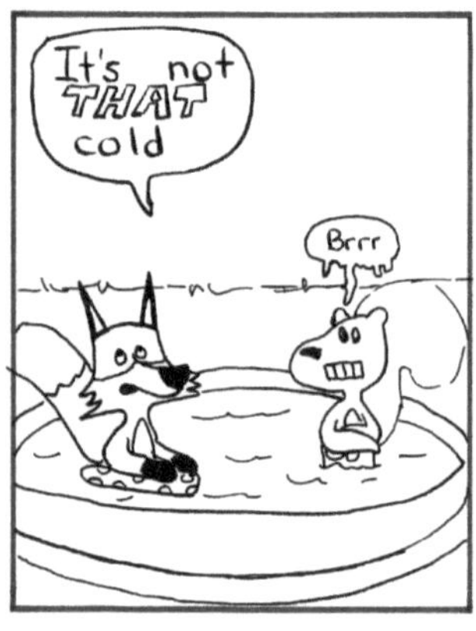
It's not THAT cold
Brrr

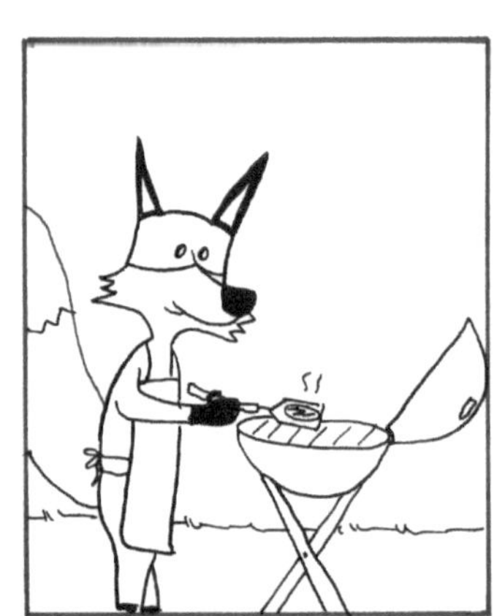

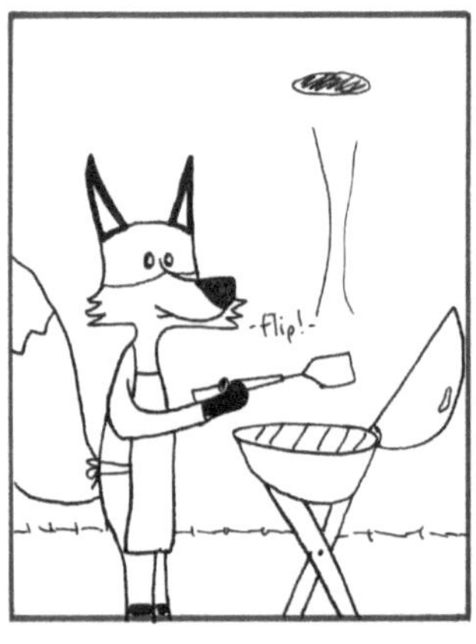
-Flip!-

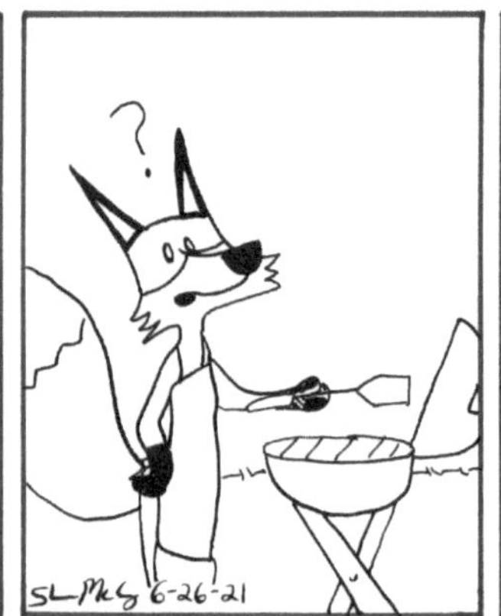
?
SL McG 6-26-21

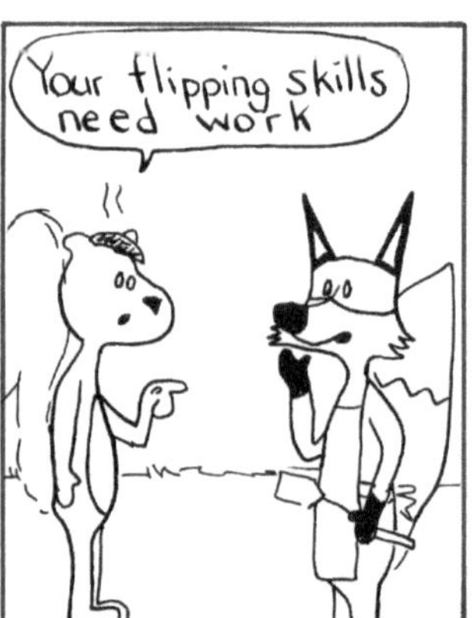
Your flipping skills need work

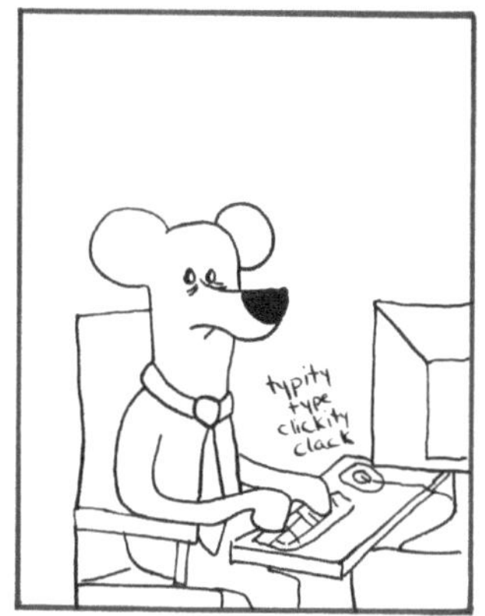
typity type clickity clack

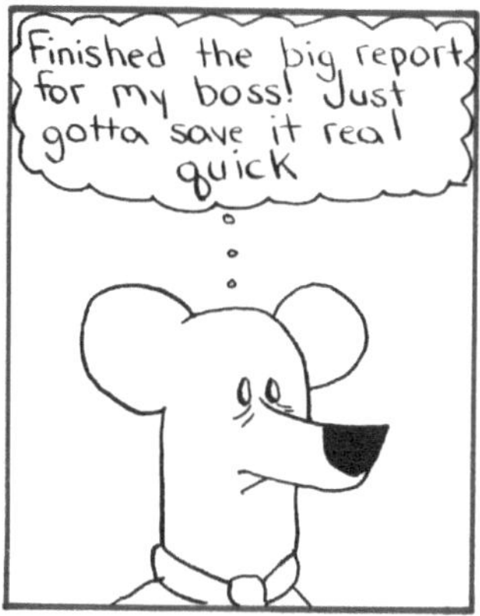
Finished the big report for my boss! Just gotta save it real quick

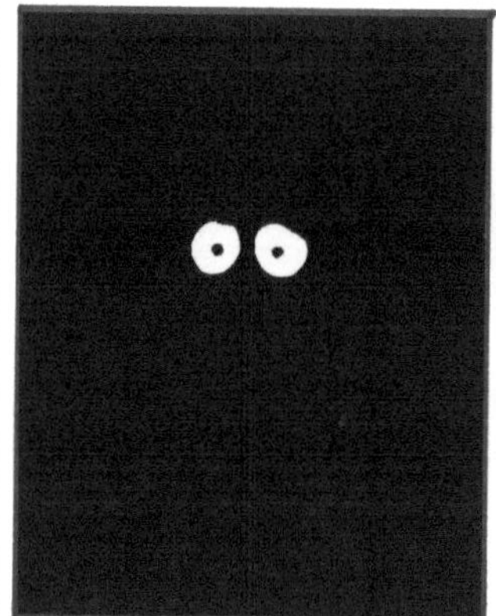

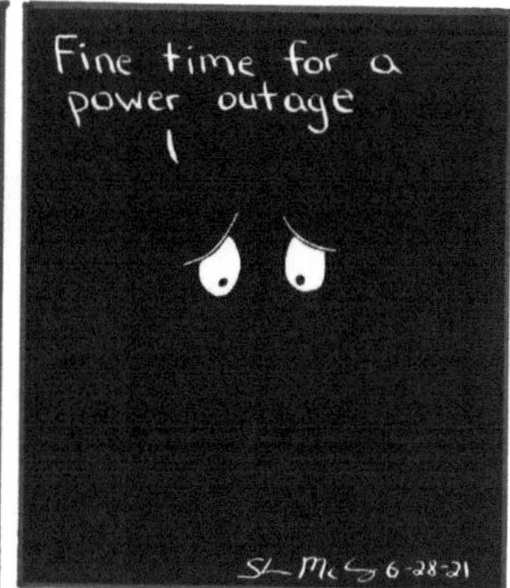
Fine time for a power outage
6-28-21

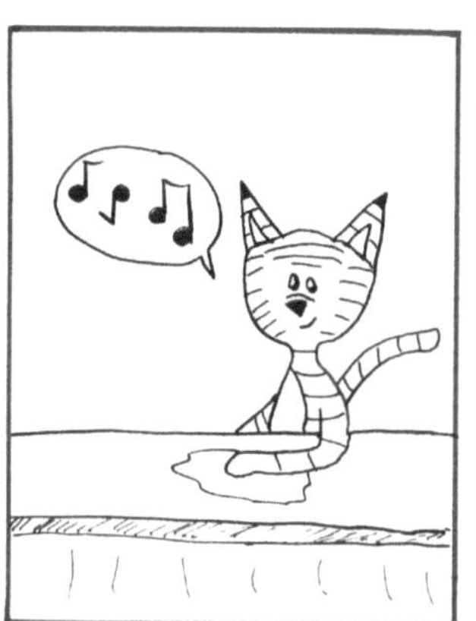

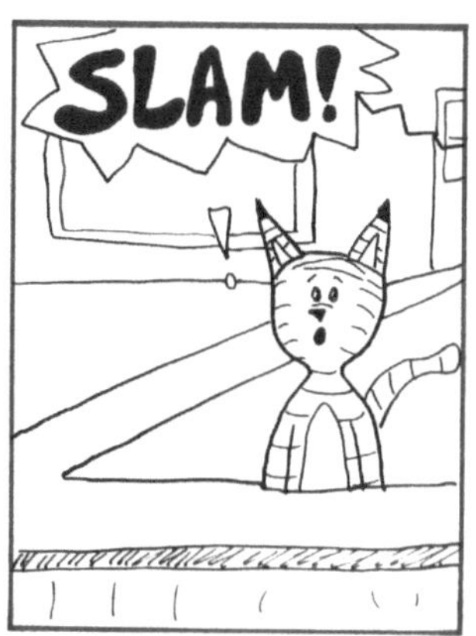
SLAM!

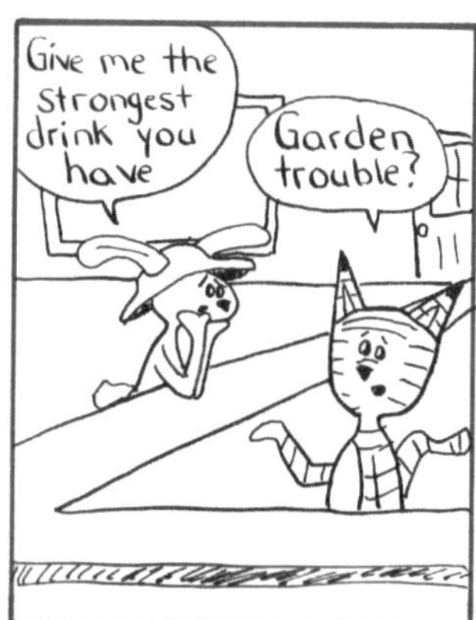
Give me the strongest drink you have
Garden trouble?

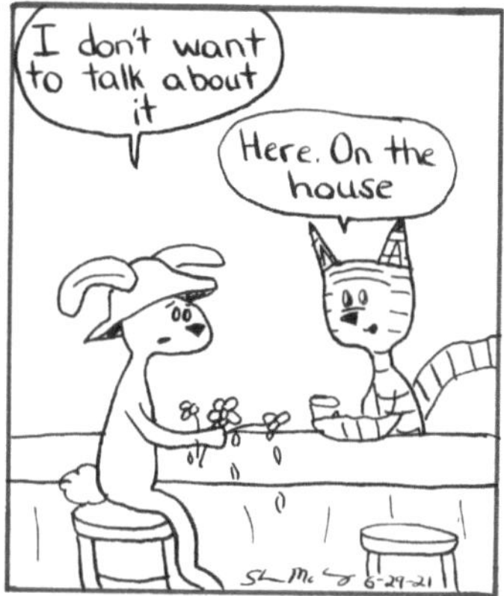
I don't want to talk about it
Here. On the house
6-29-21

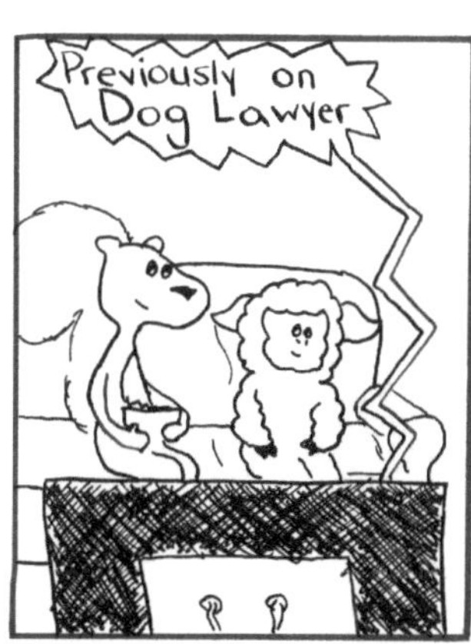
Previously on Dog Lawyer

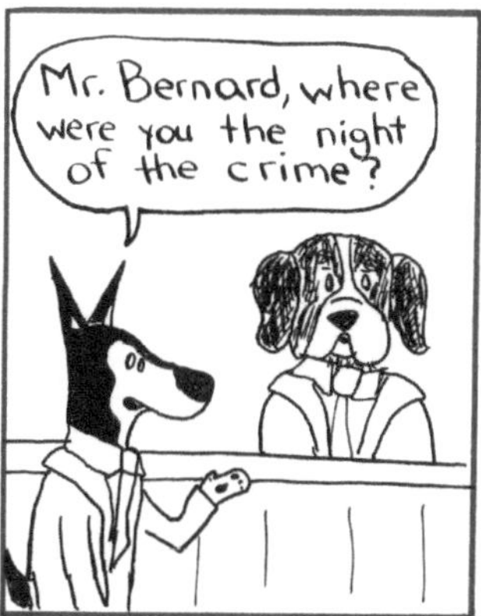
Mr. Bernard, where were you the night of the crime?

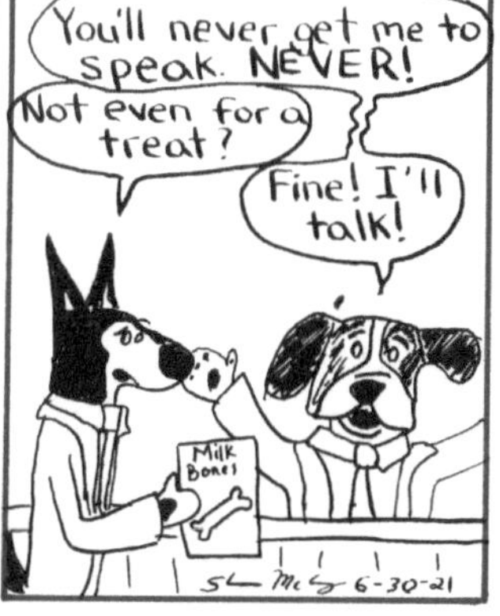
You'll never get me to speak. NEVER!
Not even for a treat?
Fine! I'll talk!
Milk Bones
6-30-21

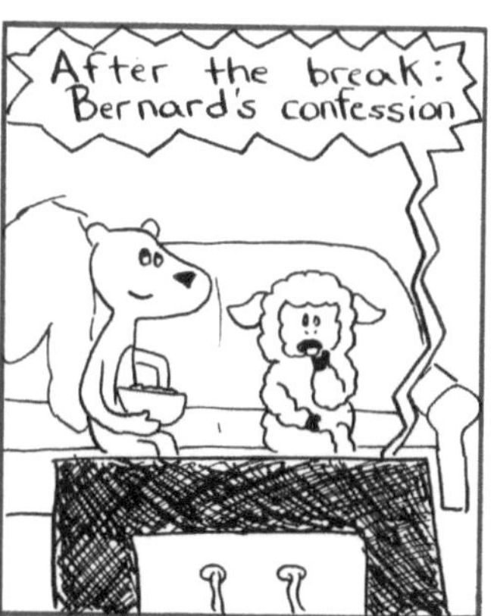
After the break: Bernard's confession

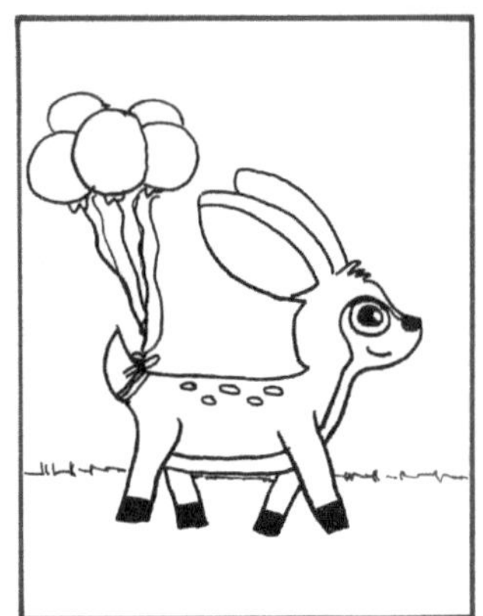

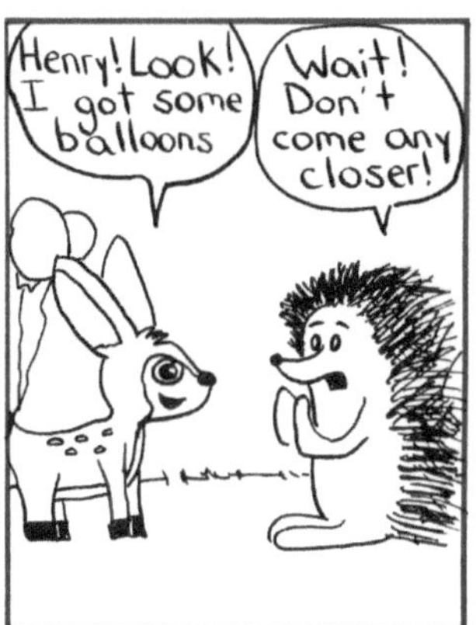
Henry! Look! I got some balloons
Wait! Don't come any closer!

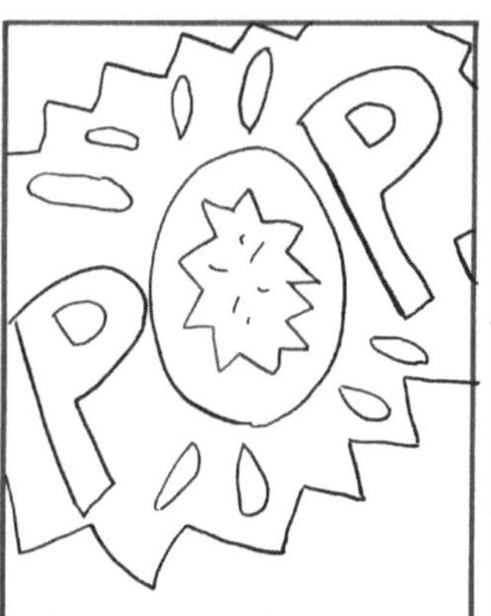
POP

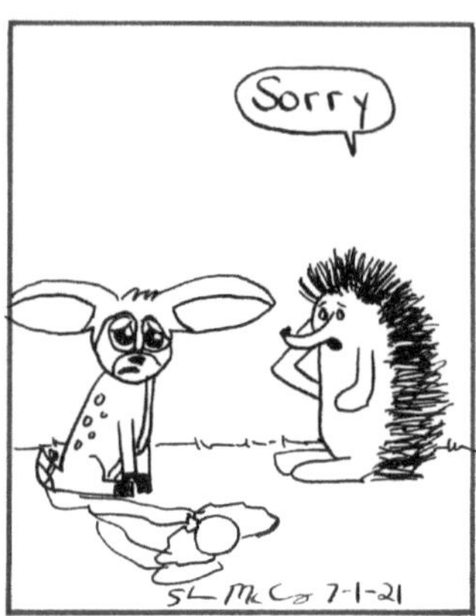
Sorry
7-1-21

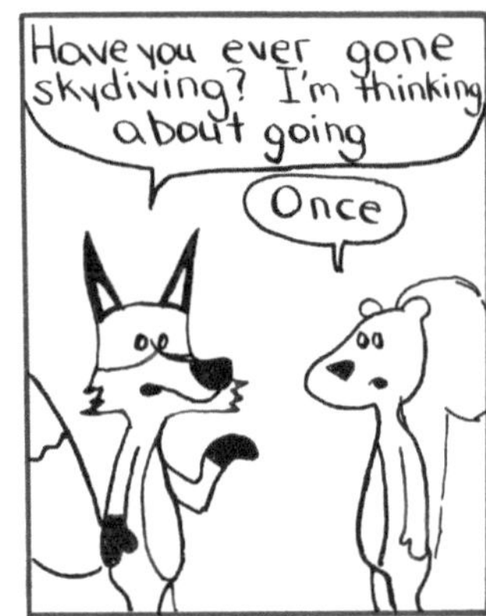
Have you ever gone skydiving? I'm thinking about going
Once

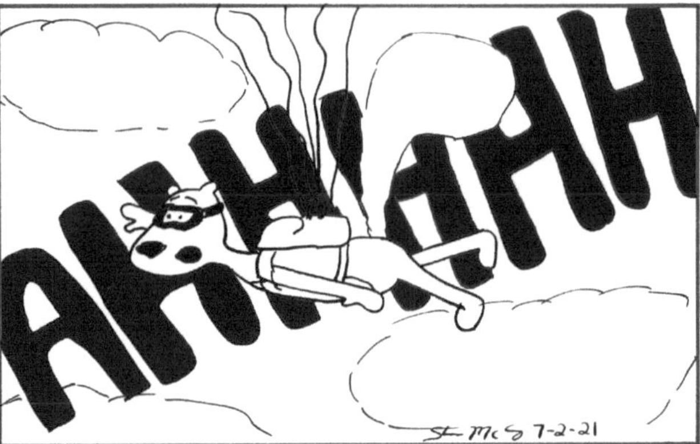
7-2-21

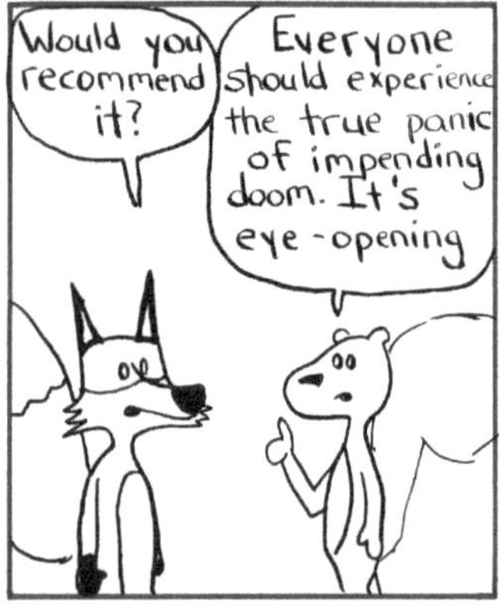
Would you recommend it?
Everyone should experience the true panic of impending doom. It's eye-opening

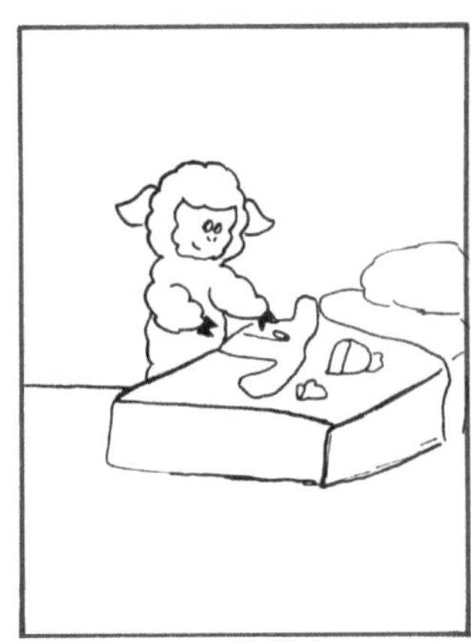

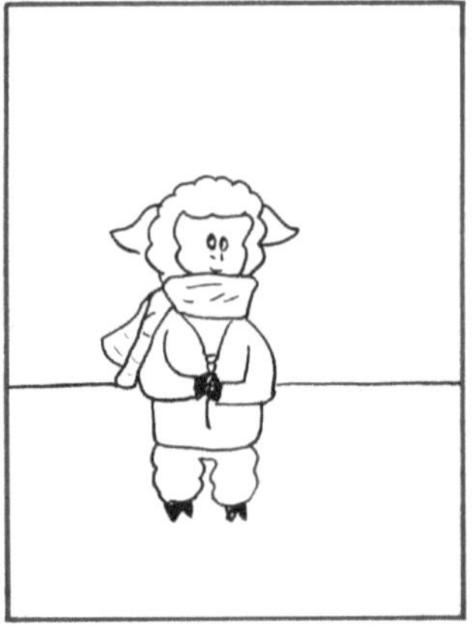

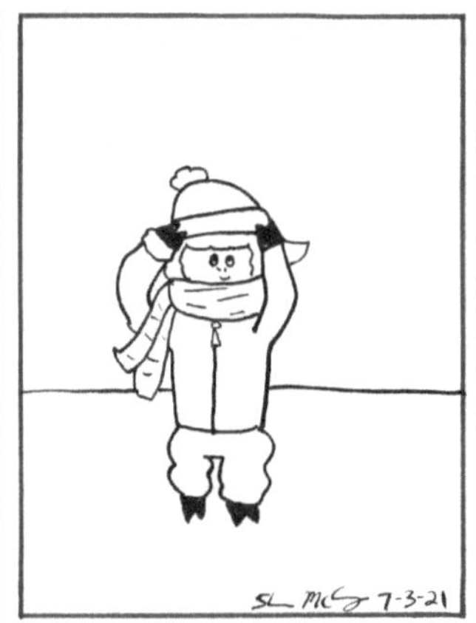
7-3-21

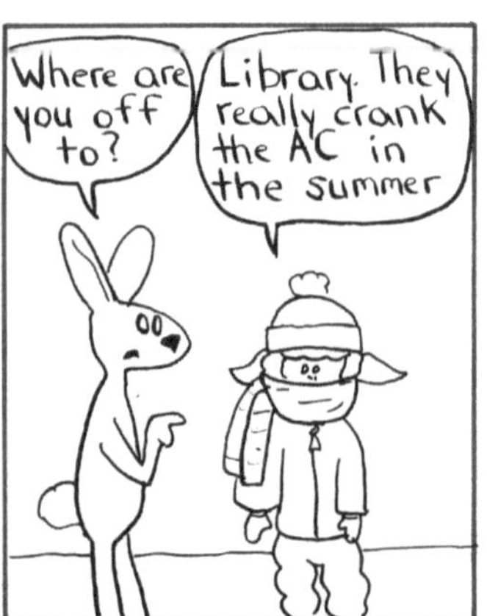
Where are you off to?
Library. They really crank the AC in the summer

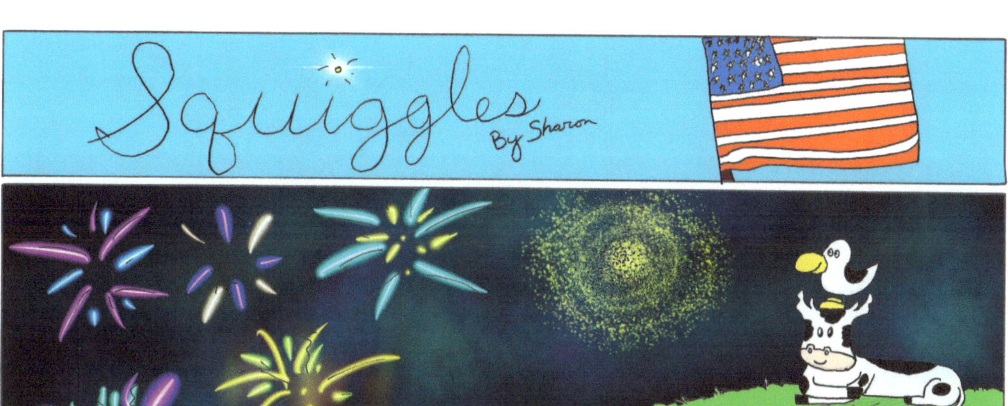
Squiggles
By Sharon

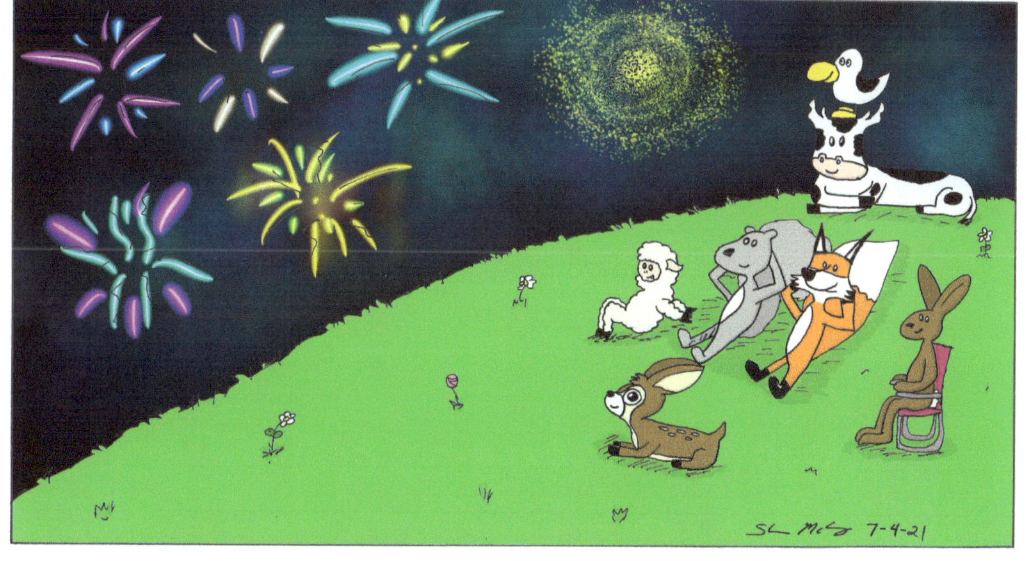
SL McG 7-4-21

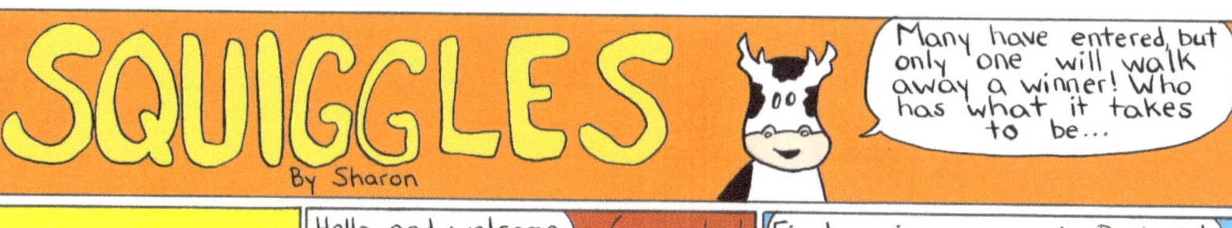
SQUIGGLES
By Sharon
Many have entered, but only one will walk away a winner! Who has what it takes to be...

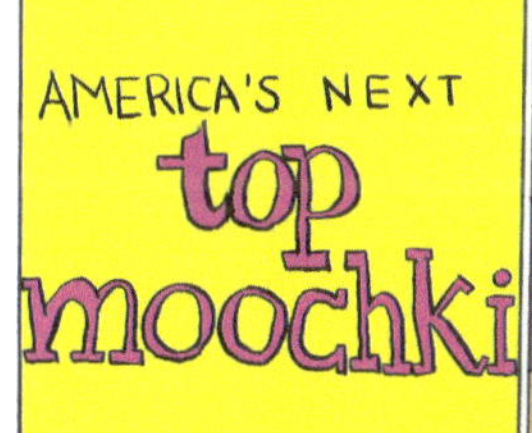
AMERICA'S NEXT
top
moochki

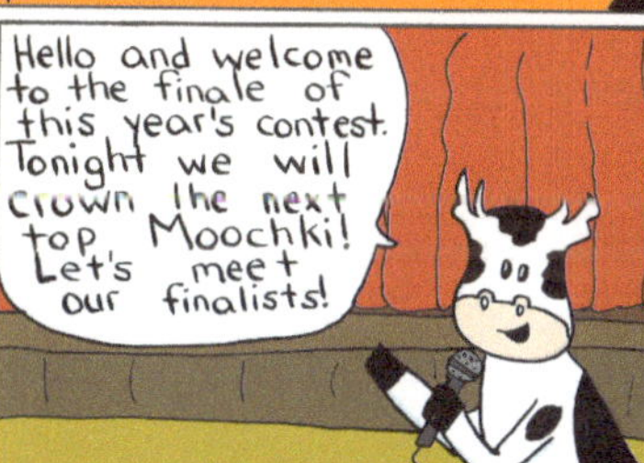
Hello and welcome to the finale of this year's contest. Tonight we will crown the next top Moochki! Let's meet our finalists!

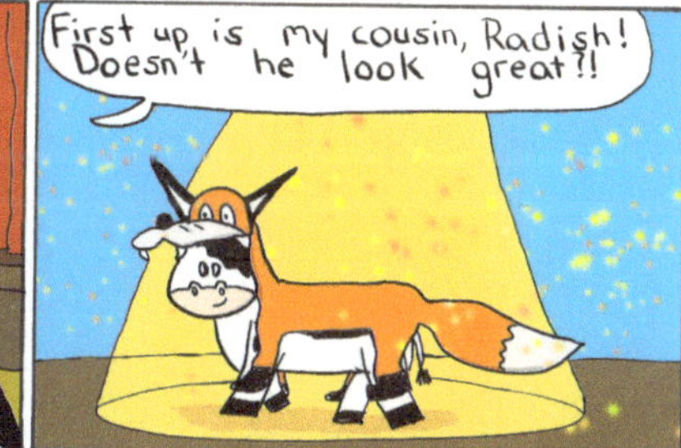
First up is my cousin, Radish! Doesn't he look great?!

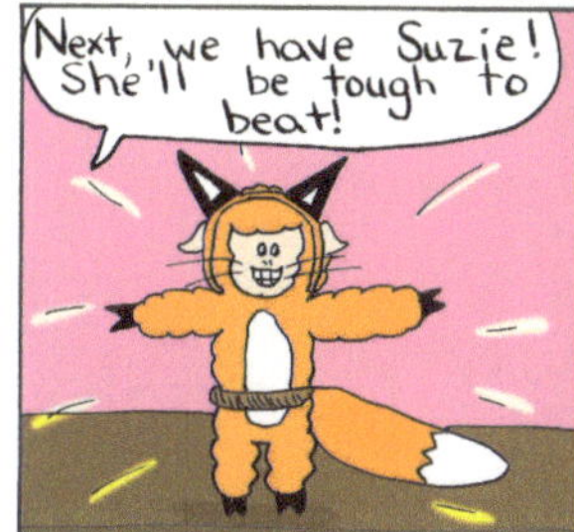
Next, we have Suzie! She'll be tough to beat!

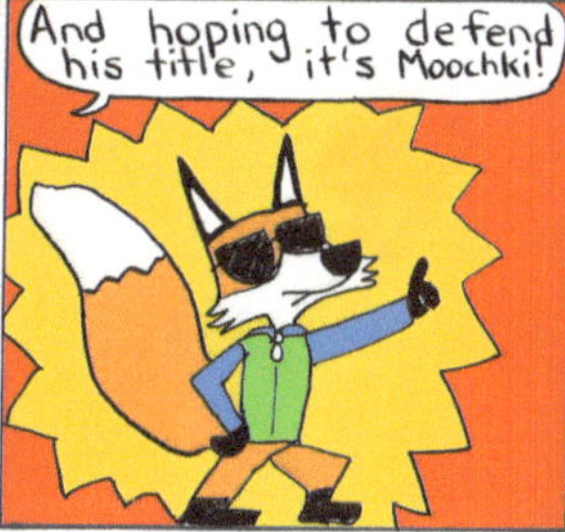
And hoping to defend his title, it's Moochki!

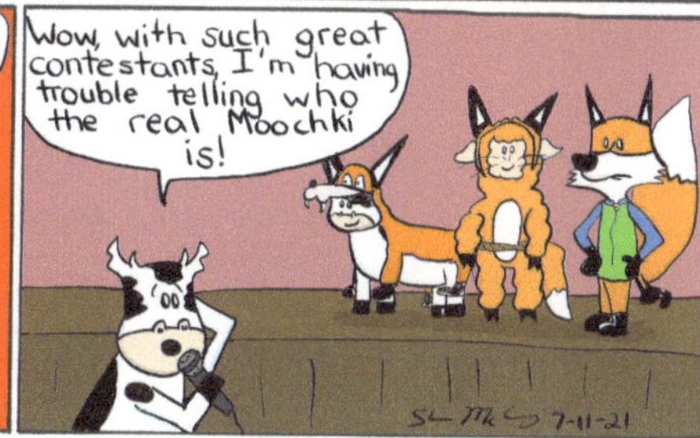
Wow, with such great contestants, I'm having trouble telling who the real Moochki is!
SL McG 7-11-21

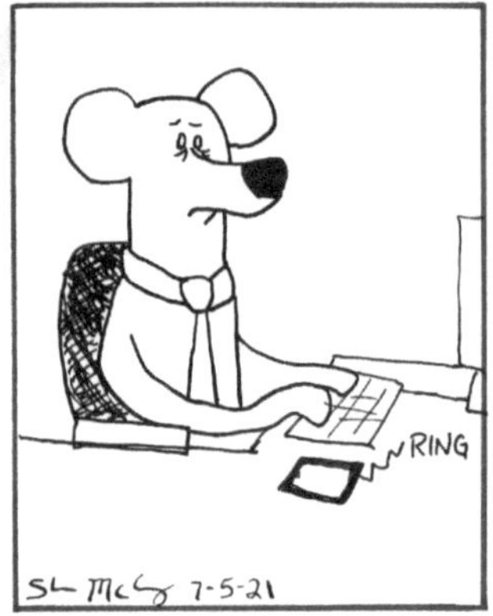
RING
SL McG 7-5-21

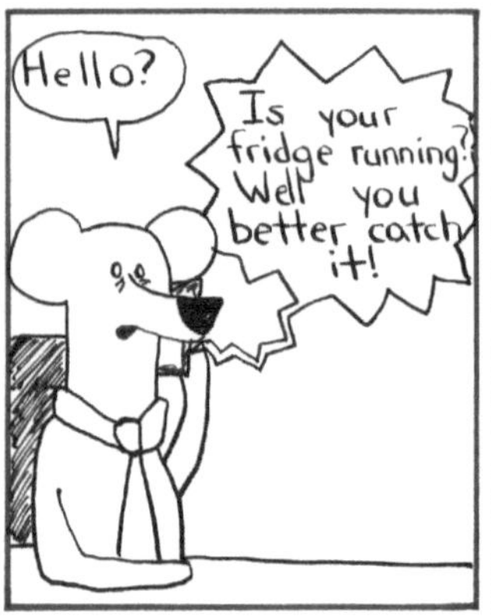
Hello?
Is your fridge running? Well you better catch it!

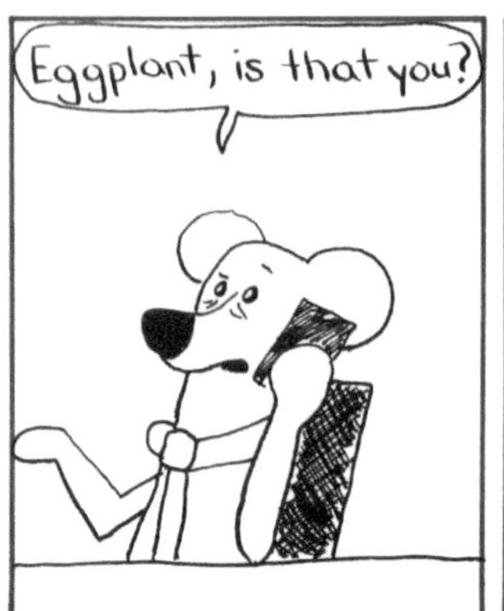
Eggplant, is that you?

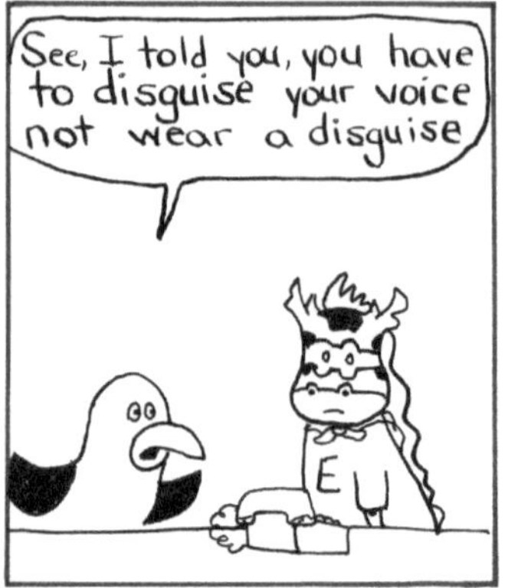
See, I told you, you have to disguise your voice not wear a disguise
E

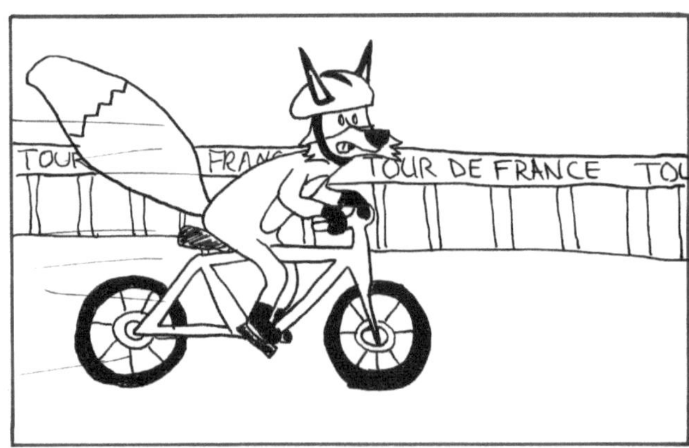
TOUR
FRAN
TOUR DE FRANCE
TOU

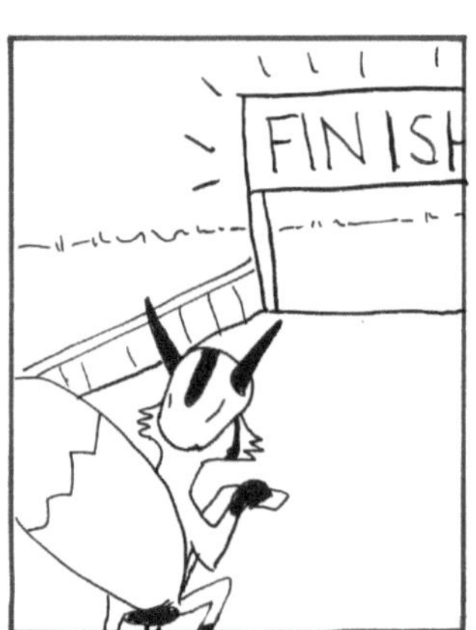
FINISH

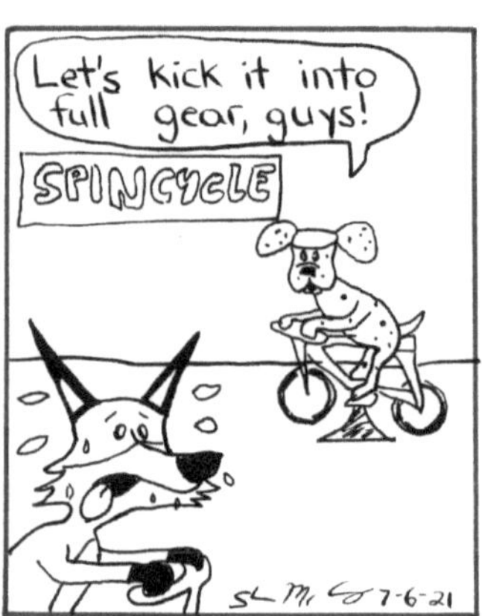
Let's kick it into full gear, guys!
SPINCYCLE
SL McG 7-6-21

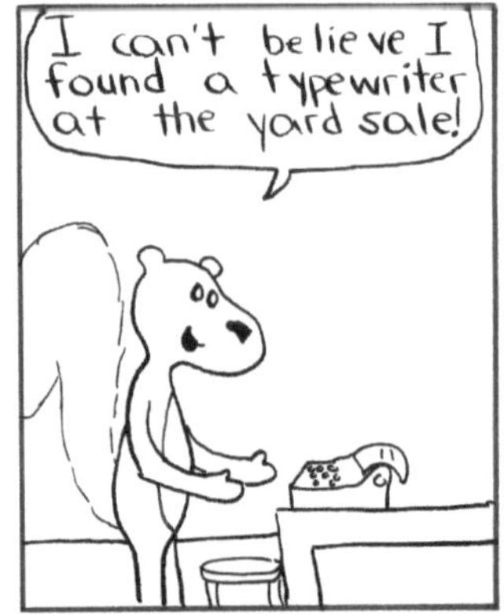
I can't believe I found a typewriter at the yard sale!

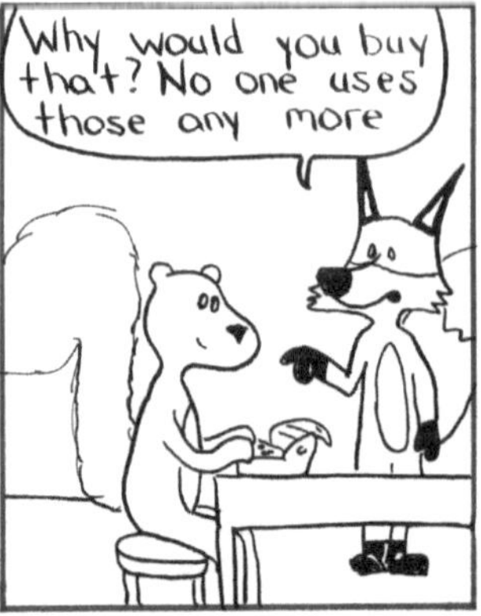
Why would you buy that? No one uses those any more

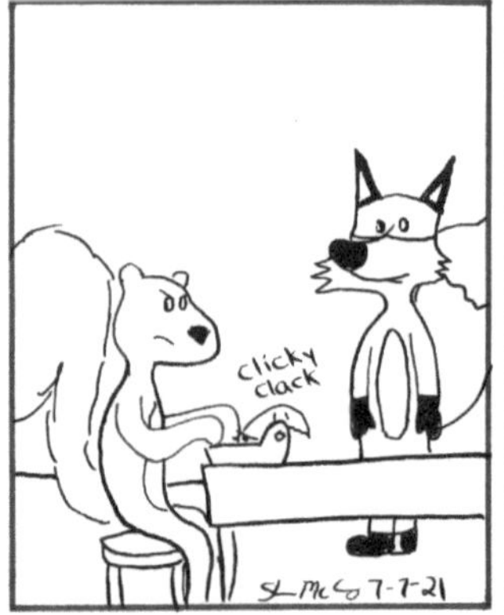
clicky clack
SL McG 7-7-21

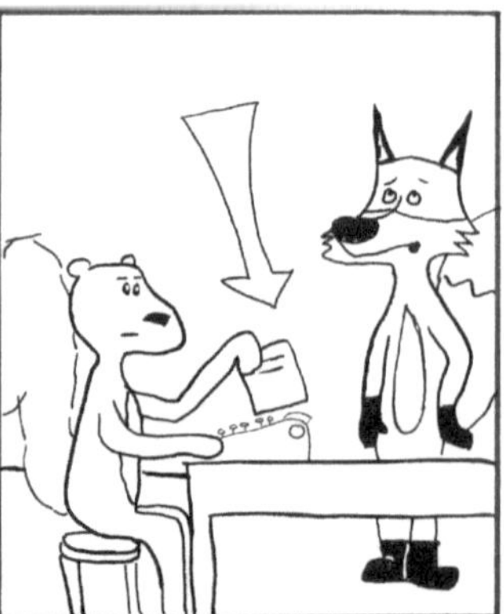

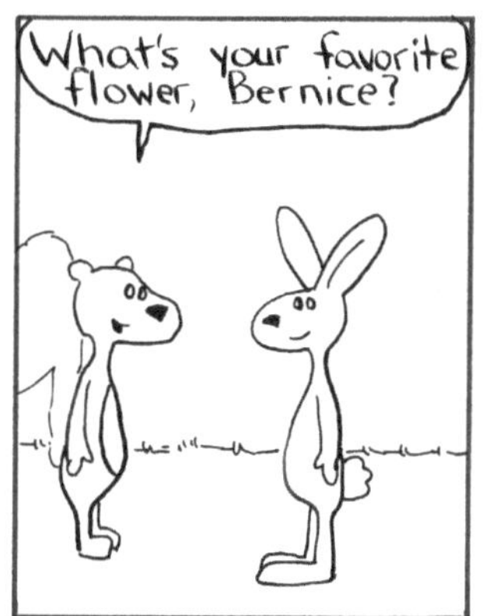
What's your favorite flower, Bernice?

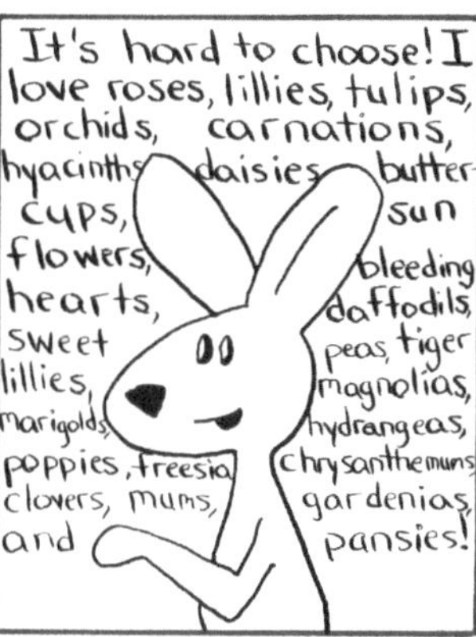
It's hard to choose! I love roses, lillies, tulips, orchids, carnations, hyacinths, daisies, buttercups, sunflowers, bleeding hearts, daffodils, sweet peas, tiger lillies, magnolias, marigolds, hydrangeas, poppies, freesia, chrysanthemums, clovers, mums, gardenias, and pansies!

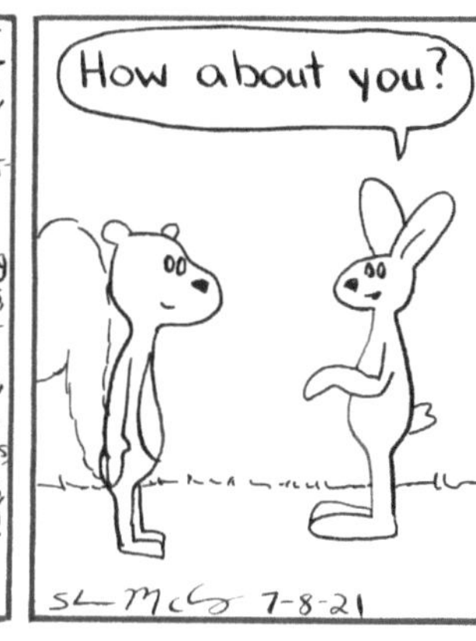
How about you?
7-8-21

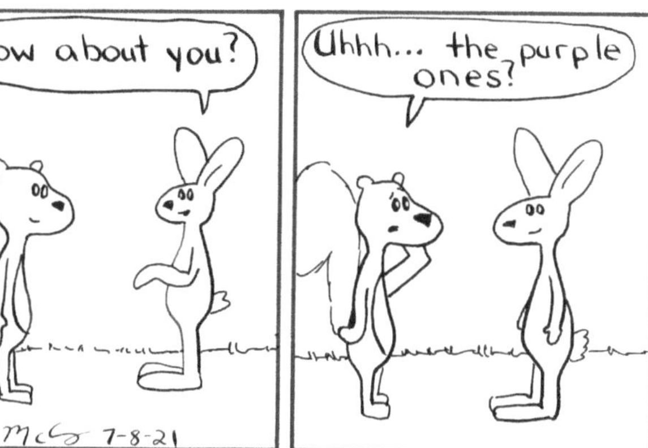
Uhhh... the purple ones?

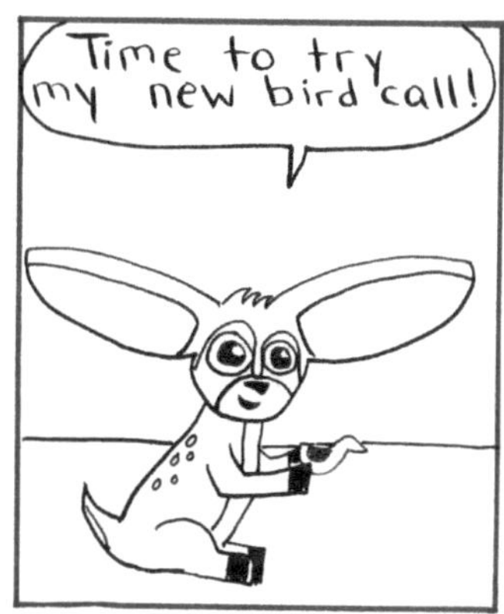
Time to try my new bird call!

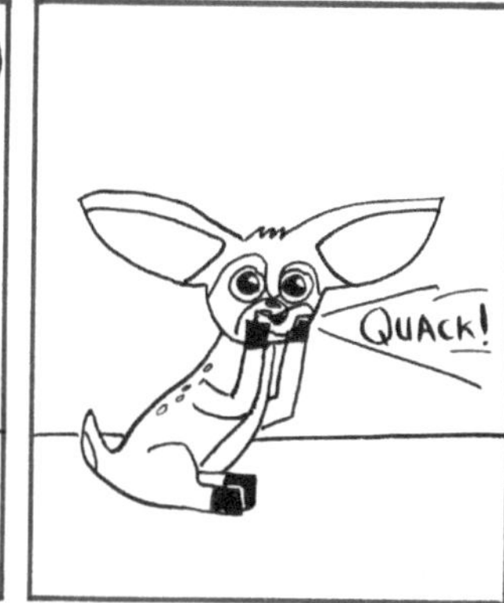
QUACK!

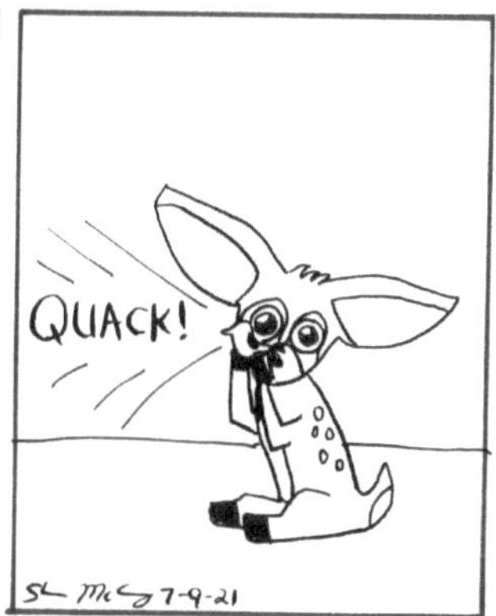
QUACK!
7-9-21

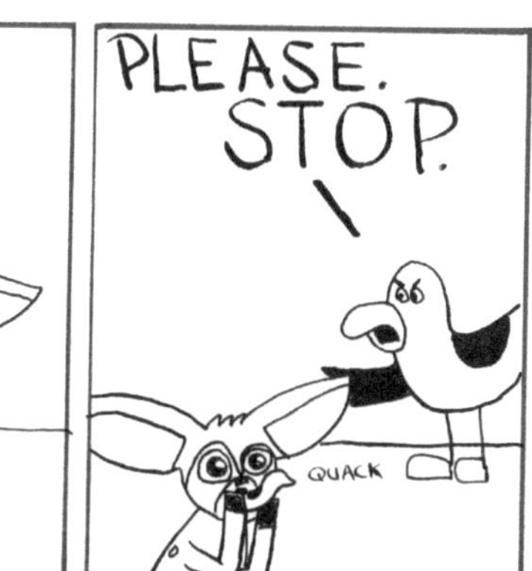
PLEASE. STOP.
QUACK

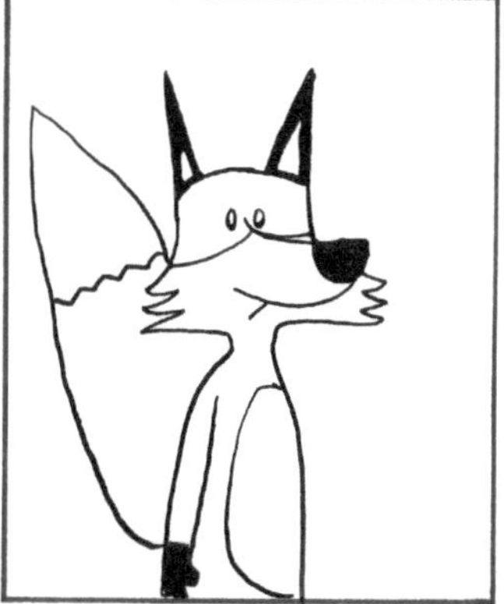

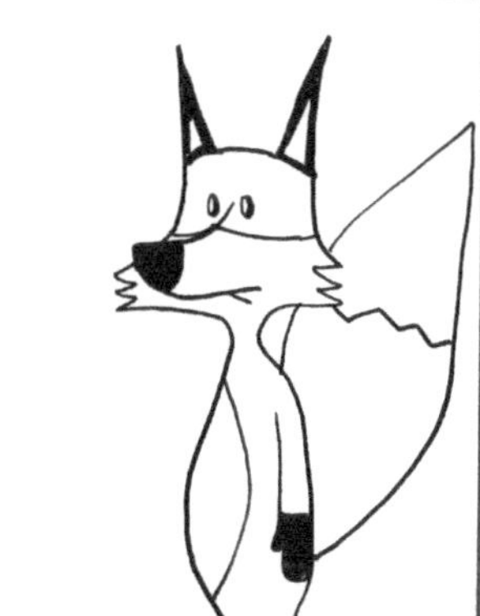

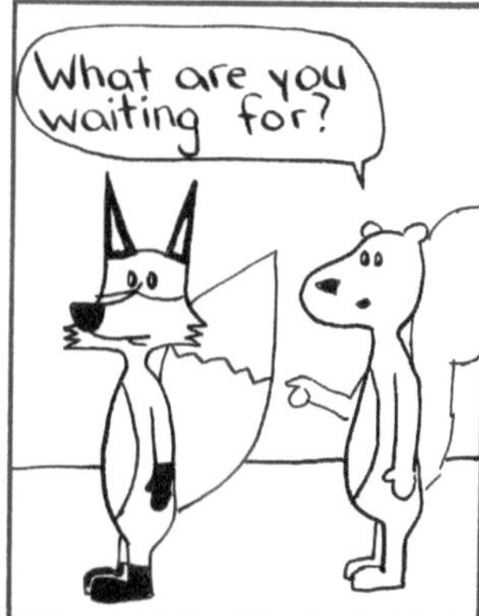
What are you waiting for?

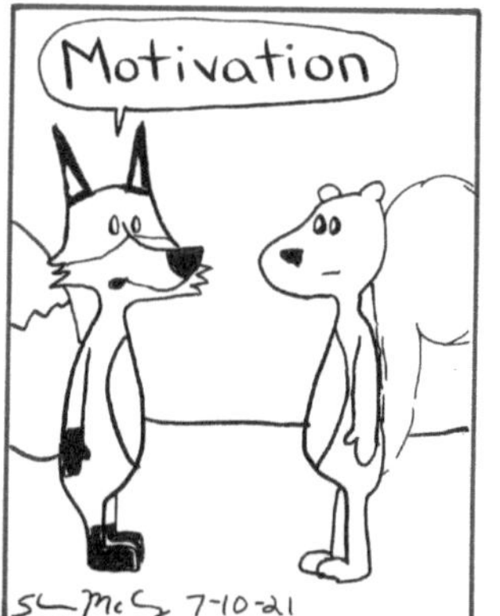
Motivation
7-10-21

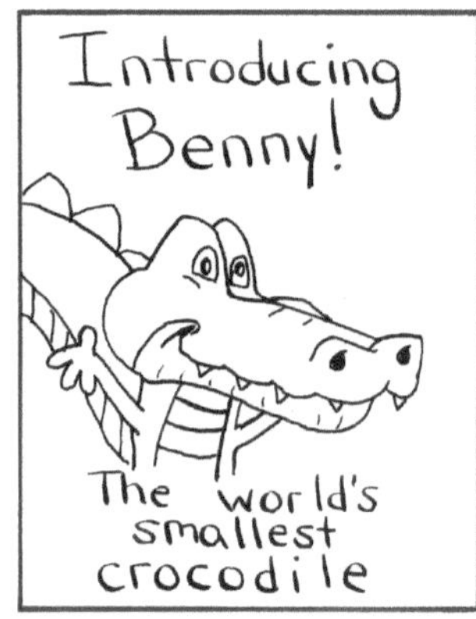
Introducing Benny!
The world's smallest crocodile

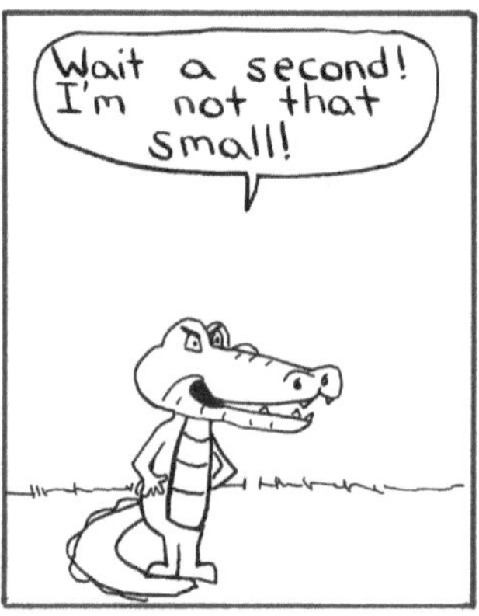
Wait a second! I'm not that small!

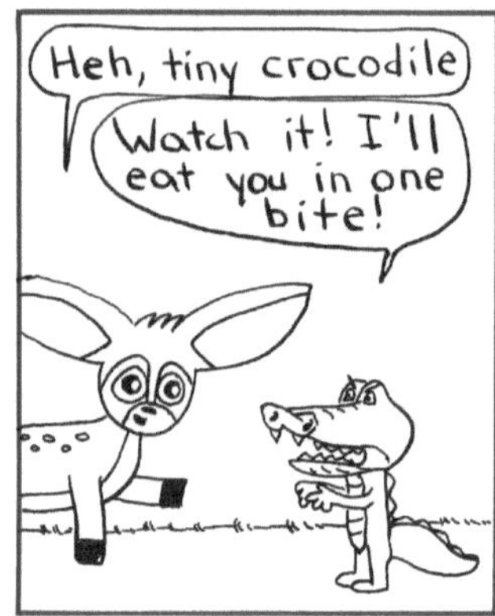
Heh, tiny crocodile
Watch it! I'll eat you in one bite!

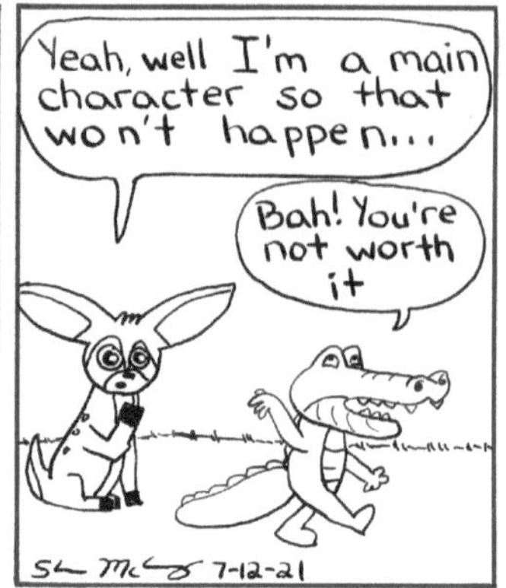
Yeah, well I'm a main character so that won't happen...
Bah! You're not worth it
7-12-21

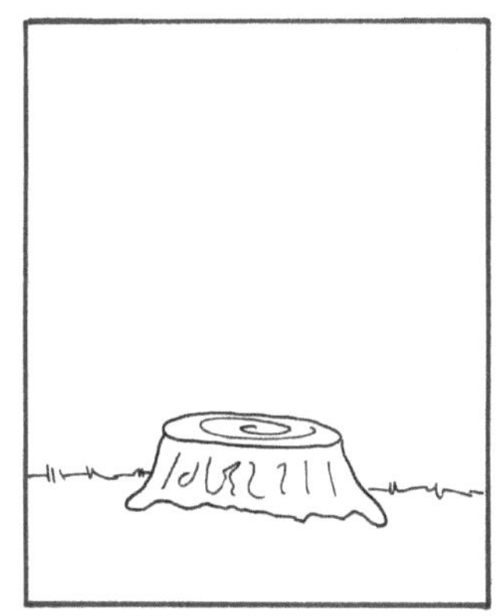

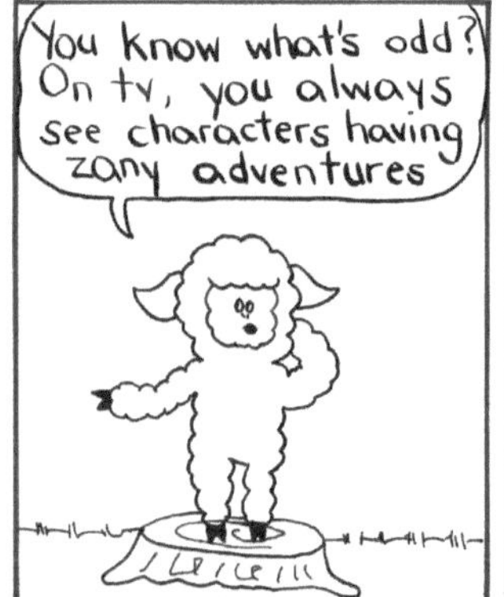
You know what's odd? On tv, you always see characters having zany adventures

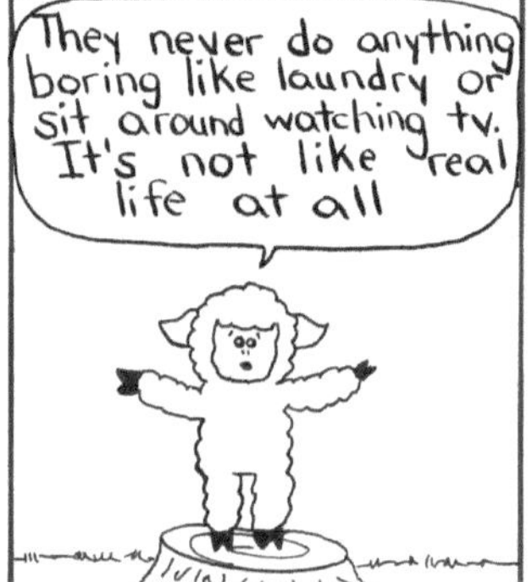
They never do anything boring like laundry or sit around watching tv. It's not like real life at all

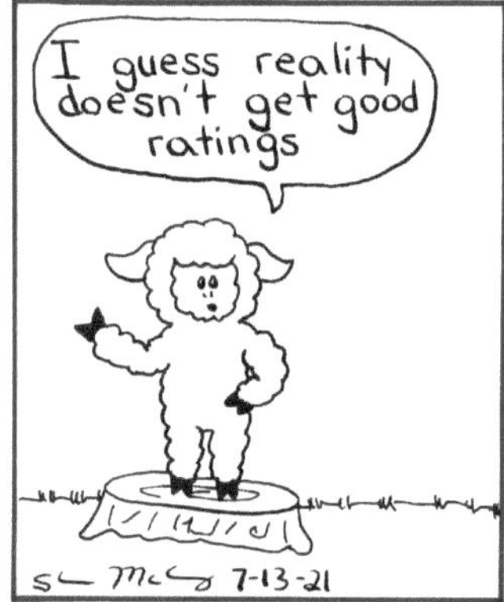
I guess reality doesn't get good ratings
7-13-21

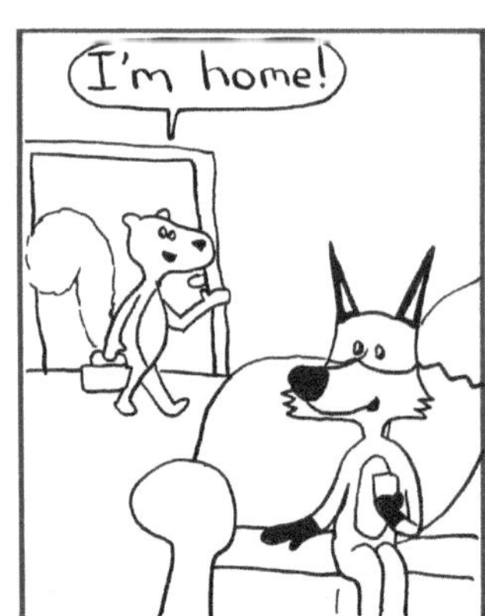
I'm home!

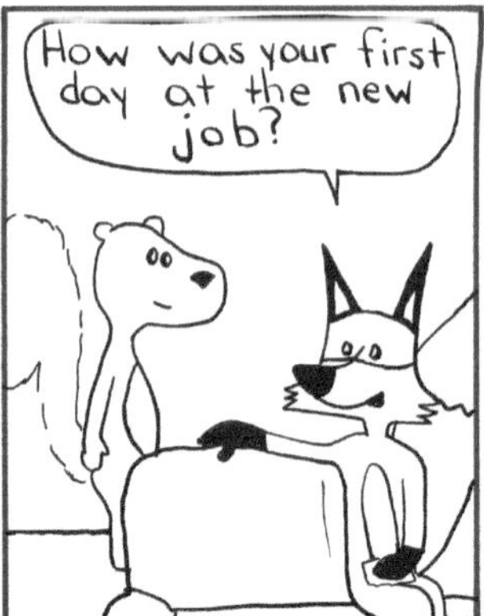
How was your first day at the new job?

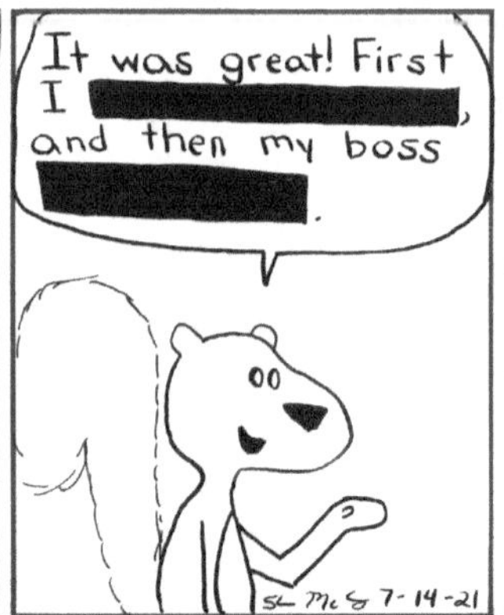
It was great! First I ██████, and then my boss ██████.
7-14-21

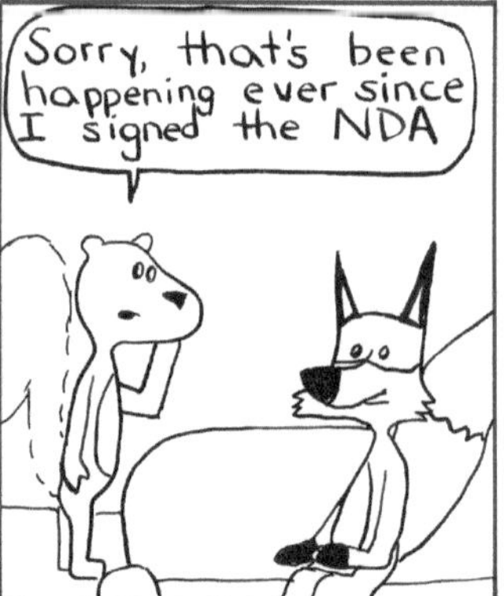
Sorry, that's been happening ever since I signed the NDA

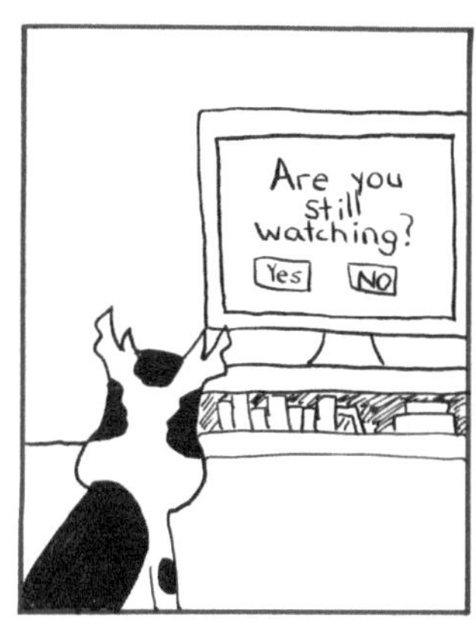
Are you still watching?
Yes NO

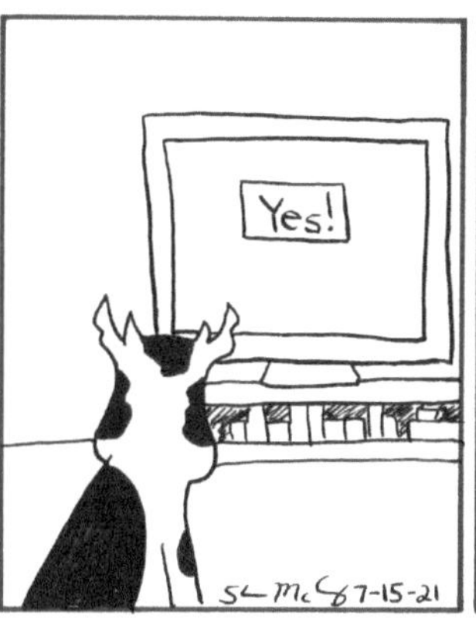
Yes!
SL McG 7-15-21

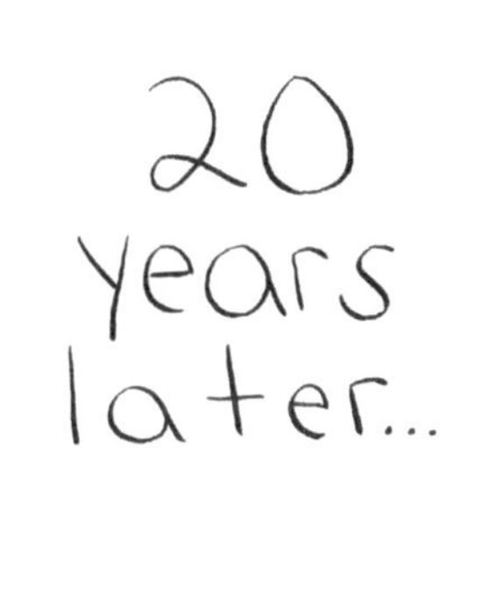
20 years later...

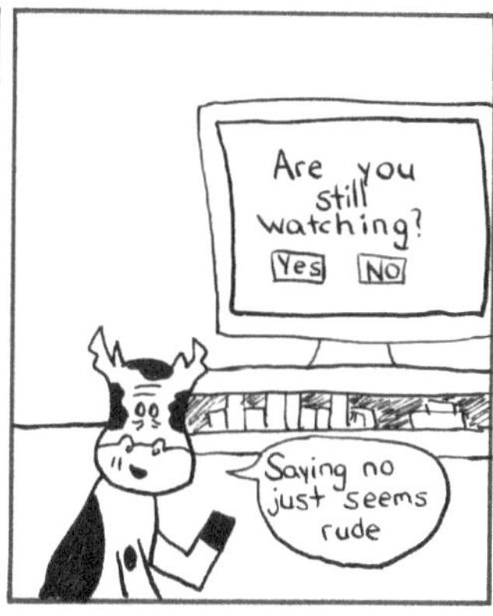
Are you still watching?
Yes NO
Saying no just seems rude

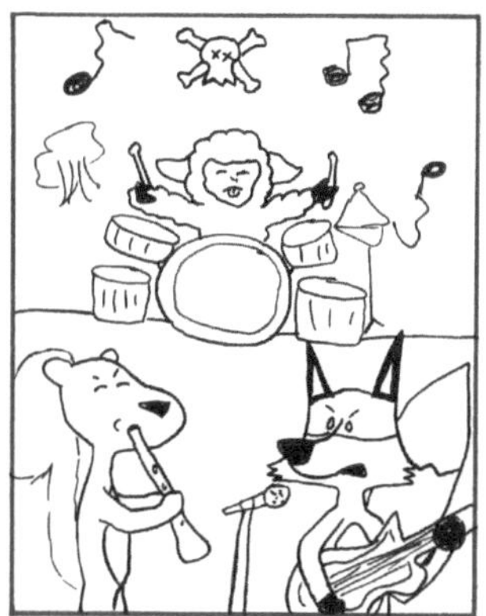

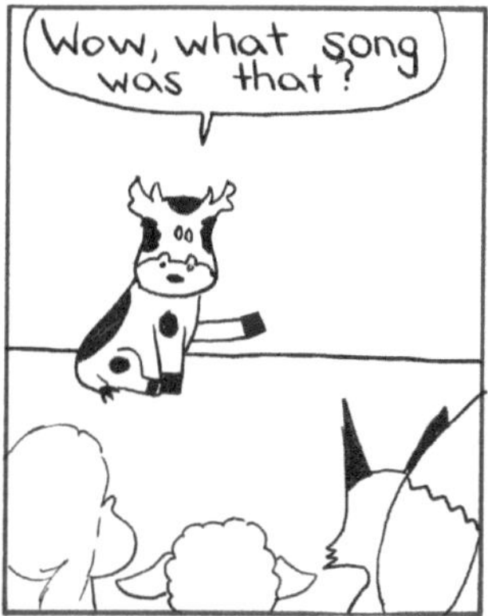
Wow, what song was that?

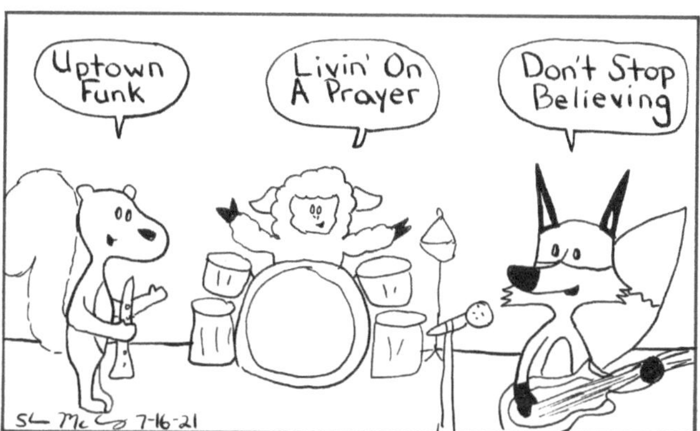
Uptown Funk
Livin' On A Prayer
Don't Stop Believing
SL McG 7-16-21

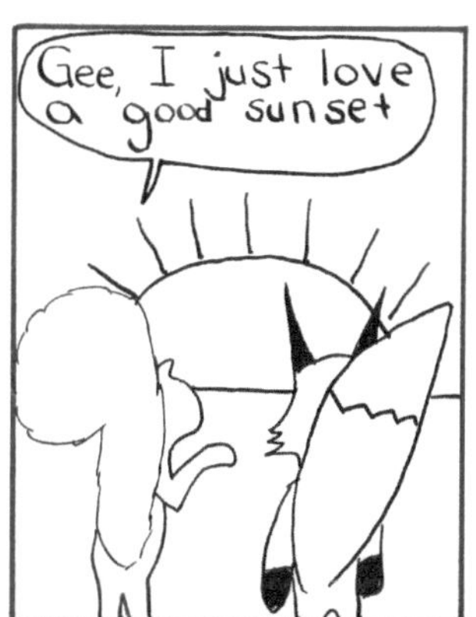
Gee, I just love a good sunset

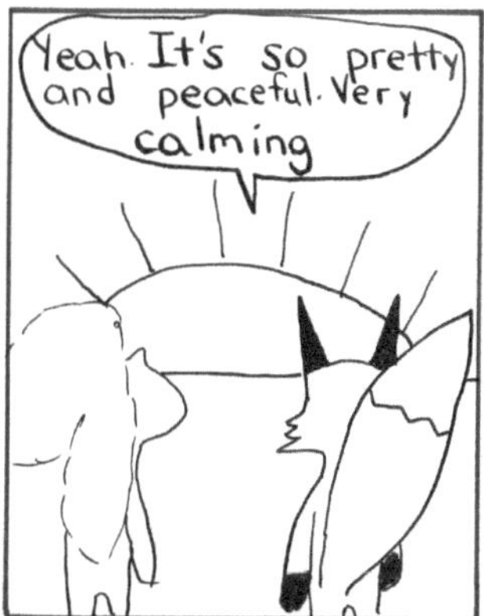
Yeah. It's so pretty and peaceful. Very calming

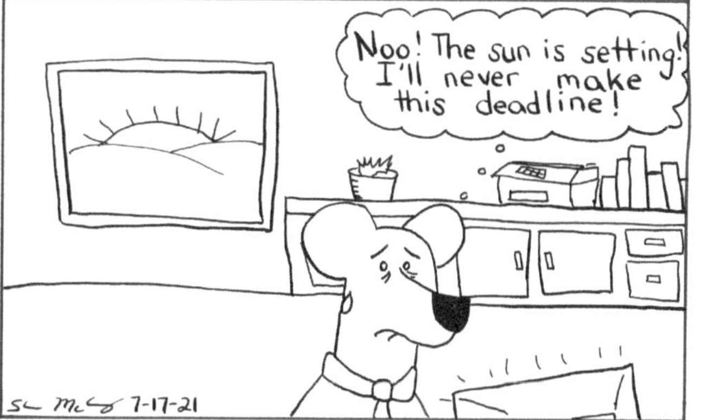
Noo! The sun is setting! I'll never make this deadline!
SL McG 7-17-21

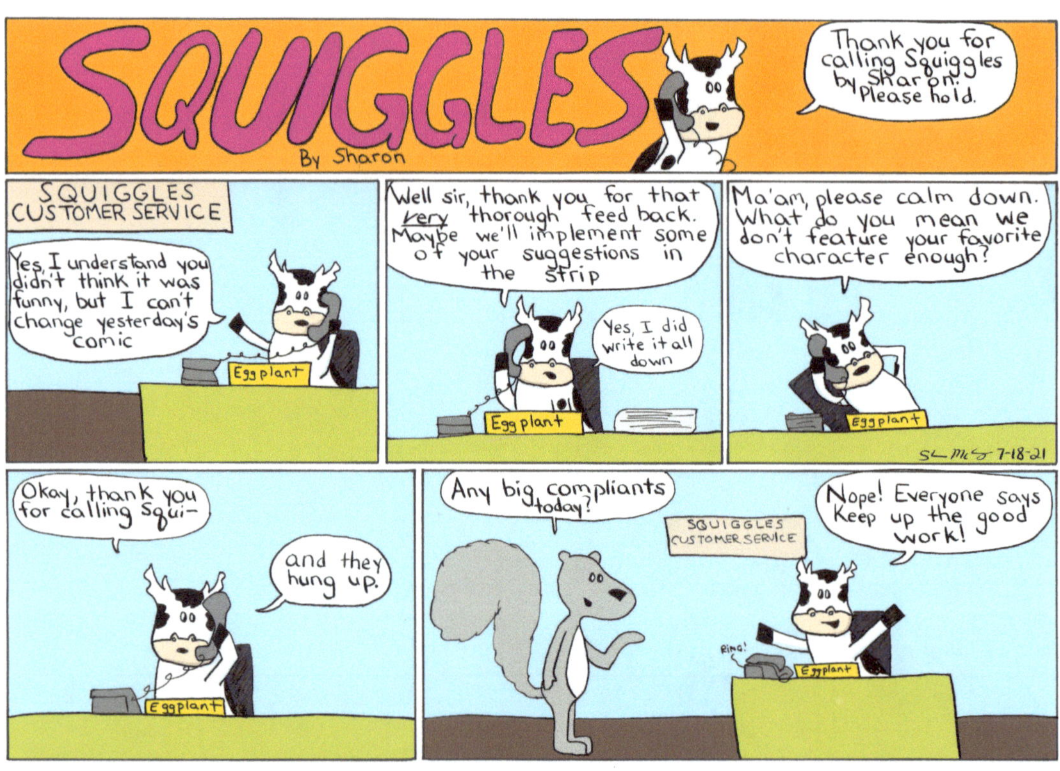
SQUIGGLES
By Sharon
Thank you for calling Squiggles by Sharon. Please hold.
SQUIGGLES CUSTOMER SERVICE
Yes, I understand you didn't think it was funny, but I can't change yesterday's comic
Eggplant
Well sir, thank you for that very thorough feed back. Maybe we'll implement some of your suggestions in the strip
Yes, I did write it all down
Eggplant
Ma'am, please calm down. What do you mean we don't feature your favorite character enough?
Eggplant
SL McS 7-18-21
Okay, thank you for calling Squi-
and they hung up.
Eggplant
Any big compliants today?
SQUIGGLES CUSTOMER SERVICE
Nope! Everyone says Keep up the good work!
RING!
Eggplant

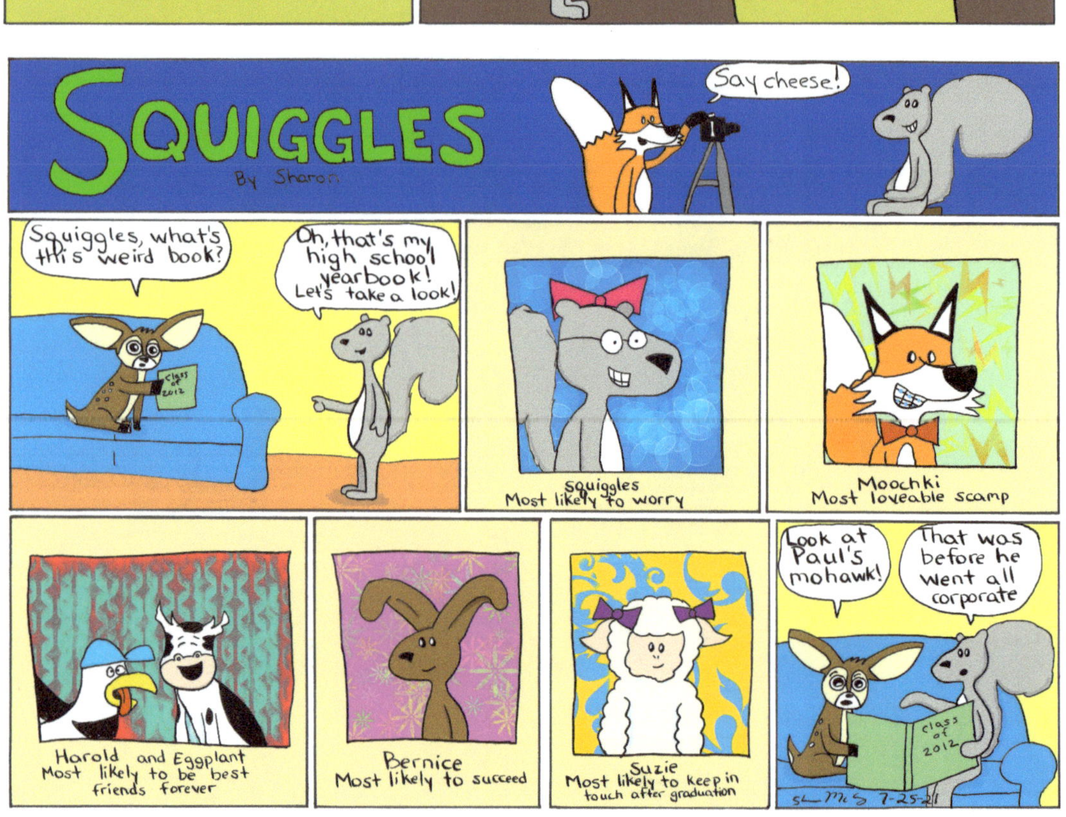
SQUIGGLES
By Sharon
Say cheese!
Squiggles, what's this weird book?
Oh, that's my high school yearbook! Let's take a look!
class of 2012
Squiggles
Most likely to worry
Moochki
Most loveable scamp
Harold and Eggplant
Most likely to be best friends forever
Bernice
Most likely to succeed
Suzie
Most likely to keep in touch after graduation
Look at Paul's mohawk!
That was before he went all corporate
class of 2012
SL McS 7-25-21

HAROLD'S SUMMER Boardwalk Tips

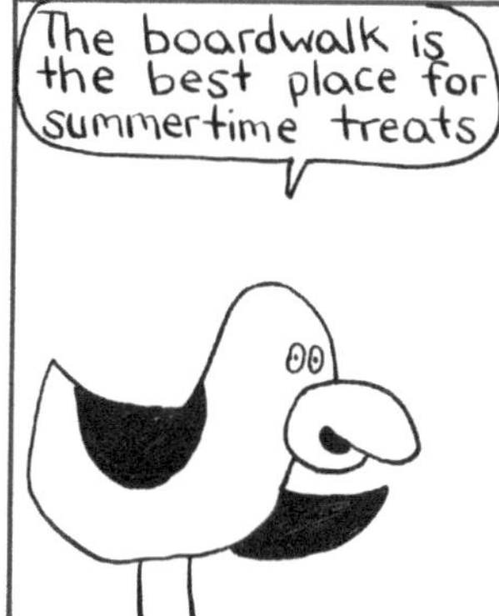

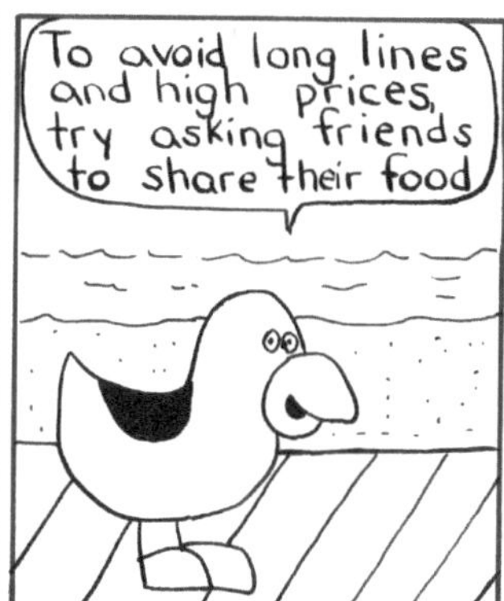

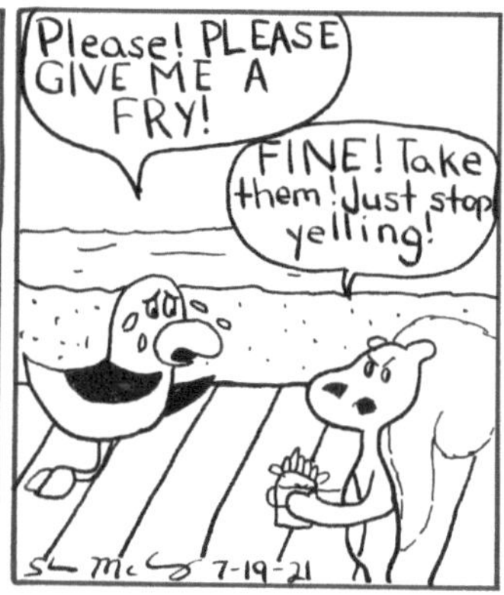

HAROLD'S SUMMER Boardwalk Tips

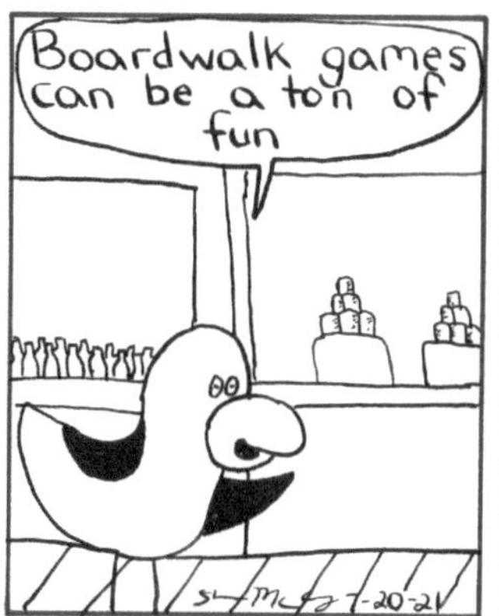

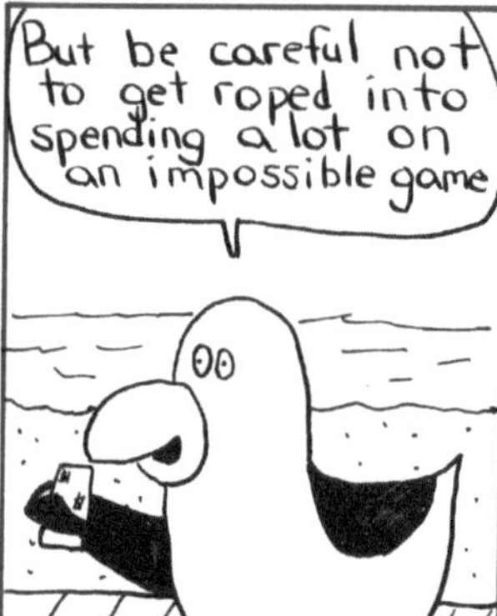

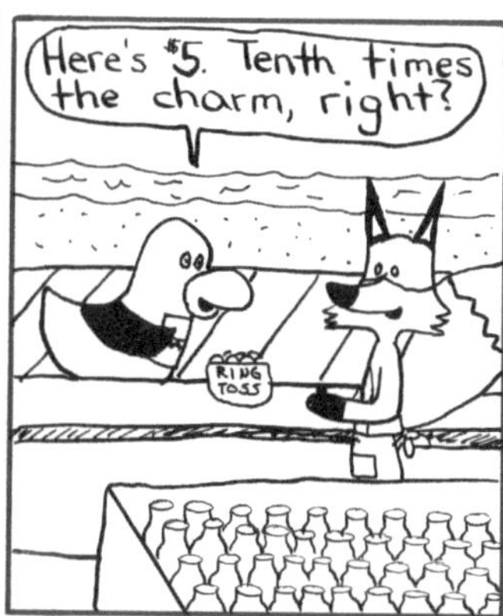

HAROLD'S SUMMER Boardwalk Tips

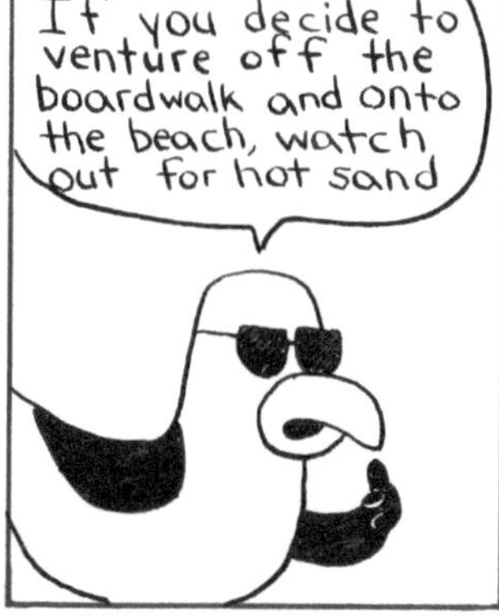

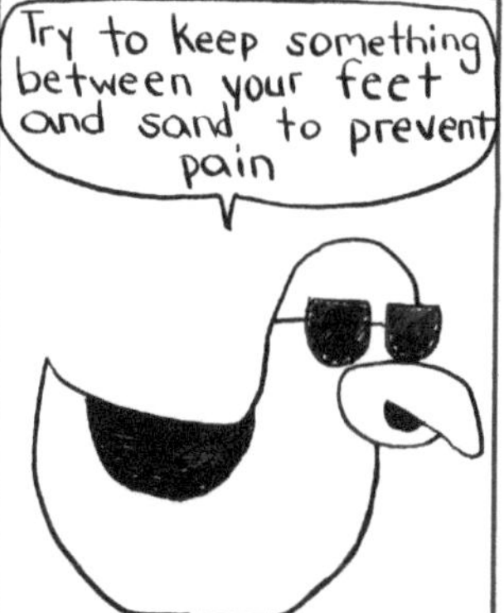

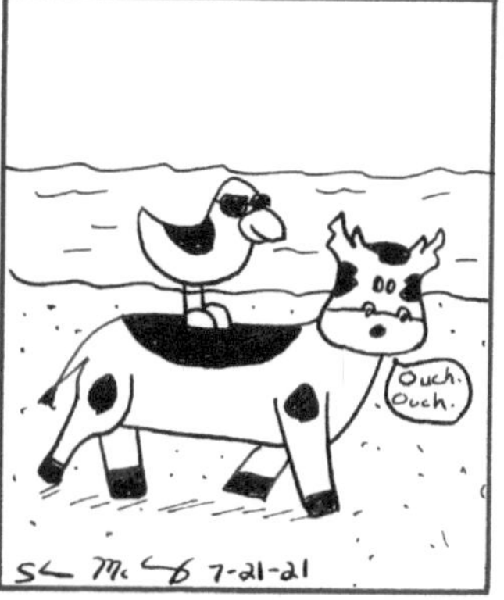

HAROLD'S SUMMER Boardwalk Tips

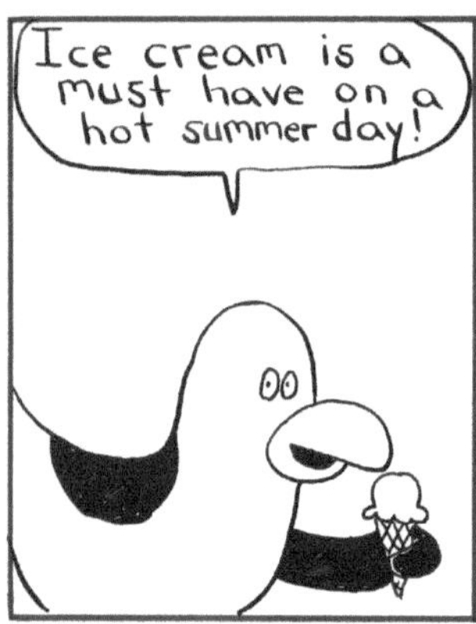

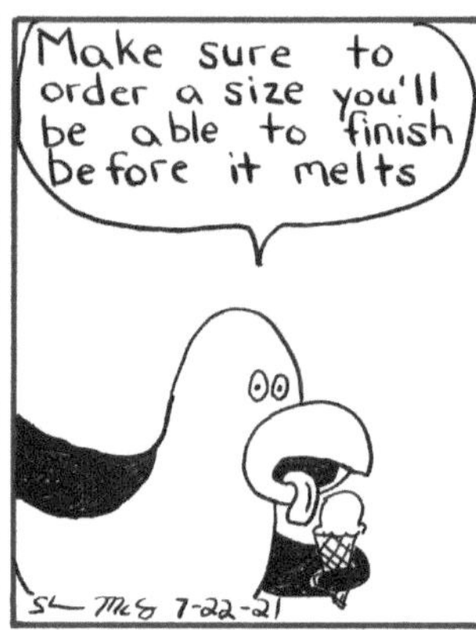

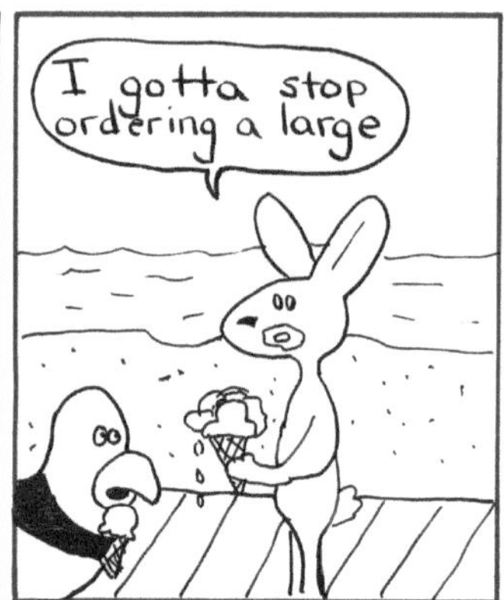

HAROLD'S SUMMER Boardwalk Tips

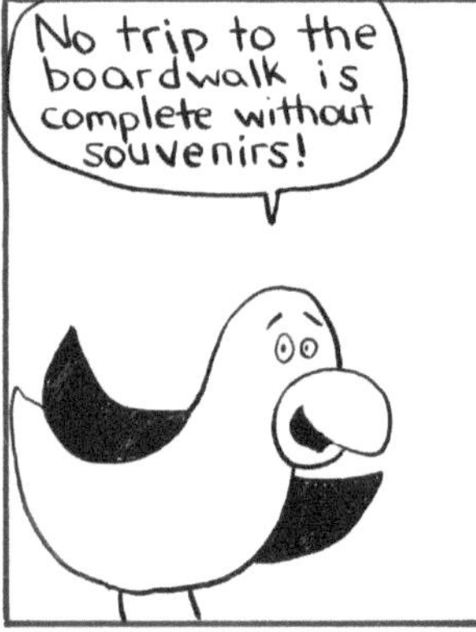

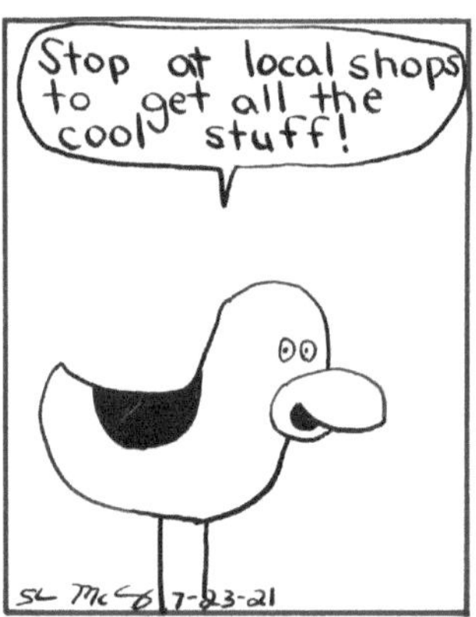

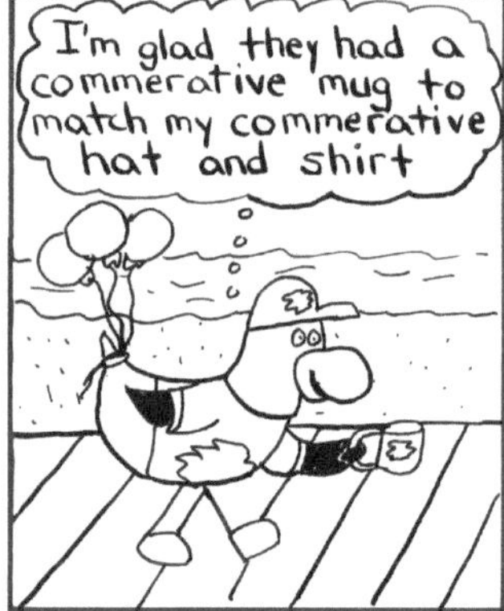

HAROLD'S SUMMER Boardwalk Tips

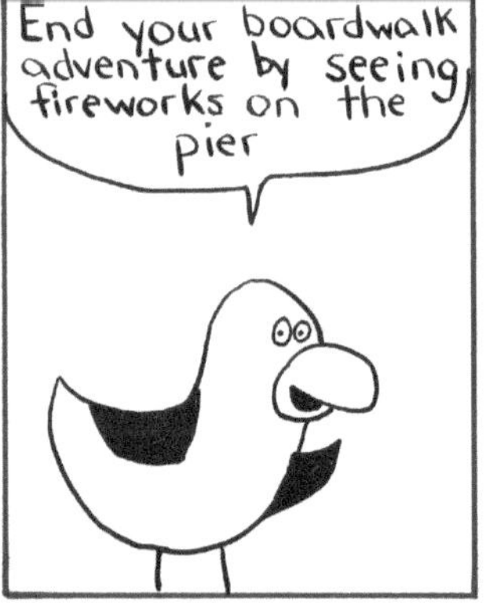

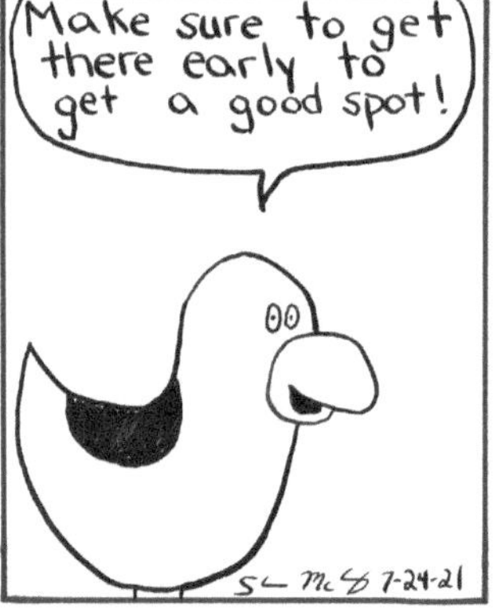

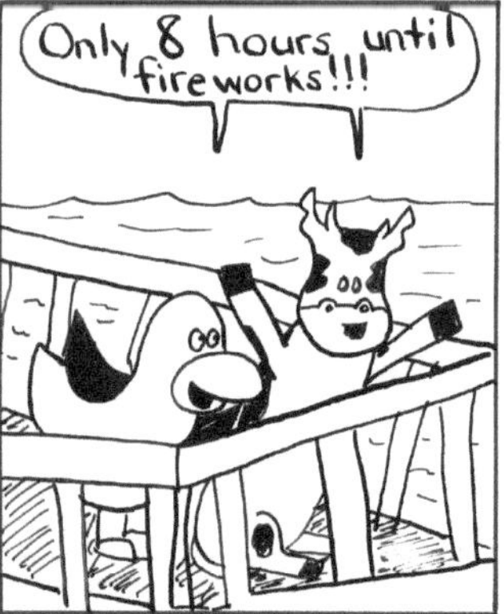

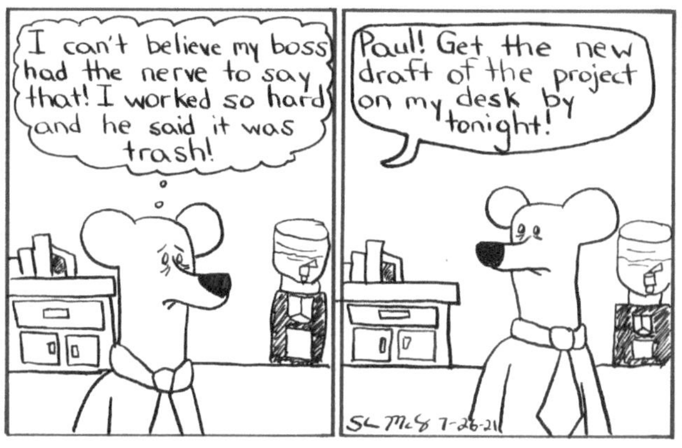
I can't believe my boss had the nerve to say that! I worked so hard and he said it was trash!
Paul! Get the new draft of the project on my desk by tonight!

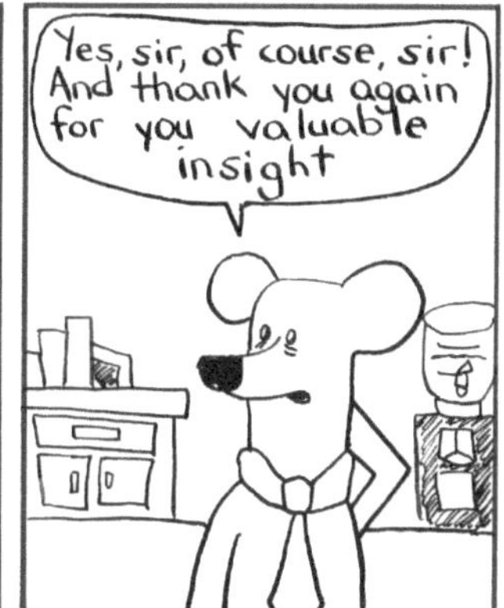
Yes, sir, of course, sir! And thank you again for you valuable insight

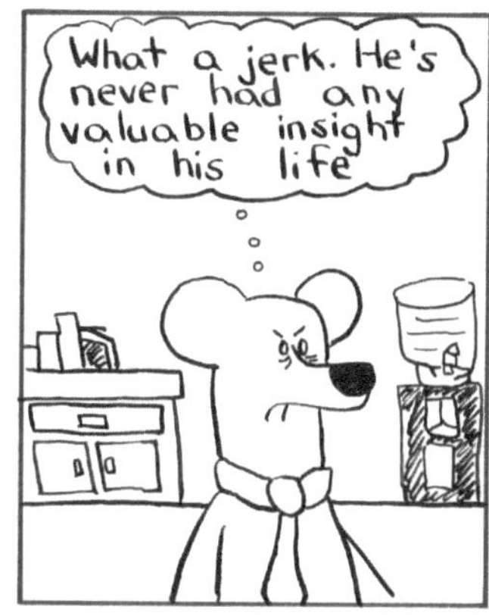
What a jerk. He's never had any valuable insight in his life

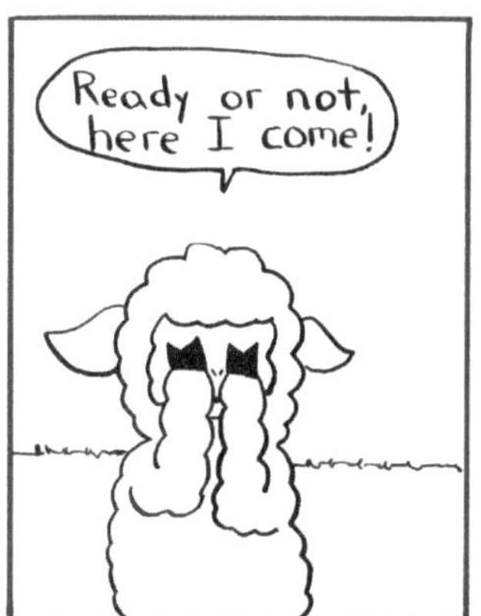
Ready or not, here I come!

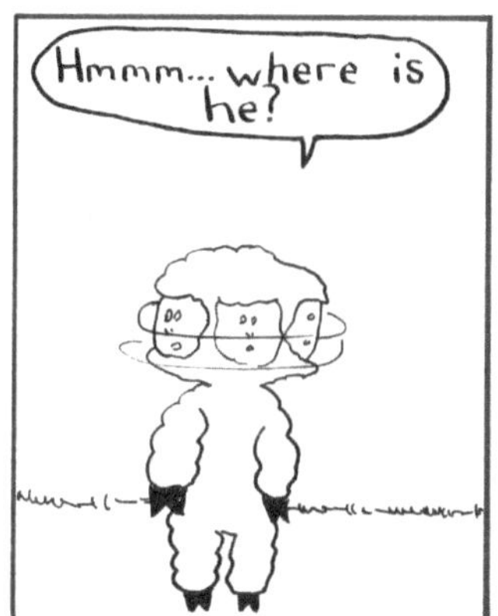
Hmmm... where is he?

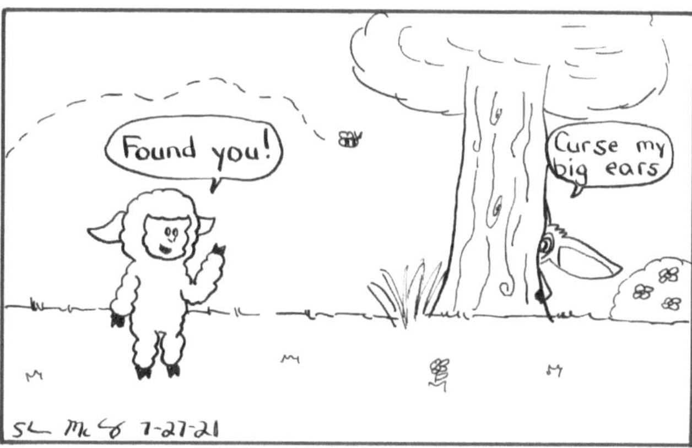
Found you!
Curse my big ears

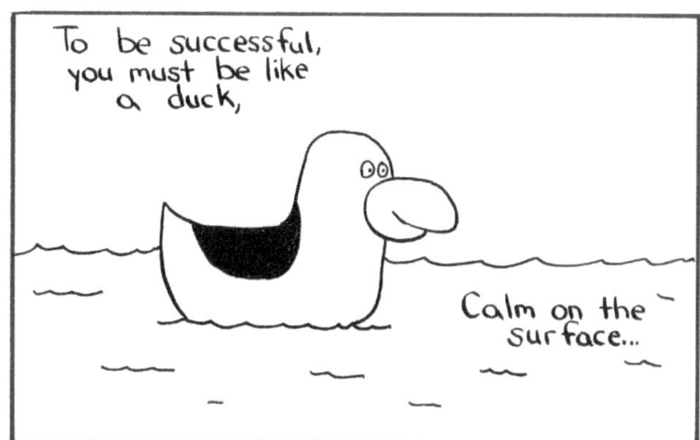
To be successful, you must be like a duck,
Calm on the surface...

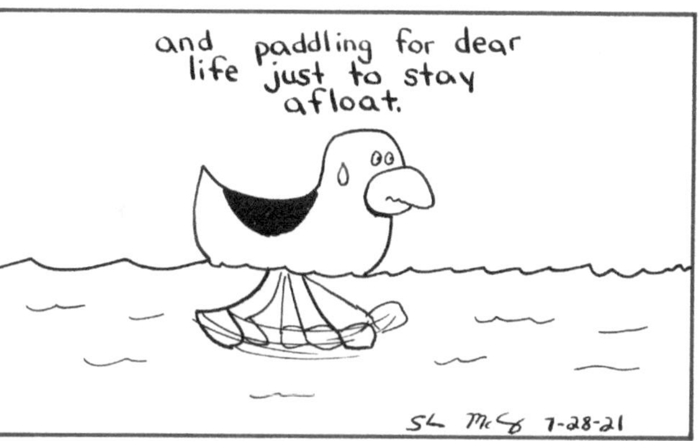
and paddling for dear life just to stay afloat.

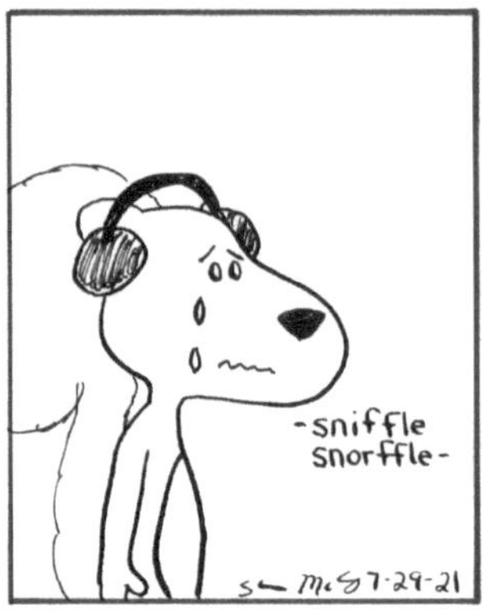
-sniffle
snorffle-
SL McG 7-29-21
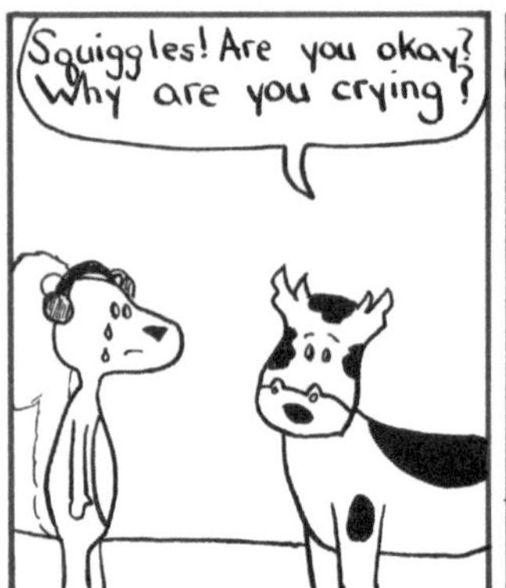
Squiggles! Are you okay? Why are you crying?
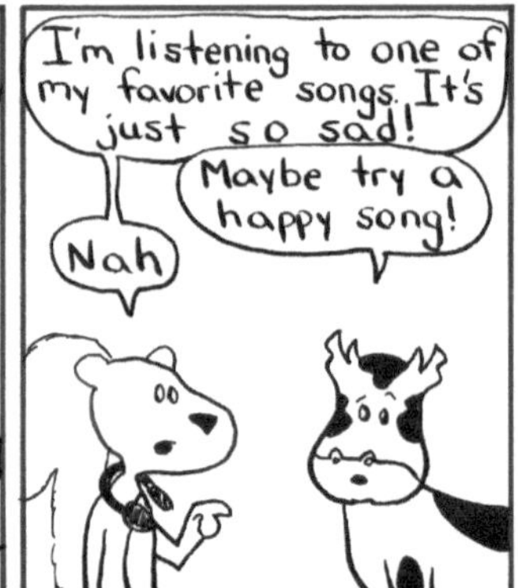
I'm listening to one of my favorite songs. It's just so sad!
Maybe try a happy song!
Nah
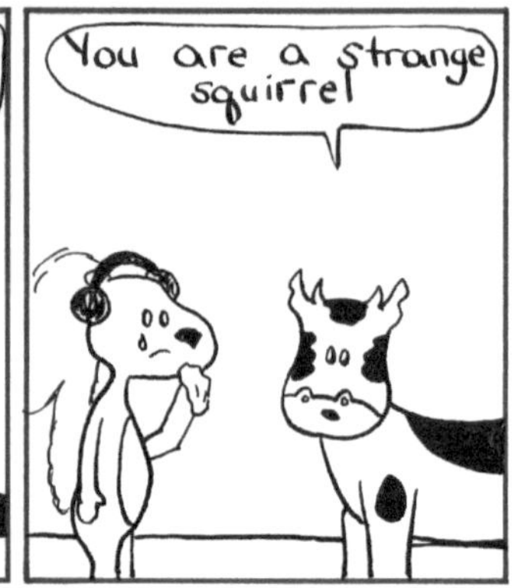
You are a strange squirrel
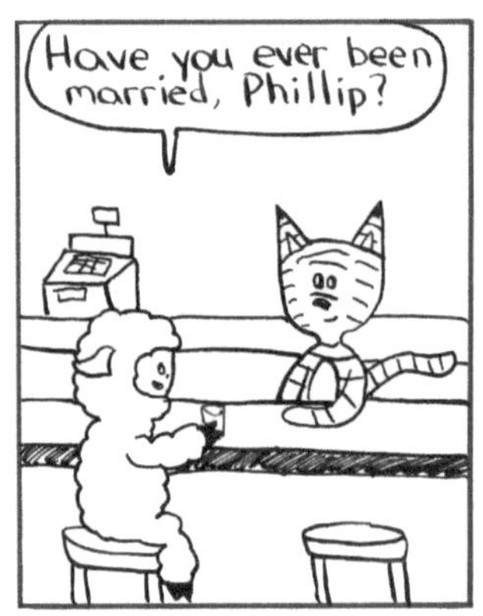
Have you ever been married, Phillip?
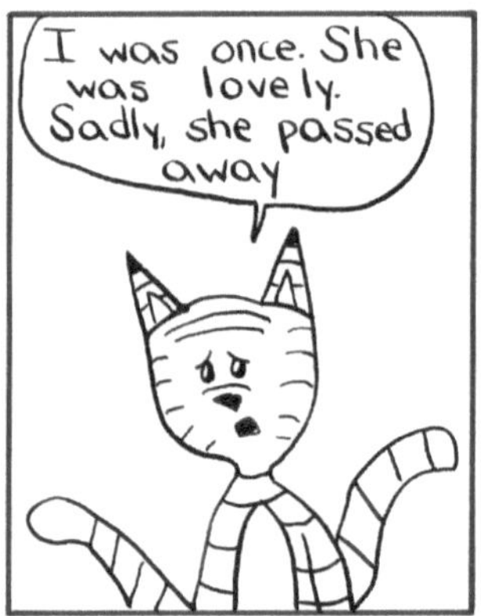
I was once. She was lovely. Sadly, she passed away
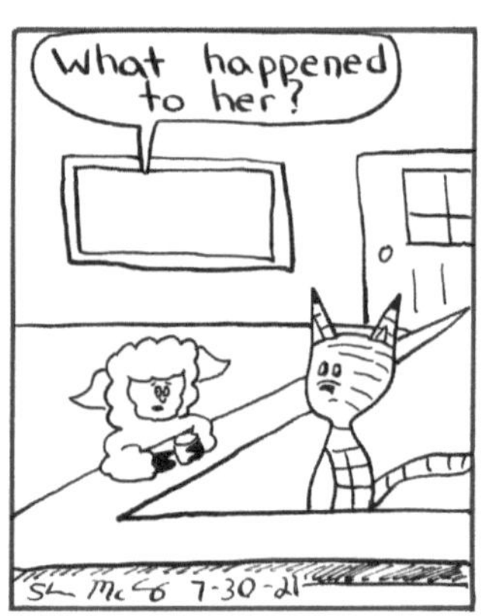
What happened to her?
SL McG 7-30-21
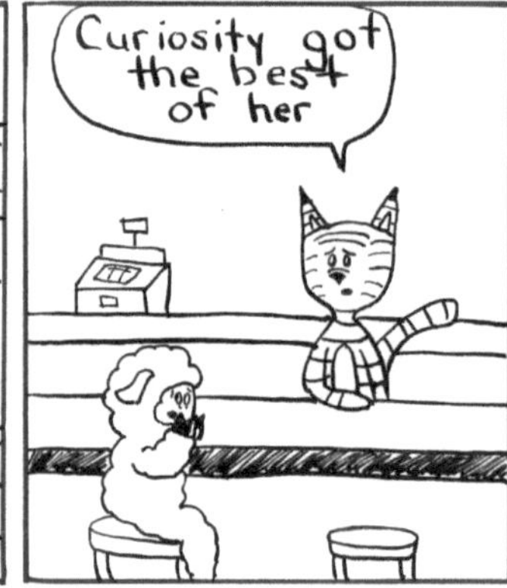
Curiosity got the best of her
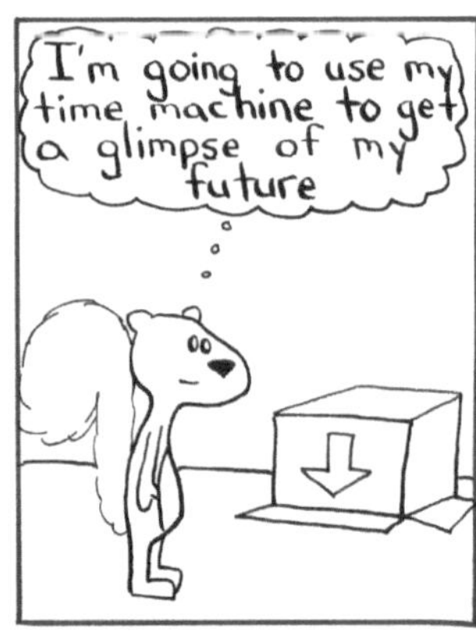
I'm going to use my time machine to get a glimpse of my future
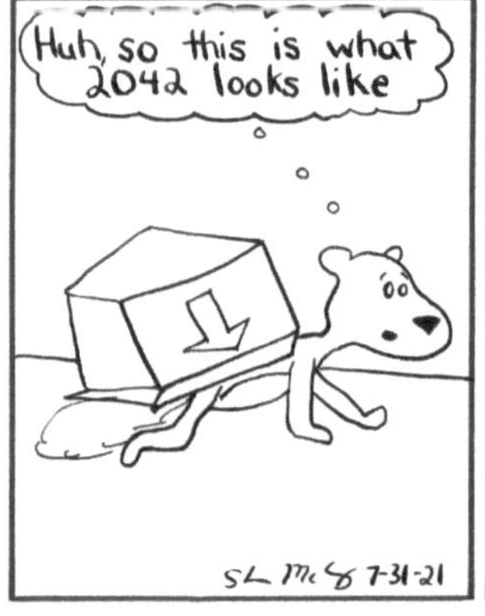
Huh, so this is what 2042 looks like
SL McG 7-31-21
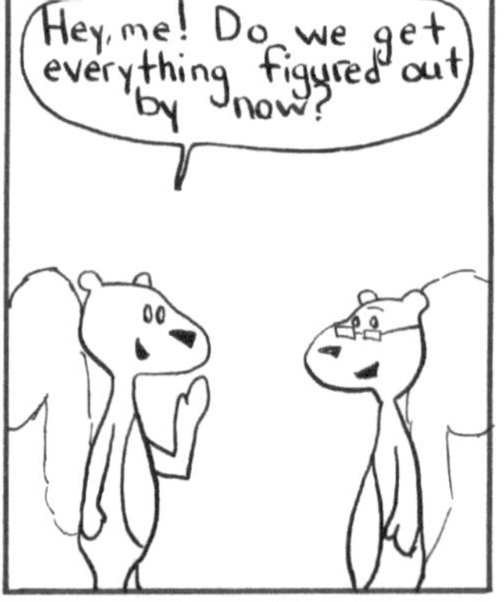
Hey, me! Do we get everything figured out by now?
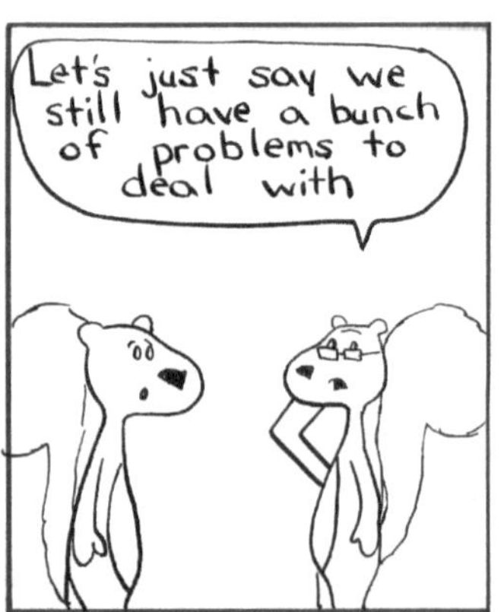
Let's just say we still have a bunch of problems to deal with

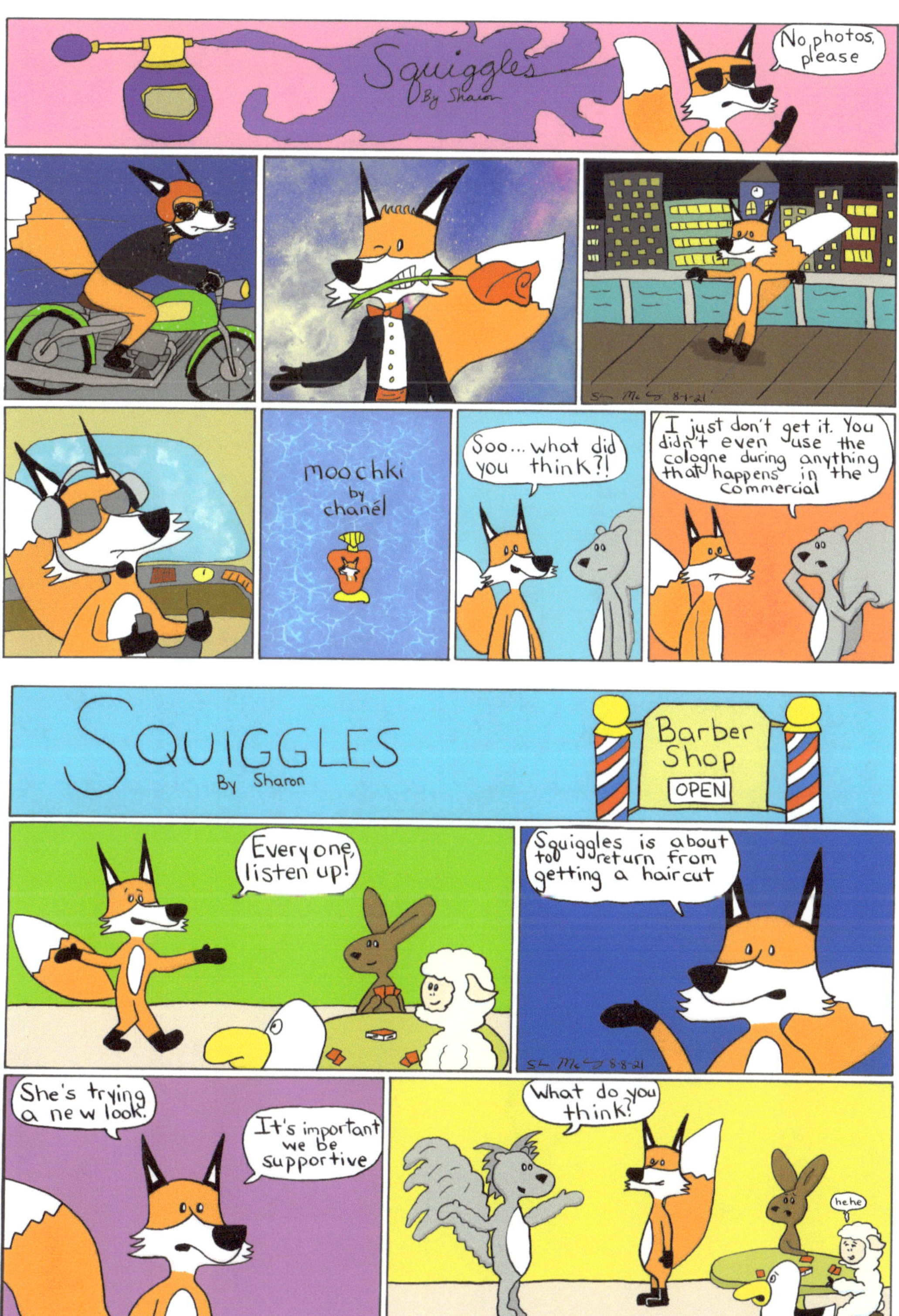
Squiggles
By Sharon
No photos, please
Sh Mc 8-1-21
Moochki
by
chanél
Soo... what did you think?!
I just don't get it. You didn't even use the cologne during anything that happens in the commercial
SQUIGGLES
By Sharon
Barber Shop
OPEN
Everyone, listen up!
Squiggles is about to return from getting a haircut
Sh Mc 8-8-21
She's trying a new look.
It's important we be supportive
What do you think?
hehe

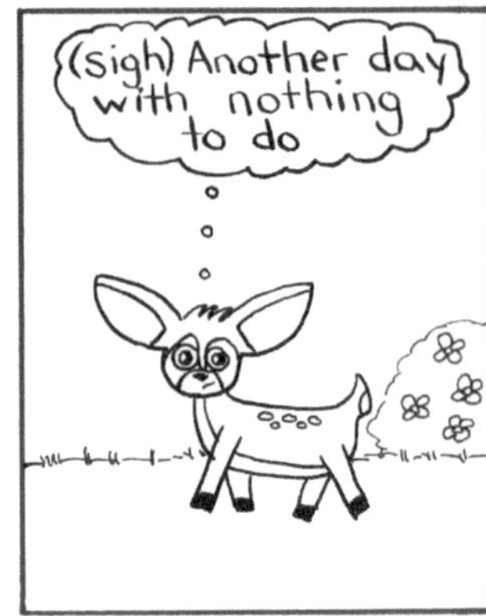
(sigh) Another day with nothing to do

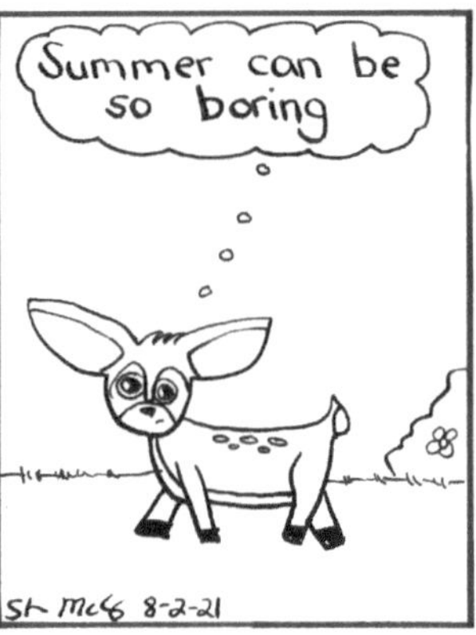
Summer can be so boring
SL McG 8-2-21

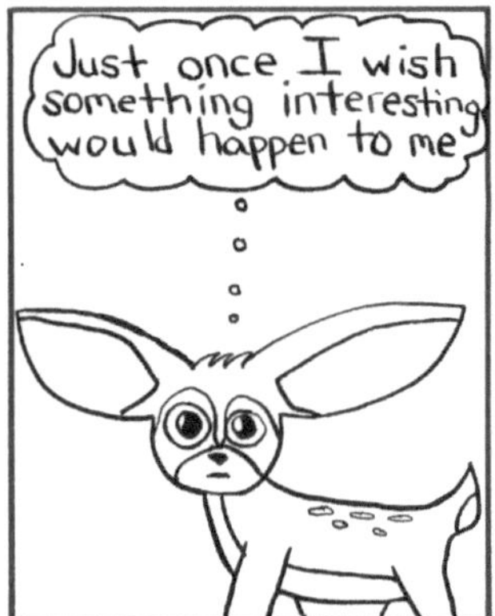
Just once I wish something interesting would happen to me

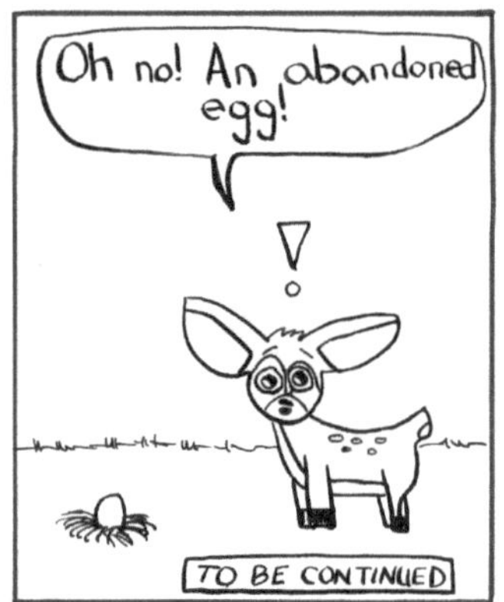
Oh no! An abandoned egg!
TO BE CONTINUED

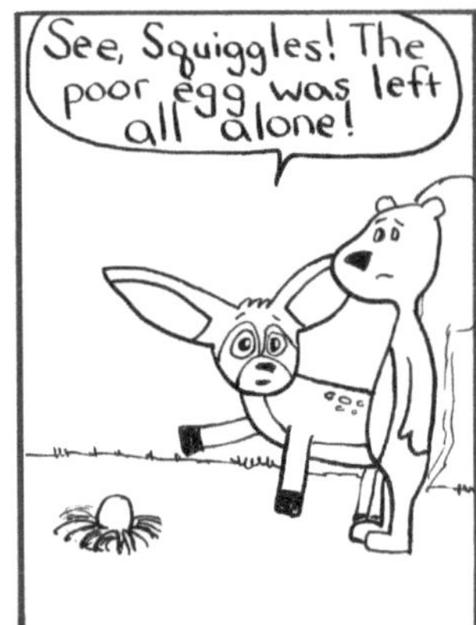
See, Squiggles! The poor egg was left all alone!

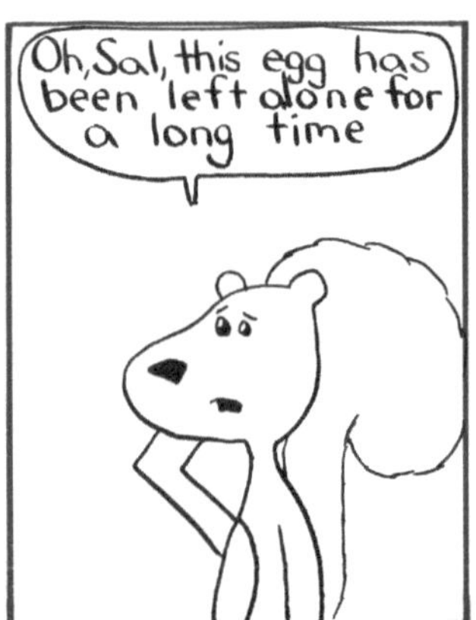
Oh, Sal, this egg has been left alone for a long time

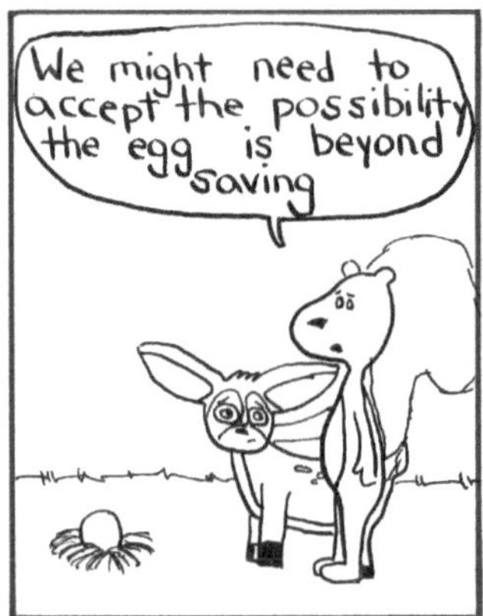
We might need to accept the possibility the egg is beyond saving

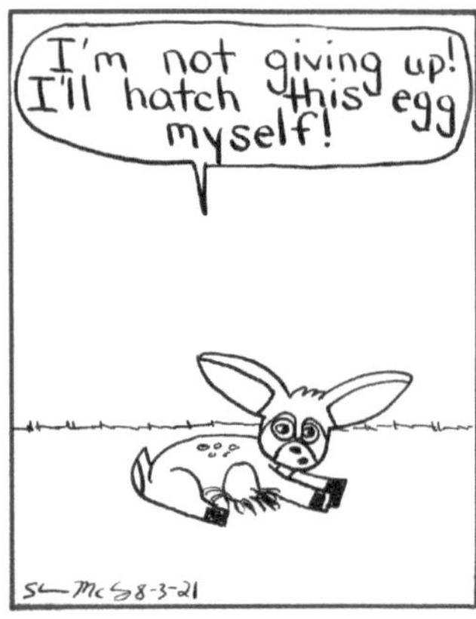
I'm not giving up! I'll hatch this egg myself!
SL McG 8-3-21

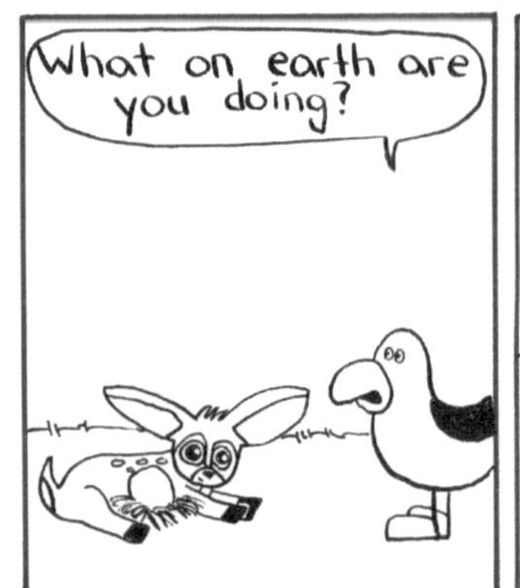
What on earth are you doing?

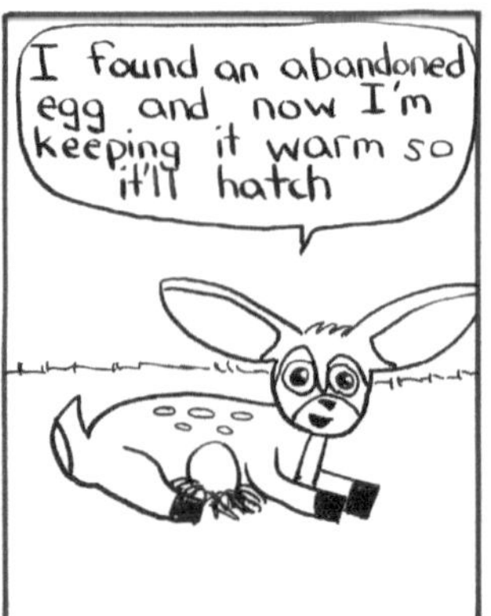
I found an abandoned egg and now I'm keeping it warm so it'll hatch

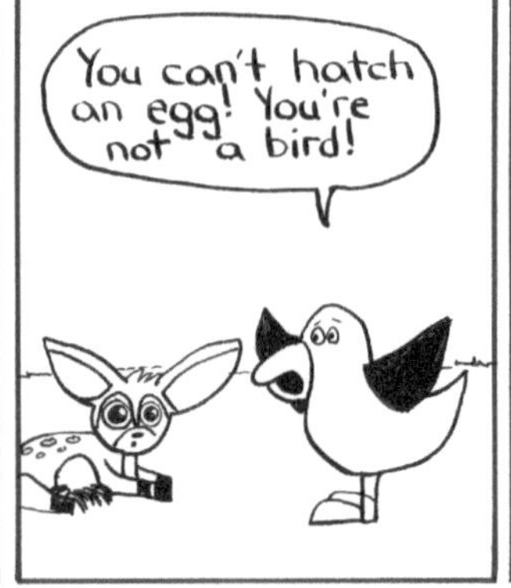
You can't hatch an egg! You're not a bird!

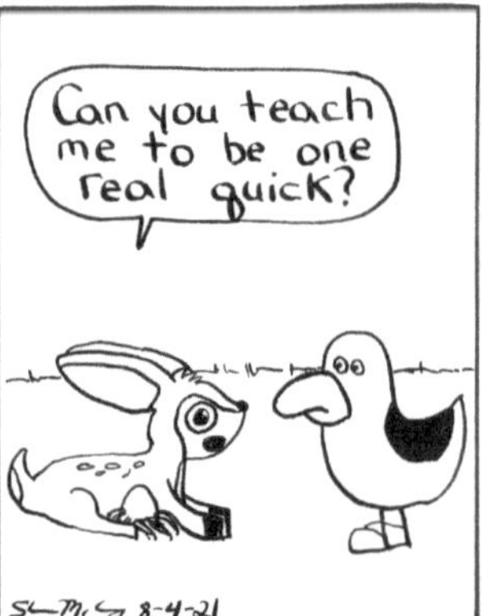
Can you teach me to be one real quick?
SL McG 8-4-21

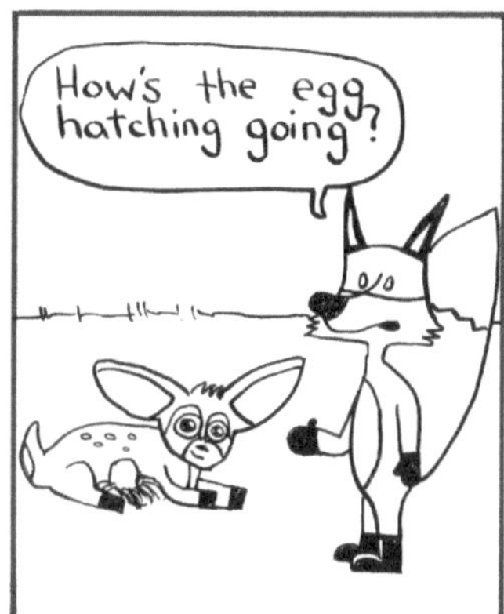
How's the egg hatching going?

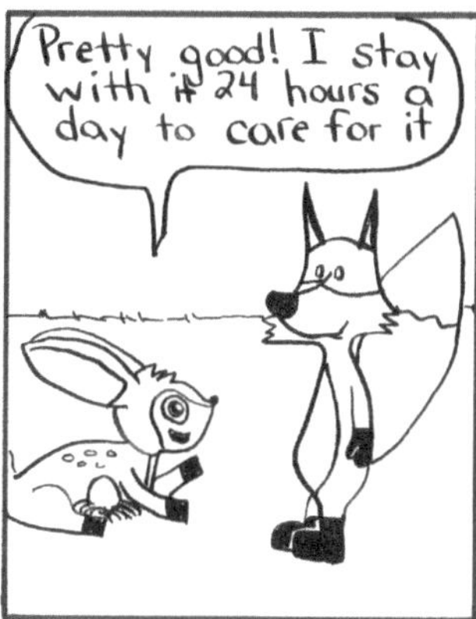
Pretty good! I stay with it 24 hours a day to care for it

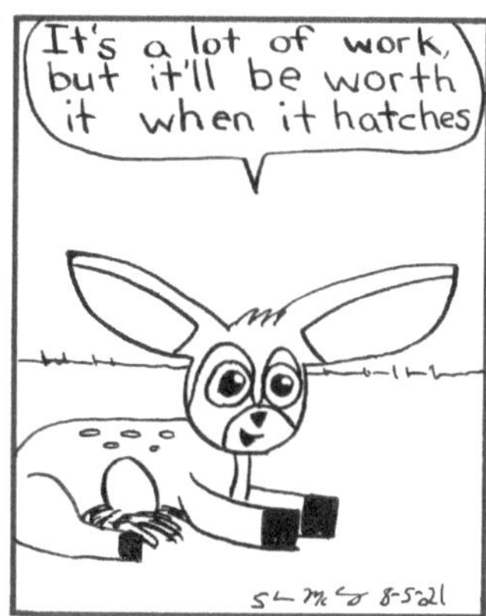
It's a lot of work, but it'll be worth it when it hatches

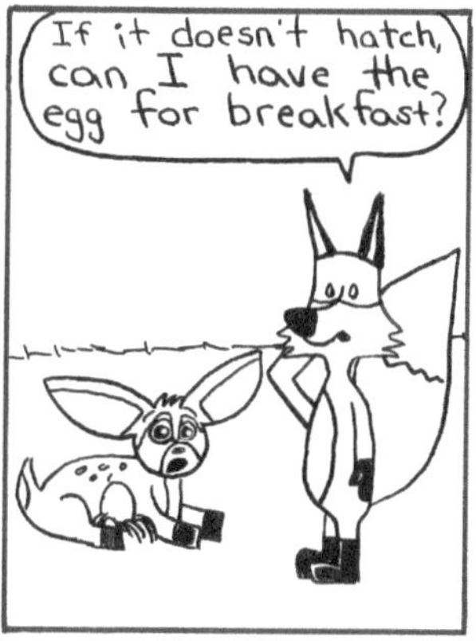
If it doesn't hatch, can I have the egg for breakfast?

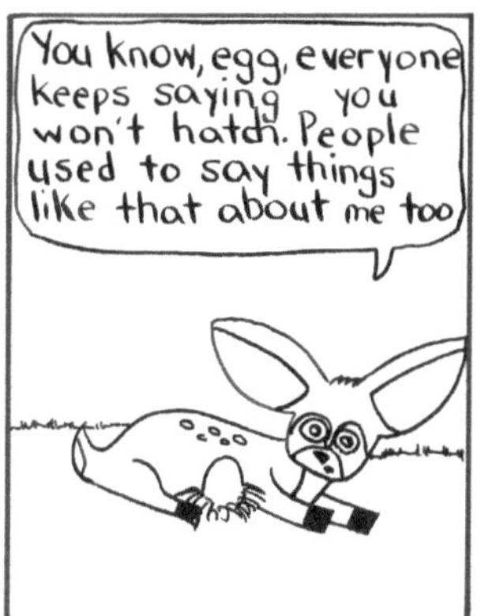
You know, egg, everyone keeps saying you won't hatch. People used to say things like that about me too

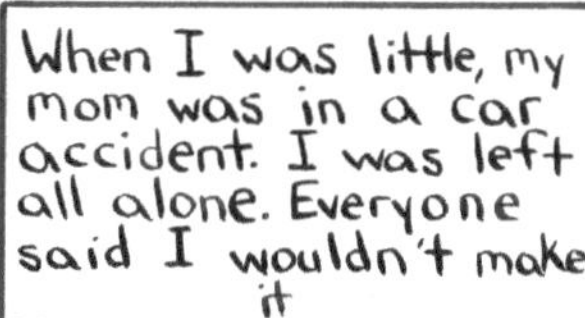
When I was little, my mom was in a car accident. I was left all alone. Everyone said I wouldn't make it

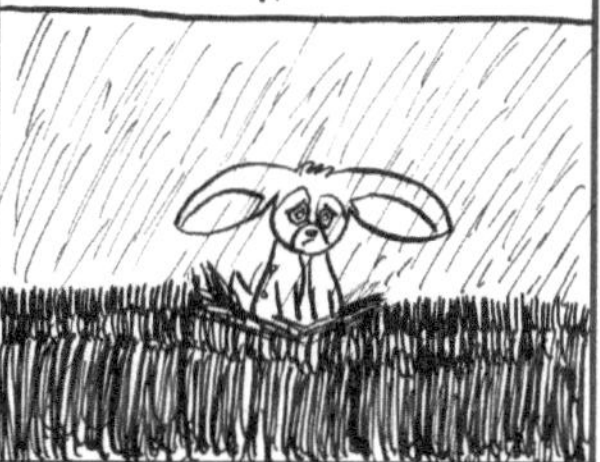

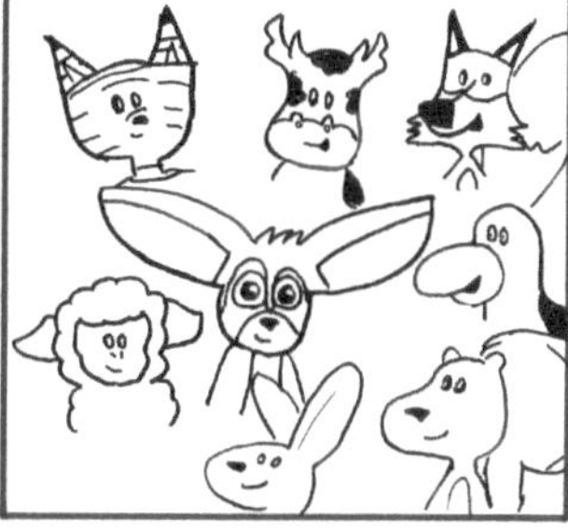
But my friends took care of me and I turned out okay

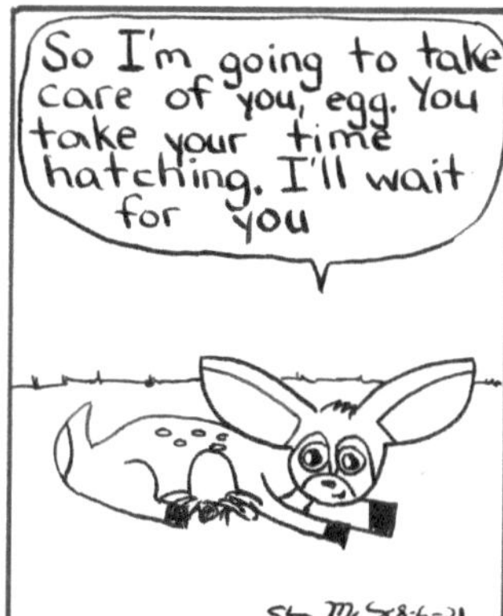
So I'm going to take care of you, egg. You take your time hatching. I'll wait for you

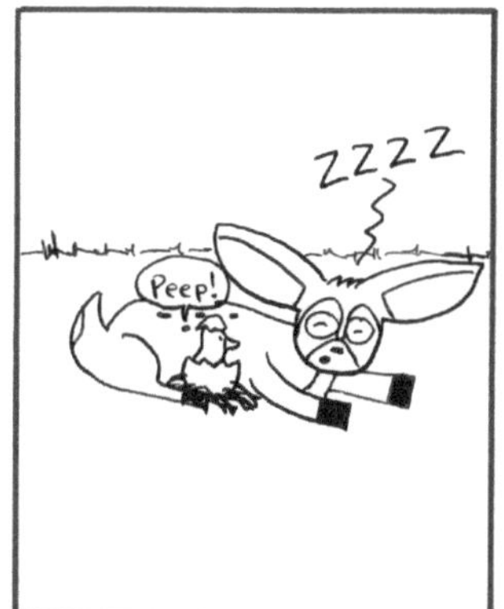
ZZZZ
Peep!

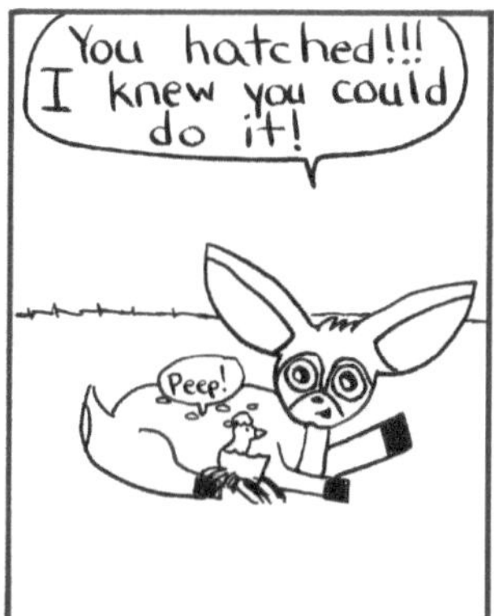
You hatched!!! I knew you could do it!
Peep!

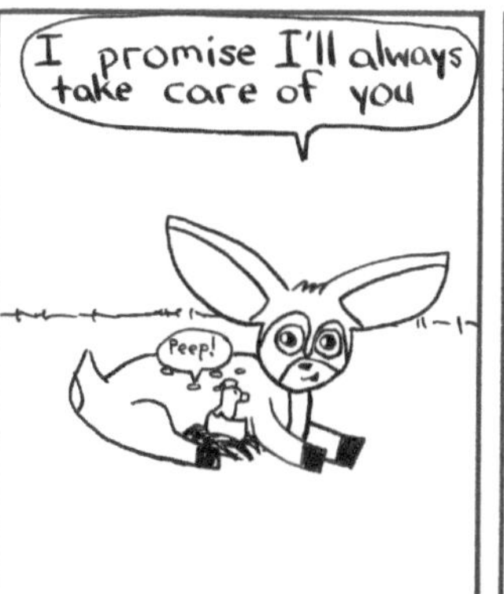
I promise I'll always take care of you
Peep!

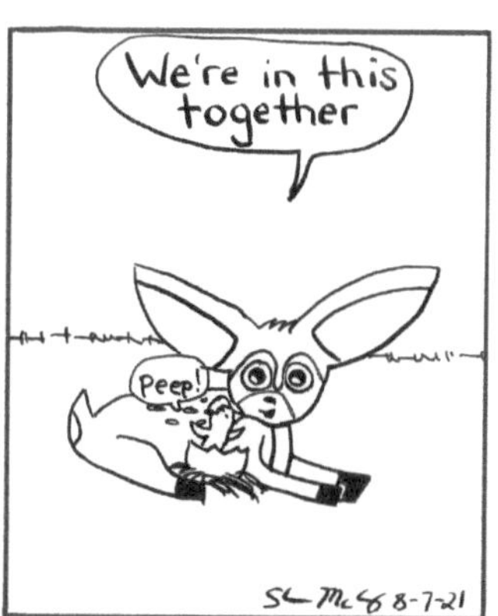
We're in this together
Peep!

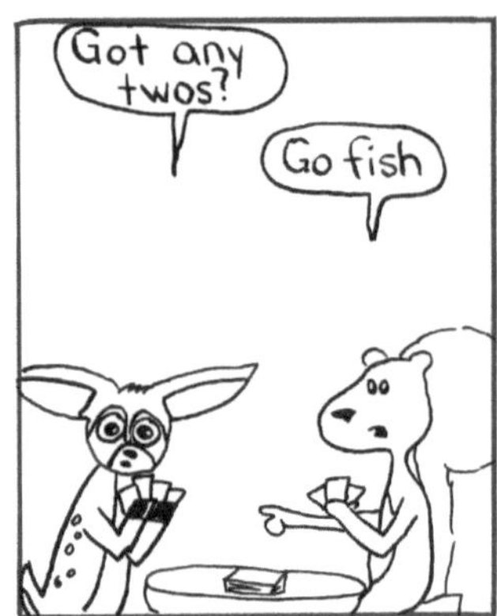
Got any twos?
Go fish

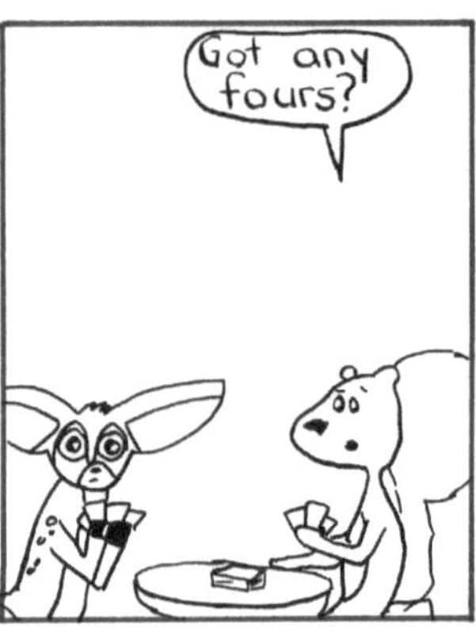
Got any fours?

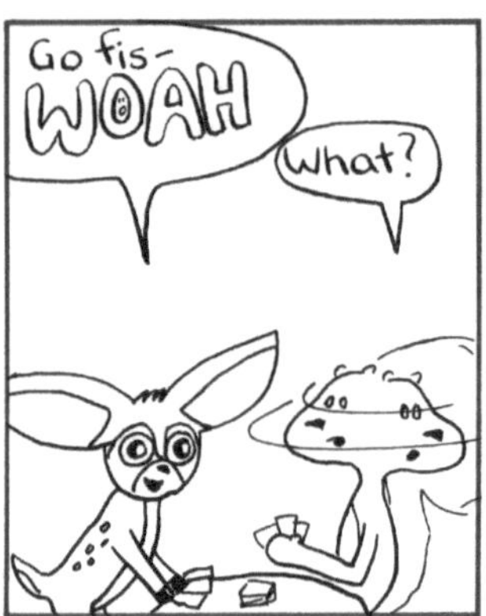
Go fis-
WOAH
What?

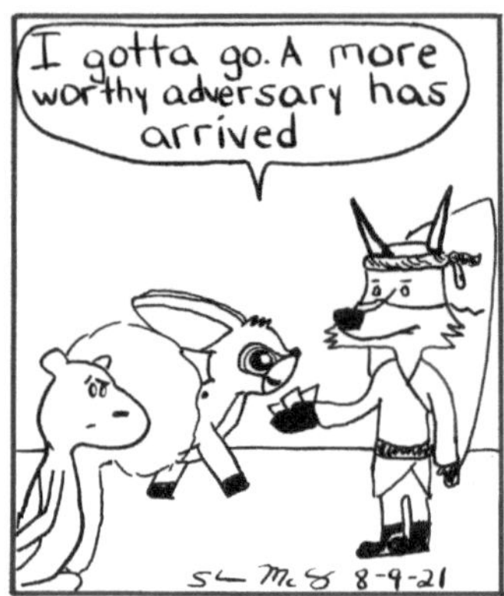
I gotta go. A more worthy adversary has arrived

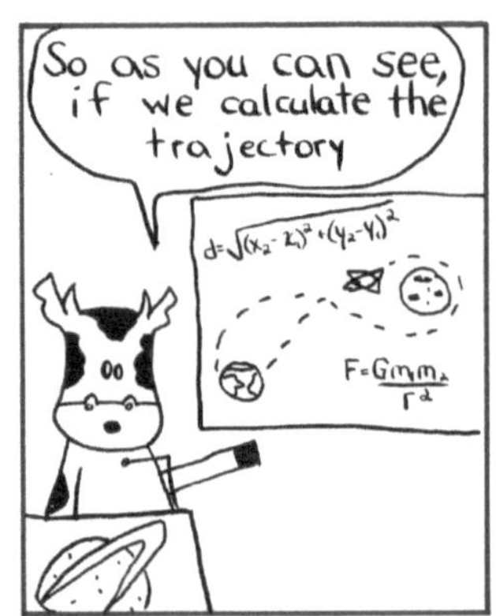
So as you can see, if we calculate the trajectory
$d=\sqrt{(x_2-x_1)^2+(y_2-y_1)^2}$
$F=\frac{Gm_1m_2}{r^2}$

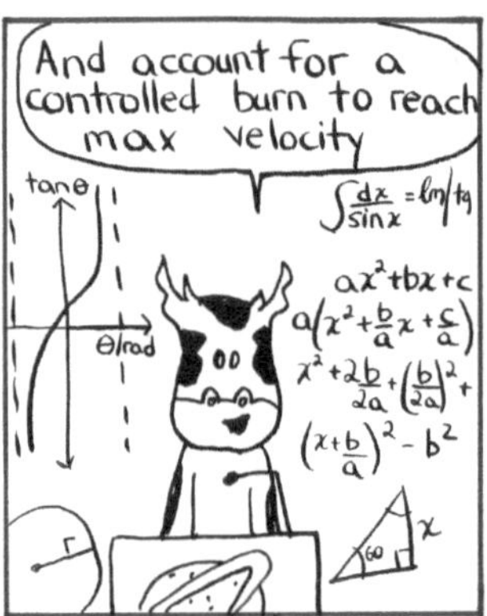
And account for a controlled burn to reach max velocity
ax^2+bx+c

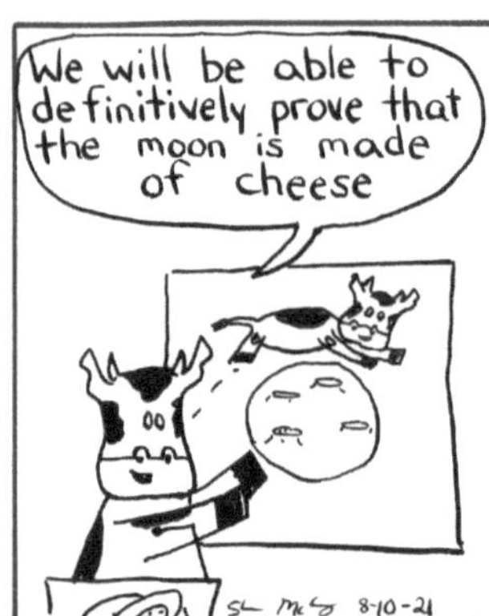
We will be able to definitively prove that the moon is made of cheese

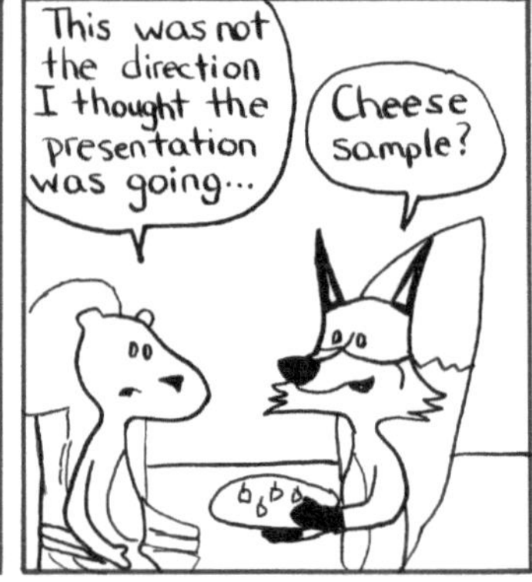
This was not the direction I thought the presentation was going...
Cheese sample?

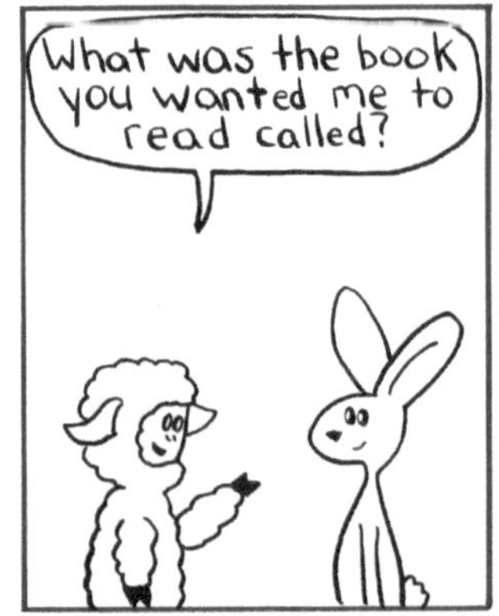
What was the book you wanted me to read called?

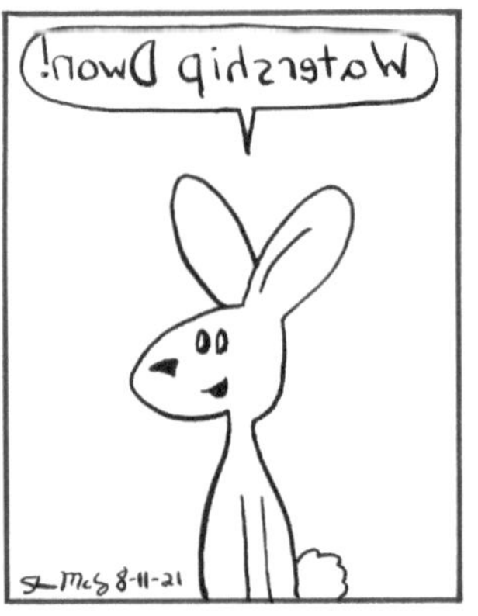
Watership Down!

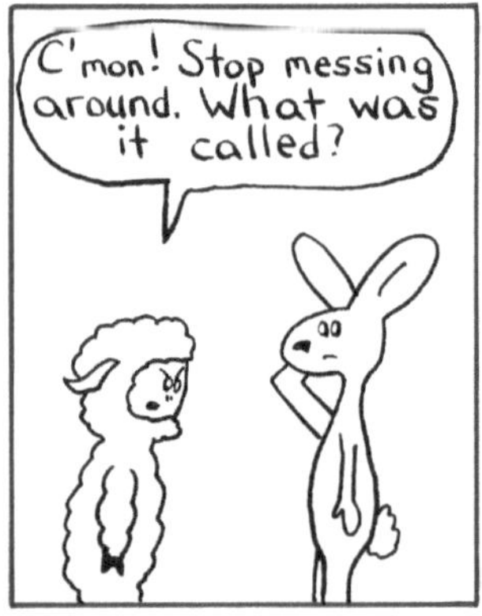
C'mon! Stop messing around. What was it called?

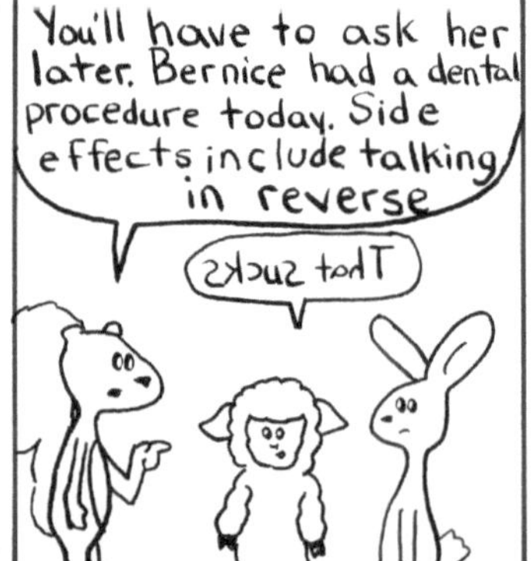
You'll have to ask her later. Bernice had a dental procedure today. Side effects include talking in reverse
That sucks

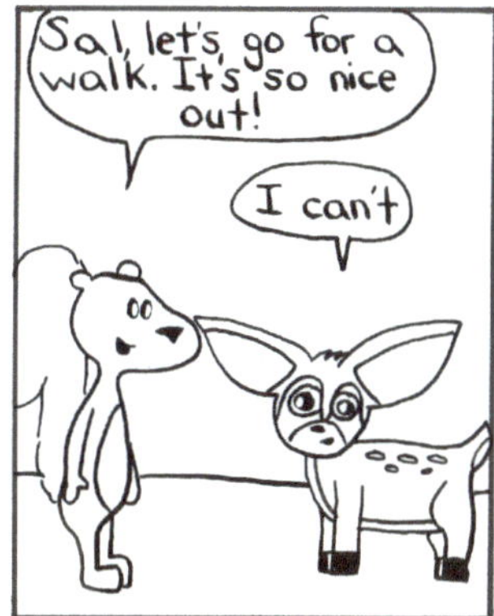
Sal, let's go for a walk. It's so nice out!
I can't

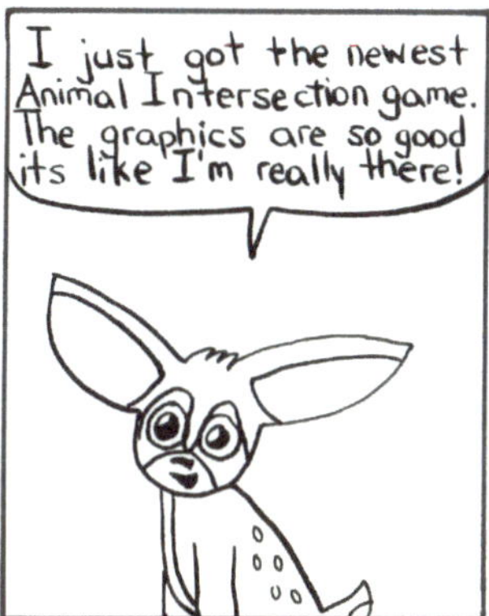
I just got the newest Animal Intersection game. The graphics are so good its like I'm really there!

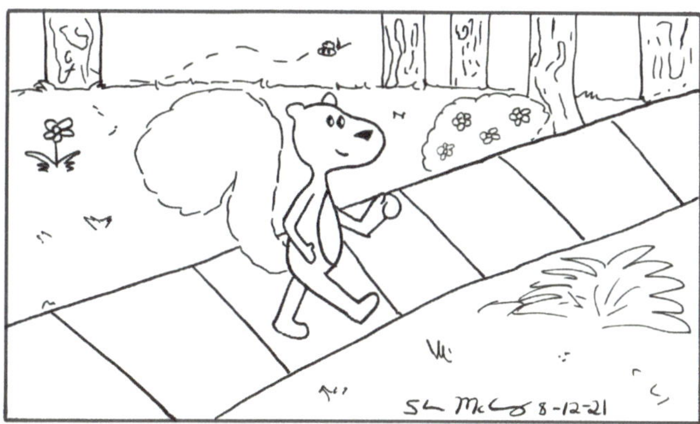
8-12-21

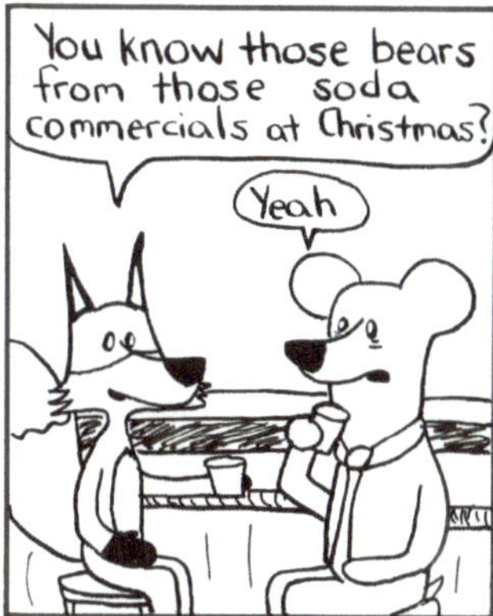
You know those bears from those soda commercials at Christmas?
Yeah

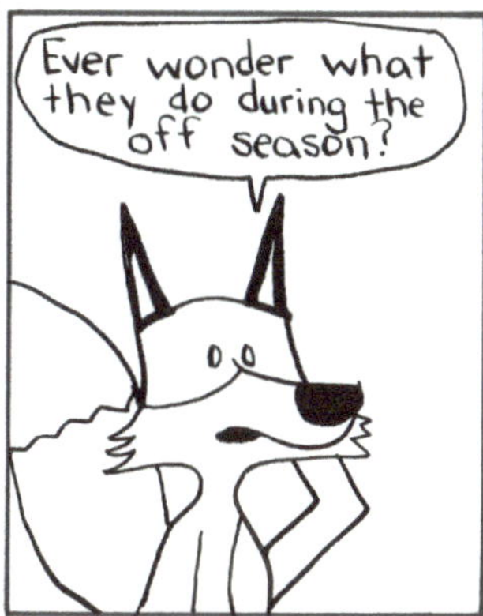
Ever wonder what they do during the off season?

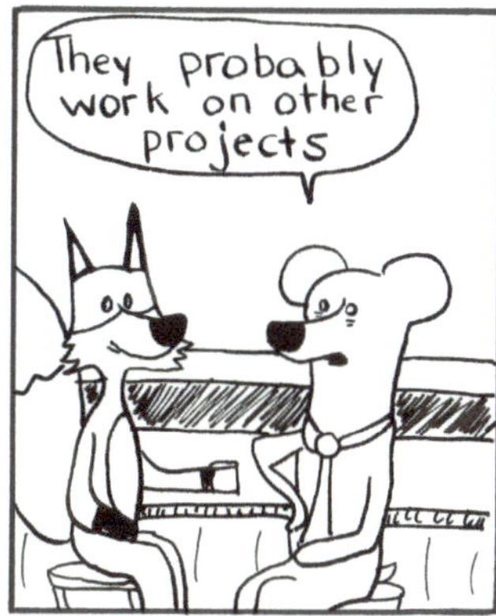
They probably work on other projects

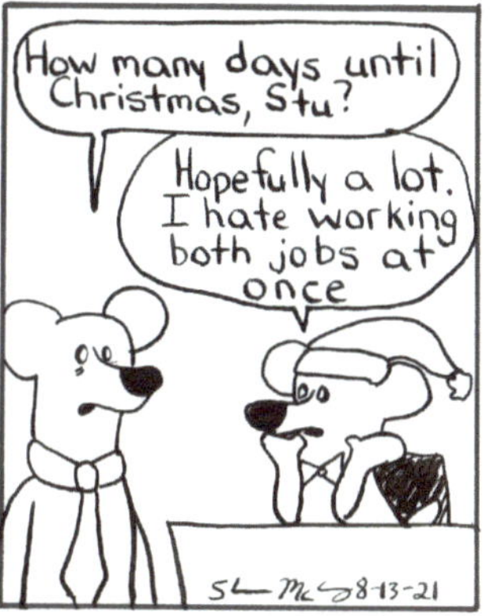
How many days until Christmas, Stu?
Hopefully a lot. I hate working both jobs at once
8-13-21

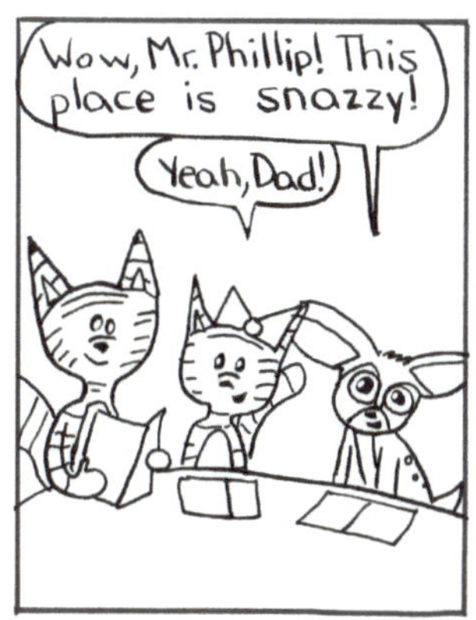
Wow, Mr. Phillip! This place is snazzy!
Yeah, Dad!

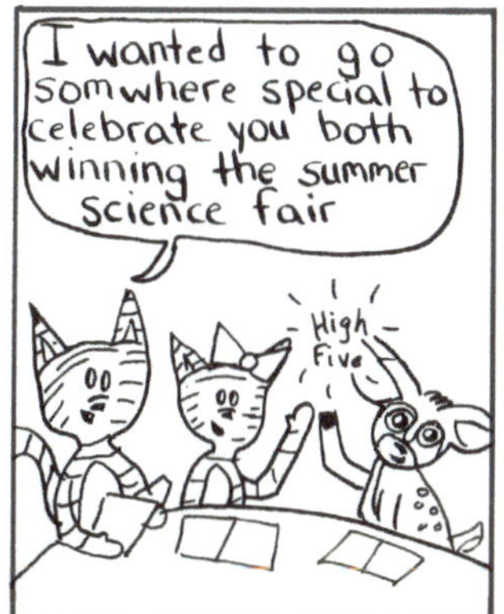
I wanted to go somwhere special to celebrate you both winning the summer science fair
High Five

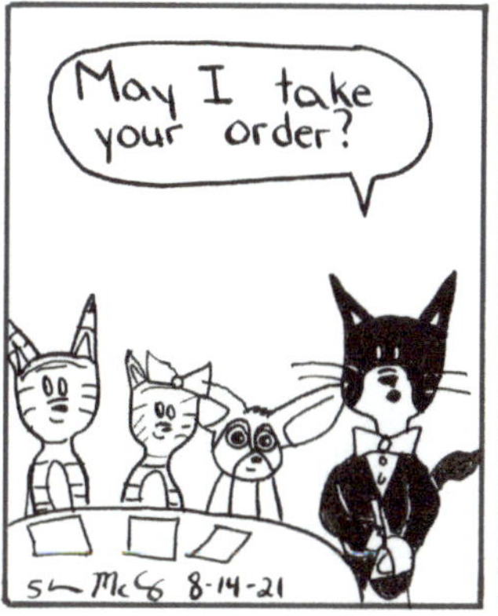
May I take your order?
8-14-21

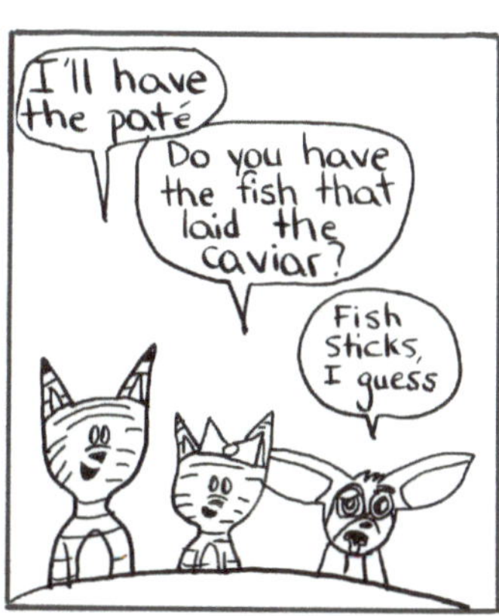
I'll have the paté
Do you have the fish that laid the caviar?
Fish sticks, I guess

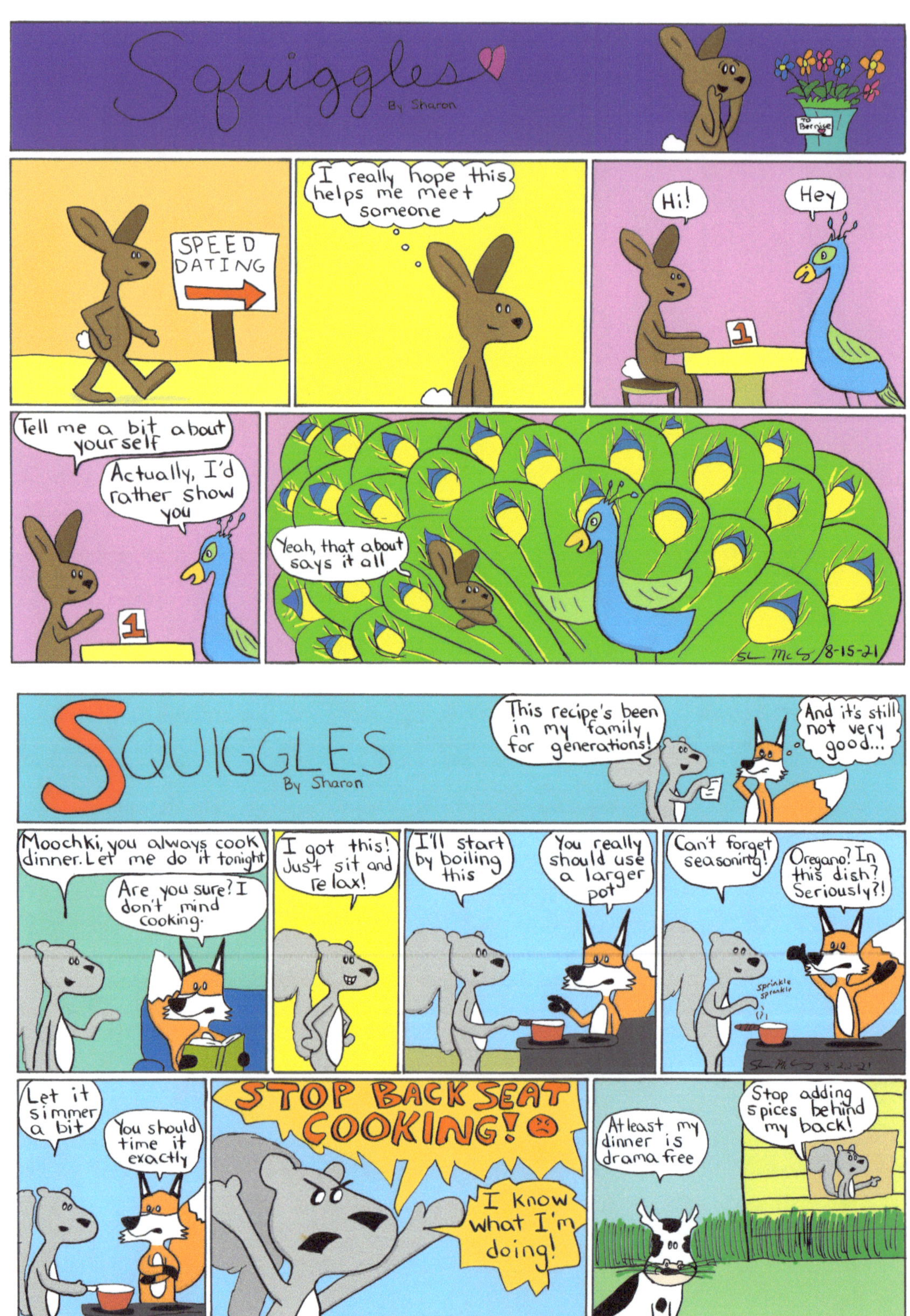
Squiggles
By Sharon
To Bernice
SPEED DATING
I really hope this helps me meet someone
Hi!
Hey
Tell me a bit about yourself
Actually, I'd rather show you
1
Yeah, that about says it all
SL McG 8-15-21
SQUIGGLES
By Sharon
This recipe's been in my family for generations!
And it's still not very good...
Moochki, you always cook dinner. Let me do it tonight
Are you sure? I don't mind cooking.
I got this! Just sit and relax!
I'll start by boiling this
You really should use a larger pot
Can't forget seasoning!
Oregano? In this dish? Seriously?!
Sprinkle sprinkle
Let it simmer a bit
You should time it exactly
STOP BACK SEAT COOKING!
I know what I'm doing!
Atleast my dinner is drama free
Stop adding spices behind my back!

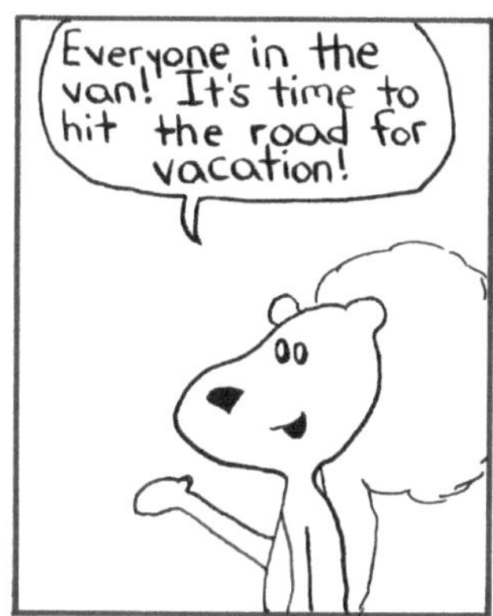
Everyone in the van! It's time to hit the road for vacation!

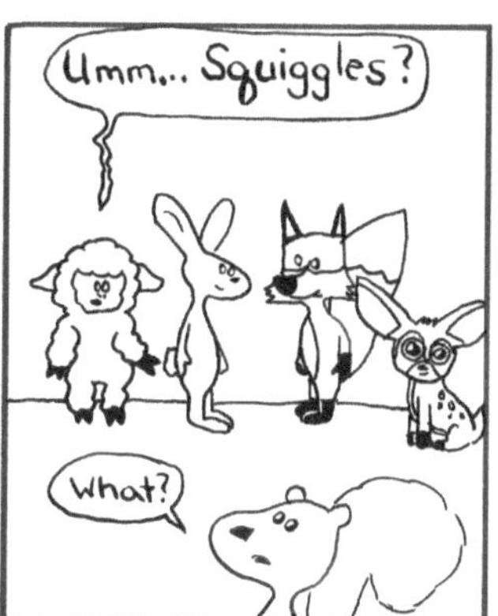
Umm... Squiggles?
What?

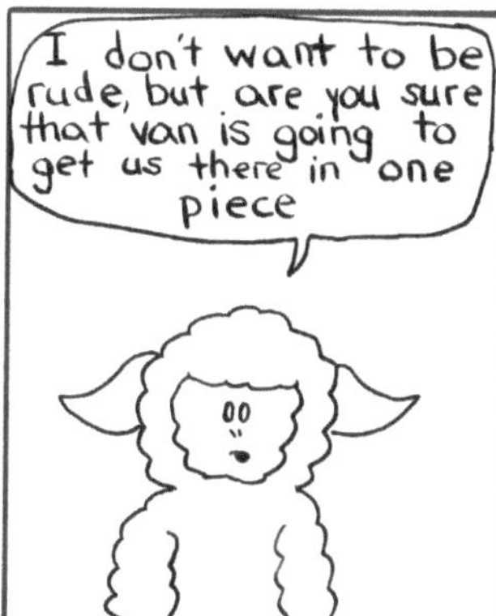
I don't want to be rude, but are you sure that van is going to get us there in one piece

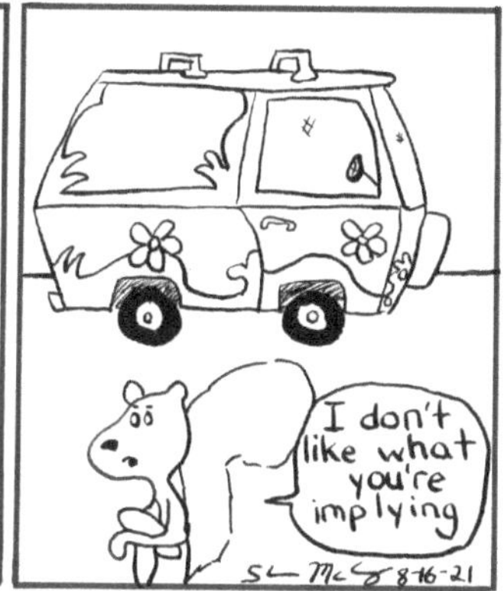
I don't like what you're implying
SL McG 8-16-21

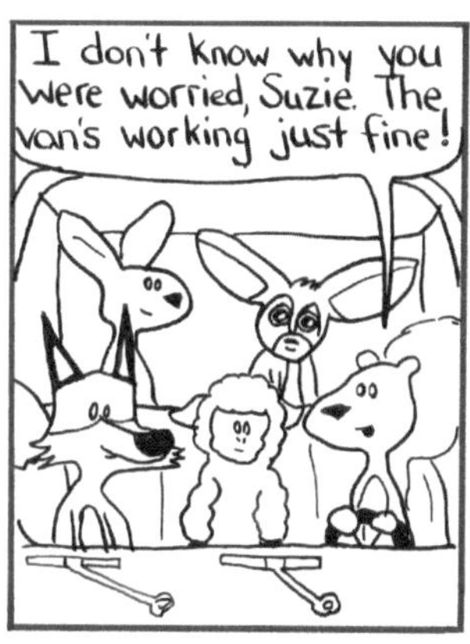
I don't know why you were worried, Suzie. The van's working just fine!

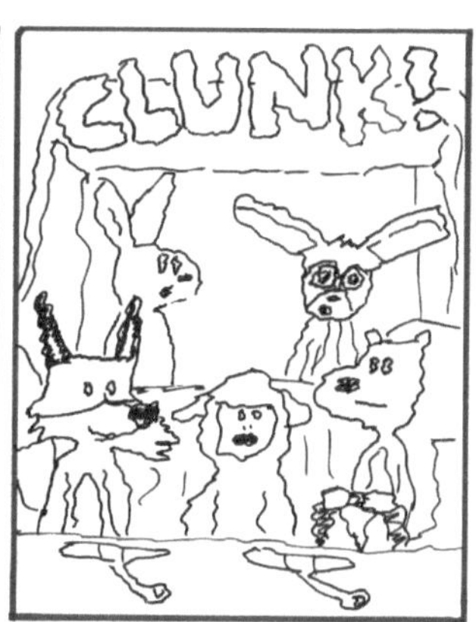
CLUNK!

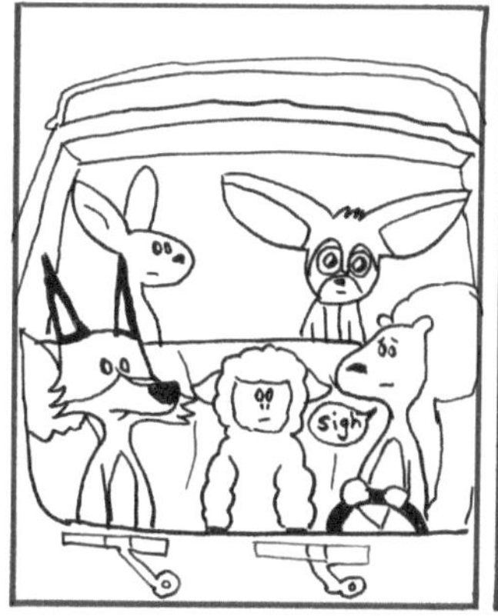
sigh

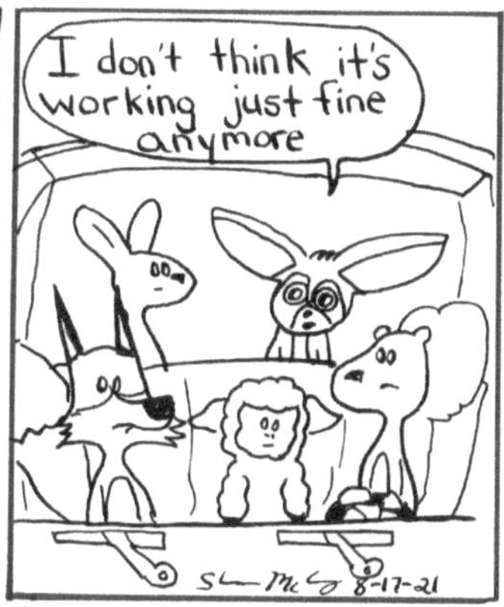
I don't think it's working just fine anymore
SL McG 8-17-21

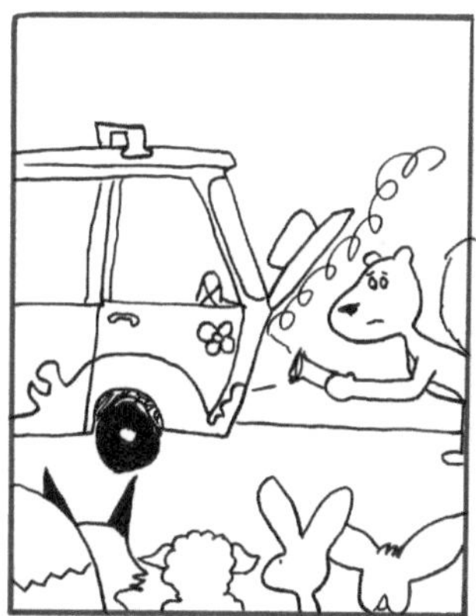

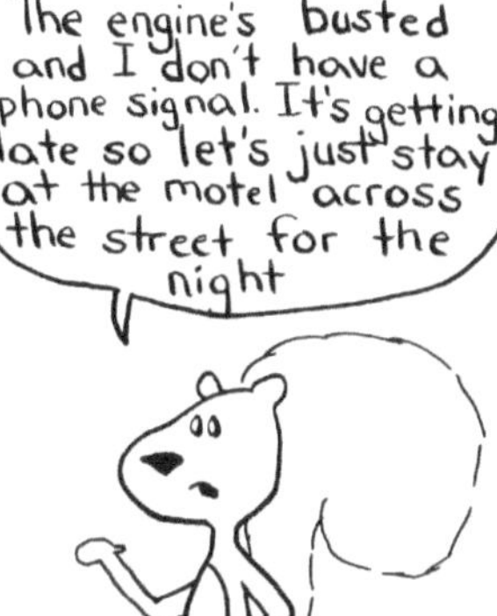
The engine's busted and I don't have a phone signal. It's getting late so let's just stay at the motel across the street for the night

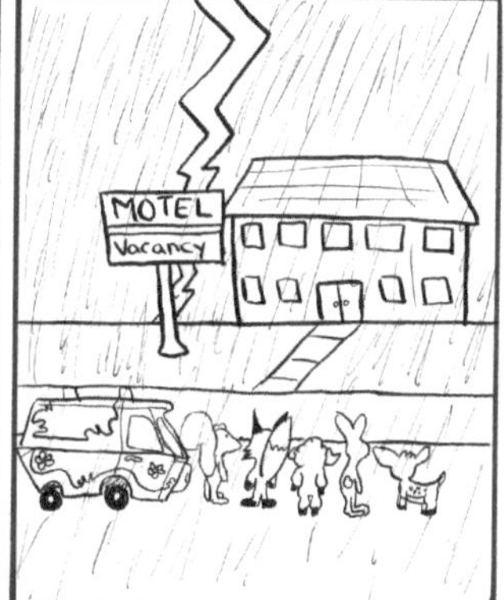
MOTEL
Vacancy

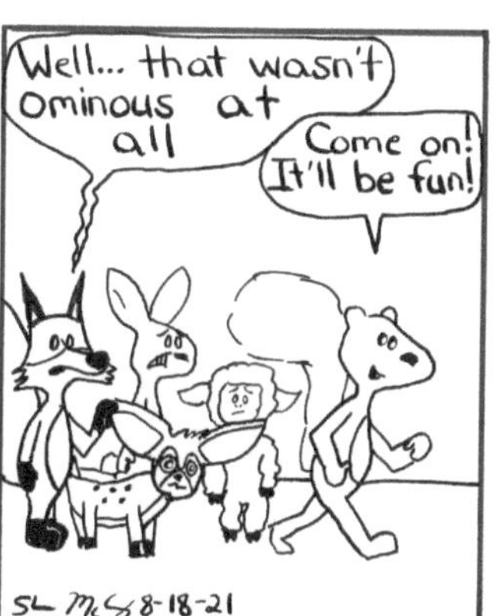
Well... that wasn't ominous at all
Come on! It'll be fun!
SL McG 8-18-21

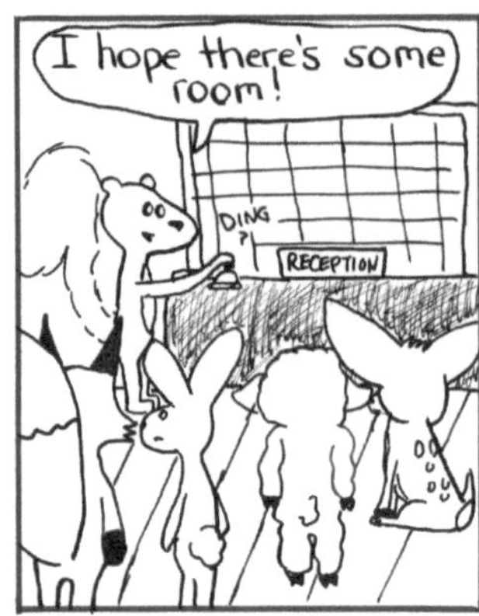
I hope there's some room!
DING
RECEPTION

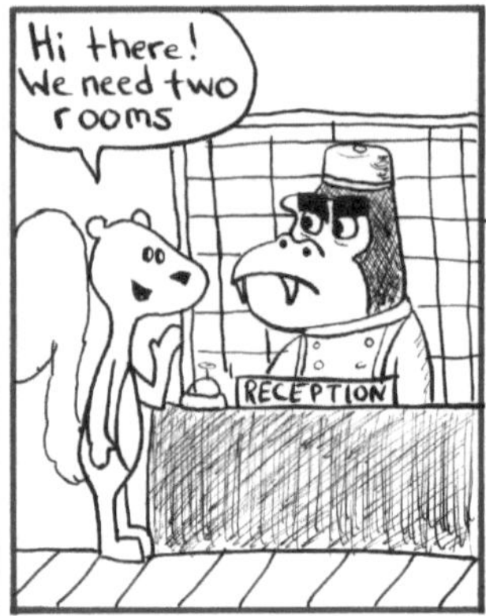
Hi there! We need two rooms
RECEPTION

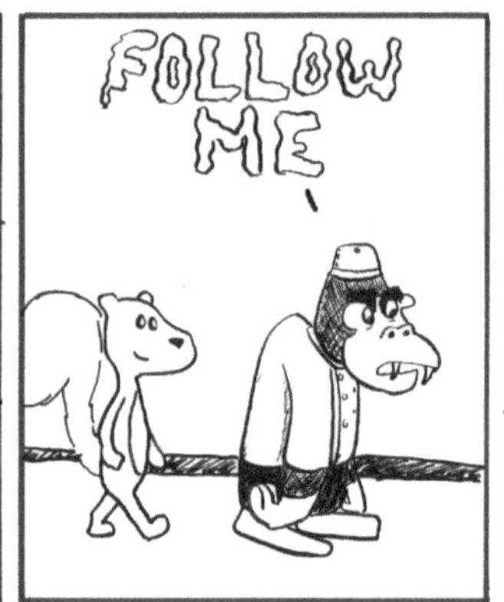
FOLLOW ME

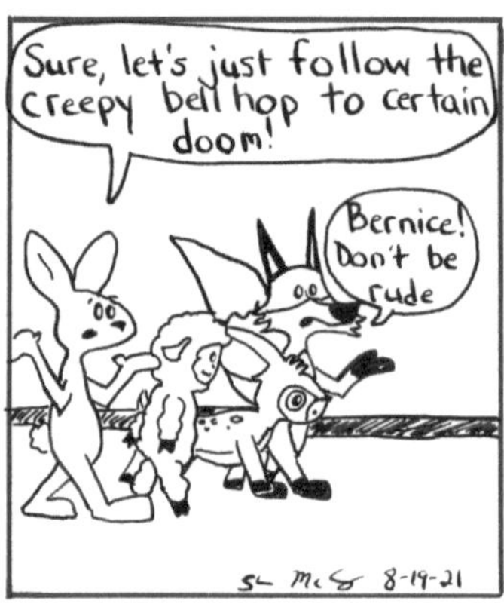
Sure, let's just follow the creepy bellhop to certain doom!
Bernice! Don't be rude
SL McS 8-19-21

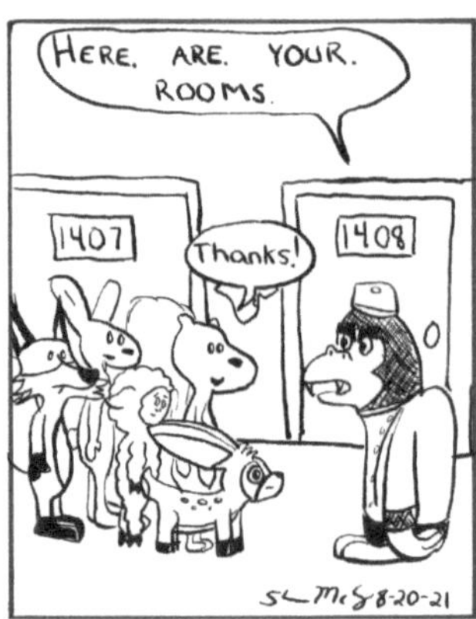
HERE. ARE. YOUR. ROOMS.
1407
Thanks!
1408
SL McS 8-20-21

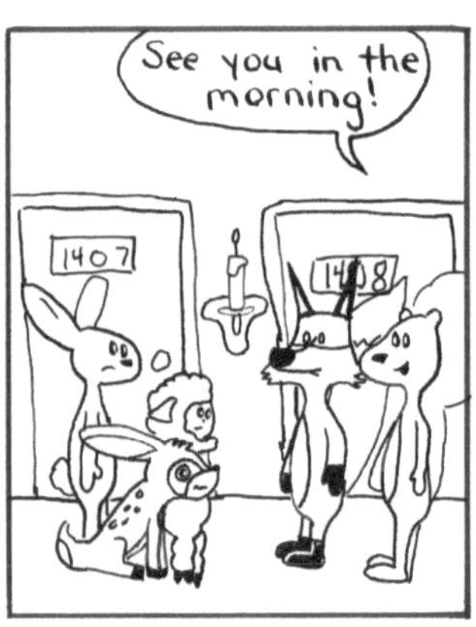
See you in the morning!
1407
1408

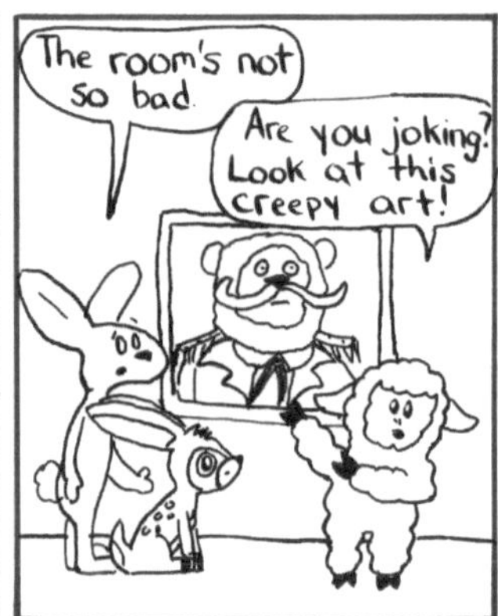
The room's not so bad.
Are you joking? Look at this creepy art!

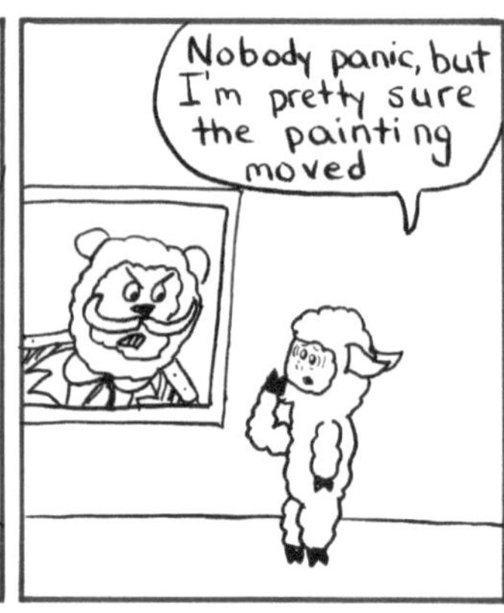
Nobody panic, but I'm pretty sure the painting moved

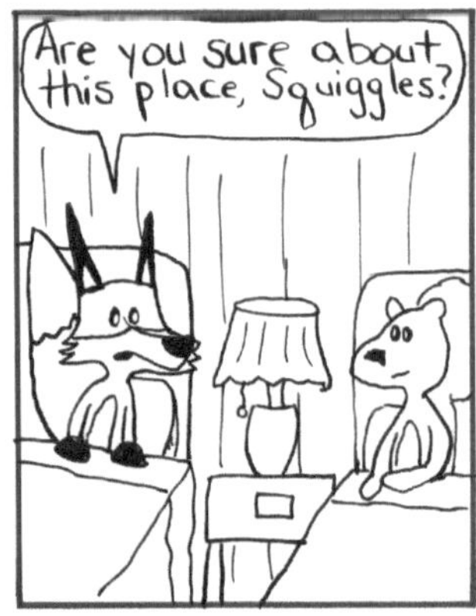
Are you sure about this place, Squiggles?

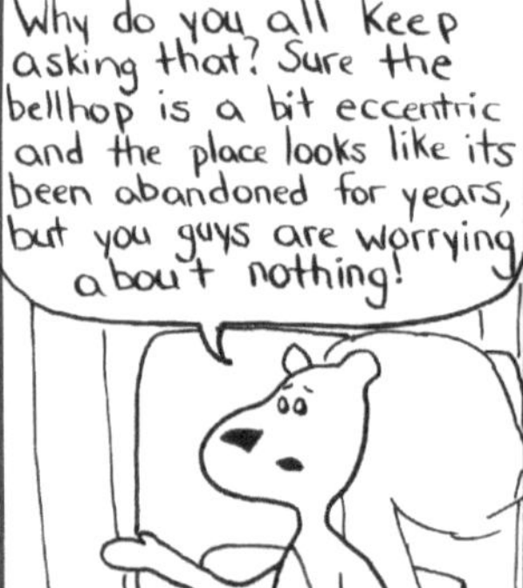
Why do you all keep asking that? Sure the bellhop is a bit eccentric and the place looks like its been abandoned for years, but you guys are worrying about nothing!

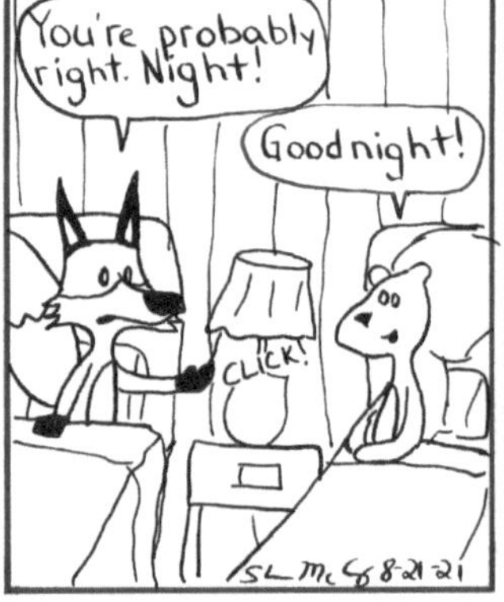
You're probably right. Night!
Goodnight!
CLICK!
SL McS 8-21-21

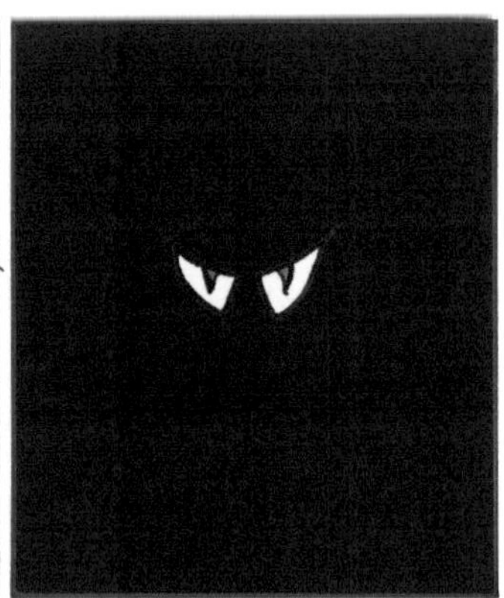

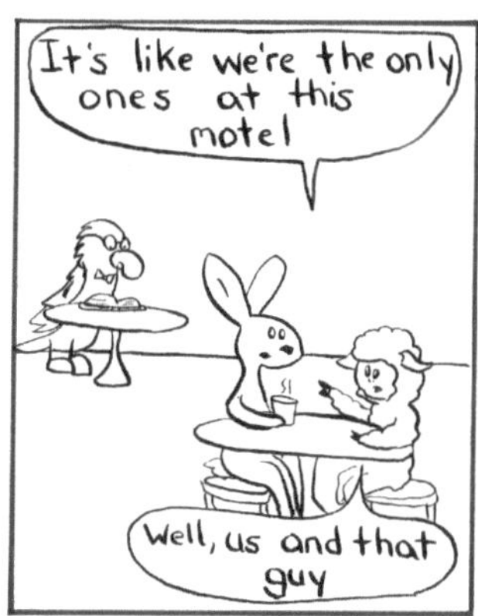
It's like we're the only ones at this motel
Well, us and that guy

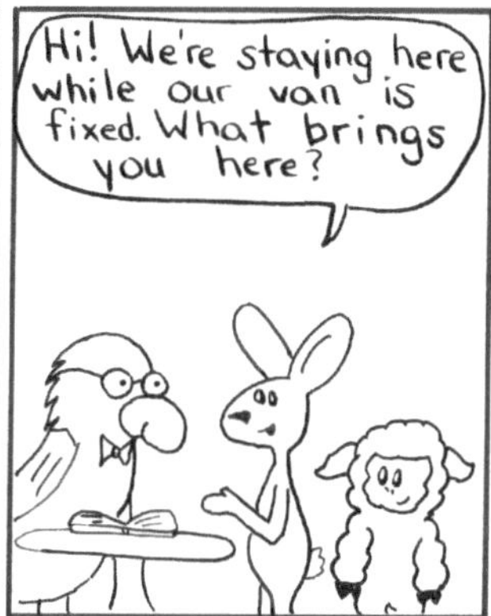
Hi! We're staying here while our van is fixed. What brings you here?

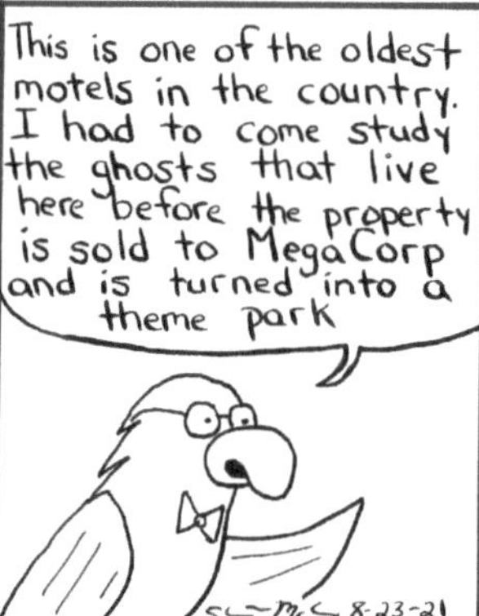
This is one of the oldest motels in the country. I had to come study the ghosts that live here before the property is sold to MegaCorp and is turned into a theme park
SL McG 8-23-21

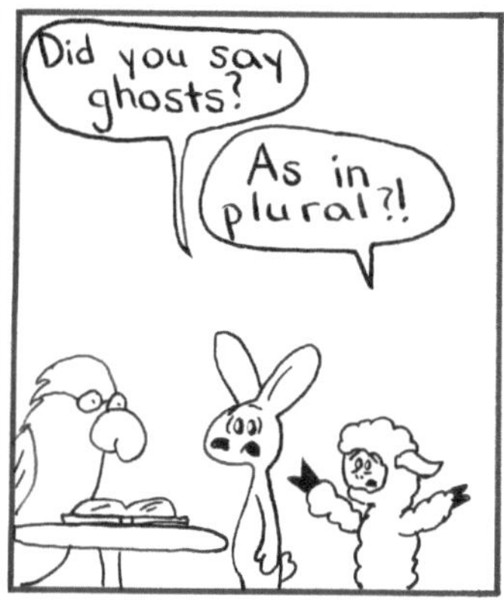
Did you say ghosts?
As in plural?!

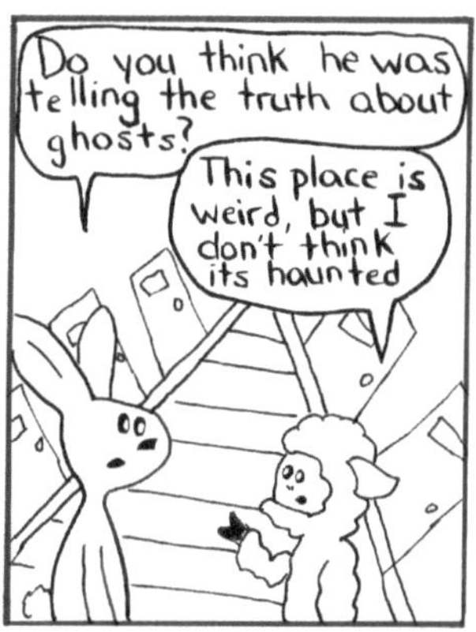
Do you think he was telling the truth about ghosts?
This place is weird, but I don't think its haunted

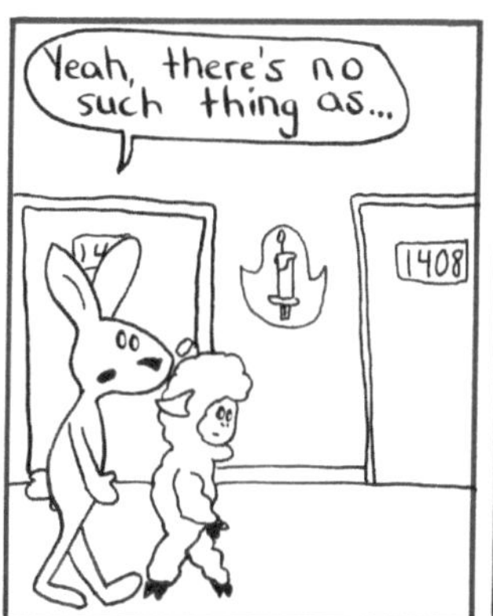
Yeah, there's no such thing as...
1408

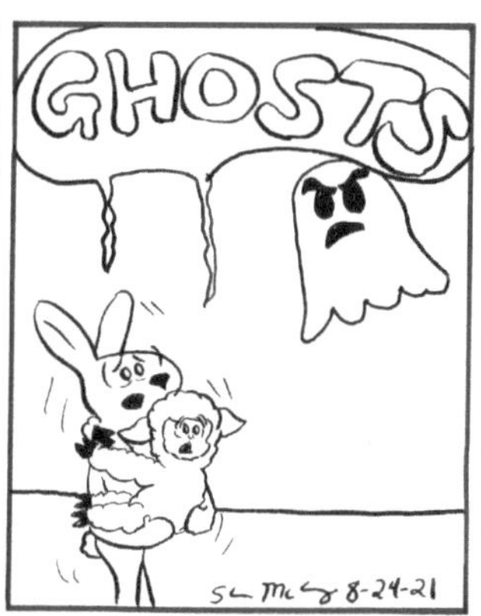
GHOSTS
SL McG 8-24-21

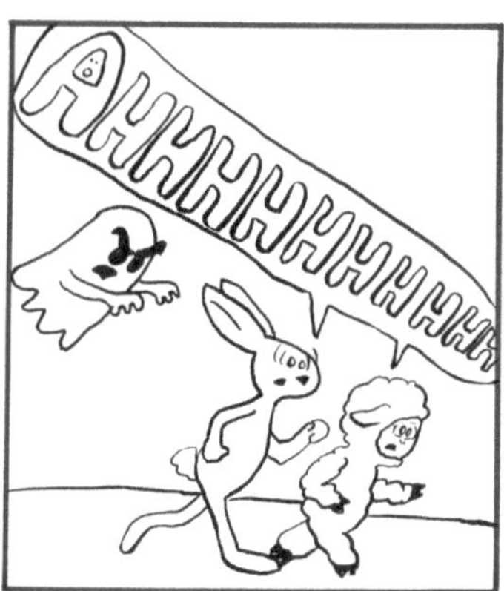
AHHHHHHHHHH

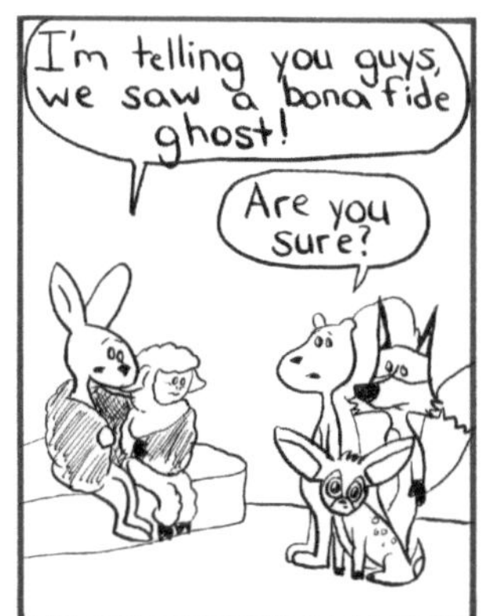
I'm telling you guys, we saw a bona fide ghost!
Are you sure?

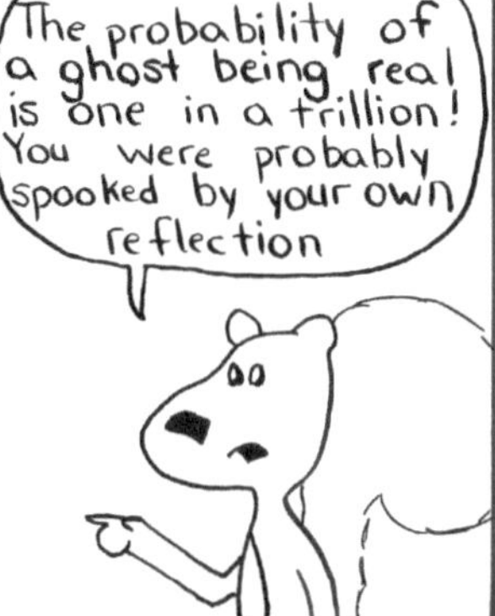
The probability of a ghost being real is one in a trillion! You were probably spooked by your own reflection

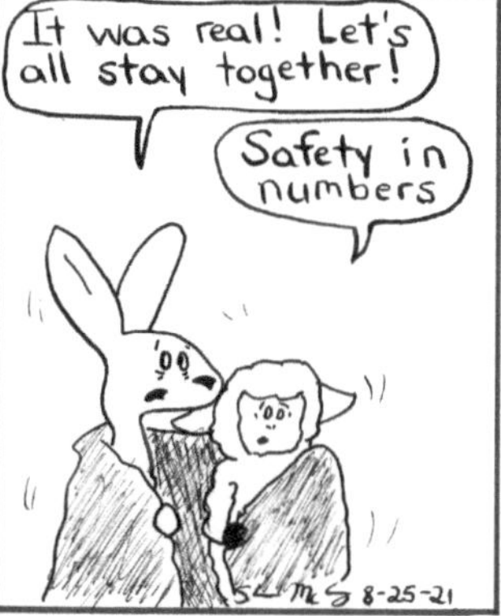
It was real! Let's all stay together!
Safety in numbers
SL McG 8-25-21

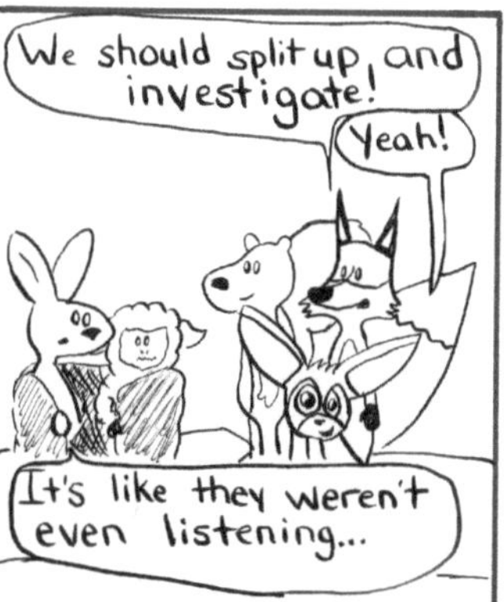
We should split up and investigate!
Yeah!
It's like they weren't even listening...

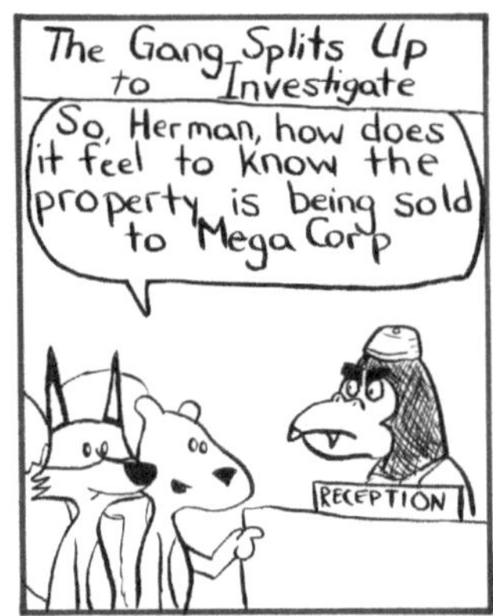
The Gang Splits Up to Investigate
So, Herman, how does it feel to know the property is being sold to Mega Corp
RECEPTION

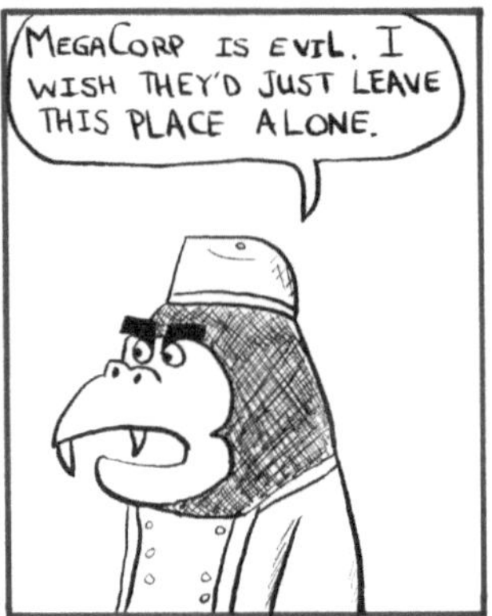
MEGACORP IS EVIL. I WISH THEY'D JUST LEAVE THIS PLACE ALONE.

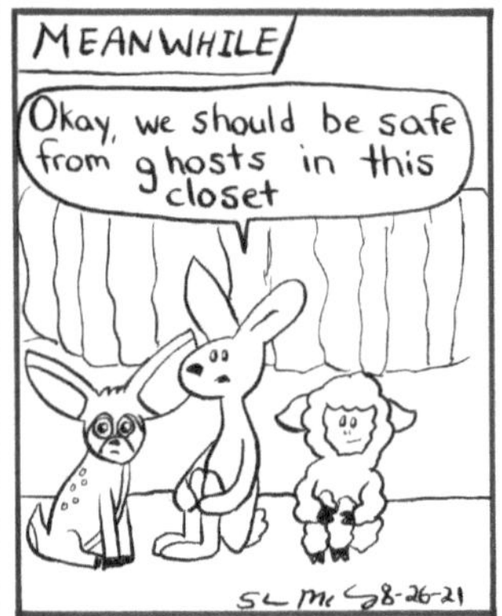
MEANWHILE
Okay, we should be safe from ghosts in this closet
SL McG 8-26-21

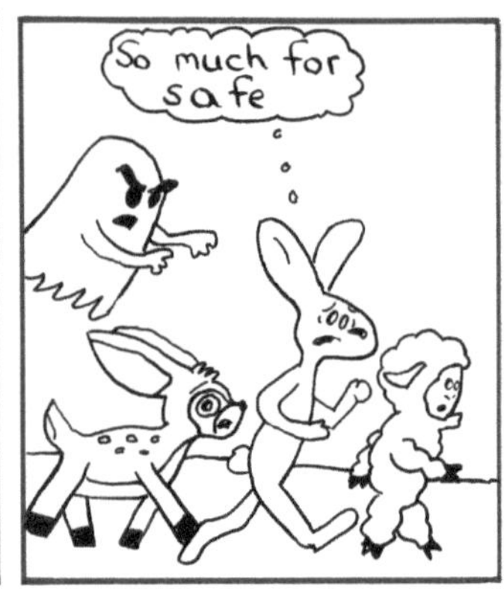
So much for safe

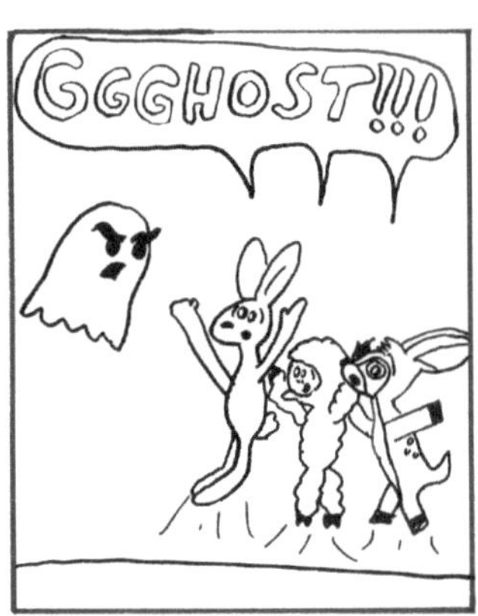
GGGHOST!!!

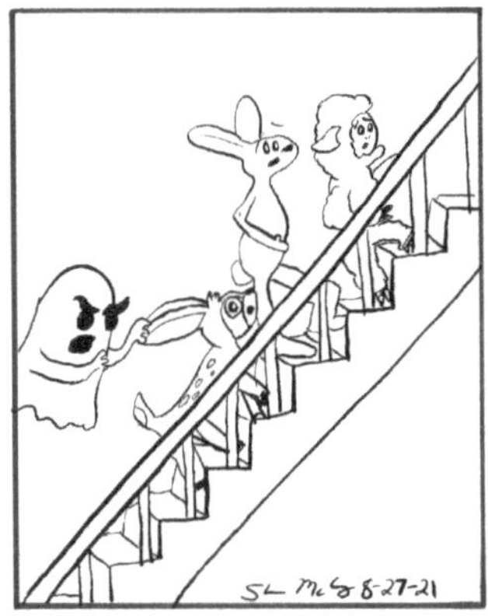
SL McG 8-27-21

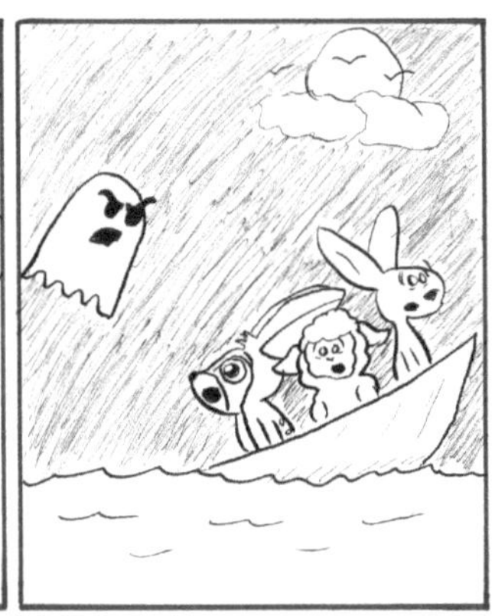

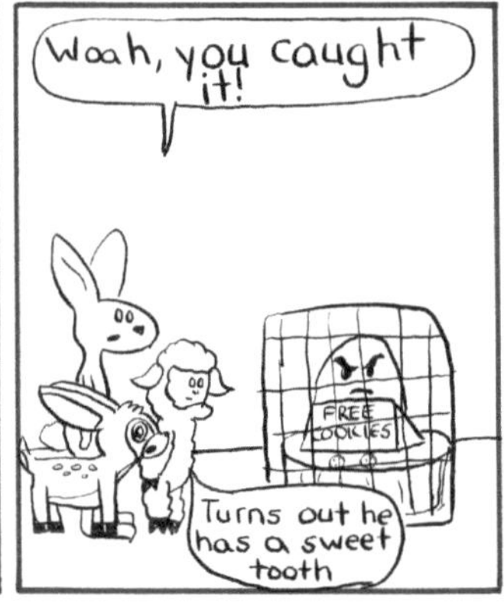
Woah, you caught it!
FREE COOKIES
Turns out he has a sweet tooth

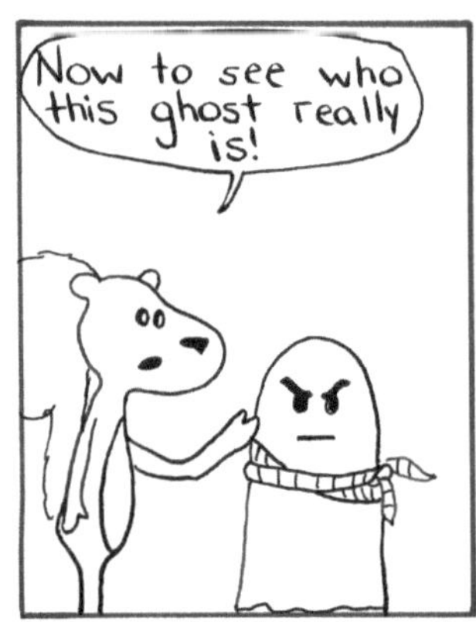
Now to see who this ghost really is!

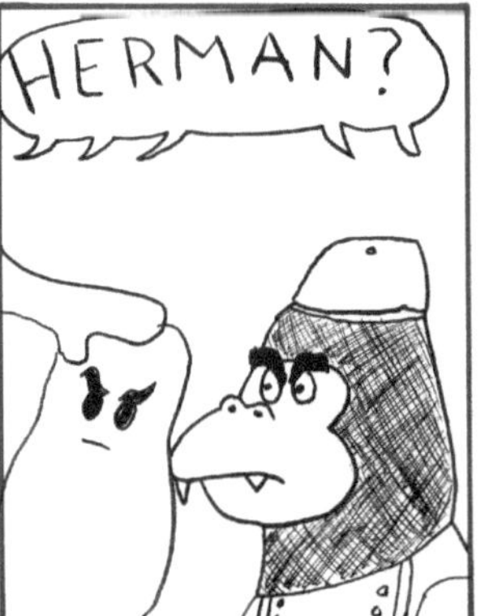
HERMAN?

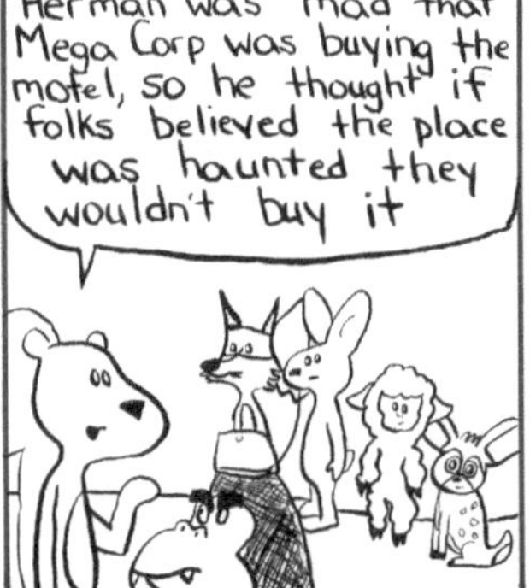
Herman was mad that Mega Corp was buying the motel, so he thought if folks believed the place was haunted they wouldn't buy it

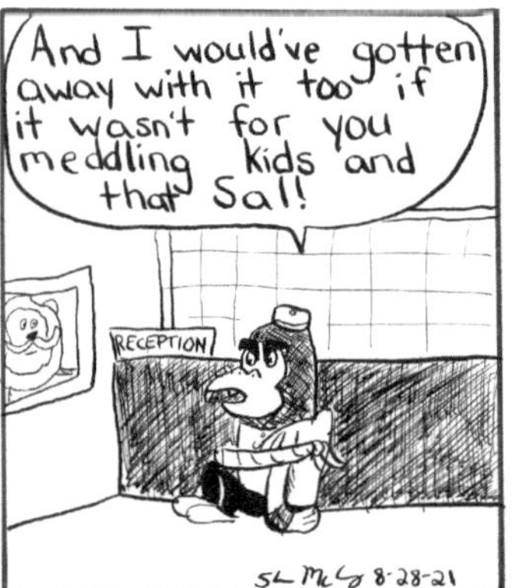
And I would've gotten away with it too if it wasn't for you meddling kids and that Sal!
RECEPTION
SL McG 8-28-21

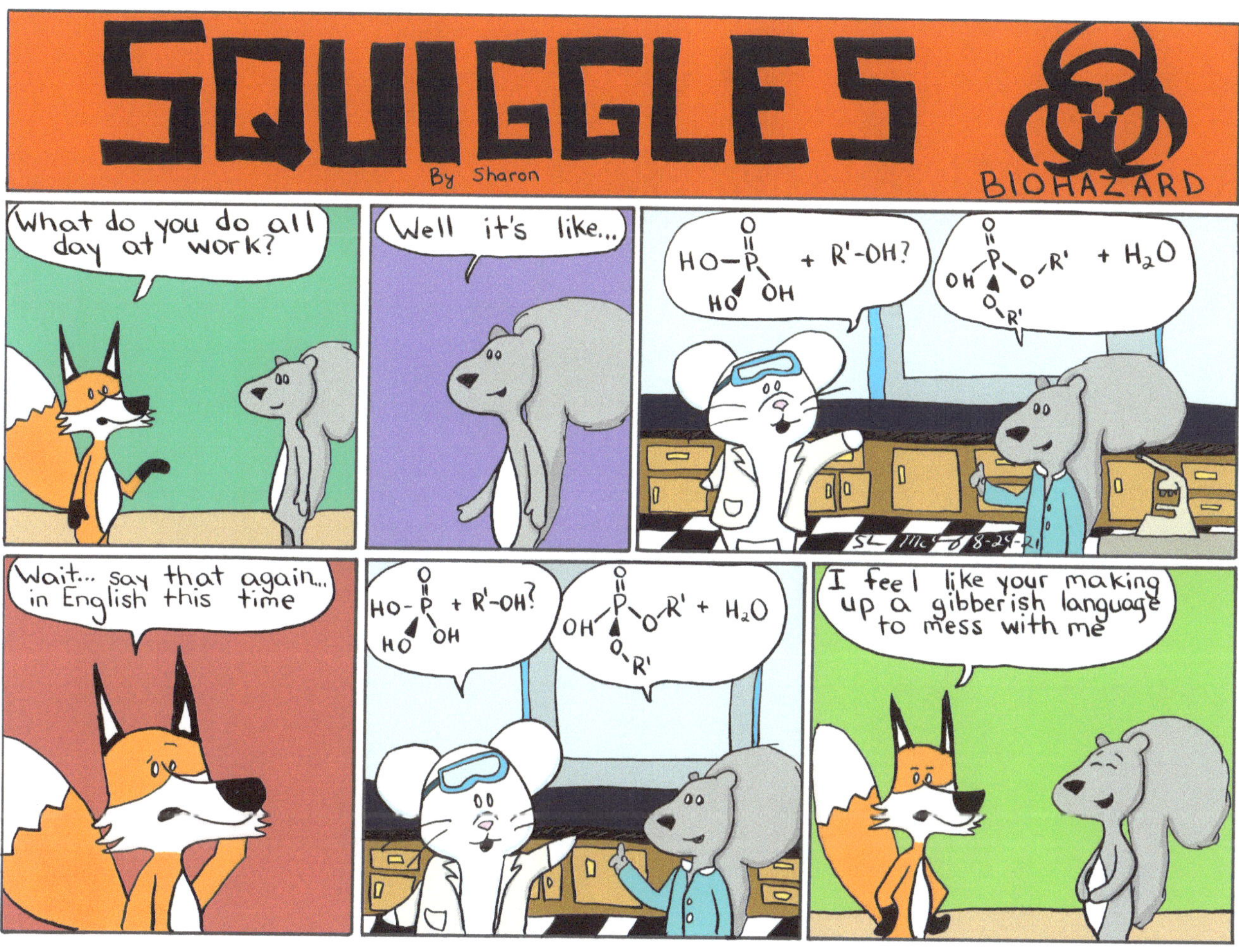
SQUIGGLES
By Sharon
BIOHAZARD
What do you do all day at work?
Well it's like...
HO—P(=O)(HO)—OH + R'-OH?
OH—P(=O)(O-R')—O-R' + H_2O
Wait... say that again... in English this time
HO-P(=O)(HO)-OH + R'-OH?
OH-P(=O)(O-R')-O-R' + H_2O
I feel like your making up a gibberish language to mess with me

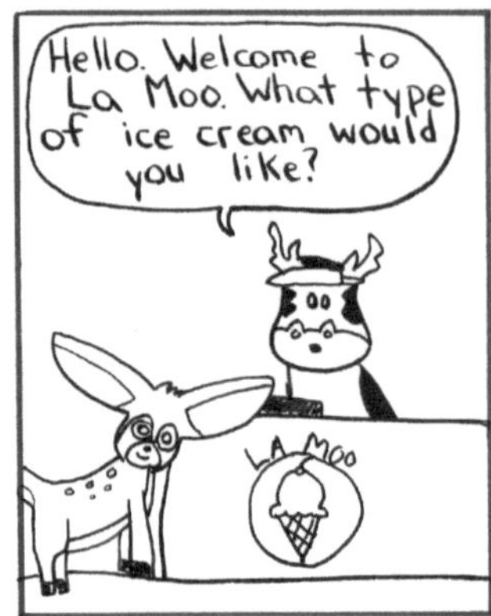
Hello. Welcome to La Moo. What type of ice cream would you like?
LA MOO
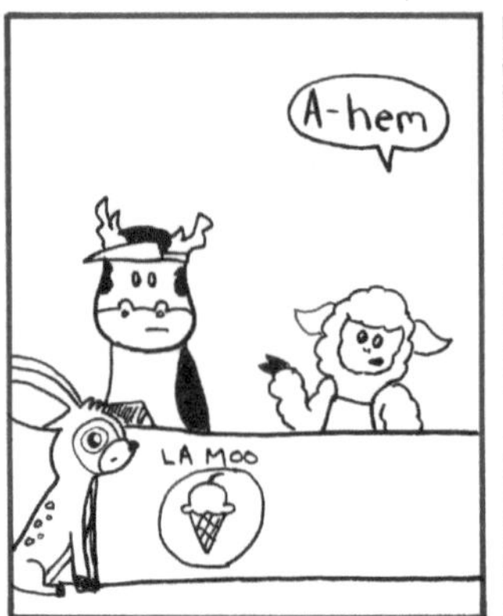
A-hem
LA MOO
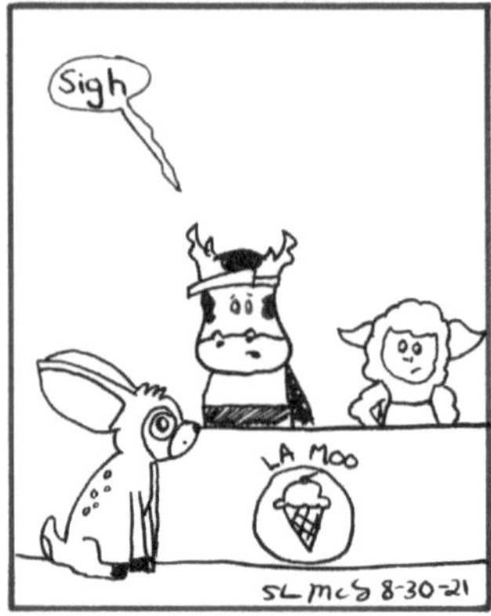
Sigh
LA MOO
SL McS 8-30-21
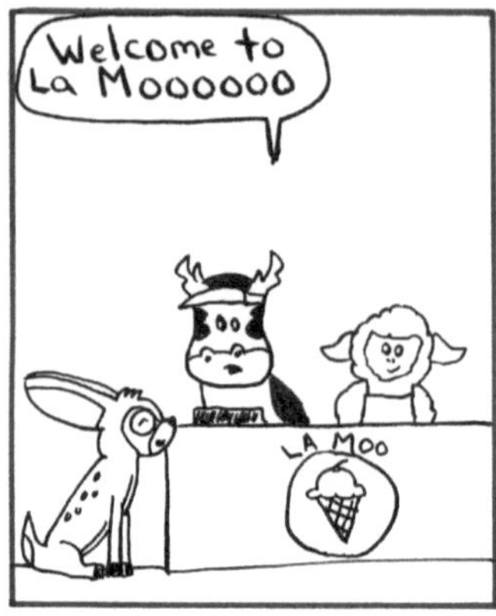
Welcome to La Moooooo
LA MOO
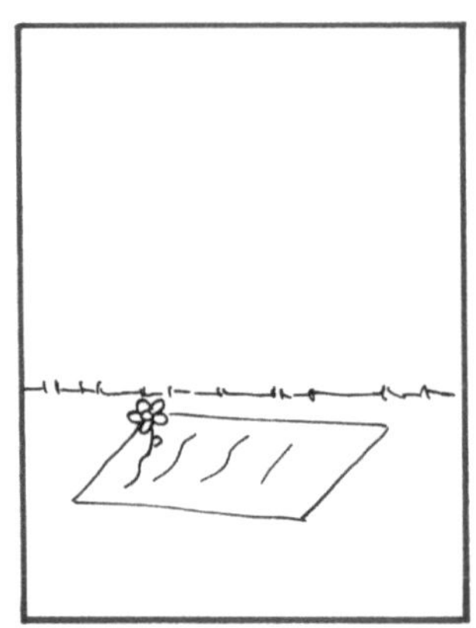
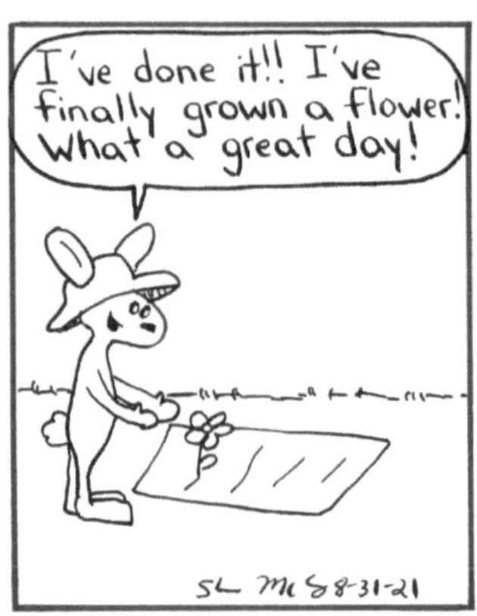
I've done it!! I've finally grown a flower! What a great day!
SL McS 8-31-21
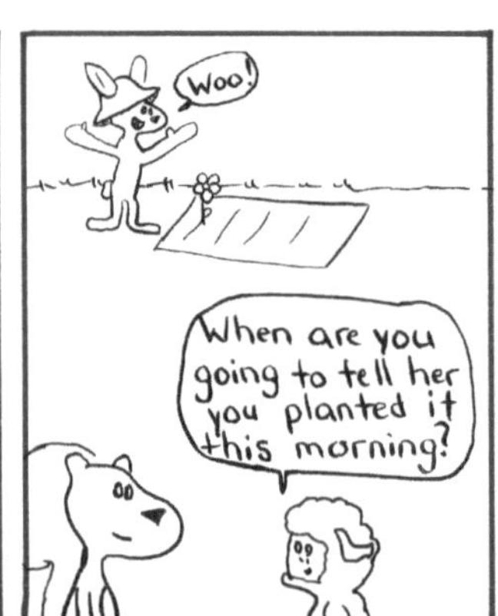
Woo!
When are you going to tell her you planted it this morning?
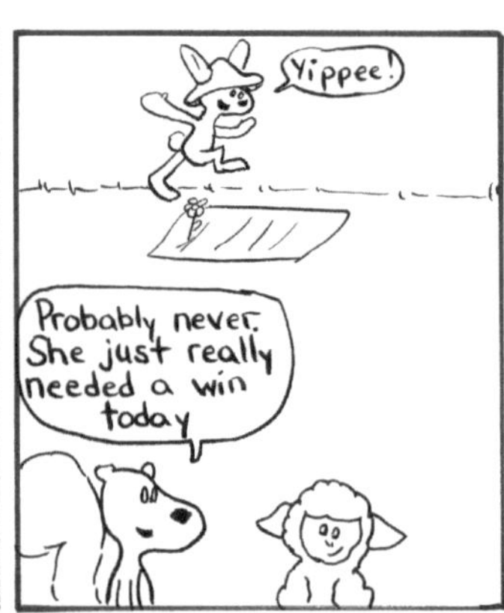
Yippee!
Probably never. She just really needed a win today
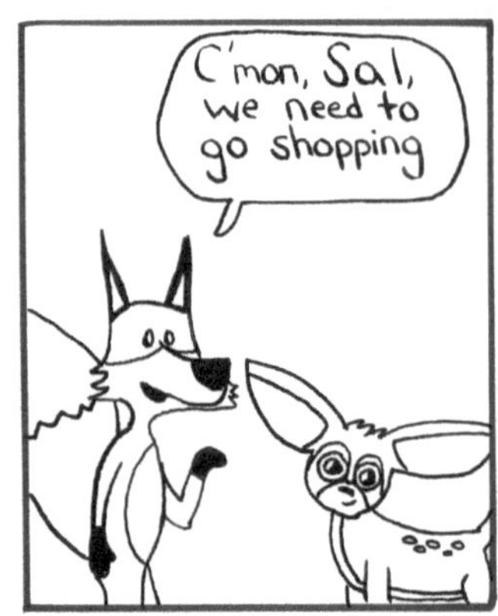
C'mon, Sal, we need to go shopping
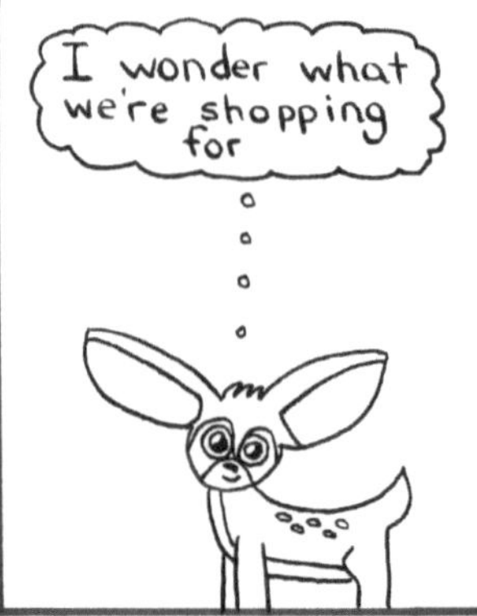
I wonder what we're shopping for
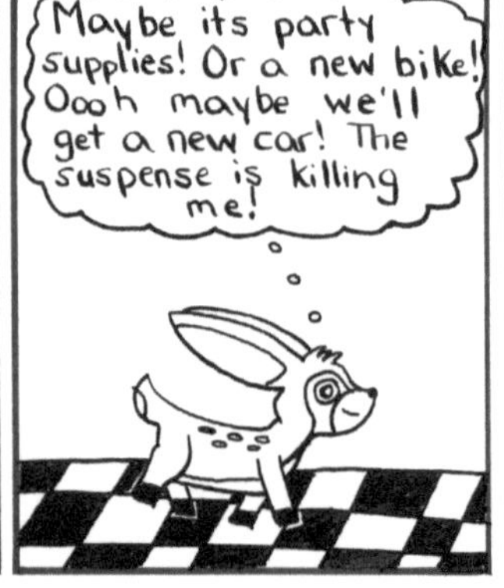
Maybe its party supplies! Or a new bike! Oooh maybe we'll get a new car! The suspense is killing me!
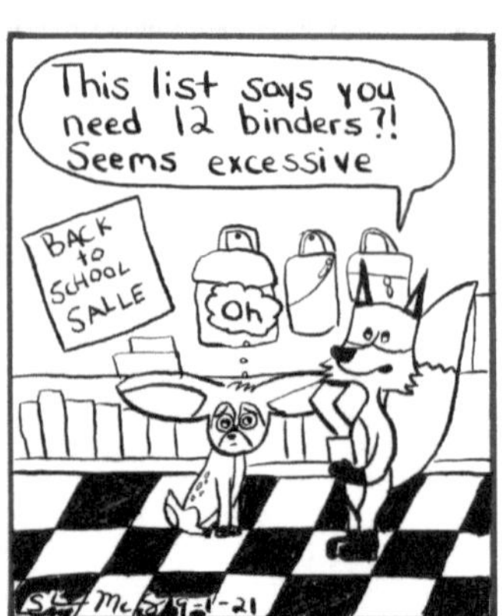
This list says you need 12 binders?! Seems excessive
BACK to SCHOOL SALLE
Oh

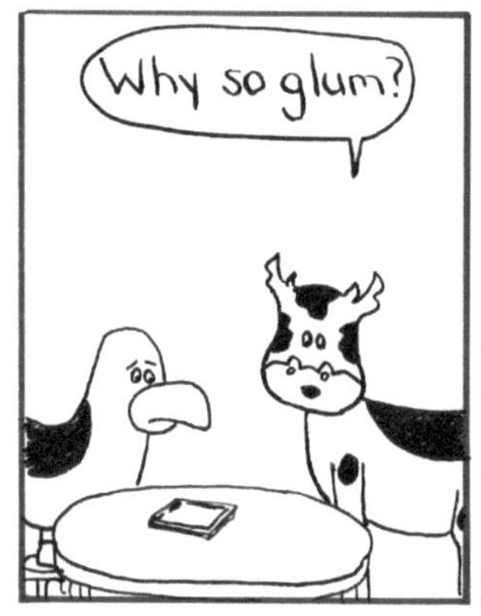
Why so glum?
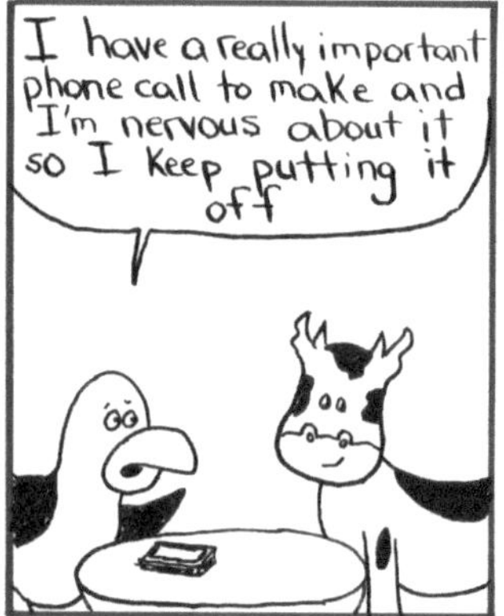
I have a really important phone call to make and I'm nervous about it so I keep putting it off
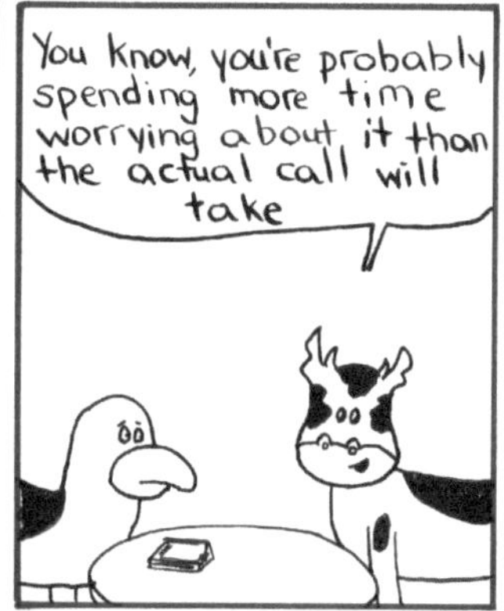
You know, you're probably spending more time worrying about it than the actual call will take
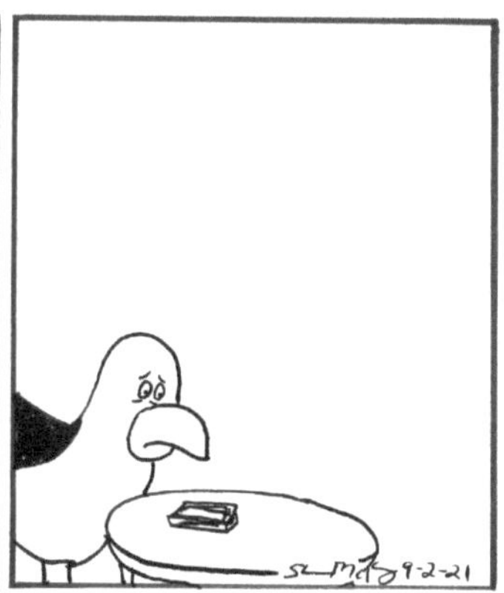
SL McG 9-2-21
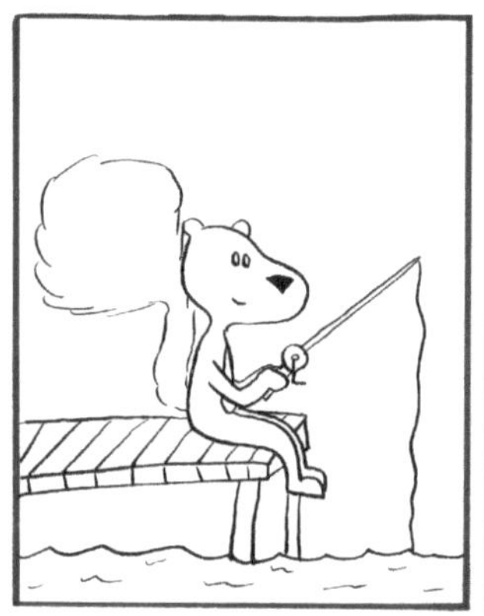
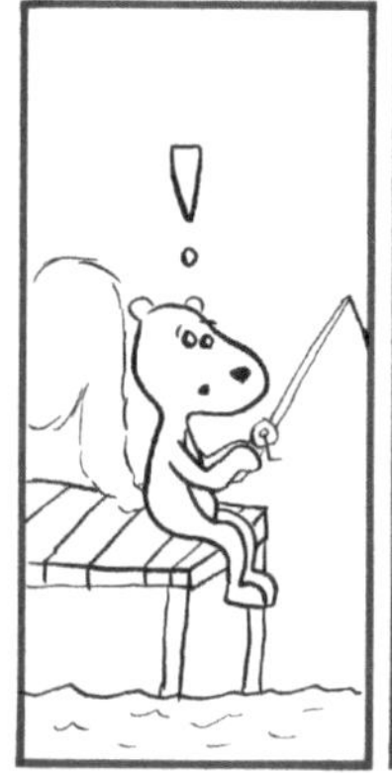
!
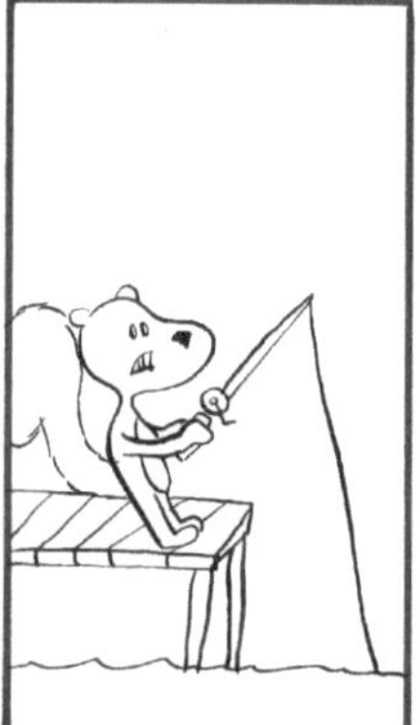
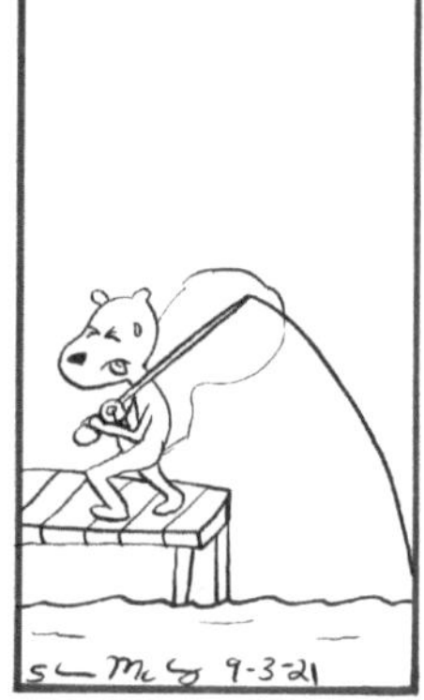
SL McG 9-3-21
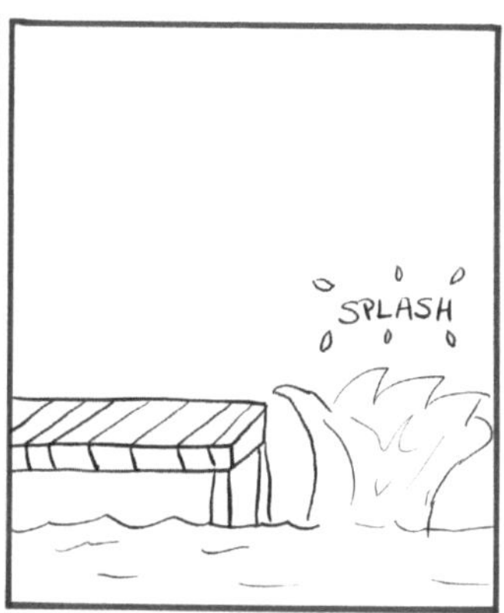
SPLASH
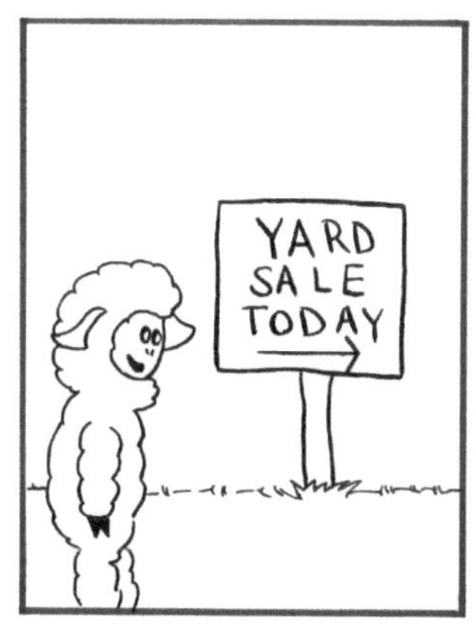
YARD SALE TODAY
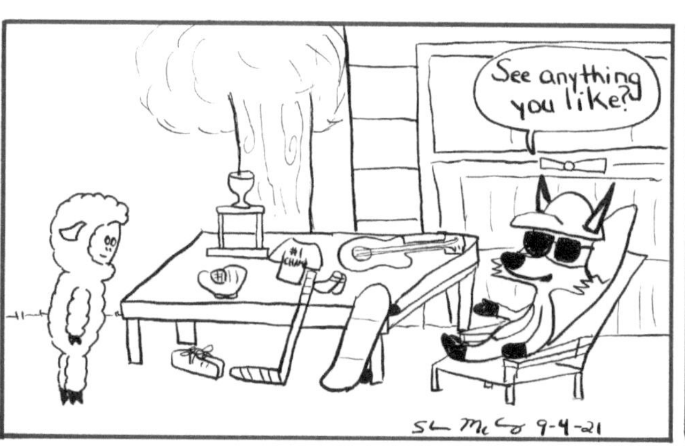
See anything you like?
#1 CHAMP
SL McG 9-4-21
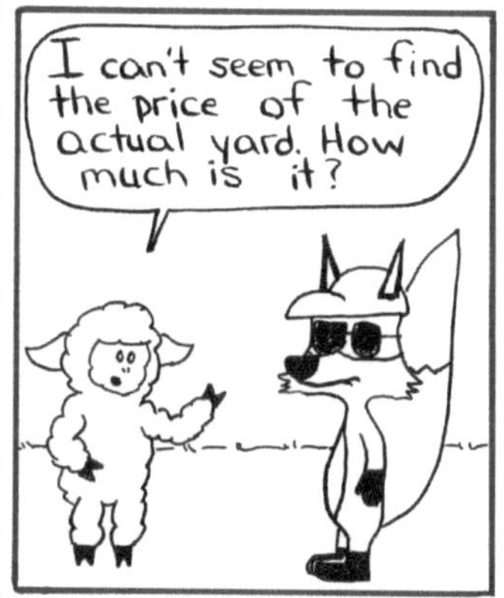
I can't seem to find the price of the actual yard. How much is it?

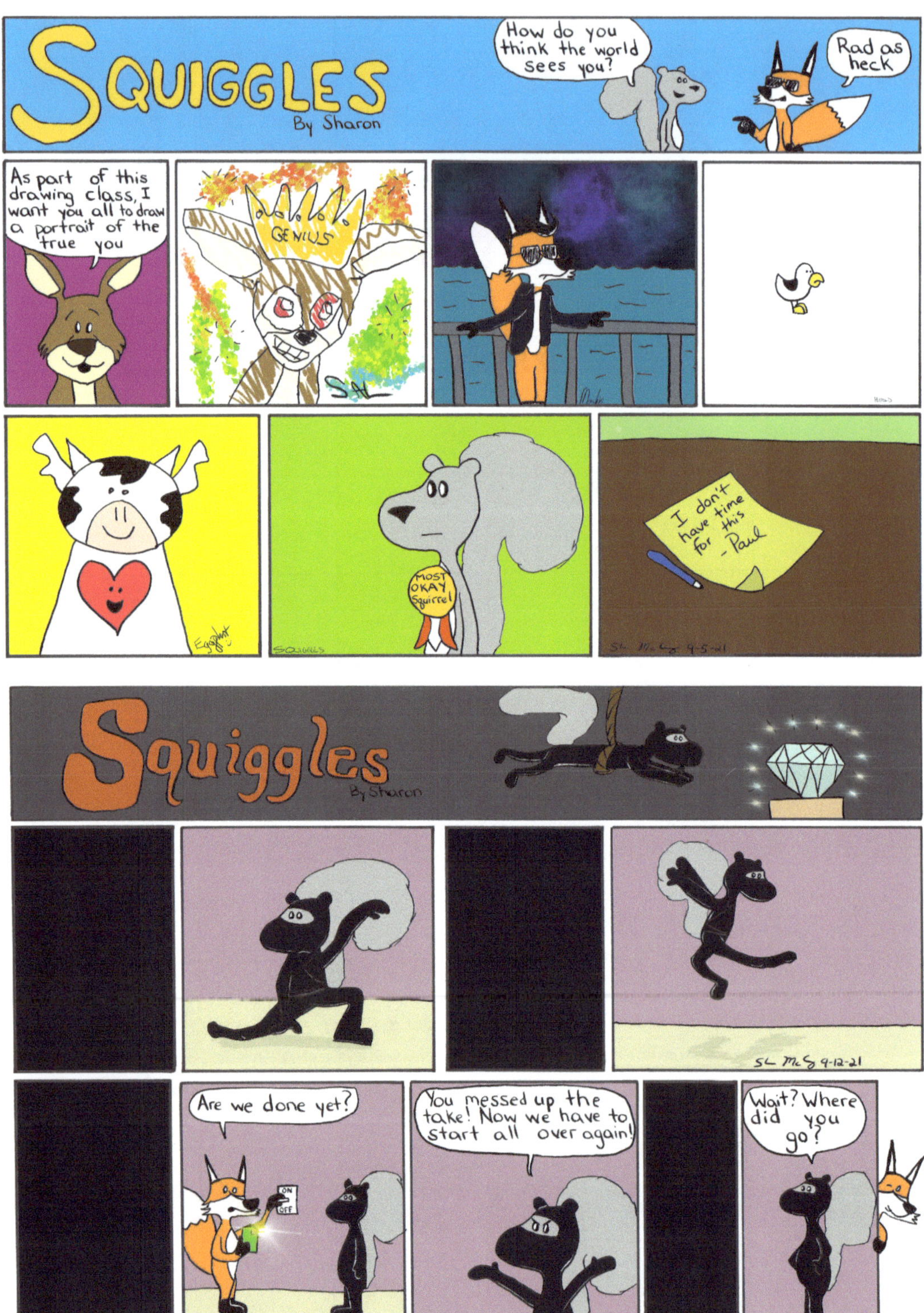
SQUIGGLES
By Sharon
How do you think the world sees you?
Rad as heck
As part of this drawing class, I want you all to draw a portrait of the true you
GENIUS
MOST OKAY Squirrel
I don't have time for this -Paul
SL McG 9-5-21
Squiggles
By Sharon
SL McG 9-12-21
Are we done yet?
ON
OFF
You messed up the take! Now we have to start all over again!
Wait? Where did you go?

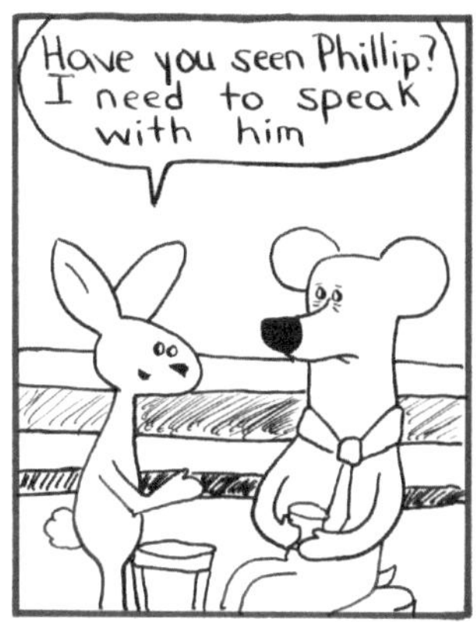
Have you seen Phillip? I need to speak with him

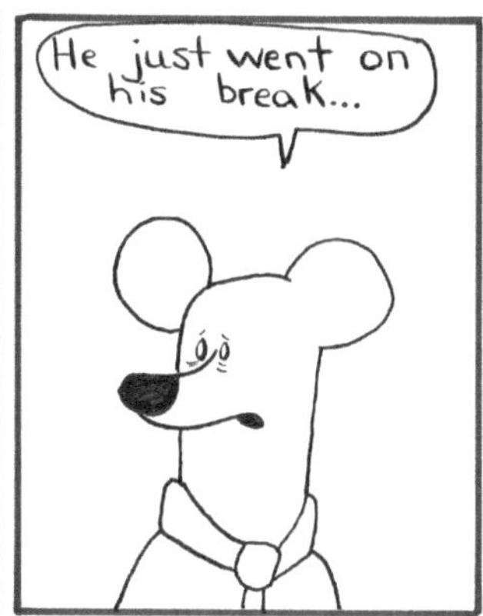
He just went on his break...

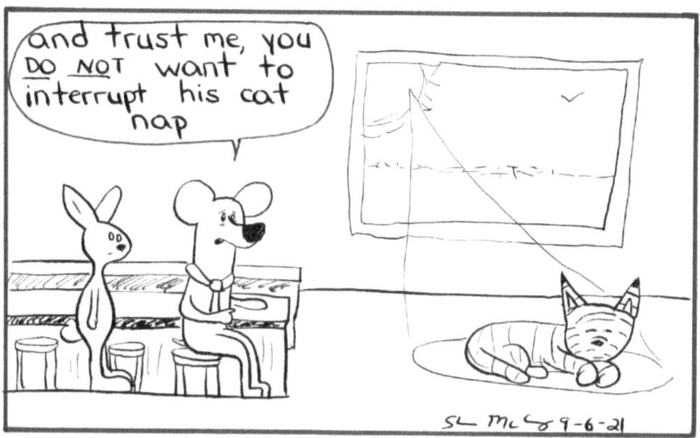
and trust me, you DO NOT want to interrupt his cat nap
SL McG 9-6-21

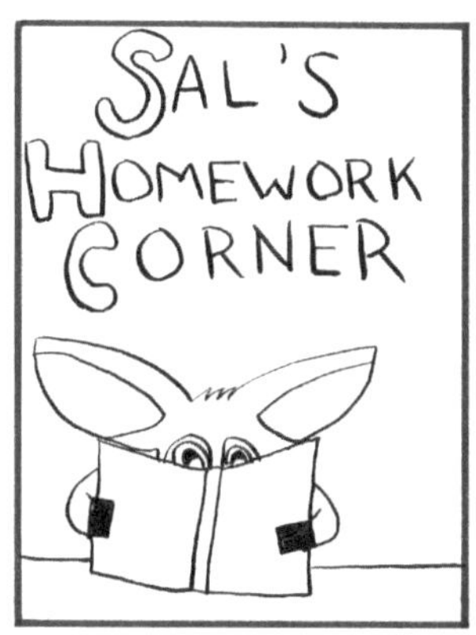
SAL'S HOMEWORK CORNER

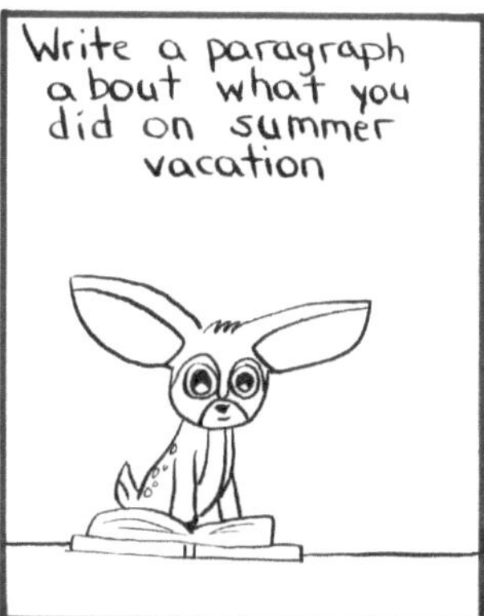
Write a paragraph about what you did on summer vacation

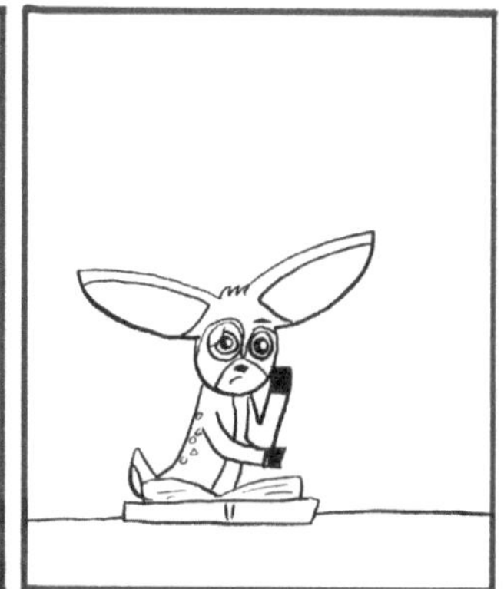

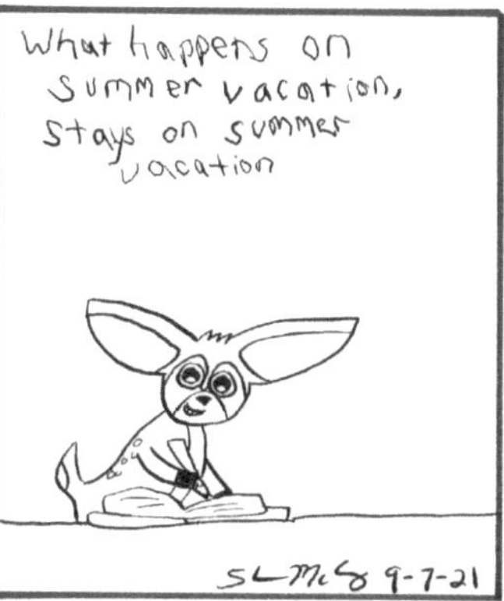
What happens on summer vacation, stays on summer vacation
SL McG 9-7-21

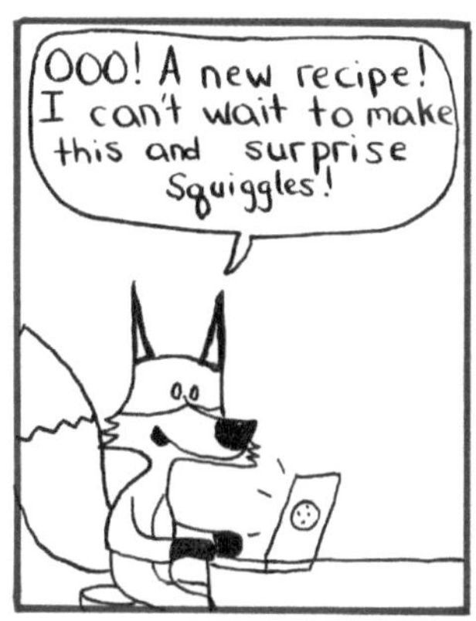
OOO! A new recipe! I can't wait to make this and surprise Squiggles!

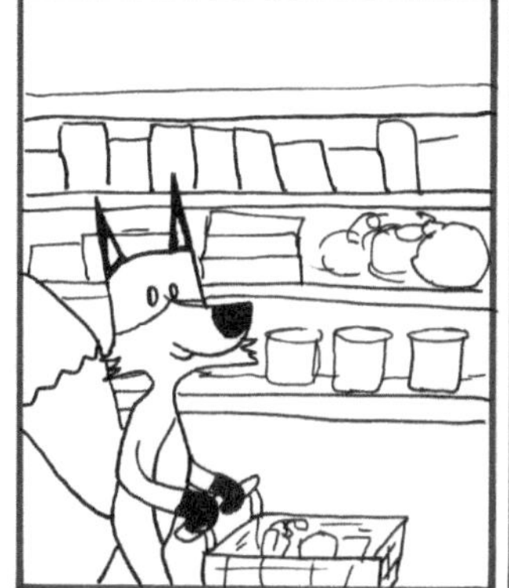

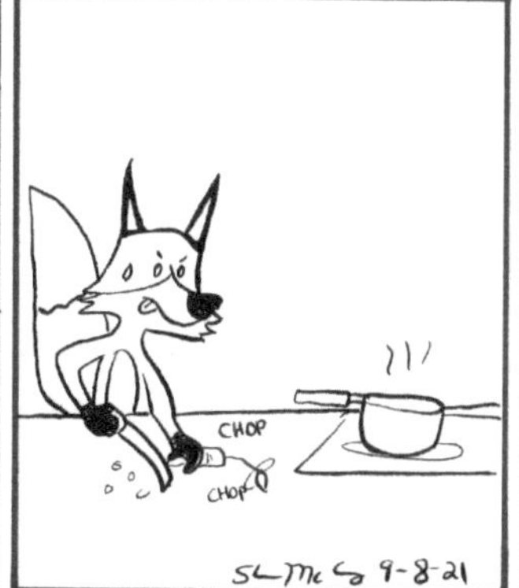
CHOP
CHOP
SL McG 9-8-21

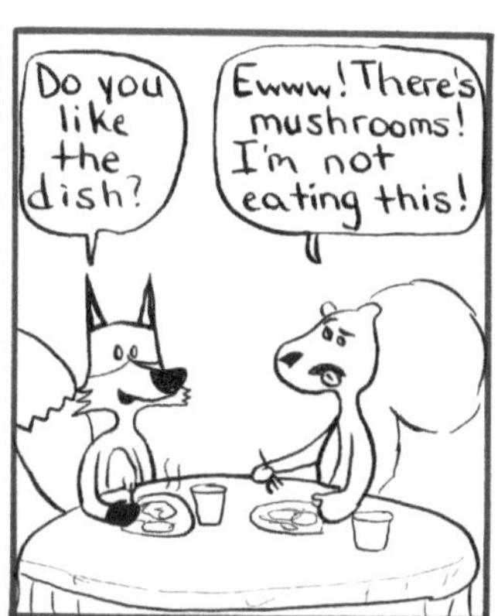
Do you like the dish?
Ewww! There's mushrooms! I'm not eating this!

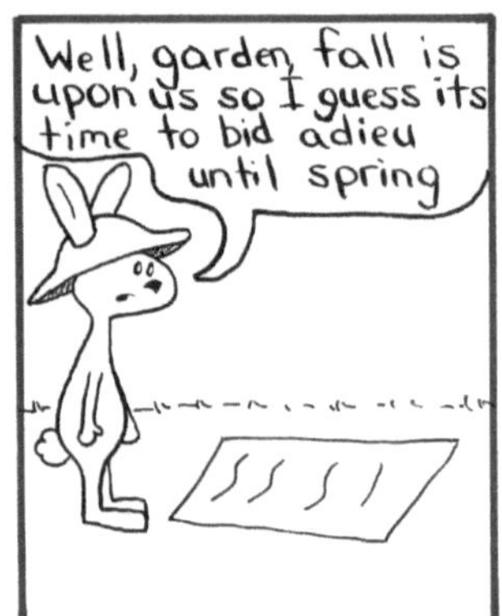
Well, garden fall is upon us so I guess its time to bid adieu until spring
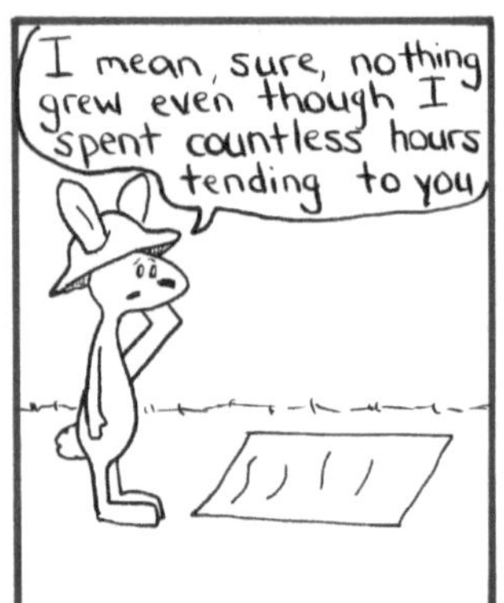
I mean, sure, nothing grew even though I spent countless hours tending to you,
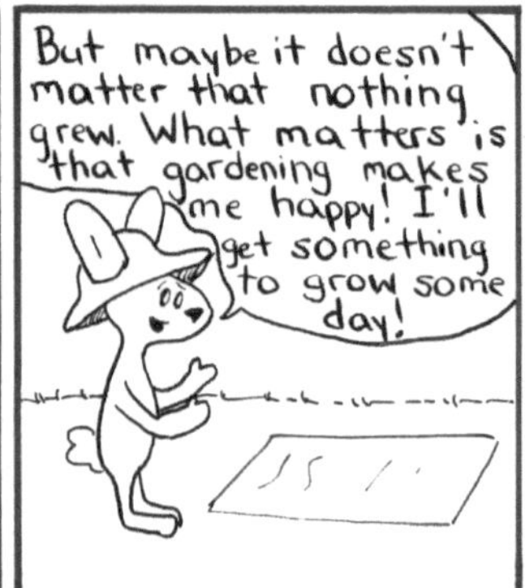
But maybe it doesn't matter that nothing grew. What matters is that gardening makes me happy! I'll get something to grow some day!
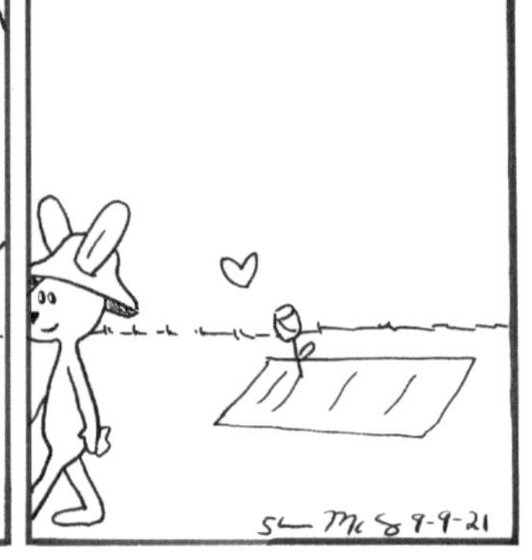
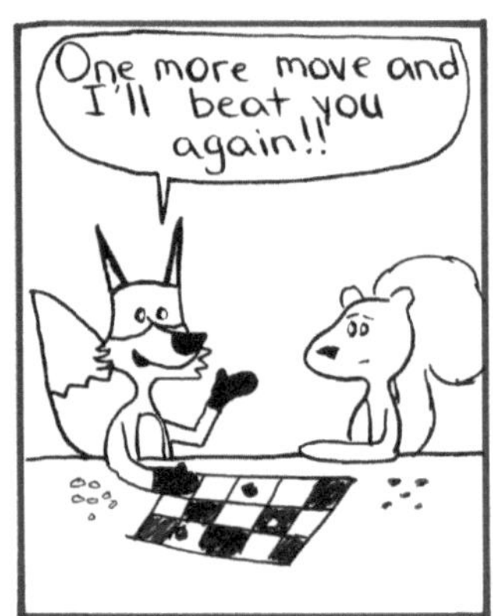
One more move and I'll beat you again!!
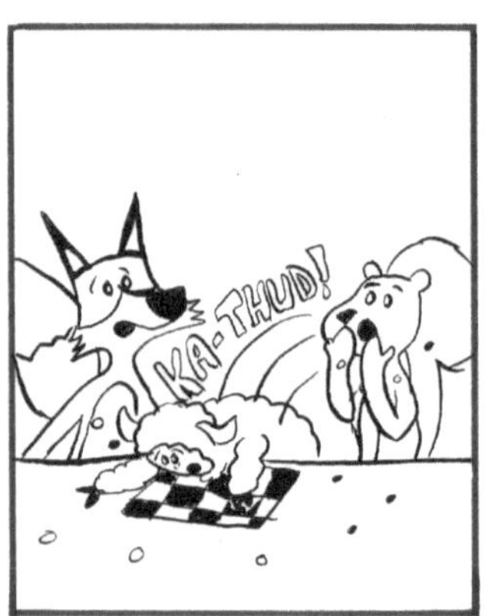
KA-THUD!
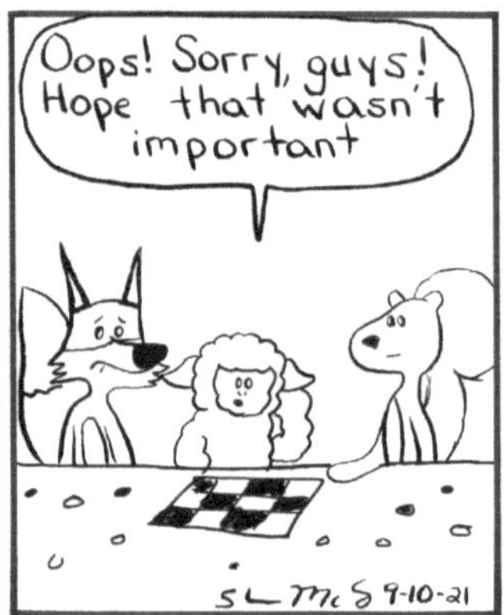
Oops! Sorry, guys! Hope that wasn't important
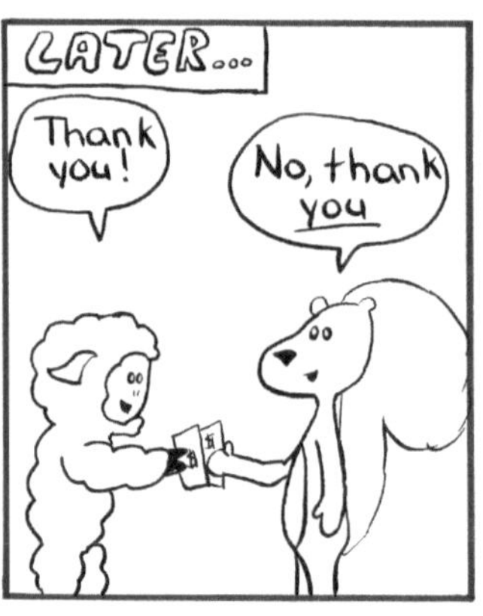
LATER...
Thank you!
No, thank you
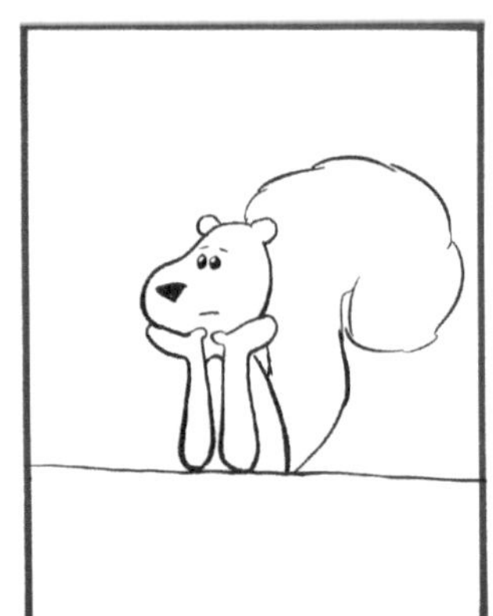
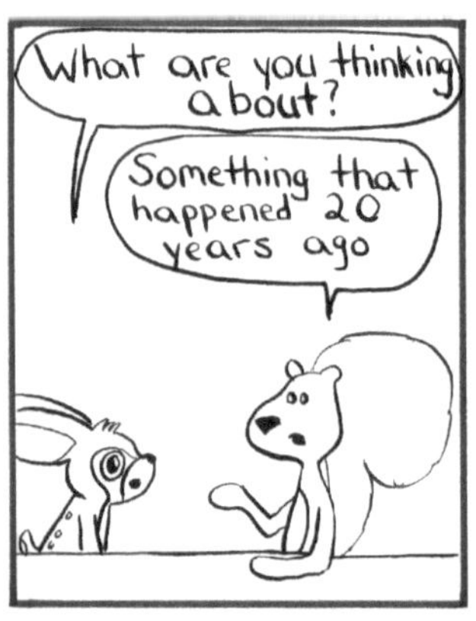
What are you thinking about?
Something that happened 20 years ago
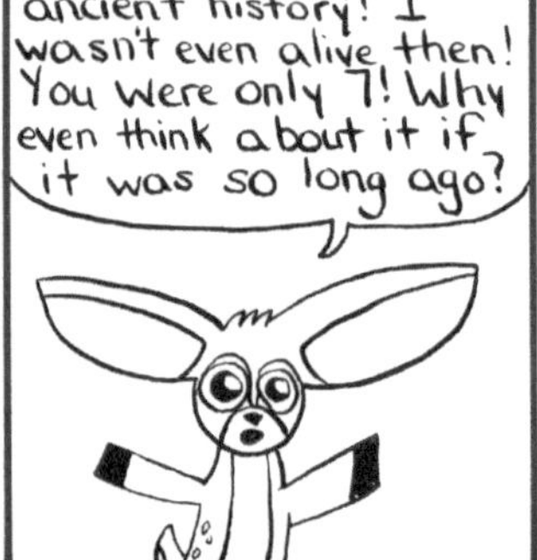
Twenty years ago?! That's ancient history! I wasn't even alive then! You were only 7! Why even think about it if it was so long ago?
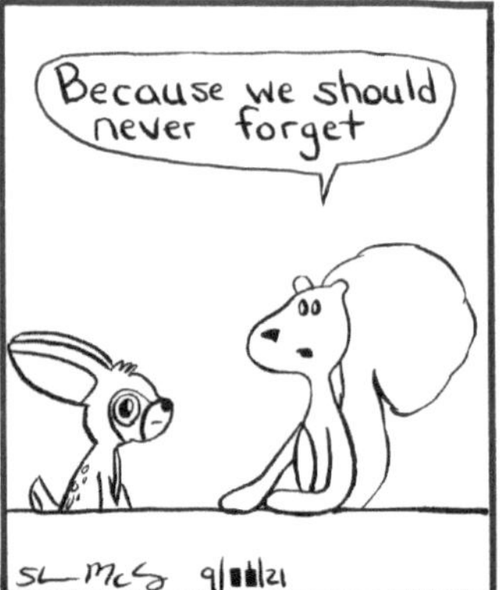
Because we should never forget

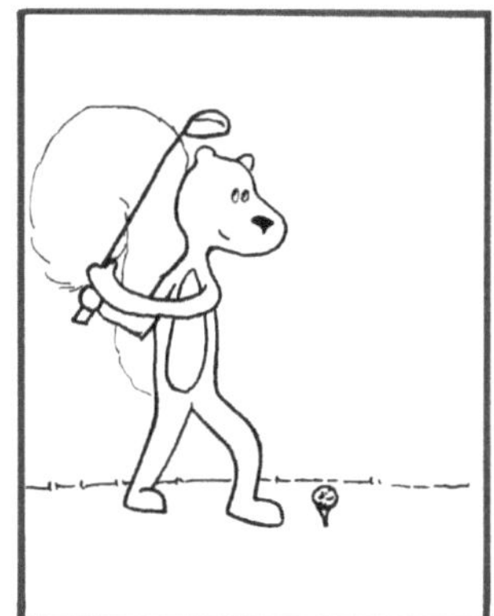

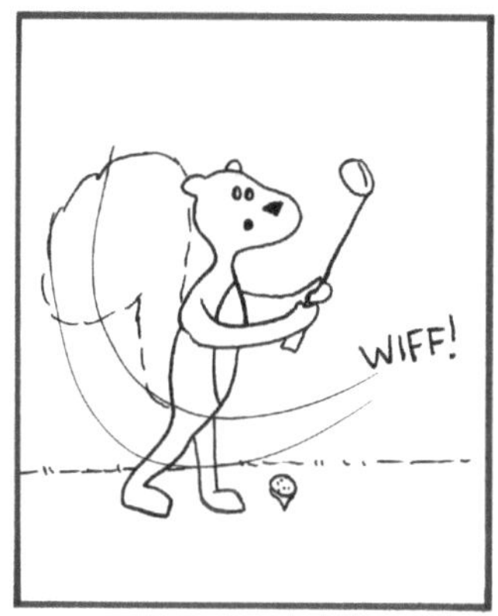
WIFF!

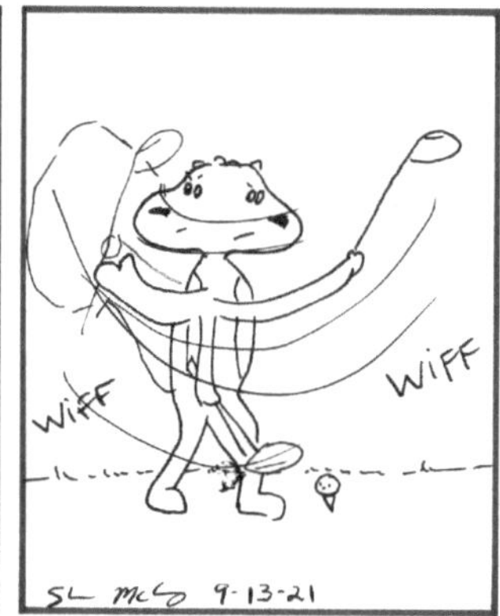
WIFF
WIFF
SL McG 9-13-21

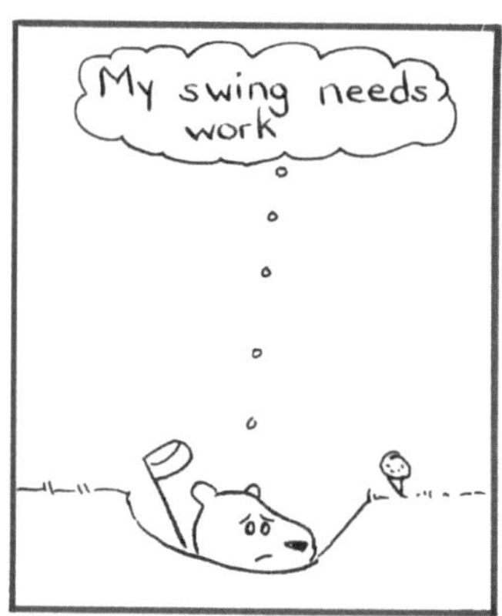
My swing needs work

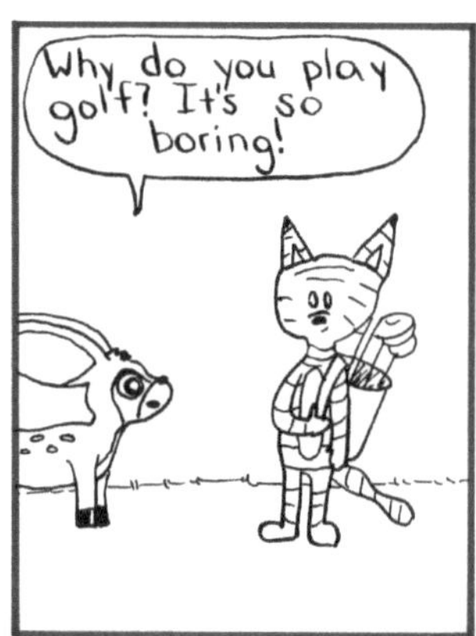
Why do you play golf? It's so boring!

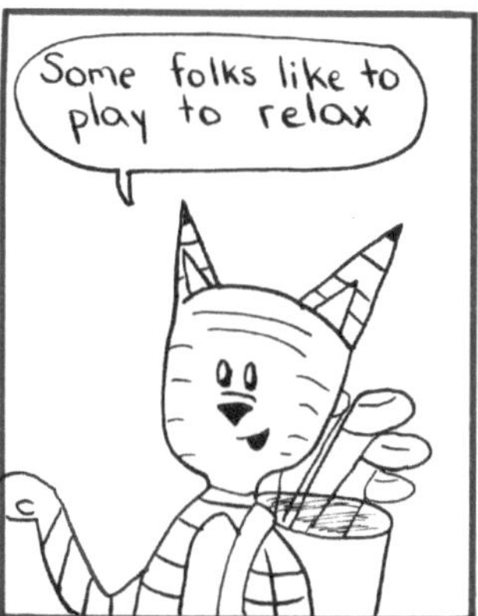
Some folks like to play to relax

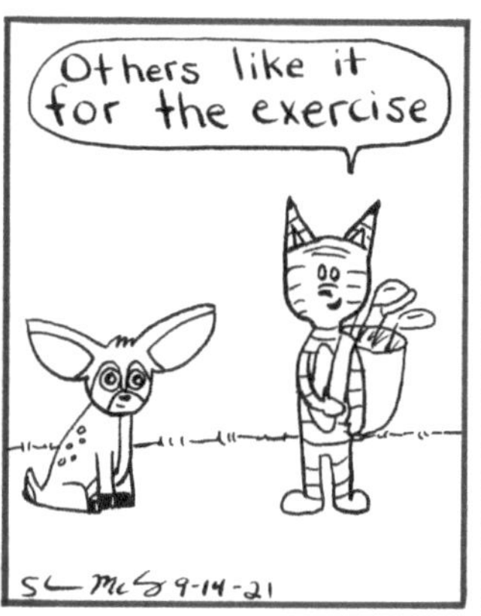
Others like it for the exercise
SL McG 9-14-21

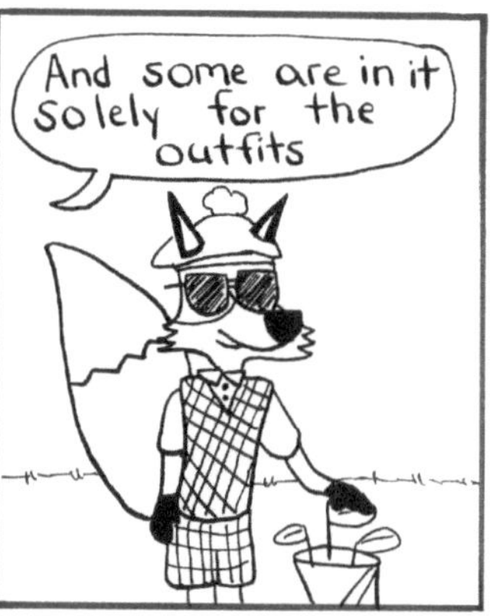
And some are in it solely for the outfits

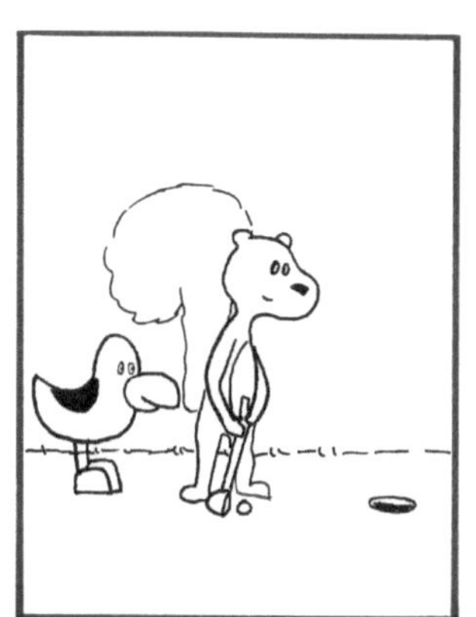

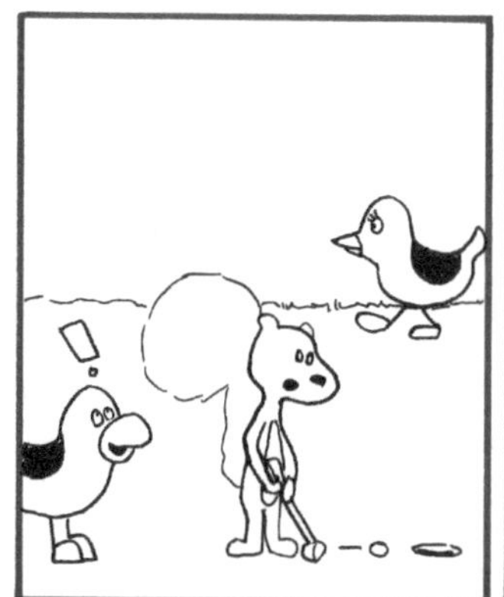
!

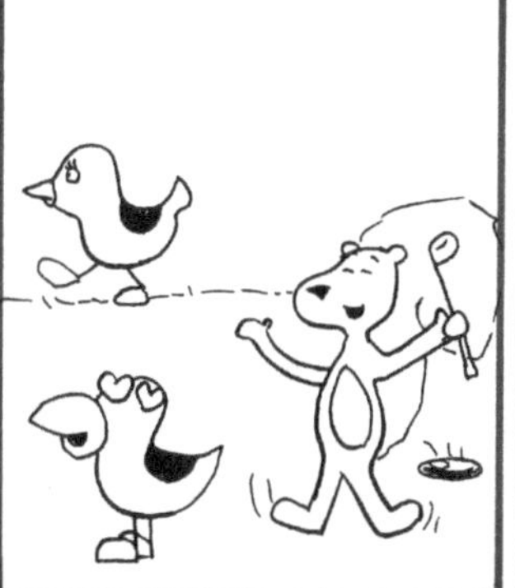

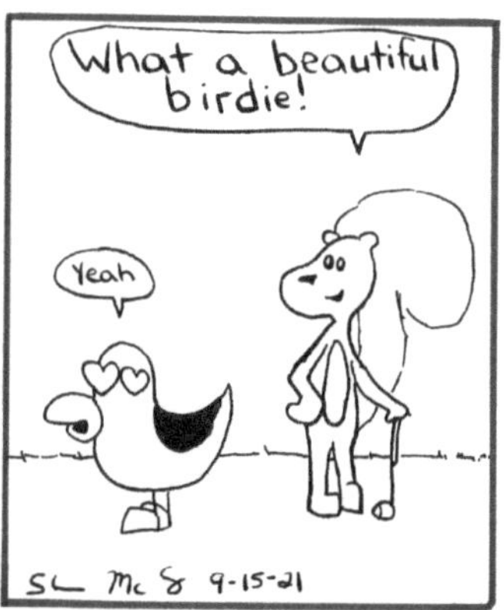
What a beautiful birdie!
Yeah
SL McG 9-15-21

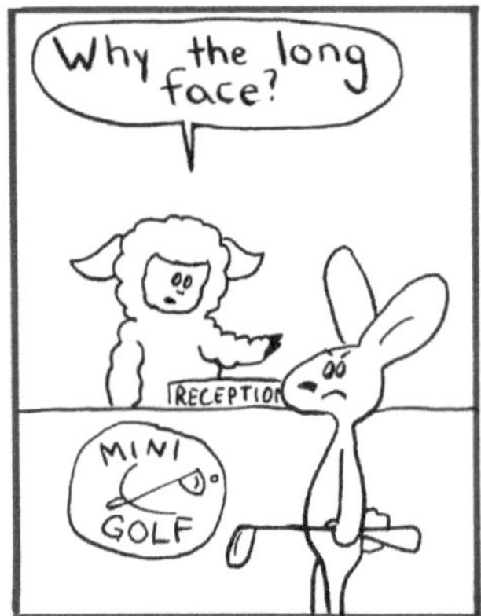
Why the long face?
RECEPTION
MINI GOLF
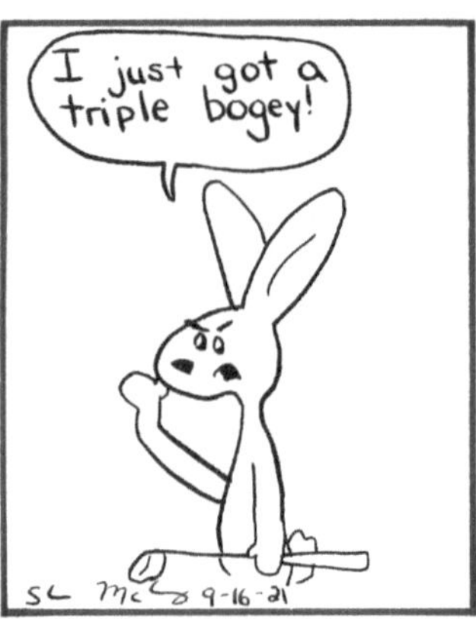
I just got a triple bogey!
SL McS 9-16-21
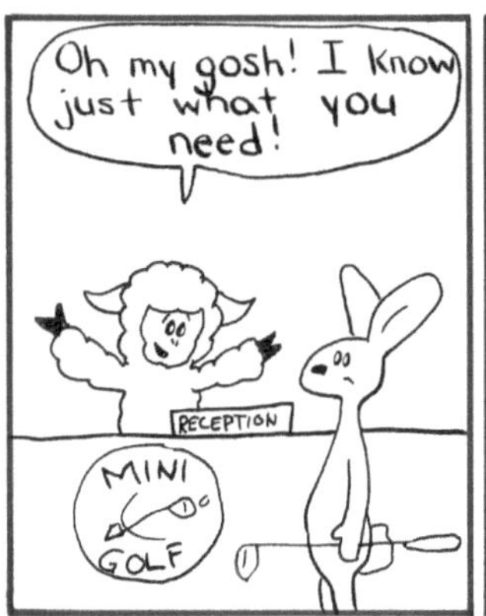
Oh my gosh! I know just what you need!
RECEPTION
MINI GOLF
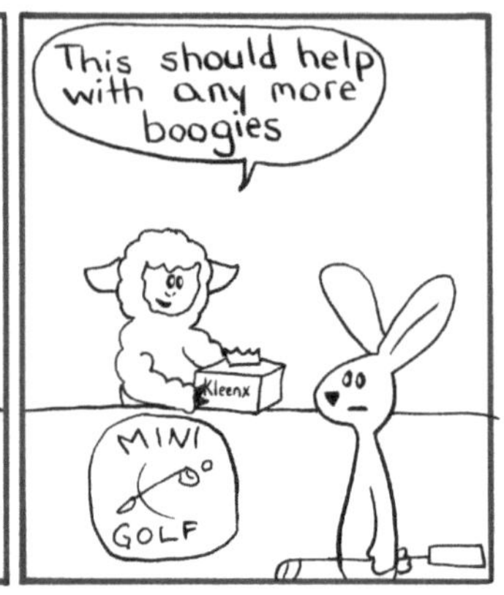
This should help with any more boogies
Kleenx
MINI GOLF
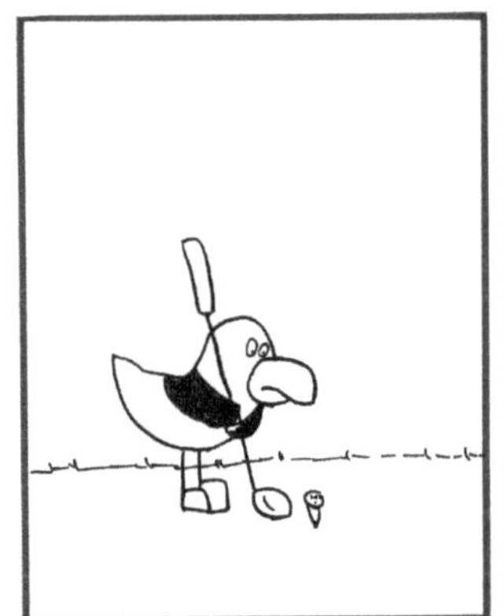
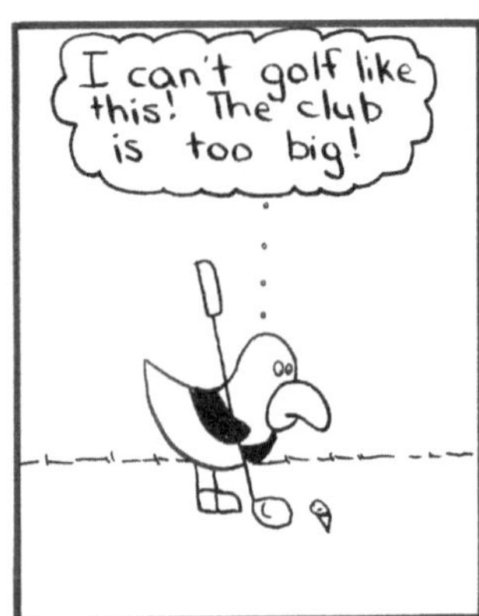
I can't golf like this! The club is too big!
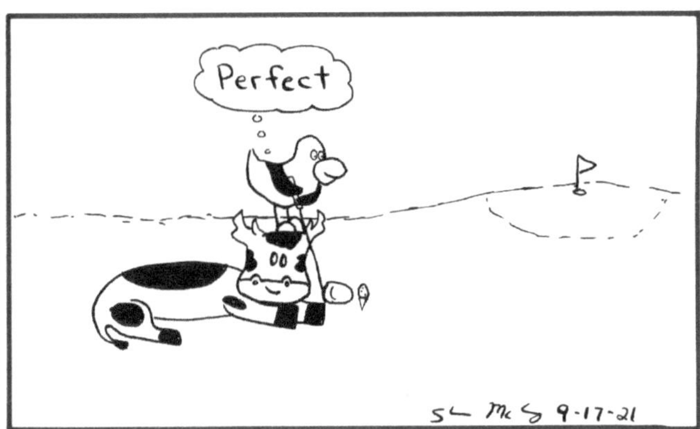
Perfect
SL McS 9-17-21
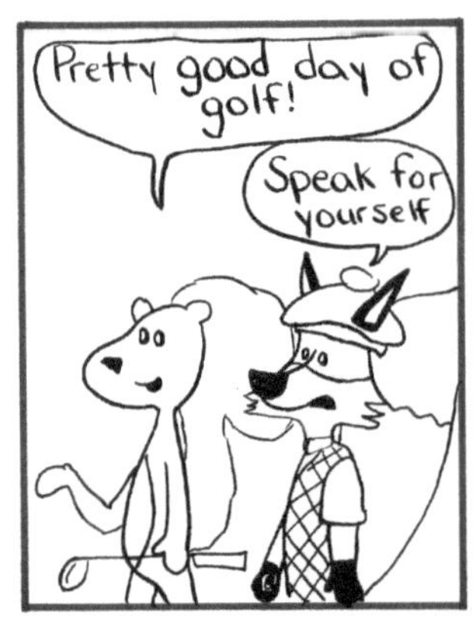
Pretty good day of golf!
Speak for yourself
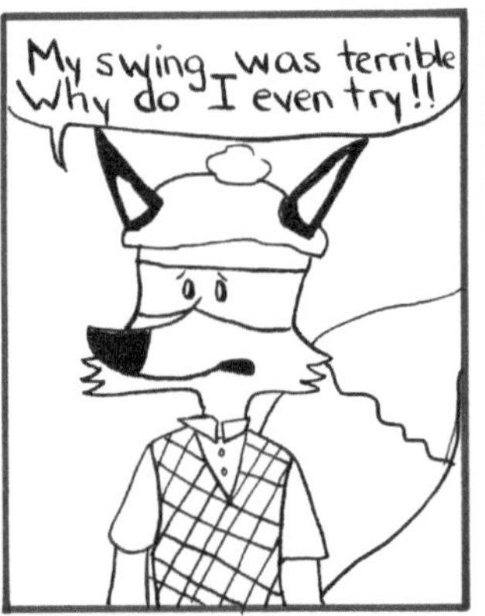
My swing was terrible Why do I even try!!
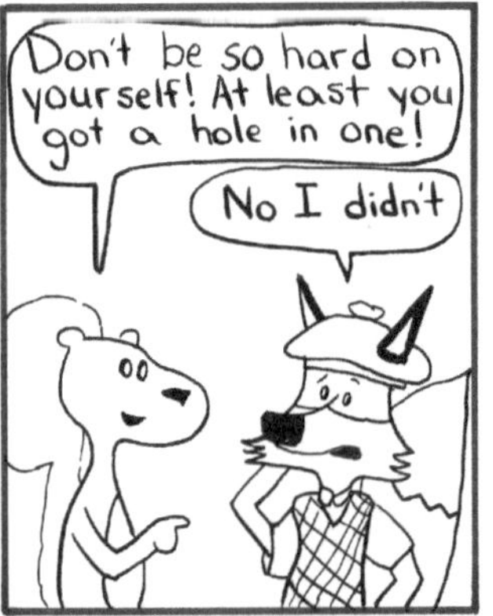
Don't be so hard on yourself! At least you got a hole in one!
No I didn't
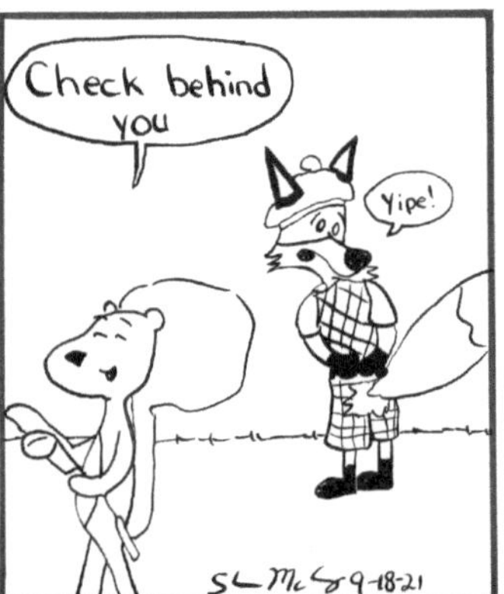
Check behind you
Yipe!
SL McS 9-18-21

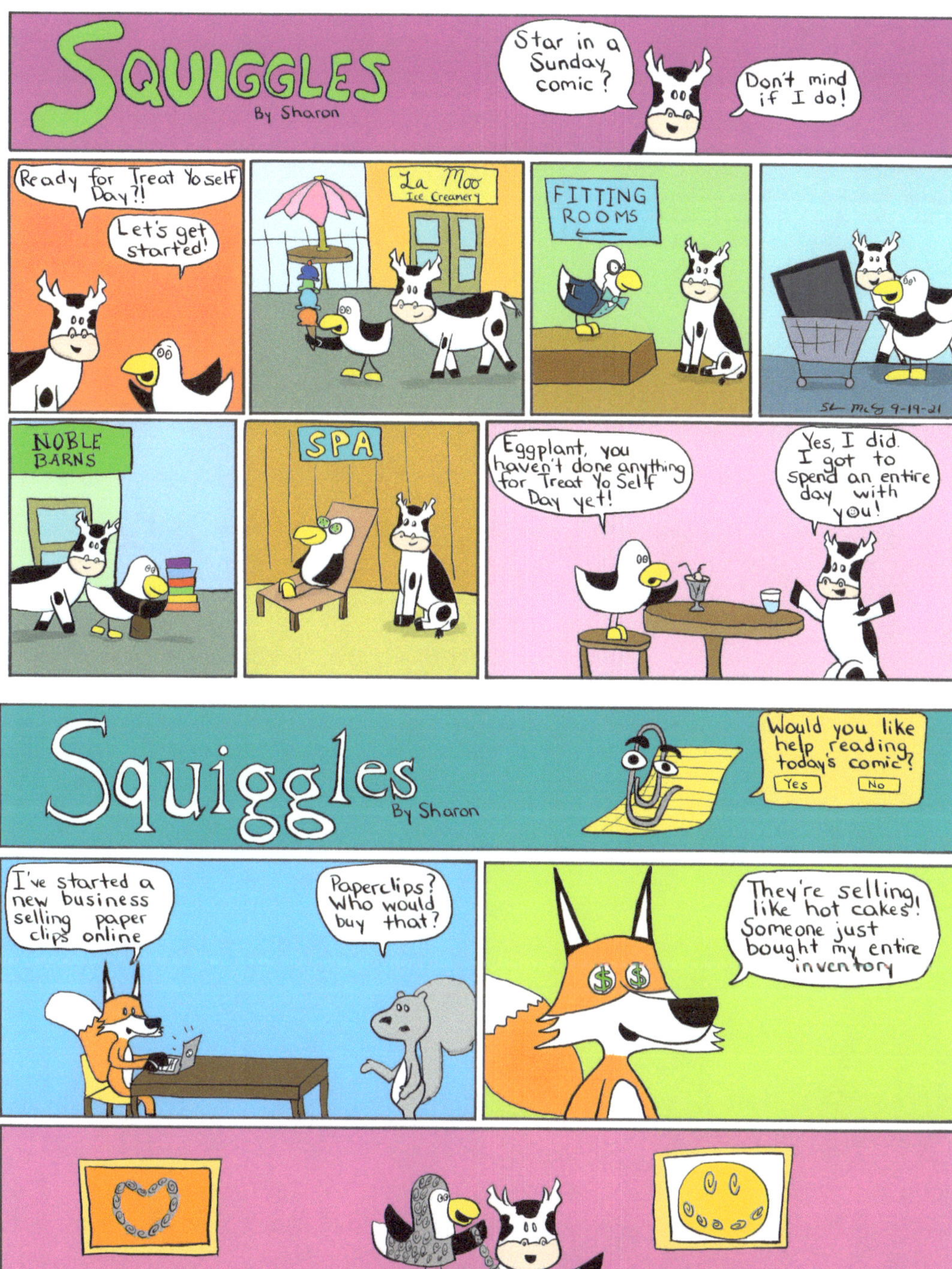
SQUIGGLES
By Sharon
Star in a Sunday comic?
Don't mind if I do!
Ready for Treat Yo self Day?!
Let's get started!
La Moo Ice Creamery
FITTING ROOMS
SL McS 9-19-21
NOBLE BARNS
SPA
Eggplant, you haven't done anything for Treat Yo Self Day yet!
Yes, I did. I got to spend an entire day with you!
Squiggles
By Sharon
Would you like help reading today's comic?
Yes
No
I've started a new business selling paper clips online
Paperclips? Who would buy that?
They're selling like hot cakes! Someone just bought my entire inventory
SLMcS 9-26-21

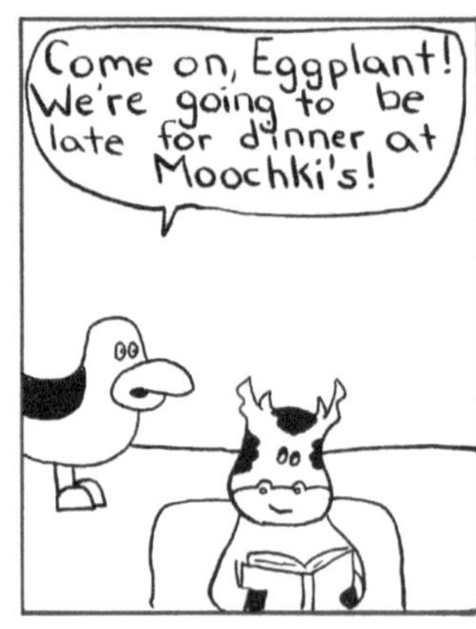
Come on, Eggplant! We're going to be late for dinner at Moochki's!

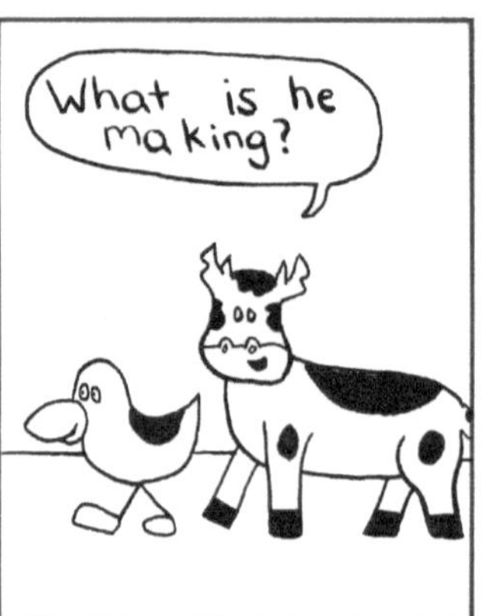
What is he making?

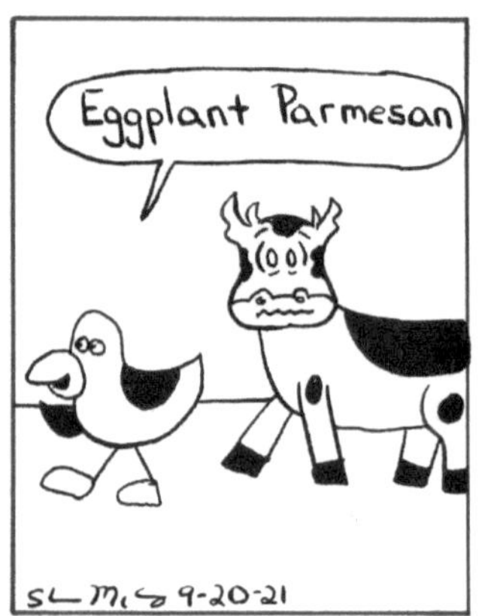
Eggplant Parmesan
SL McG 9-20-21

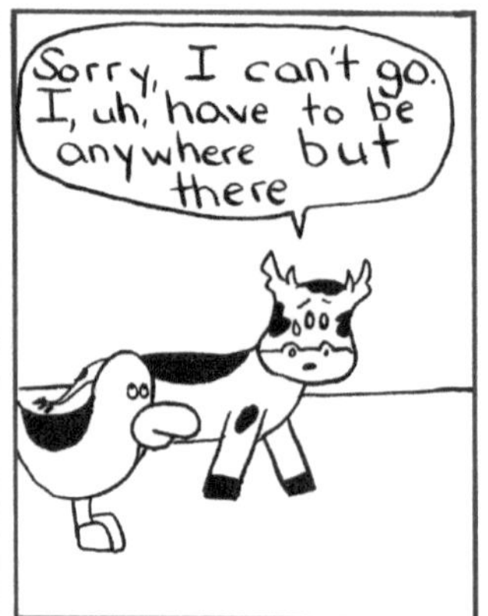
Sorry, I can't go. I, uh, have to be anywhere but there

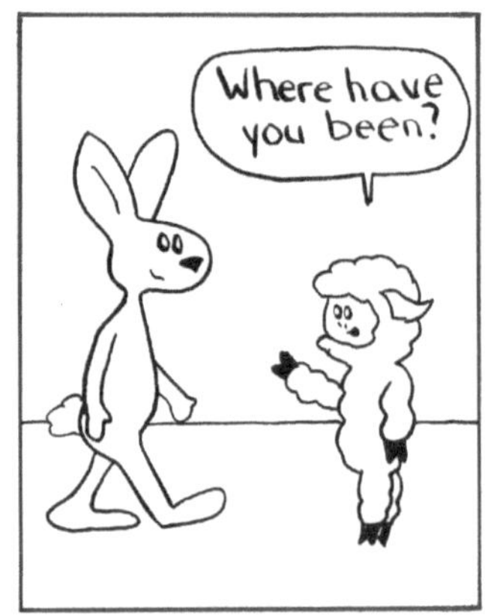
Where have you been?

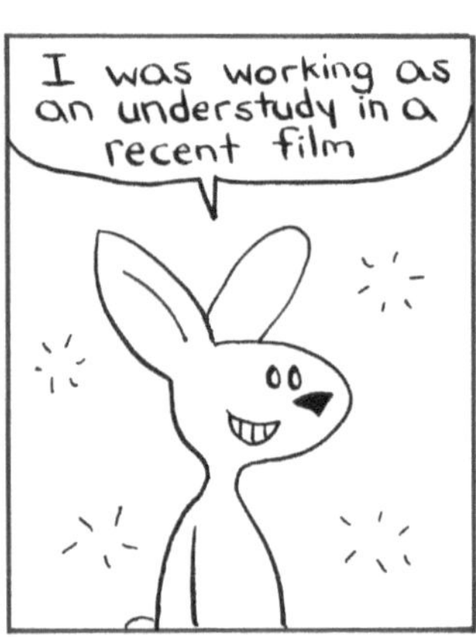
I was working as an understudy in a recent film

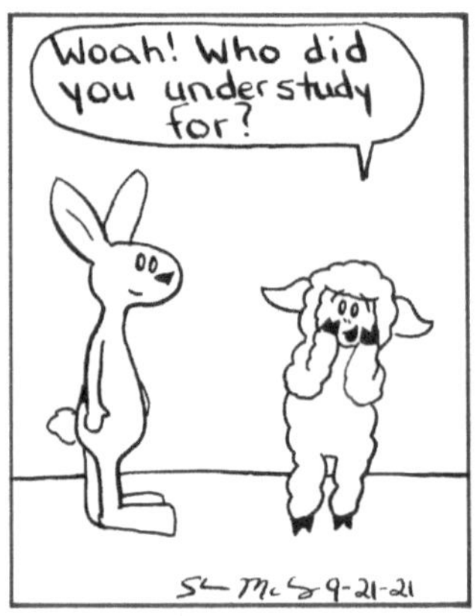
Woah! Who did you understudy for?
SL McG 9-21-21

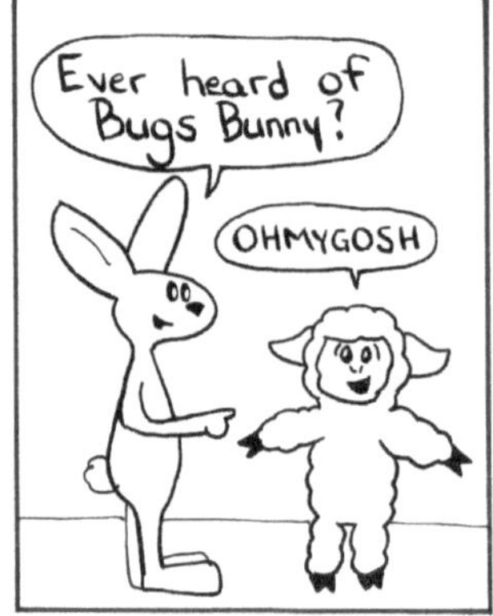
Ever heard of Bugs Bunny?
OHMYGOSH

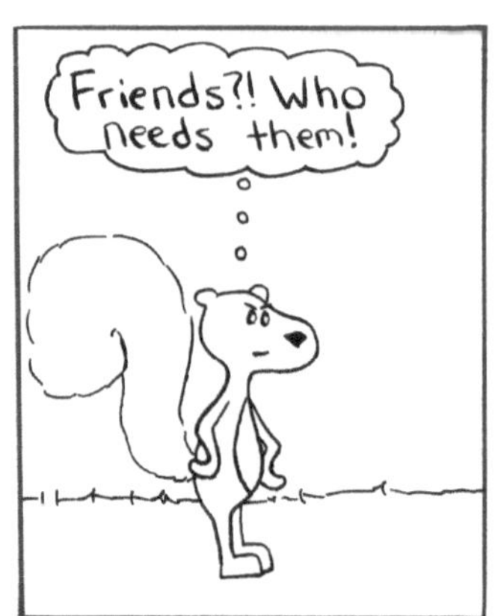
Friends?! Who needs them!

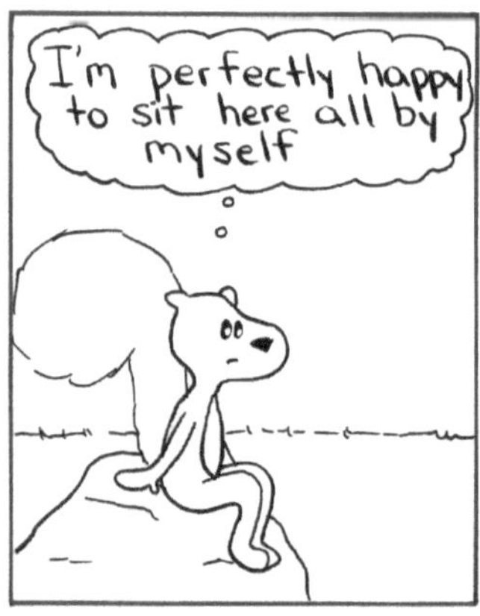
I'm perfectly happy to sit here all by myself

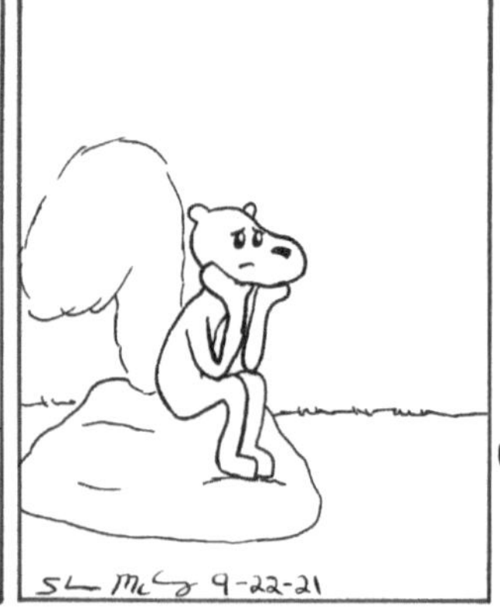
SL McG 9-22-21

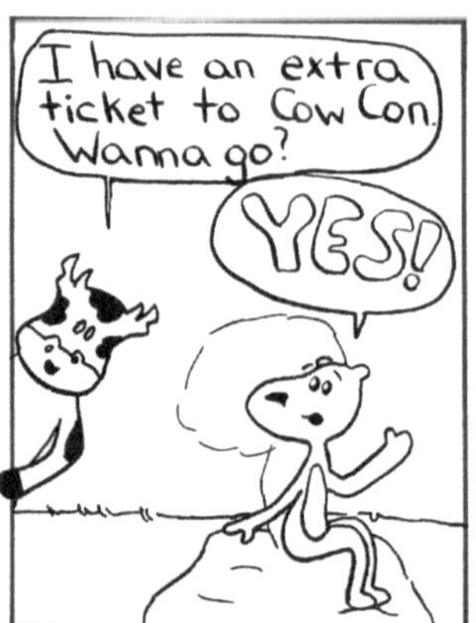
I have an extra ticket to Cow Con. Wanna go?
YES!

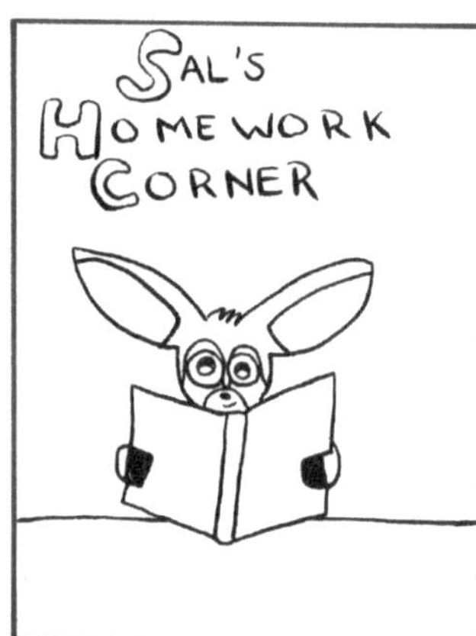
SAL'S
HOMEWORK
CORNER
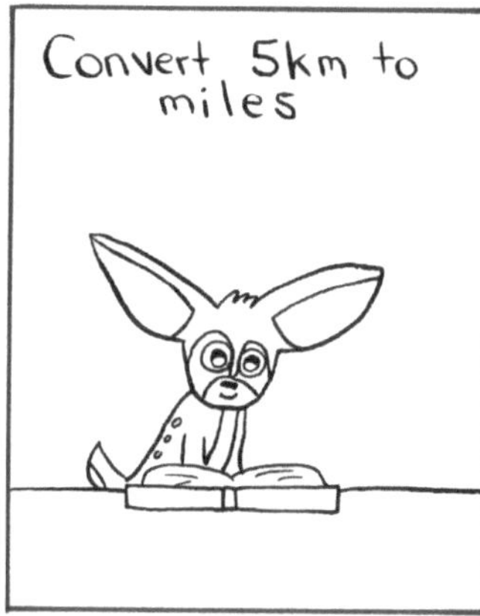
Convert 5km to miles
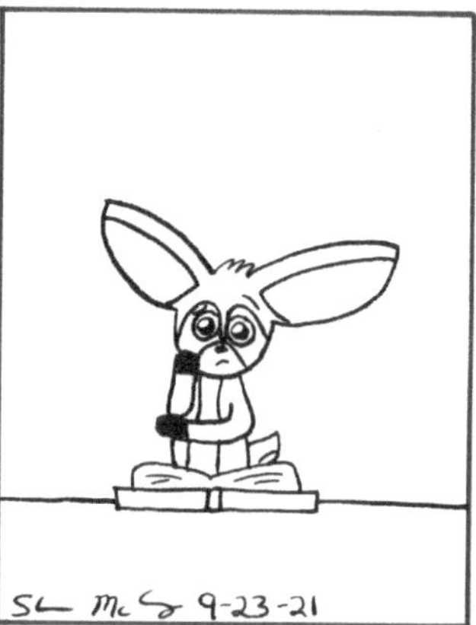
SL McS 9-23-21
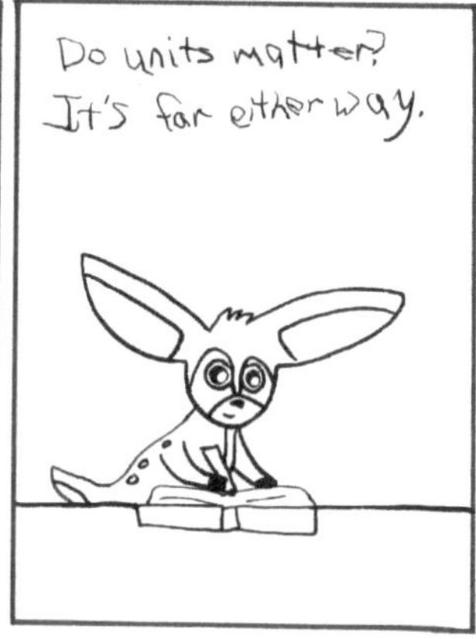
Do units matter?
It's far either way.
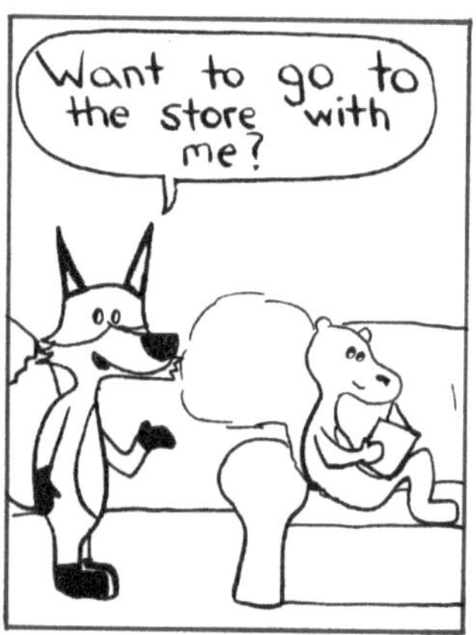
Want to go to the store with me?
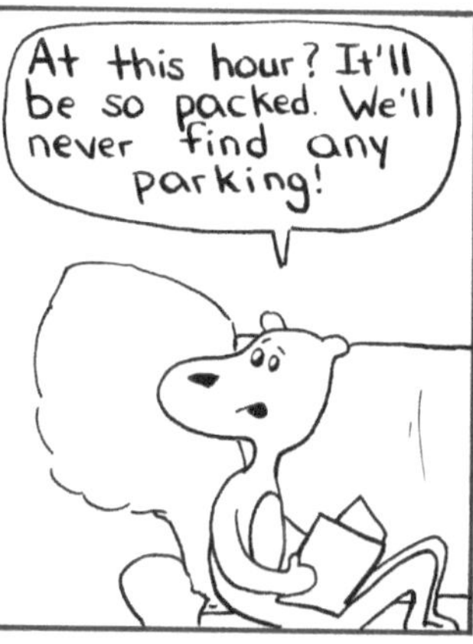
At this hour? It'll be so packed. We'll never find any parking!
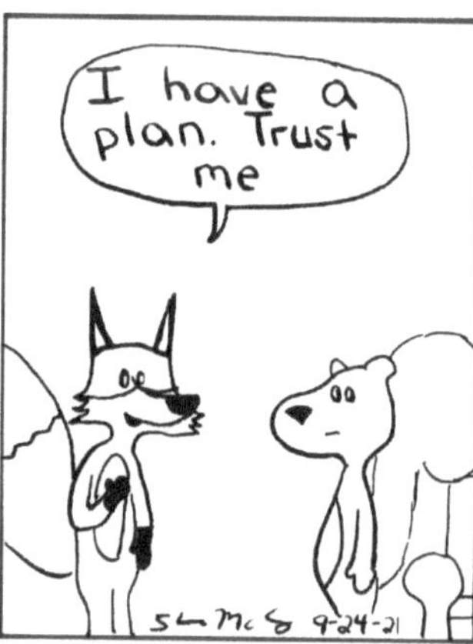
I have a plan. Trust me
SL McS 9-24-21
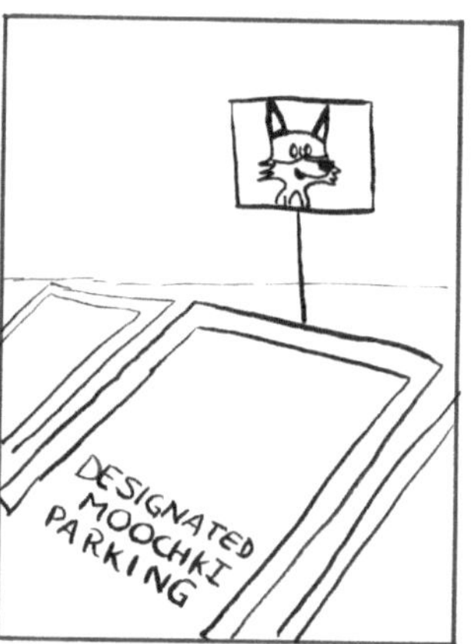
DESIGNATED MOOCHKI PARKING
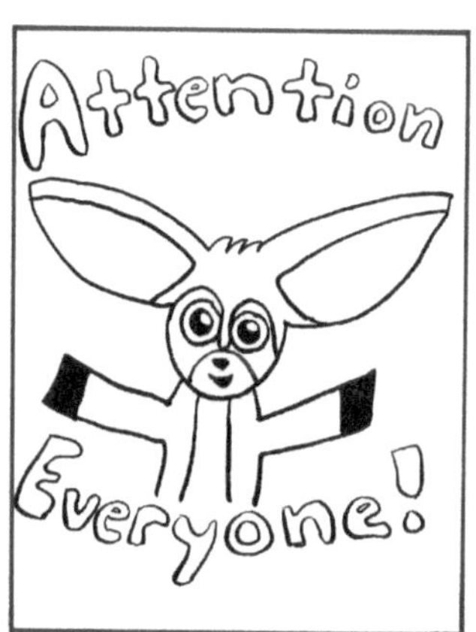
Attention
Everyone!
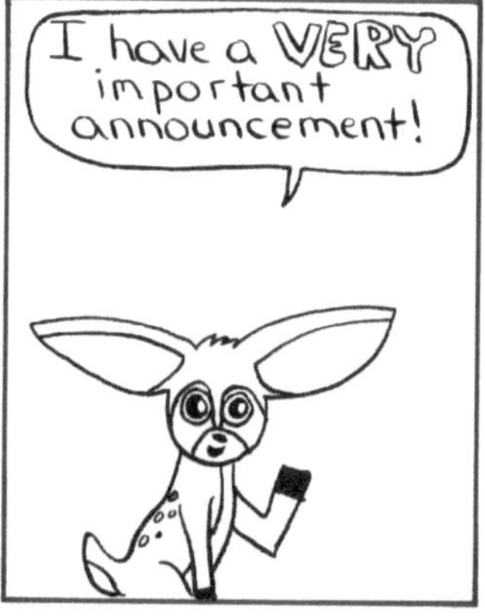
I have a VERY important announcement!
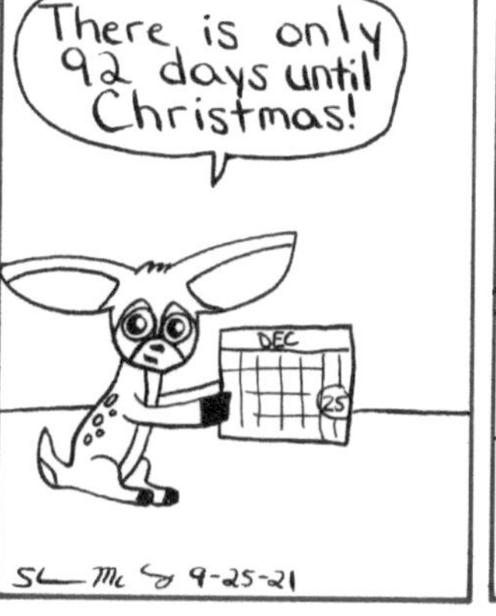
There is only 92 days until Christmas!
DEC
25
SL McS 9-25-21
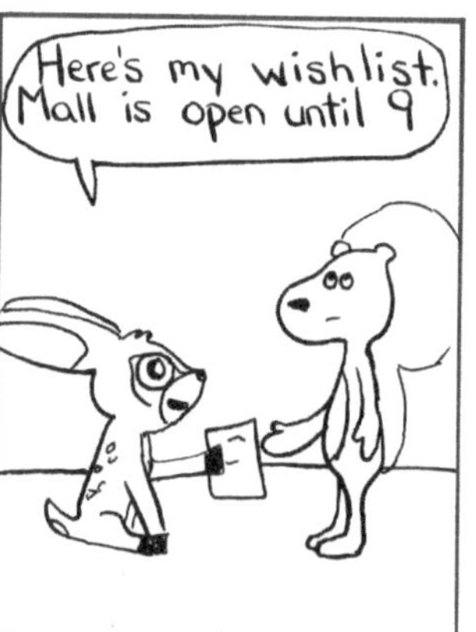
Here's my wishlist. Mall is open until 9

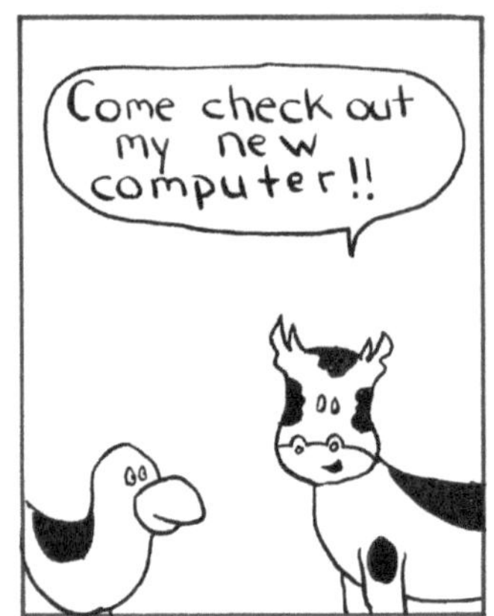
Come check out my new computer!!

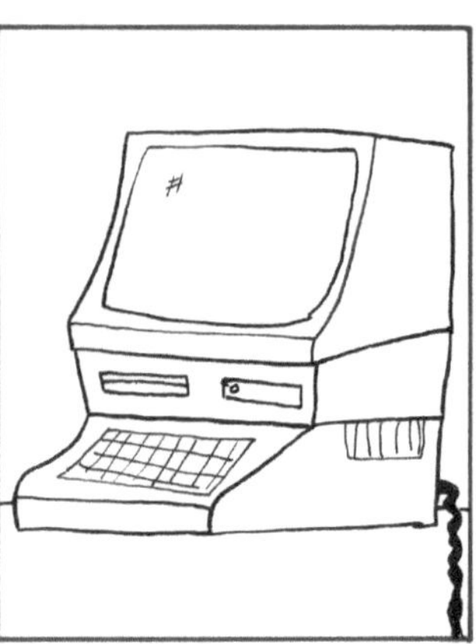

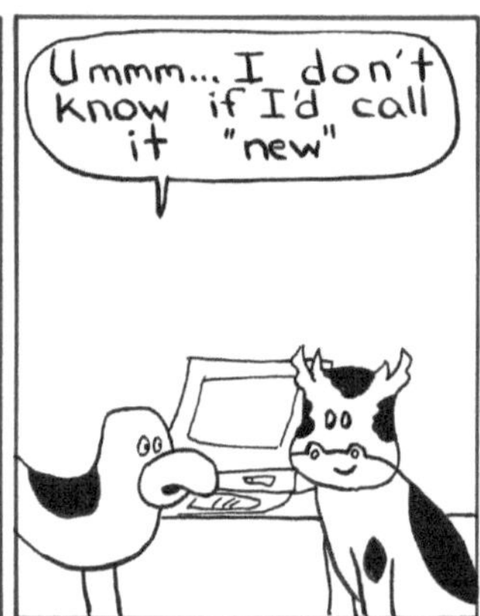
Ummm... I don't know if I'd call it "new"

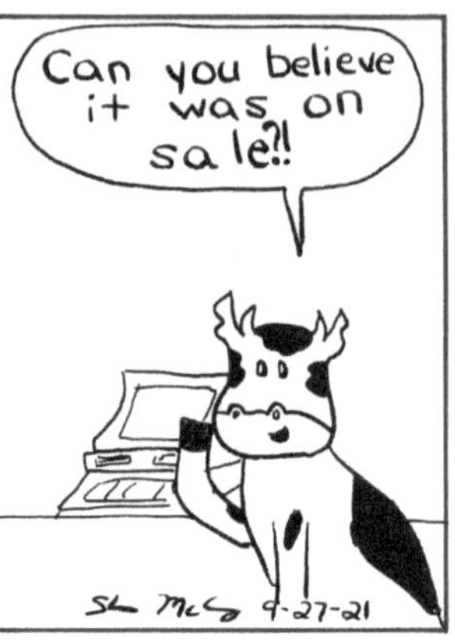
Can you believe it was on sale?!
SL McG 9-27-21

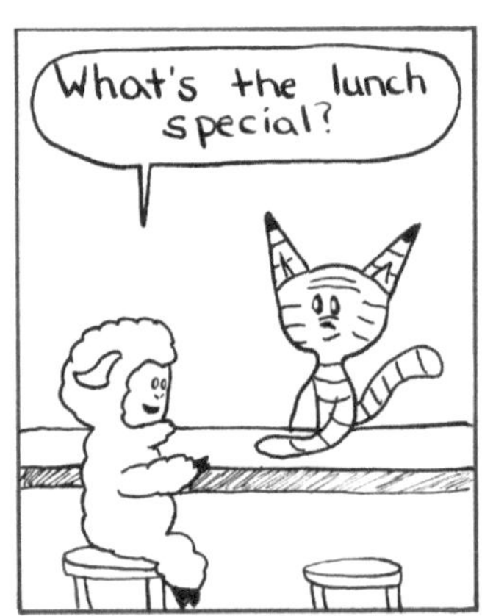
What's the lunch special?

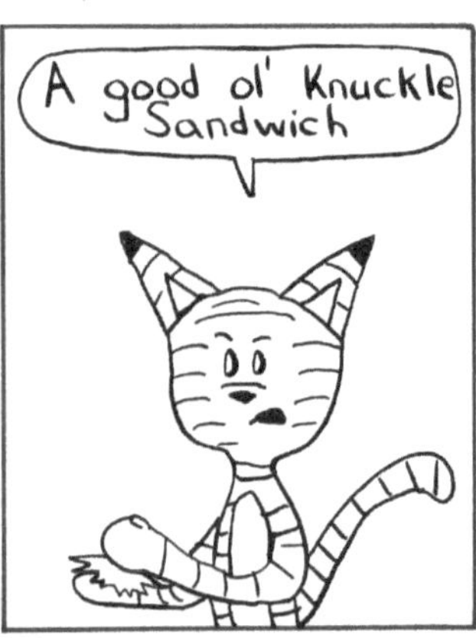
A good ol' Knuckle Sandwich

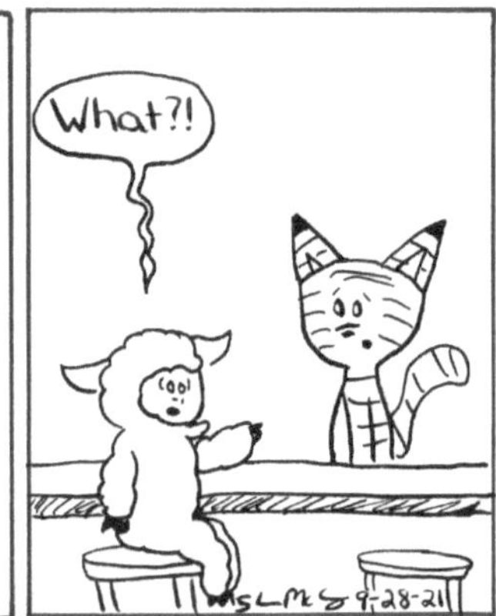
What?!
SL McG 9-28-21

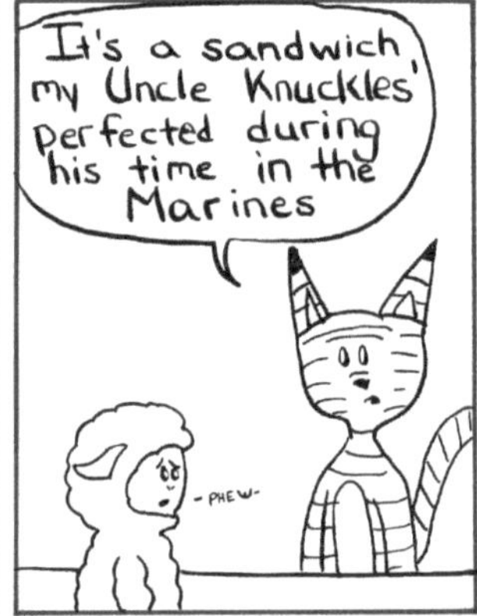
It's a sandwich my Uncle Knuckles' perfected during his time in the Marines
-PHEW-

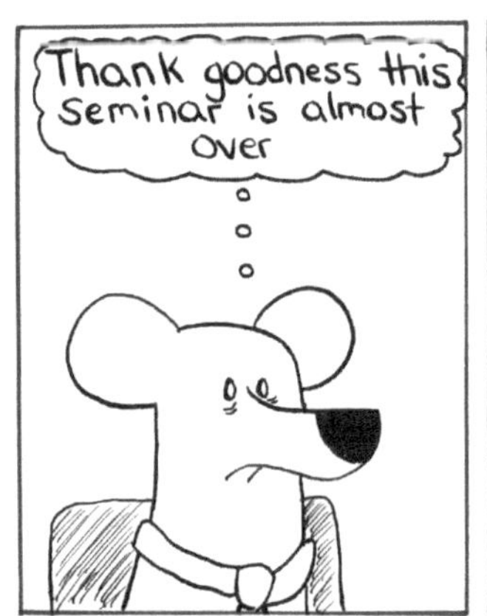
Thank goodness this seminar is almost over

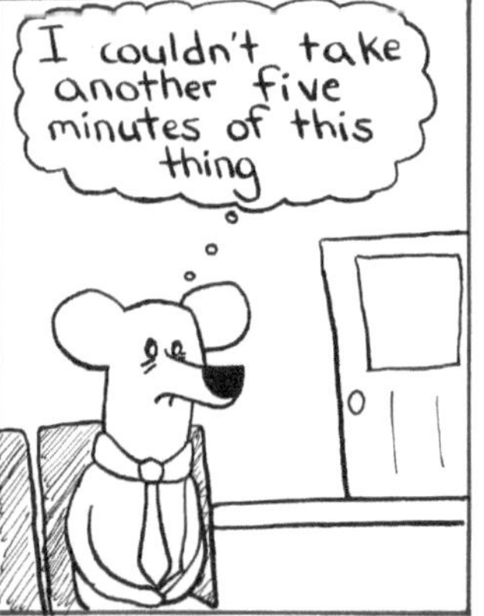
I couldn't take another five minutes of this thing

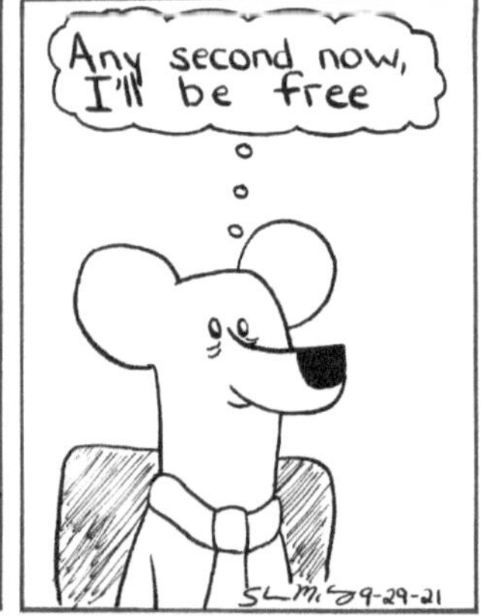
Any second now, I'll be free
SL McG 9-29-21

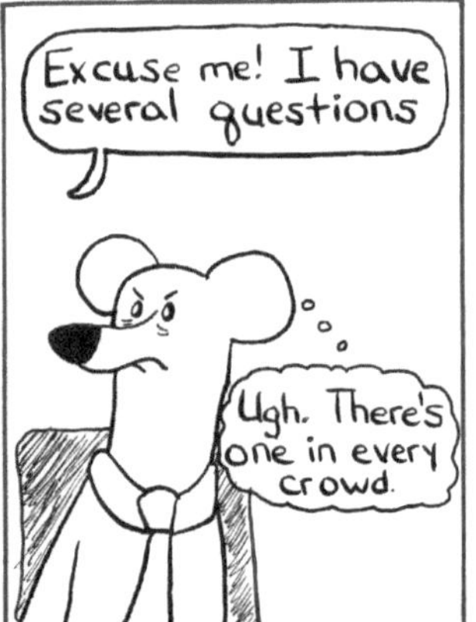
Excuse me! I have several questions
Ugh. There's one in every crowd.

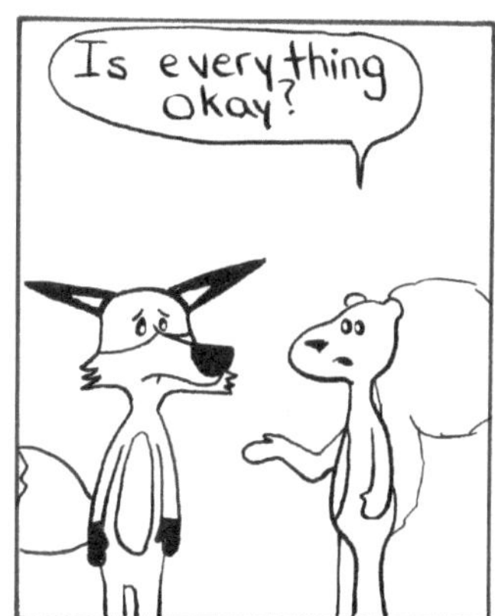
Is everything okay?

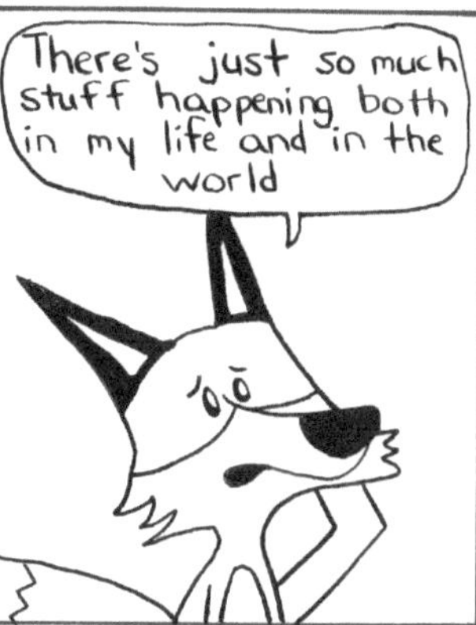
There's just so much stuff happening both in my life and in the world

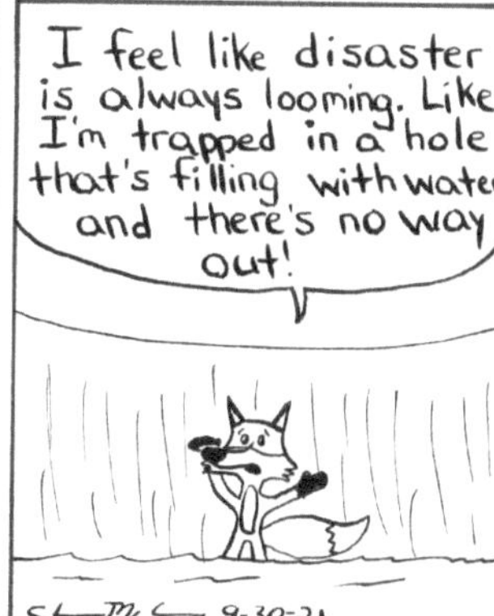
I feel like disaster is always looming. Like I'm trapped in a hole that's filling with water and there's no way out!
SL McG 9-30-21

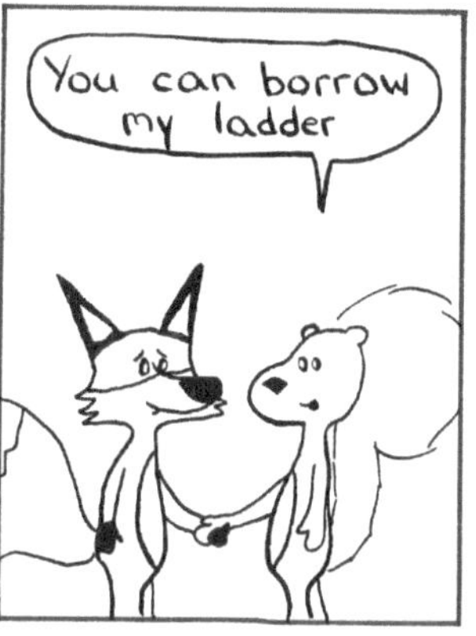
You can borrow my ladder

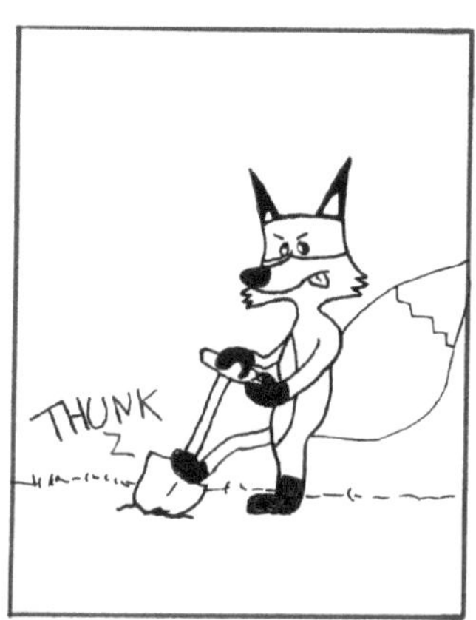
THUNK

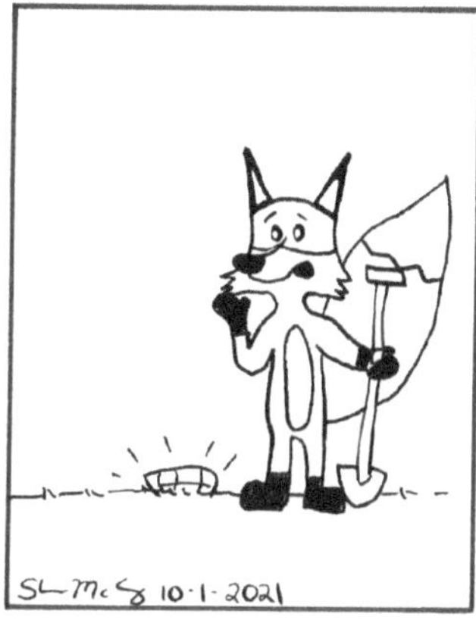
SL McG 10-1-2021

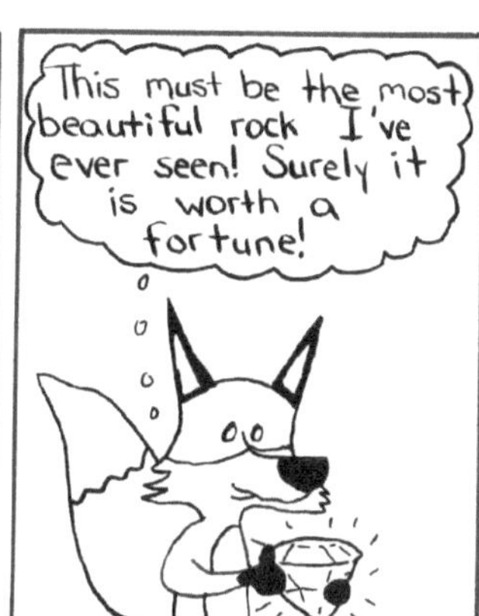
This must be the most beautiful rock I've ever seen! Surely it is worth a fortune!

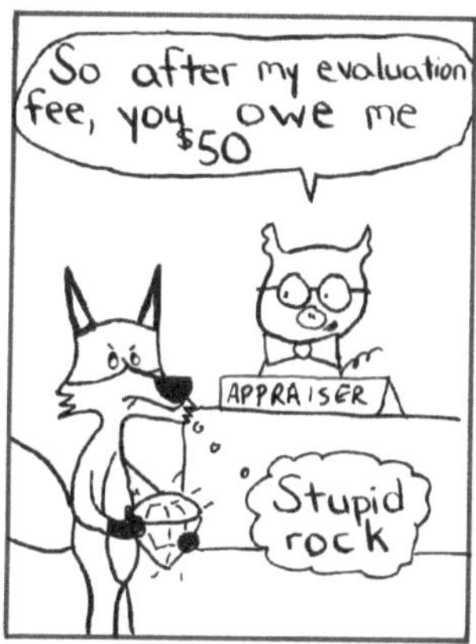
So after my evaluation fee, you owe me $50
APPRAISER
Stupid rock

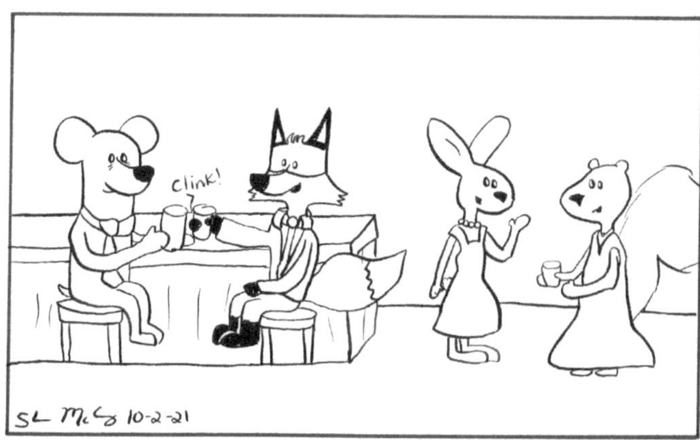
clink!
SL McG 10-2-21

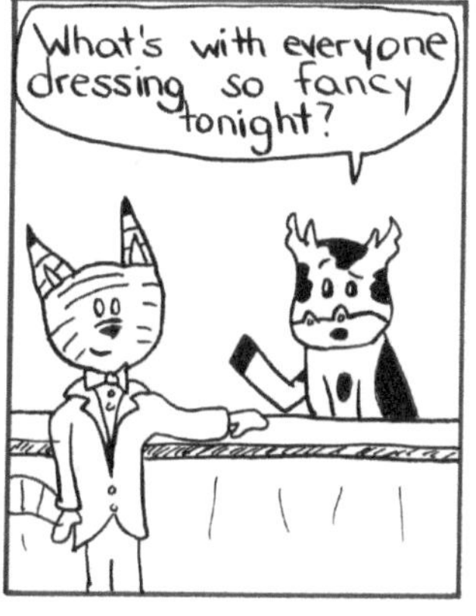
What's with everyone dressing so fancy tonight?

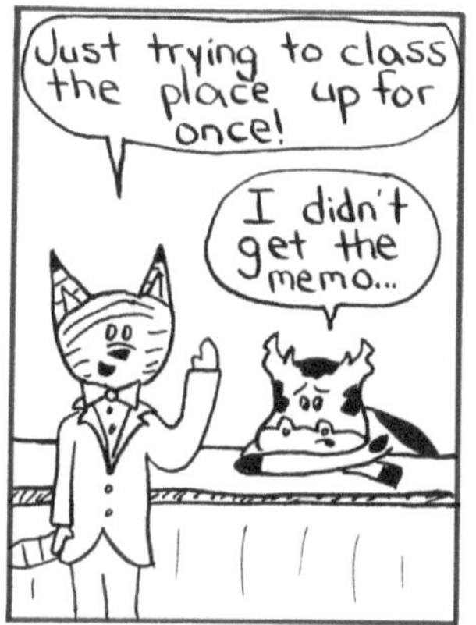
Just trying to class the place up for once!
I didn't get the memo...

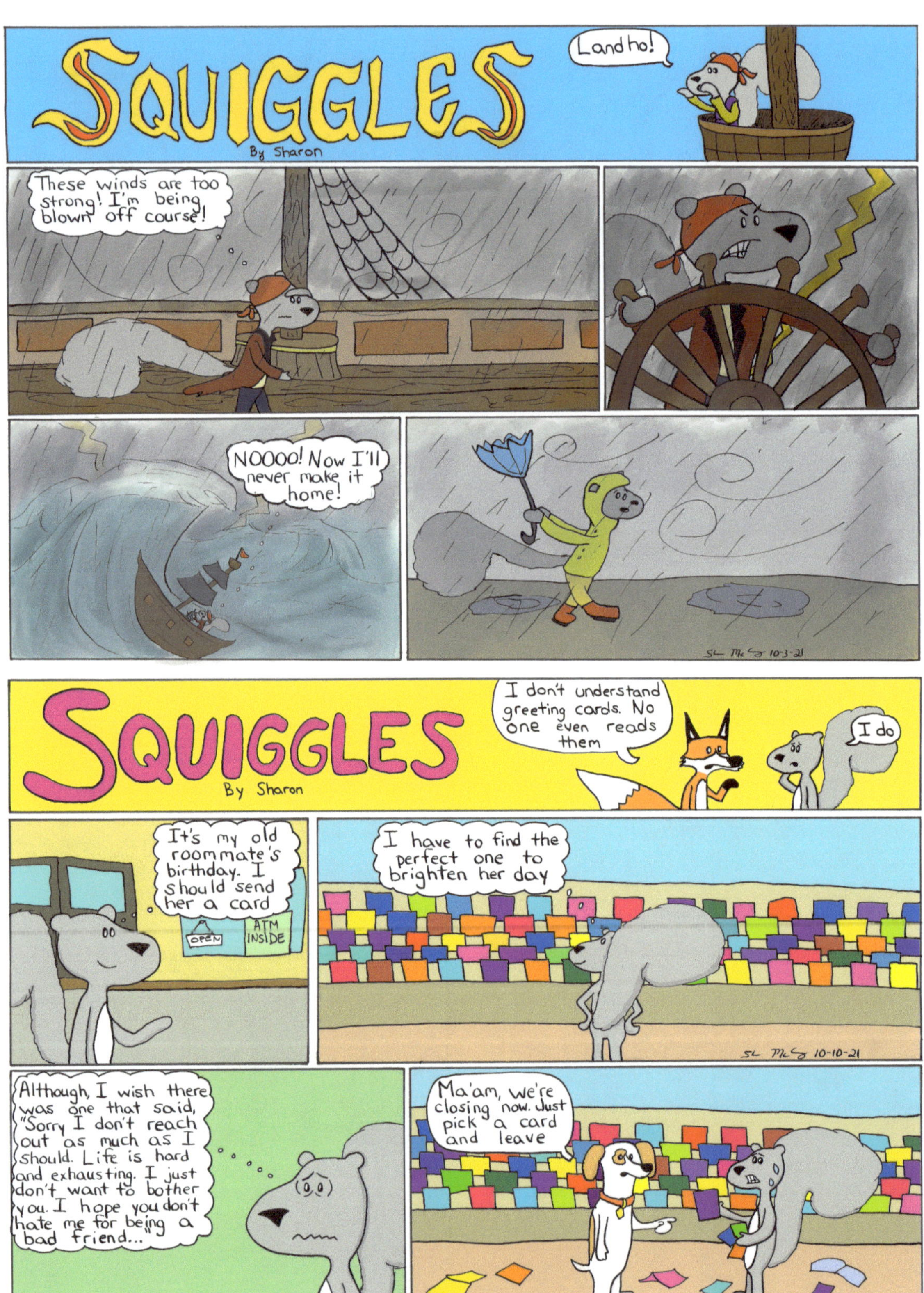
SQUIGGLES
By Sharon
Land ho!
These winds are too strong! I'm being blown off course!
NOOOO! Now I'll never make it home!
SL McG 10-3-21
SQUIGGLES
By Sharon
I don't understand greeting cards. No one even reads them
I do
It's my old roommate's birthday. I should send her a card
OPEN
ATM INSIDE
I have to find the perfect one to brighten her day
SL McG 10-10-21
Although, I wish there was one that said, "Sorry I don't reach out as much as I should. Life is hard and exhausting. I just don't want to bother you. I hope you don't hate me for being a bad friend..."
Ma'am, we're closing now. Just pick a card and leave

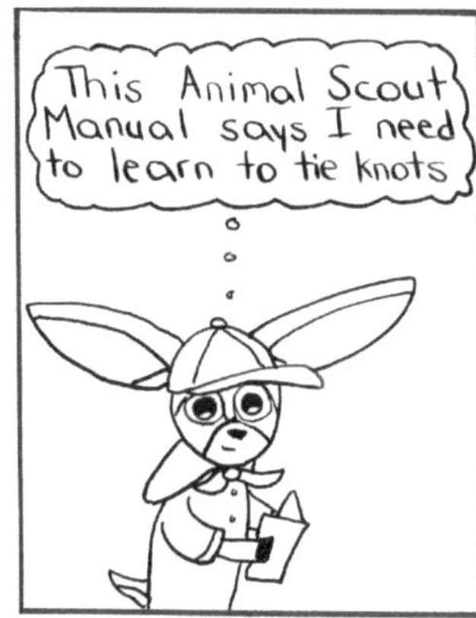
This Animal Scout Manual says I need to learn to tie knots

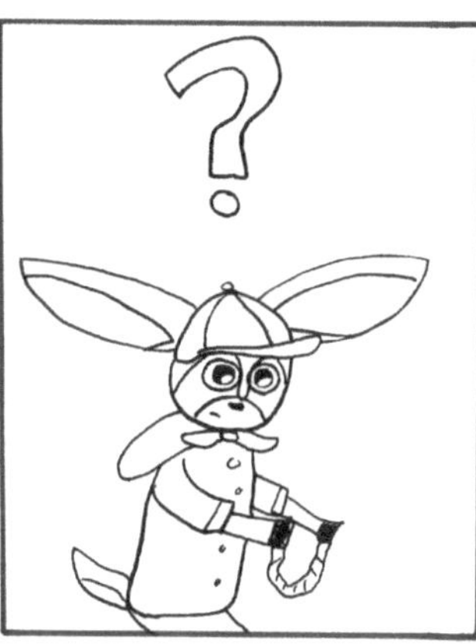
?

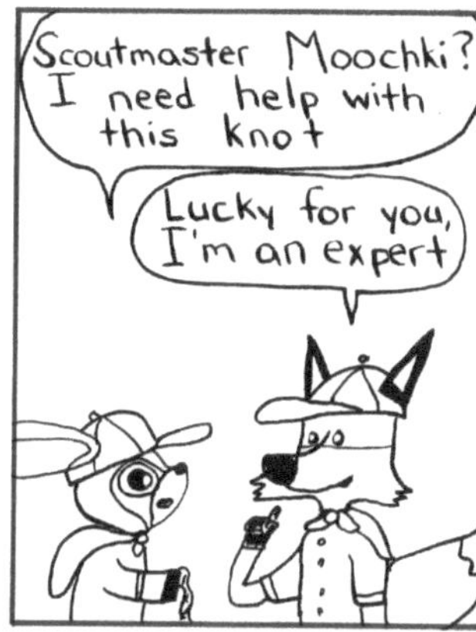
Scoutmaster Moochki? I need help with this knot
Lucky for you, I'm an expert

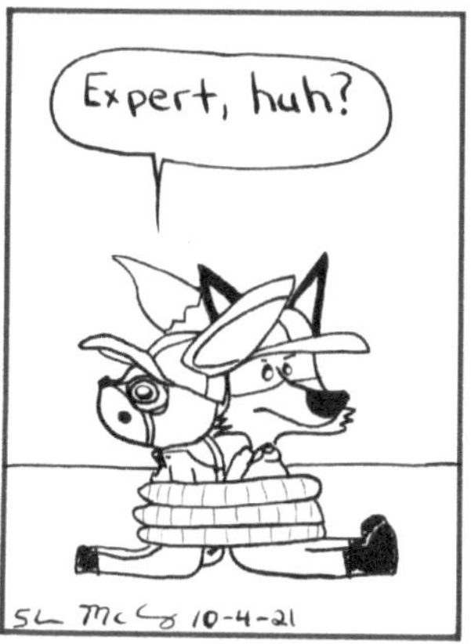
Expert, huh?

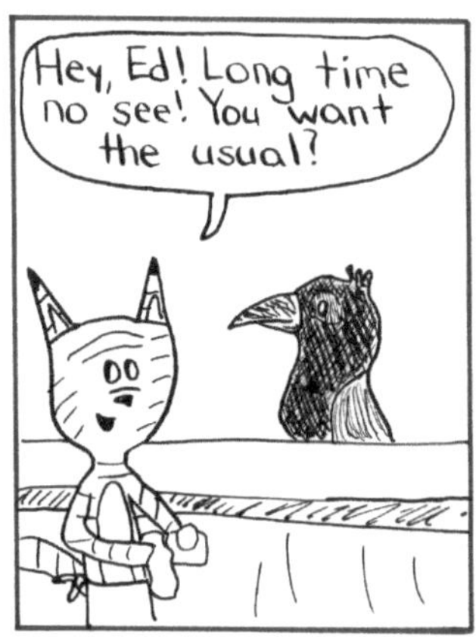
Hey, Ed! Long time no see! You want the usual?

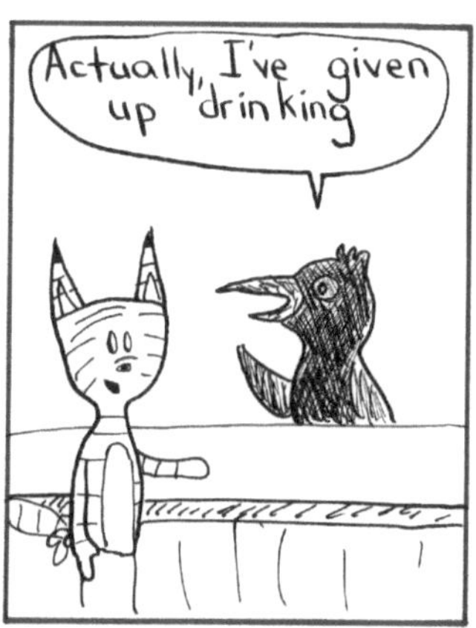
Actually, I've given up drinking

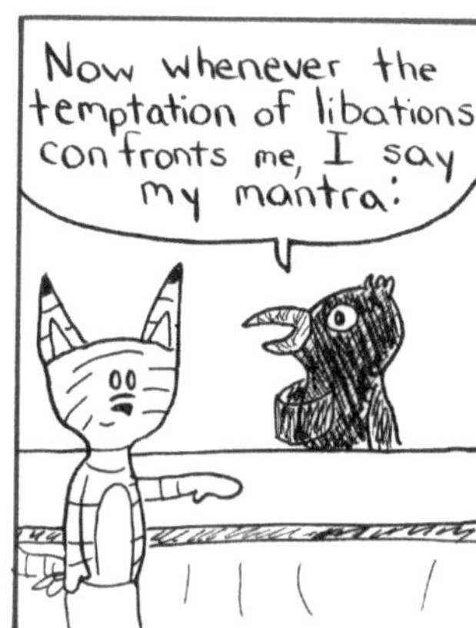
Now whenever the temptation of libations confronts me, I say my mantra:

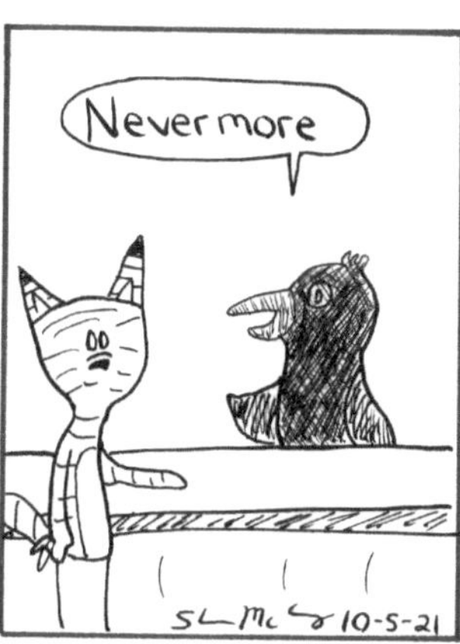
Nevermore

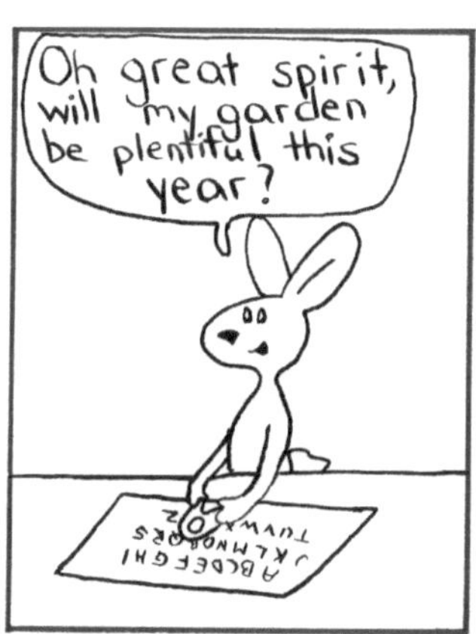
Oh great spirit, will my garden be plentiful this year?

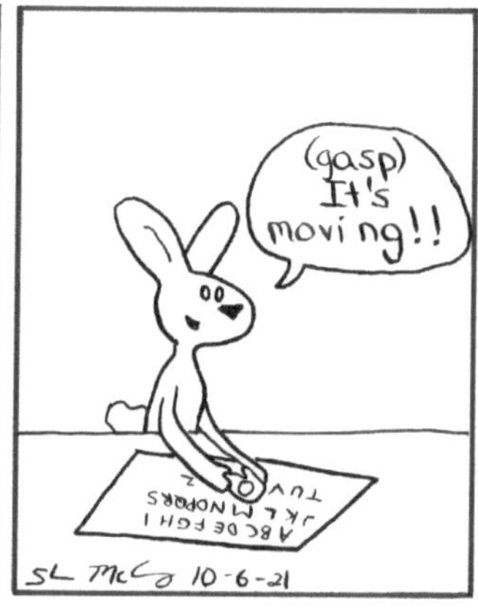
(gasp) It's moving!!

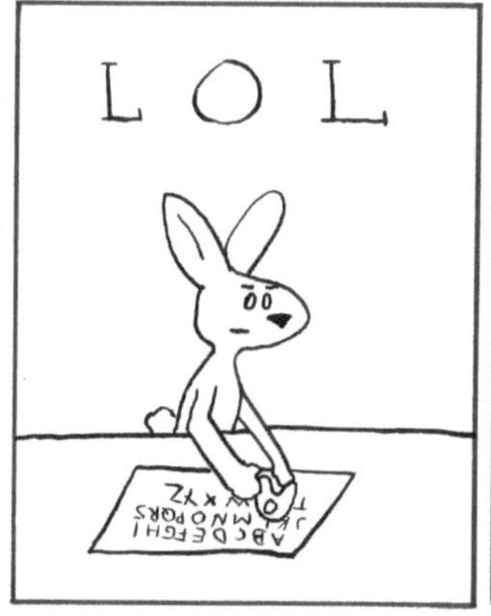
LOL

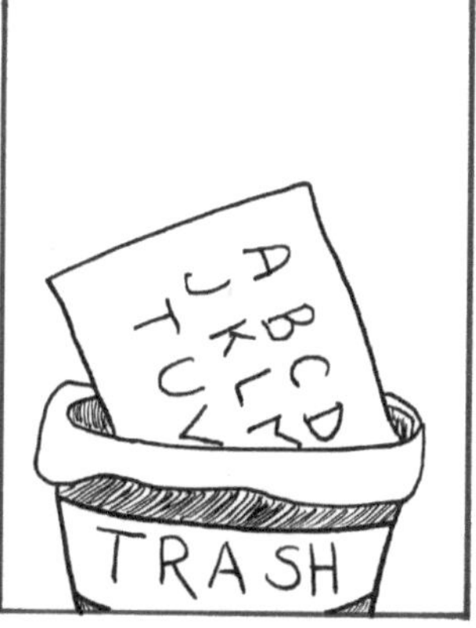
TRASH

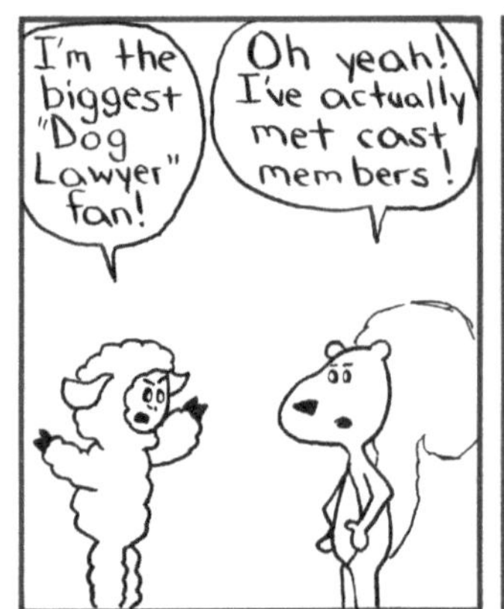
I'm the biggest "Dog Lawyer" fan!
Oh yeah! I've actually met cast members!

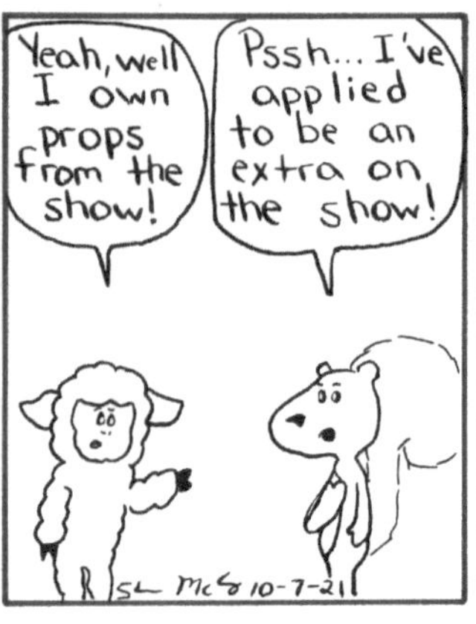
Yeah, well I own props from the show!
Pssh... I've applied to be an extra on the show!

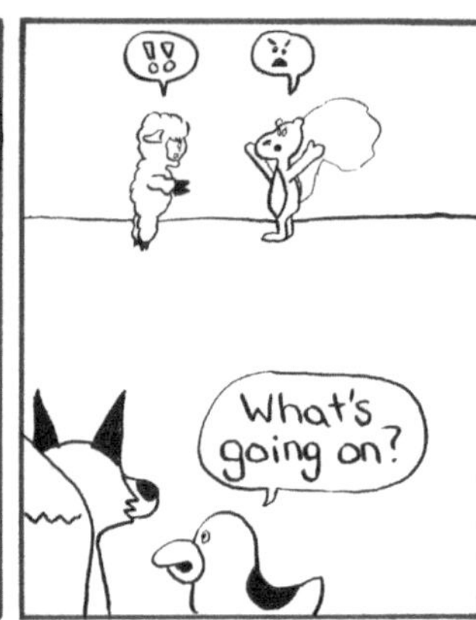
!!
What's going on?

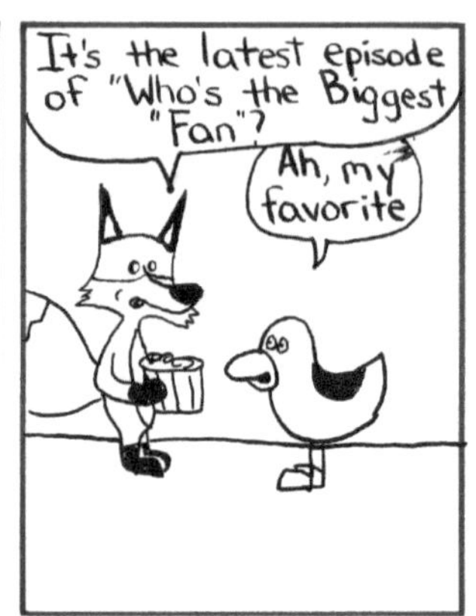
It's the latest episode of "Who's the Biggest "Fan"?
Ah, my favorite

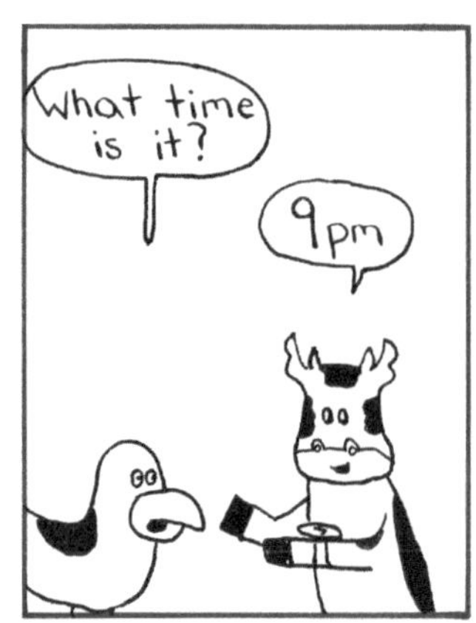
What time is it?
9pm

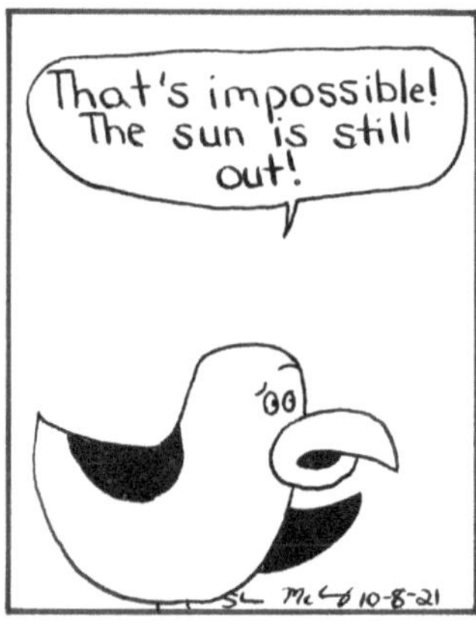
That's impossible! The sun is still out!

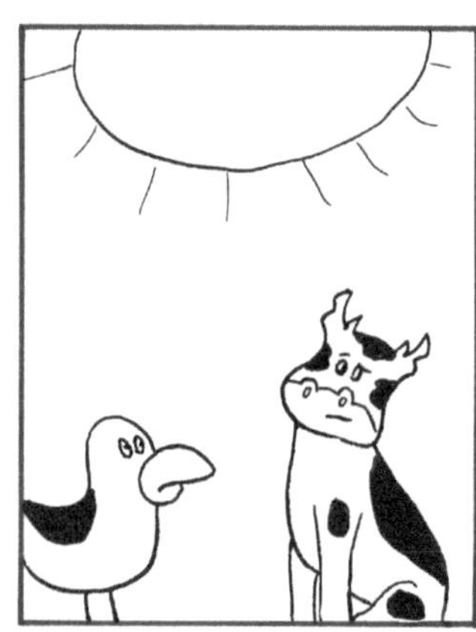

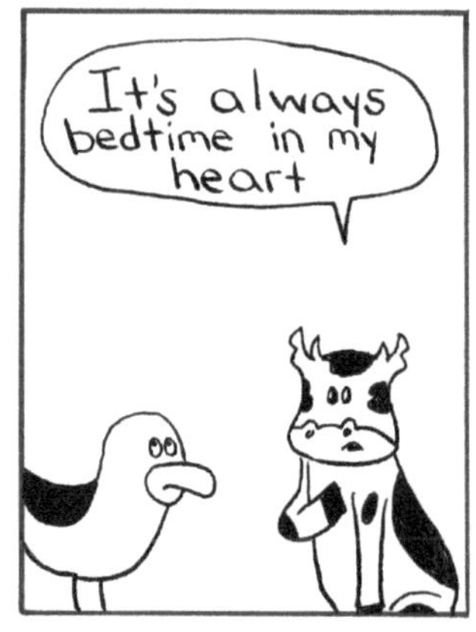
It's always bedtime in my heart

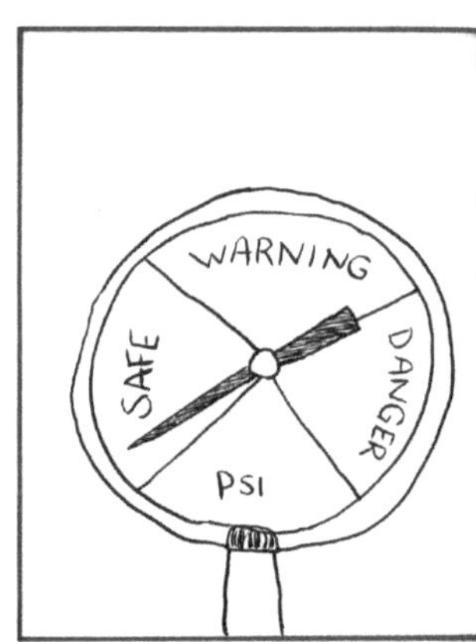
WARNING
SAFE
DANGER
PSI

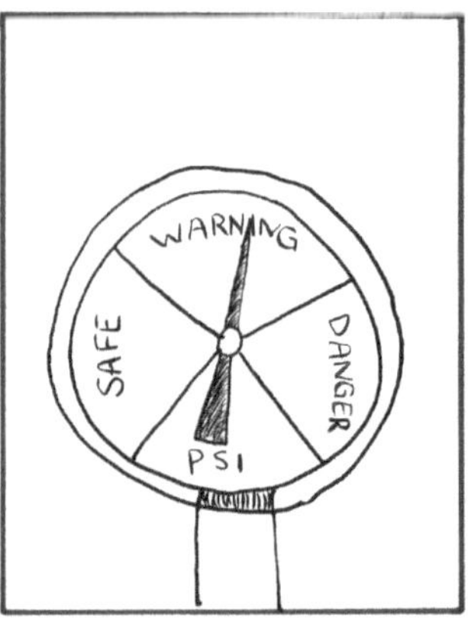
WARNING
SAFE
DANGER
PSI

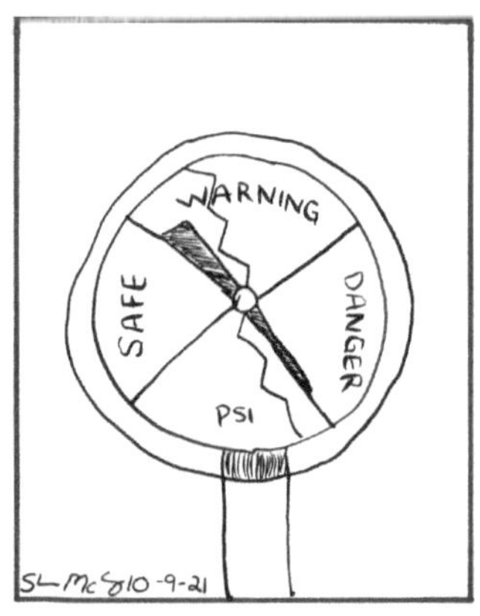
WARNING
SAFE
DANGER
PSI

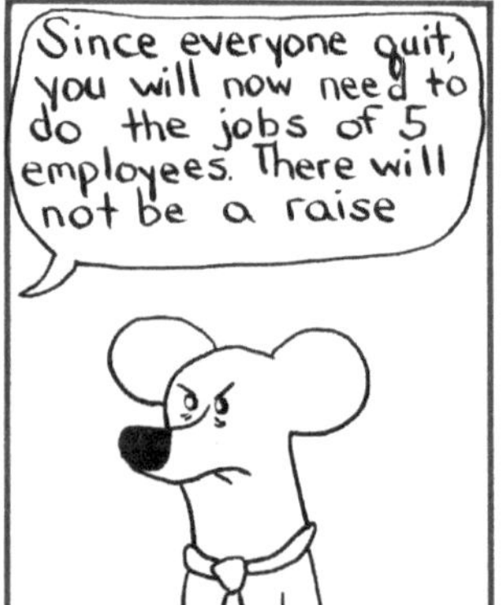
Since everyone quit, you will now need to do the jobs of 5 employees. There will not be a raise

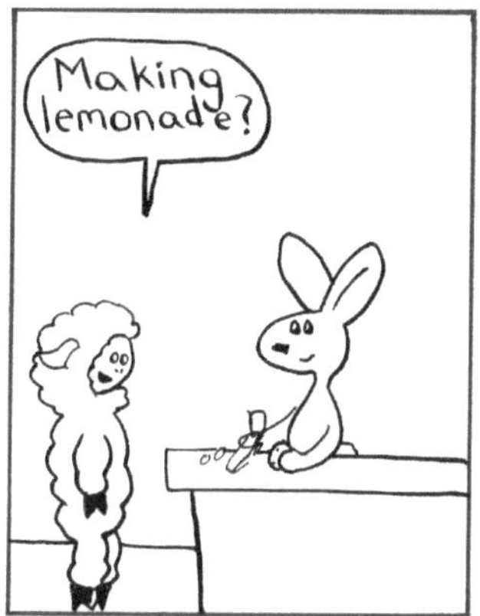
Making lemonade?

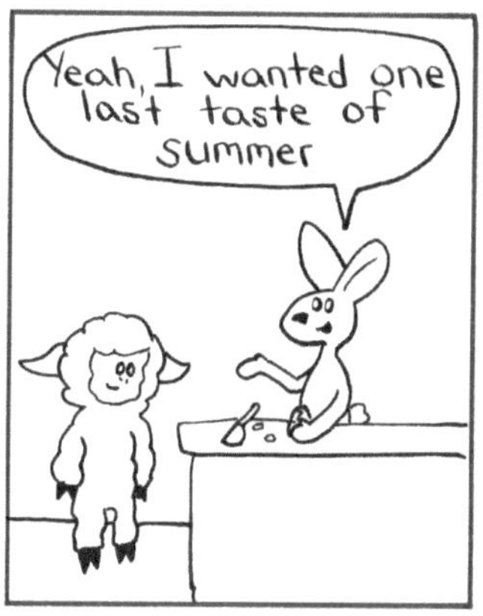
Yeah, I wanted one last taste of summer

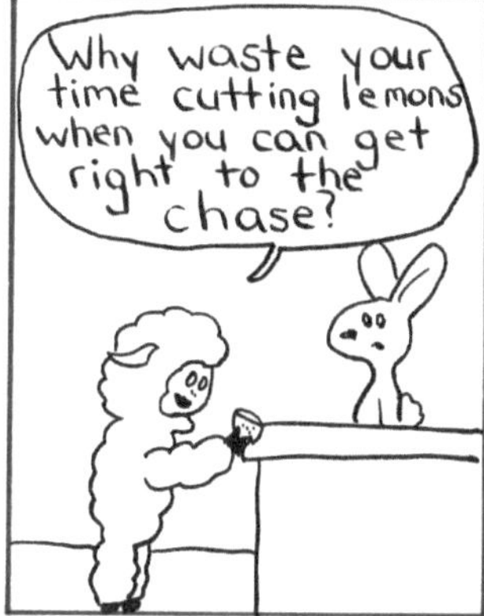
Why waste your time cutting lemons when you can get right to the chase?

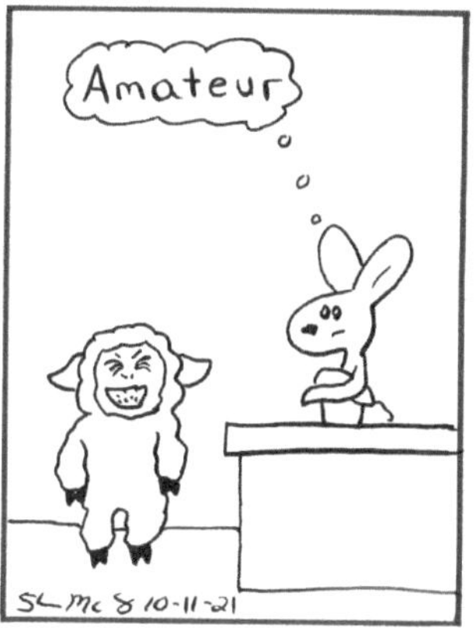
Amateur
SL McS 10-11-21

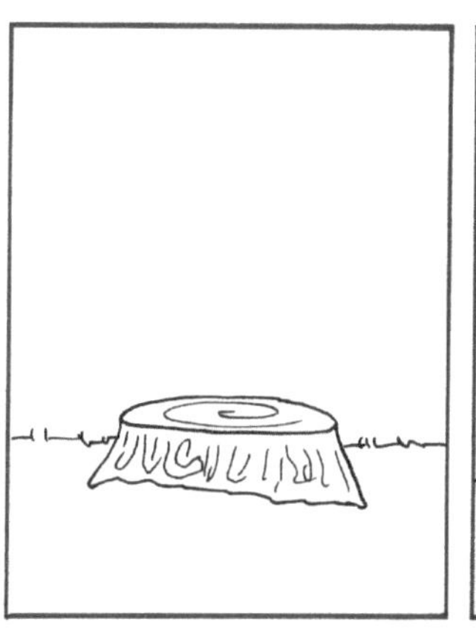

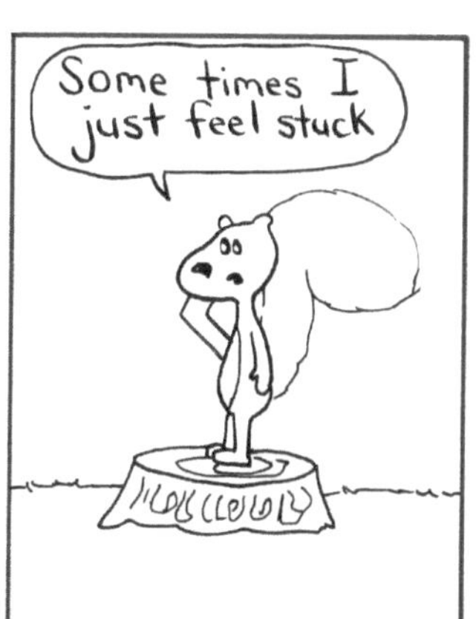
Some times I just feel stuck

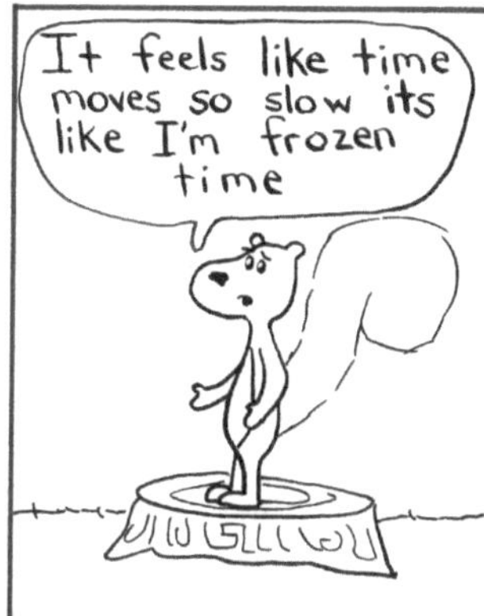
It feels like time moves so slow its like I'm frozen time

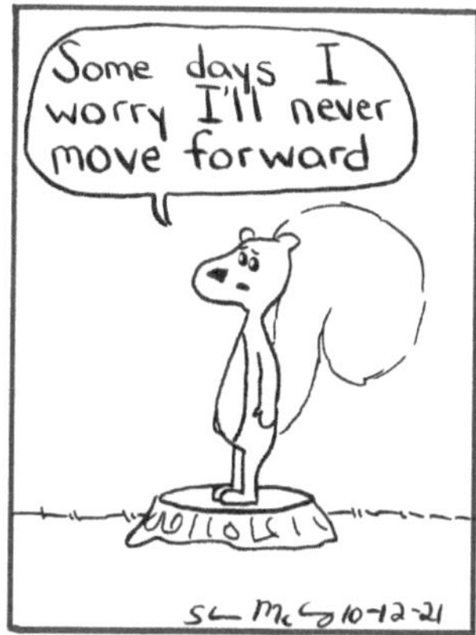
Some days I worry I'll never move forward
SL McS 10-12-21

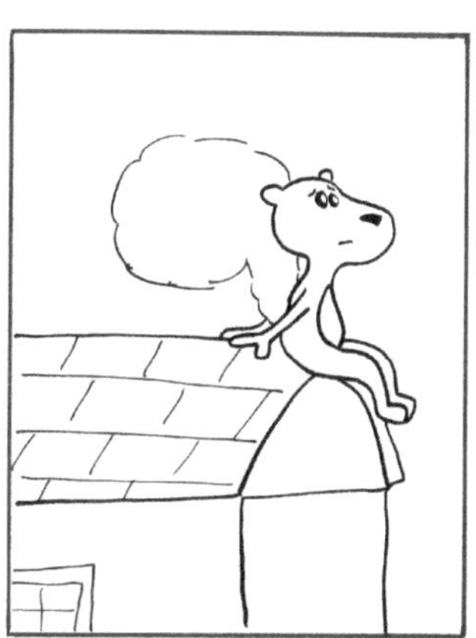

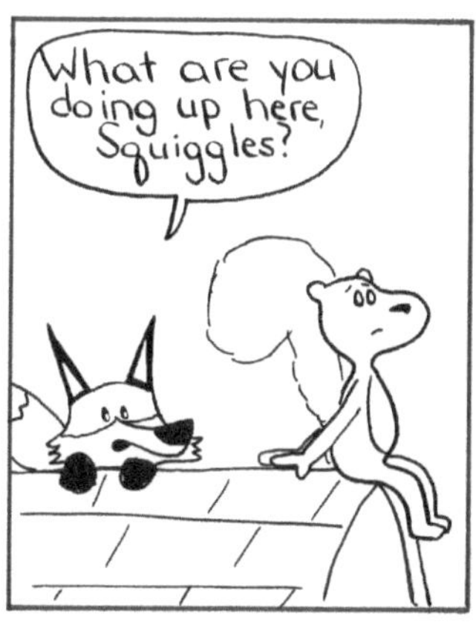
What are you doing up here, Squiggles?

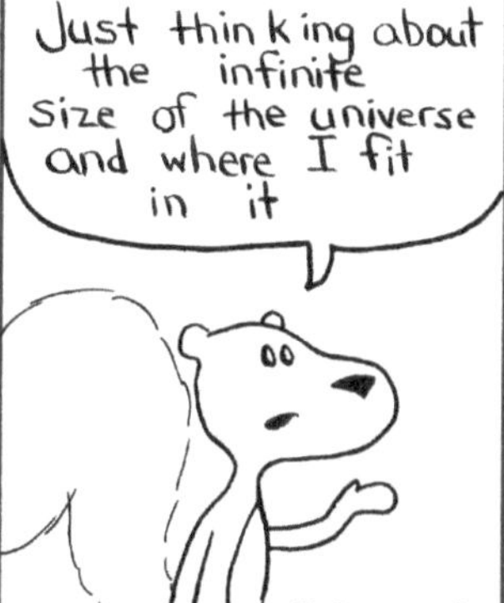
Just thinking about the infinite size of the universe and where I fit in it
SL McS 10-13-21

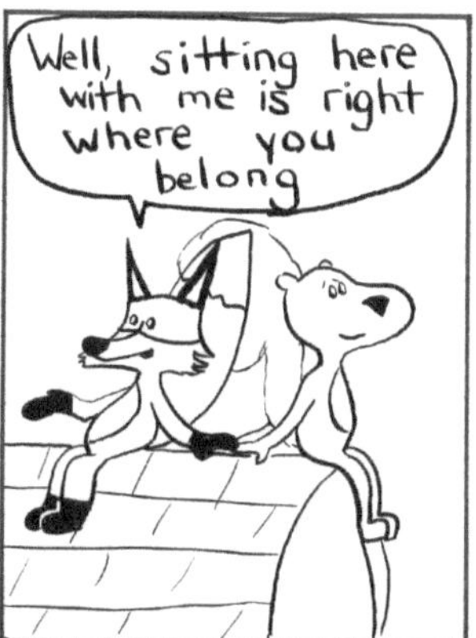
Well, sitting here with me is right where you belong

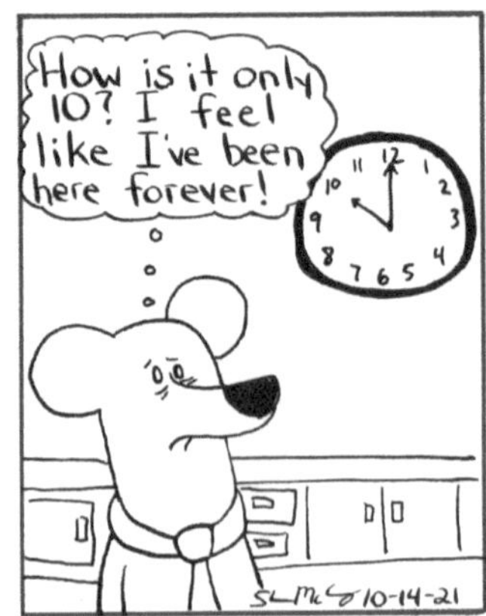
How is it only 10? I feel like I've been here forever!
12 1 2 3 4 5 6 7 8 9 10 11
SLMcG 10-14-21

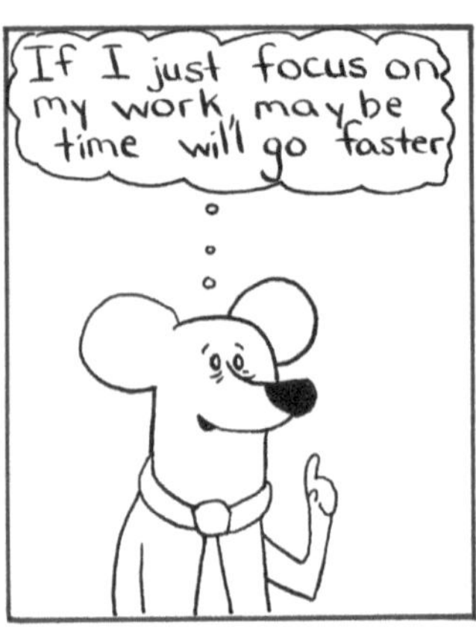
If I just focus on my work maybe time will go faster

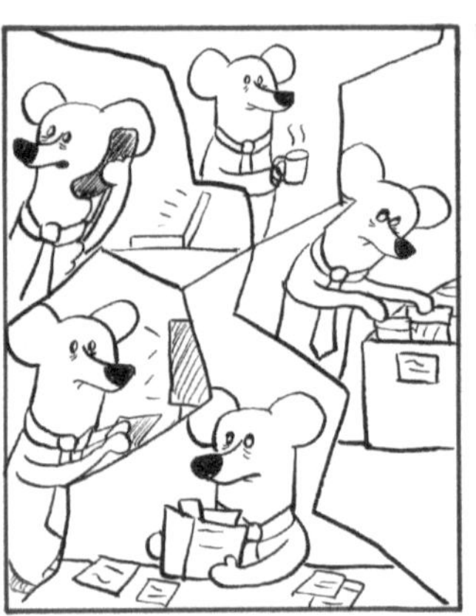

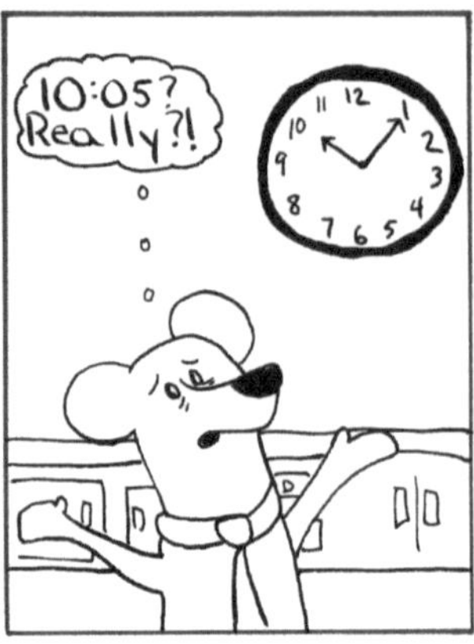
10:05? Really?!
12 1 2 3 4 5 6 7 8 9 10 11

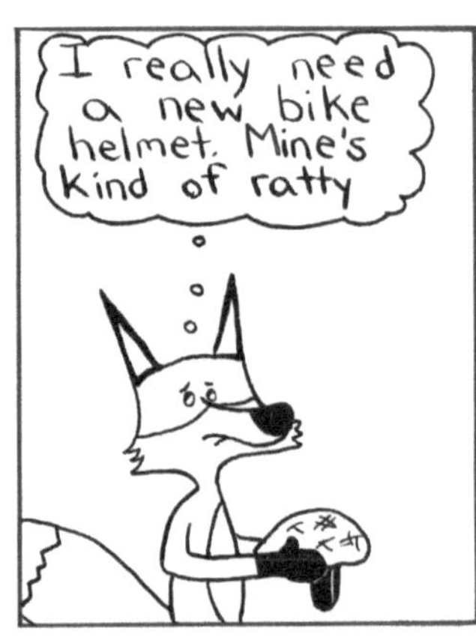
I really need a new bike helmet. Mine's kind of ratty

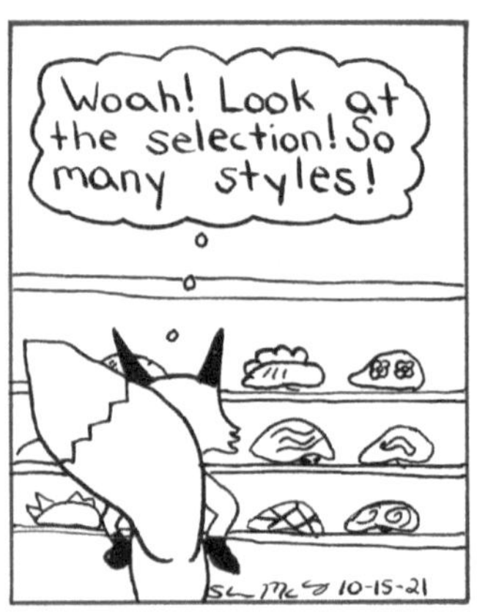
Woah! Look at the selection! So many styles!
SLMcG 10-15-21

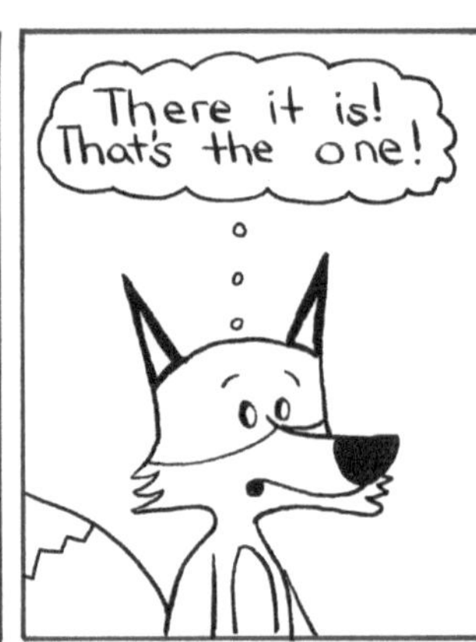
There it is! That's the one!

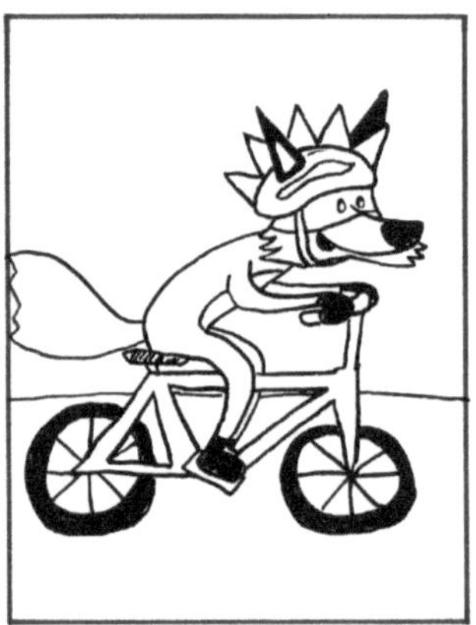

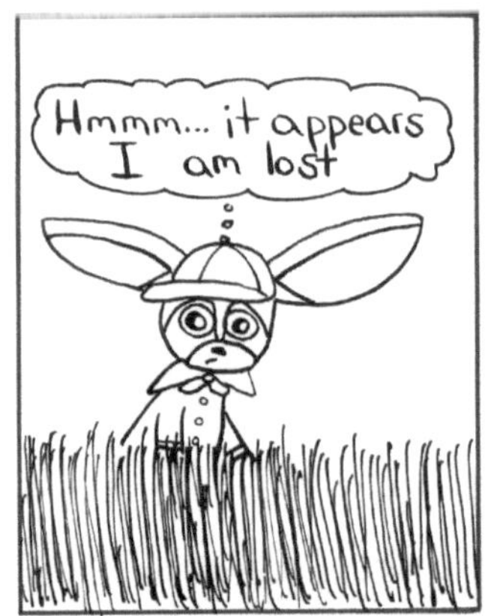
Hmmm... it appears I am lost

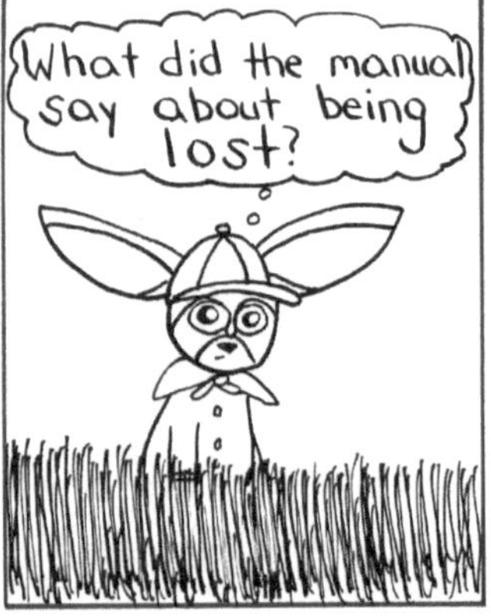
What did the manual say about being lost?

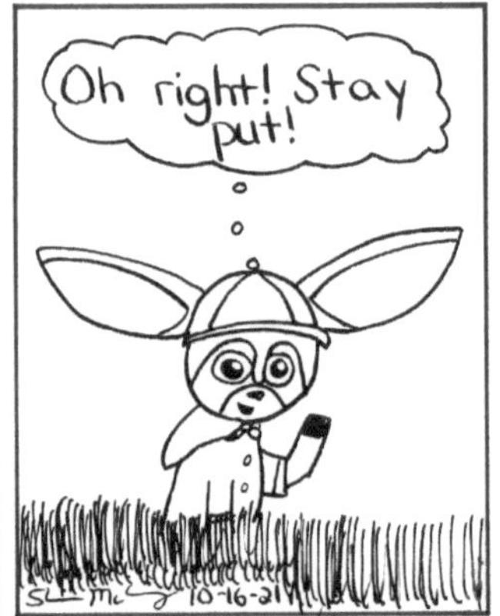
Oh right! Stay put!
SLMcG 10-16-21

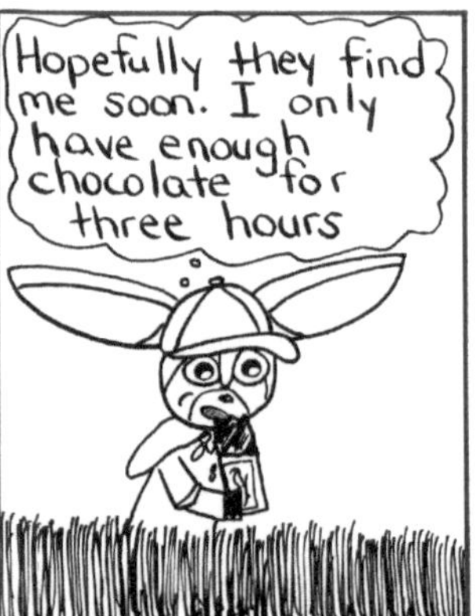
Hopefully they find me soon. I only have enough chocolate for three hours

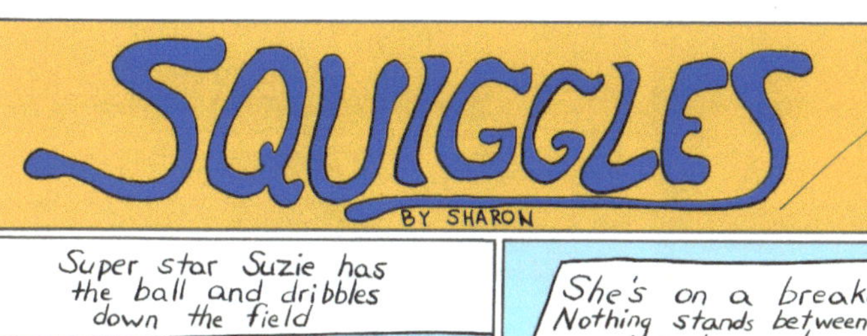
SQUIGGLES
BY SHARON

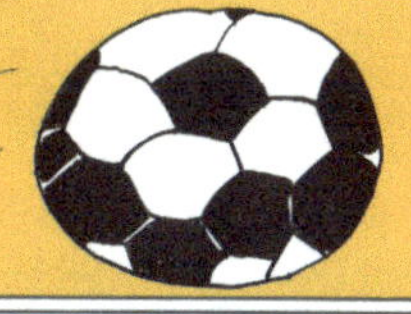

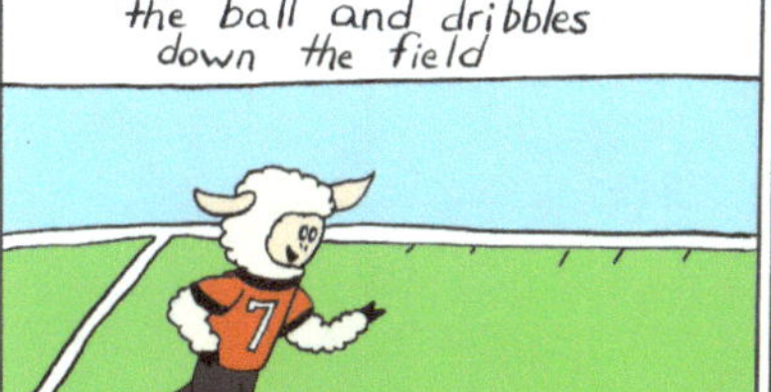
Super star Suzie has the ball and dribbles down the field

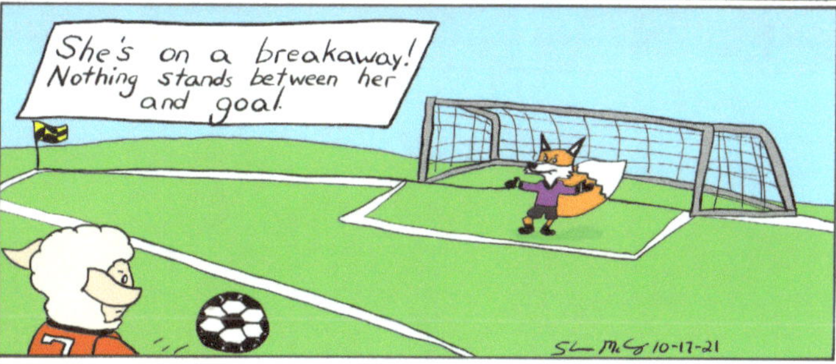
She's on a breakaway! Nothing stands between her and goal.
SL McG 10-17-21

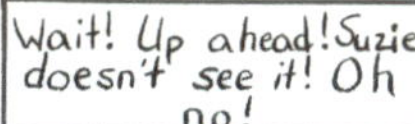
Wait! Up ahead! Suzie doesn't see it! Oh no!

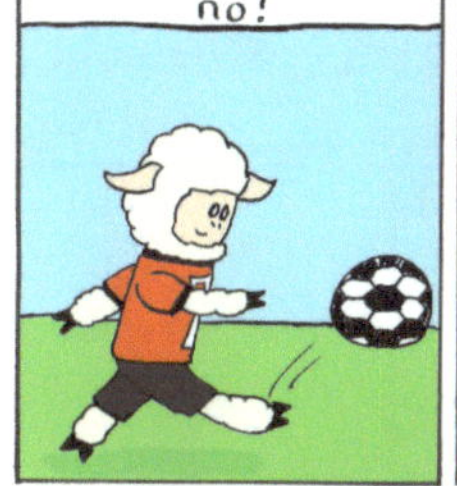

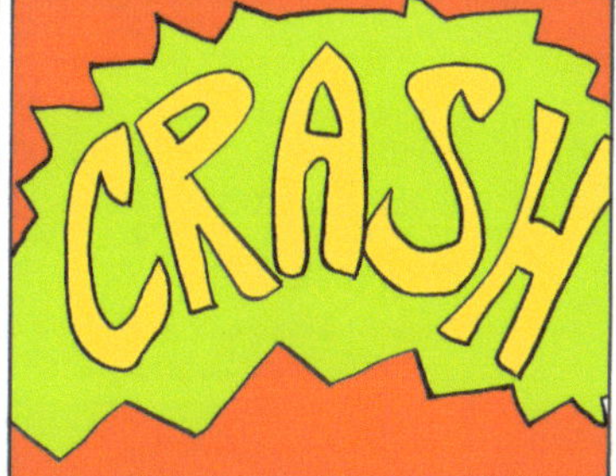
CRASH

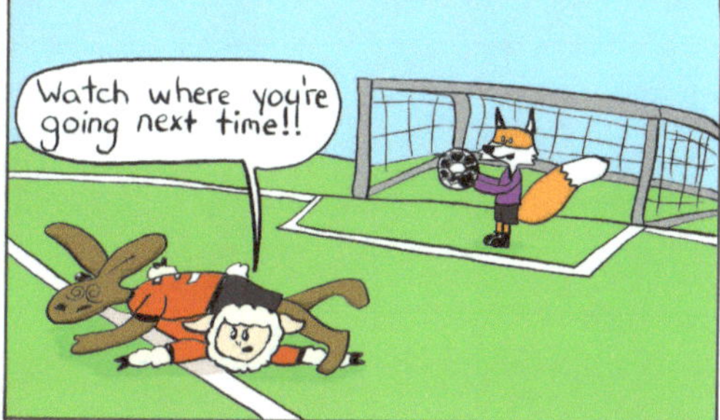
Watch where you're going next time!!

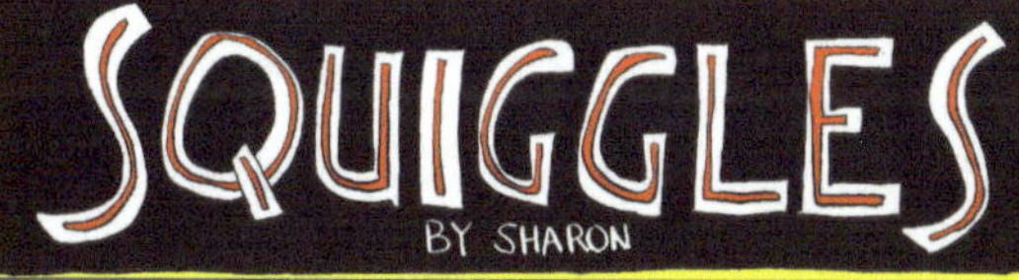
SQUIGGLES
BY SHARON

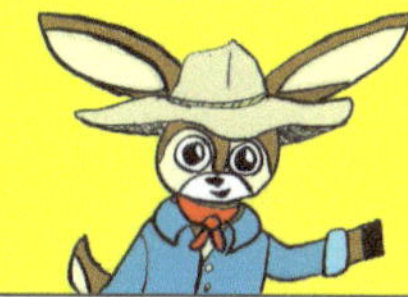
Welcome to Salassic Park

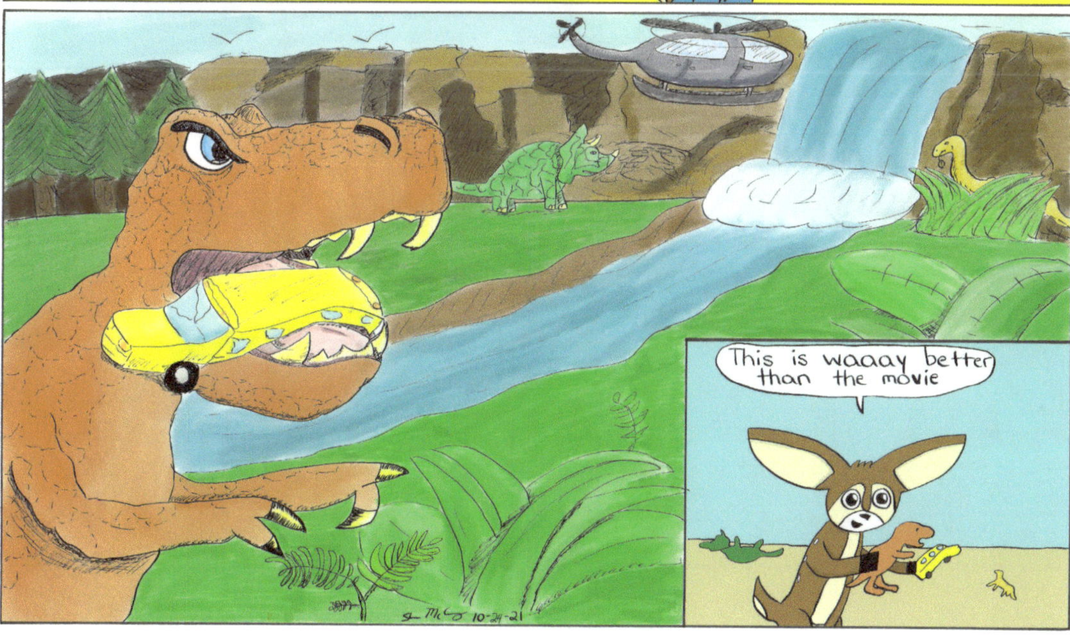
This is waaay better than the movie
SL McG 10-29-21

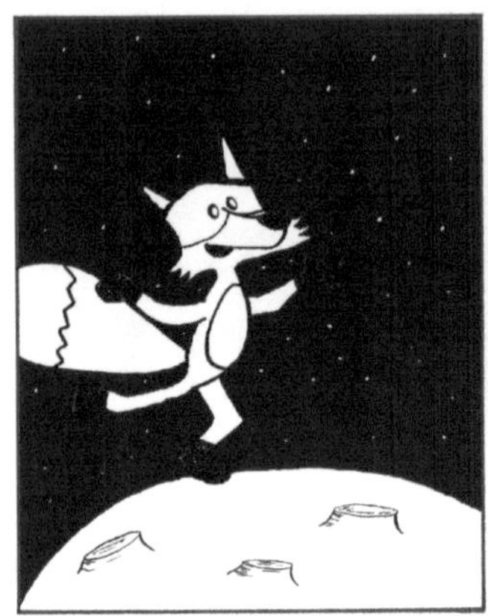
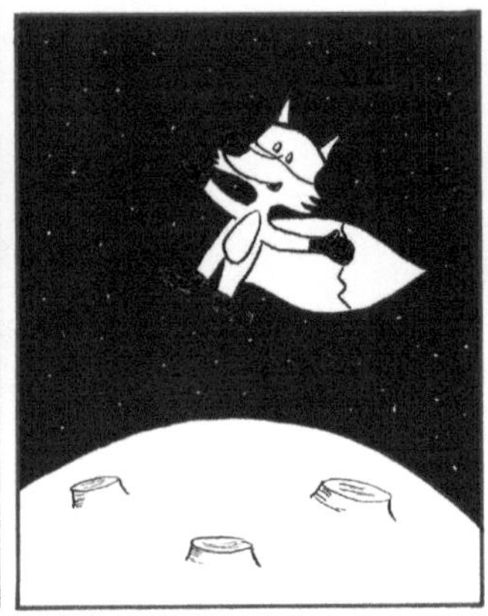
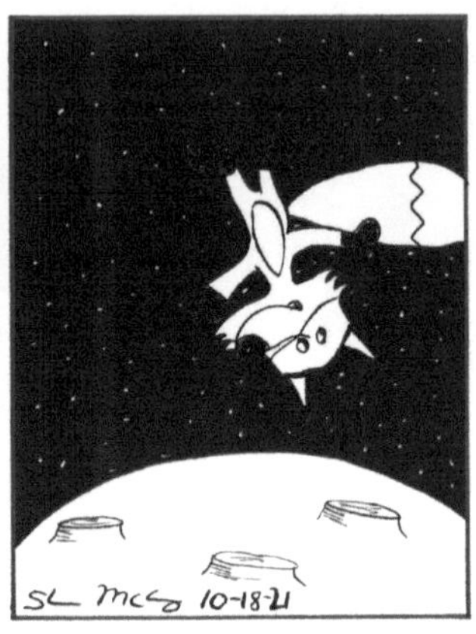
SL McG 10-18-21
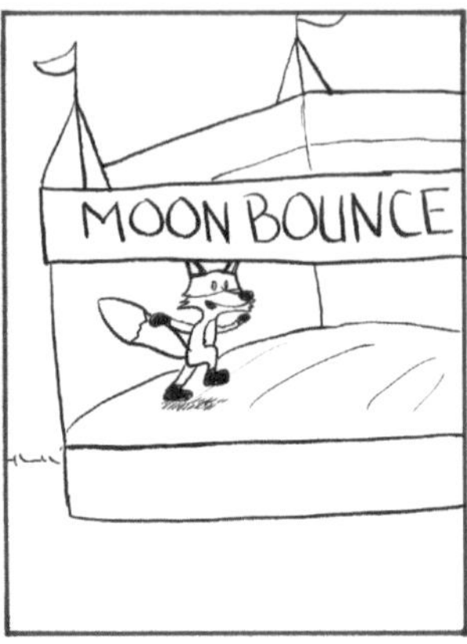
MOON BOUNCE

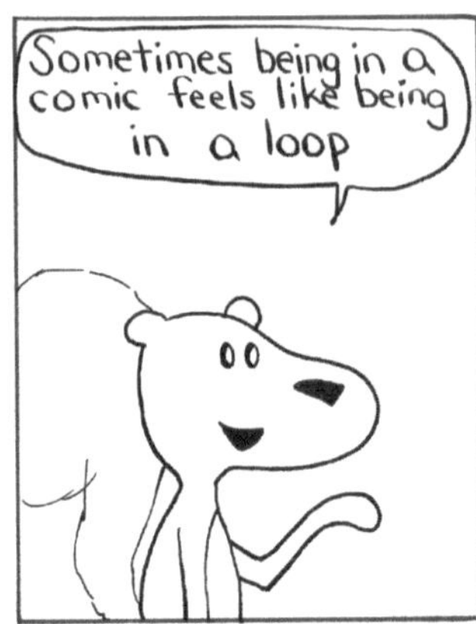
Sometimes being in a comic feels like being in a loop
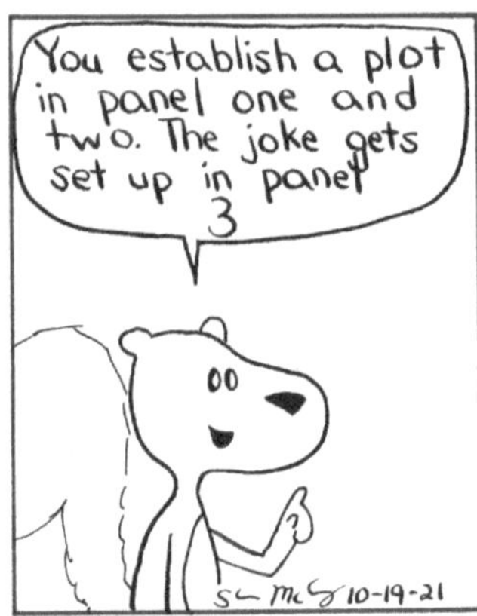
You establish a plot in panel one and two. The joke gets set up in panel 3
SL McG 10-19-21
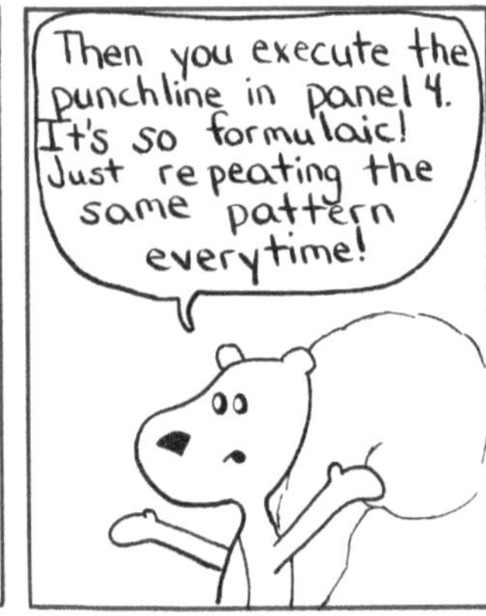
Then you execute the punchline in panel 4. It's so formulaic! Just repeating the same pattern everytime!
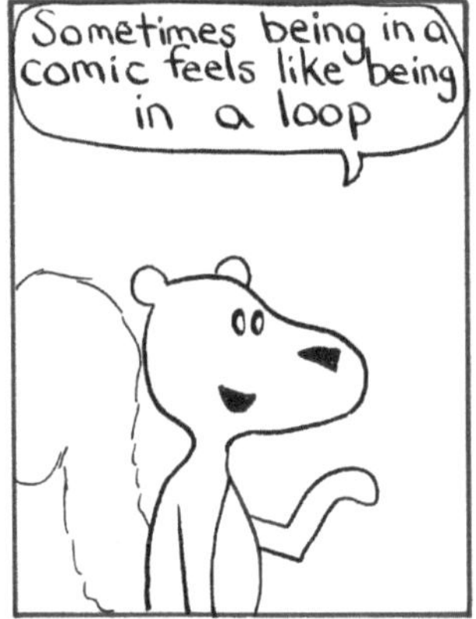
Sometimes being in a comic feels like being in a loop

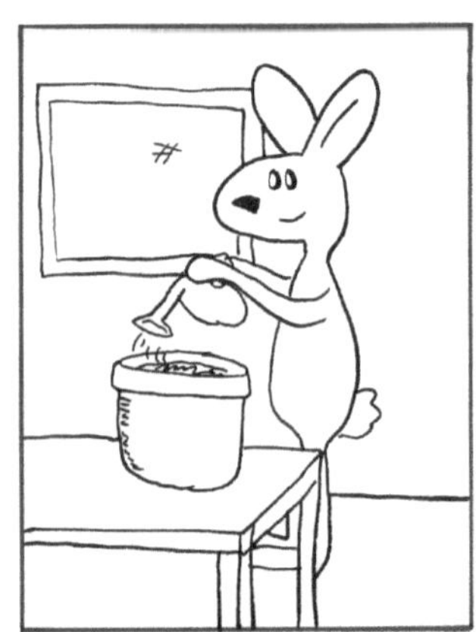
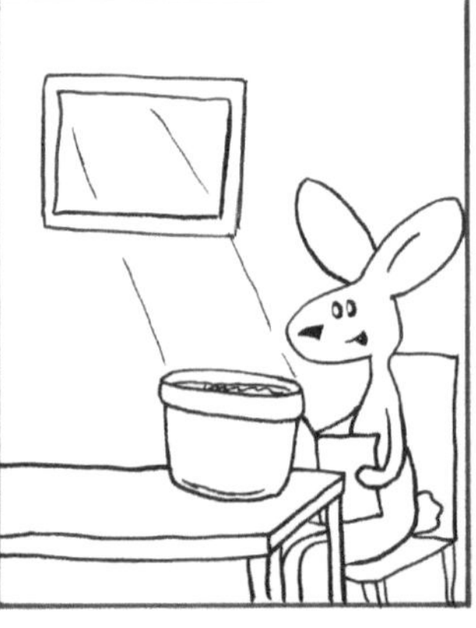
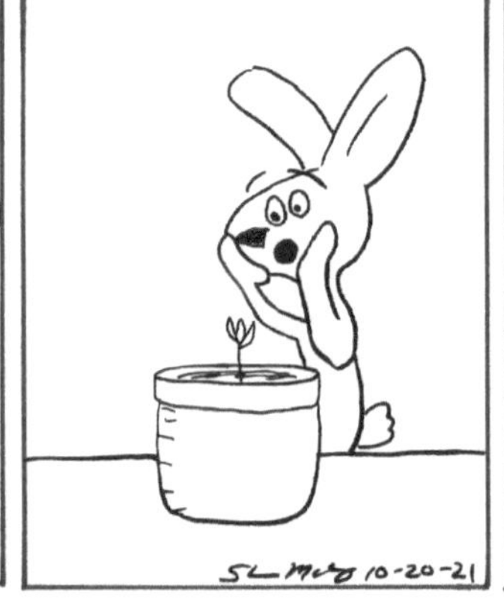
SL McG 10-20-21
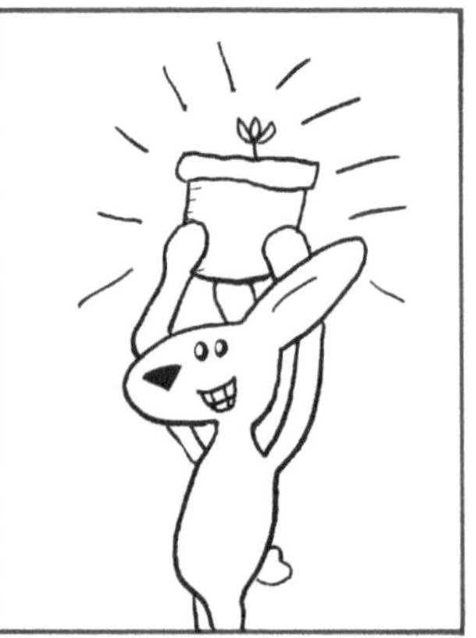

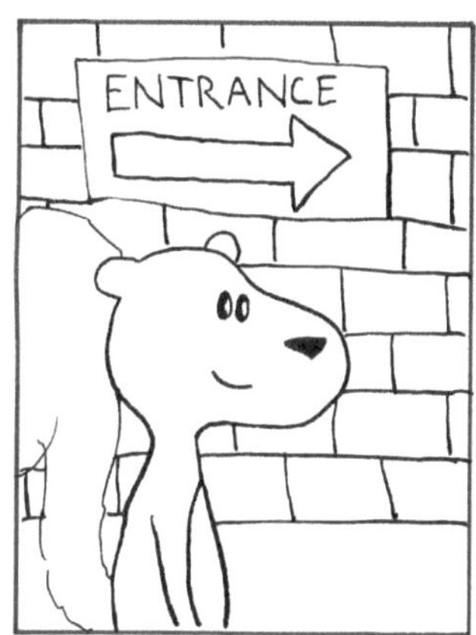
ENTRANCE

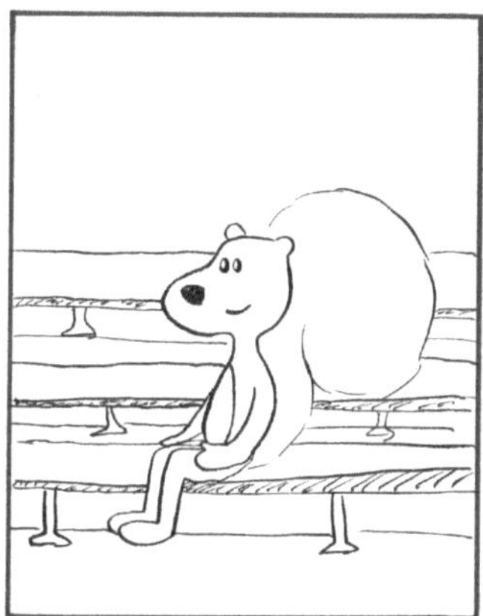

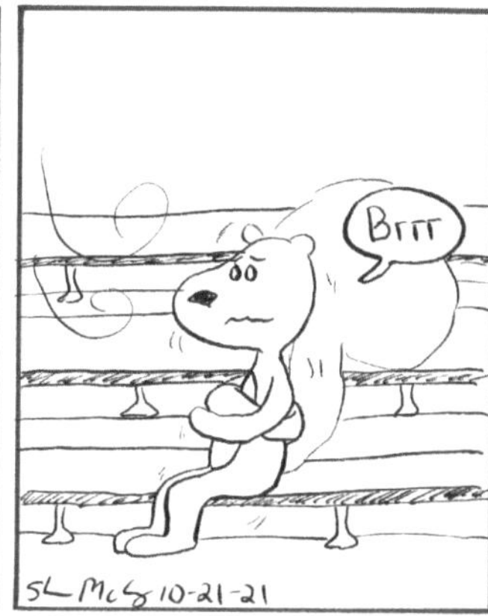
Brrr
10-21-21

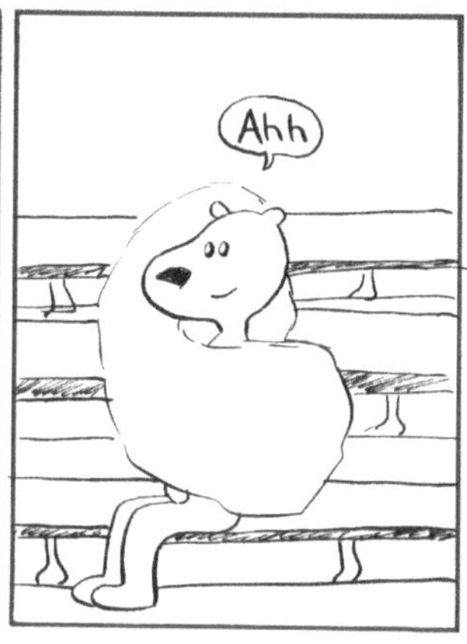
Ahh

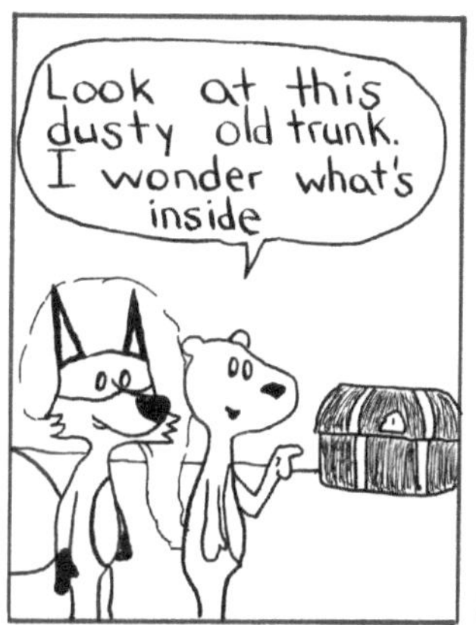
Look at this dusty old trunk. I wonder what's inside

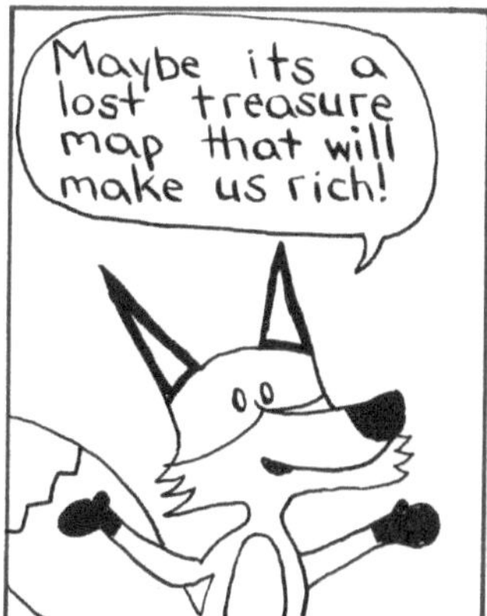
Maybe its a lost treasure map that will make us rich!

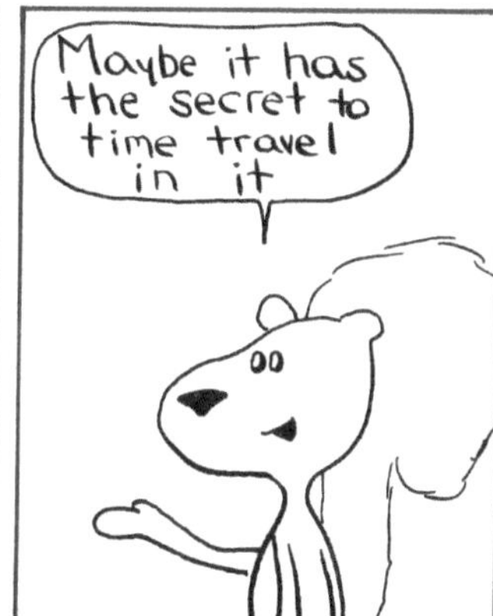
Maybe it has the secret to time travel in it

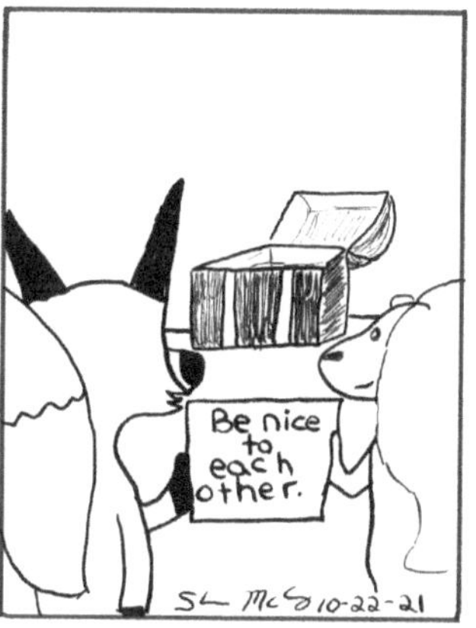
Be nice to each other.
10-22-21

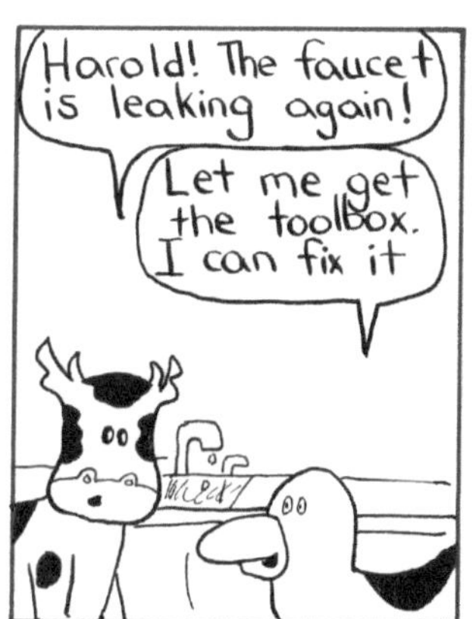
Harold! The faucet is leaking again!
Let me get the toolbox. I can fix it

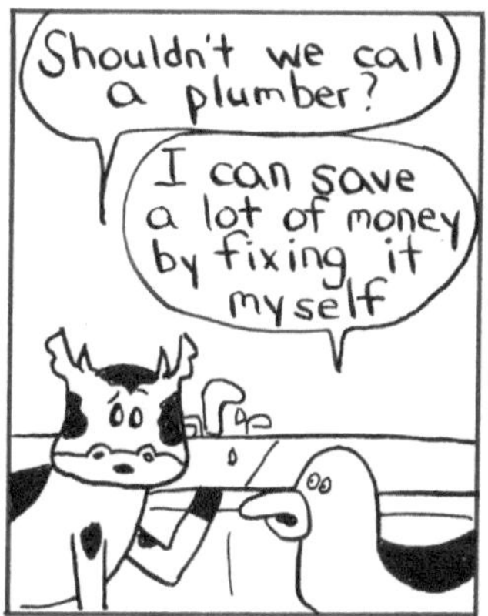
Shouldn't we call a plumber?
I can save a lot of money by fixing it myself

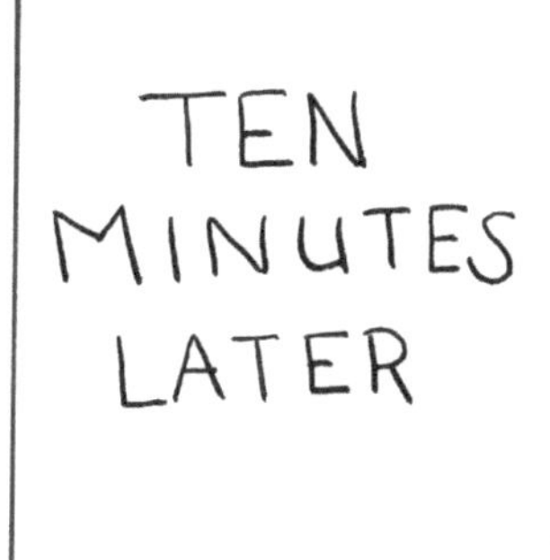
TEN MINUTES LATER

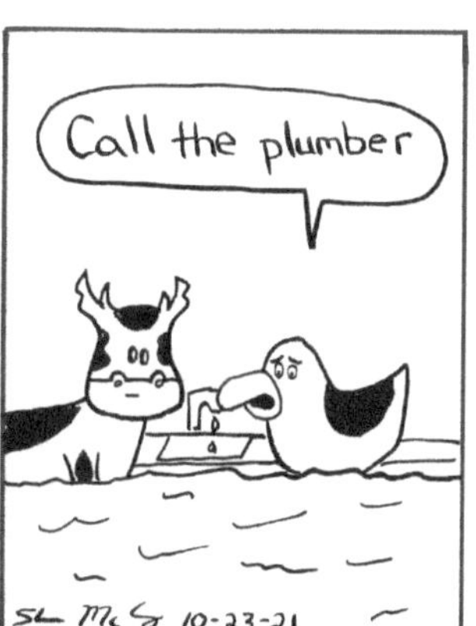
Call the plumber
10-23-21

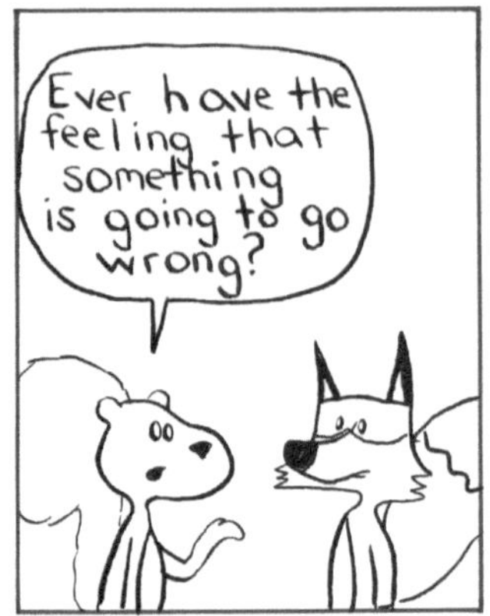

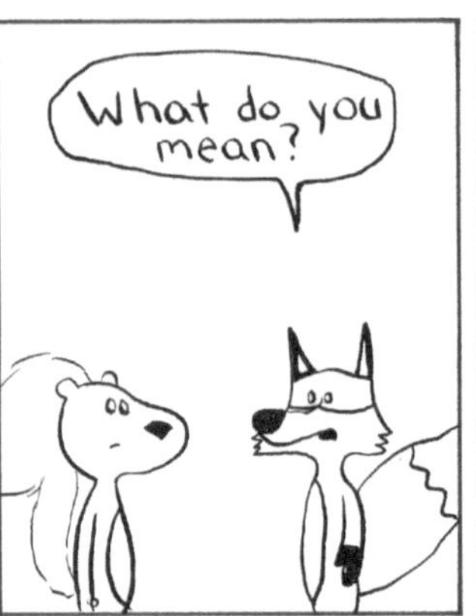

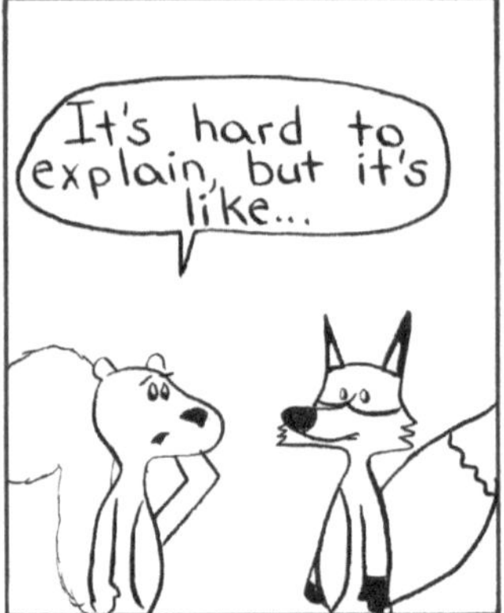

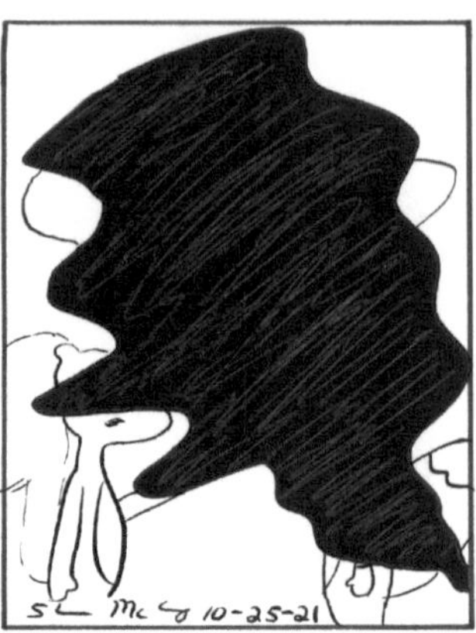

Welcome to today's interactive edition of Squiggles by Sharon.

Connect the dots to draw your favorite characters

SL Mc 10-26-21

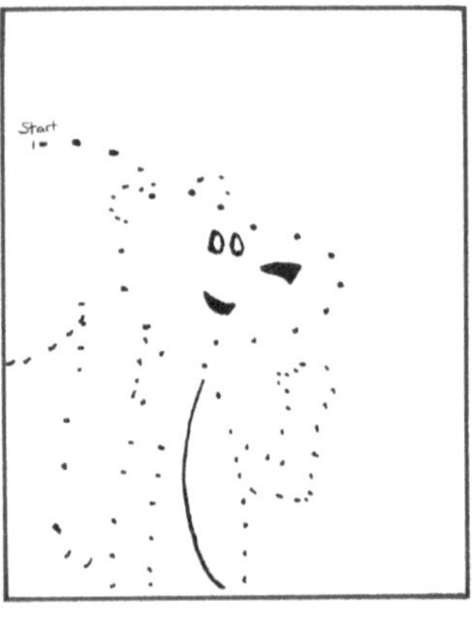

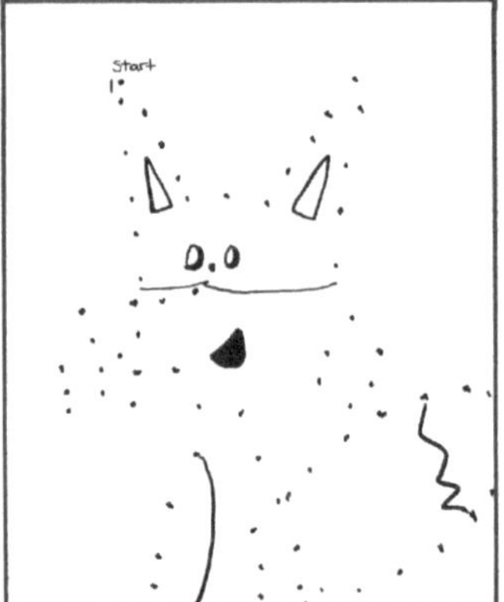

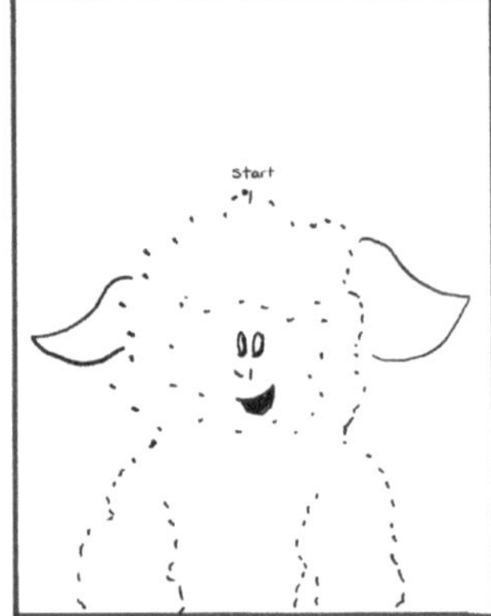

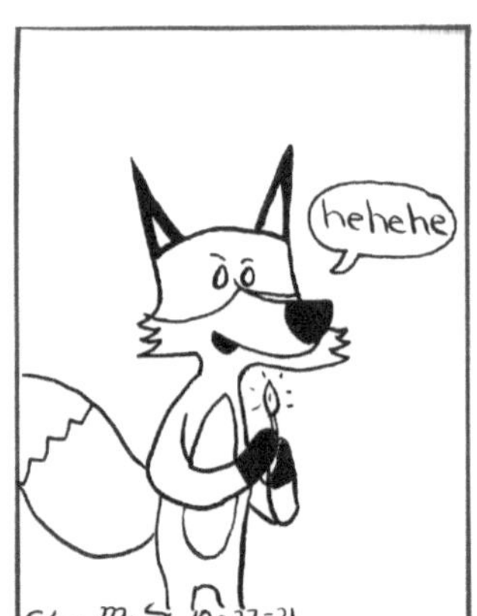

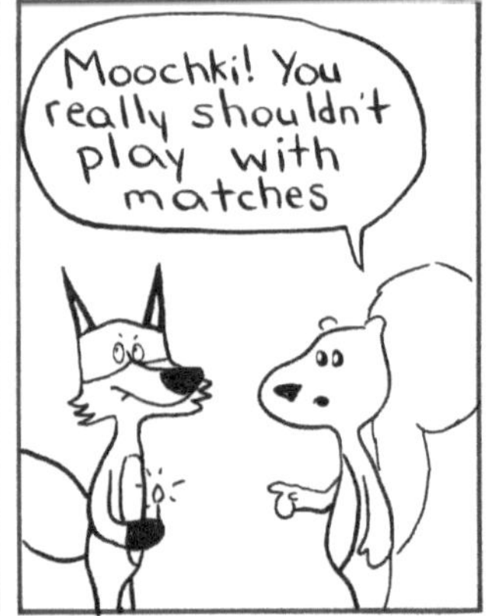

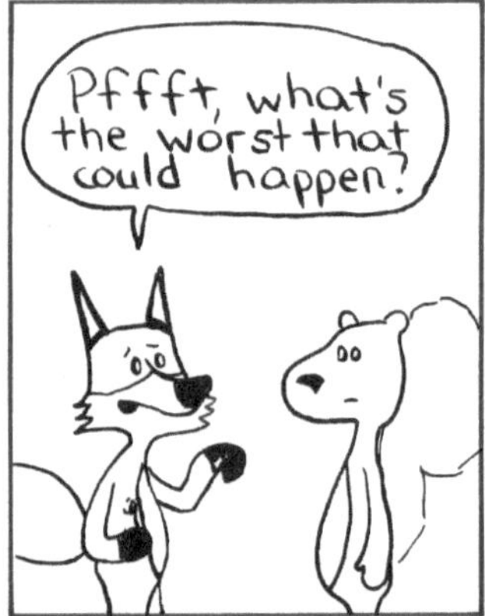

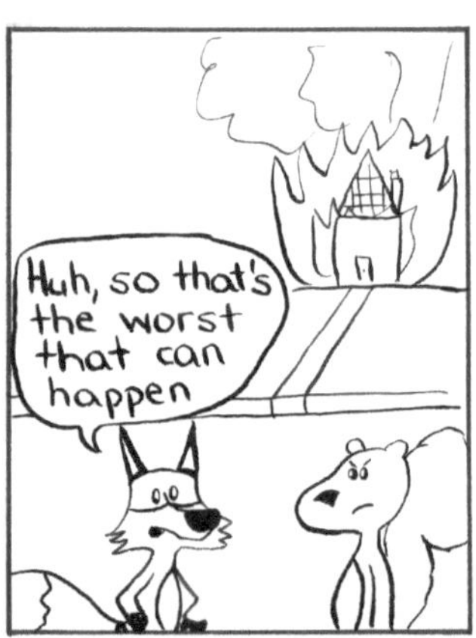

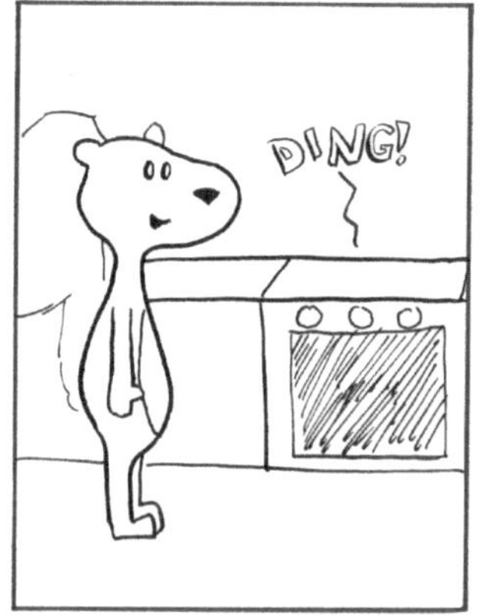
DING!

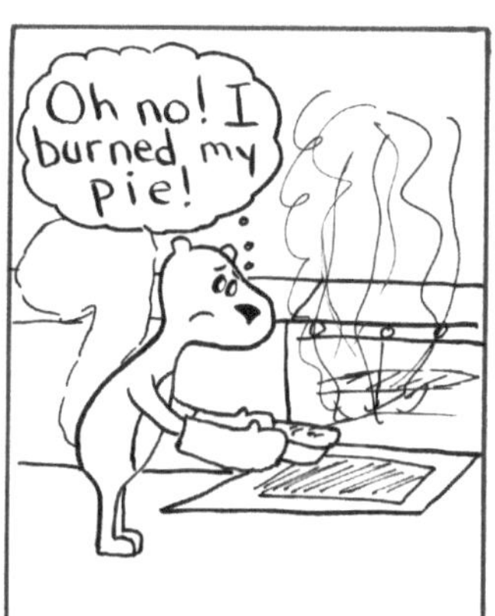
Oh no! I burned my pie!

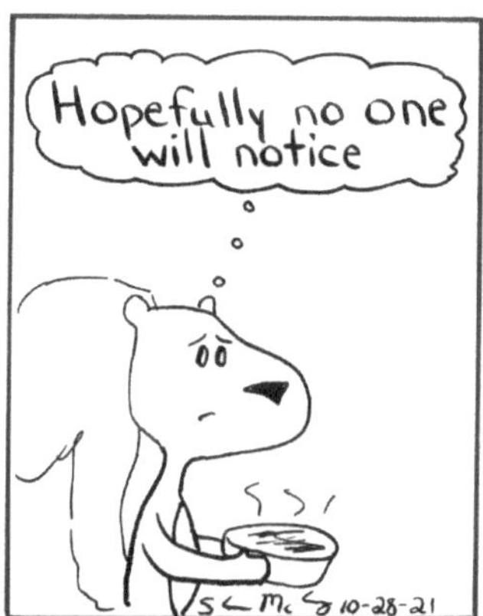
Hopefully no one will notice
10-28-21

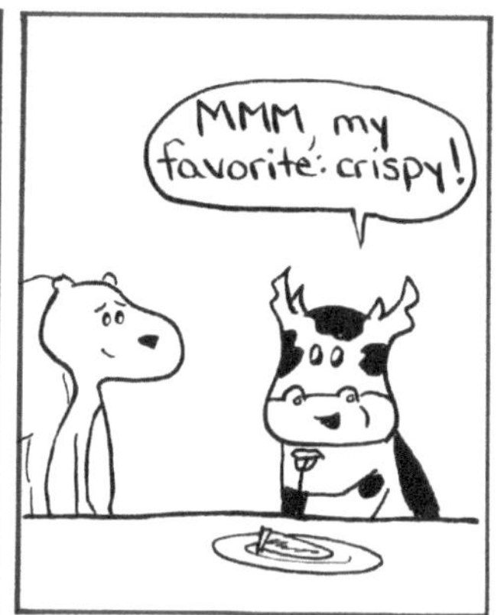
MMM, my favorite: crispy!

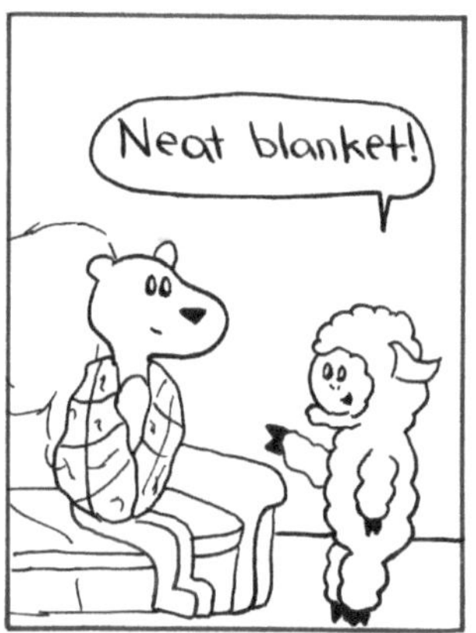
Neat blanket!

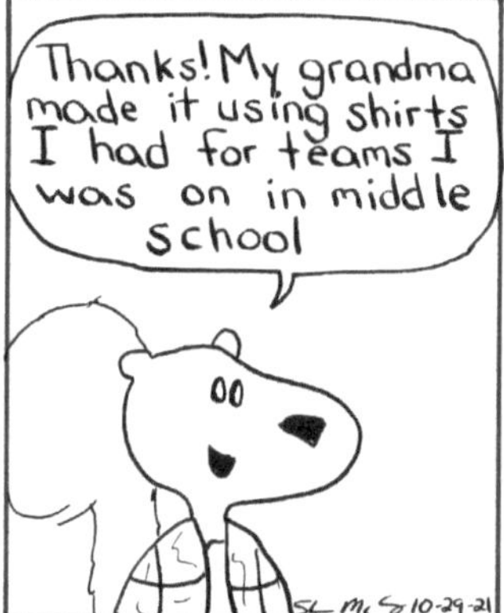
Thanks! My grandma made it using shirts I had for teams I was on in middle school
10-29-21

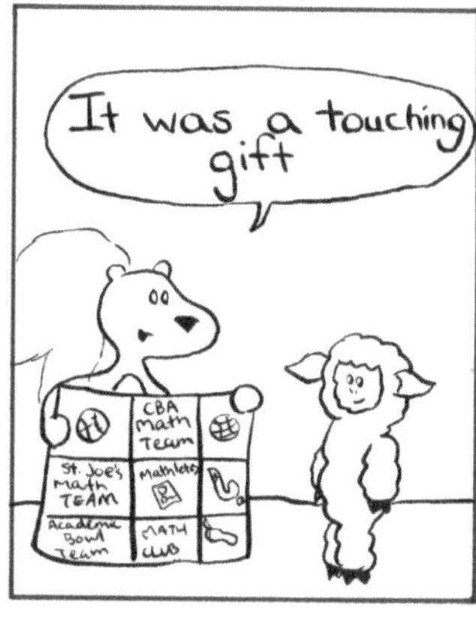
It was a touching gift
CBA Math Team
St. Joe's Math TEAM
Mathletes
Academic Bowl Team
MATH Club

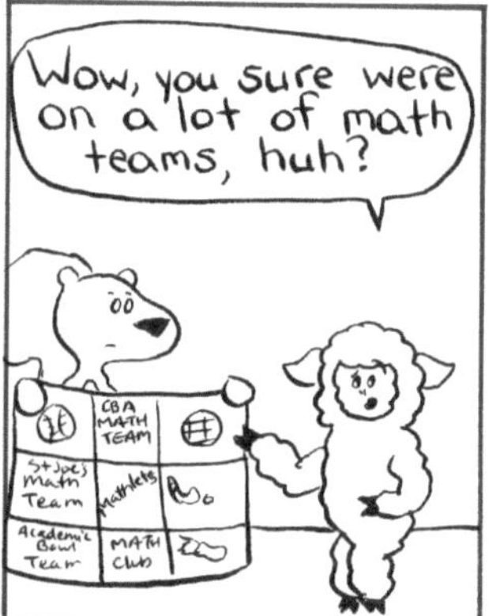
Wow, you sure were on a lot of math teams, huh?
CBA MATH TEAM
St. Joe's Math Team
Mathletes
Academic Bowl Team
MATH Club

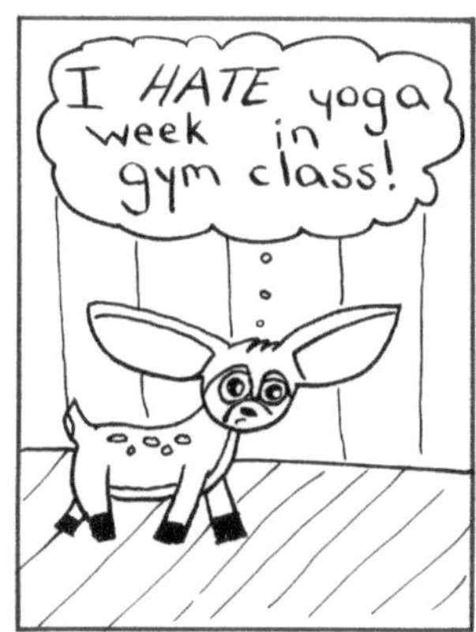
I *HATE* yoga week in gym class!

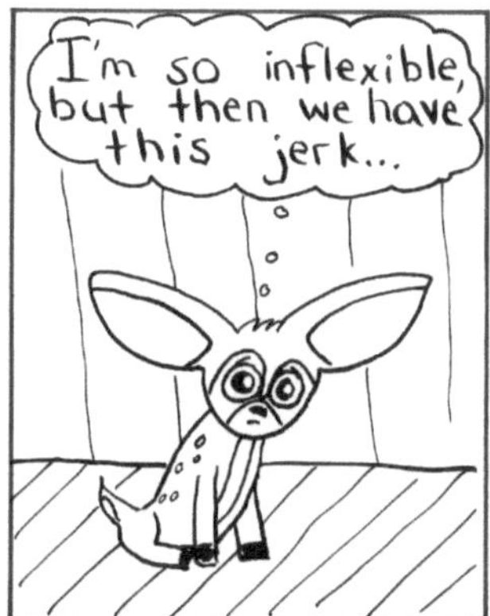
I'm so inflexible, but then we have this jerk...

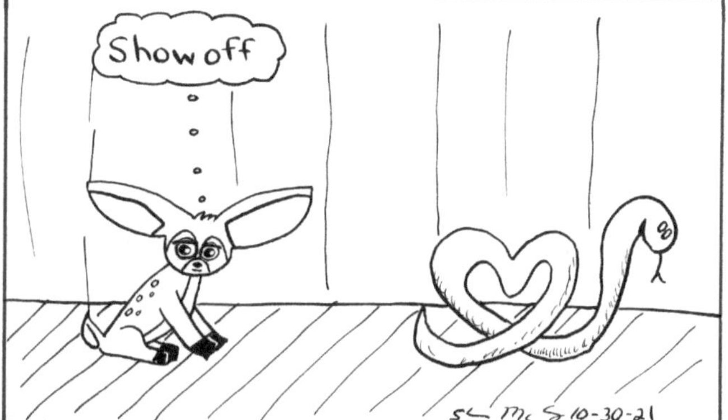
Showoff
10-30-21

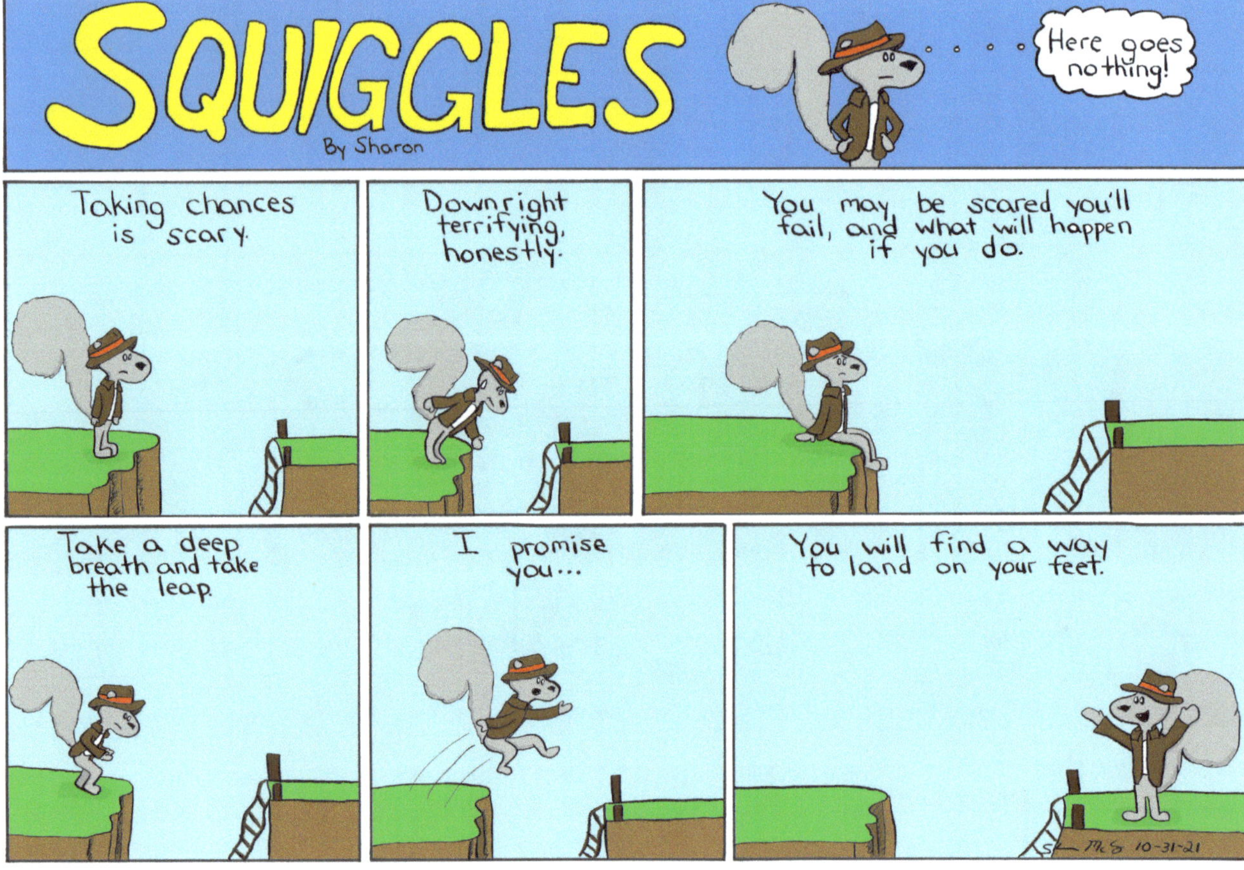
SQUIGGLES
By Sharon
Here goes nothing!
Taking chances is scary.
Downright terrifying, honestly.
You may be scared you'll fail, and what will happen if you do.
Take a deep breath and take the leap.
I promise you...
You will find a way to land on your feet!
SK McS 10-31-21

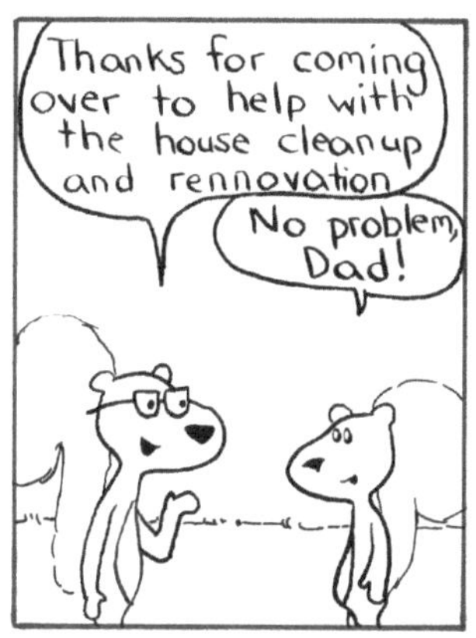
Thanks for coming over to help with the house cleanup and rennovation
No problem, Dad!

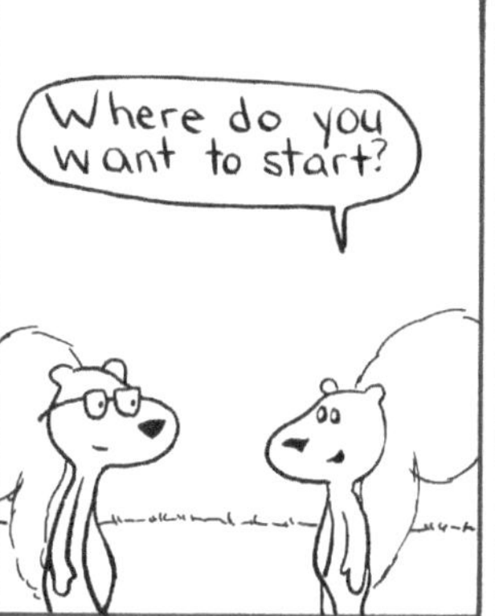
Where do you want to start?

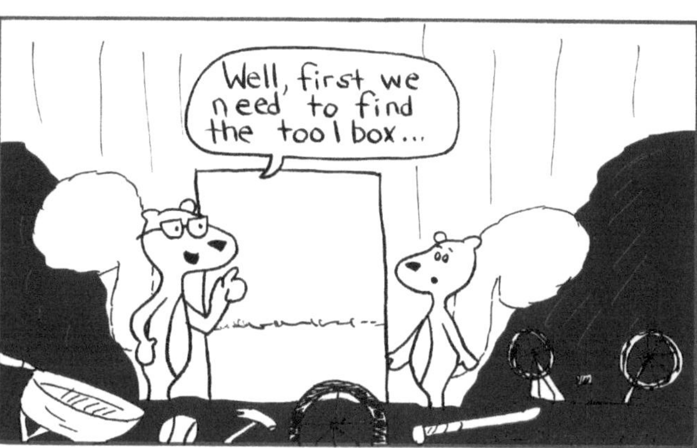
Well, first we need to find the tool box...

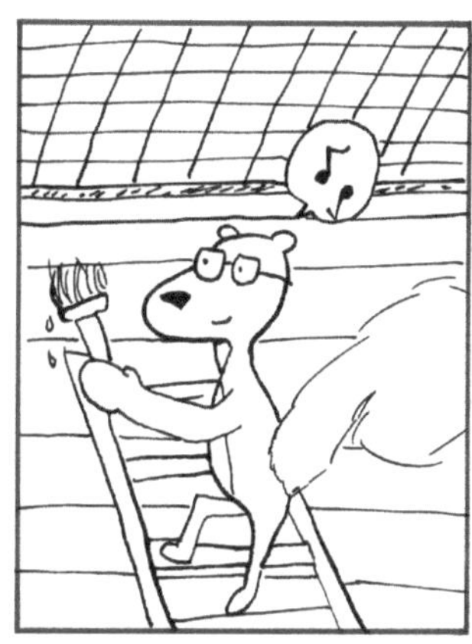

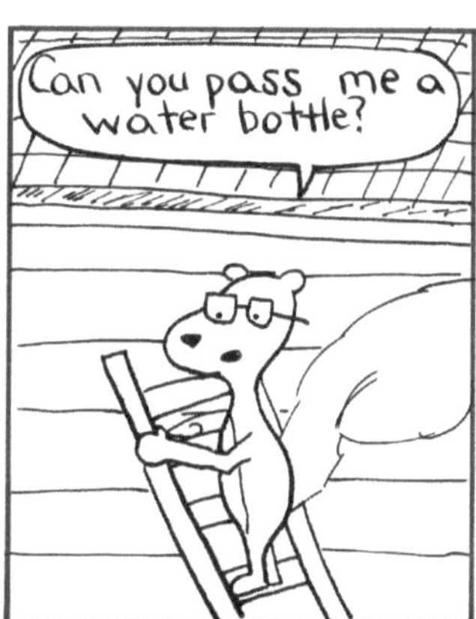
Can you pass me a water bottle?

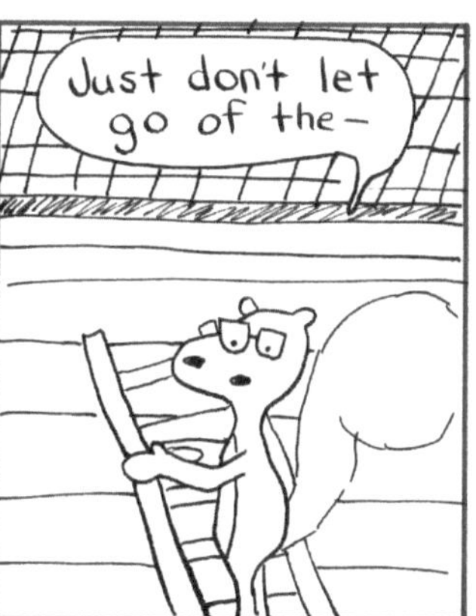
Just don't let go of the-

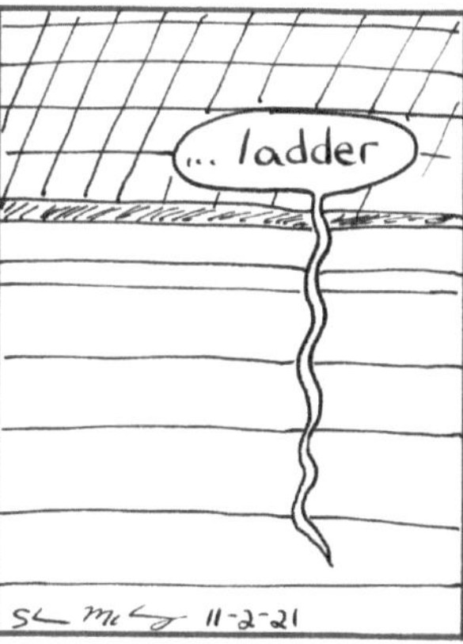
... ladder
SL McG 11-2-21

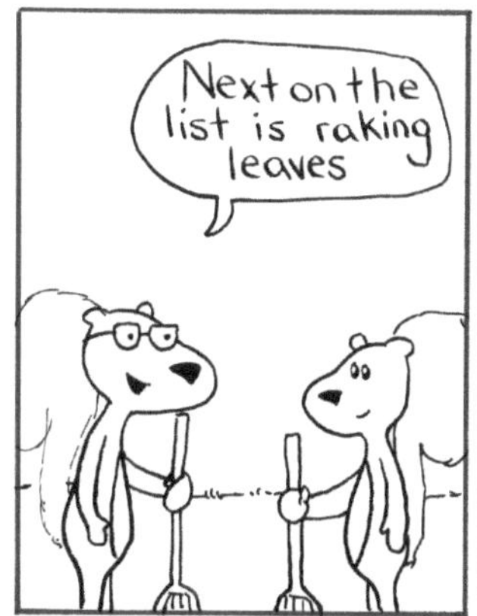
Next on the list is raking leaves

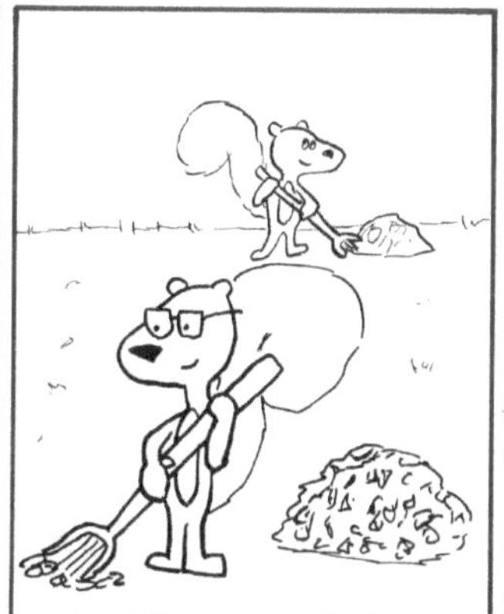

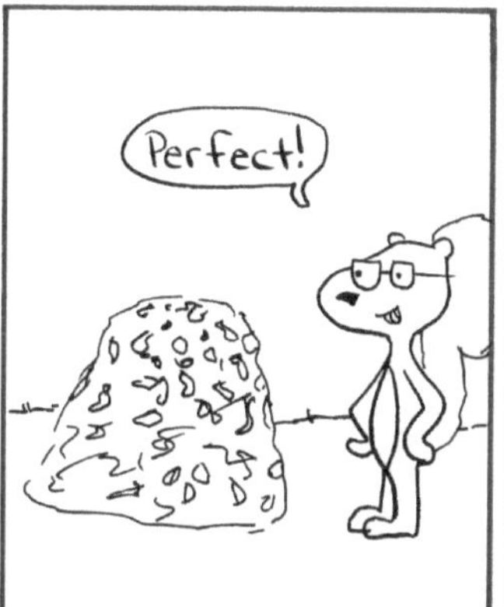
Perfect!

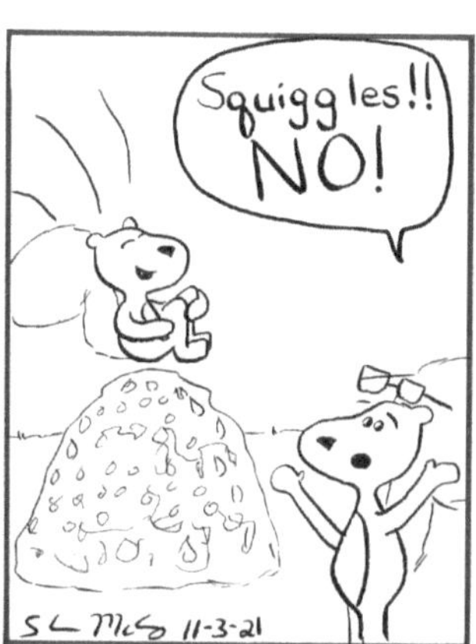
Squiggles!! NO!
SL McG 11-3-21

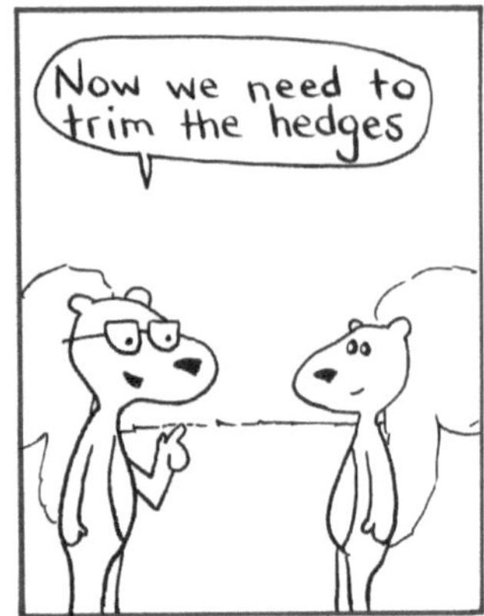
Now we need to trim the hedges
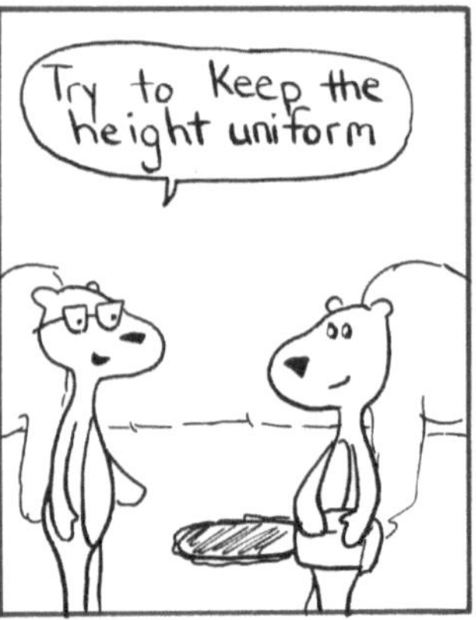
Try to Keep the height uniform
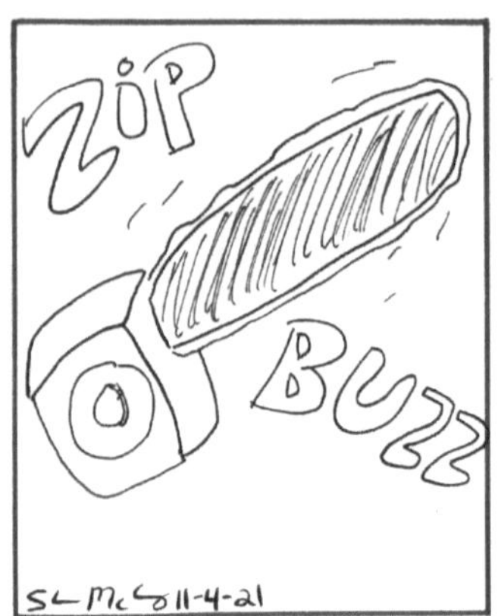
ZIP
BUZZ
SL McG 11-4-21
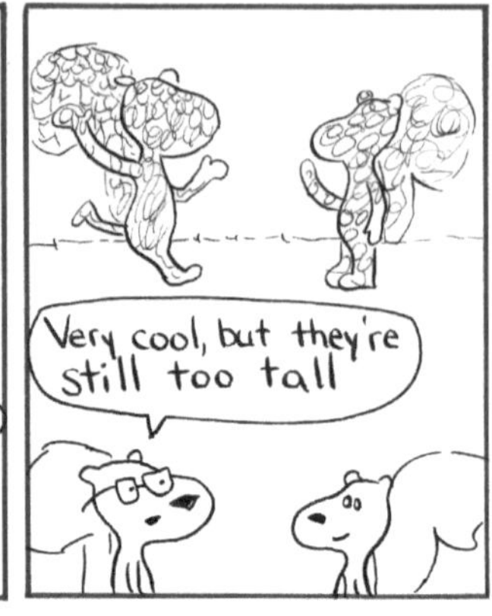
Very cool, but they're still too tall
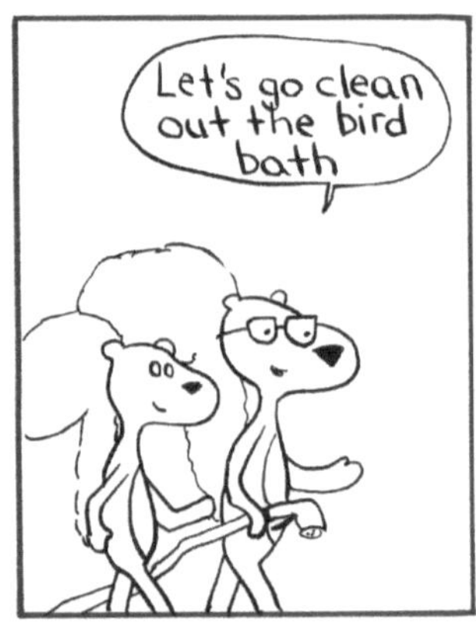
Let's go clean out the bird bath
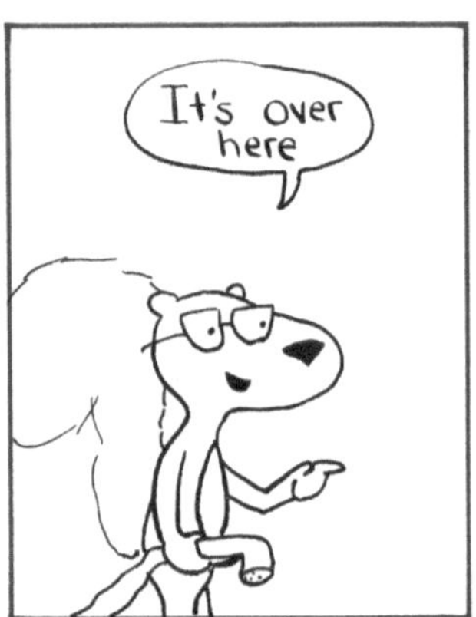
It's over here
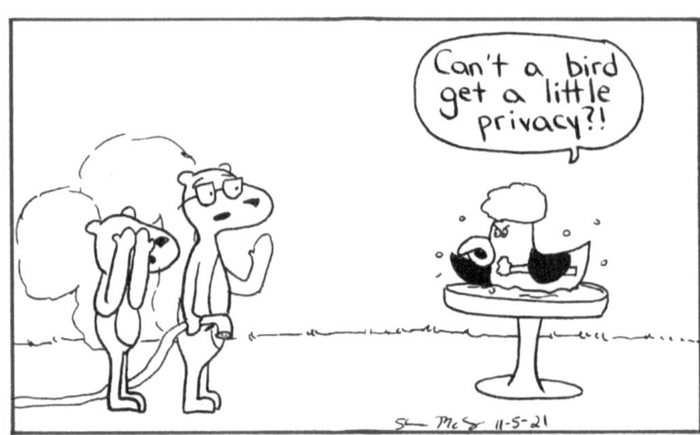
Can't a bird get a little privacy?!
SL McG 11-5-21
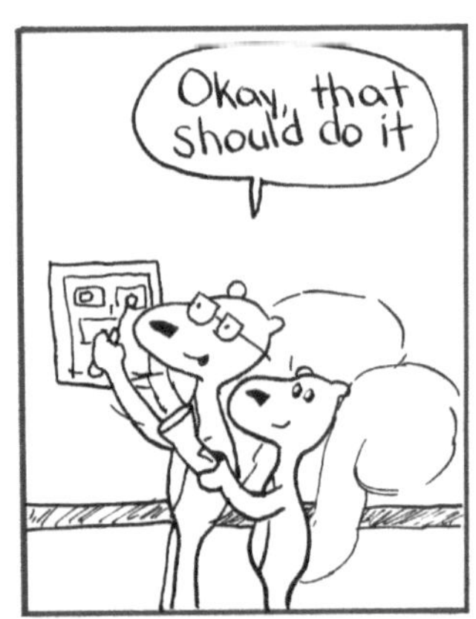
Okay, that should do it
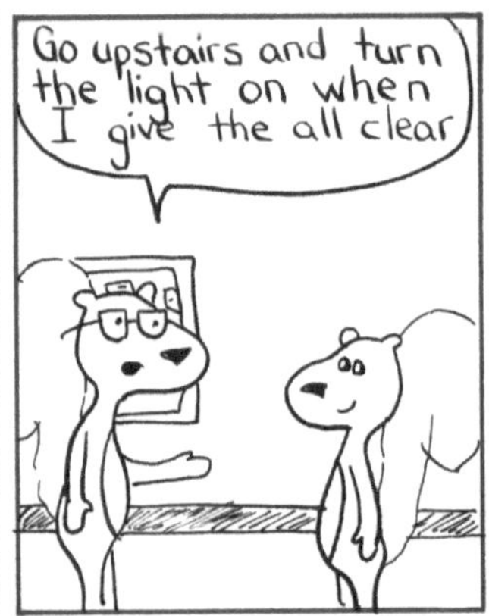
Go upstairs and turn the light on when I give the all clear
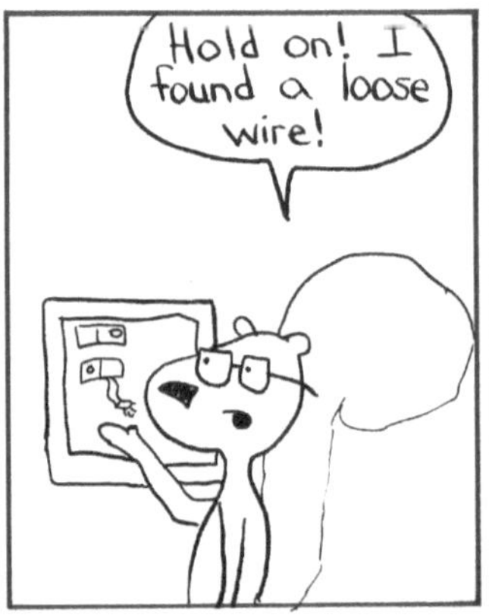
Hold on! I found a loose wire!
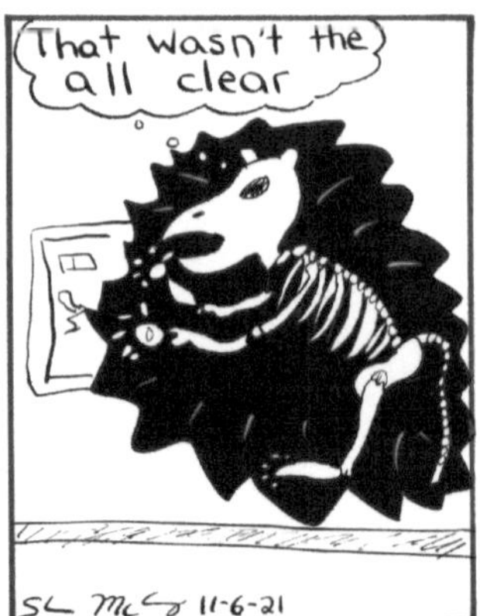
That wasn't the all clear
SL McG 11-6-21

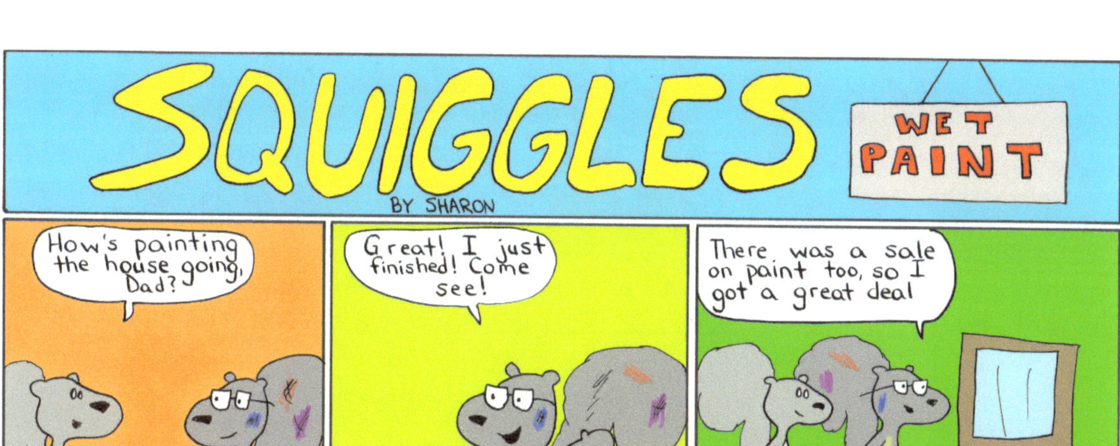

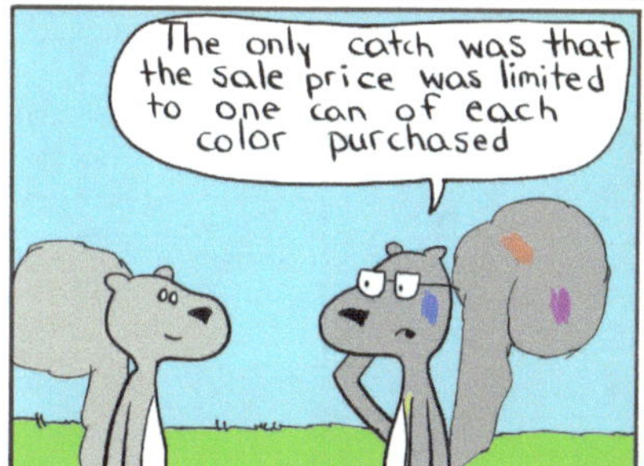

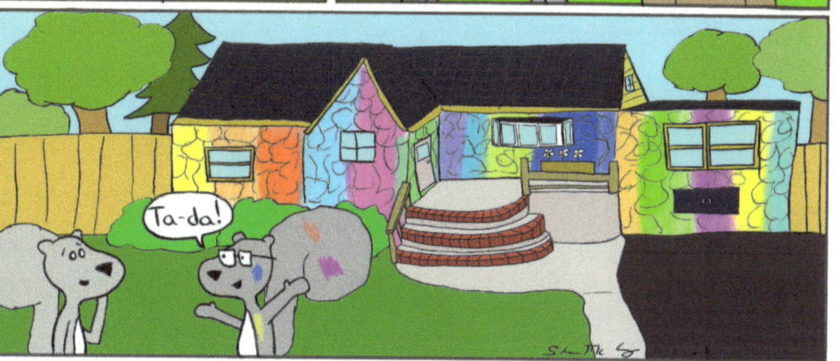

The only catch was that the sale price was limited to one can of each color purchased

Ta-da!

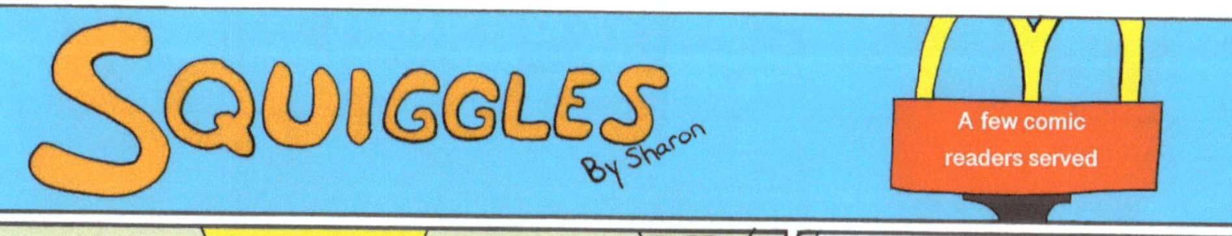

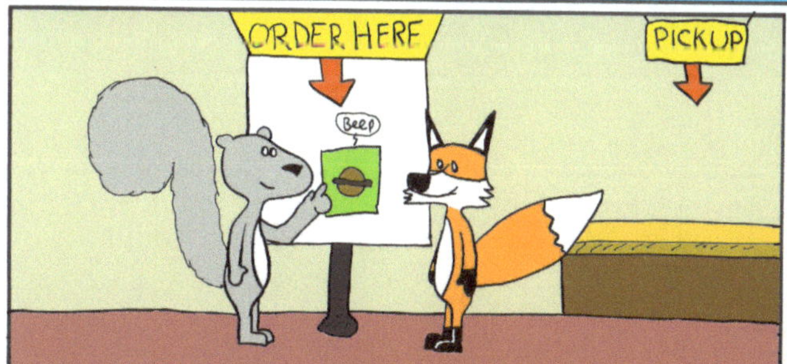

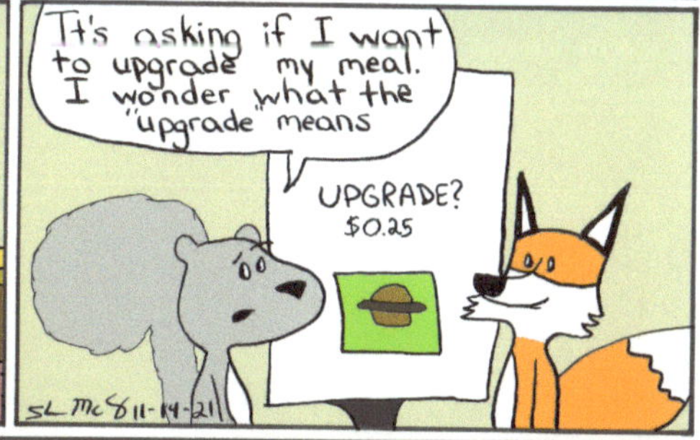

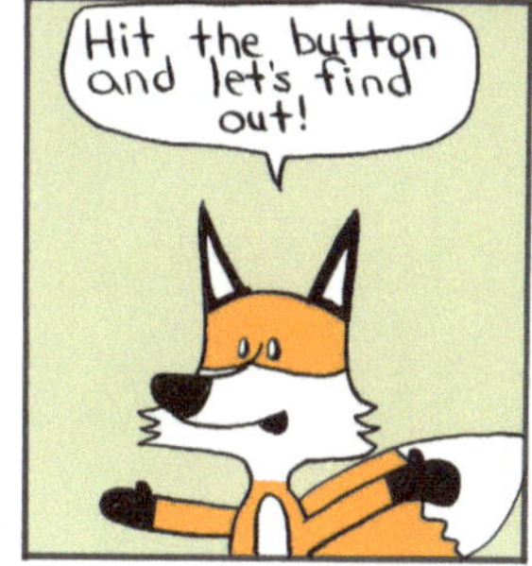

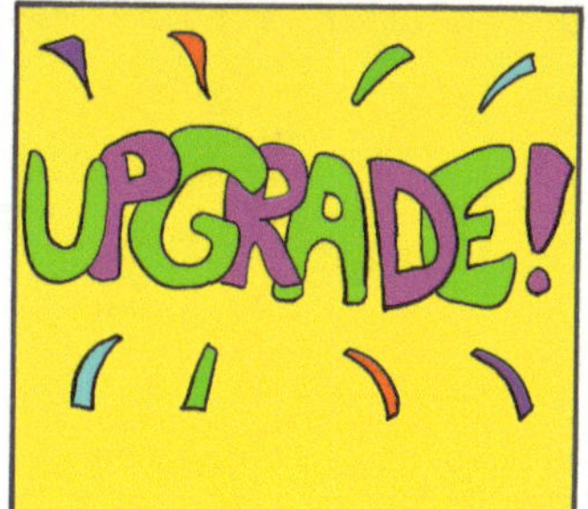

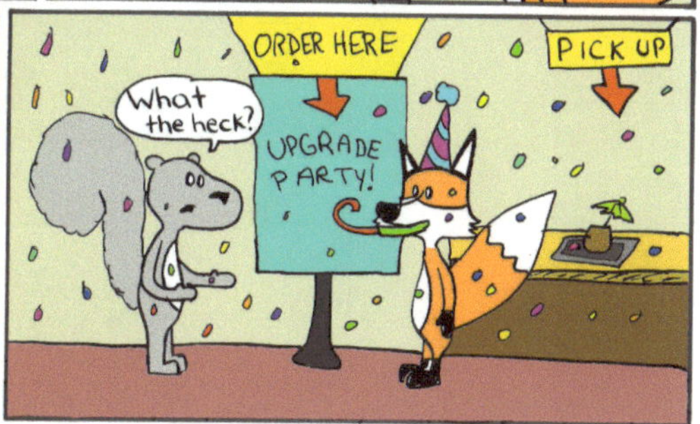

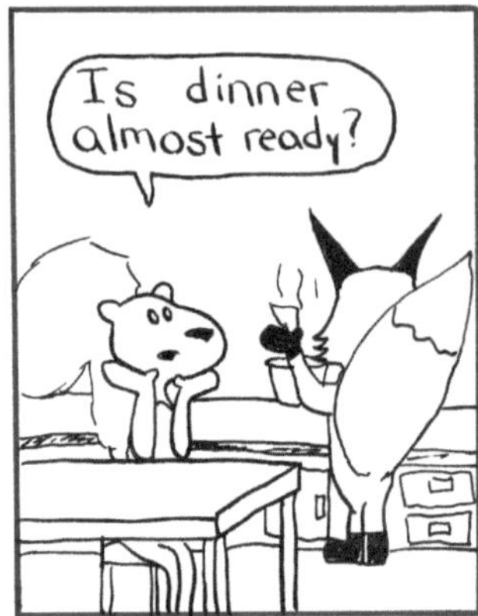

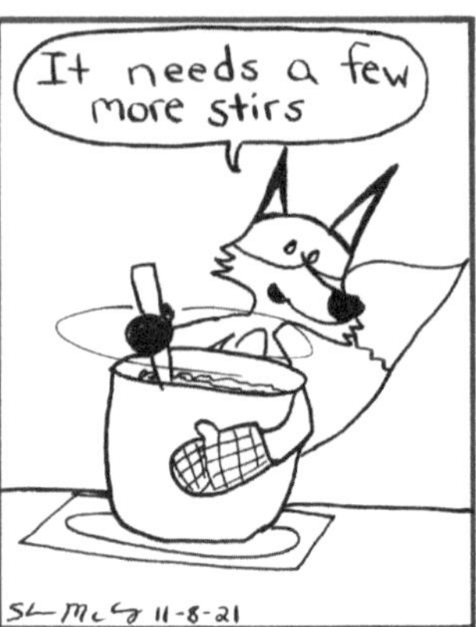

Exactly 7,214 stirs later...

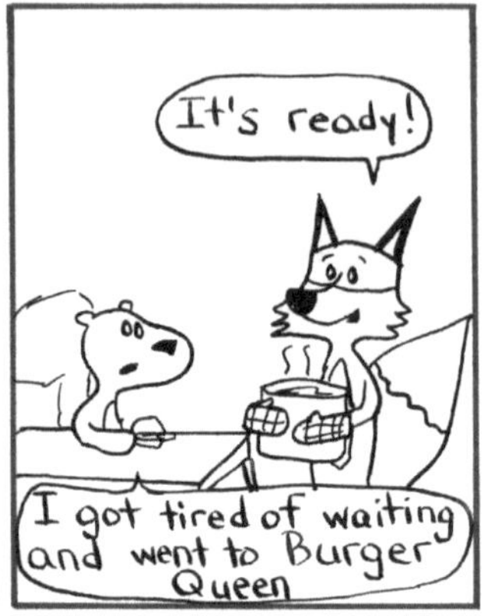

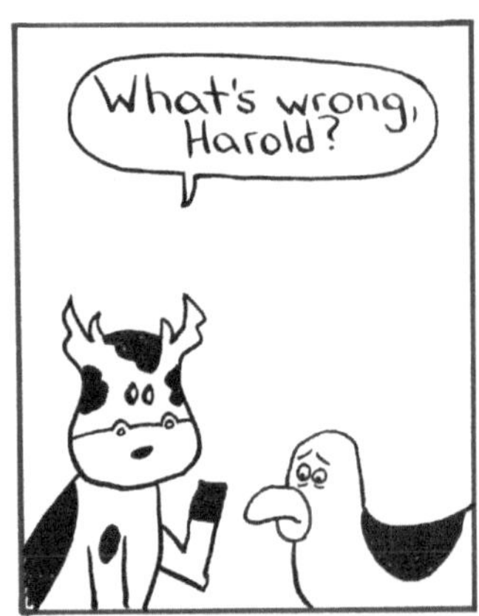

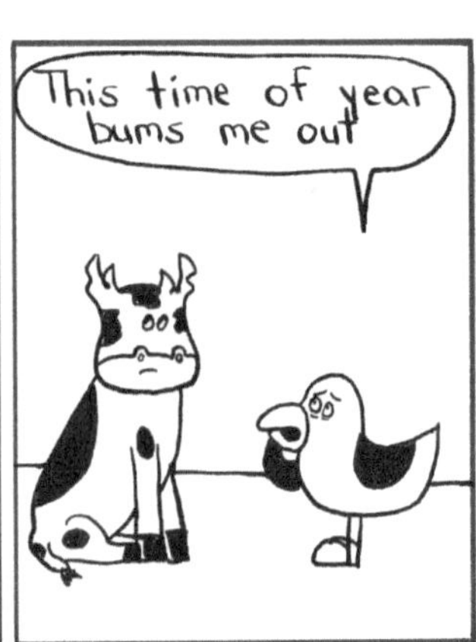

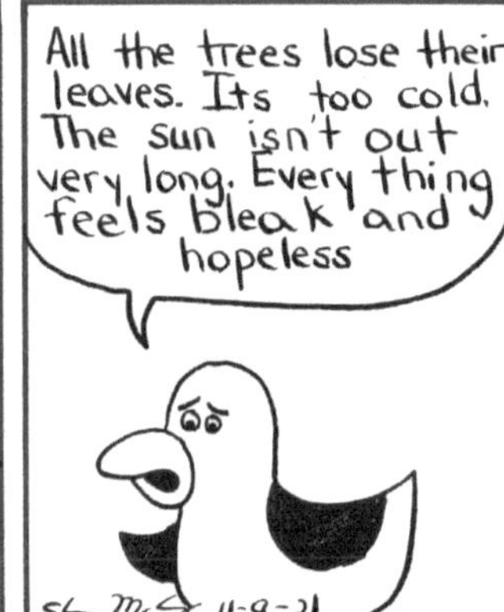

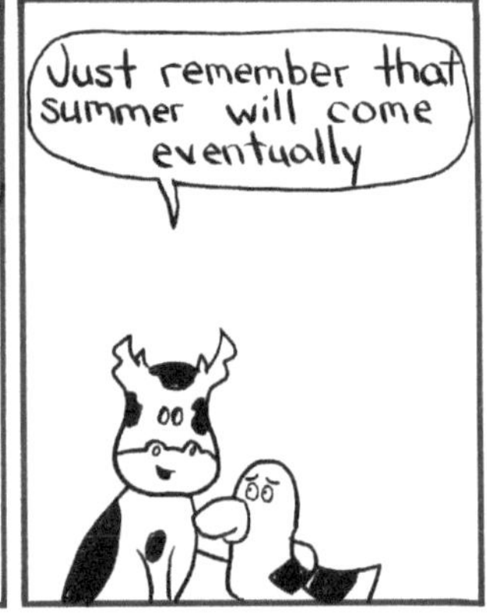

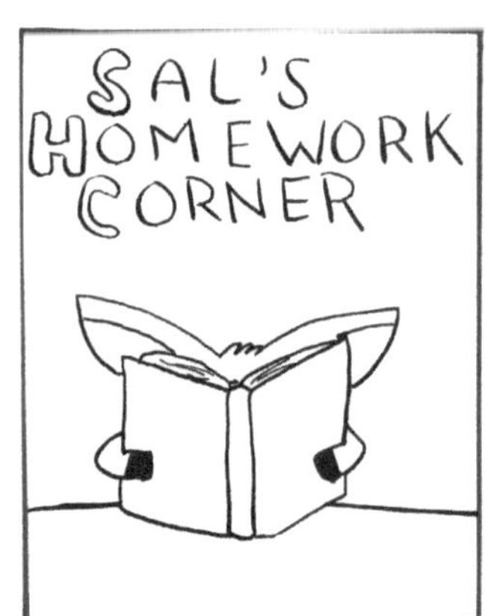

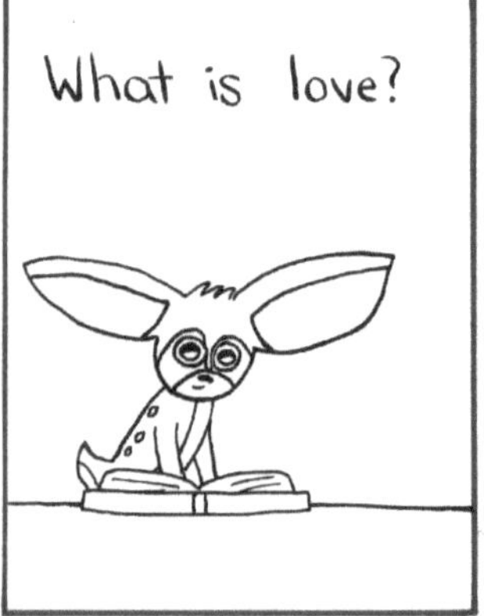

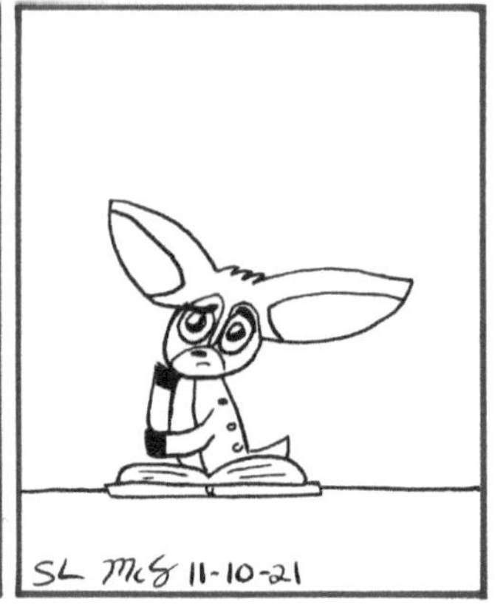

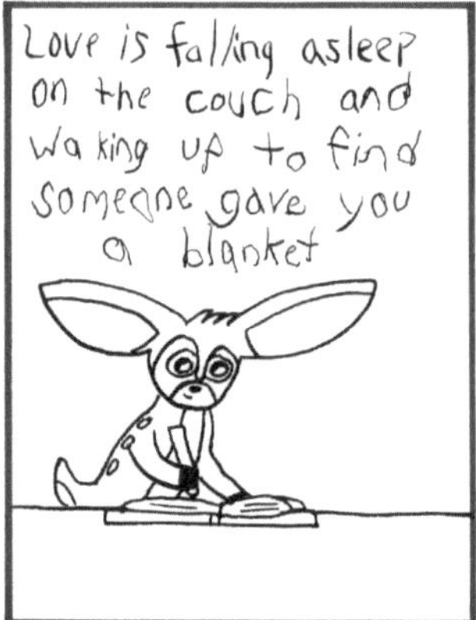

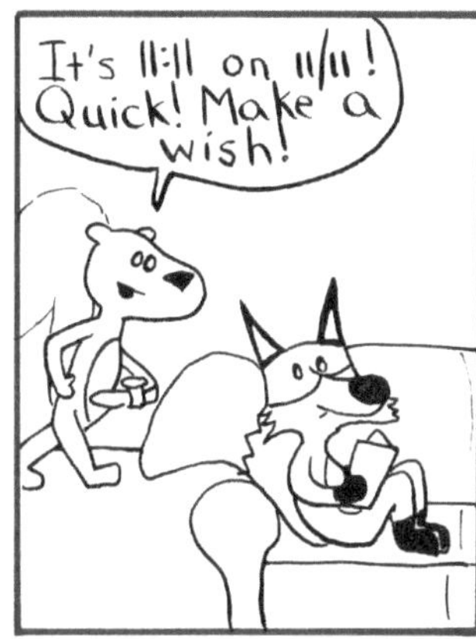
It's 11:11 on 11/11! Quick! Make a wish!

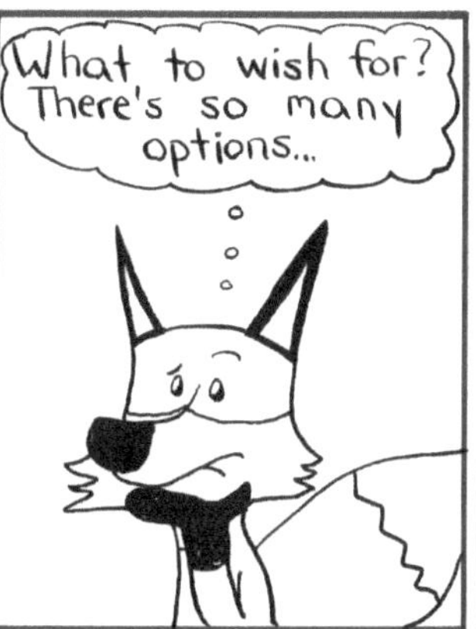
What to wish for? There's so many options...

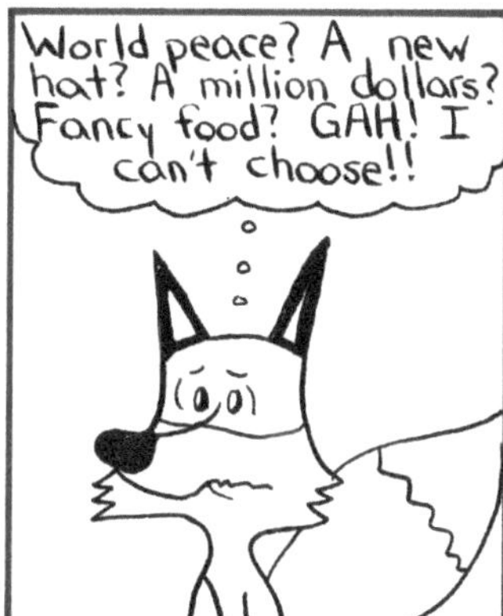
World peace? A new hat? A million dollars? Fancy food? GAH! I can't choose!!

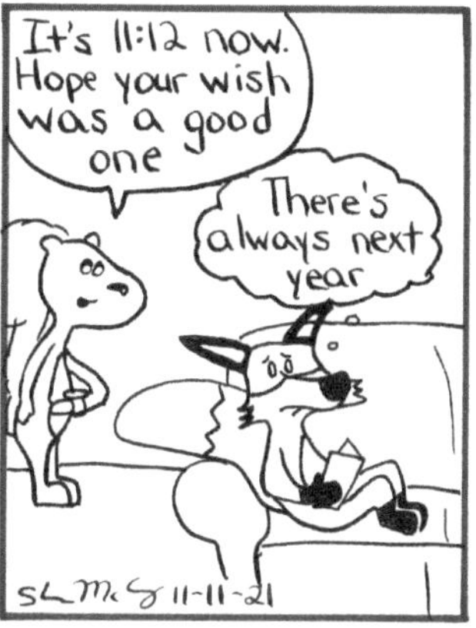
It's 11:12 now. Hope your wish was a good one
There's always next year
SL McG 11-11-21

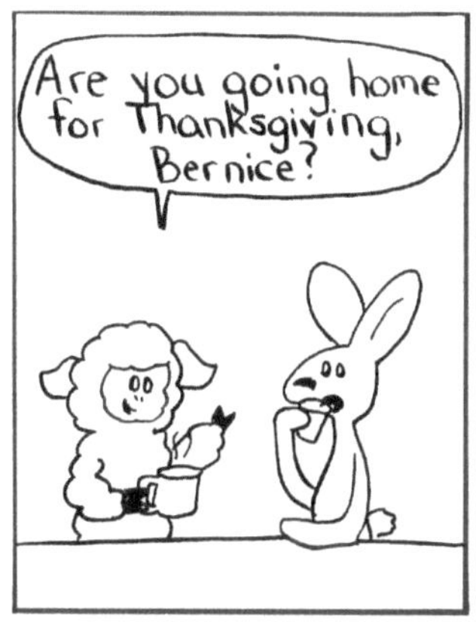
Are you going home for Thanksgiving, Bernice?

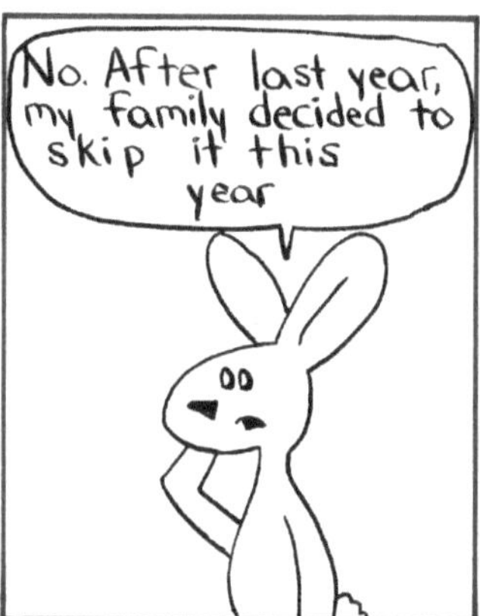
No. After last year, my family decided to skip it this year

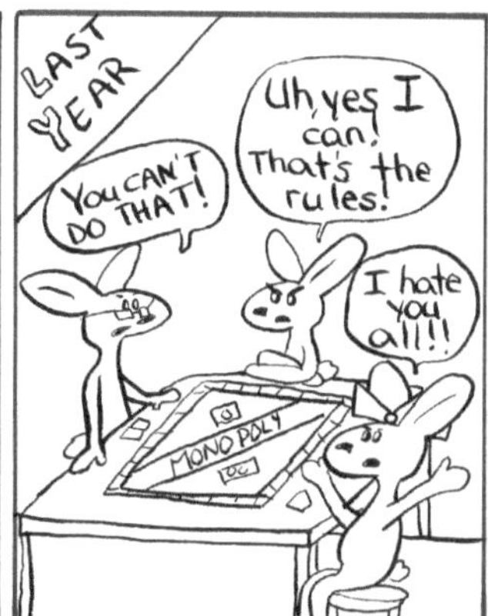
LAST YEAR
You CAN'T DO THAT!
Uh, yes I can! That's the rules!
I hate you all!!
MONOPOLY

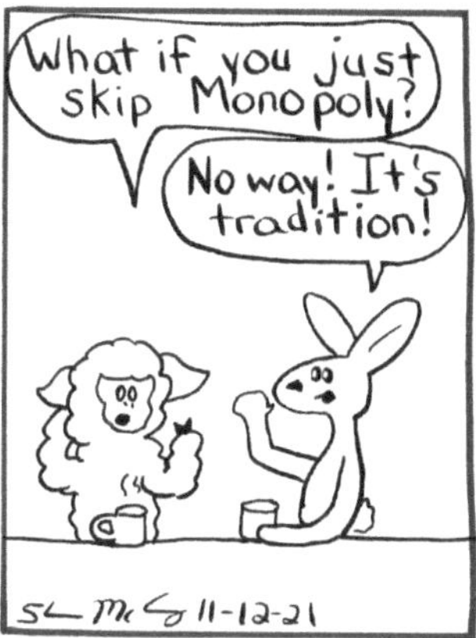
What if you just skip Monopoly?
No way! It's tradition!
SL McG 11-12-21

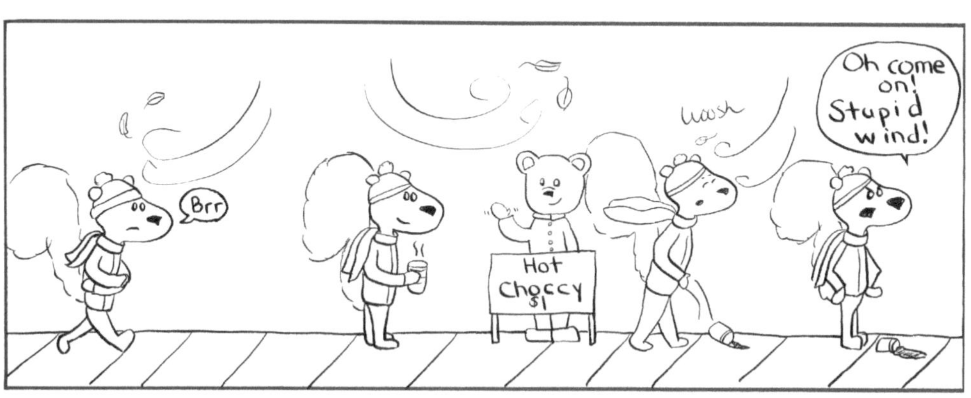
Brr
Hot Choccy $1
woosh
Oh come on! Stupid wind!

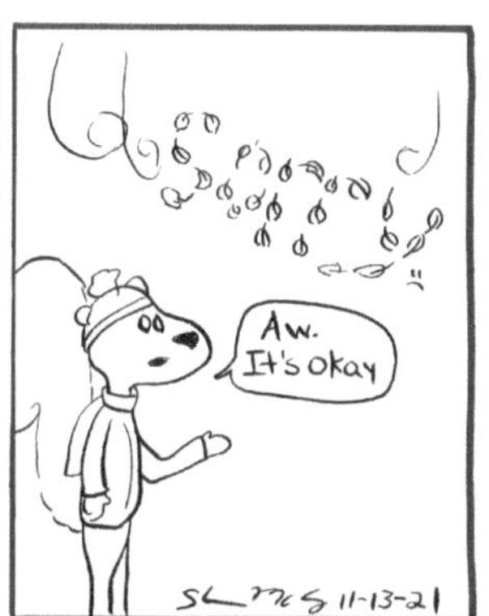
Aw. It's okay
SL McG 11-13-21

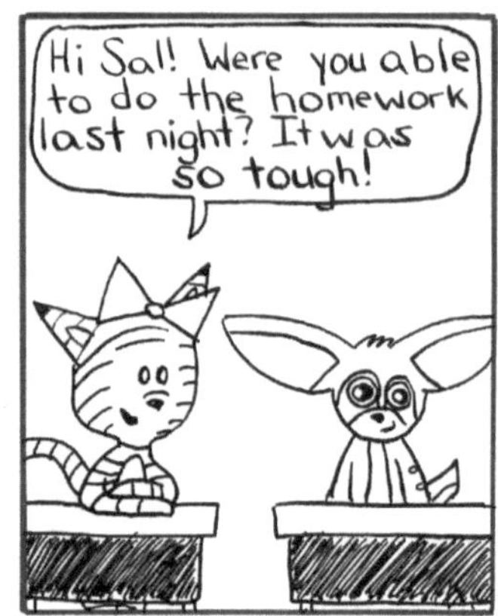
Hi Sal! Were you able to do the homework last night? It was so tough!

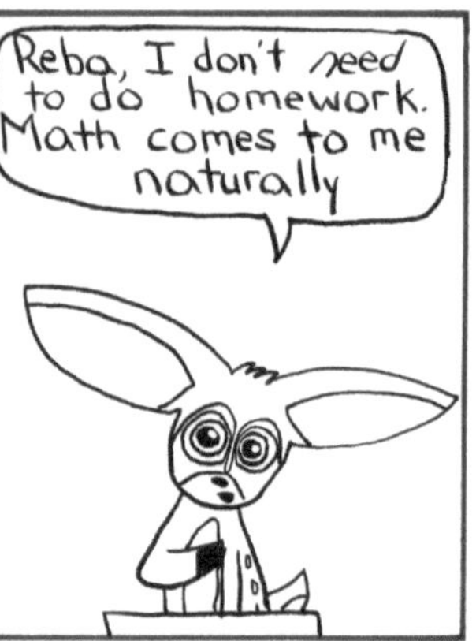
Reba, I don't need to do homework. Math comes to me naturally

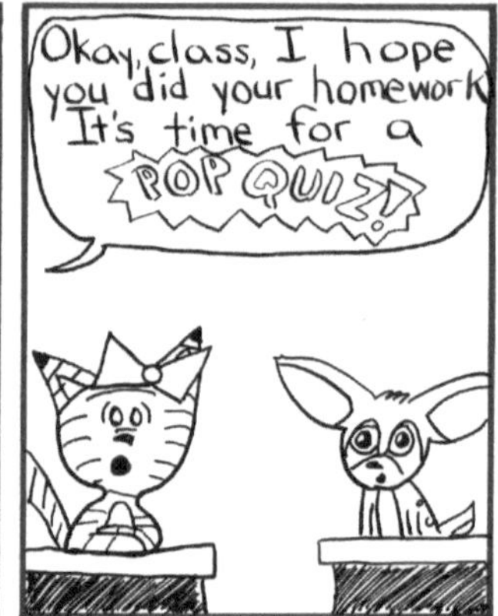
Okay, class, I hope you did your homework. It's time for a
POP QUIZ!

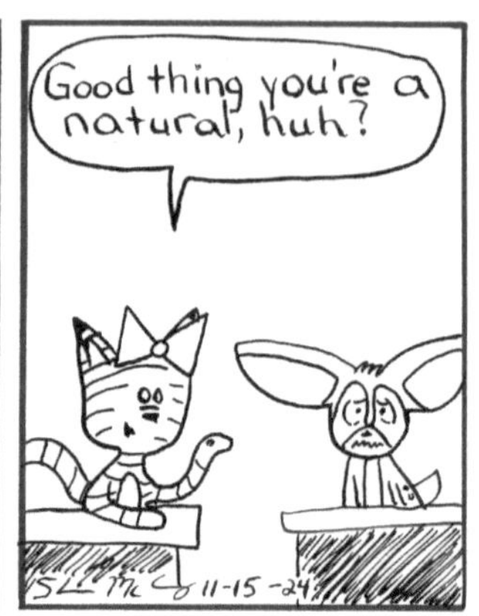
Good thing you're a natural, huh?
SL Mc 11-15-21

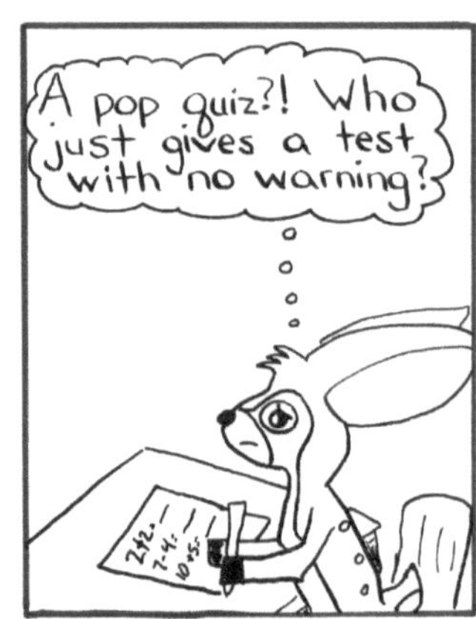
A pop quiz?! Who just gives a test with no warning?

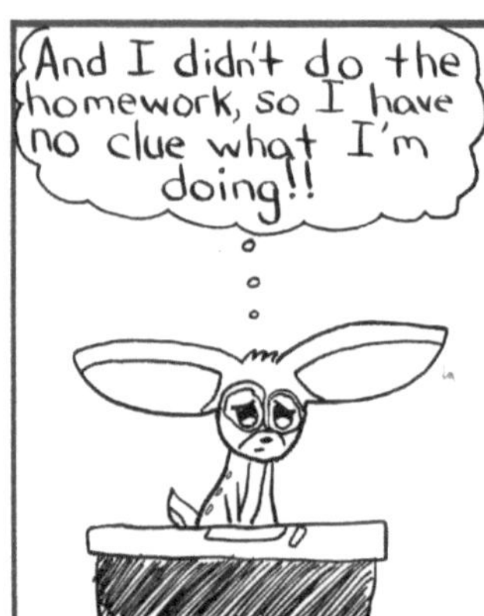
And I didn't do the homework, so I have no clue what I'm doing!!

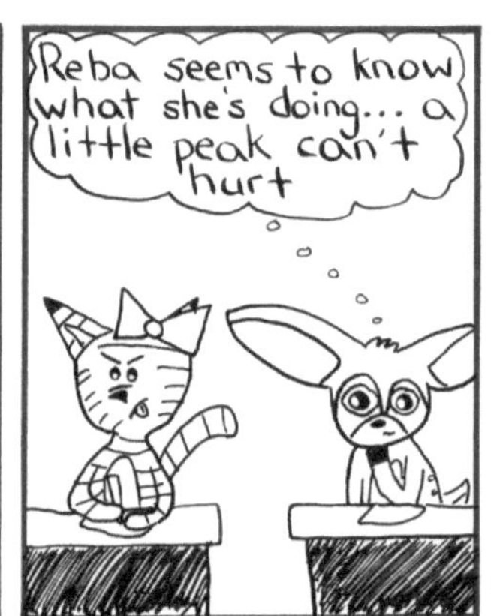
Reba seems to know what she's doing... a little peak can't hurt

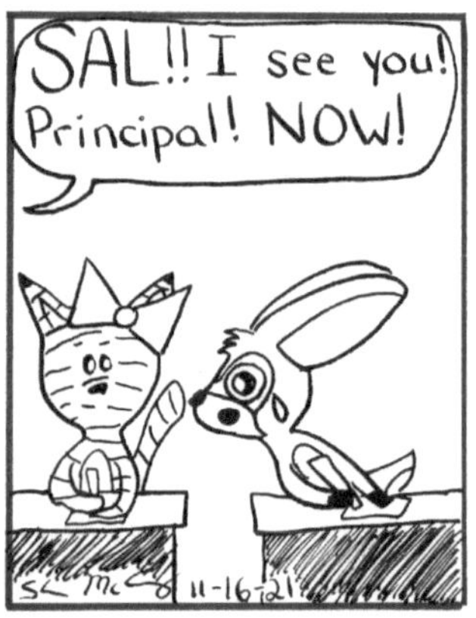
SAL!! I see you! Principal! NOW!
SL Mc 11-16-21

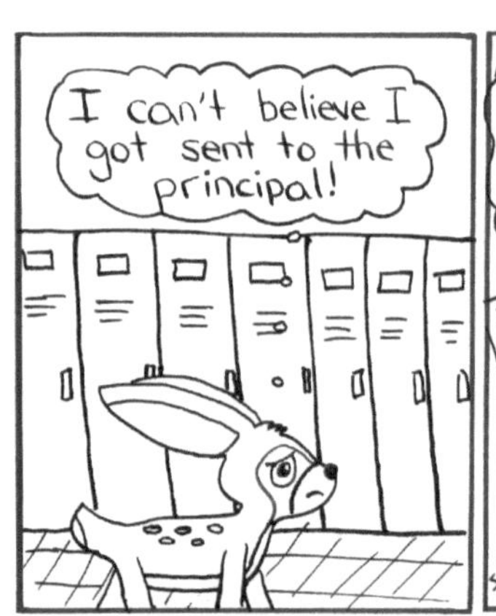
I can't believe I got sent to the principal!

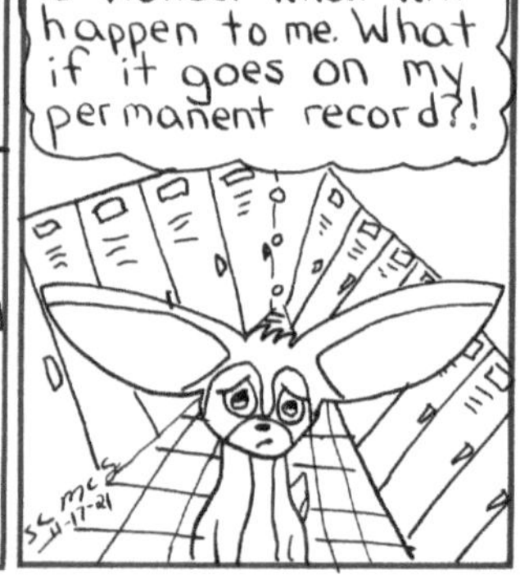
I wonder what will happen to me. What if it goes on my permanent record?!

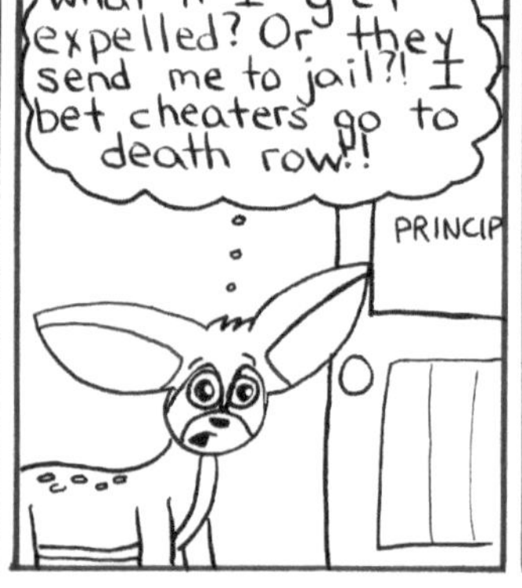
What if I get expelled? Or they send me to jail?! I bet cheaters go to death row!!
PRINCIP

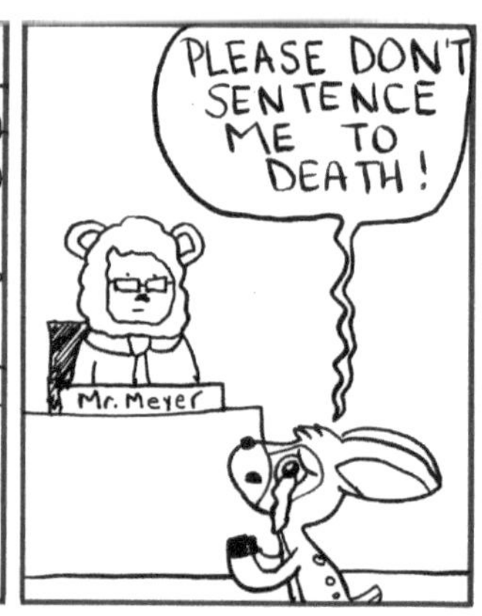
PLEASE DON'T SENTENCE ME TO DEATH!
Mr. Meyer

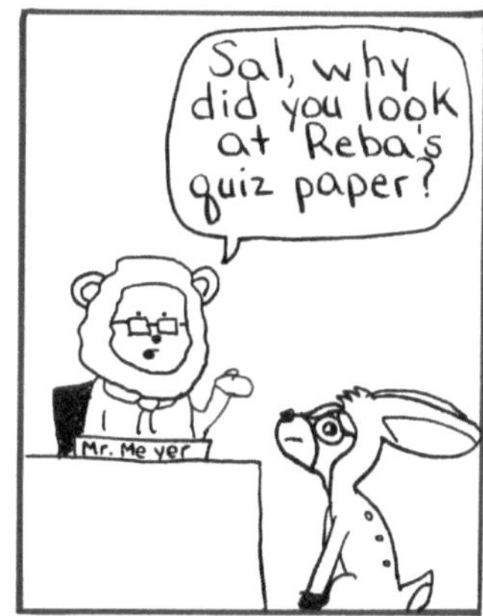
Sal, why did you look at Reba's quiz paper?
Mr. Meyer

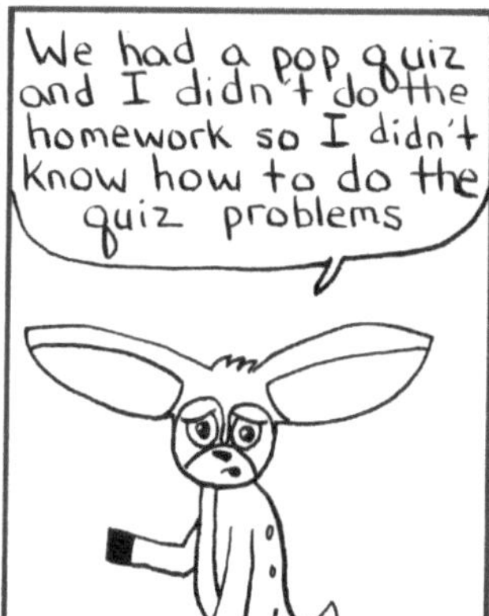
We had a pop quiz and I didn't do the homework so I didn't know how to do the quiz problems

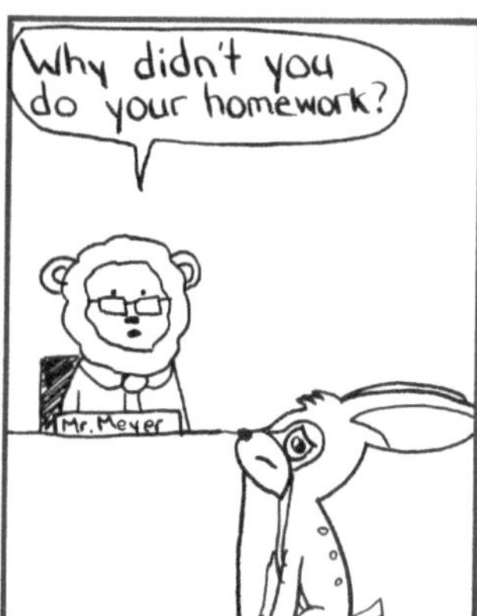
Why didn't you do your homework?
Mr. Meyer

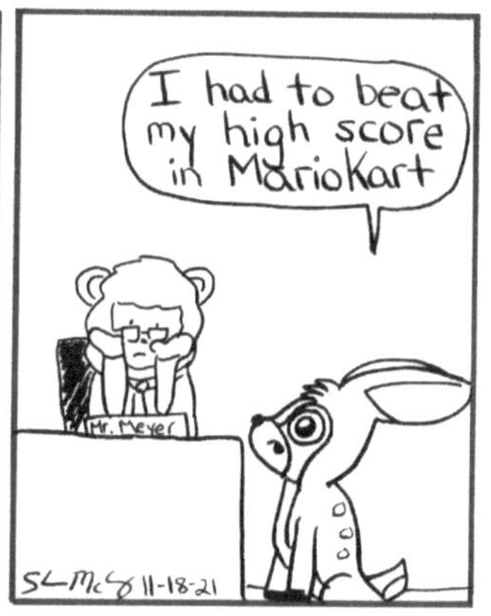
I had to beat my high score in MarioKart
Mr. Meyer
SL McS 11-18-21

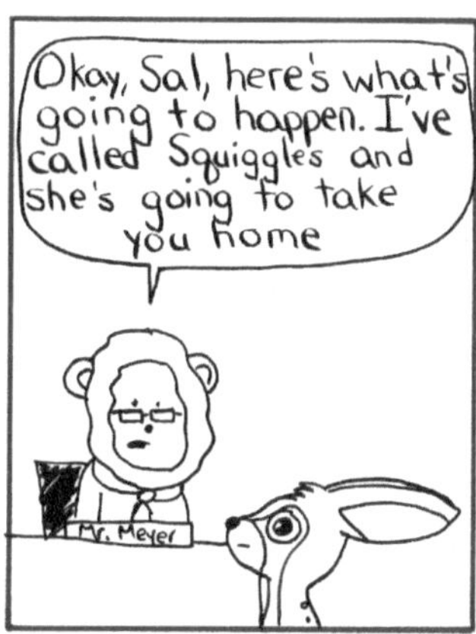
Okay, Sal, here's what's going to happen. I've called Squiggles and she's going to take you home
Mr. Meyer

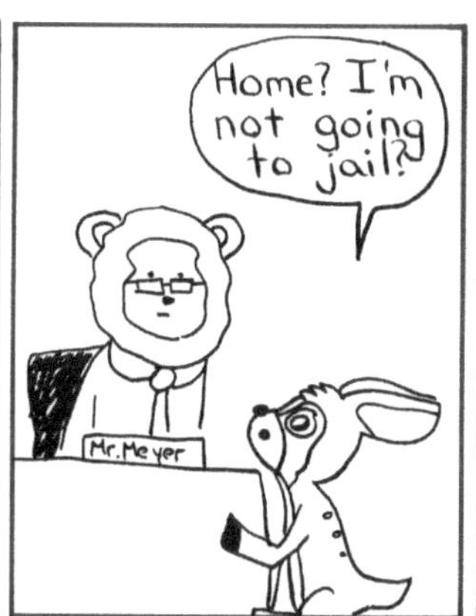
Home? I'm not going to jail?
Mr. Meyer

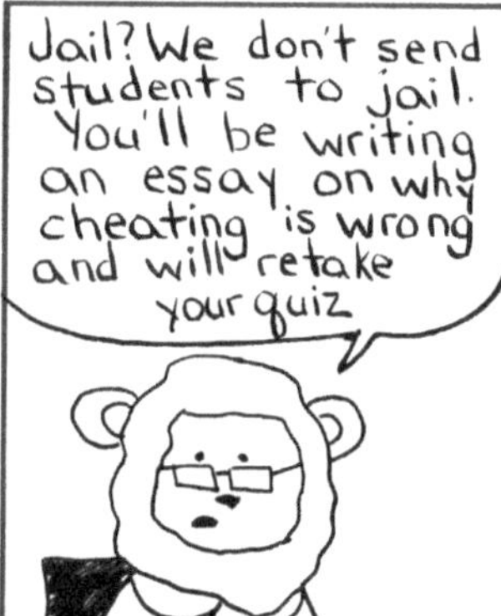
Jail? We don't send students to jail. You'll be writing an essay on why cheating is wrong and will retake your quiz

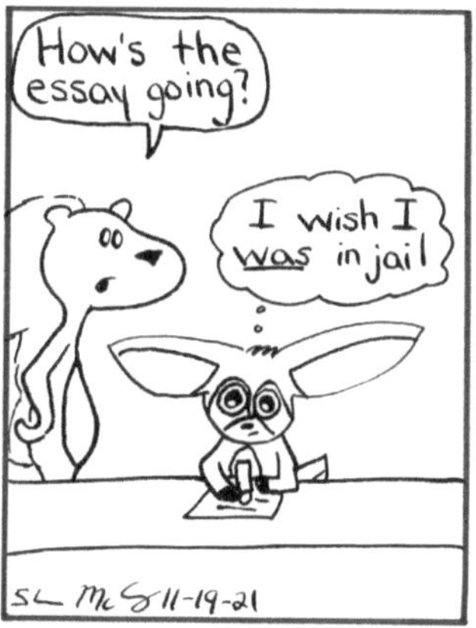
How's the essay going?
I wish I was in jail
SL McS 11-19-21

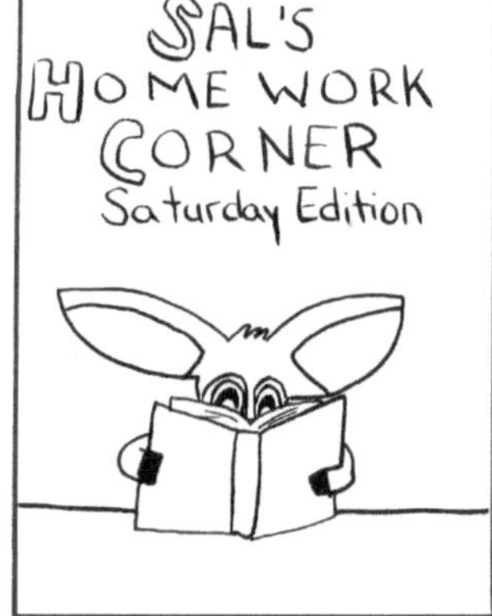
SAL'S HOME WORK CORNER
Saturday Edition

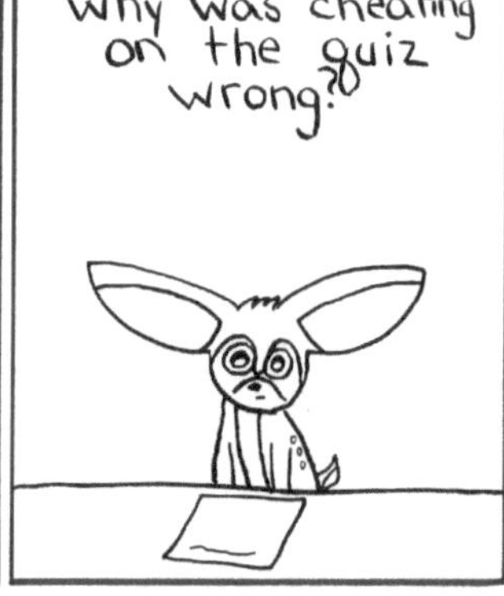
Why was cheating on the quiz wrong?

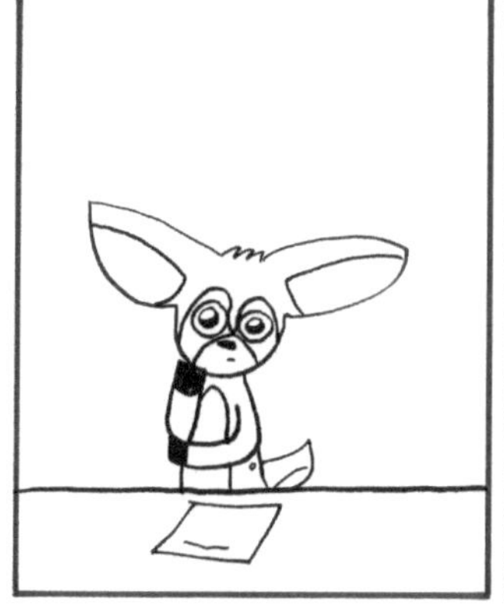

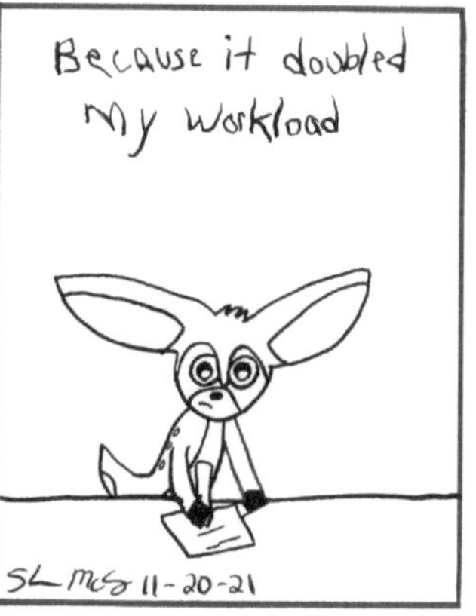
Because it doubled my workload
SL McS 11-20-21

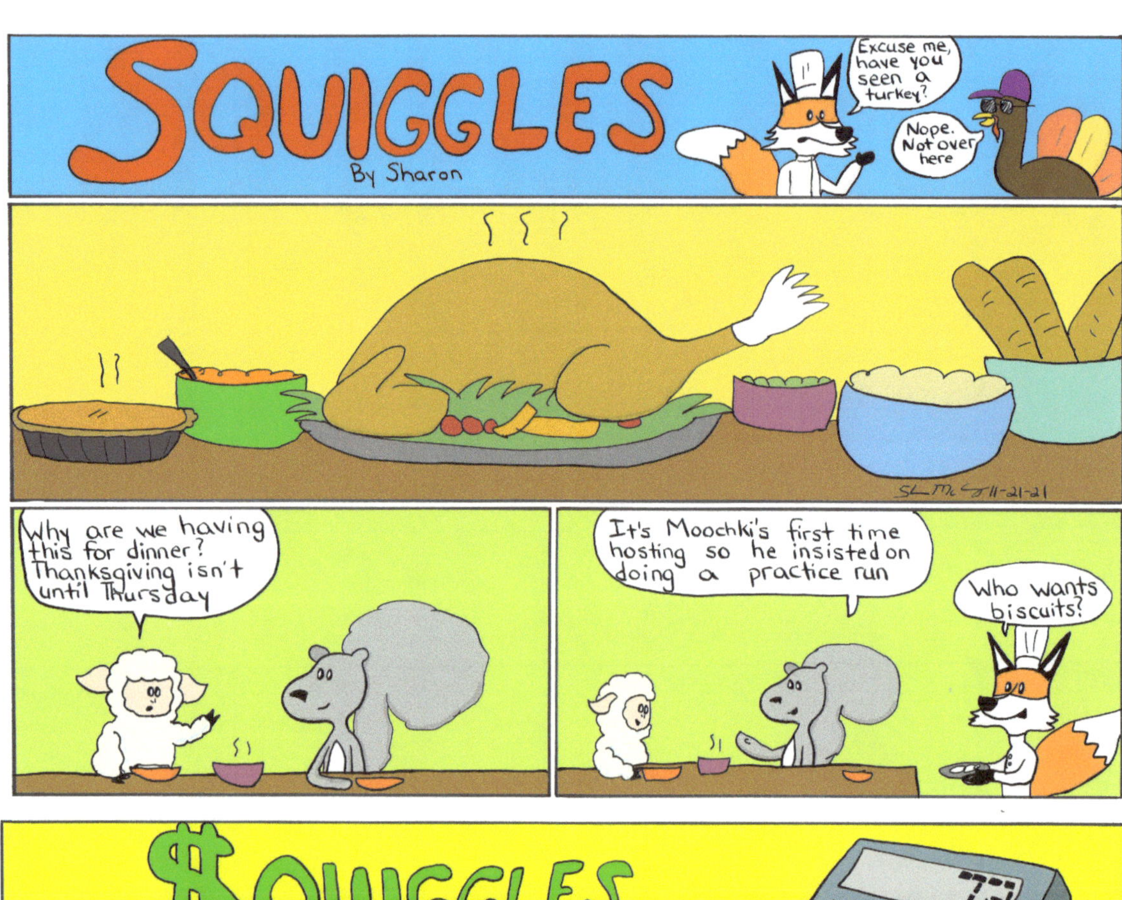
SQUIGGLES
By Sharon
Excuse me, have you seen a turkey?
Nope. Not over here
Why are we having this for dinner? Thanksgiving isn't until Thursday
It's Moochki's first time hosting so he insisted on doing a practice run
Who wants biscuits?

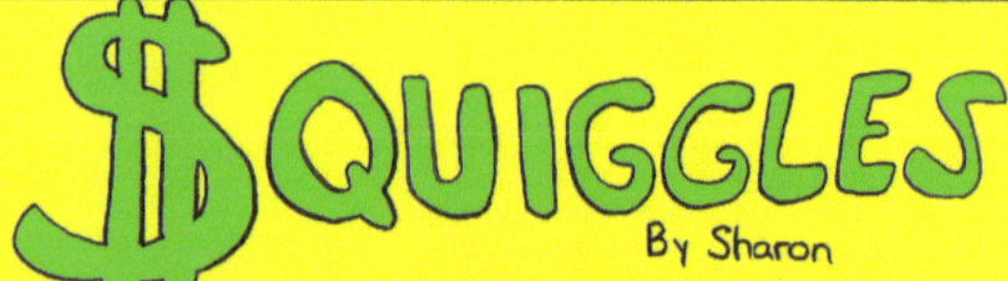
$QUIGGLES
By Sharon

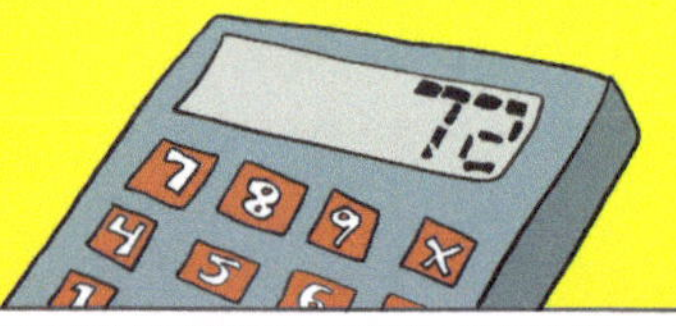

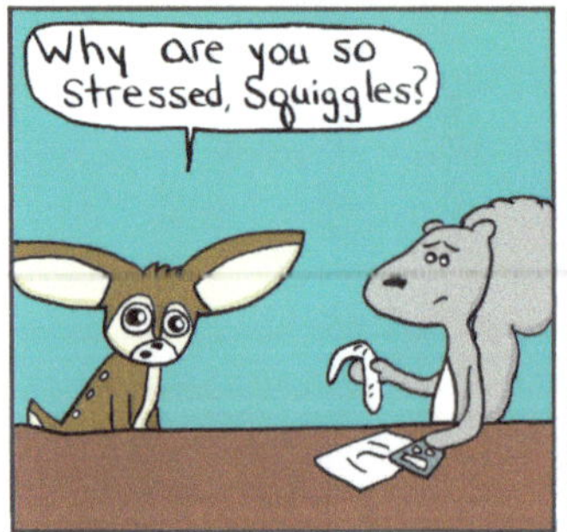
Why are you so stressed, Squiggles?

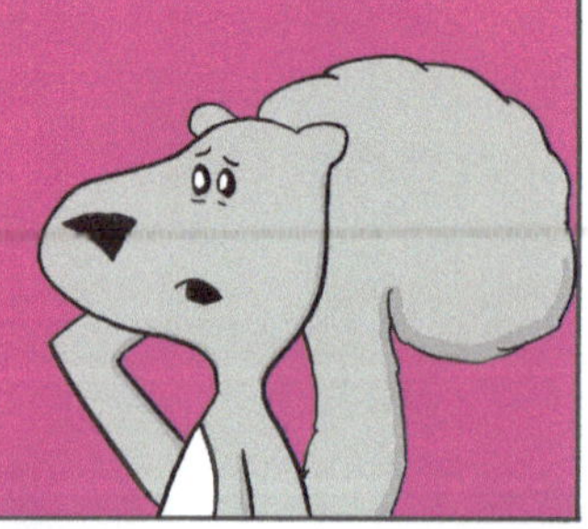
I'm paying the bills. We have a lot of expenses this month so I need to take some money from savings. (sigh) Never enough money to go around

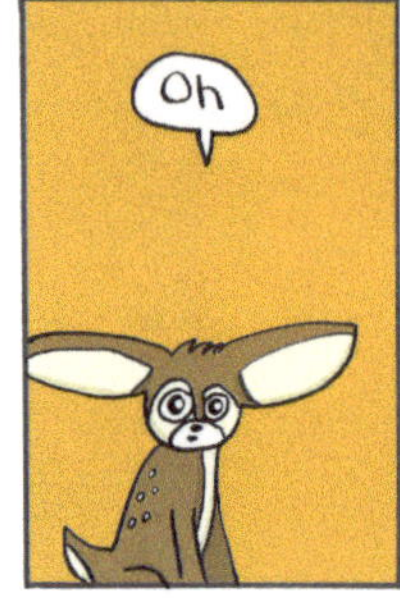
Oh

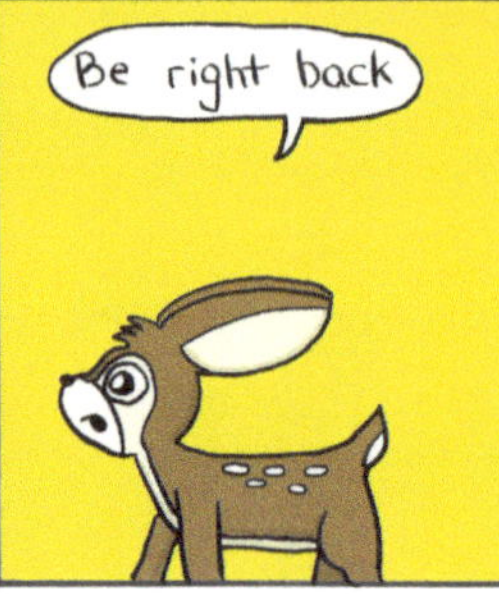
Be right back

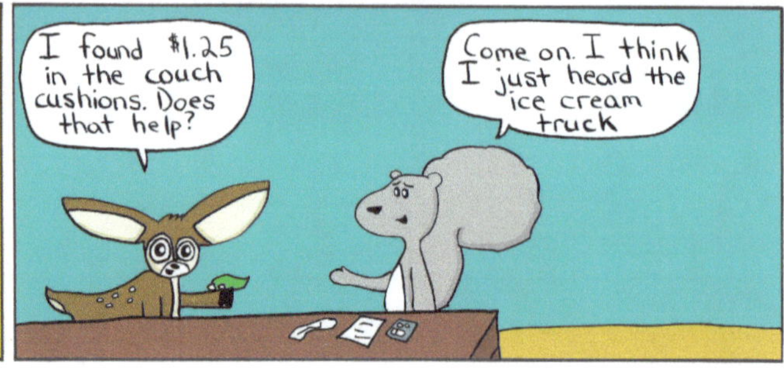
I found $1.25 in the couch cushions. Does that help?
Come on. I think I just heard the ice cream truck

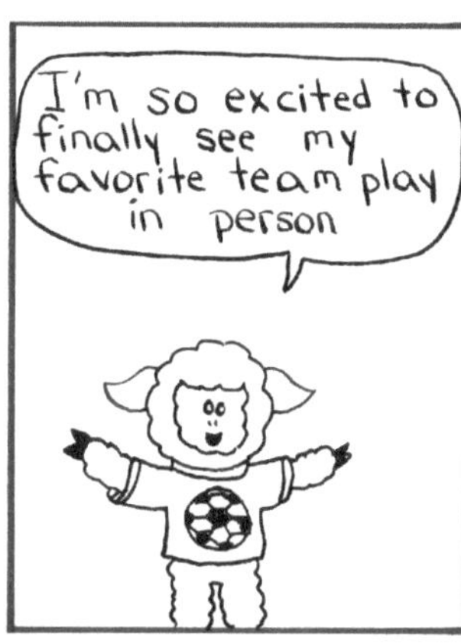
I'm so excited to finally see my favorite team play in person
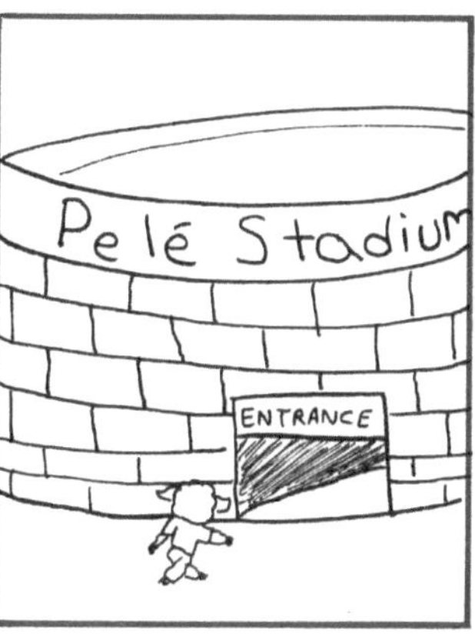
Pelé Stadium
ENTRANCE
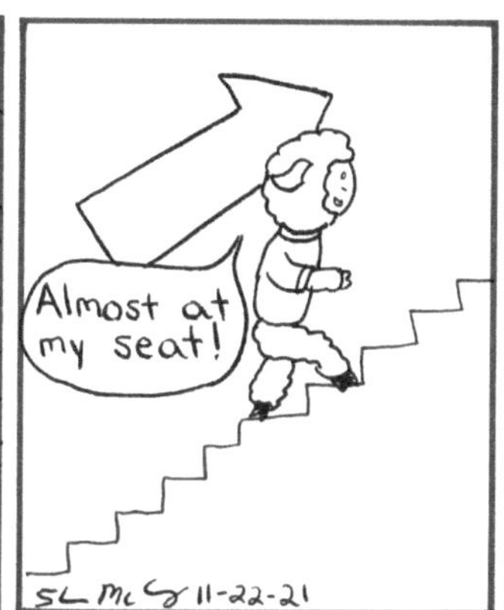
Almost at my seat!
SLMcG 11-22-21
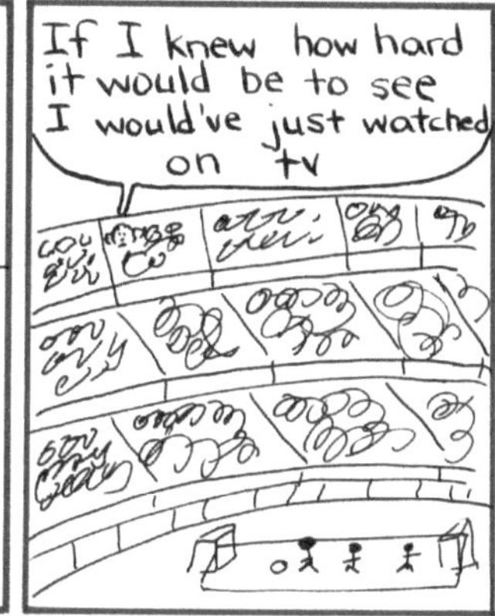
If I knew how hard it would be to see I would've just watched on tv
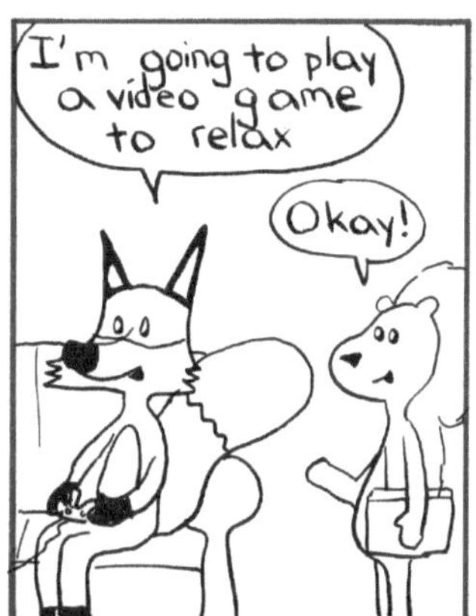
I'm going to play a video game to relax
Okay!
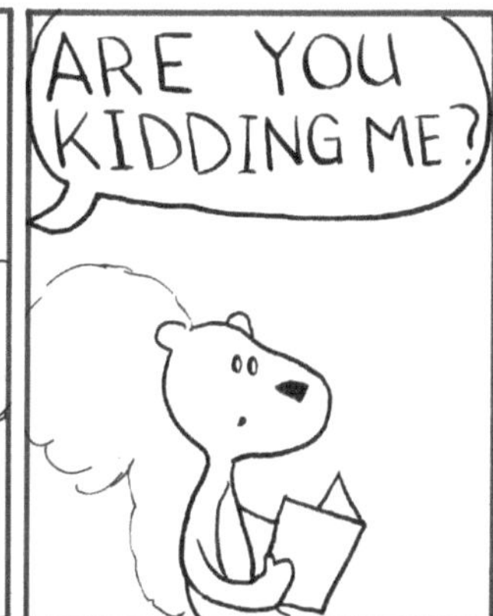
ARE YOU KIDDING ME?
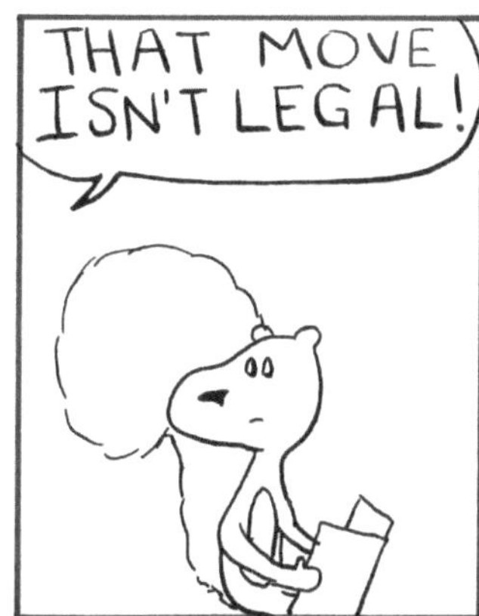
THAT MOVE ISN'T LEGAL!
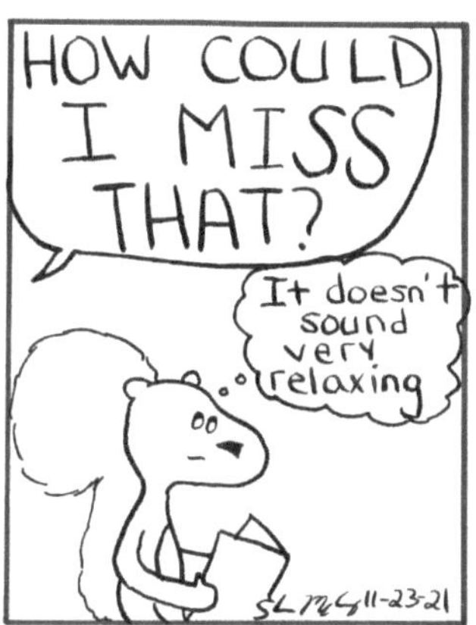
HOW COULD I MISS THAT?
It doesn't sound very relaxing
SLMcG 11-23-21
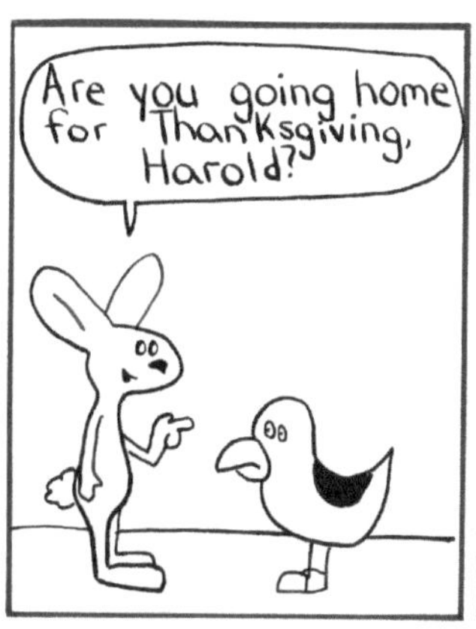
Are you going home for Thanksgiving, Harold?
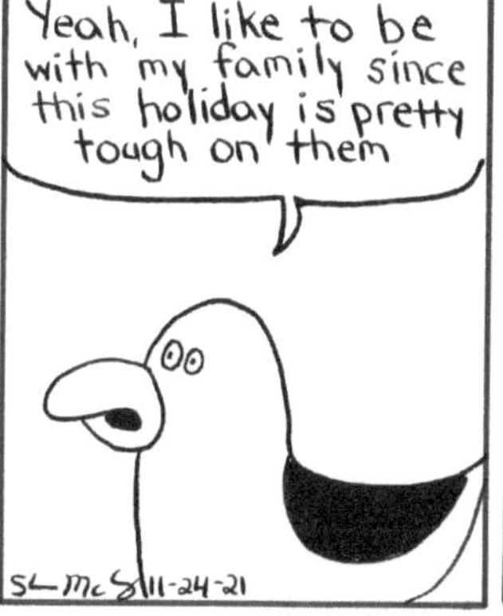
Yeah, I like to be with my family since this holiday is pretty tough on them
SLMcG 11-24-21
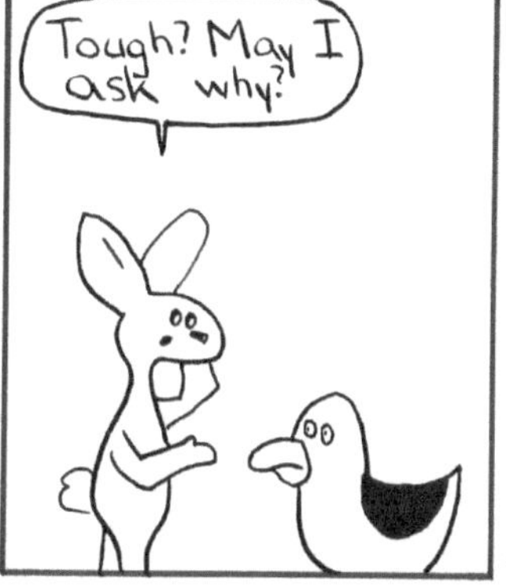
Tough? May I ask why?
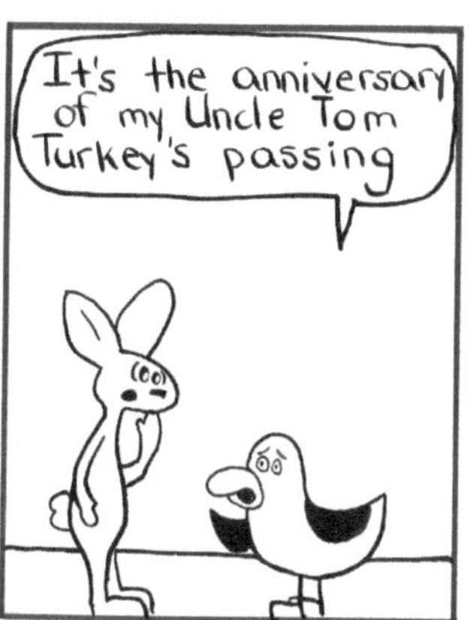
It's the anniversary of my Uncle Tom Turkey's passing

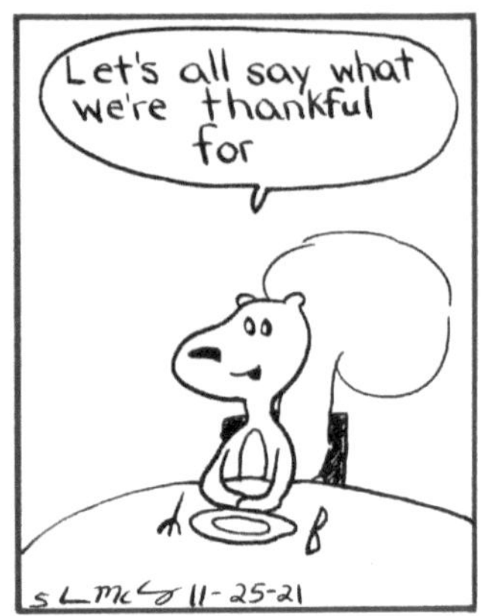
Let's all say what we're thankful for
SLMcG 11-25-21

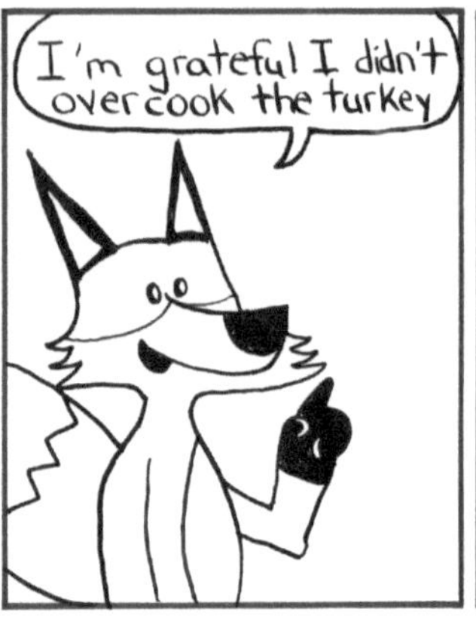
I'm grateful I didn't overcook the turkey

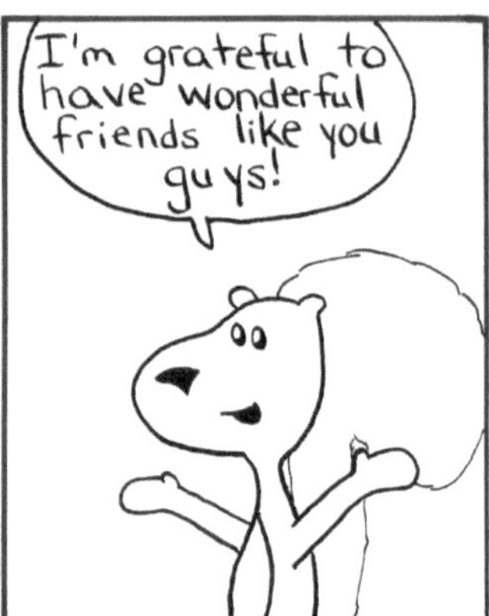
I'm grateful to have wonderful friends like you guys!

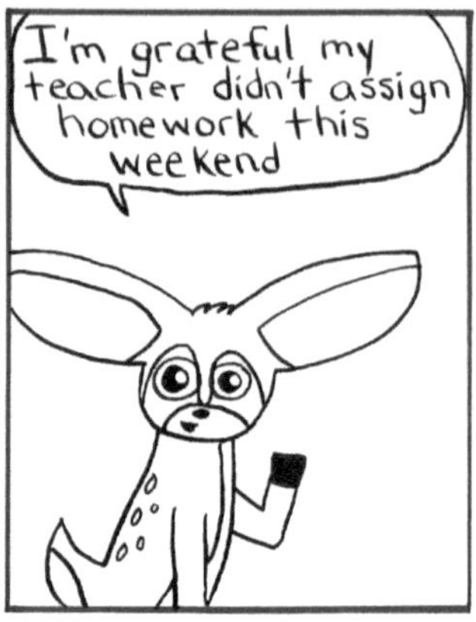
I'm grateful my teacher didn't assign homework this weekend

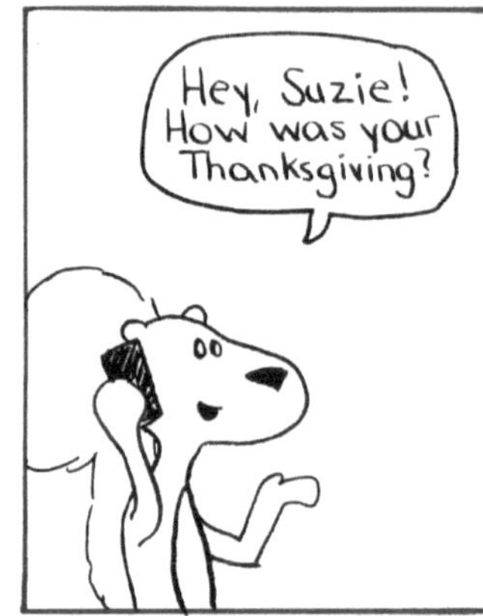
Hey, Suzie! How was your Thanksgiving?

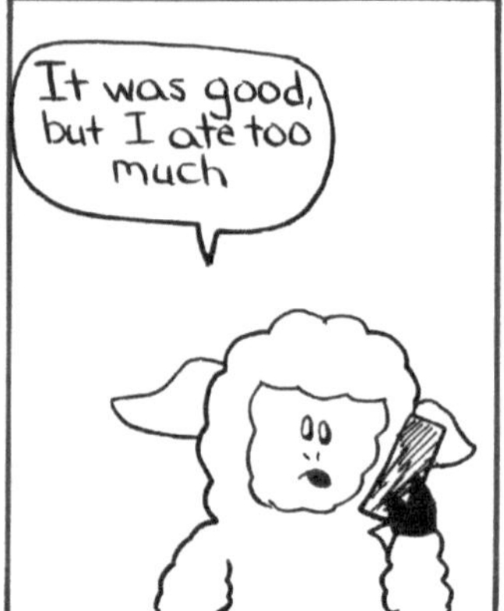
It was good, but I ate too much

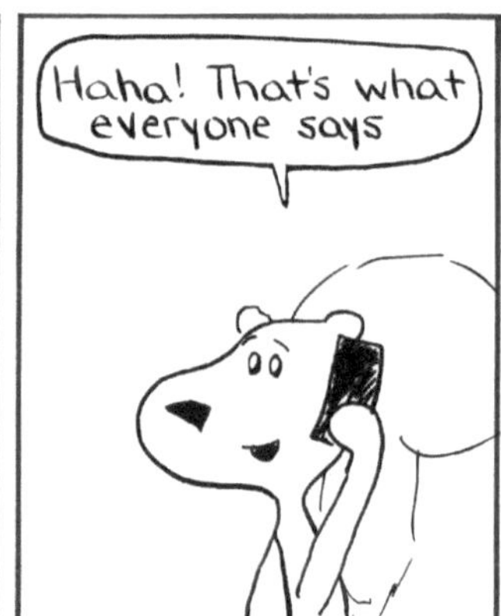
Haha! That's what everyone says

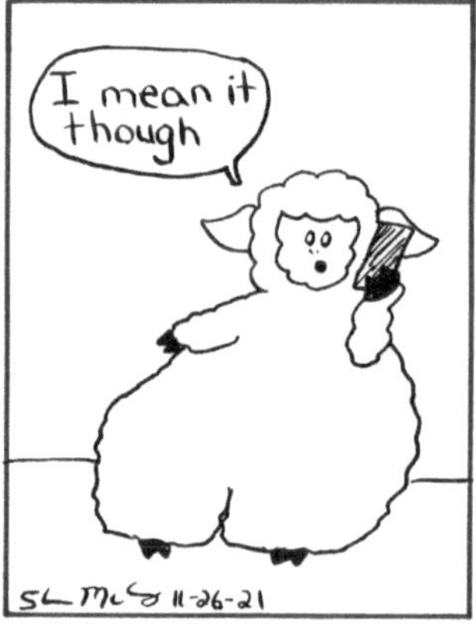
I mean it though
SLMcG 11-26-21

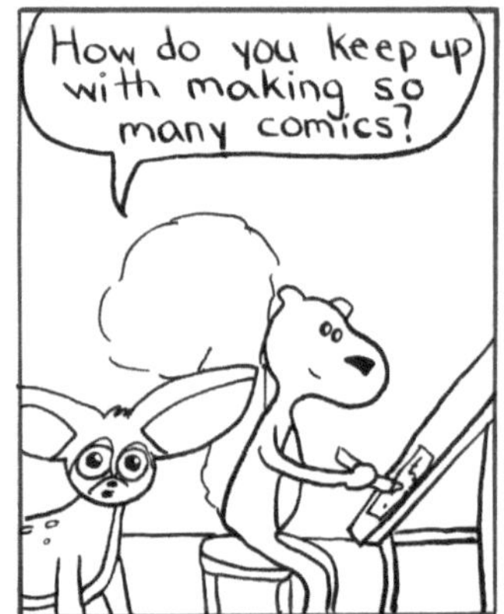
How do you keep up with making so many comics?

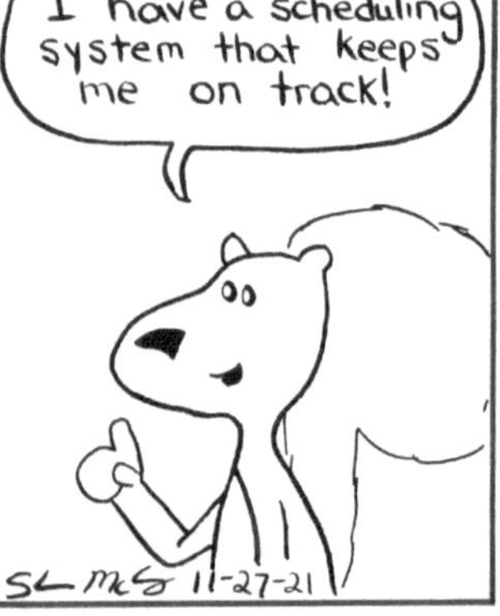
I have a scheduling system that keeps me on track!
SLMcG 11-27-21

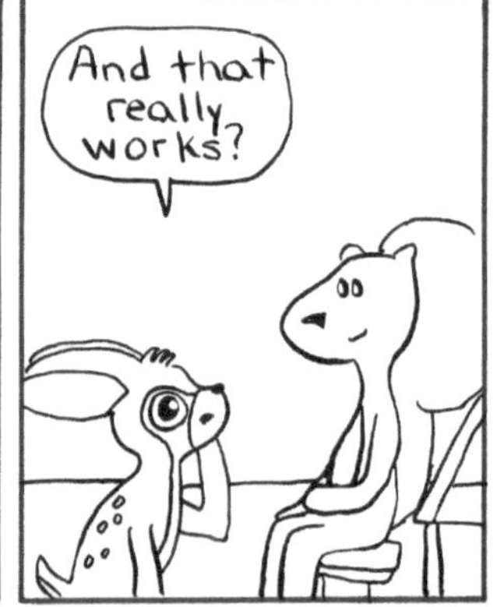
And that really works?

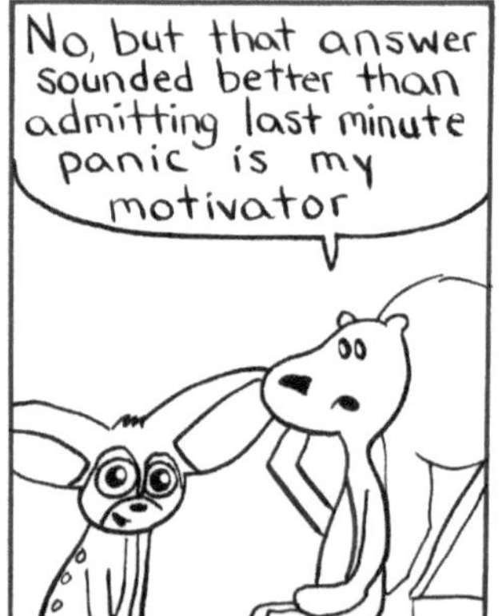
No, but that answer sounded better than admitting last minute panic is my motivator

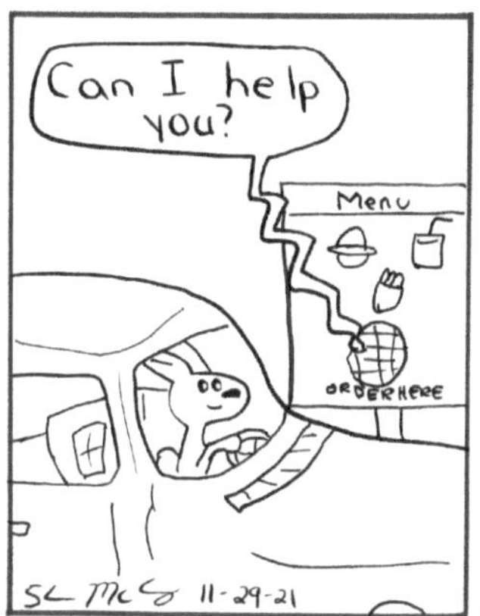
Can I help you?
Menu
ORDER HERE
SL McG 11-29-21

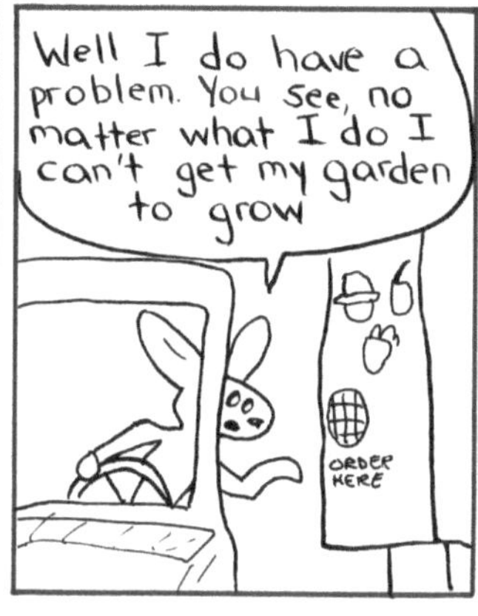
Well I do have a problem. You see, no matter what I do I can't get my garden to grow
ORDER HERE

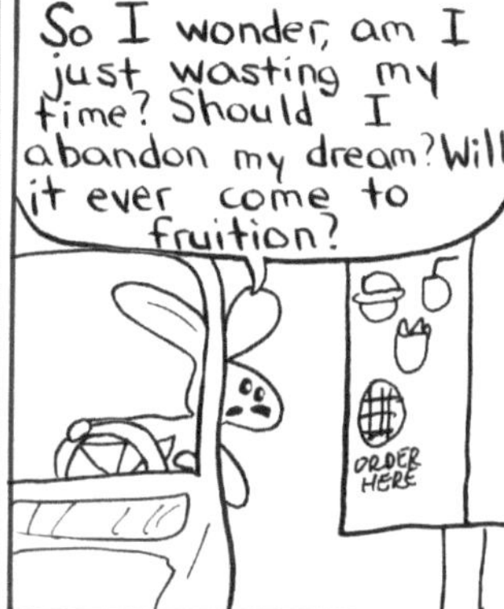
So I wonder, am I just wasting my time? Should I abandon my dream? Will it ever come to fruition?
ORDER HERE

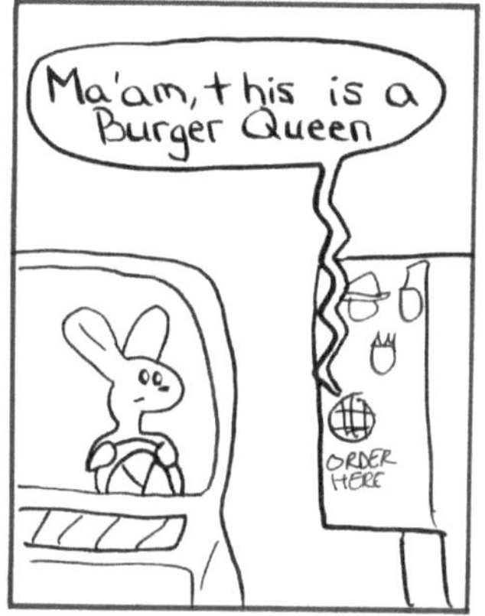
Ma'am, this is a Burger Queen
ORDER HERE

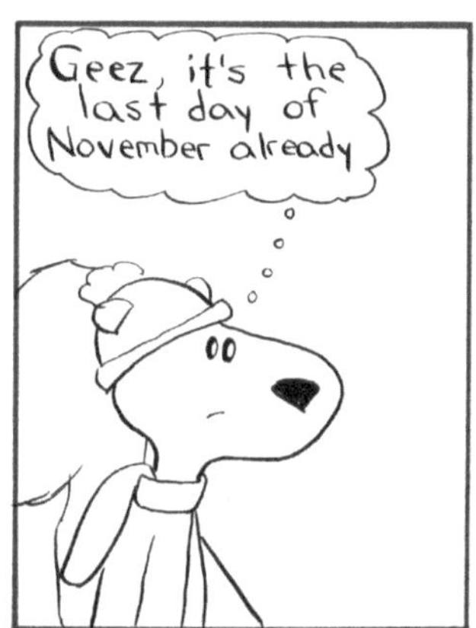
Geez, it's the last day of November already

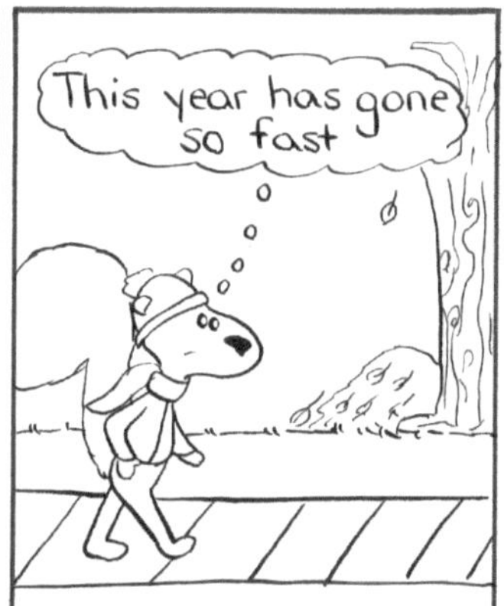
This year has gone so fast

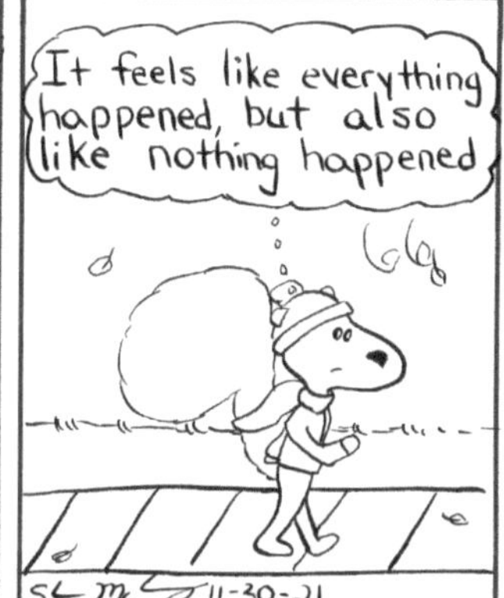
It feels like everything happened, but also like nothing happened
SL McG 11-30-21

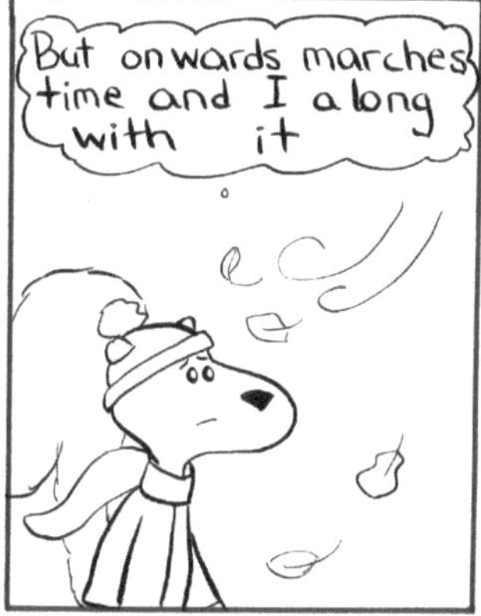
But onwards marches time and I along with it

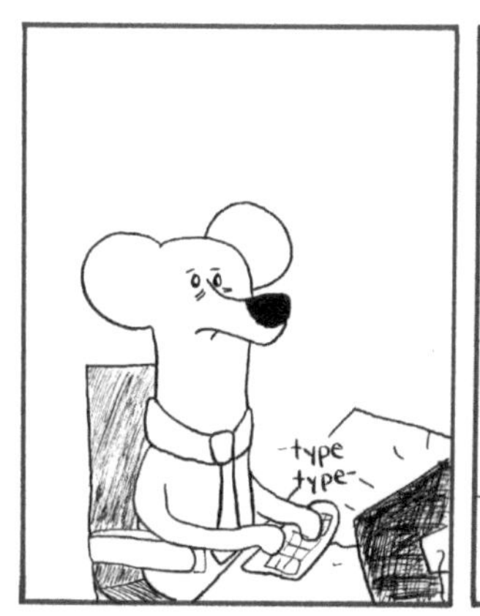
-type type-

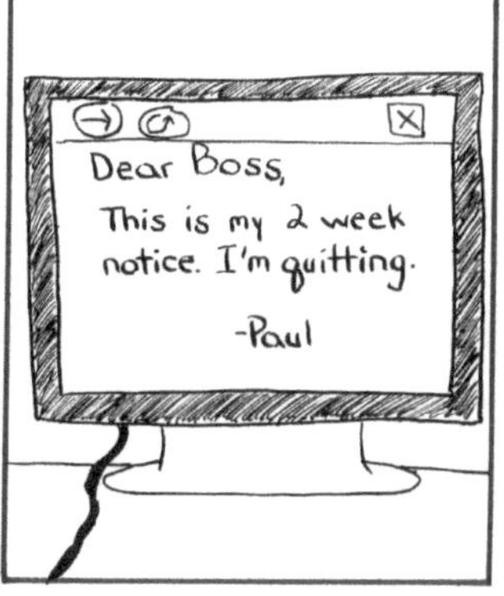
Dear Boss,
This is my 2 week notice. I'm quitting.
-Paul

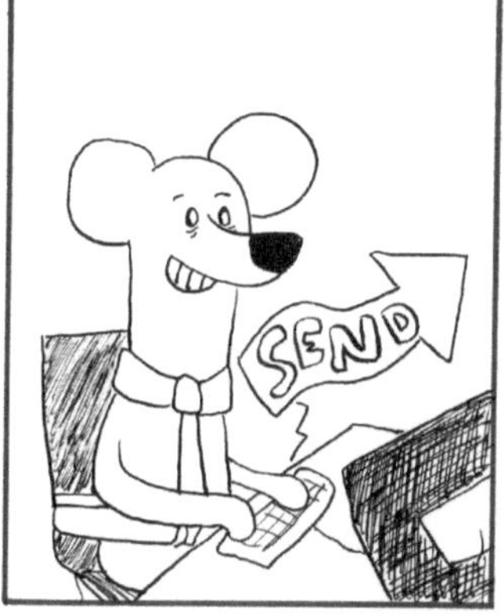
SEND

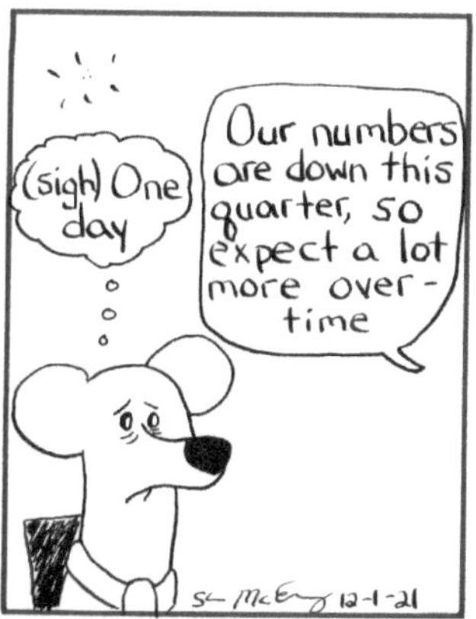
(sigh) One day
Our numbers are down this quarter, so expect a lot more over-time
SL McG 12-1-21

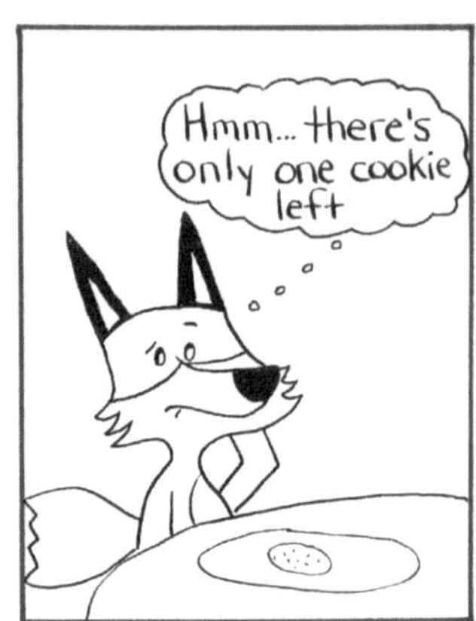
Hmm... there's only one cookie left

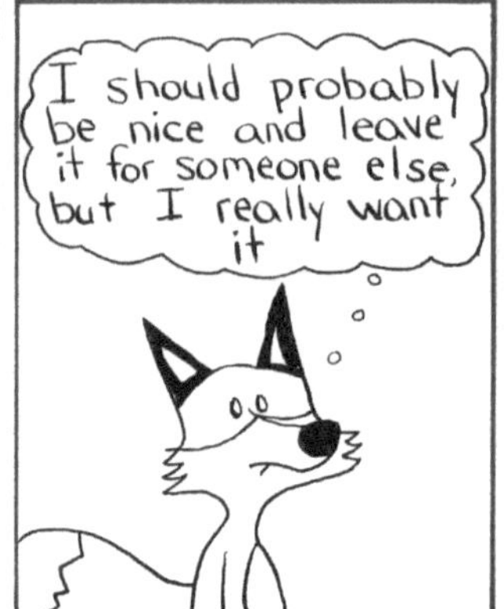
I should probably be nice and leave it for someone else, but I really want it

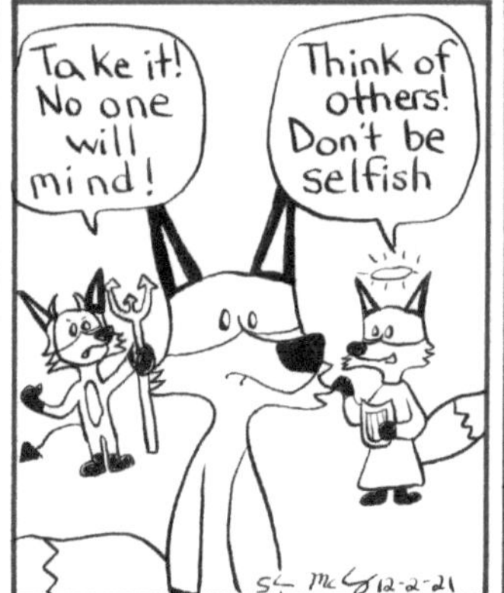
Take it! No one will mind!
Think of others! Don't be selfish
SL McS 12-2-21

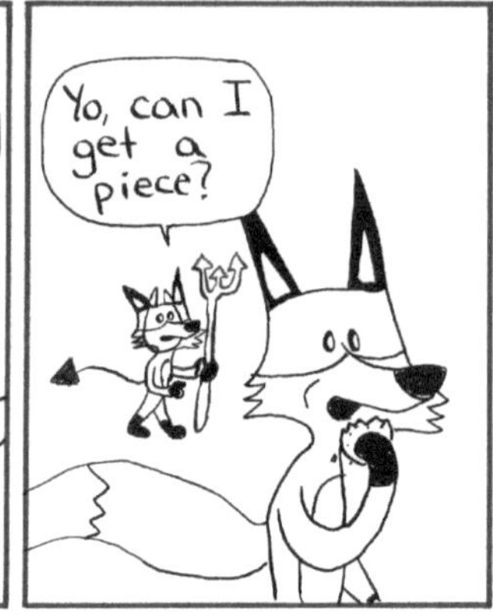
Yo, can I get a piece?

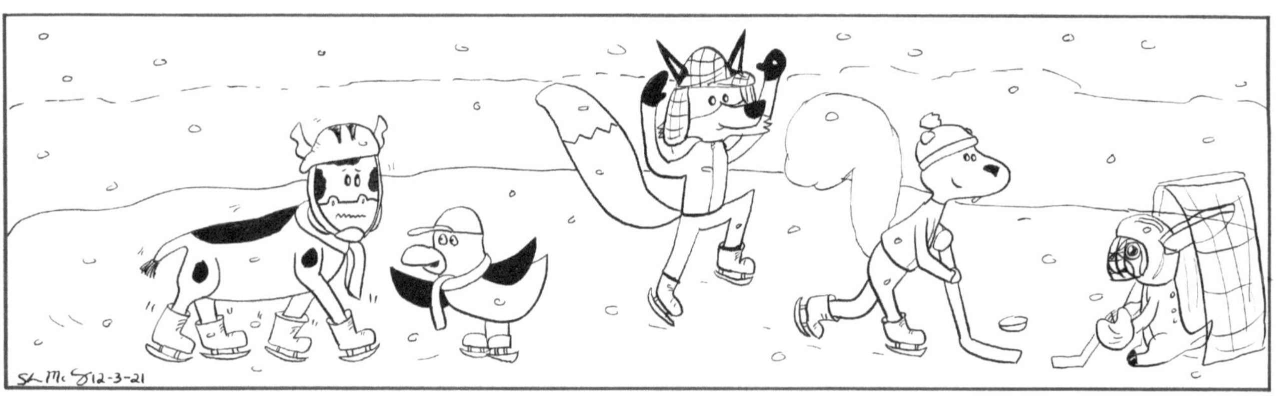
SL McS 12-3-21

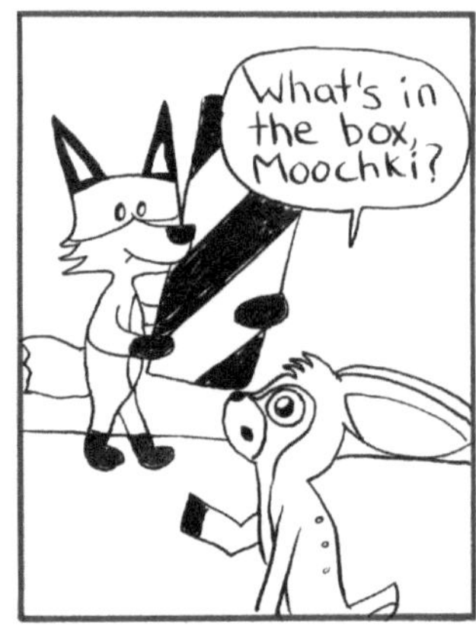
What's in the box, Moochki?

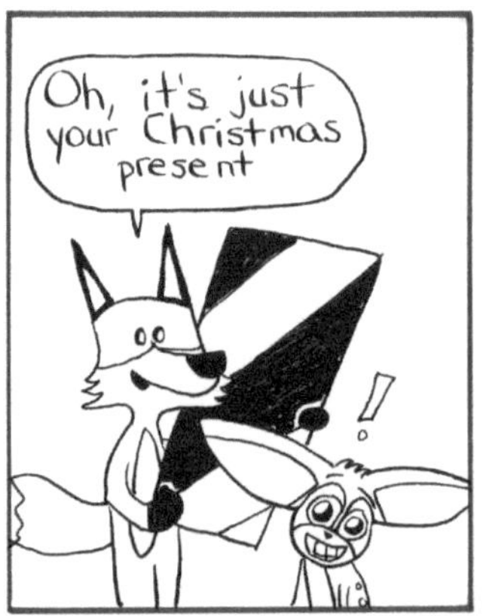
Oh, it's just your Christmas present
!

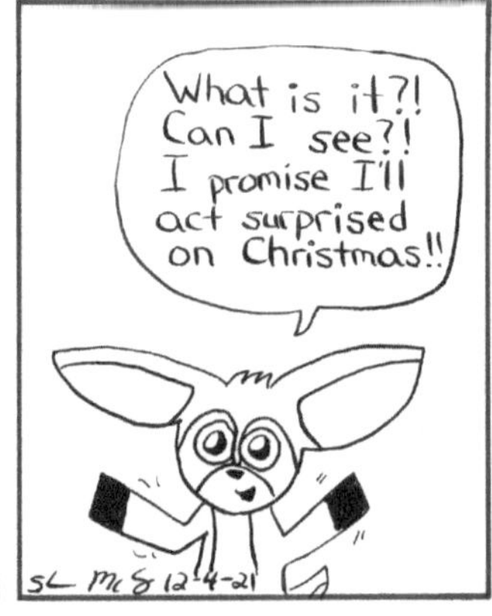
What is it?! Can I see?! I promise I'll act surprised on Christmas!!
SL McS 12-4-21

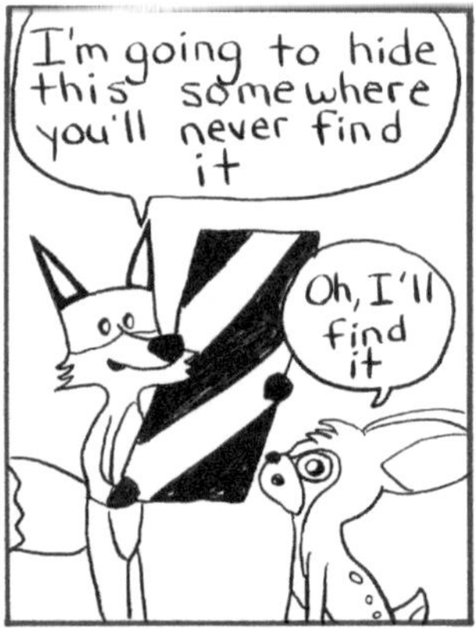
I'm going to hide this somewhere you'll never find it
Oh, I'll find it

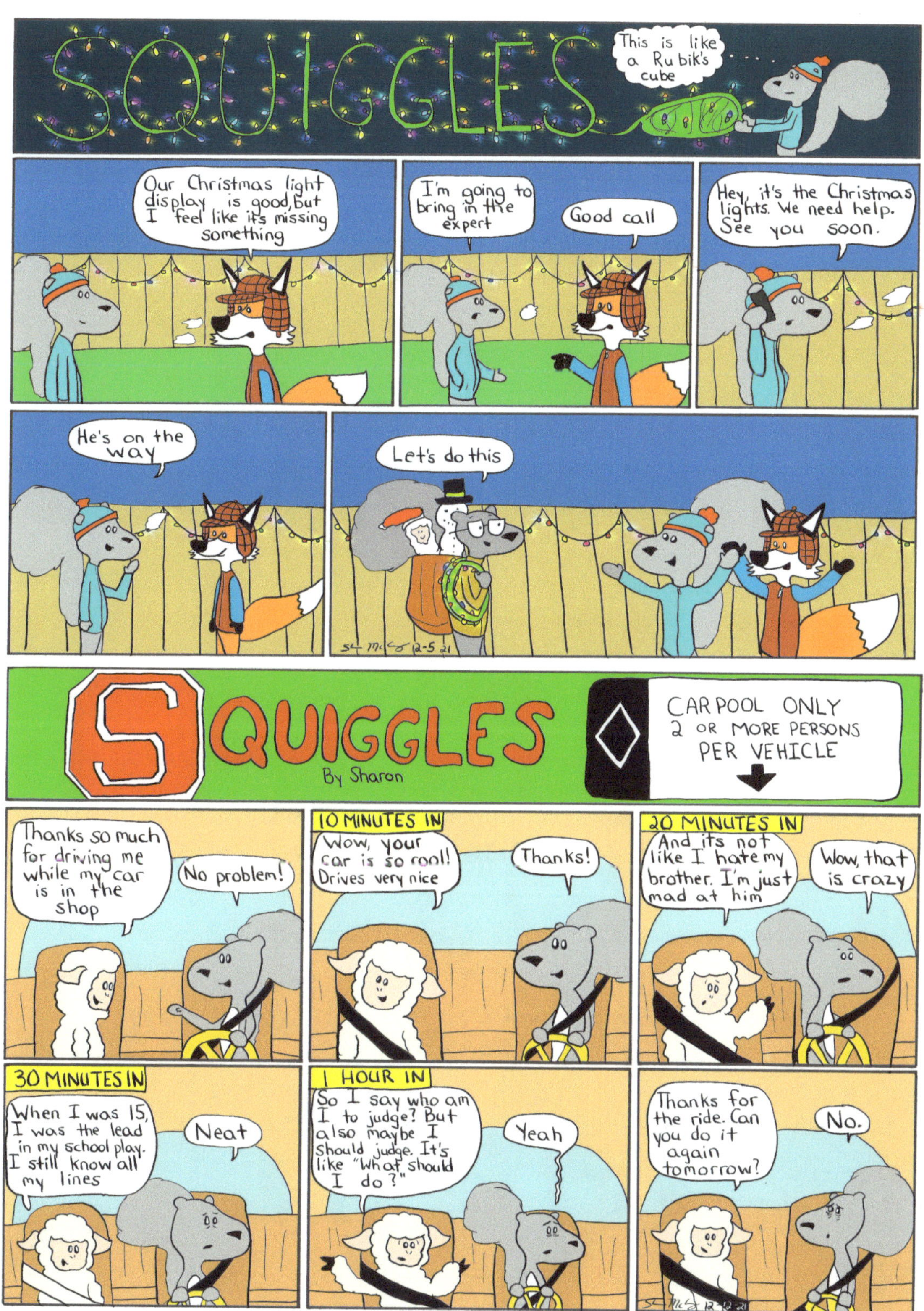
SQUIGGLES
This is like a Rubik's cube
Our Christmas light display is good, but I feel like it's missing something
I'm going to bring in the expert
Good call
Hey, it's the Christmas lights. We need help. See you soon.
He's on the way
Let's do this
SQUIGGLES
By Sharon
CAR POOL ONLY
2 OR MORE PERSONS PER VEHICLE
Thanks so much for driving me while my car is in the shop
No problem!
10 MINUTES IN
Wow, your car is so cool! Drives very nice
Thanks!
20 MINUTES IN
And its not like I hate my brother. I'm just mad at him
Wow, that is crazy
30 MINUTES IN
When I was 15, I was the lead in my school play. I still know all my lines
Neat
1 HOUR IN
So I say who am I to judge? But also maybe I should judge. It's like "What should I do?"
Yeah
Thanks for the ride. Can you do it again tomorrow?
No.

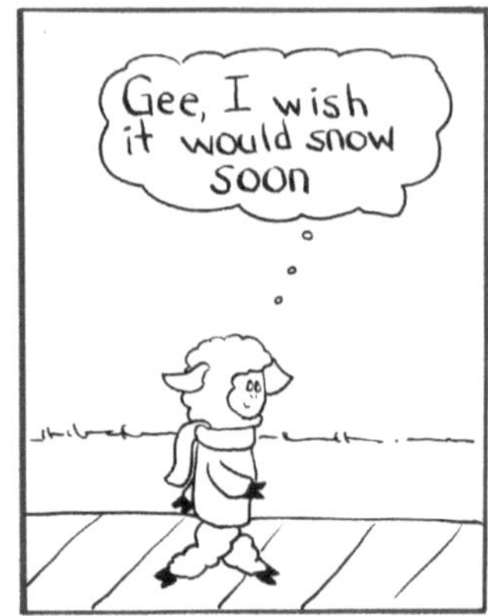
Gee, I wish it would snow soon
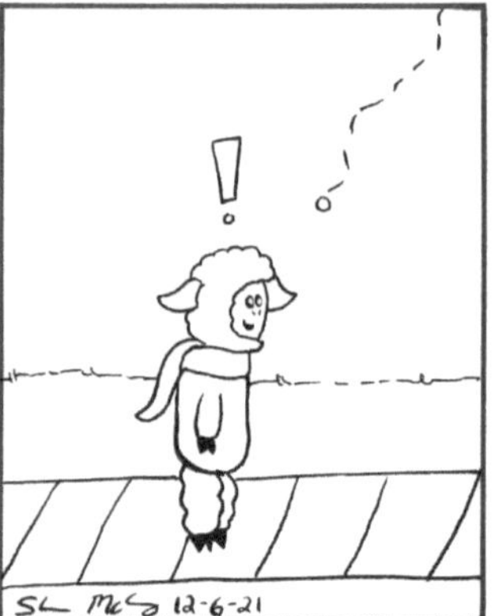
!
SL McG 12-6-21
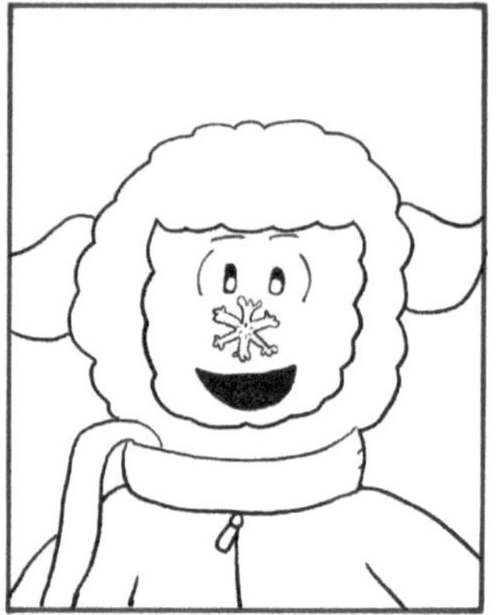
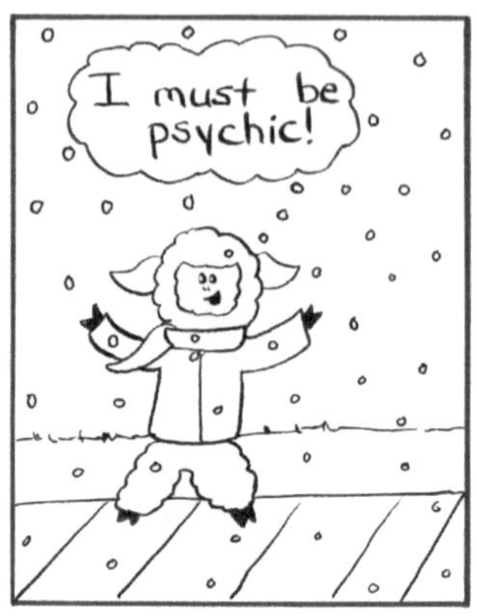
I must be psychic!
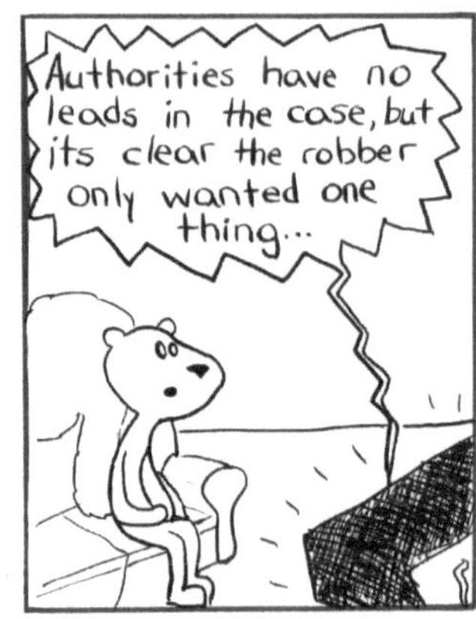
Authorities have no leads in the case, but its clear the robber only wanted one thing...
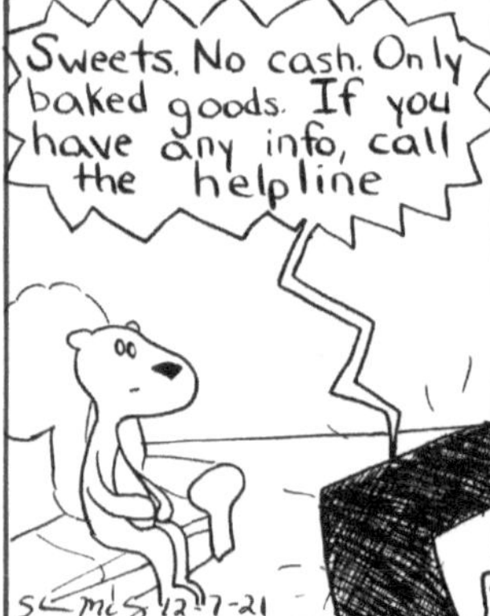
Sweets. No cash. Only baked goods. If you have any info, call the helpline
SL McG 12-7-21
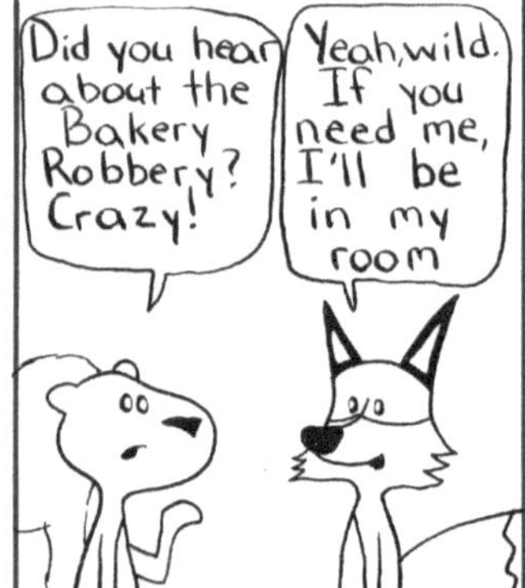
Did you hear about the Bakery Robbery? Crazy!
Yeah, wild. If you need me, I'll be in my room
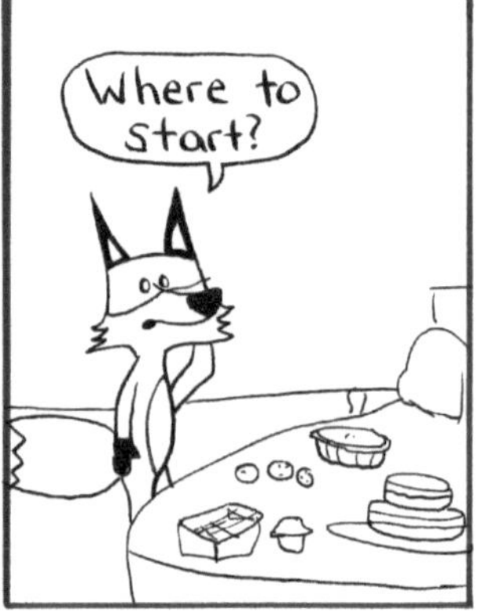
Where to start?
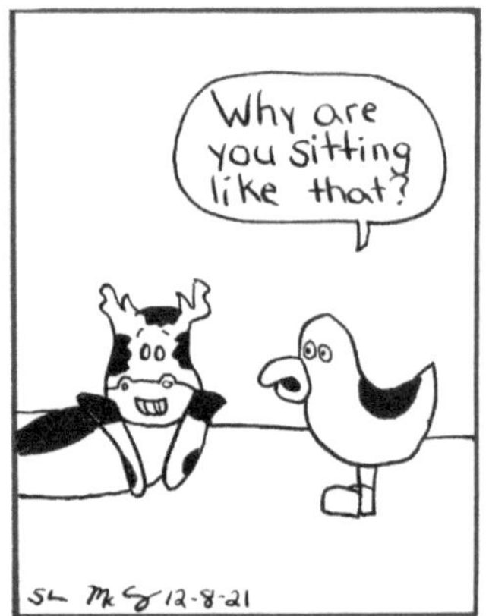
Why are you sitting like that?
SL McG 12-8-21
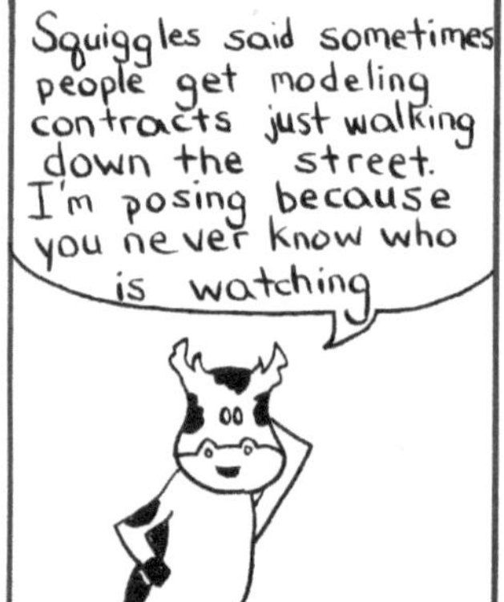
Squiggles said sometimes people get modeling contracts just walking down the street. I'm posing because you never know who is watching
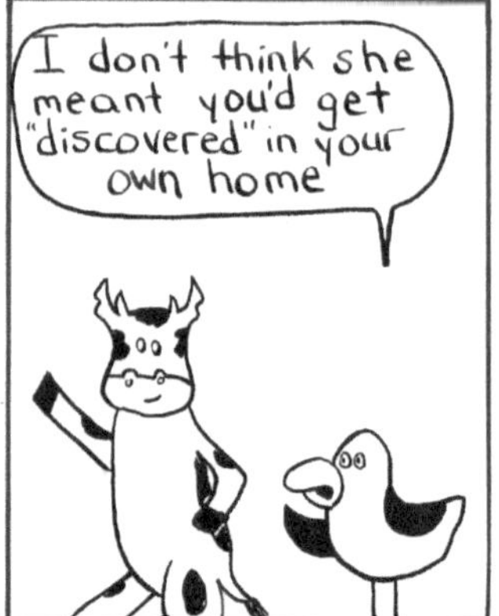
I don't think she meant you'd get "discovered" in your own home
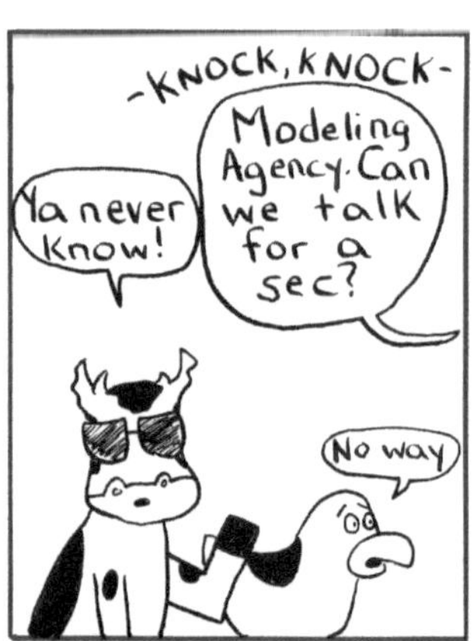
-KNOCK, KNOCK-
Ya never know!
Modeling Agency. Can we talk for a sec?
No way

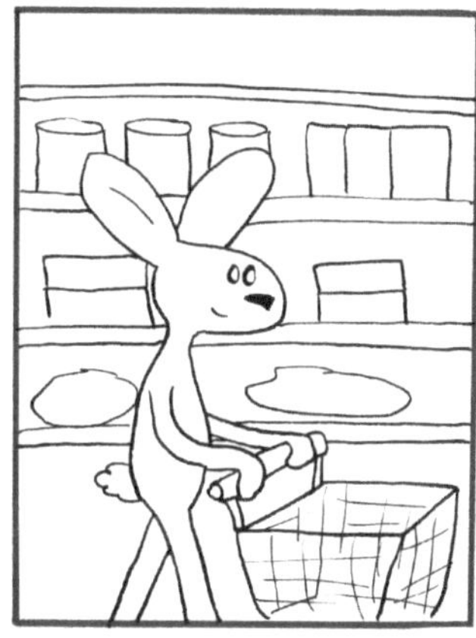
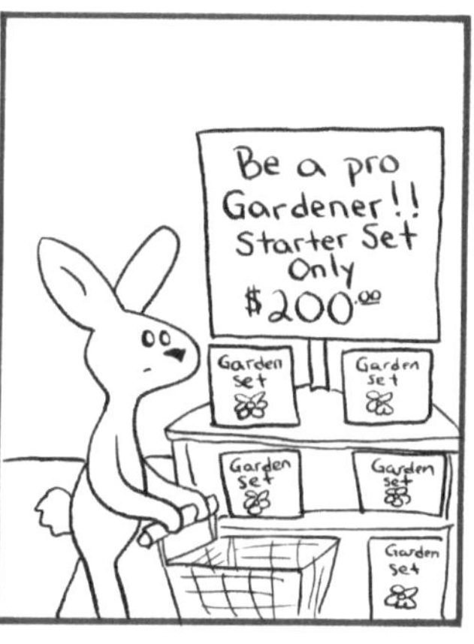
Be a pro Gardener!! Starter Set Only $200.00
Garden set
Garden set
Garden set
Garden set
Garden set
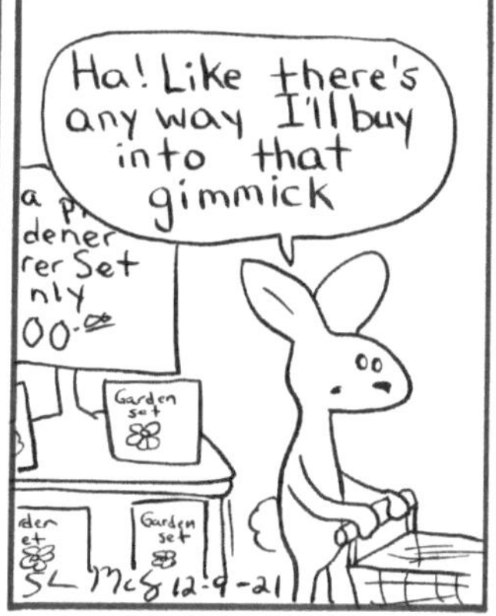
Ha! Like there's any way I'll buy into that gimmick
Garden set
Garden set
SL McS 12-9-21
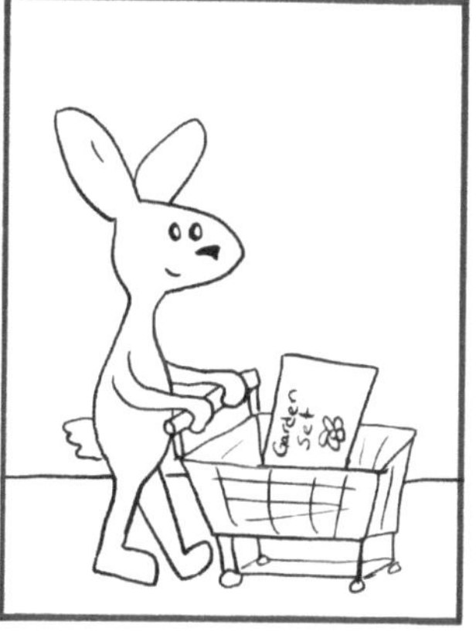
Garden set
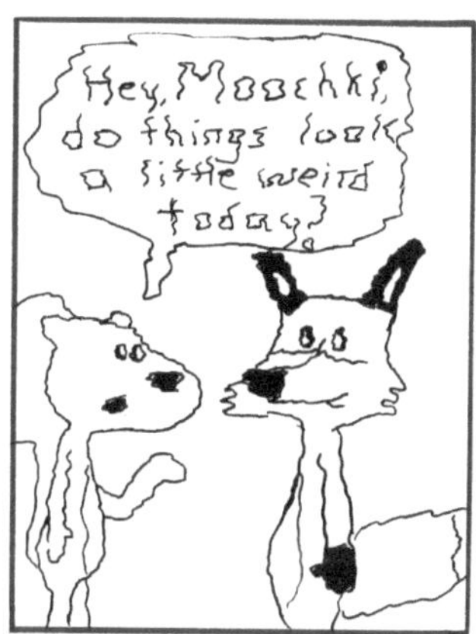
Hey, Moochki, do things look a little weird today?
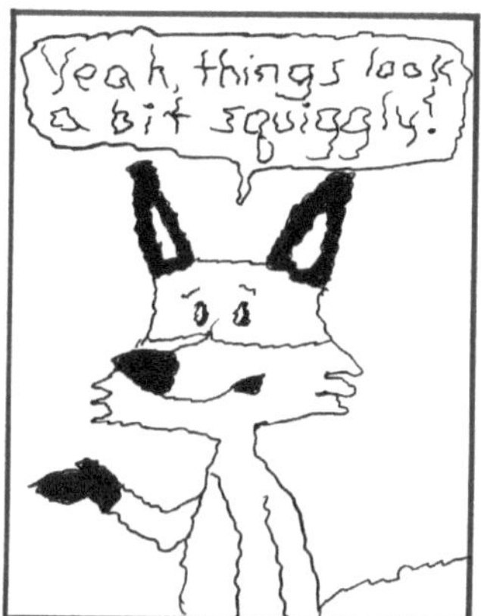
Yeah, things look a bit squiggly!
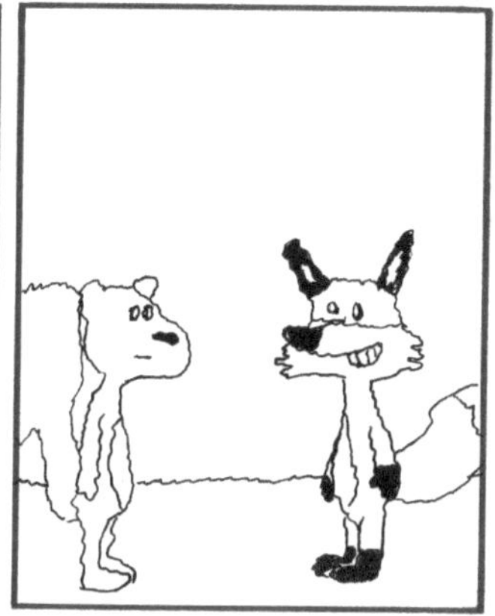
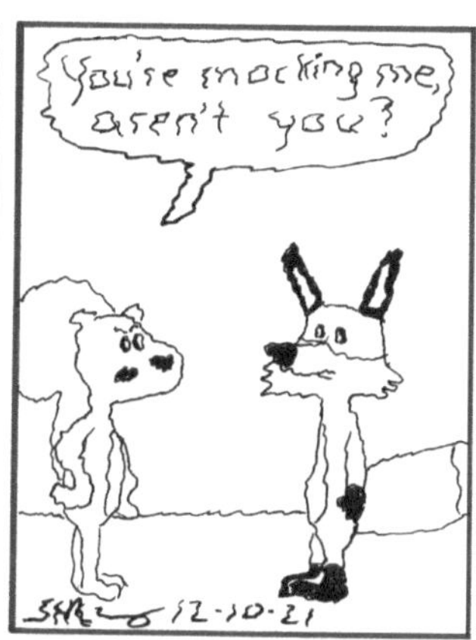
You're mocking me, aren't you?
12-10-21
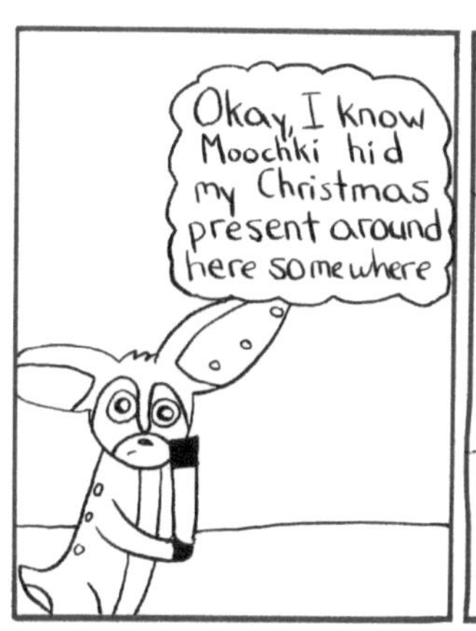
Okay, I know Moochki hid my Christmas present around here somewhere
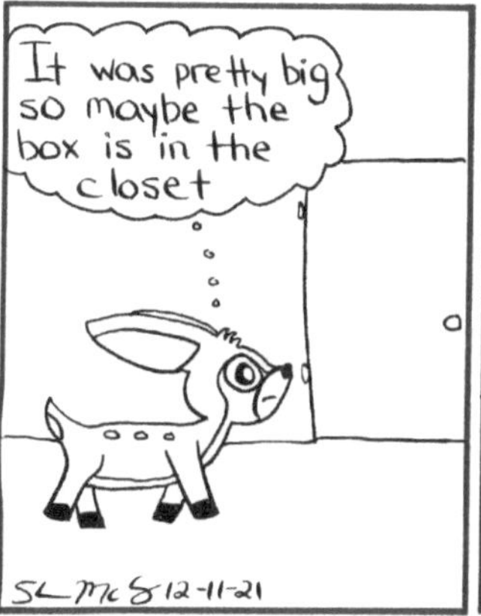
It was pretty big so maybe the box is in the closet
SL McS 12-11-21
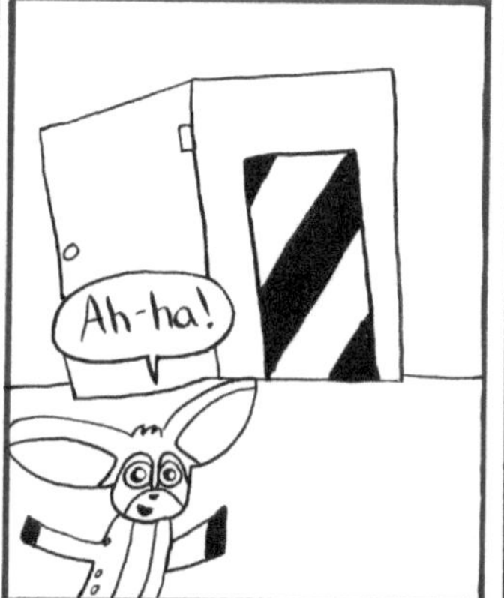
Ah-ha!
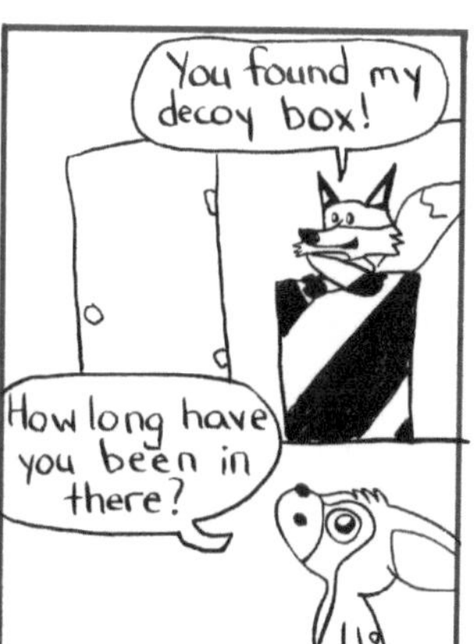
You found my decoy box!
How long have you been in there?

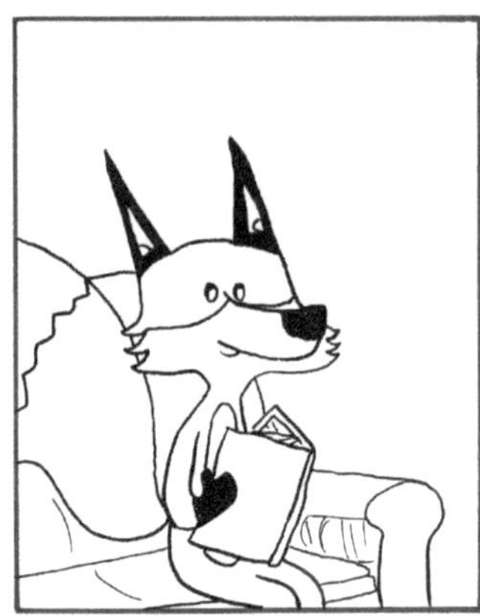
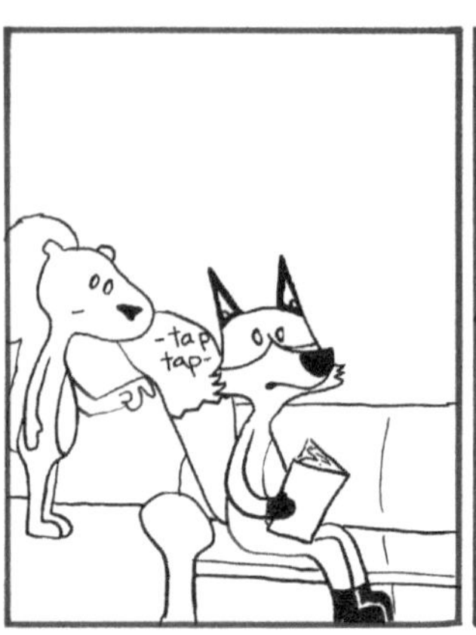
-tap tap-
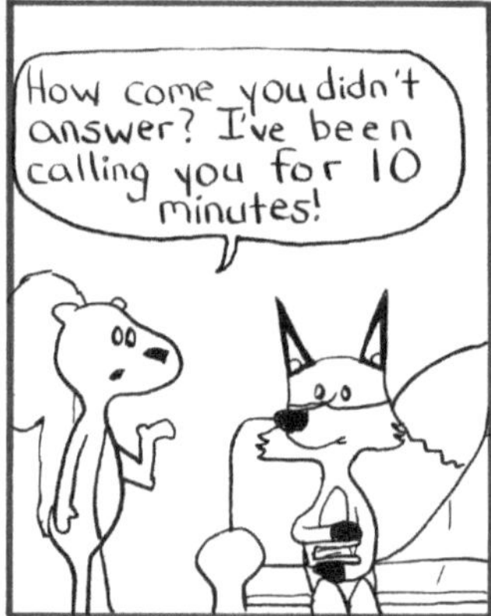
How come you didn't answer? I've been calling you for 10 minutes!
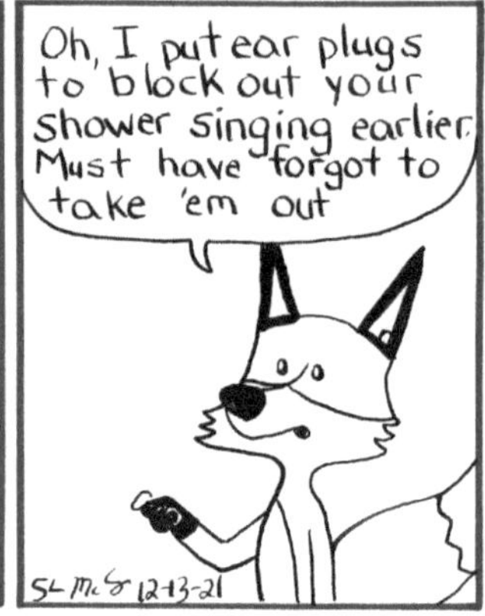
Oh, I put ear plugs to block out your shower singing earlier. Must have forgot to take 'em out
SL McS 12-13-21
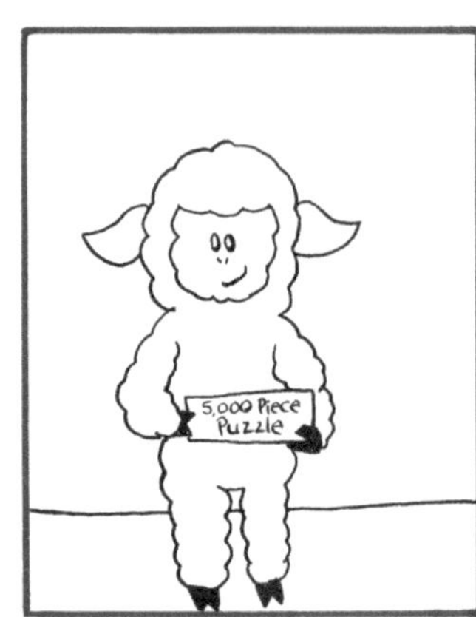
5,000 Piece Puzzle
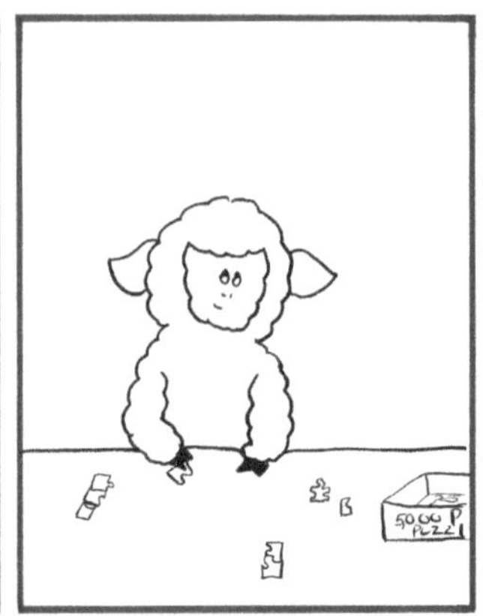
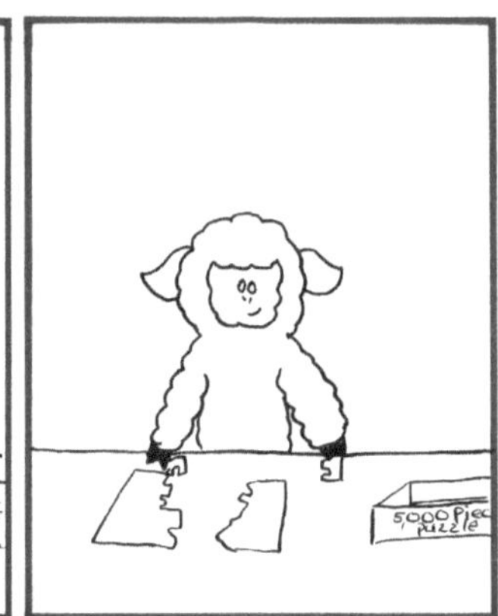
5,000 Piece Puzzle
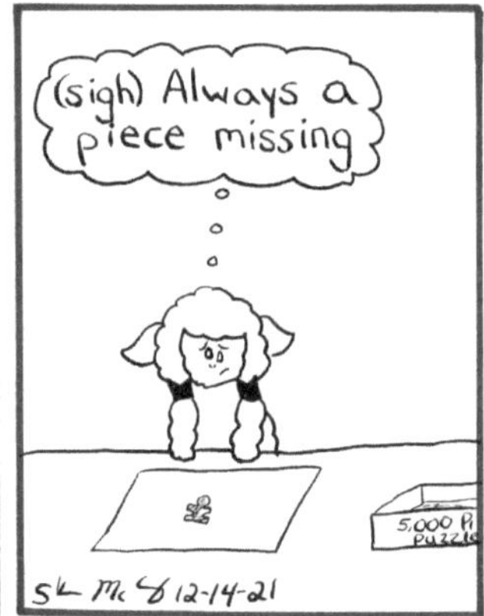
(sigh) Always a piece missing
SL McS 12-14-21
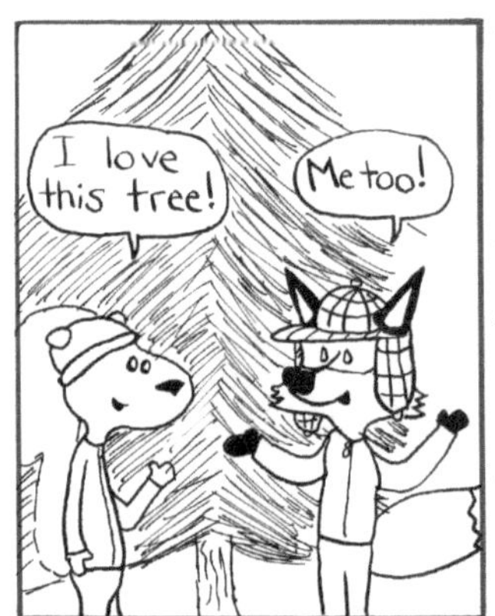
I love this tree!
Me too!
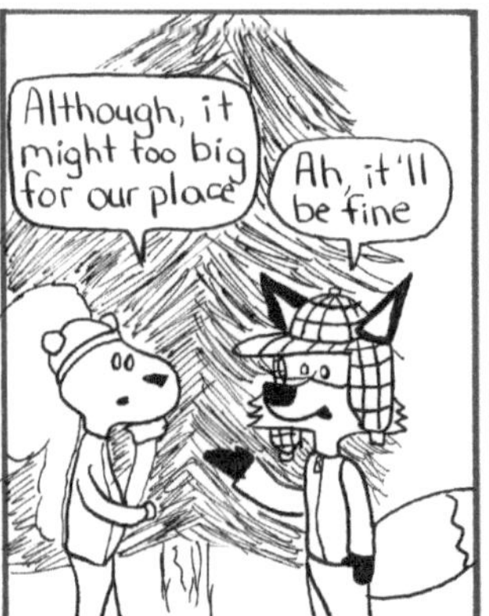
Although, it might too big for our place
Ah, it'll be fine
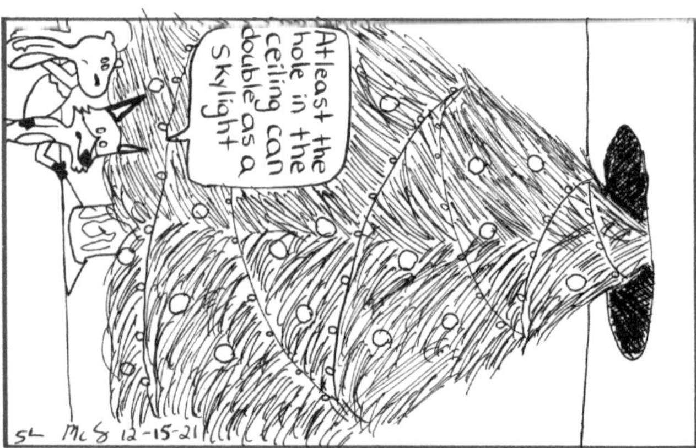
At least the hole in the ceiling can double as a skylight
SL McS 12-15-21

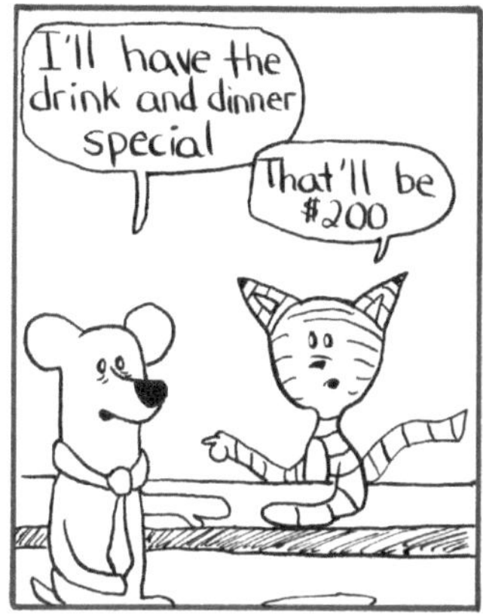
I'll have the drink and dinner special
That'll be $200
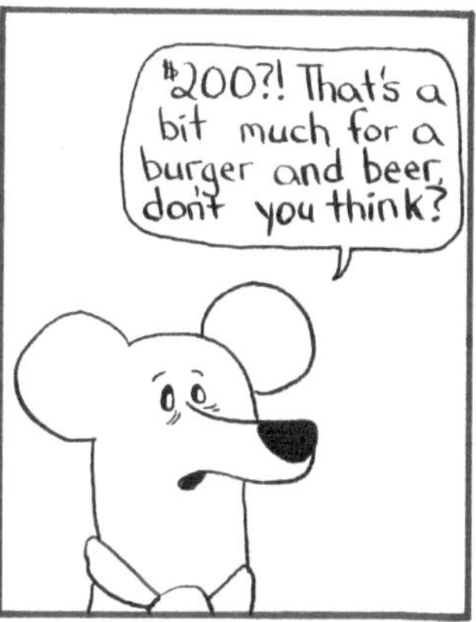
$200?! That's a bit much for a burger and beer, don't you think?
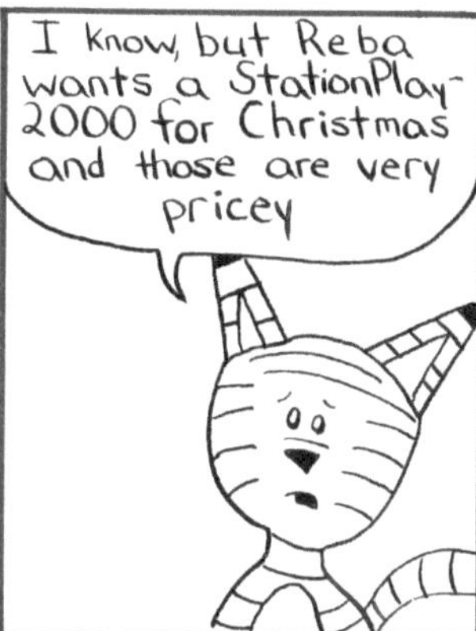
I know, but Reba wants a StationPlay-2000 for Christmas and those are very pricey
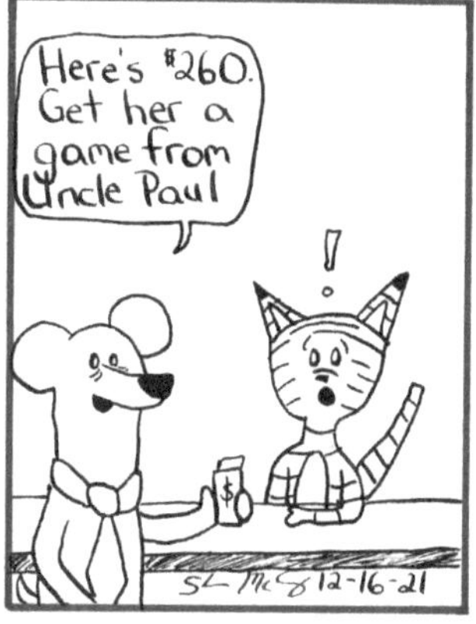
Here's $260. Get her a game from Uncle Paul
!
SL McG 12-16-21
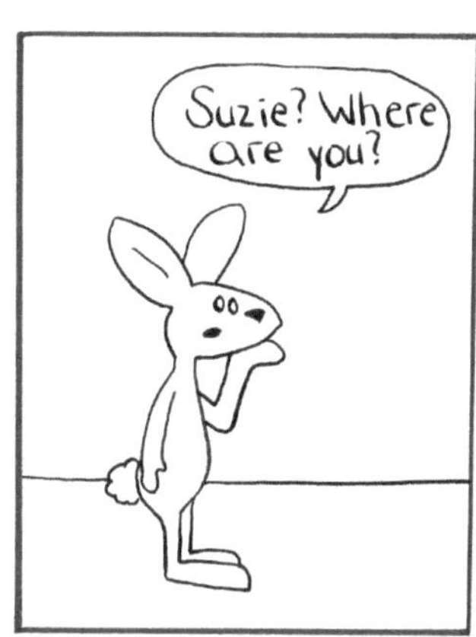
Suzie? Where are you?
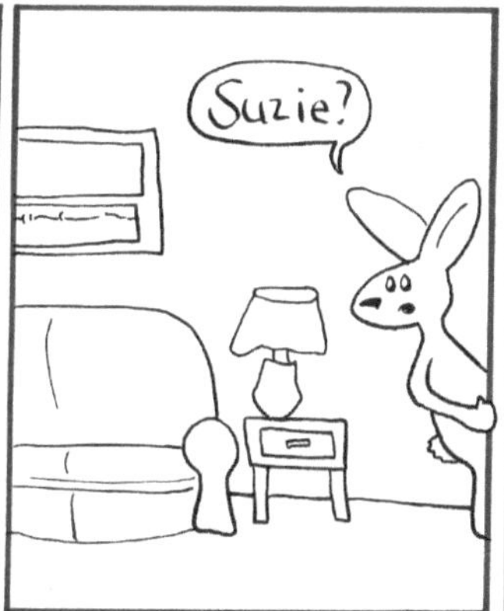
Suzie?
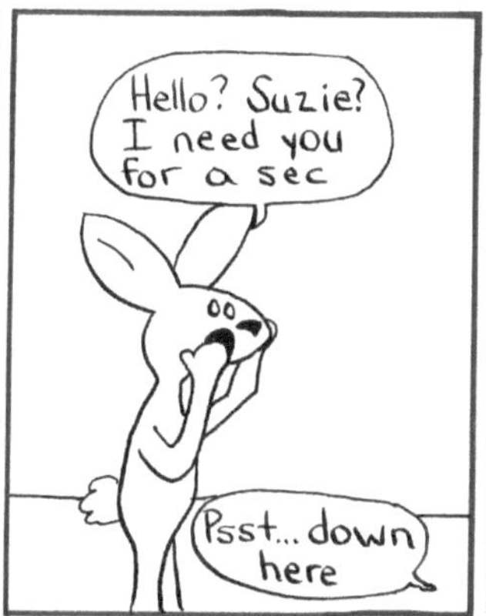
Hello? Suzie? I need you for a sec
Psst... down here
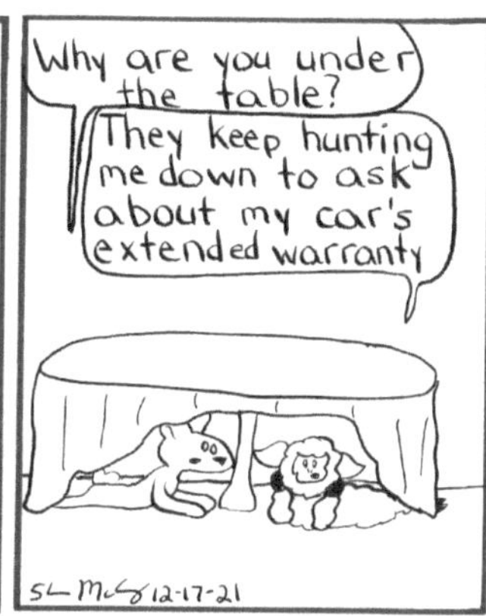
Why are you under the table?
They keep hunting me down to ask about my car's extended warranty
SL McG 12-17-21
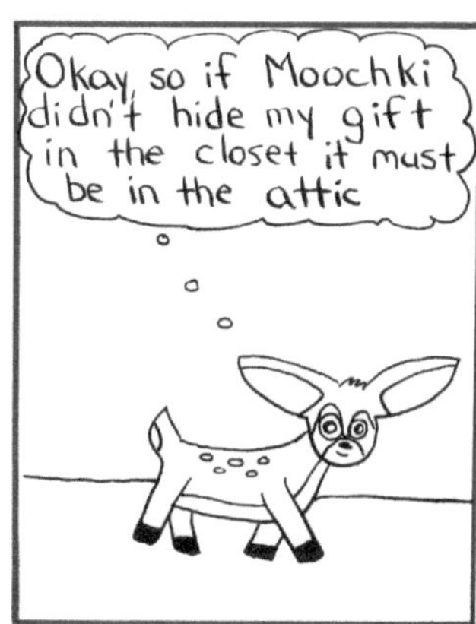
Okay, so if Moochki didn't hide my gift in the closet it must be in the attic
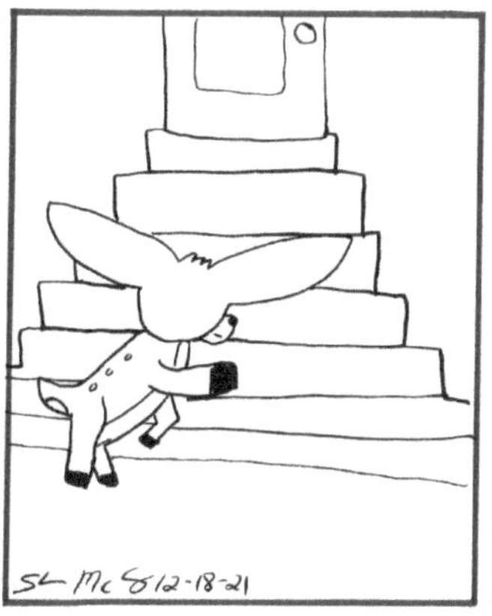
SL McG 12-18-21
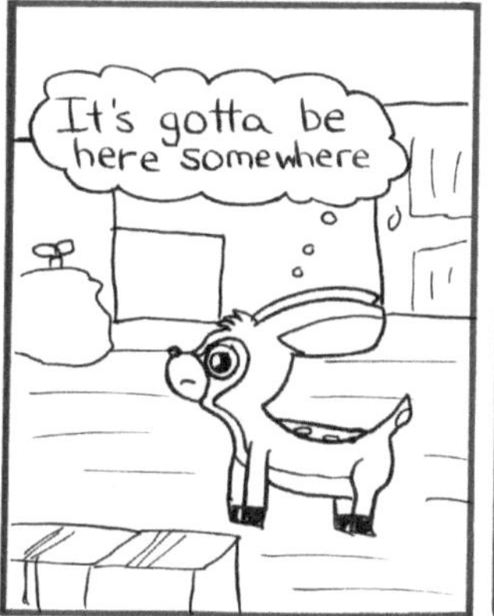
It's gotta be here somewhere
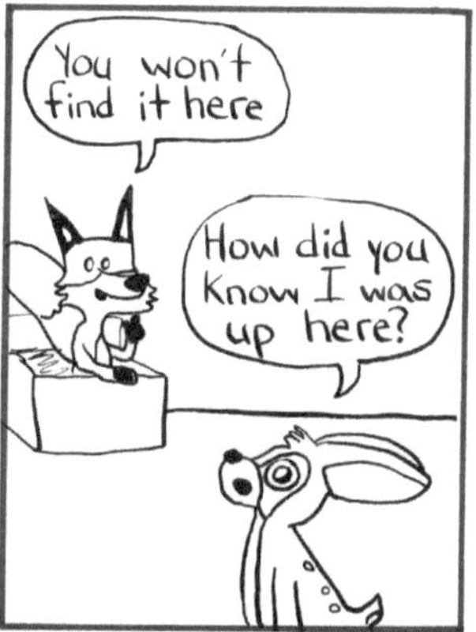
You won't find it here
How did you know I was up here?

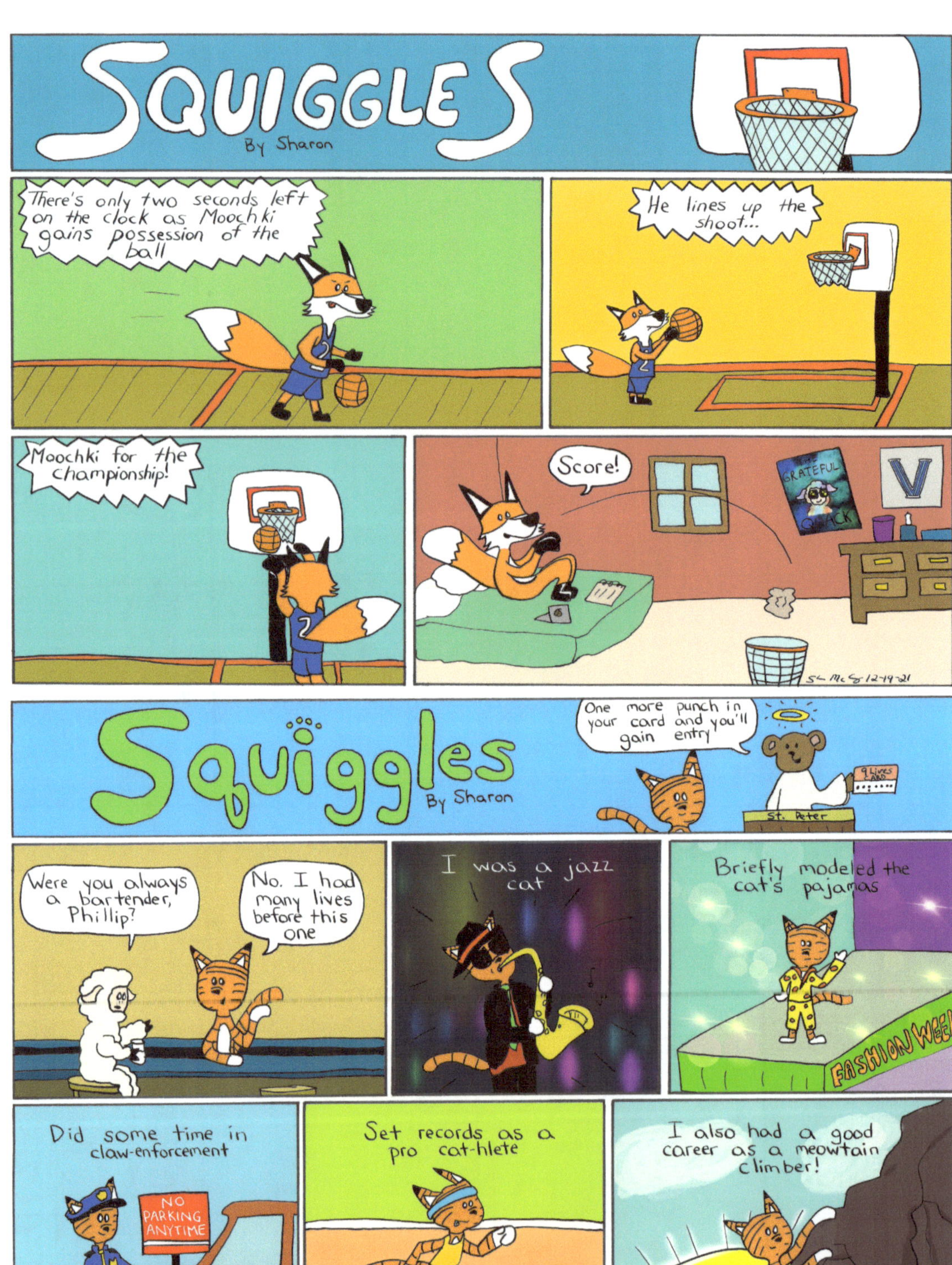
SQUIGGLES
By Sharon
There's only two seconds left on the clock as Moochki gains possession of the ball
He lines up the shoot...
Moochki for the championship!
Score!
GRATEFUL
QUACK
V
Sh McG 12-19-21
Squiggles
By Sharon
One more punch in your card and you'll gain entry
9 Lives
St. Peter
Were you always a bartender, Phillip?
No. I had many lives before this one
I was a jazz cat
Briefly modeled the cat's pajamas
FASHION WEEK
Did some time in claw-enforcement
NO PARKING ANYTIME
Set records as a pro cat-hlete
Sh McG 12-26-21
I also had a good career as a meowtain climber!

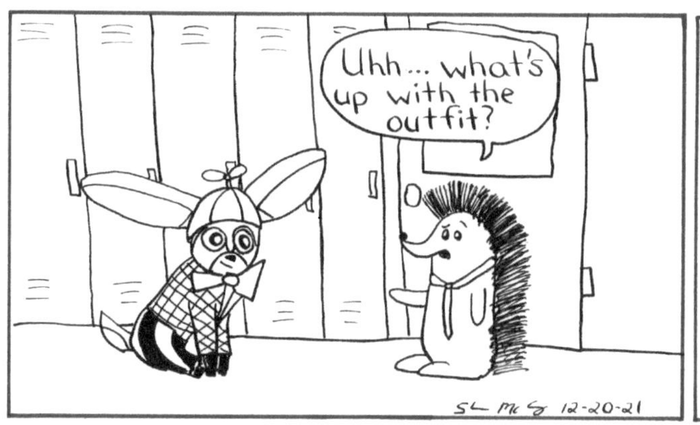
Uhh... what's up with the outfit?
SL McG 12-20-21

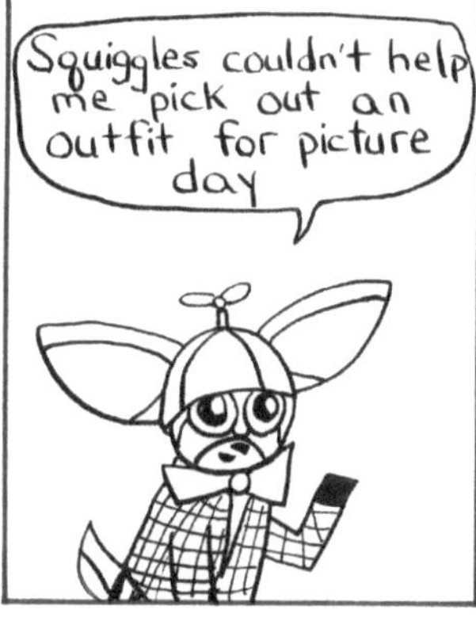
Squiggles couldn't help me pick out an outfit for picture day

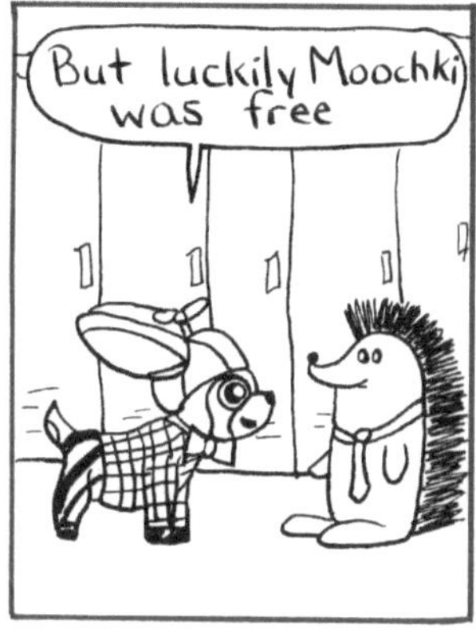
But luckily Moochki was free

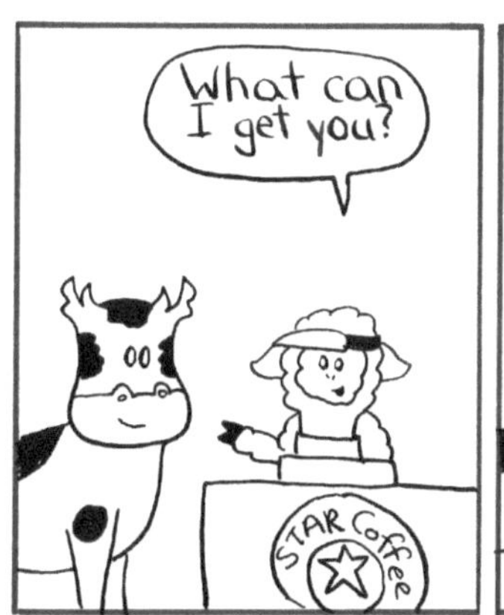
What can I get you?
STAR Coffee

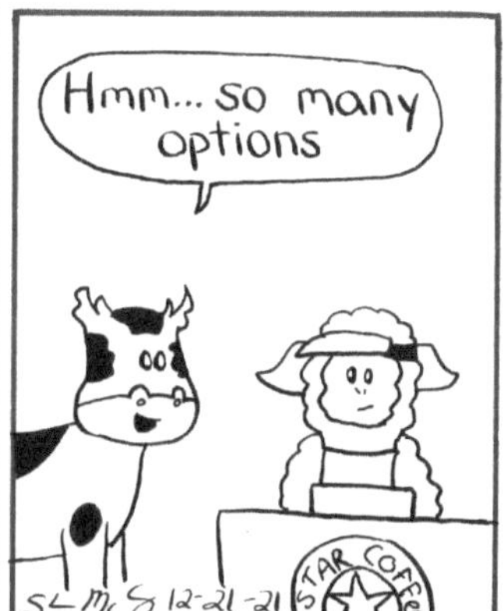
Hmm... so many options
SL McG 12-21-21
STAR Coffee

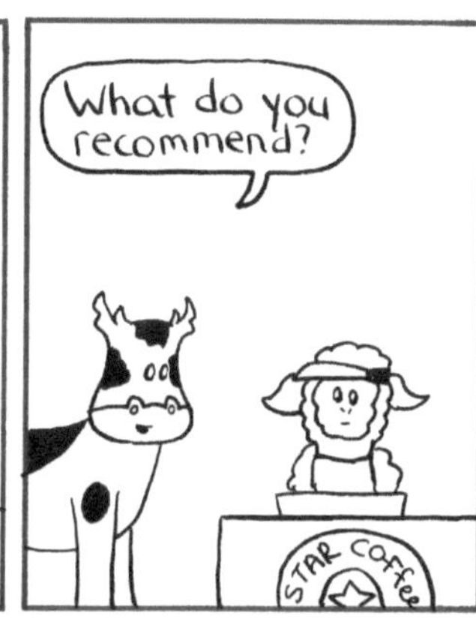
What do you recommend?
STAR Coffee

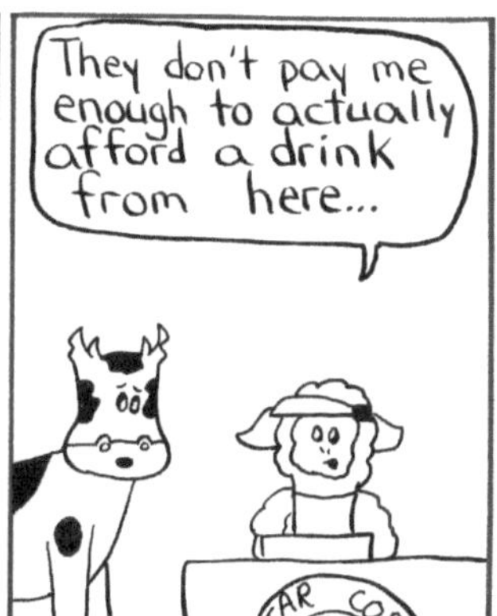
They don't pay me enough to actually afford a drink from here...

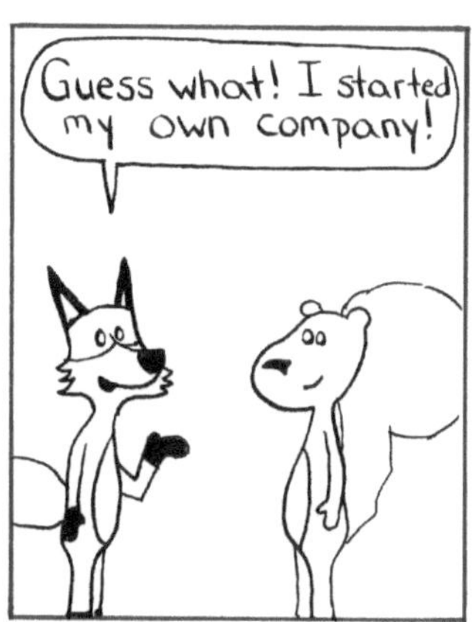
Guess what! I started my own company!

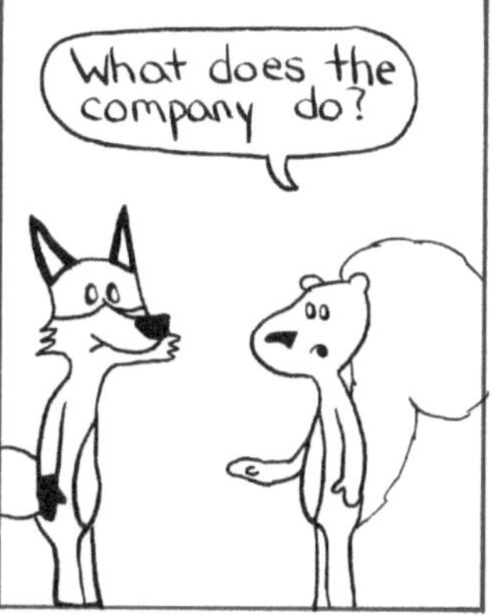
What does the company do?

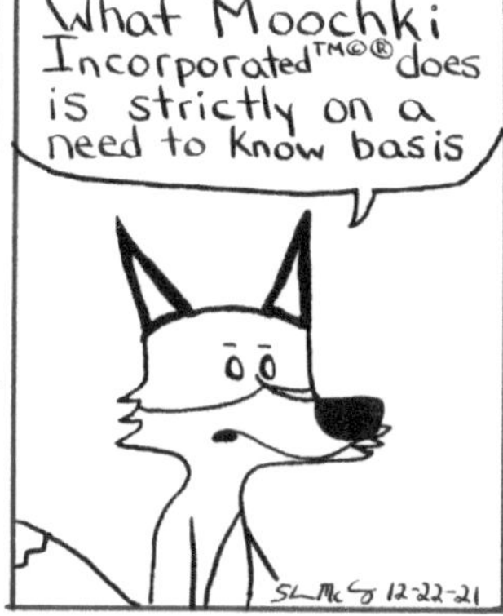
What Moochki Incorporated™©® does is strictly on a need to know basis
SL McG 12-22-21

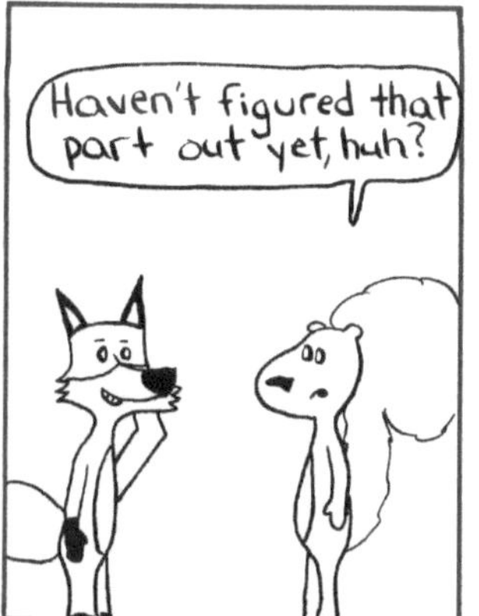
Haven't figured that part out yet, huh?

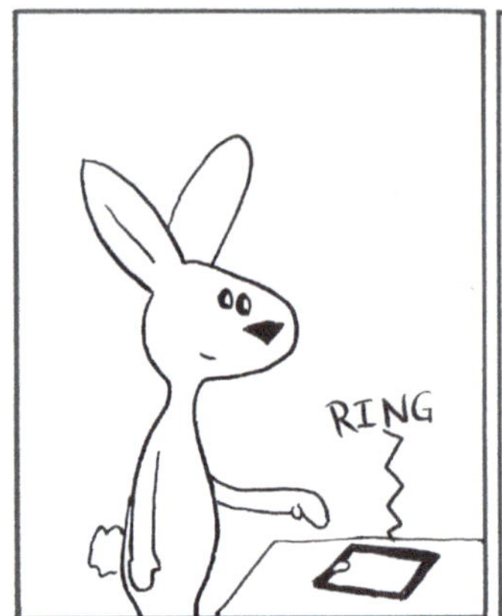
RING

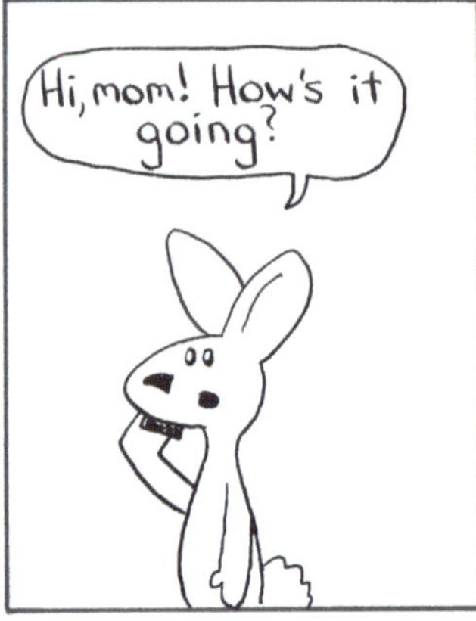
Hi, mom! How's it going?

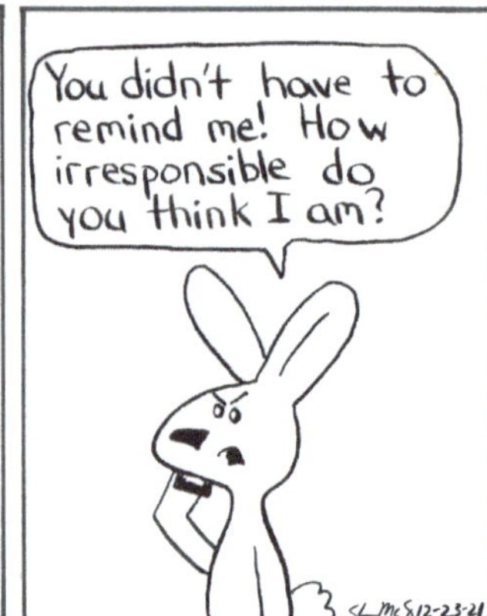
You didn't have to remind me! How irresponsible do you think I am?
SLMcS 12-23-21

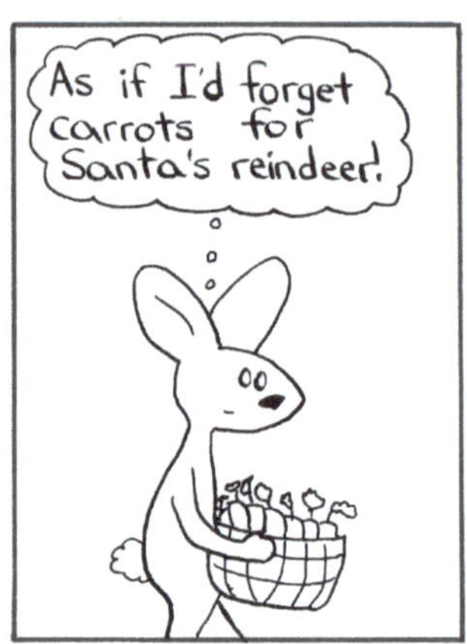
As if I'd forget carrots for Santa's reindeer!

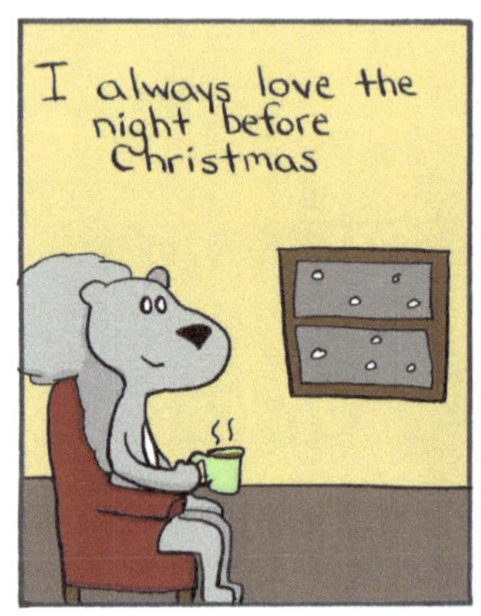
I always love the night before Christmas

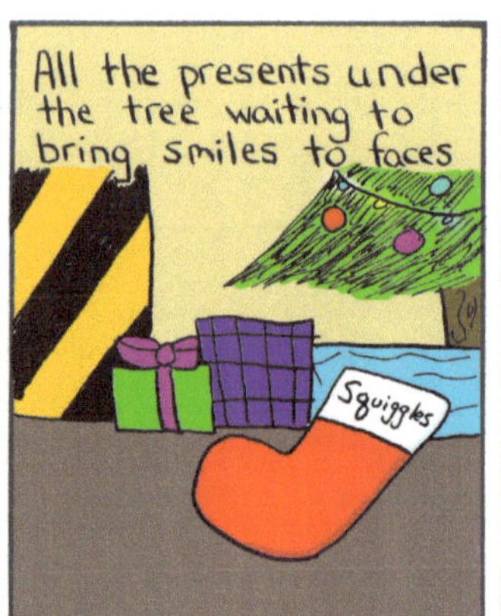
All the presents under the tree waiting to bring smiles to faces
Squiggles

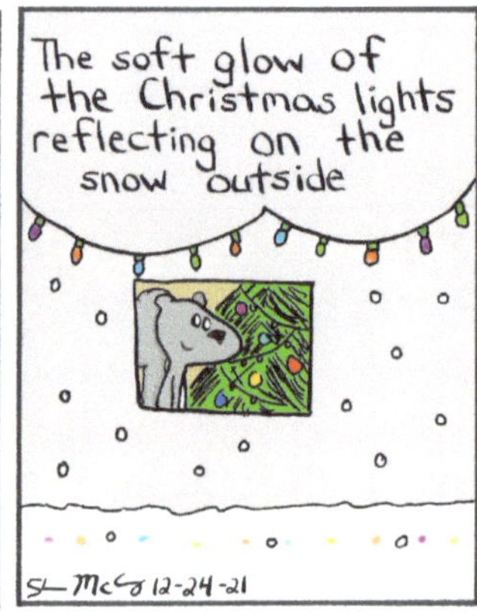
The soft glow of the Christmas lights reflecting on the snow outside
SLMcS 12-24-21

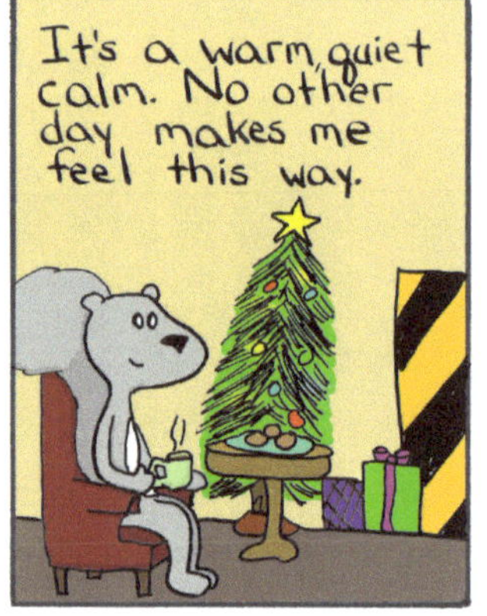
It's a warm, quiet calm. No other day makes me feel this way.

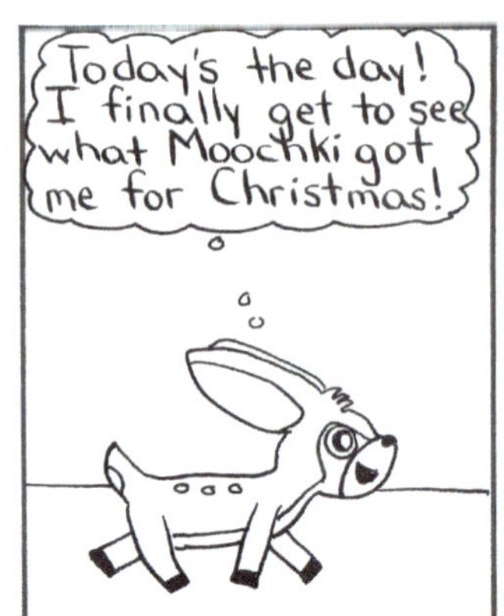
Today's the day! I finally get to see what Moochki got me for Christmas!

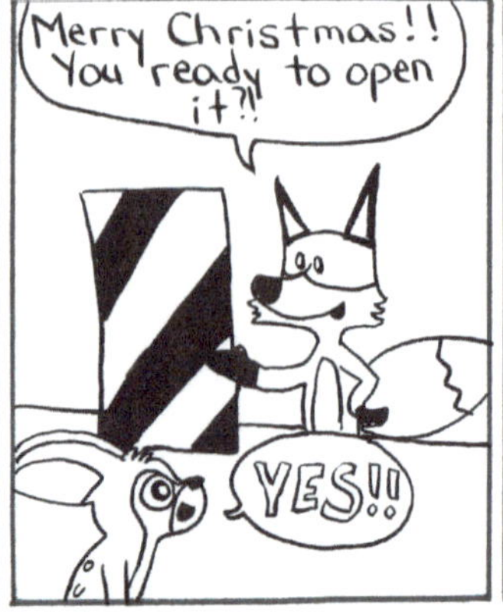
Merry Christmas!! You ready to open it?!
YES!!

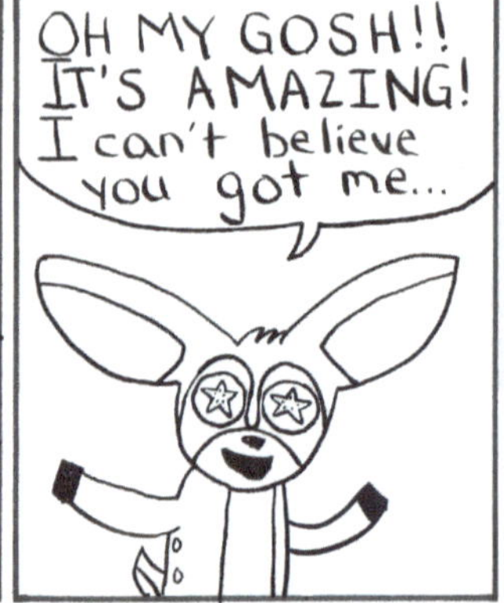
OH MY GOSH!! IT'S AMAZING! I can't believe you got me...

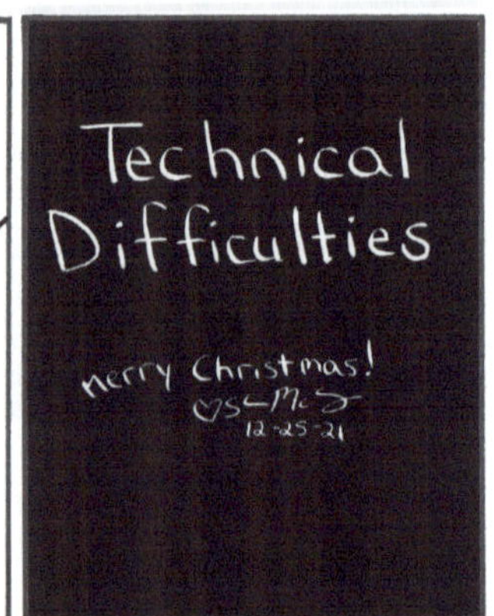
Technical Difficulties
Merry Christmas!
SLMcS
12-25-21

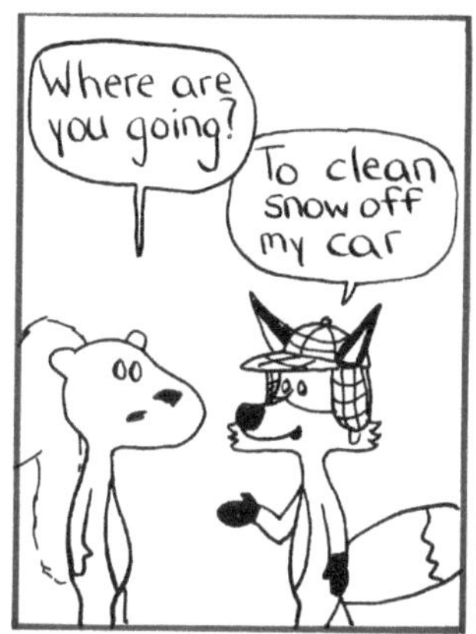
Where are you going?
To clean snow off my car
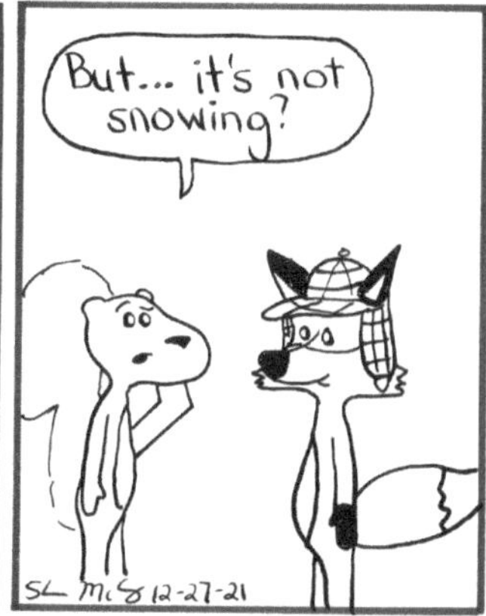
But... it's not snowing?
SL McG 12-27-21
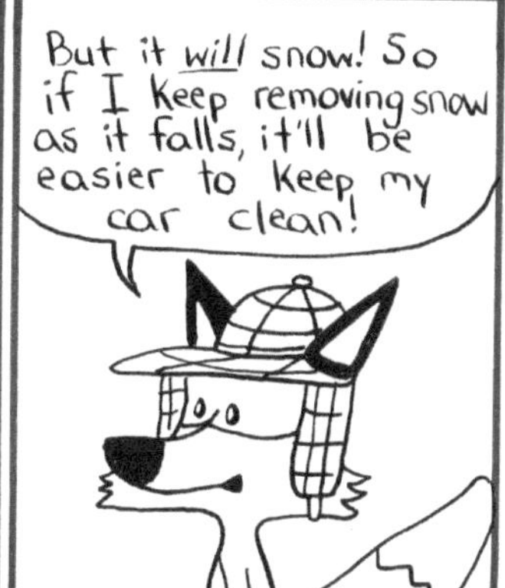
But it *will* snow! So if I keep removing snow as it falls, it'll be easier to keep my car clean!
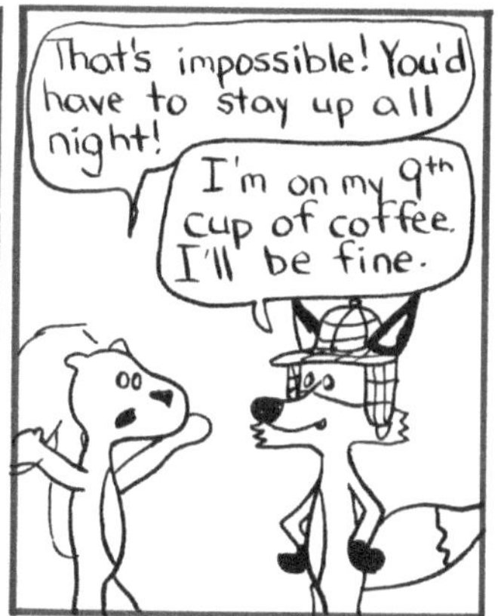
That's impossible! You'd have to stay up all night!
I'm on my 9th cup of coffee. I'll be fine.
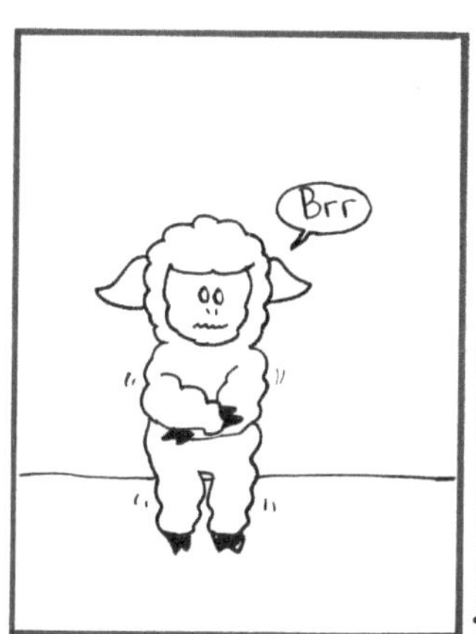
Brr
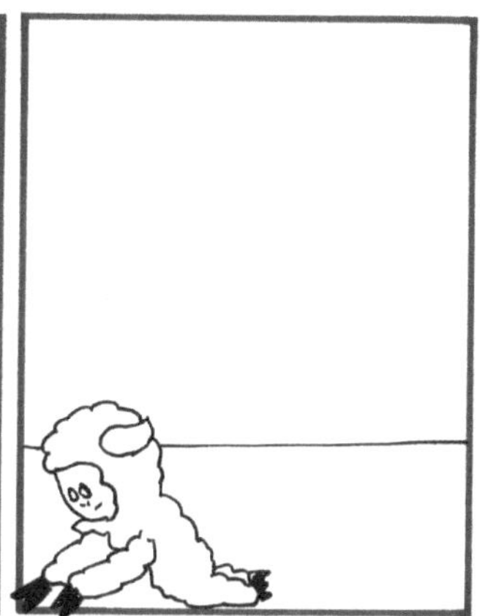
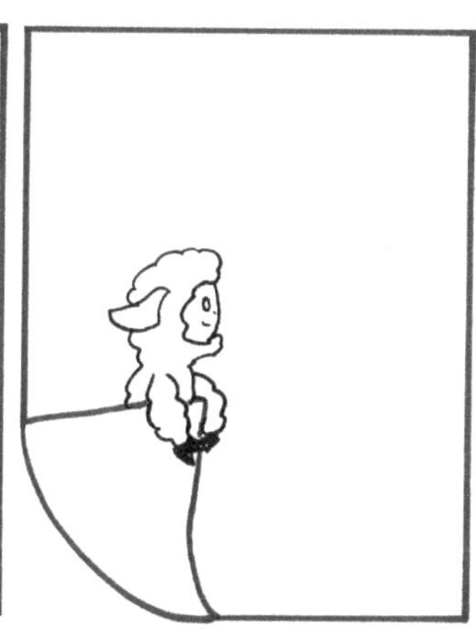
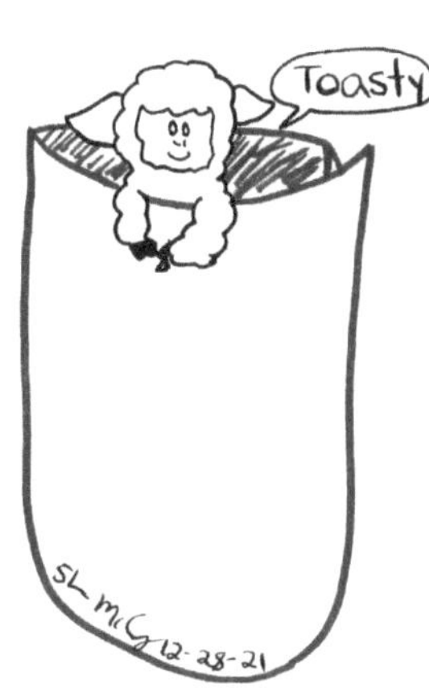
Toasty
SL McG 12-28-21
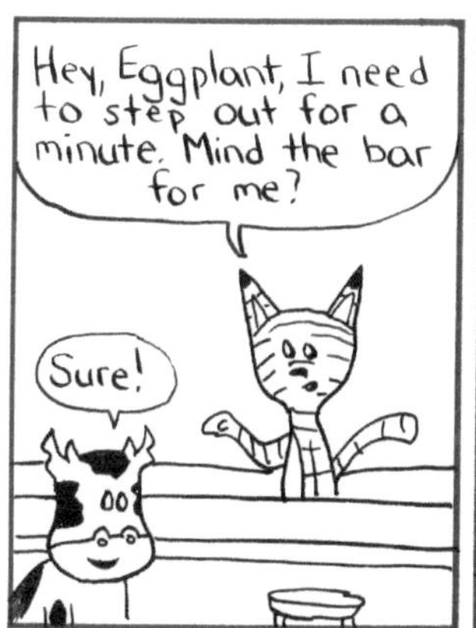
Hey, Eggplant, I need to step out for a minute. Mind the bar for me?
Sure!
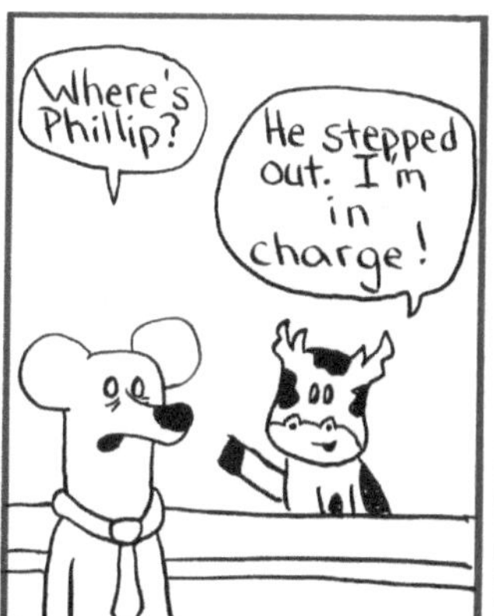
Where's Phillip?
He stepped out. I'm in charge!
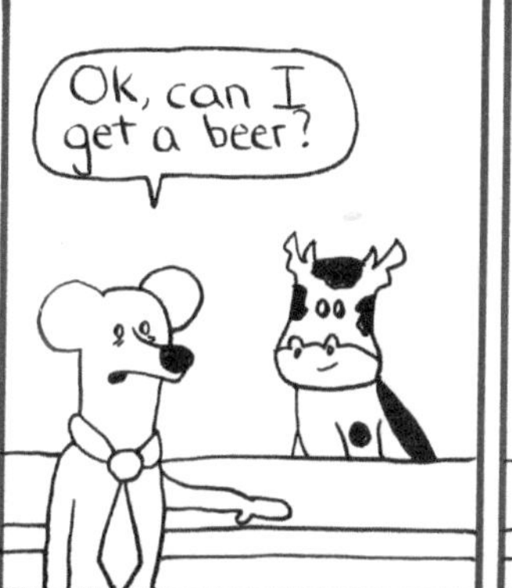
Ok, can I get a beer?
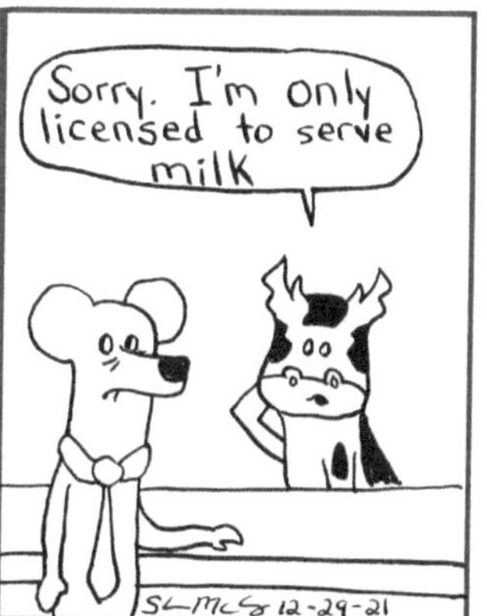
Sorry. I'm only licensed to serve milk
SL McG 12-29-21

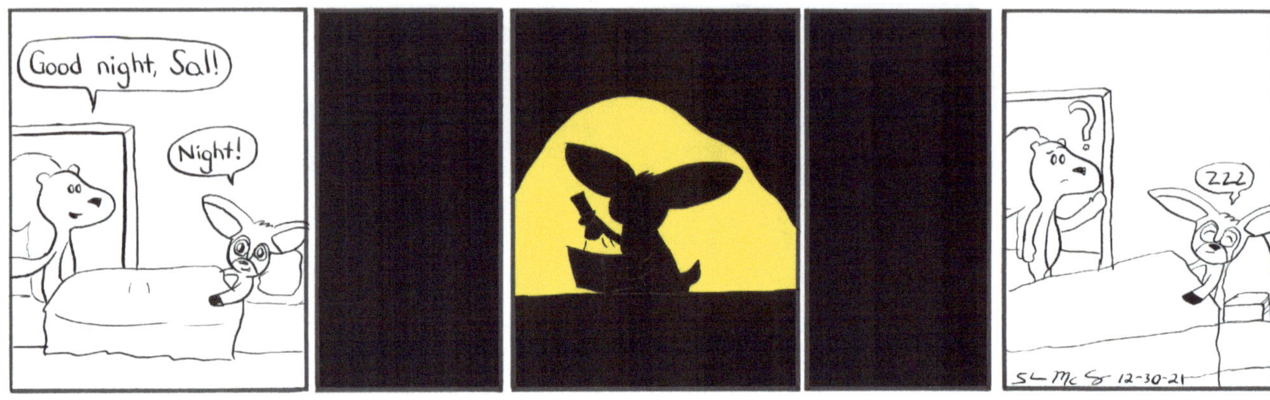
Good night, Sal!
Night!
?
ZZZ
SL McS 12-30-21

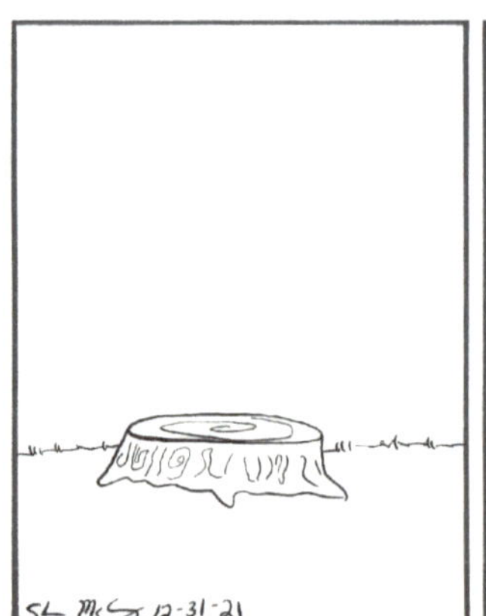
SL McS 12-31-21

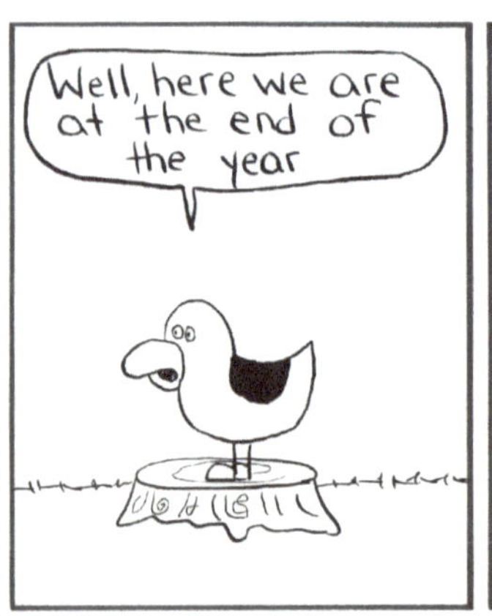
Well, here we are at the end of the year

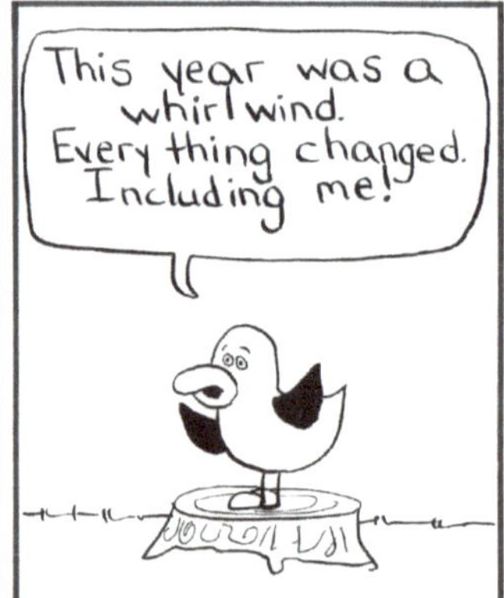
This year was a whirlwind. Everything changed. Including me!

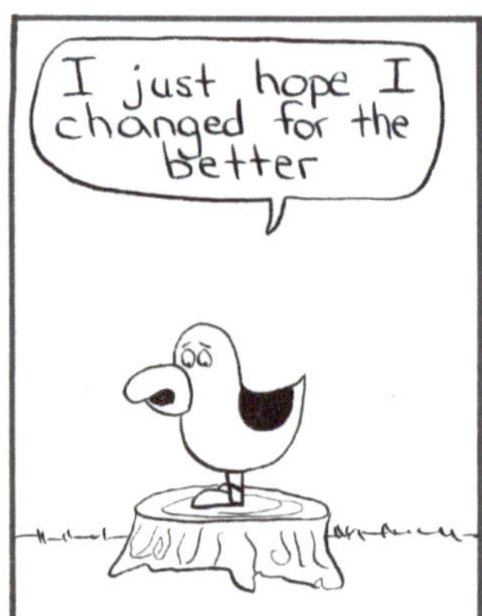
I just hope I changed for the better

About the Author

Sharon McEnearney is a scientist by morning and a cartoonist by evening. She loves squirrels, Scooby Doo, and pop-punk bands. Sharon lives in Arlington, VA with her fiancé, Jack, and their cat, Reba.

CPSIA information can be obtained
at www.ICGtesting.com
Printed in the USA
LVHW072219150622
721315LV00002B/95

* 9 7 8 1 7 3 6 8 3 1 8 4 7 *